MW00928540

THE MEMOIRS OF DETECTIVE VIDOCQ

THE MEMOIRS OF DETECTIVE VIDOCQ

PRINCIPAL AGENT OF THE FRENCH POLICE UNTIL 1827

COMPLETE AND UNABRIDGED

By

EUGÈNE FRANÇOIS VIDOCQ

The Parisian Press
2018

© Copyright 2018 by The Parisian Press.

This book or any portion thereof may not be reproduced or used in any manner whatsoever without the express written permission of the publisher except for the use of brief quotations in a book review or scholarly journal. All rights reserved.

Published by The Parisian Press, Los Angeles.

FIRST PRINTING 2018.

ISBN-13: 978-1721937578.

ISBN-10: 1721937579.

Contents

Chapter I

I WAS BORN AT ARRAS ON JULY 23, 1715, in a house adjoining that in which Robespierre was born, sixteen years previously. It was night; the rain fell, lightning flashed, the thunder rolled; and a relation, who was both midwife and clairvoyant, foretold that my life would be a stormy one.

However that may be, we will presume that the sky was not troubled on my account; and although there is always something attractive in the sublime, I am far from thinking that the turbulence of the elements had much to do with my birth.

I had a most robust constitution, and there was a lot of me, so much so that people took me for a child of two years; and I gave signs of that athletic figure, that colossal form, which has since struck terror into the most hardened criminals. My father's house being situated in the Place d'Armes, the haunt of local rogues, I had my muscles tested early in scuffles with local boys, whose parents were always complaining of me to my father and mother.

At home, nothing was talked of but torn-ears, black-eyes, and ripped garments. At eight years old, I was the terror of all the dogs, cats, and children of the neighborhood; at thirteen, I handled a foil with no little skill. My father, seeing that I associated chiefly with the military of the garrison, was concerned, and instructed me to prepare myself for receiving Holy Communion, and that he had employed two devotees to prepare me for this solemn duty. At the same time, I was to learn the trade of a baker, which was my father's business, in which he intended that I should succeed him, although I had an elder brother.

My job primarily consisted in carrying bread through the city. During my rounds, I made frequent visits to the fencing rooms, of which my parents were not long in ignorance; but the cooks all gave such testimony of my politeness and punctuality, that they winked at this trifling prank. This went on until they discovered a deficiency in the till, of which they never took away the key. My brother, who visited it in the same manner as myself, was detected in the very act, and sent off in a hurry to a baker at Lille. The day after this event, which had not been explained to me, I was about to explore, as had become habit, the convenient drawer, when I perceived that it was carefully closed. The same day, my father instructed me to use more alacrity in my rounds, and to return at a certain hour. It was evident that from that day forward I should be equally deprived of liberty and money. I bewailed this twofold calamity, and hastened to impart it to a comrade named Poyant, who was older than myself.

As a hole was cut in the counter to drop the money through, he first advised me to try using a feather dipped in glue; but this clever idea only yielded small coins, and it became necessary for me to procure a fake key, which was made for me by a blacksmith's son. It worked and we spent together the fruits of this pilfering at a public-house, where we had established our headquarters.

Here there congregated, attracted by the master of the house, a great many well-known rogues, and some unfortunate young fellows, who, to replenish their pockets, used the same expedient as me. I soon joined the society of the these abandoned vagabonds, and they initiated me into all their villainies. Such was the honorable society in the bosom of which I spent my leisure hours, until one day my father surprised me, as he had done my brother, took away my key, heartily thrashed me, and took such precautions as totally cut off all my hopes of ever again getting a dividend from the receipts therein deposited.

My only recourse now was to draw a wage directly from the baked goods. Occasionally, I pilfered a loaf or two; but as in disposing of them I was compelled to sell them very cheaply. I scarcely by their sale obtained sufficient funds to keep myself in tarts and honey. Necessity makes us active. I had an eye for everything; all was agreeable to me; wine, sugar, coffee and liquor. My mother had never known her provisions to disappear so quickly, and perhaps would not have discovered so soon, but two chickens which I had resolved on disposing of to my own peculiar profit, raised their voices to accuse me.

Hid in my breeches pocket, and concealed by my baker's apron, they thrust out their heads and crowed; and my mother, thus informed of their intended fate, came out to prevent it. She gave me several cuffs on the head, and sent me to bed without supper. I did not sleep a wink, and it was, I think, the evil spirit that kept me tossing; all I know is, that I rose with the determination to lay hands on all the silver. One thing alone gave me uneasiness. On each piece the name of VIDOCQ was engraved in large letters. Poyant, to whom I broached the matter, overruled all difficulties; and the same day, at dinner time, I swept off ten forks and as many coffee spoons. Twenty minutes afterwards the whole was pawned, and the next day I had not a farthing left of the hundred and fifty francs which I had borrowed on them.

I didn't come home for three days, and on the third evening I was arrested by two police officers who conveyed me to the Baudets, a place which housed the insane, together with those awaiting trial, and incorrigible villains of the district. I was thrown into a dungeon for ten days, without being told the cause of my arrest, and then the jailer told me that I had been imprisoned at the desire of my father! After I recovered from the shock, the information comforted me. It was a paternal correction that was inflicted on me, and I accordingly judged that its continuance would not be rigorous.

My mother came to see me the next day, and I was pardoned. Four days later, I was set free, and I returned to work with a determination to conduct myself irreproachably from now on. Oh, vain resolve!

I soon resumed my old habits, except extravagance; and I had excellent reasons for no more playing the prodigal son; for my father, who had before been rather lax with me, his youngest son, now exercised a vigilance that would have done credit to the commandant of a cadet training camp. If he left the post at the counter, my mother relieved guard. It was impossible for me to approach it, although I was constantly on the lookout. This put me in despair.

At last, one of my drinking companions took pity on me; it was Poyant again; that thorough rogue, of whose abilities in this way the citizens of Arras no doubt still remember. I confided my sorrows to his friendly ear.

"What a precious fool you are," he said. "What business has a lad of your age to be short of a farthing? Ah! Were I in your place, I know what I would do."

"What?"

"Your parents are rich, and a thousand crowns, more or less, would not hurt them. The old misers! They are fair game, and we must carry it off."

"I understand, we must grasp at once what we cannot get piece by piece."

"Exactly; and then we will be off, neither seen nor known."

"Yes, but the police."

"Hold your tongue! Are you not their son? And your mother is too soft for you."

This consideration of my mother's love, united to the remembrance of her kindness after my recent transgressions, was powerfully persuasive. I blindly adopted a project which smiled on my audacity. It only remained to put the plan in motion, and I didn't have to wait long

One evening, whilst my mother was at home alone, a confidant of Poyant came kindly to tell her that, engaged in a debauch with some girls, I was fighting everybody, and breaking and destroying everything in the house; and that, if I were not stopped, there would be at least a hundred francs to pay for the damage done.

At this moment, my mother was seated in her chair knitting; the stocking dropped from her hand, she arose with haste, and ran with great alarm to the place of the pretended affray, which had been fixed on at the extremity of the city.

Her absence could not be of long continuance, and we hastened to profit by it. A key which I had stolen from the old lady procured us admittance into the shop. The till was closed. I was almost glad to meet with this obstacle; I recalled the memory of my mother's love for me, not as an inducement to commit the act with impunity, but as exciting feelings of coming remorse. I was going to retire. Poyant held me; his infernal eloquence made me blush for what he called my weakness; and when he presented me with a crowbar, with which he had the foresight to bring along, I seized it almost with enthusiasm. The chest was forced. It contained nearly 2000 francs, which we shared, and half an hour afterward I was alone on the road to Lille.

Knowing the trouble which this affair must have thrown me into, I walked at first very quickly, so that when I reached Lens I was much fatigued. A return chaise passed, into which I got, and in less than three hours arrived at the capital of French Flanders, whence I immediately started for Dunkirk, being excessively anxious to place myself beyond the reach of pursuit.

I had resolved on visiting the new world. My fate forbade this project. The port of Dunkirk was empty, I reached Calais, intending to embark immediately, but they asked me more than the whole sum in my possession. I was induced to hope that at Ostend the fare would be less; and on going there found the captains not more reasonable than at Calais. Thus disappointed I fell into that adventurous disposition, which induces us to throw ourselves voluntarily into the arms of the first enterprise that offers. Whilst I was walking, I was accosted by a person whose benevolent appearance gave me rather a favorable impression of him. The first words he addressed to me were questions. He had learnt that I was a stranger; he told me that he was a shipbroker; and when he learnt the cause of my coming to Ostend, he offered his services.

"Your countenance pleases me," said he. "I like an open face; there is in your features the air of frankness and joviality, which I like, and I will prove it to you by procuring for you a passage for almost nothing."

I spoke of my gratitude. "No thanks, my friend; that will be soon enough when your business is completed, which I hope will be soon; but surely you will be tired of waiting about in this manner?" I said that certainly I was not very much amused. "If you will accompany me to Blakemberg, we will sup there together, with some jolly fellows, who are very fond of Frenchmen."

The broker was so polite, and asked me so cordially, that I thought it would be ungentlemanly to refuse, and therefore accepted his invitation. He conducted me to a house where some very agreeable young ladies welcomed us with all that ancient hospitality which did not confine itself only to feasting.

At midnight, probably—I say, probably, for we took no account of hours—my head became heavy, and my legs would no longer support me; there was around me a complete chaos, and things whirled in such a manner, that without perceiving that they had undressed me, I thought I was stripped to my shirt in the same bed with one of the Blakembergian nymphs; it might be true, but all that I know is, that I soon fell soundly asleep. On waking, I found myself cold; instead of the large green curtains, which had appeared to me in my sleep, my heavy eyes only gazed on a forest of masts, and I heard the watchful cry which only echoes in the seaports. I endeavored to rise, and my hand touched a heap of cordage, against which I was leaning.

Did I dream then, or had I dreamt the previous evening? I felt about, I got up, and when on my feet I found that I did not dream, and what was worse, that I was not one of the small numbers of those personages whom fortune favors while sleeping. I was half-naked, and except two crowns and six livres, which I found in one of my breeches pockets, I was penniless. It was then but too clear to me, as the broker had said, "my business had soon been done." I was greatly enraged, but what did that avail me?

I was even unable to point out the spot where I had been thus plundered. I made up my mind and returned to the inn, where I had some clothes which remedied the deficiencies of my attire. I had no occasion to tell my misfortune to the landlord.

"Ah, ah!" said he to me, as far off as he could see me, "here comes another. Do you know, young man, that you have got off well? You are with all your limbs, which is lucky when one gets into such a hornet's nest; you now know what a land shark is; they were certainly beautiful sirens! All pirates are not on the sea, you observe, nor all the sharks within it; I will wager that they have not left you a farthing." I drew my two crowns from my pocket to show them the innkeeper. "That will be," said he, "just enough to pay your bill," which he then presented. I paid it and took leave of him, without however quitting the city.

The sea was open to me as a profession, and I resolved to betroth myself to it, at the risk of breaking my neck thirty times a day, by climbing, for eleven francs a month, up the rigging of a ship. I was ready to enter like a novice, when the sound of a trumpet suddenly arrested my attention; it was not that of a regiment, but of Paillasse (a clown) and his master, who, in front of a show bedecked with the emblem of an itinerant menagerie, were awaiting the mob which never hisses the vulgar exhibitions.

I saw the beginning; and whilst a large crowd was testifying its gratification by loud shouts of laughter, it occurred to me that the master of Paillasse might give me employment. Paillasse appeared to be a good fellow, and I was desirous of securing his protection; and as I knew that one good turn deserves another, when he got down from his platform, on saying *"follow the crowd,"* thinking that he might be thirsty, I devoted my last shilling in offering him half a pint of gin. Paillasse, sensible of this politeness, promised instantly to speak for me, and as soon as our half-pint was finished, he presented me to the director. He was the famous Cotte-Comus: he called himself the first physician of the world, and in traversing the country, had united his talents to those of the naturalist Garnier, the learned preceptor of General Jacquet, whom all Paris saw In the square of the Fountains before and after the Revolution. These gentlemen had with them a troop of rope-dancers.

Comus, as soon as I appeared before him, asked me what I could do.

"Nothing," said I.

"In that case," said he, "they will teach you; there are greater fools than you, and then besides, you have not a clumsy appearance. We shall see if you have a taste for the stage; then I will engage you for two years; the first six months you shall be well fed, and clothed; at the end of that time you shall have a sixteenth of the profits; and the year following, if you are bright, I will give you a share like the others; in the meantime, my friend, I will find occupation for you."

Thus was I introduced, and then went to partake of the flock-bed of the obliging merry-andrew clown. At the break of day, we were awakened by the sonorous voice of our master. Leading me to a kind of small room, whilst showing me the lamps and wooden chandeliers, he said, "There is your job; you must clean these and put everything in proper order; do you understand? And afterward you must clean out the cages of the animals, and sweep the floors."

I went about my job which did not greatly please me; the tallow disgusted me, and I was not quite at my ease with the monkeys, who, enraged to see a fool to whom they were not accustomed, made inconceivable efforts to tear my eyes out. But I yielded to iron necessity. My duty performed, I appeared before the director, who said that I was an apt pupil, and that if I was assiduous he would do something for me. I rose early, and was very hungry; it was ten o'clock, but no signs of breakfast were visible, and yet it was agreed that I should have bed and board. I was sinking from want, when they gave me a piece of brown bread, so hard, that being unable to get through with it, although gifted with sharp teeth, and a famous appetite, I threw the greater portion amongst the animals. I was obliged to light up in the evening, and as, from want of practice, I did not evince in my occupation all possible dispatch, the director, who was a brute, administered to me a slight correction, which he renewed the next and following days.

A month had not elapsed, before I was in a wretched condition; my clothes, spotted with grease and torn by the monkeys, were in rags; I was devoured by vermin; hard diet had made me so thin, that no one would have recognized me; and then it was that there arose in all imaginable bitterness the regrets for my paternal home, where good food, soft bed, and excellent clothing were mine, and where I had no monkeys to make clean and feed.

I was in this mood, when one morning Comus told me, that after due consideration he was convinced that I should make an admirable tumbler. He then placed me under the tuition of Sieur Balmate, called the "little devil," with orders to train me. My master just escaped breaking my loins at the first bend which he compelled me to make. I took two or three lessons daily. In less than three weeks, I was able to execute with much skill the monkey's leap, the drunkard's leap, the coward's leap, etc.

My teacher, delighted at my progress, took pains to forward me; a hundred times I thought that in developing my powers he would dislocate my limbs. At length we reached the difficulties of the art, which became more and more complicated. At my first attempt at the grand fling, I nearly split myself in two; and in the chair-leap, I broke my nose. Bruised, maimed, and tired of so perilous a business, I determined on telling Comus that I had no desire to become a vaulter. "Oh, you do not like it," said he; and without objecting to my refusal gave me a sound thumping. I then left Balmate and returned to my lamps.

Comus had given me up, and it was now for Garnier to give me a turn. One day, after having beaten me more than usual, (for he shared this pleasing office with Comus), Garnier, measuring me from head to foot, and viewing with a marked delight the dilapidation of my doublet, through which my flesh was visible, said to me, "I like you; you have reached the point that pleases me. Now, if you are obedient it remains with yourself to be happy; from today you must let your nails grow; your hair is already of a sufficient length; you are nearly naked, and a decoction of walnut tree leaves will do the rest."

I did not understand what Garnier meant, when he called my friend Paillasse and desired him to bring the tiger-skin and club. Paillasse obeyed.

"Now," said Garnier, "we will go through the performance. You are a young savage from the South Seas, and moreover a cannibal; you eat raw flesh, the sight of blood puts you in a fury, and when you are thirsty, you introduce into your mouth flints which you crack; you utter only broken and shrill sounds, you open your eyes widely, your motions are violent; you only move with leaps and bounds; finally, take for your model the orangutan who is in cage number one."

During this lesson, a jar full of small stones quite round was placed at my feet, and near it a cock which was tired with having its legs tied together; Garnier took it, and offered it to me, saying, "Gnaw away at this." I would not bite it; he threatened me. I rebelled, and demanded to be released; to which he replied by a dozen cuffs of the ear. But he did not get off scot-free; irritated at this usage, I seized a stake, and should assuredly have knocked the naturalist on the head, if the whole troop had not fallen on me, and thrust me out at the door with a shower of blows from the fists and kicks of the feet.

Some days afterward, I was at the same public-house, with a showman and his wife, who exhibited puppets in the open street. We made acquaintance, and I found that I had inspired them with some feelings of interest. The husband pitied me for having been condemned to what he termed the society of beasts. He compared me with Daniel in the lions' den. We may see that he was learned, and intended for something better than to play "Punch." At a later period he superintended a provincial theatrical company, and perhaps superintends it still. I shall conceal his name.

The little manager was very witty, though his wife did not perceive it; he was very ugly, which she plainly perceived. She was one of those smart brunettes with long eyelashes, whose hearts are of the most inflammable material, which deserves a better destiny than to light a fire of straw. I was young, and so was the lady: she was only sixteen, her husband thirty-five. As soon as I found myself out of place, I went to see this couple; it struck me that they would advise me correctly. They gave me some dinner, and congratulated me on having dared to free myself from the despotic yoke of Garnier.

"Since you are your own master," said the husband to me, "you had better accompany us: you will assist us; at least, when we are three in number, we shall have no lost time between the acts; you will move the actors, whilst Eliza goes around with the hat; thus the public will be attracted and not go off, and the profits will be more abundant. What say you, Eliza?"

Eliza answered, that she would do in this respect all he might desire, and besides, she entirely agreed with him; and at the same time gave me a look which bespoke that she was not displeased, and that we should soon understand each other. I accepted the new employment with gratitude, and at the next representation I was installed in my office. The situation was infinitely superior to Garnier's. Eliza, who, despite my leanness, had discovered that I was not so badly made as I was clothed, made a thousand secret advances, to which I was not backward in reply. At the end of three days she said she loved me. I was not ungrateful; we were happy, and constantly together.

At home, we only laughed, played, and joked. Eliza's husband took all that for child's sport; when at work we were side by side under a narrow cabin, formed of four cloth rags, dignified by the splendid title of 'Theatre of Amusing Varieties.' Eliza was on the right of her husband, and I on her right hand, and filled her place when she was not there to superintend the entrances. One

Sunday the play was in full representation, and there was a crowded audience around the stage. Punch had beaten everybody, and our master having nothing more to do with one of his personages (the Serjeant of the Watch) wished it to be removed, and called for his assistant. We heard him not. "Assistant, assistant," he repeated with impatience, and at the third time turning round he saw us enfolding each other in a close embrace. Eliza, surprised, sought for an excuse, but the husband, without listening, cried out again, "Assistant," and thrust against his eye the hook which served to suspend the serjeant. At the same moment the blood flowed, the representation was interrupted, and a battle ensued between the two married people; the show was overturned, and we were exposed in the midst of a numerous crowd of spectators, from whom this scene drew a lengthened peal of applause and laughter.

This disaster again threw me on the wide world, without a home to shelter my head. If I had had a decent appearance, I might have procured a situation in a respectable family, but my appearance was so wretched that no one would have anything to say to me. In my situation I had but one resource, that of returning to Arras: but then how to exist on the road? I was a prey to these perplexities, when a person passed near me whom I took by his appearance to be a peddler. I entered into conversation with him, and he told me he was going to Lille; that he sold powders, opiates, and elixirs, cut corns, relieved bunions, and sometimes extracted teeth. "It is a good trade," added he, "but I am getting old, and want somebody to carry my pack; it is a stiff-backed fellow like you that I need, with a firm foot, and steady eye; so if you like we will tramp it together."

"Willingly," was my reply, and without any further stipulation, we went on our way together. After an eight hours' walk, night drew on, and we could scarcely see our way, when we halted before a wretched village inn. "Here it is," said the itinerant doctor, knocking at the door.

"Who is there?" cried a hoarse voice.

"Father Godard with his pack," answered my guide; and, the door immediately opening, we found ourselves in the midst of a crowd of peddlers, tinkers, quack-doctors, umbrella-venders and showmen who hailed my new master, and ordered a plate to be brought for him. I thought they would do me equal honor, and I was about to seat myself at table, when the host, striking me familiarly on the shoulder, asked me if I was not mountebank of father Godard.

"Who do you call a mountebank?" said I with astonishment.

"A clown, then."

I confess that, despite the recent reminiscences of the menagerie, and the Theatre of Amusing Varieties, I felt mortified at such an appellation. But I had a devil of an appetite, and as I thought that supper would follow the interrogation, and that, after all, my situation with father Godard had not been accurately defined, I consented to pass for his mountebank.

On my answering, the host led me at once to a neighboring spot, a sort of barn, where a dozen fellows were smoking, drinking, and playing at cards. He said that they would send me in something to eat. Soon afterward a stout wench brought me in a mess in a wooden bowl, on which I fed with the utmost avidity. A loin of mutton was swimming in a sea of pot-liquor with stringy turnips: I cleared the whole up in a twinkling. This done, I laid myself down with the other packmen's valets on some piles of straw, which we shared with a camel, two muzzled bears, and a crowd of learned dogs. The vicinity of such bedfellows was not the most pleasing; but it was necessary to put up with it. I did not close my eyes, whilst all the others snored away most gloriously.

Father Godard paid for all, and however bad were the beds and the fare, as we drew near Arras, it was necessary that I should not quit him. At length we reached Lille, which we entered on a market day. By way of losing no time, father Godard went straight to the principal square, and desired me to arrange his table, his chest, his vials, and packets, and then proposed that I should go and announce his arrival round the place. I had made a good breakfast, and the proposition disgusted me; I could put up with sleeping with a dromedary, and carrying his baggage from Ostend to Lille, but to go round in parade, at ten leagues from Arras—No!

I bade adieu to father Godard, and then set out toward my native city, of which the clock soon became visible. Having reached the foot of the ramparts, before the closing of the gates, I trembled at the idea of the reception I should meet with: one moment I was tempted to beat a retreat, but fatigue and hunger could not allow that: rest and food were vital. I wavered no longer, and ran toward my paternal roof. My mother was alone in the shop: I entered, and throwing myself at her feet, wept, whilst I entreated her forgiveness. The poor old woman, who hardly recognized me, so greatly was I altered, was softened. She had no power to repulse me, and even appeared to have forgotten all. She reinstated me in my old chamber, after having supplied all my wants. But it was necessary to tell my father of my return. She did not have the courage to face his first bursts of anger: a priest of her acquaintance, the almoner of the regiment of Anjou, garrisoned at Arras, undertook to be the bearer of the words of peace; and my father, after having vowed fire and flames, consented to pardon me. I trembled lest he should prove inexorable, and when I learnt that he had yielded, I jumped for joy. The almoner brought the news to me, and followed it up with a moral application, which was no doubt very touching, but I do not remember a word of it; I only recollect that he quoted the parable of the Prodigal Son, which was in truth a history similar to my own.

My adventures had made some noise in the city; everybody was anxious to hear them from my own lips. But no one, except one actress of the Arras company, took more interest in them than two milliners of the Rue de Trois Visages: I paid them frequent visits. However, the actress soon obtained the exclusive privilege of my attention, and an intrigue followed, in which, disguised as a young girl, I renewed at her house some scenes from the romance of Faublas. A sudden journey to Lille with my conquest, her husband, and a very pretty little maidservant, who passed me off for her sister, proved to my father that I had soon forgotten the troubles of my first campaign. My absence was not of long continuance: three weeks had scarcely elapsed, when, from want of money, the actress refused any longer to allow me to form part of the baggage. I returned quietly to Arras, and my father was confounded at the straightforward way with which I asked his consent to enter the army. The best he could do was to comply, which he did; and the next day I was clad in the uniform of the Bourbon regiment.

My height, good figure, and skill in arms, procured for me an appointment in a company of chasseurs. Some old veterans took offense at it, and I sent two to the hospital in consequence, where I soon joined them myself, on being wounded by one of their comrades. This commencement gave me notoriety, and they took a malicious pleasure in reviewing my past adventures; so that at the end of six months, 'Reckless'—for they bestowed that name upon me—had killed two men and fought fifteen duels. In other respects, I enjoyed all the pleasure of a garrison life. I mounted guard at the cost of some good shopkeepers, whose daughters took on themselves the charge of making me as comfortable as possible. My mother added to these liberalities, and my father made me an allowance; and besides, I found means to run into debt: thus I really cut a figure, and scarcely felt anything of the troubles of discipline.

Once only I was sentenced to a fortnight's imprisonment, because I had not answered to three summonses. I underwent my punishment in a dungeon beneath one of the bastions, where one of my comrades was confined with me, a soldier in the same regiment. He was accused of various robberies, which he had confessed. Scarcely were we alone when he told me the grounds of his detention fully. Doubtless the regiment would give him up, and this idea, joined to the dread of dishonoring his family, threw him into despair. I pitied him, and seeing no remedy for so deplorable a case, I counseled him to evade punishment either by escape or suicide. He determined to try the former ere he resolved on the latter; and, aided by a young friend who came to visit me, I prepared all for his flight.

At midnight, two bars of iron were broken, and we conducted the prisoner to the ramparts, and then I said to him, "Go: you must either jump or hang."

He calculated the height, and hesitating, determined rather to run the chance of his sentence than to break his legs. He was preparing to return to his dungeon: at a moment when he least expected it, we gave him a push over: he shrieked out whilst I bid him be silent.

I then returned to my cell; when on my straw, I tasted the repose which the consciousness of a good deed always brings. The next day, on the flight of my companion being discovered, I was questioned, and dismissed on saying that I knew nothing of the affair. Some years afterward, I met this unfortunate fellow, who looked on me as his liberator. Since his fall he had been lame, but had become an honest man.

I could not remain eternally at Arras. War had been declared against Austria, and I set out with the regiment, and soon after was present at the rout of Marquain, which ended at Lille by the massacre of the brave and unfortunate general Dillon. After this, we were ordered against the camp at Maulde, and then in that of de la Lune, when, with the infernal army under the command of Kellerman, I was engaged in the battle against the Prussians of the 30th of October.

The next day I was made corporal of grenadiers: thereupon it became necessary to baptize my worsted lace, and I acquitted myself with much credit at the drinking booth, when, I know, not how or why, I quarreled with the sergeant-major of the regiment which I had just left. An honorable meeting, which I proposed, was agreed upon, but when on the ground, my adversary pretended that the difference in rank would not allow of his measuring weapons with me. I sought to compel him by violence, he went to make complaint of me, and the same evening I was, together with my second, placed under arrest.

Two days afterward, we were informed that we were to be tried by court-martial, and I thereupon determined to desert. My comrade in his waistcoat only, with a cap on his head, like a soldier about to undergo punishment, walked before me, who had on a hairy cap, my knapsack and musket, at the end of which was a large packet sealed with red wax, and inscribed, "To the citizen commandant of the quarters at Vitry-le-Francais." This was our passport, and we reached Vitry in safety, and procured citizens' habits from a Jew. At this period the walls of every city were covered with placards, in which all Frenchmen were invited to fly to the defense of their country. At such a juncture, the first comers were enrolled. A quartermaster of the 11th Chasseurs received us, gave us our route, and we immediately started for the depot at Philippeville.

My companion and I had but little cash, when fortunately a lucky windfall was awaiting us at Chalons. In the same inn with us was a soldier of Beaujolais, who invited us to drink. He was an open-hearted countryman of Picardy, and as I conversed with him in the provincial dialect of his country, whilst the glass was circulating, we grew such great friends, that he showed us a portfolio filled with assignats, which he said he had found near Chateau-l'Abbaye. "Comrades," said he, "I cannot read; but if you will tell me what these papers are worth, I will give you a share." The man could not have asked anyone better able to inform him, and in bulk he had much the greater quantity; but he had no suspicions that we had retained in value nine-tenths of the sum. This little supply was not useless during the remainder of car journey, which we finished with much glee.

Arrived at our place of destination, we had still enough left to keep the pot boiling. A short time afterward we were sufficiently skilled in horsemanship to be appointed to one of the squadrons on service, and we reached the army two days before the battle of Jemappes. It was not the first time that I had smelled powder, and I was no coward; indeed, I had reason to know that I had found favor in the eyes of my officers, when my captain informed me that, having been discovered to be a deserter, I should be most certainly arrested. The danger was imminent, and that same evening I saddled my horse, intending to go over to the Austrians. I soon reached their outposts, and on asking to be admitted, was incorporated at once with the cuirassiers of Kinski. What I most feared was lest I should be compelled next day to cross swords with the

French, and I hastened to avoid any such necessity. A pretended illness enabled me to be left at Louvain, where after passing some days in the hospital, I offered to give the officers in the garrison lessons in fencing. They were delighted with the proposal, and supplied me with masks, gloves and foils; and an assault, in which I disarmed two or three pretended German masters, was enough to give them the highest opinion of my skill. I soon had many pupils, and reaped a good harvest of florins.

I was too much elated with my success, when at the end of it brisk attack on a brigadier, I was condemned to undergo twenty stripes of the cat, which, according to custom, were given to me on parade. This transported me with rage, and I refused to give another lesson. I was ordered to continue, with a choice of giving lessons or a fresh flogging. I decided on the former; but the cat annoyed me, and I resolved to dare try to escape from it. Being informed that a lieutenant was about to join the army under General Schroeder, I begged to accompany him as his servant, to which he agreed, under the idea that I should make a St. George of him; but he was mistaken; for as we approached Quesnoy I took French leave, and directed my journey toward Landrecies, where I passed for a Belgian who had left the Austrian banner. They wished me to enter a cavalry regiment, but the fear of being recognized and shot, if ever I should be brigaded with my old regiment, made me give the preference to the 14th Light Regiment (the old Chasseurs of the Barriers.)

The army of the Sambre and Meuse was then marching toward Aix-la-Chapelle; the company to which I belonged received orders to follow it. We set out, and on entering Rocroi, I saw the chasseurs of the 11th. Myself up for lost, when my old captain, with whom I could not avoid an interview, gave me courage. This worthy man, who had taken an interest in me ever since he had seen me cut a way amongst the hussars of Saxe-Teschen, told me that as an amnesty would henceforward place me out of the reach of all pursuit, he should have much pleasure in again having me under his orders. I told him how glad it would make me; and he, undertaking to arrange the affair, I was once more reinstated in the 11th. My old comrades received me with pleasure, and I was not less pleased to find myself once again amongst them; and nothing was wanting to complete my happiness, when love, who is always busy, determined on playing one of his tricks. It will not be thought surprising that at seventeen I captivated the housekeeper of an old gentleman.

Manon, for that was her name, was near twice my age, but then she loved me very tenderly, and proved it by making every sacrifice to me unhesitatingly. I was, to her taste—the handsomest of chasseurs because I was hers, and she wished that I should also be the most dashing. She had already given me a watch, and I was proudly adorned with various jewels, proofs of the love with which I inspired her, when I learned that Manon was accused by her master of robbery. Manon confessed the fact, but at the same time, to assure herself that after her sentence I should not pass into another's arms, she pointed me out as her accomplice, and even asserted that I had proposed the theft to her. It had the appearance of probability, and I was consequently implicated, and should have extricated myself with difficulty if chance had not brought to light some letters of hers which established my innocence. Manon, conscience-stricken, retracted. I had been shut up in the house of confinement at Stenay, whence I was set at liberty, and sent back as white as snow.

My captain, who had never thought me guilty, was delighted at seeing me again; but the chasseurs could not forgive my being even suspected; and in consequence of various allusions and comments, I had no less than six duels in as many days. In the last I was badly wounded, and was conveyed to the hospital, where I remained for a month before I recovered. On going out, my officer, convinced that these quarrels would be renewed if I did not go away for a time, gave me a furlough for six weeks. I went to Arras, where I was much astonished to find my father in a public employment. As an old baker, he had been appointed to watch over the supplies of the commissariat. He opposed the distribution of bread at a time of scarcity; and this discharge of his duty, although he performed it gratis, was so offensive, that he would assuredly have been conducted to the guillotine had he not been protected by citizen (now lieutenant-general) Souham, commandant of the 2nd Battalion of Correze, into which I was temporarily drafted.

My furlough being out, I rejoined my regiment at Givet, whence we marched for the county of Namur. We were quartered in the villages on the banks of the Meuse; and as the Austrians were in sight, not a day passed without some firing on both sides. At the termination of an engagement more serious than usual, we were driven back almost under the cannon of arrest; and in the retreat I received a ball in my leg, which compelled me to go again to the hospital, and afterward to remain at the depot; and I was there when the Germanic legion passed, principally composed of a party of deserters, fencing-masters, etc. One of the chief officers proposed that I should enter this corps, offering the rank of quartermaster. "Once admitted," said he, "I will answer for you; you shall be safe from all pursuit." The certainty of not being asked for, joined to the remembrance of the disagreeables of my intimacy with Manon, decided me. I accepted the offer, and the next day was with the legion on the road to Flanders. No doubt, in continuing to serve in this corps, where promotion was very rapid, I should have been made an officer, but my wound opened afresh, with such bad symptoms, that I determined to ask for leave again, which on obtaining, I was six days afterward once more at the gates of Arras.

CHAPTER II

ON ENTERING THE CITY, I WAS STRUCK WITH THE AIR of consternation which every countenance wore; some persons whom I questioned looked at me with contempt, and left me without making any reply. What extraordinary business was being transacted?

Penetrating the crowd, which was thronging in the dark and winding streets, I soon reached the fish market. Then the first object which struck my sight was the guillotine, raising its blood-red boards above the silent multitude. An old man, whom they had just tied to the fatal plank, was the victim; suddenly I heard the sound of trumpets. On a high place which overlooked the orchestra, was seated a man, still young, clad in a Carmagnole of black and blue stripes. This person, whose appearance announced monastic rather than military habits, was leaning carelessly on a cavalry sabre, the large hilt of which represented the Cap of Liberty; a row of pistols ornamented his girdle, and his hat, turned up in the Spanish fashion, was surmounted by a large tricolored cockade: I recognized Joseph Lebon.

At this moment his mean countenance was animated with a horrid smile; he paused from beating time with his left foot; the trumpets stopped; he made a signal, and the old man was placed under the blade. A sort of clerk, half drunk, then appeared at the side of the 'Avenger of the People,' and read with a hoarse voice a bulletin of the army of the Rhine and Moselle. At each paragraph the orchestra sounded a chord; and when the reading was concluded, the head of the wretched old man was stricken off amidst shouts of "Vive la Republique!" repeated by the satellites of the ferocious Lebon. I shall never forget, nor can I adequately depict the impression of this horrible sight. I reached my father's house almost as lifeless as the miserable being whose agony had been so cruelly prolonged; and then I learnt that he was M. de Mongon, the old commandant of the citadel, condemned as an aristocrat. A few days before, they had executed at the same place, M. de Vieux-Pont, whose only crime was that of having a parrot, in whose chatterings there were some sounds like the cry of "Vive le Roi!"

The parrot had escaped the fate of his master; and it was said that it had been pardoned at the entreaty of the citizeness Lebon, who had undertaken to convert it. The citizeness Lebon had been a nun of the abbey of Vivier: with this qualification added to many others, she was the fitting consort of the ex-curate of Neuville, and exercised a powerful influence over the members of the commission at Arras, in which were seated, as judges or jurymen, her brother-in-law and three uncles. The ex-nun was no less greedy of gold than blood. One evening at the theatre, she ventured to make this address to the crowded auditory:

"Ah, Sans Culottes, they say it is not for you that the guillotine is at work? What the devil, must we not denounce the enemies of the country? Do you know any noble, any rich person, any aristocratical shopkeeper? Denounce him and you shall have his money bags."

The atrocity of this monster was only equaled by that of her husband, who abandoned himself to the greatest excesses. Frequently after his orgies he was seen running through the city making bestial propositions to one young person, brandishing a sabre over another's head, and firing pistols in the ears of women and children.

An old woman, with a red cap and sleeves tucked up to the shoulders, carrying a long stick of hazel-wood, usually attended him in his walks, and they were frequently met arm-in-arm together. This woman, called mother Duchesne, in allusion to the famous father Duchesne, figured as the Goddess of Liberty in several democratic solemnities. She regularly assisted at the sittings of the commissions, for which she prepared the arrests by her speeches and denunciations. She thus brought to the guillotine all the inhabitants of one street, which was left entirely desolate.

I have often asked myself how, in the midst of such deplorable scenes, the taste for pleasure and amusement lost none of its relish. The fact is, that Arras continued to offer to me the same dissipations as ever; the ladies were as accessible; and I was easily convinced of that, as in a very few days I rose gradually in my amours from the young and pretty Constance, only child of corporal Latulipe, canteen-keeper of the citadel, to the four daughters of the notary, who had an office at the corner of the Rue des Capucines.

Lucky should I have been had I confined myself to that, but I began to pay my homage to a beauty of the Rue de la Justice; and one day I met my rival in my walks. He, who was the old musician of the regiment, was one of those men who, without boasting of the success which they have obtained, hint in plain terms that they have experienced refusals. I charged him with boasting in this way, and he became enraged; I provoked him the more, and the more angry he grew: I had forgotten my own cause of anger with him, when I remembered that I had good grounds of offense. I demanded an explanation, which was useless; and he only consented to meet me after I had inflicted on him the most degrading humiliation. The rendezvous was fixed for the next morning. I was punctual; but scarcely had I arrived when I was surrounded by a troop of gendarmes and police officers, who demanded my sword and ordered me to follow them. I obeyed, and was soon enclosed within the walls of the Baudets, whose use had been changed since the terrorists had put the population of Arras in a state of periodical decapitation.

The jailer, Beaupre, covered with an enormous red cap, and followed by two large black dogs, who never quitted him, conducted me to a vast garret, where he held in his keeping the principal inhabitants of the country.

There, deprived of all communications from without, they scarcely received nourishment, and not even that until it had literally been overhauled by Beaupre, who carried his precaution so far as to plunge his filthy dirty hands in the broth, to assure himself that there were no arms or keys. If anybody complained, he said to him, "Umph! you are very difficult to please for the time you have left to live. How do you know that it will not be your turn tomorrow? Oh, by the way, what is your name?"

"So and so."

"Ah! By my faith it is your turn tomorrow!" And the predictions of Beaupre were the less likely to fail as he himself pointed out the individuals to Joseph Lebon, who, after his dinner, consulted him, saying, "Whom shall we bathe tomorrow?"

Amongst the gentry shut up with us, was the Count de Bethune. One morning they sent for him to the tribunal. Before leading him out to the forecourt, Beaupre said to him abruptly, "Citizen Bethune, since you are going down there, am not I to have all you leave behind you?"

"Certainly, M. Beaupre," answered the old man tranquilly.

"There are no ministers now," said the grinning wretch of a jailer, "we are all citizens;" and at the gate he again cried out to him, "Adieu, citizen Bethune!"

M. de Bethune was however acquitted. He was brought back to prison as a suspected person. His return rejoiced us all; we thought him saved, but the next day he was again called up. Joseph Lebon, during whose absence the sentence of acquittal had been passed, arrived from the country: furious at being deprived of the blood of so worthy a man, he had ordered the members of the commission to assemble immediately, and M. de Bethune, condemned at the next sitting, was executed by torchlight.

This event, which Beaupre announced to us with ferocious joy, gave me serious uneasiness; every day they condemned to death men who were ignorant even of the cause of their arrest, and whose fortune or situation in society never intended them for political commotion; and on the other hand I knew that Beaupre, very scrupulous as to the number, thought not of the quality; and that frequently, not seeing immediately the number of individuals pointed out, sent the first who came to hand, that the service of the state might suffer nothing from delay. Every moment then might place me in the clutch of Beaupre, and you may believe that this idea was not the most satisfactory in the world.

I had been already detained sixteen days, when a visit from Joseph Lebon was announced; his wife accompanied him, and he had in his train the principal terrorists of the country, amongst whom, I recognized my father's old barber, and an emptier of wells, called Delmotte, or Lantilette. I asked them to say a word for me to the representative, which they promised; and I augured the better of it as they were both in good estimation.

However, Joseph Lebon went through the rooms, questioning the prisoners in a brutal manner, and pretending to address them with frightful harshness. When he came to me, he stared at me, and said in a tone half severe and half jesting, "Ah ha! Is it you, Francois? What, you an aristocrat? You who speak ill of the Sans Culottes and regret your old Bourbon regiment? Take care, for I can send you to be cooked (guillotined). But send your mother to me."

I told him, that being so strictly immured (au secret) I could not see her. "Beaupre," said he to the jailer, "let Vidocq's mother come in;" and went away, leaving me full of hope, as he had evidently treated me with marked amenity.

Two hours afterward I saw my mother, who told me, what I knew not before, that the musician whom I had challenged had denounced me. The denunciation was in the hands of a furious Jacobin, the terrorist Chevalier, who out of friendship to my rival, would certainly have been much against me, if his sister, at the persuasion of my mother, had not prevailed on him to exert himself to procure my discharge. Having left prison, I was conducted with great state to the patriotic society, where they made me take the oath of fidelity to the republic and hatred to tyrants. I swore all they desired. What sacrifices will not a man make to procure his freedom!

These formalities concluded, I was replaced in the depot, where my comrades testified much pleasure at seeing me again. After what had passed, I should have been deficient in gratitude had I not looked on Chevalier as my deliverer; I went to thank him, and expressed to his sister how much I was touched at the interest which she had so kindly testified to a poor prisoner. This lady, who was the most amorous of brunettes, but whose large black eyes did not compensate for their ugliness, thought that I was in love because I was polite; she construed literally some compliments which I paid her and from the first interview she so greatly misinterpreted my sentiments as to cast her regards upon me. Our union was talked of, and my parents were questioned on the point, who answered that eighteen was too young for marriage, and so the matter went on.

Meanwhile, battalions were formed at Arras, and being known as an excellent driller, I was summoned, with seven other subaltern officers, to instruct the 2nd Battalion of Pas-de-Calais, to which belonged a corporal of grenadiers of the regiment of Languedoc, named Caesar, now garde champetre at Colombre or Pateux, near Paris. Afterward, I was promoted to the rank of sublieutenant on arriving at St. Sylvestre-Capelle, near Bailleul, where we quartered. Caesar had been fencing-master in his own regiment, and my prowess with the advanced guard of Kinski's cuirassiers was well known. We resolved to teach the practice as well as the theory of fencing to the officers of the battalion, who were much pleased at such an arrangement.

Our lessons produced us some money, but not enough for our wants, or if you please, the desire of men of our abilities. It was particularly in good living that we were found wanting. What increased our regrets and appetites was, that the mayor with whom we lodged, kept an excellent table. We sought in vain the means of increasing our supplies; an old domineering servant, named Sixca, always defeated our intentions, and disturbed our gastronomic plans. We were disheartened and starving.

At length, Caesar found out the secret of breaking the charm which kept us from the table of the municipal functionary. At his suggestion, the drummajor came one morning to beat the morning call under the mayor's windows. Judge of the disturbance. It may be surmised that the old Maegara did not fail to request an intervention in putting a stop to this uproar. Caesar promised, with a mild air, to use all his influence to put a stop to the noise, and then ran to beg the drum-major to renew the cause of complaint; and the next morning there was a row sufficient to awaken the dead from the adjacent churchyard; and at length, not to do things by halves, he sent the drum-major to practice with his boys at the back of the house; a pupil of the Abbey Sicard could not have endured it. The old woman came to us, and invited the cunning Caesar and me very graciously; but that was not enough. The drummers continued their concert, which only concluded when their respectable chief was admitted, as well as ourselves, to the municipal banquet. From that time, no more drums were heard at St. Sylvestre-Capelle, except when detachments were passing by, and everybody was at peace except myself, whom the old woman began to threaten with her obliging favors. This unfortunate passion brought on a scene which must still be remembered in that part of the country, where it made much noise at the time.

It was the village feast: dancing, singing, drinking went on; and I bore my part so ably that they were compelled to lead me to bed. The next day I awoke before daybreak; as after all similar orgies, I had a giddy head, my mouth parched, and my stomach disordered; I wanted something to drink; and on rising I felt a hand as cold as a well-rope encircling my neck; my head was still wandering and weak from the overnight's debauch, and I shrieked out lustily.

The mayor, who slept in an adjoining chamber, ran with his brother and an old servant, both armed with cudgels. Caesar had not returned, and reflection had convinced me that the nocturnal visitor could only be Sixca; and pretending to be greatly alarmed, I told them that some hobgoblin had come to my side, and had glided out at the foot of the bed. They then laid on several blows with their sticks; and Sixca, perceiving that she would soon be killed, cried out, "Gentlemen, do not strike, it is I—it is Sixca. I walked in my sleep to the officer's bed." At the same time, she showed her head, and did well; for although they recognized her voice, yet the superstitious Flemings were about to renew the application of the bastinado. This affair made much noise throughout the place. It spread even to Cassel, and procured me many intrigues. I had, amongst others, one with a pretty barmaid, whom I should not allude to if she had not taught me, that at the counter of some coffee-houses a good-looking fellow may get change for cash which he has not paid.

We had been quartered for three months when the division was ordered to Stinward. The Austrians had given tokens of an intention to proceed to Poperingue, and the second battalion of the Pas-de-Calais was placed in the first rank. The night after our arrival the enemy surprised our outposts, and penetrated to the village of Belle, which we occupied, and we formed in battle array in the greatest haste. In this nocturnal maneuver our young recruits evinced that intelligence and alacrity which are only to be found in Frenchmen.

About six o'clock in the morning, a squadron of Wurmser hussars debouched on our left, and charged us without being able to break through our ranks. A column of infantry which followed them, attacked us at the same time with the bayonet; and it was only after a brisk encounter that our inferiority of numbers compelled us to fall back upon Stinward, our headquarters.

On arriving there, I received the congratulations of General Tandomme, and a billet for the hospital of St. Omer, for I had had two sabre cuts in fighting with an Austrian hussar, who was killed whilst crying, *"Ergib dich! Ergib dich!* (Surrender, surrender)."

My wounds were not very severe, since at the end of two months I was enabled to rejoin the battalion which was at Hazebrouck. I then saw the strange corps called the Revolutionary Army.

The men with pikes and red caps, who composed it, took with them everywhere the guillotine. The convention had not, they said, found any better way of securing the fidelity of the officers of the fourteen armies which it had on foot, than by placing before their eyes the instrument of punishment reserved for traitors. All that I can say is, that this mournful sight almost killed with fear the inhabitants of the country through which it passed. It did not much flatter the military, and we had many quarrels with the Sans Culottes, who were called 'The Bodyguard of the Guillotine.' I beat one of the party, who took upon himself to censure my gold epaulettes, when the regulation only ordered those of worsted. My fine array would have brought misfortune on me, and I should have paid dearly for my disregard of the sumptuary law, if I had not been allowed to start for Cassal, where I was joined by my battalion, which was then arrayed like the other regiments. These officers became plain soldiers, and it was in that capacity that I was directed to enter the 28th Battalion of Volunteers, which formed part of the army destined to drive the Austrians from Valenciennes and Conde.

Shortly afterward, the battalion was quartered at Fresnes. In the farmhouse in which I was billeted, there arrived one day the whole family of a pilot, consisting of the husband, wife, and two children, one of whom was a girl of eighteen, who was remarkably handsome. The Austrians had taken the boat, laden with grain, which was their whole fortune; and these poor people, reduced to the garments which covered them, had in resource left but to take refuge with my host, their relation. This circumstance, their pitiable condition, and the beauty of the young girl Delphine, touched my heart.

During a foraging party, I discovered their boat, which the enemy were only gradually unlading and measuring out, I proposed to a dozen of my comrades to carry off the spoils from the Austrians. They acceded to the proposition; our colonel gave his consent; and on a stormy night, we approached the vessel without being observed by the officers in charge, whom we dispatched, to feed the fish of the Escaut, with five strokes of the bayonet. The wife of the pilot, who would follow us, instantly ran for a bag of florins, which she had concealed in the grain, and gave them to my charge. We then loosened the boat, to let it float to a point where we had an entrenched post, but at the moment it got into the stream, we were surprised by the challenge of a guard, whom we had not observed amongst the bulrushes, which concealed him. At the report of his gun which accompanied his second call to us, the next piquet flew to arms, and in a moment the bank was covered with soldiers who fired a shower of balls at the boat, which we were compelled to quit. My comrades and I cast ourselves on a sort of raft which we had, and the woman did the same; but the pilot, forgotten in the confusion, or stopping with a hope of escape, was taken by the Austrians, who were not sparing of their blows and kicks. This experiment had besides lost us three men, and I had two fingers broken by a musket-ball. Delphine loaded me with caresses.

Her mother having set out for Ghent, where she knew her husband had been sent as a prisoner of war, we betook ourselves to Lille. I there passed my time of convalescence. As Delphine had a portion of the money found in the grain, we led a very pleasant life. We talked of marriage, and the affair was so far arranged that I started one morning for Arras, whence I was to return with the license and my parents' consent. Delphine had already procured that of her parents, who were still at Ghent. A league from Lille, I remembered that I had forgotten my hospital billet, which it was indispensably necessary to produce before the municipality of Arras, and I returned for it. Arrived at the hotel, I went to the room we occupied and knocked; no one answered. It was impossible that Delphine could be out so early, it being scarcely six o'clock. I knocked again, and Delphine opened the door, stretching her arms and rubbing her eyes like someone who has been suddenly awakened. To prove her, I proposed that she should go with me to Arras, that I might present her to my parents; and she very tranquilly agreed. My suspicions were disappearing, and yet something whispered to me that she was deceiving me. I at length perceived that she frequently glanced toward the wardrobe. I pretended a desire to open it, which my chaste betrothed opposed, and gave me one of those excuses which a woman always has ready.

But I was determined; and at length opened the closet, where I found concealed, beneath a heap of dirty linen, the doctor who had attended me during my convalescence. He was old, ugly, and misshapen. The first feeling was the humiliation of having such a rival: and yet I should have been more enraged at finding a good-looking fellow, but this I leave for the decision of the numerous lovers who have been similarly circumstanced. As for me, I wished to begin by knocking out the brains of the intriguing Esculapius, but (which seldom happened to me) reflection restrained me. We were in a town of war, where they might play me some trick about my leave of absence. Besides Delphine was not my wife; I had no right over her, I determined on kicking her out; after which, I threw her from the window her clothes, and money enough to take her to Ghent. I allowed myself to retain the remainder of the money, which I thought I had lawfully acquired, since I had directed the splendid expedition which had rescued it from the clutches of the Austrians. I forgot to say that I allowed the doctor to return unmolested.

Having got rid of my faithless she, I determined on remaining at Lille until the time of my furlough should expire; but it is as easy to conceal oneself in this city as at Paris, and my residence would have been undisturbed but for an affair of gallantry of which I shall spare the details. It will suffice to say, that being arrested in female attire, at the moment I was flying from the rage of a jealous husband, I was taken to the police office, where I at first obstinately refused to give an account of myself; for in fact, by speaking, I should either destroy the female who had been kind to me, or announce myself as a deserter. Some hours' confinement changed my resolution; a superior officer, to whom I had appealed to receive my declaration, and to whom I candidly stated the facts, seemed to take some interest for me. The commandant-general of the division wished to hear from my own lips this recital, which made him laugh to excess. He then gave orders that I should be set at liberty; and caused a line forthwith to be given to me to rejoin the 28th Battalion at Brabant: but instead of following this destination, I went to Arras, determined only to enter the service again at the last extremity.

My first visit was to the patriot Chevalier. His influence with Joseph Lebon made me hope that I should obtain through his interest an extension of leave, which he procured for me, and I was again introduced to the family of my benefactor. His sister, whose kind intentions toward me are already known, redoubled her kindness; and on the other hand, the habit of seeing her daily familiarized me with her ugliness.

In short, matters came to such a point that I was not at all surprised one day to hear that she was pregnant. She made no mention of marriage, not even pronouncing the word; but I saw too clearly that to this complexion it must come at last, lest I should incur the vengeance of her brother, who would not have hesitated to denounce me as an aristocrat, and moreover a deserter. My parents, struck with all these considerations, and conceiving the hope of keeping me near them, gave their consent to the marriage, which the Chevalier family were very anxious about. It was at last settled, and I became a husband at eighteen years of age. I thought myself also almost the father of a family; but scarcely had a few days elapsed, when my wife confessed that her pretended pregnancy was the result of a plan to induce me to marry her. The excessive satisfaction which such an avowal gave me may be conceived; but the same motives which had decided me on contracting the alliance, compelled me to be silent; and I determined to keep my own counsel, enraged as I was. A mercer's shop, which my wife had opened, turned out very badly. I thought that I found the cause of it in the repeated absence of my wife, who was all day at her brother's. I made my observations, and received orders to rejoin my regiment at Tournay. I might have complained of this expeditious mode of getting rid of a troublesome husband, but I was so much tired of the joke of Chevalier, that I resumed with joy my uniform, which I had cast off with so much pleasure.

At Tournay, a veteran officer of the Bourbon regiment, then adjutant-general, attached me to his office as a deputy, and particularly in the serving out of clothing. Business soon demanded that a man of trust should be dispatched to Arras. I set out at once, and arrived in the city at eleven o'clock at night. As I was charged with orders, the gates were opened to me, and by an impulse, for which I cannot account, I was induced to run to my wife's abode. I knocked for a long time and no one answered. A neighbor, at length, opened the door, and I ran upstairs with all speed to my wife's chamber. On approaching, I heard the clank of a falling sabre, then a window opened, and a man leaped out into the street. It is, needless to say, that they recognized my voice. I went downstairs with great haste, and soon overtook my Lovelace, in whom I recognized an adjutant-major of the 11th Horse Chasseurs, quartered at Arras. He was half-naked. I led him back to my conjugal domicile, when he finished his toilette, and we then separated, on agreeing to fight the next day.

This scene had roused the whole neighborhood. The greater part of the people, assembled at their windows, had seen me seize on the guilty adjutant, who had been found guilty of the fact in their presence. I had no lack of witnesses to prove and obtain the divorce, and that was what I intended to do; but the family of my chaste wife, who were desirous of keeping a protector for her, exerted themselves to check my measures, or at least to paralyze them. The next day, before I could meet the adjutant-major, I was arrested by the police, who spoke of placing me in the Baudets. Fortunately for me, I plucked up courage, as I saw that there was nothing discouraging in my situation. I demanded to be carried before Judge Lebon, which could not be denied me. I appeared before the representative of the people, whom I found surrounded by an enormous pile of letters and papers.

"What, is it you," said he to me, "who come here without permission; and for maltreating your wife, too?"

I saw what course I should pursue. I produced my orders. I called for the testimony of my neighbors against my wife, and that of the adjutant-major himself, who could not gainsay the facts. Indeed, I so clearly explained the affair, that Joseph Lebon was forced to confess that the wrongs were not of my committing; but out of regard, however, to his friend Chevalier, he made me promise not to remain long at Arras; and as I feared the wind might veer against me, as I had seen it with many others, I undertook to comply with his request as promptly as possible. Having completed my mission, I bade farewell to all my friends, and the next morning found me on the road to Tournay.

Chapter III

I DID NOT FIND THE ADJUTANT-GENERAL AT TOURNAY; he had set out for Brussels, and I set out on the following day by the diligence to join him there. At the first glance, I recognized amongst the travelers those Individuals whom I had known at Lille, as passing the whole day at the public-houses, and living in a very suspicious manner. To my great astonishment, I found them clothed in uniforms of different regiments, one having the epaulettes of lieutenant-colonel, the others those of captain or lieutenant. How can they have got them, thought I, for they have never seen service.

I was lost in conjecture. On their side, they appeared at first much confused at the rencontre; but soon recovering, they testified a mutual surprise at finding me only a plain soldier. When I had explained to them how the regulation of the battalion had deprived me of my rank, the lieutenant-colonel promised me his protection, which I accepted, although scarcely knowing what to think of my protector. I saw clearly, however, that he had plenty of money, and paid for all at the table d'hôte, where he testified a violent republican feeling, at the same time affecting to have sprung from an ancient family.

I was not more fortunate at Brussels than at Tournay; the adjutant-general, who seemed to fly from me, had gone to Liege, for which place I set out, relying on not taking a useless journey this time; but on arriving, I learnt that my man had taken the road to Paris on the previous evening, having been summoned to appear at the bar of the Convention. His absence would not be longer than a fortnight. I waited, but no one arrived. Another month passed, and still no adjutant. My cash was sensibly diminishing, and I resolved on returning to Brussels, where I hoped to find some means of extricating myself from my embarrassment. To speak with that candor on which I pique myself in giving this history of my life, I must confess that I had begun not to be over-scrupulous in my choice of these means; my education had not made me a very precise man in such matters, and the injurious society of a garrison, which I had been used to from my childhood, had corrupted a naturally honorable mind.

It was then, without doing much violence, to my delicacy, that I saw myself installed, at Brussels, with a gay lady of my acquaintance, who, after having been patronized by General Van-de-Nott, had fallen a little lower into public society. Idle, as are all who have but a precarious mode of existence, I passed whole days and nights at the Café Turc, or the Café de la Monnaie, the rendezvous of knights of the post, and professed gamblers.

These fellows spent liberally, and played the devil's games; and as they had no ostensible means of living, I could not divine how they managed to carry on the war. A young fellow with whom I had associated myself, and whom I questioned on this subject, appeared struck at my inexperience, and I had the greatest difficulty in persuading him that I was really a novice.

"The men whom you see there every day, and all day," said he, "are sharpers; those who only come once, and do not appear again, are dupes, who lose their money."

Thus instructed, I made many remarks, which till then had escaped me; I saw tricks of sleight of hand almost incredible; and what proved that there was still something good within me, I was often tempted to tell the pigeon whom they plucked. What happened to me will prove that my intentions were guessed.

A party was one evening engaged at the Café Turc; the dupe (le gonse) lost fifty louis, and demanding his revenge on the next day, went away. Scarcely had he gone out, when the winner, whom I now see daily in the streets of Paris, approached me, and said with an air of simplicity, "On my word, sir, we have played with luck, and you were right to bet on me; I have won ten games, which, at four crowns a game, will make your share ten louis—here they are." I told him that he was mistaken, and that I had not interested myself in his play; he made me no answer, but put the ten louis in my hand.

"Take it," said the young man who had initiated me into these mysteries, and who was sitting next to me, "take it and follow me."

I obeyed mechanically, and when we reached the street, my mentor added, "They have discovered that you watch the games, and fear lest you should blow the concern; and as there are no means of intimidating you, because they know that you have a strong arm and a mischievous hand, they have resolved on giving you a slice of the cake, so you have a good means of existence before you, the two coffee-houses will be milch cows to you, whence you may draw your four or six crowns a day."

In spite of the accommodating propensity of my conscience, I was desirous of replying and making some observations.

"You are a child," said my honorable friend; "we do not talk of robbery here—it is fortune only; and believe me, matters pass in the drawing-room as they do at the tavern—there they bubble, that is the word; and the merchant, who in the morning whilst at his desk would think it a crime to rob you of an hour's interest, would very quietly cheat you at the gaming-table in the evening."

How could I answer such unanswerable arguments? I had nothing to reply but to keep the money, which I did.

These small dividends, joined to a remittance of a hundred crowns from my mother, enabled me to dash a little, and to show my gratitude to Emily, whose devotion to me I was not insensible of. Matters were in this agreeable train when I was one evening arrested at the Theatre du Parc, by several police officers, and ordered to produce my papers. This would have been a dangerous exhibition, and I said that I had none. They conducted me to the Madelonettes; and the next morning, at my examination, I found that I was unknown, and they had mistaken me for another person. I said that my name was Rousseau, born at Lille, and added, that I had come to Brussels on pleasure, and had not thought it expedient to provide myself with papers. I then asked to be conducted to Lille, at my own expense, by two gendarmes, which was granted, and for a few crowns my escort agreed that poor Emily should accompany me.

Having left Brussels, I was so far safe; but it was still more important that I should not reach Lille, where I should be certainly recognized as a deserter. Escape must be made at all risks, and this was Emily's opinion when I communicated my intention to her, and we executed our preconcerted plan on reaching Tournay. I told the gendarmes that before they left me at Lille the next day, where I should be at once set at liberty, I wished to treat them with a good supper. Already taken with my liberality and mirth, they accepted the invitation with much willingness, and in the evening, whilst they were sleeping on the table, stupefied with rum and beer, thinking me in the same condition, I descended by the sheets from the second-floor window.

Emily followed, and we struck into the crossroads, where they would not think of pursuing us. We thus reached the suburbs of Notre-Dame at Lille, when I dressed myself in the cloak of the horse-chasseurs, taking the precaution to put a black patch on my left eye, which made it impossible to recognize me. But I did not judge it prudent to remain long in a city so near my birthplace, and we started for Ghent. There, by a rather romantic incident, Emily found her father, which determined her to return to her family. It is true that she would not consent to part from me, but with an express stipulation that I should rejoin her as soon as matters which I said called me to Brussels, should be arranged.

My business at Brussels was to begin again to levy rates on the Café Turc and the Café de la Monnaie. But to present myself at this city, I wanted papers which should prove that I was really Rousseau, born at Lille, as I had said at my examination before I made my escape. A captain of Belgian carabineers in the French service, named Labbre, undertook for fifteen louis to supply me with the necessary credentials. At the end of three weeks he brought me a copy of my register of birth, a passport, and a certificate of half-pay in the name of Rousseau, all done better than I ever saw them executed by any other forger. Thus protected, I went to Brussels; the commandant of the place, an old comrade of Labbre's, undertook to make all right.

Quieted in this particular, I hastened to the Café Turc. The first persons whom I saw in the room were the pretended officers with whom I had traveled They received me with acclamation; and judging from the recital of my adventures that my situation was not over splendid, proposed that I should take the rank of sub-lieutenant of horse chasseurs, doubtless because they saw the cloak I wore. So advantageous a promotion was not to be refused; and it was then conferred on me: and when I said Rousseau was only an assumed name, the worthy lieutenant-colonel told me to take any one which I preferred. It was impossible to be more obliging. I resolved on keeping the name of Rousseau, on which they gave me, not a brevet, but a line of route for a sub-lieutenant of the 6th Chasseurs, traveling with his horse, and being entitled to lodgings and rations.

I thus found myself incorporated with the roving army (armée roulante) composed of officers without brevet, and without troops, and who, furnished with false certificates and false lines of march, imposed the more easily on the commissaries at war, as there was less method at this period in the military arrangements. It is certain that, during a tour which we made through the Netherlands, we got all our allowances without the least demur. Yet the roving army was not then composed of less than two thousand adventurers, who lived like fishes in water. What is still more curious is, that they promoted themselves as rapidly as circumstances would allow: an advancement was the more profitable, as an increase of rank meant an increase of allowances.

I passed in this manner to be captain of hussars; one of my comrades became chief of a battalion; but what most astonished me was, the promotion of Auffray, our lieutenant-colonel, to the rank of brigadier-general. It is true, that if the importance of the rank and the notoriety of a promotion of this kind rendered it more difficult to keep up the deception, yet the very audacity of such a step bade defiance to suspicion.

Returned to Brussels, we showed our billets, and I was sent to a rich widow, the Baroness d'I____.

I was received in the manner in which all Frenchmen were welcomed at Brussels at this period, that is, with open arms. A very handsome bedchamber was placed at my sole disposal, and my hostess, delighted at my reserved conduct, assured me in the most gracious manner, that if her hours suited me, a place at her table would always be prepared for me. It was impossible to resist such pressing politeness, and I was profuse in my thanks, and I took my seat at her board the same day with three other guests, who were ladies, older than the baroness, who was about fifty. They were all charmed with the prepossessing manners of the captain of hussars.

At Paris I should have felt somewhat awkward in such society, but I did very well at Brussels for a young man whose premature introduction to the world had necessarily injured his education. The baroness doubtlessly made some such reflections, for she paid me such little attention as gave me much food for thought.

As I was sometimes absent to dine with the general, whose invitations I told her it was impossible to refuse, she desired me to present him and my other friends to her. At first, I was not overly desirous of introducing my associates to the society of this lady, who saw much company, and might have guests at her home who might guess our little speculations. But the baroness insisted on it, and I consented, at the same time stipulating that the general should only meet a small party, as he was desirous of keeping up a sort of incognito. He came; and the baroness, who received him with marked attention, seated him near her, and talked to him for so long a time in an undertone that I was rather piqued. To disturb this tête-à-tête, I imagined that it would be a good plan to ask the general to sing us something, and accompany himself on the piano. I knew that he could not make out a note, but I relied that the usual persuasions which guests make on such occasions would at least occupy his attention for some minutes. My stratagem only half succeeded; the lieutenant-colonel, who was of the party, seeing that the general was so much pressed, kindly offered himself as a substitute, and accordingly seated himself at the piano, and sung some little ditties with sufficient taste to procure him universal approbation, whilst I all the time wished him at the devil.

At last this interminable evening concluded, and each person withdrew, I raging with anger and plotting revenge against the rival who I imagined was about to carry off from me, I will not say the love, but the kind attentions of the baroness. Full of this idea, I went to my general at his rising, who was much surprised to see me so early. "Do you know," said he, without giving me time to break in upon his conversation, "do you know, my friend, that the baroness is..."

"Who spoke of the baroness?" interrupted I, abruptly, "it is no matter what she is or what she is not."

"So much the worse," he replied; "if you are not speaking of her, I have nothing to understand." And, continuing thus to puzzle me for some time, he ended by telling me that his conversation with the baroness was concerning me only, and that he had so far pushed my interest, that he believed that she was quite disposed to—to marry me.

I at first thought that my poor comrade's head was turned. That one of the richest women of rank in the United Provinces would marry an adventurer, of whose family, fortune, and ancestors she knew nothing, was an idea that would have staggered the most credulous. Ought I, moreover, to engage in a deceit which must be discovered, sooner or later, and must ruin me? Besides, was I not really and actually married at Arras? These objections, and many others, which the remorse I must experience at deceiving the excellent woman who had treated me so kindly, excited in my mind, did not for an instant stop my comrade, who thus answered them:

"All you say is very fine, and I am quite of your opinion; and to follow my natural bias for virtuous behavior, I only want £10,000 a year. But I see no reason for being scrupulous in your case. What does the baroness want? A husband, and a husband to her liking. Are you not that husband? Are you not determined to pay her every attention, and to treat her as a person who is necessary to you, and of whom you have had no cause to complain? You talk of the inequality of your fortunes,—the baroness thinks not of that. You only want, to complete the matter, one single thing—a title of rank, which I will give you,—yes, I will give it to you! Why do you stare so? Listen, and do not interrupt me. You must be acquainted with some young nobleman of your own age and country; you are he, and your parents have emigrated and are now at Hamburg. You entered France to endeavor to recover a third of the value of your paternal property, and to carry off the plate, and a thousand double-louis concealed beneath the flooring of the drawing-room at the breaking out of the revolution: the presence of some strangers, the haste of departure, which an arrest issued against your father would not allow you to delay, has prevented you from getting this treasure. Arrived in this country, disguised as a journeyman tanner, you were denounced by the very person who had pledged himself to aid your enterprise; outlawed by the sentence of the republican authorities, you were nearly losing your head on the scaffold, when I fell in with you, half dead from inquietude and necessity. An old friend of the family, I procured for you the brevet of an officer of hussars, under the name of Rousseau, until an opportunity should offer of rejoining your noble parents at Hamburg. The baroness already knows all this; yes all, except your name, which, for appearances' sake, I did not tell her; but in fact, because I did not know what appellation you might choose to assume. That is a confidence which I left for yourself to communicate.

"Thus the affair is quite settled, and you are a gentleman, nothing can be said against that. Say nothing to me of your jade of a wife; you were divorced at Arras under the name of Vidocq, and you are married at Brussels under the name of Count B___. Now listen to me. So far, our business has gone on well, but that may be entirely marred at any moment. We have already met with some very inquisitive commissaries, and we may find others still less civil, who may cut off our supplies and send us to the fleet at Toulon. You understand me, I know. The best that can happen to you will be to take up your knapsack and accoutrements in your old regiment, or else be shot as a deserter; but by marrying, you acquire the means of a splendid life, and will be enabled to assist your friends. Since we have come to the point, let us understand each other; your wife has a hundred thousand florins a year; there are three of us, and you shall give us each a pension of a thousand crowns, payable in advance, and I shall expect besides a premium of thirty thousand francs for having mad; a count of a baker's son."

I was quite stupefied; but this harangue, in which the general had so skillfully stated all the difficulties of my situation, overcame all my opposition, which, to say the truth, was not very obstinate. I agreed to everything, and then returned to the baroness. The Countess de B___ fell at her feet: and the scene was so well played, and, though it may be scarcely be said, I entered so completely into the spirit of my part that I even for a moment surprised myself— which I am told sometimes happens to impostors. The baroness was charmed at the allies and sentiments with which my situation inspired me. The general was rejoiced with my success, as was every other person. Several expressions escaped me which savored a little of the canteen, but the general had told the baroness that political events had caused my education to be strangely neglected, and this explanation was satisfactory to her.

Subsequently, Marshal Suchet was no less easily satisfied, when Coignard addressing him as "M. le Duque d'Albufera," excused himself by the plea, that having emigrated when very young, he could consequently have but a very imperfect knowledge of the French language.

We sat down to table and dined in high spirits. After the dessert the baroness whispered me thus, "I know, my dear sir, that your fortune is in the hands of the Jacobins, and your parents at Hamburg may be in some difficulty, oblige me by remitting to them a bill for three thousand florins, which my banker will send you tomorrow morning." I was about to express my thanks, when she rose from table and went into the drawing-room. I took the opportunity of telling the general what had just occurred.

"Well, simpleton," said he, "do you think you are telling me any news? Was it not I who hinted to the baroness that your parents must be in want of money? We are at this moment your parents. Our funds are low; and to run any risk in procuring more, would be to hazard too foolishly the success of this adventure; I will undertake to negotiate the bill. At the same tIme I suggested to the baroness that a supply of cash was needed for you to make some figure before your marriage, and it is understood that from now until the consummation of the marriage you shall have five hundred florins a month."

I found the next day this sum on my dressing-table, where also was placed a handsome dressing-case and some trinkets.

Yet the register of my birth, as Count de B___, whose name I had assumed, and which the general wished to procure, thinking that the other credentials might be forged, did not arrive; but the baroness, whose blindness must appear inconceivable, to those who are not in a situation to know to what extent credulity can go, and the audacity of some rogues, consented to marry me under the name of ROUSSEAU.

I had all the necessary papers to justify my claim to that. Nothing was wanting but my father's consent; that was easily procured through the instrumentality of Labbre, whom we had under our thumb; but although the baroness had consented to marrying me under a name which she knew was not my own, yet she felt some repugnance at being as it were an accomplice in a falsehood, for which the only excuse was, that it saved my head from the block.

Whilst we were planning means for avoiding this, we learnt the number of the *armée roulante* had become so considerable, that the eyes of government were opened, and that the most severe orders had been issued to check the abuse. We divested ourselves of uniforms, believing that we should have nothing to fear, but the inquiries were so active that the general was compelled to set out suddenly for Namur, where he thought he should be less liable to detection. I explained his abrupt departure to the baroness, by attributing it to the general's having been in fear of a reprimand for having procured me a commission under an assumed name. This circumstance made her very uneasy for me, and I could only calm her fears by setting out for Breda, to which place she would accompany me.

I am not very well calculated to play the sentimental, and it would compromise the tact and finesse, for which I have some credit, if I made a parade and fuss, but I just may be believed when I say so much attachment affected me. The whispers of remorse, to which we cannot be always deaf at nineteen, were heard; I saw the abyss into which I was leading an admirable woman who had been so generous toward me; I pictured her as driving from her with horror the deserter, the vagabond, the bigamist, the forger; and this idea determined me to tell her all. Away from those who had drawn me into this imposture, and who had just been arrested at Nainur, I decided on the measures I would adopt;

and one evening, after supper, I determined on breaking the ice. Without detailing my adventures, I told the baroness, that circumstances which I could not explain compelled me to appear at Brussels under the two names by which she knew me, but that neither was the real one. I added, that events forced me to quit the Netherlands without the power of contracting a union which would have ensured my happiness, but that I should forever preserve the recollection of the kindness which she had so generously evinced for me.

I spoke long, and with an emotion which increased my utterance and warmth of manner—and I am now astonished at the facility of my own eloquence when I think of it—but I feared to hear the reply of the baroness. Motionless, pale, and with a glazing eye, she heard me without interruption; then looking at me with a glance of horror, she rose abruptly and ran and shut herself up in her room. I never saw her again.

Enlightened by my confession, and by some words which without doubt fell from me in the embarrassment of the moment, she saw all the dangers from which she had escaped, and unjustly suspected me perhaps of being more culpable than I was; she might think that she had escaped from some vile criminal, whose hands might have been imbued in blood! On the other hand, if this complication of disguises might render her more apprehensive, the spontaneous avowal that I had made was sufficient to have quelled her fears; and this idea probably took hold of her, for the next day when I arose, the landlord gave me a casket, containing fifteen thousand francs in gold, which the baroness had left for me before her departure, at one o'clock in the morning, which I was glad to hear of, as her presence would have troubled me. Nothing now detaining me at Breda, I packed my trunks, and some hours afterward set out, for Amsterdam.

I have already said, and now repeat, that certain portions of this adventure may appear unnatural, and some may call them altogether false, but nothing is more true. The initials I have given will suffice to explain it to any person who knew Brussels thirty years ago. Besides, there is nothing uncommon in the affair, nothing more than is read of in the commonest romance. If I have entered into minute details, it is not to ensure a melodramatic effect, but with the intention of putting too credulous persons on their guard against a species of deception more frequently employed, and with more success than may be generally thought, in all classes of society; and such is the aim of these Memoirs. Let them be reflected on in every particular, and who knows but some fine morning the duties of attorney-general, judge, gendarme, and agent of police, may be discovered to have become sinecures.

My stay at Amsterdam was very short. Having converted into cash two bills of those left me by the baroness, I set out, and on the 2nd of March, made my entrance into the capital, where at a future day my name was destined to make some noise. I put up at the Hotel du Gaillard-Bois in Rue de l'Echeile, and first employed myself in changing my ducats into French money, and in selling a quantity of small jewelry and trinkets, now superfluous to me, as I resolved on establishing myself in some village in the environs, and entering into some business; but this project was not to be realized. One evening, one of those persons who are always to be found in hotels seeking acquaintance with travelers, proposed to present me at a house where there was a party. I unfortunately consented, confiding in my experience of the Café Turc and the Café de la Monnaie; but I soon found the gamblers that of Brussels were but bunglers in comparison with these gentlemen, of whose society I now formed one. Now the games of chance are better managed and more equal; but at this time, the police tolerating those places, called *étouffoirs*, they were not contented with slipping a card or managing the suits as they liked—sometimes at M. Lafittes, Messrs. de S, Jan., and A. de la Rock's—the knowing ones had conventional signs so combined that they must succeed. Two sittings cleared me of a hundred louis; I had enough to spare still but it was decreed that the money of the baroness should soon leave my company. The destined agent of its dissipation was a very pretty woman, whom I met at a table d'hôte which I sometimes frequented. Rosine, for that was her name, at first showed an exemplary disinterestedness. A month afterwards I was her acknowledged lover, without having spent anything but for dinners, theatres, coach-hire, gowns, ribands, flowers, all which things *cost nothing* at Paris, when we do not pay for them.

More and more enamored of Rosine, I never left her. One morning, whilst at breakfast, I found her thoughtful. I pressed her with inquiries, which she resisted, and finished by avowing to me that she was troubled about a little trifle due to her milliner and upholsterer. I offered my services instantly, which were refused with remarkable magnanimity, and I could not even learn the names of her two creditors. Many very excellent people would have left the matter here; but, like a true knight, I had not a moment's rest until Divine, the waiting-maid, had given me the desired addresses.

From the Rue Vivienne, where Rosine lived, who was called Madame de Saint Michel, I ran to the upholsterer, in the Rue de Clery. I told him the purpose of my visit, and he immediately overwhelmed me with politeness, as is usually the case under such circumstances. He handed me the bill, which, to my consternation, amounted to twelve hundred francs! But I was too far gone to recede now. At the milliner's, the same scene took place, with an additional hundred francs. It was sufficient to have intimidated the boldest; and yet matters had not reached their climax. Some days after I had paid the creditors, they brought me jewels to purchase, to the amount of two thousand francs; and other similar expenses perpetually occurred. I saw my money fly away in this way; but, fearing that it would not be so easily replenished, I parted with it less freely from day to day.

However, I went on, and found that at the end of two months I had spent the moderate sum of fourteen thousand francs. This discovery made me serious, and Rosine immediately perceived it. She guessed that my finances were getting low. Women have great tact in this respect, and are but rarely deceived; and without being exactly cold toward me, she yet showed a kind of reserve, and on my manifesting astonishment, she answered me with singular abruptness, "that private matters put her out of temper." That was a trick; but I had been too deeply a sufferer already by my interference in these private matters to proffer again to arrange them, and I advised her with an air of coolness to have patience. She became only more contemptuous, passed some days in pouting, and then the storm burst.

At the conclusion of some trifling discussion, she said with a very flippant tone, "that she did not choose to be crossed; and that those who could not put up with her ways had better remain at home." That was plain speaking; but I was weak enough to appear not to understand her. New presents brought back a temporary renewal of kindness, which, however, could no longer impose upon me. Then knowing all that she could get from my blind infatuation, Rosine soon returned to the charge for cash for a letter of credit for two thousand francs, which she had to pay or else go to prison. Rosine in prison! The idea was insupportable, and I was about to discharge the debt at once, when chance placed in my way a letter which opened my eyes.

It was from the platonic friend of Rosine, who was staying at Versailles, and this interesting personage asked "when the pigeon would be quite plucked," that he might make his appearance. I intercepted this agreeable missive in the hands of Rosine's porter. I went to the perfidious woman, but she was absent; and, enraged and humiliated at the same time, I could not restrain myself. I was in the bedroom, and at one kick I overthrew a stand covered with china, and a cheval glass was shivered to atoms. Divine, the waiting-maid, who had followed me, went down on her knees and begged me to pause from what would cost me so dear. I looked at her and hesitated, and a remnant of common sense induced me to think that she was right. I questioned her, and the poor girl, who had always been gentle and attentive, told me all about her mistress. It is the more in place to mention her statement, as the same things occur daily at Paris.

When Rosine met me she had not had anybody for two months; and thinking me fair game, from the extravagant way I spent my money, conceived the plan of profiting by it; and her lover, whose letter I had intercepted, had consented, and went to Versailles to stay until my money should be exhausted. It was in the name of this lover that the proceedings had been carried on for the bill of exchange which I had formerly taken up; and the debts of the milliner and upholsterer were equally false.

Although cursing my egregious folly, I was yet astonished not to see the honorable lady, who had so well tricked me, return. Divine told me that most probably the porter had told her that I had got the letter, and that she would not very speedily appear. This conjecture was well founded. On learning the catastrophe which had prevented her from plucking the last feather from my wing, Rosine had set out in a hackney-coach for Versailles to rejoin her friend. The finery, which she left in her furnished apartments, was not sufficient to pay for the two months' lodging due to the landlord, who, when I was going out, compelled me to pay for the china and cheval glass which I had broken in my first transports of anger.

Such violent inroads had dreadfully reduced my finances. Fourteen hundred francs alone remained of the ducats of the baroness! I left the capital with horror, as it had been so unpropitious to me, and resolved to regain Lille, where, knowing the localities, I might at least find resources which I should in vain seek for at Paris.

CHAPTER IV

LILLE, AS A FORTIFIED AND FRONTIER TOWN, offered great advantages to all who, like myself, were likely to find there useful acquaintances, either amongst the military of the garrison, or that class of persons who, with one foot in France and the other in Belgium, have really no home in either; and I relied a little on this for recovering myself, and my hope was not groundless. In the 13th chasseurs I met several officers of the south, and amongst the rest a lieutenant named Villedien, whom we shall presently hear more of. All these persons had only known me in the regiment under one of those noms de guerre, which it was the custom at this time to assume, and were therefore not astonished at seeing me bear the name of Rousseau. I spent the day with them at the café or fencing rooms, but this was not lucrative, and I actually began to be in want of money. At this juncture a visitor of the café, whom they called Rentier, from his regular life, and who had made me many compliments, of which he was very prodigal to all the world, inquired with some interest into my affairs, and asked me to travel with him.

To travel was all very well; but in what quality? I was no longer of an age to engage myself as Merry Andrew or valet-de-chambre of monkeys and bears, and nobody would doubtless make me such a proposition: but yet it was necessary to know in what capacity. I asked my new protector very modestly what duties I had to perform in his service. "I am an itinerant doctor," said this man, whose bushy eyebrows and sunburnt skin gave him a singular physiognomy; "I cure secret diseases with an infallible recipe. I cure animals, and lately restored the horses of a squadron of the 13th chasseurs, whom the veterinary surgeon had given over."

"Well," said I to myself, "once more a doctor." But there was no backing down now: we agreed to start next morning, and to meet at five a.m. at the gate leading to the Paris road.

I was punctual at the rendezvous, and my friend, who was equally punctual, seeing my trunk strapped at the back of a lad, said that it would be useless to take it, as we should be only three days away, and must go on foot. At this observation I sent my goods back to the inn, and we walked on at a brisk rate, having, as my guide said, to make five leagues before mid-day. About this time we reached a solitary farmhouse, where he was received with open arms and saluted by the name of Caron, which was strange to me who had always heard him called Christian.

After a few words, the master of the house went into his chamber and returned with two or three bags of crowns, which he spread on the table. My friend took them, and examining them singly with an attention which appeared to me affected, put aside one hundred and fifty, and counted out a like sum for the farmer in different money, with a premium of six crowns: I understood nothing of this operation, which was carried on in a Flemish dialect, of which I understood but very little. I was then much astonished when on leaving the farm, where Christian had said he would soon return, he gave me three crowns, saying that I ought to have a share of the profits. I could not learn what the profits were, and said so. "That is my secret," said he, with a mysterious air; "you shall know it at a future time, if I am satisfied with you." I told him that he might rely on my discretion since I knew nothing, only that he had changed crowns for another coin. He told me that this was the only point on which I ought to be silent, to avoid difficulties, and I therefore took the money without knowing what was to result from all this.

For four days we made similar excursions to various farms, and every evening I touched two or three crowns. Christian, whom they all called Caron, was well known in this part of Brabant, but only as a doctor; for, although he everywhere carried on his change of moneys, the conversation was always about healing man or beast. I found besides that he had a reputation for removing the charms cast on animals. A proposal which he made me as we entered the village of Wervique, initiated me into this species of magic—

"May I rely on you?" said he to me, stopping suddenly—

"Certainly," said I; "but for what and how?"

"Listen, and learn."

He took from a sort of game-bag four square packets made up like those of chemists, and apparently containing some specifics; he then said, "You see those four farms, situated at some distance from each other, you can enter them the back way, taking care that no one sees you; get into the stable, and throw into the manger the powder of one of these packets. Take great care that you are not discovered—I will take care of the rest."

I objected to this, as I might be surprised at the moment I was climbing the gate and they would seize me, and perhaps put some awkward questions. I refused point-blank, in spite of the perspective of the crowns, and all Christian's eloquence failed in persuading me. I even said that I would quit him at once, unless he would disclose to me his real condition and the mystery of his exchange of money, which seemed to me extremely suspicious. This declaration seemed to embarrass him, and, as we may learn, he endeavored to draw me off the scent, in making me a half confidant.

"My country?" said he, answering my latter question, "I have none. My mother, who was hanged last year at Temeswar, belonging to a gang of gypsies (Bohemian) who were traversing the frontiers of Hungary and Bannat, where I was born in a village on the Carpathian mountains. I say Bohemians that you may understand, for this is not our proper name, we call ourselves Roma-michels, in a language which we are forbidden to teach to any person; we are also forbidden to travel alone, and that is the reason why we are generally in troops of fifteen or twenty. We have had a long run through France, curing charms and spells of cattle, but this business is pretty well destroyed at present. The countryman has grown too cunning, and we have been driven into Flanders, where they are not so cunning, and the difference of money gives us a finer opportunity for the exercise of our industry. As for me, I have been at

Brussels on private business which I have just settled, and in three days I rejoin the troop at the fair of Malines. It is at your pleasure to accompany me: you may be useful to us. But we must have no more nonsense now!"

Half embarrassed as to where I should shelter my head, and half curious to see the termination of this adventure, I agreed to go with Christian, without at all understanding how I could be useful to him. The third day we reached Malines, whence he told me we should return to Brussels. Having traversed the city we stopped in the Faubourg de Louvain, before a wretched-looking house with blackened walls, furrowed with wide crevices, and many bundles of straw as substitutes for window-glass. It was midnight, and I had time to make my observations by the moonlight, for more than half an hour elapsed before the door was opened by one of the most hideous old hags I ever saw in my life.

We were then introduced to a long room, where thirty persons of both sexes were indiscriminately smoking and drinking, mingling in strange and licentious positions. Under their blue loose frocks, ornamented with red embroidery, the men wore blue velvet waistcoats with silver buttons, like the Andalusian muleteers; the clothing of the women was all of one bright color: there were some ferocious countenances amongst them, but yet they were all feasting. The monotonous sound of the drum, mingled with the howling of two dogs tied under the table, accompanied the strange songs, which I mistook for a funeral psalm. The smoke of tobacco and wood, which filled this den, scarcely allowed me to perceive in the midst of the room a woman who, adorned with a scarlet turban, was performing a wild dance with the most wanton postures.

On our entrance there was a pause in the festivity; the men came to shake hands with Christian and the women to embrace him, and then all eyes were turned on me, who felt much embarrassed at my present situation. I had been told a thousand strange stories of the Bohemians, which did not increase my comfortable feelings: they might take offense at any scruples I should make, and might get rid of me before it was even known where I had gone to, since no one could trace me to such a haunt.

My disquietude became sufficiently apparent to attract the attention of Christian, who thought to assure me by saying that we were at the house of the duchess, (a title which is equivalent to that of mother amongst such comrades) and that we were in perfect safety. My appetite decided me on taking my part at the banquet. The gin bottle was often filled and emptied, when I felt an inclination to go to bed. At the first word that I said Christian conducted me to a neighboring closet, where were already on clean straw several Bohemians. It did not suit me to be particular; but I could not prevent myself from asking my patron why he, who had always before selected such good quarters, had made choice of so bad a sleeping place? He told me that in all towns, where there was a house of the Romamichels, they were constrained to lodge, under pain of being considered as a false brother, and as such punished by a council of the tribe. Women and children all slept in this military bed; and the sleep which soon overtook them, proved that it was a familiar couch.

At break of day everybody was on foot, and the general toilet was made. But for their prominent features, without their raven-black tresses and that oily and tanned skin, I should scarcely have recognized my companions of the preceding evening. The men, clad in rich jockey holland vests, with leathern sashes like those worn by the inhabitants of Poissy, and the women covered with ornaments of gold and silver, assumed the costume of Zealand peasants; even the children, whom I had seen covered with rags, were neatly clothed, and had an entirely different appearance. All soon left the house and took different directions, that they might not reach the marketplace all together, where the country people were assembling in crowds. Christian, seeing that I was preparing to follow him, told me that he should not have need of me the whole day, and that I might go wherever I pleased until evening, when we were to meet at the house of the duchess. He then put some crowns in my hand and left me.

As in our conversation of the previous evening he had told me that I was not compelled to lodge with the troop, I began by ordering a bed at the inn. Then, not knowing how to kill time, I went to the fair, and had scarcely gone round it four or five times, when I met face to face, an old officer of the recruiting battalions, named Margaret, whom I had known as making one of the gambling set at the Café Turc at Brussels. After the first salutations, he asked me why I was staying at Malines. I told him a history, and he was equally communicative about his travels; and we were thus content, each thinking that he had imposed on the other. Having taken some refreshments we returned to the fair, and every part where there was a crowd I met some of the lodgers of the duchess. Having told my companion that I had no acquaintance at Malines, I turned my head that they might not recognize me, for I did not much care to confess that I had such friends; but I had too cunning a fox to deal with. "Look," said he to me, eyeing me full in the face, "look at those people who are regarding you so attentively. Pray, do you know them?" Without turning my head I replied that I had never seen them before, and did not even know who they were. "Who they are!" replied my companion, "I will tell you—supposing you to be ignorant—they are robbers!"— "Robbers!" I replied. "How do you know it?" "In the same way that you shall soon know if you will follow me, for it is a fair bet that we shall not have far to go without finding them at work. Come along—here they are."

Raising my eyes towards a crowd in front of a menagerie, I perceived one of the false jockeys taking the purse of a fat grazier, whom we saw the next moment seeking for it in his pocket: the Bohemian then entered a jeweler's shop, where were already two of the pretended Zealand peasants, and my companion assured me that he would not come out until he had pilfered some of the jewels that were shown to him. We then left our post of observation to go and dine together: and, at the end of the repast, seeing my companion disposed to talk, I pressed him to tell me precisely who the people were whom he had pointed out to me, assuring him that, in spite of appearances, I knew but very little of them. He complied, and told me as follows:

"It was in the prison (Rasphuys) of Ghent, where I passed six months, some years since, at the end of a game at which some doctors (loaded dice) were discovered, that I made acquaintance with two men of the troop now at Malines. We were in the same cell, and as I passed myself off for an accomplished thief, they told me, without distrust, all their light-fingered tricks: and even gave me the minutest details of their singular existence. These people come from the country about Moldavia, where a hundred and fifty thousand of them were, like the Jews in Poland, without the power of fulfilling any office but that of executioner. Their name changes with their change of country; they are Zigeuners in Germany, gypsies in England, zingari in Italy, gitanos in Spain, and Bohemians in France and Belgium. They thus traverse all Europe, exercising the lowest and most dangerous trades. They clip dogs, tell fortunes, mend crockery, repair saucepans, play wretched music at the public-house doors, speculate in rabbit-skins, and change foreign money which they find out of the usual circulation.

"They sell specifics against the illness of cattle, and to promote the business, they dispatch trusty envoys, who, under pretenses of making purchases, get into the stables, and throw drugs into the mangers, which make the cattle sick. They then present themselves, and are received with open arms, and knowing the nature of the malady, they easily remove it, and the farmer hardly knows how to be adequately grateful. This is not all; for before they quit the farm, they learn whether the husbandman has any crowns of such and such a year, or such and such a stamp, promising to give a premium for them. The interested countryman, like all persons who but seldom find an opportunity of getting money, spreads his coin before them, of which they invariably contrive to pilfer a portion. What is almost incredible is, that they are seen to repeat with impunity the same trick frequently at the same house. Indeed, what is most villainous of all in their transactions, is, that they profit by these circumstances, and their knowledge of the localities of the country, to point out to burglars the detached farms in which there is money, and the means of getting at it, and it is needless to add, that they come in for their share of the spoil."

Malgaret gave further details concerning the Bohemians, which determined me on quitting their dangerous society as speedily as possible.

He was speaking thus, looking into the streets from time to time from the window near which we were seated, when suddenly I heard him exclaim, "Oh, the devil! My friends of the Rasphuys at Ghent!"—I looked out, and saw Christian walking very fast, and with an air of busy import. I could scarcely help exclaiming aloud. Malgaret, profiting by the trouble into which his explanation had thrown me, had not much difficulty in extracting from me how I was associated with the Bohemians. Seeing me resolved on quitting their company, he proposed that I should accompany him to Coutrai, where, he said, he had some game in view. After having taken from the inn the few things I had brought from the house of the duchess I set out with my new associate, but we did not find at Coutrai the friends Malgaret had relied on meeting there, and it was our cash, and not theirs, that was spent. Despairing of their appearance, we returned to Lille; I had still one hundred francs left, and Malgaret gambled with them on our mutual account, and lost them, together with what he had of his own, and I afterward learnt that he had confederated with his antagonist to cheat me out of what I had left.

In this extremity, I had recourse to my abilities; and some fencing-masters, to whom I spoke of my situation, gave me a benefit at a fencing match, which produced me a hundred crowns. Set up with this sum, which for a time secured me from want, I frequented public places, balls, etc. I then formed an intimacy, of which the circumstances and consequences decided the destiny of my whole life. Nothing could be more simple than the commencement of this important episode of my history. I met at the Bal de la Montague with a young lady, with whom I was soon on good terms. Francine, for that was her name, appeared much attached to me, and at every moment made me protestations of fidelity, which did not, however, prevent her from giving private interviews to a captain of engineers.

I one day surprised them supping at a tavern in the place Riourt, and transported with rage, I heartily thumped the astonished pair. Francine, with her hair hanging loose, fled; but her partner remained, and making a charge against me, I was arrested and conducted to prison of Petit Hotel. Whilst my trial was preparing, I was visited by many females of my acquaintance, who made it a duty to offer me their consolations. Francine learnt this, and her jealousy aroused, she dismissed the unfortunate captain, withdrew the charge against me which she had made at the same time with his, and beseeching me to receive her, I weakly consented. The judges heard of this fact, which was tortured into a premeditated plan between me and Francine, and I was sentenced to three months' imprisonment. From the Petit Hotel I was transferred to St. Peter's Tower, where I obtained a chamber called the Bull's-eye. Francine remained with me there for a part of the day, and the remainder I passed with the other prisoners, amongst whom were two old sergeant-majors, Grouard and Herbeaux, the latter son of a bootmaker at Lille, both condemned for forgeries; and a laborer, named Boitel, condemned for six years' confinement for stealing garden tools; this latter, who was the father of a large family, was always bewailing his imprisonment, which, he said, deprived him of the means of working a small farm, which he only knew how to turn to advantage. In spite of the crime he had committed, much interest was evinced in his favor, or rather toward his children, and many inhabitants of his district had drawn up and presented petitions in his favor, which were as yet unanswered, and the unfortunate man was in despair, often repeating that he would give such and such a sum for his liberty. Grouard and Herbaux, who were in St. Peter's Tower, waiting to be sent to the gallies, thought they could get him pardoned by means of a memorial, which they drew up, or rather plotted together; a plan which was ultimately injurious to me.

Grouard began to complain that he could not work quietly in the midst of the uproar of the common room, in which were eighteen prisoners singing, swearing, and quarreling all day, Boitel, who had done me some little kind offices, begged me to lend my chamber to the compilers of his memorial, and I consented, although very unwillingly, to give it up to them for four hours a day. From the next morning they were there installed, and the jailer frequently went there secretly. These comings and goings, and the mystery which pervaded them, would have awakened suspicions in a man accustomed to the intrigues of a prison, but ignorant of their plans, and occupied in drinking with the friends who visited me, I interested myself but too little with what was going on in the Bull's-eye.

At the end of eight days, they thanked me for my kindness, telling me that the memorial was concluded, and that they had every reason to hope for the pardon of the petitioner, without sending it to Paris, from the influence of the representations of the people at Lille. All this was not very clear to me, but I did not give it much attention, thinking it no business of mine; and there was no occasion for me to concern myself. But it took a turn which threw blame on my carelessness, for scarcely had forty-eight hours elapsed after the finishing of the memorial, when two brothers of Boitel arrived by express, and came to dine with him at the jailer's table. At the end of the repast, an order arrived, which being opened by the jailer, he cried, "Good news, by my faith! It is an order for the liberation of Boitel!" At these words, they all arose in confusion, embraced him, examined the order, and congratulated him; and Boitel, who had sent away his clothes, etc. the previous evening, immediately left the prison without bidding adieu to any of the prisoners.

Next day, about ten o'clock in the morning, the inspector of the prisons came to visit us; and on the jailers showing him the order for Boitel's liberation, he cast his eye over it, said that it was a forgery, and that he should not allow the prisoner to depart until he had referred to the authorities. The jailer then said that Boitel had left on the previous evening. The inspector testified his astonishment that he should have been deceived by an order signed by persons whose names were unknown to him, and at last placed him under a guard. He then took the order away with him, and soon made himself certain that, independently of the forgery of the signatures, there were omissions and errors in form which must have struck any person at all familiar with such papers.

It was soon known in the prison, that the inspector had placed the jailer under arrest, for having allowed Boitel to go out under a false order, and I began to surmise the truth. I desired Grouard and Herbaux to tell me the whole, observing indistinctly, that the affair might compromise me; but they swore most solemnly that they had done nothing but draw up the memorial, and were themselves astonished at its prompt success. I did not believe a word of this, but having no opposing proofs, I was compelled to wait for the event. The next day I was summoned to the court, before the judge, and answered, that I knew nothing of the framing of the forged order, and that I had only lent my room, as the only quiet place in the prison, for the preparation of the justificatory memorial. I added, that all these facts could be corroborated by the jailer who frequently went into the room during their work, appearing to be much interested for Boitel. Grouard and Herbaux were also interrogated, and then placed in solitary confinement, whilst I returned to my chamber. Scarcely had I entered it, when Boitel's bedfellow came to me, and told me the whole plot, which I had only before suspected.

Grouard, hearing Boitel so often repeat that he would willingly give a hundred crowns to procure his liberty, had planned with Herbaux the means of getting him out, and they had devised no mode so simple as that of forging a false order. Boitel was let into the plot, as may be supposed. They only told him that, as there were many persons to gain over, he must give four hundred francs. It was then that they applied for my chamber, which was indispensable for the due concoction and forging of the order, without being perceived by the other prisoners. Moreover, the jailer was in their confidence, to judge by his frequent visits, and by the circumstances which had preceded and followed the departure of Boitel. The order had been brought by a friend of Herbaux, named Stofflet. He appeared besides only to decide Boitel on giving four hundred francs, which the forger had persuaded him was to be shared with me, although I rendered him no other service than that of lending my room.

Thus instructed, I at first wished the person who had given me these particulars to make a declaration of them, but he obstinately refused, saying that he would not reveal to justice a secret confided to his oath; and besides, he did not feel desirous of being knocked on the head by the prisoners for turning nose, -- *pour avoir mange le morceau.* He dissuaded me even from informing the judge, telling me that I was in no danger.

But on arresting Boitel in the country, and bringing him to Lille, and putting him into solitary confinement, he named as the aiders and abettors of his escape, Grouard, Herbaux, Stofflet and Vidocq. On this confession, we were questioned at the tower, and I persisted in my first declaration, although I could have extricated myself in a moment by disclosing all that Boitel's bedfellow had told me; but I was so fully convinced that it was impossible to substantiate any charge against me, that I was thunderstruck when, at the expiration of my three months, I was prevented from quitting the prison by an entry stating me as arraigned as an "accomplice in the forgery of authentic and public documents."

CHAPTER V

I THEN BEGAN TO THINK THAT THIS AFFAIR MIGHT TURN out badly for me; but any other statement, without proof, would be more dangerous to me than silence, which it was now too late to think of breaking. All these reflections affected me so much that I had a severe illness, during which time Francine attended me most carefully. I was scarcely convalescent, when, unable to support the state of incertitude in which I found my affairs, I resolved on escaping, and to escape by the door, although that may appear a difficult step. Some particular observations made me prefer this method in preference to any other. The wicket-keeper at St. Peter's Tower was a galley slave from the Bagne (place of confinement) at Brest, sentenced for life.

After the revision of the penal laws and the code of 1791, he had obtained a commutation of six years' confinement in the prison at Lille, where he had made himself useful to the jailer, who, persuaded that a man who had passed four years at the Bagne must be as watchful as an eagle, since he must know every method of escape, promoted him to the office of gatekeeper, which he thought he could not confide to more trustworthy hands. It was, however, on the stupidity of this prodigy of cunning that I relied for the success of my project; and it appeared the more easy to deceive him, as he was so confident in his own sagacity. In a word, I relied on passing by him in the disguise of a superior officer, charged with visiting St. Peter's Tower, which was used as a military prison, twice a week.

Francine, whom I saw daily, got me the requisite clothing, which she brought me in her muff. I immediately tried them on, and they suited me exactly. Some of the prisoners who saw me thus attired, assured me that it was impossible to detect me. I was the same height as the officer whose character I was about to assume, and I made myself appear twenty-five years of age. At the end of a few days he made his usual round, and whilst one of my friends occupied his attention, under pretext of examining his food, I disguised myself hastily, and presented myself at the door, which the jail keeper, taking off his cap, opened, and I went out into the street. I ran to a friend of Francine's, as agreed on in case I should succeed, and she soon joined me there.

I was there perfectly safe, if I could resolve on keeping concealed; but how could I submit to a slavery almost as severe as that of St. Peter's Tower. As for three months I had been enclosed within four walls, I was now desirous to exercise the activity so long repressed. I announced my intention of going out; and, as with me an inflexible determination was always the auxiliary of the most capricious fancy, I did go. My first excursion was safely performed, but the next morning, as I was coming to the Rue Ecremoise, a serjeant named Louis, who had seen me during my imprisonment, stopped me, and asked if I was free. He was a severe, practical man, and by a motion of his hand could summon twenty persons. I said that I would follow him; and begging him to allow me to bid adieu to my mistress, who was in a house of Rue de l'Hospital, he consented, and we really met Francine, who was much surprised to see me in such company; and then I told her that having reflected that my escape might injure me in the estimation of my judges, I had decided on returning to St. Peter's Tower to await the result of the process.

Francine did not at first comprehend why I had expended three hundred francs, to return at the end of four months to prison. A sign put her on her guard, and I found an opportunity of desiring her to put some cinders in my pocket whilst Louis and I took a glass of rum, and then set out for the prison. Having reached a deserted street, I blinded my guide with a handful of cinders, and regained my asylum with all speed.

Louis having made his declaration; the gendarmes and police officers were on the full cry after me; and there was one Jacquard amongst them who undertook to secure me if I were in the city. I was not unacquainted with these particulars, and instead of being more circumspect in my behavior, I affected a ridiculous bravado. It might have been said that I ought to have had a portion of the premium promised for my apprehension. I was certainly hotly pursued, as may be judged from the following incident.

Jacquard learned one day that I was going to dine in Rue Notre Dame. He immediately went with four assistants, whom he left on the ground floor, and ascended the staircase to the room where I was about to sit down to table with two females. A recruiting serjeant, who was to have made the fourth, had not yet arrived. I recognized Jacquard, who, never having seen me, had not the same advantage, and besides my disguise would have bid defiance to any description of my person. Without being at all uneasy, I approached, and with the most natural tone I begged him to pass into a closet, the glass door of which looked on the banquet room.

"It is Vidocq whom you are looking for," said I; "if you will wait for ten minutes you will see him. There is his cover, he cannot be long. When he enters, I will make you a sign; but if you are alone, I doubt if you can seize him, as he is armed and resolved to defend himself."

"I have my gendarmes on the staircase," answered he, "and if he escapes ..."

"Take care how you place them then," said I, with affected haste. "If Vidocq should see them he would mistrust some plot, and then farewell to the bird."

"But where shall I place them?"

"Oh, why in this closet—mind, no noise, that would spoil all; and I have more desire than yourself that he should not suspect anything." My commissary was now shut up in four walls with his agents. The door, which was very strong, closed with a double lock. Then, certain of time to escape, I cried to my prisoners, "You are looking for Vidocq—well, it is he who has caged you; farewell." And away I went like a dart, leaving the party shouting for help, and making desperate efforts to escape from the unlucky closet.

Two escapes of the same sort I put in motion, but I was soon arrested and carried back to St. Peter's Tower, where, for greater security, I was placed in a dungeon with a man named Calendrin, who was also thus punished for two attempts at escape. Calendrin, who had known me during my first confinement in the prison, imparted to me a fresh plan of escape, which he had devised by means of a hole worked in the wall of the dungeon of the galley slaves, with whom we could communicate. The third night all was managed for our escape, and eight of the prisoners who first went out were so fortunate as to avoid being detected by the sentinel, who was only a short distance off.

Seven of us still remained, and we drew straws, as is usual in such circumstances, to determine which of the seven should first pass. I drew the short straw, and undressed myself that I might get with greater ease through the hole, which was very narrow, but, to the great disappointment of all, I stuck fast, without the possibility of advancing or receding. In vain did my companions endeavor to pull me out by force; I was caught as if in a trap, and the pain of my situation was so extreme, that not expecting further help from within, I called to the sentry to render me assistance. He approached with the precaution of a man who fears a surprise, and presenting his bayonet to my breast, forbade me to make the slightest movement. At his summons the guard came out, the porters ran with torches, and I was dragged from my hole, not without leaving behind me a portion of my skin and flesh. Torn and wounded as I was, they immediately transferred me to the prison of Petit Hotel, where I was put into a dungeon, fettered hand and foot.

Ten days afterward I was placed among the prisoners, through my entreaties and promises not to attempt again to escape. Up to this time I had lived with men who were sharpers, robbers, and forgers; but here I found myself in the midst of most hardened villains, and of this number was one of my fellow townsmen, named Desfosseux, a man of wonderful ingenuity, prodigious strength, and who, condemned to the galleys from the age of eighteen, had escaped from the Bagne three times, whence he was to be sent again with the next chain of convicts. He told all his exploits and hairbreadth escapes with much coolness, and said that no doubt "one day or other the guillotine would make sausage meat of his flesh." In spite of the secret horror with which this man inspired me, I took a pleasure in conversing with him of the wild life he had led, and what most induced me to make so many inquiries of him was, that I hoped he would be able to aid me with some means of escape. With the same motive I associated with many individuals imprisoned as part of a band of forty or fifty Chauffeurs, who infested the adjacent districts, under the command of the famous Sallambier. They were named Chopiue (called the Nantzman), Louis (of Douay), Duhamel (called Lilleman), Auguste Poissard (called the Provencal), Caron, the younger, Caron the Humpback, and Bruxellois (called the Daring), an appellation which he deserved for an act of courage which is seldom heard of even in bulletins.

At the moment of entering a farm with six of his comrades he thrust his left hand through an opening in the shutter to lift the latch, but when he was drawing it back, he found that his wrist had been caught in a slip-knot. Awakened by the noise, the inhabitants of the farm had laid this snare, although too weak to go out against a band of robbers which report had magnified as to numbers. But the attempt being thus defeated, day was fast approaching, and Bruxellois saw his dismayed comrades looking at each other with doubt, when the idea occurred to him that to avoid discovery they would knock out his brains. With his right hand he drew out his clasp-knife with a sharp point, which he always had about him, and cutting off his wrist at the joint, fled with his comrades without being stopped by the excessive pain of this horrid wound. This remarkable deed, which has been attributed to a thousand different spots, really occurred in the vicinity of Lille, and is well authenticated in the northern districts, where many persons yet remember to have seen the hero of this tale, who was thence called Manchot (or one-armed), executed.

Introduced by so distinguished a worthy as my townsman Desfosseux, I was received with open arms in the circle of bandits, where from morning to night the means of escape was our only theme. Under these circumstances, as in many others, I remarked that with prisoners, the thirst for liberty, becoming the engrossing idea, produced plots inconceivable by the man who discusses them at his ease. Liberty! In this word all is centered, this thought pursues the prisoner throughout the tedious day, and during the wintry nights spent in utter darkness, when abandoned to all the tormenting impulses of impatience. Enter any prison you will hear shouts of noisy mirth, and you may almost imagine yourself at a place of entertainment; approach—mouths grin horribly a ghastly smile, but the eyes betray no pleasure, they are stern and haggard; this assumed gayety is forced in its hideous yells, like that of the jackal, which dashes against its cage, striving to burst the bars.

Well knowing what men they had to guard, our jailers watched us with a care that marred all our plans; the only opportunity which gave a chance of success now offered itself, and I seized on it before my companions, cunning as they were, had even thought of it. We were about eighteen of us in the ante-room of the examining judge, where we had been conducted for the purpose of being interrogated, which was guarded by soldiers, and two gendarmes, one of whom had laid down his hat and cloak near me, whilst he went to the bar, whither his companion was summoned by the ring of a bell. I put his hat on my head instantly, and wrapping myself in his cloak, took a prisoner under my arm as if I was taking him out for a pressing necessity; I went to the door, which the corporal of the guard immediately opened, and we got out once more. But what could we do without money or papers? My comrade went into the province, and I, at the risk of being retaken, returned to Francine, who, overjoyed at seeing me, determined on selling her furniture, and flying with me to Belgium. This was determined on, when a most unexpected event, attributable only to my incredible carelessness, completely overthrew our plan.

The night before our intended departure, I met in the dusk of the evening a woman of Brussels, named Eliza, with whom I had been on intimate terms. She embraced me, and begged me to go and sup with her, and, conquering my weak objections, kept me with her until the next day. I persuaded Francine, who had sought me everywhere, that, pursued by police officers, I had been compelled to take refuge in a house which I could not quit till daybreak. She was at first satisfied; but having by accident discovered that I had passed the night with a female, her jealousy burst forth in overwhelming and tearful reproaches against my ingratitude, and in her rage she swore that she would have me arrested. To put me in prison was certainly the best mode of putting a stop to my infidelities; but Francine was a woman of her word, and I deemed it prudent to allow her anger to evaporate, intending to return after some time, and start with her as we had agreed on. However, as I needed my clothes, and did not like to ask for them, for fear of a fresh burst of temper, I went alone to our chamber, of which she had the key, and forcing a shutter, I took out what I wanted, and left the house.

At the end of five days, clothed like a countryman, I left the place I had inhabited in the suburbs, and going into the city, I went to the house of a seamstress, a friend of Francine's, on whose mediation I relied for reconciling us. This woman seemed so greatly embarrassed, that fearing I should implicate her, I only begged her to go and seek my mistress. "Yes," said she, with a very remarkable air, and without looking at, me. She went out, and I was left alone to reflect on my' strange reception.

A knock at the door was heard, which I hastened to open, thinking that I should receive Francine in my arms, when a crowd of gendarmes and police officers appeared, who seizing me I was carried before the magistrate, who began by asking me where I had been during the last five days. My answer was brief, as I never implicated those who sheltered me. The magistrate observed, that my obstinacy in refusing him any explanation would go much against me, and that my head was in jeopardy, etc., I only laughed, as imagining this remark to be a trap to force me to confess through fear. I persisted in my silence, and was remanded to the Petit Hotel.

Scarcely had I set foot in the street, when all eyes were fixed on me. People called to each other and whispered, which I thought was caused by my disguise, and I scarcely heeded it. They made me enter a cell, where I was left alone in the straw, heavily ironed. At the end of two hours the jailer came, who, pretending to pity me, and take an interest in me, told me that my resolution not to confess where I had spent the last five days, would injure me in the estimation of the judges; but I was immovable, and two more hours elapsed, when the jailer returned with a turnkey, who took off my fetters, and desired me to go down to the office, where two judges were in attendance. I was again questioned, and made a similar reply, and they then stripped my clothes entirely off, and stamped on my right shoulder a blow that would have killed an ox, which was to mark me; my clothes were taken away, after being described in the procés-verbal and I was sent back to my cell, covered with a shirt of sailcloth, in a surtout half black and half grey, in rags which had served at least two generations of prisoners.

All this gave me food for reflection. It was evident that the seamstress had denounced me, but for what? She had no complaint to make of me. In spite of her fury, Francine would have reflected twice before she denounced me; and if I had withdrawn for some days, it was rather because I did not wish to irritate her by my presence, than from any fear of consequences. Why these reiterated inquiries, these mysterious words of the jailer, and this description of my attire? I was lost in a labyrinth of conjecture, and for twenty-five hours I was kept in the strictest solitary confinement; I then underwent an examination which informed me of all.

"What is your name?"

"Eugene Francois Vidocq."

"What is your profession?"

"Military."

"Do you know the girl Francine Longuet?"

"Yes; she is my mistress."

"Do you know where she is at this moment?"

"She should be at a friend's house, for she sold her own furniture."

"What is the name of this friend?"

"Madame Bourgeois."

"Where does she live?"

"At a baker's in the Rue St. Andre."

"How long had you left the woman Longuet when you were arrested?"

"Five days."

"Why did you leave her?"

"To avoid her anger; she knew that I had passed the night with another female, and in a fit of jealousy threatened to have me arrested.

"Who was the woman with whom you passed the night?"

"A former mistress."

"What is her name?"

"Eliza—I only know her by that name."

"Where does she live?"

"At Brussels, whither, I believe, she has returned."

"Where are the things which you had in the house of the woman."

"In a place that I can point out if need be."

"How could you get them, having quarreled with her, and not wishing to see her?"

"After our quarrel in the Café, where she found me, she threatened to call for the guard to seize me: knowing her perverseness, I ran down the bystreets, and reached the house before her, which I had hoped to do, and wanting some clothes, I forced a shutter to affect my entrance, and then took out what I wanted. You just now asked me where these things are, and I will now tell you; they at the house of Duboc who will corroborate, this."

"You do not speak true—before you left Francine at her house, you had a great quarrel; it is said that you struck her."

"That is false; I did not see Francine at her own home after the quarrel, and consequently I could not have maltreated her. She can corroborate this."

"Do you know this knife?"

"Yes; it is the one I generally use at my meals."

"You see the blade and shaft are covered with blood. Does not the sight of it make any impression upon you? You are agitated!"

"Yes," I replied with emotion; "but what has happened to France? Tell me, and I will give every possible explanation."

"Did nothing particular happen to you when you carried off your clothes?"

"Nothing that I can call to mind."

"You persist in your declarations?"

"Yes."

"You are imposing on justice; that you may have time for reflection on your position, and the consequences of your obstinacy, I shall now delay the remainder of your examination until tomorrow. Gendarmes, watch this man most carefully. Go!"

It was late when I returned to my cell, where they brought me my allowance, which the trouble I experienced from the result of the interrogatory would not allow me to eat; I could not sleep, and passed the whole night without closing an eye. Some crime had been committed, but on whom? By whom? Why was I inculpated? I had asked myself that question a thousand times, without getting at any rational solution, when they came to fetch me on the following morning to renew my examination. After the usual question, a door was opened, and two gendarmes entered, supporting a female. It was Francine—Francine pale, and altered so as to be scarcely recognizable. On seeing me she fainted; and when I wished to approach her, I was withheld by the gendarmes. They took her away, and I alone remained with the examining judge, who asked me if the sight of the unfortunate woman did not prompt me to confess all? I protested my innocence, asserting that I did not know till that instant that Francine was ill. I was led back to the prison, but not to solitary confinement, and I could then hope that I might be informed of all the events of which I was so singularly the victim. I questioned the jailer, but he would not answer me; I wrote to Francine, although I was told that the letters would be detained by the judge, and that she was dismissed. I was on thorns, and had just determined on sending for counsel, who, after having learnt the accusation, told me that I was charged with attempting to assassinate Francine. On the very day I left her, she had been found expiring, stabbed with a knife in five places, and bathed in blood. My precipitate flight—the secret carrying away of my clothes, which it was known that I had taken from one place to another as if to elude the search of justice—the broken shutter in my room—the footmark which resembled mine,—all tended to confirm the suspicions of my guilt, and my disguise still more corroborated it.

It was thought that I only disguised myself and returned, to learn whether she had died without accusing me. One particular, which would have been in my favor under any other circumstances, now aggravated the charge against me; as soon as the physicians would allow Francine to speak, she declared that she had stabbed herself, in despair, at finding that she was abandoned by a man for whom she had sacrificed all. But her attachment to me rendered her testimony suspected, and it was believed that she only spoke thus to save me.

My counsel had terminated this narrative at least a quarter of an hour, and I was still listening like a man oppressed with the nightmare. At the age of twenty I was suffering under the weight of the twofold accusation of forgery and assassination, without having even dreamt of committing such crimes. I even reflected whether I would not hang myself at the bars of my cell with a straw rope. I was losing my senses, but at last collected myself sufficiently to detail all the facts requisite for my exculpation. In the post-examination, they insisted strongly on the blood which the porter, who had carried my luggage, stated he had seen on my hands. This blood had flowed from a cut inflicted by the glass of a window which I had broken to remove the shutter, and I could produce two witnesses of this fact. My counsel, to whom I told all my grounds of defense, assured me, that united with the testimony of Francine, which alone had been of no avail, I should be acquitted, which was the case a few days afterward. Francine, although still very weak, came immediately to see me, and confirmed all the particulars which the examination had first acquainted me with.

I was thus relieved of an enormous weight, without being yet entirely freed from uneasiness. My repeated escapes had delayed the decision of the accusation of forgery, in which I had been implicated, and nothing indicated its termination, for Grouard had also escaped. The result of the charge from which I had just been freed, had, however, given me a hope, and I thought nothing of attempting to escape, when an opportunity presented, which I seized, as it were, by instinct. In the chamber in which I was placed were the temporary prisoners, and on fetching away two of them one morning, the jailer forgot to close the door, which I perceived, and descending to the ground floor, found, on looking about me, that I had a chance. It was scarcely daybreak, and the prisoners were all asleep. I had met no one on the staircase, and there was no one at the gate, which I cleared; but the jailer, who was drinking a dram at a public-house opposite the prison, pursued me, crying loudly, "Stop him! Stop him!" He cried in vain, for the streets were empty, and the desire of liberty gave me wings. In a few minutes, I got out of sight of the jailer, and soon reached a house in Rue Saint Sauveur, where I was very certain they would not come to seek for me. I was now compelled to quit Lille as quickly as possible, as I was too well known there to be safe for long.

At nightfall all were on the lookout, and I learned that all the gates were closed, and no one was let out but through the wicket, where police officers and disguised gendarmes were stationed to examine all comers. The gates thus closed on me, I resolved on descending the ramparts, and knowing the spot well, I went at ten o'clock at night to the bastion of Notre Dame, which I judged the most propitious place for the execution of my project. Having tied to a tree a cord, which I had procured for the purpose, I began to slide down; but the weight of my body impelling me more rapidly than I anticipated, the friction of the cord made my hands so hot that I was compelled to let go about fifteen feet from the ground, and fell so heavily on my right foot that I sprained it, and in endeavoring to get out of the ditch I thought I should never be able to affect it. Unheard of efforts at length extricated me, but on reaching the plain I could move no further.

There I was, swearing most emphatically against all ditches, ropes and sprains; but this did not relieve my embarrassment, when a man passed me with one of those cars so common in Flanders. A crown-piece, my only one, prevailed on him to place me on his car, and convey me to the next village. On reaching his house he laid me on a bed, and rubbed my foot with brandy and soap, whilst his wife assisted him very efficiently, although staring with wonder at my clothes, stained with the mud of the ditch.

They did not ask for any explanation, but I thought it expedient to give one; and to prepare myself for it, I pretended that I was greatly in want of sleep, and my host left me. At the end of two hours I called them, like a man just waking, and told them in a few words that, in conveying smuggled tobacco up the ramparts, I had fallen, and my comrades, pursued by the customs officers, had been compelled to leave me in the ditch; and I added, that I left myself in their hands to do as they pleased with me. These good creatures, who hated the customs officers as cordially as the inhabitant of any frontier town ever does, assured me that they would not for the world betray me. To try them, I asked if there was no means of conveyance to my father's house, who lived at the other side, and they said that such a step would expose me, and that it would be better to wait a few days until I was well. I consented; and to remove all suspicions, it was agreed that I should pass for a relative on a visit. No one, however, made the least observation.

Quieted on this head, I began to reflect on my next step, and what I must do. I determined on leaving these parts and going into Holland. But to execute this plan money was indispensable, and except my watch, which I had offered to my host, I possessed only four shillings and ten pence. I might go to Francine, but then, of course, she was closely watched; and to send her any message, would infallibly hazard her safety. At least, I must wait until the heat of the first pursuit was over. I did wait, and at the end of a, fortnight I determined to write to Francine, which I entrusted to my host, telling him that, as this female was the go-between of the smugglers, he must use much caution in visiting her. He fulfilled his commission with much care, and brought me next day one hundred and twenty francs in gold. The next day I bade farewell to my friends, whose charges were extremely moderate, and at the end of six days reached Osterid.

My intention, as at my first visit to this city, was to go to America or India, but I only met with Danish and Dutch skippers, who refused to take me without credentials. The little cash which I had brought from Lille diminished rapidly, and I was approaching that situation with which we become more or less familiarized, but which is not less disagreeable on that account. Money certainly does not produce wit, nor talents, nor understanding; but the quiet of mind which it superinduces, the equanimity which it affords, amply supply the place of these qualities; whilst in the absence of this equanimity these gifts are of no avail with many who possess them.

I had heard much of the adventurous and lucrative life of the coasting smugglers, of whom the prisoners had boasted with enthusiasm; for this profession was often followed through inclination, by individuals whose fortune and situation did not compel them to adopt so perilous a life. I confess, for my part, that I was not seduced by the prospect of passing whole nights under cliffs, in the midst of rocks, exposed to all winds, and, above all, to the shots of the custom house officers.

It was with real repugnance that I went to the house of a man named Peters, to whom I was directed, as one deeply engaged in the pursuit, and able to introduce me to it. A seagull nailed on his door with extended wings, like the owls and weasels that we see on barns, guided me. I found the worthy in a sort of cellar, which by the ropes, sails, oars, hammocks, and barrels which filled it, might have been taken for a naval depot. From the midst of a thick atmosphere of smoke which surrounded him, he viewed me at first with a contempt which had not a good appearance, and my conjectures were soon realized, for I had scarcely offered my services than he fell upon me with a shower of blows. I could certainly have resisted him effectually, but astonishment had in a measure deprived me of the power of defense; and I saw besides, in the courtyard, half a dozen sailors and an enormous Newfoundland dog, which would have been powerful odds. Turned into the street, I endeavored to account for this singular reception, when it occurred to me that Peters had mistaken me for a spy, and treated me accordingly.

This idea determined me on returning to a dealer in Hollands, who had told me of him, and he, laughing at the result of my visit, gave me a password that would procure me free access to Peters. Thus empowered, I again went to his formidable abode, having first filled my pockets with large stones, which in case of a second attack, might protect my retreat. Fortunately, I had no need of them. At the words "Beware of the sharks" (customs officers), I was received in a most amicable manner, for my strength and activity made me a valuable acquisition to the fraternity, who are often compelled to carry with speed, from one spot to another, the most oppressive loads. A Bordeaux man, who was one of the gang, undertook to initiate me, and teach me the stratagems of the profession, which, however, I was called on to put in practice before my tuition had progressed very far.

I slept at Peters' house with a dozen or fifteen smugglers, Dutch, Danish, Swedish, Portuguese, and Russian; there were no Englishmen, and only two Frenchmen. The day after my installation, as we were all getting into our hammocks, or flock-beds, Peters entered suddenly into our chamber, which was only a cellar contiguous to his own, and so filled with barrels and kegs that we could scarcely find room to sling our hammocks. Peters had put off his usual attire, which was that of ship-caulker, or sailmaker, and had on a hairy cap, and a long red shirt, closed at the breast with a silver-pin, firearms in his belt, and a pair of thick large fisherman's boots, which reach the top of the thigh, or may be folded down beneath the knee.

"Ahoy! Ahoy!" cried he at the door, striking the ground with the butt-end of his carbine, "Down with the hammocks, down with the hammocks! We will sleep some other day. The *Squirrel* has made signals for a landing this evening, and we must see what she has in her, muslin or tobacco. Come, come, turn out my sea-boys."

In a twinkling everybody was ready. They opened an arms-chest, and every man took out a carbine or blunderbuss, a brace of pistols, and a cutlass or boarding-pike, and we set out, after having drunk so many glasses of brandy and arrack that the bottles were empty. At this time there were not more than twenty of us, but we were joined or met, at one place or another, by so many individuals, that on reaching the seaside we were forty-seven in number, exclusive of two females and some countrymen from the adjacent villages, who brought hired horses, which they concealed in a hollow behind some rocks.

It was night, and the wind was shifting, whilst the sea dashed with so much force that I did not understand how any vessel could approach without being cast on shore. What confirmed this idea was, that by the starlight I saw a small boat rowing backward and forward, as if it feared to land. They told me afterward that this was only a maneuver to ascertain if all was ready for the unloading, and no danger to be apprehended. Peters now lighted a reflecting lantern, which one of the men had brought, and immediately extinguished it; the *Squirrel* raised a lantern at her mizzen, which only shone for a moment, and then disappeared like a glow-worm on a summer's night. We then saw it approach, and anchor about a gun-shot off from the spot where we were. Our troop then divided into three companies, two of which were placed five hundred paces in front, to resist the revenue officers if they should present themselves. The men of these companies were then placed at intervals along the ground, having at the left arm a packthread which ran from one to the other; in case of alarm, it was announced by a slight pull, and each being ordered to answer this signal by firing his gun, a line of firing was thus kept up, which perplexed the revenue officers. The third company, of which I was one, remained by the seaside, to cover the landing and the transport of the cargo.

All being thus arranged, the Newfoundland dog already mentioned, and who was with us, dashed at a word into the midst of the waves and swam powerfully in the direction of the *Squirrel,* and in an instant afterward returned with the end of a rope in his mouth. Peters instantly seized it, and began to draw it toward him, making us signs to assist him, which I obeyed mechanically. After a few tugs, I saw that at the end of the cable were a dozen small casks, which floated toward us. I then perceived that the vessel thus contrived to keep sufficiently far from the shore, not to run a risk of being stranded.

In an instant the casks, smeared over with something that made them waterproof, were unfastened and placed on horses, which immediately dashed off for the interior of the country. A second cargo arrived with the same success; but as we were landing the third, some reports of firearms announced that our outposts were attacked. "There is the beginning of the ball," said Peters, calmly; "I must go and see who will dance;" and taking up his carbine, he joined the outposts, which had by this time joined each other. The firing became rapid, and we had two men killed, and others slightly wounded. At the fire of the revenue officers, we soon found that they exceeded us in number, but alarmed, and fearing an ambuscade, they dared not to approach, and we affected our retreat without any attempt on their part to prevent it. From the beginning of the fight the *Squirrel* had weighed anchor, and stood out to sea, for fear that the noise of the firing should bring down on her the government cruiser. I was told that most probably she would unload her cargo in some other part of the coast, where the owners had numerous agents.

On the return to Peters' house, at break of day, I threw myself into my hammock, and did not leave it for eight-and-forty hours; the fatigue of the night, the moisture which penetrated my clothes, whilst exercise had made me perspire profusely, and the uneasiness of my new situation, all combined to make me ill, and a fever seized me. When it left me, I told Peters that I found the employment too hard, and that I should be glad if he would allow me to go. He agreed more quietly than I expected, and gave me a hundred francs. I have since learnt that he had me followed for several days, to be assured whether or not I took the road to Lille, which I had told him was my intention.

I did go to that city, led by a childish wish to see Francine, and take her with me to Holland, where I had formed a plan of a small establishment. But my imprudence was soon punished; for two gendarmes, who were drinking in a pot-house, saw me crossing the street, and they resolved on following me to ask for my papers. They overtook me at a turning, and the trouble which their appearance caused me, determined them on apprehending me. They took me to the brigade prison, where I was already looking out for means of escape, when I heard someone say to the gendarmes, "Here is the guard of Lille; is there anyone for the prison?"

Two men of the Lille brigade came to the prison and asked if there was any game for the trap? "Yes," said the fellows who took me, "we have one named Leger (my assumed name), whom we found without a passport." They opened the door, and the brigadier of Lille, who had often seen me at the Petit Hotel, cried, "By Jove, 'tis Vidocq!" I was compelled to confess it, and setting out, I entered Lille a few hours afterward, between my two bodyguards.

CHAPTER VI

I FOUND AT THE PETIT HOTEL THE GREATER NUMBER of the prisoners who had been emancipated before my escape. Some of them had made but a very short absence, and were speedily apprehended, charged with fresh crimes, or fresh offenses.

Amongst them was Calandrin, whom I have spoken about: enlarged on the 11th, he was retaken on the 13th, charged with burglary and being an accomplice of the Chauffeurs, whose name alone inspired universal dread. On the strength of the reputation which my various escapes had procured for me, these men looked on me as one on whom they might rely. On my side, I could scarcely separate myself from them. Accused of capital offenses, they had a powerful motive for being secret concerning our attempts, whilst the unfortunate "petty larceny rascal" might denounce us, in the dread of being accused of being privy to our designs. This is the logic of the prison. This escape, however, was not so very easy a matter, as may be surmised when I say that our dungeons, seven feet square, had walls six feet thick, strengthened with planking crossed and riveted with iron; a window, two feet by one, closed with three iron gratings placed one after the other, and the door eased with wrought iron. With such precautions, a jailer might depend on the safe keeping of his charge, but yet we overcame it all.

I was in a cell on the second floor with Duhamel. For six francs, a prisoner, who was also a turnkey, procured us two files, a ripping chisel, and two turn screws. We had pewter spoons, and our jailer was probably ignorant of the use which prisoners could make of them. I knew the dungeon key; it was the counterpart of all the others on the same story; and I cut a model of it from a large carrot; then I made a mound with crumb of bread and potatoes. We wanted fire, and we procured it by making a lamp with a piece of fat and the rags of a cotton cap. The key was at last made of pewter, but it was not yet perfect; and it was only after many trials and various alterations that it fitted at last. Thus masters of the doors, we were compelled to work a hole in the wall, near the barns of the town-hall. Sallambier, who was in the dungeons below, found a way to cut the hole, by working through the flanking. All was ready for our escape, and it was fixed for the evening, when the jailer told me that my term of dungeon imprisonment had expired, and I should be placed again with the other prisoners.

A favor was never less welcome; I saw all my preparations useless, and I might wait for a long time for circumstances as favorable. I was, however, compelled to follow the jailer, whom I wished at the devil with his congratulations. This disappointment affected me so greatly that all the prisoners saw it. One of them having learnt my secret from me, made some very just observations on the danger I ran in escaping with such men as Sallambier and Duhamel, who would, perhaps, not be out of prison twenty-four hours, without committing a murder. He even made me promise to let them go, and wait myself for some other opportunity. I followed his advice, and it was well that I did so; I even took the precaution of telling Duhamel and Sallambier that they were suspected, and that they had not a moment to spare in saving themselves. They followed my advice literally, and two hours afterward they had joined a band of forty-seven Chauffeurs, of whom twenty-eight were executed the following month at Bruges.

The escape of Duhamel and Sallambier made a great noise in the prison and throughout the city. They found some extraordinary circumstances belonging to it, but the jailer was the more astonished that I had not made one of the party. It was necessary to repair the breach they had made, and workmen came; and they stationed at the bottom of the staircase a guard with orders not to let anyone pass. The thought came to me of deceiving the sentinel, and getting out by the breach which was to have aided my escape before.

Francine, who came every day to see me, brought me three ells of tricolored ribbon, which I had requested her to procure. With one piece I made a belt, and ornamenting my hat with the rest, I passed, muffled up, by the soldier; who, taking me for a municipal officer, presented his arms. I ascended the staircase quickly—reached the opening, which I found guarded by two sentinels, one in the granary of the town-hall, and the other in the passage of the prison. I told the latter that it was impossible for a man to pass through this opening; he insisted on the contrary; and his comrade, as if plotting with me, said that I could get through with my clothes on. I said I would try; and creeping through the hole, I got into the barn. Pretending that I had hurt myself in passing, I told my two men that as I was on that side I should go round by another way. "In this case," said he who was in the granary, "wait whilst I open the door;" and putting the key in the lock, I jumped at two bounds down the staircase of the town hall and got into the street with my ribbon still on, and which would again have caused my arrest had not the day been drawing to a close.

I was scarcely out, when the jailer, who rarely lost sight of me, said, "Where is Vidocq?" They told him that I was taking a turn in the yard; but when he went there to convince himself, he sought me everywhere in vain, calling loudly over all parts of the prison (an official search would not have been more successful), no prisoner had seen me go out. It was soon known that I was no longer in the prison; but how then could I have escaped? Of this no one knew anything—not even Francine, who most ingenuously declared that she knew nothing of how I had liberated myself, for she had brought me the ribbon without knowing the purpose for which I intended it. She was however confined; but this revealed nothing, the soldiers, who had allowed me to pass, taking good care not to implicate themselves.

Whilst they were thus punishing the pretended authors of my escape, I left the city and reached Courtrai, where the juggler Olivier and the quack Devoye enrolled me in their troop to play pantomime. I saw there many prisoners who had escaped, whose acting costume, which they always wore (because they had no other), served greatly to mystify the police. From Courtrai we returned to Ghent, whence we were soon to depart for the fair of Enghien. We were in this latter city for five days: and the receipts, of which I had a share, were very good; when one evening, as I was about to go on the stage, I was arrested by the police officers, to whom I had been betrayed by the merry-andrew, out of malice at seeing me fill the chief characters. I was again taken back to Lille, where I learned, to my great grief, that my poor Francine had been sentenced to six months' confinement for having aided my escape. The turnkey Baptiste—whose only crime was that of having taken me for a superior officer, and having allowed use in this capacity to quit St. Peter's Tower—the unlucky Baptiste was also imprisoned for the same fault. The terrible charge against him was, that the prisoners (overjoyed at an opportunity of revenging themselves) declared that a hundred crowns had made him take a young man of nineteen for an old soldier on the shady side of fifty.

As for me, I was sent to the prison of the department of Douai, where I was treated as a dangerous man; that is to say, I was thrust into a dungeon with my hands and legs in fetters. I found there my townsman Desfosseux and a young man named Doyenette, condemned to chains for sixteen years for a burglary effected with his father, mother, and two brothers under fifteen years of age. They had been four months in the dungeon where I was put, lying on straw, eaten up with vermin, and living on bean bread and water. I ordered my provisions, which were soon consumed; we then talked over our business, and my fellow prisoners told me that for the last fortnight they were making a hole under the pavement of the dungeon which would open at the level of the Scarpe, which washed the prison walls. I at first regarded the enterprise as difficult, as it was necessary to pierce a wall five feet thick and yet avoid the observation of the jailer, whose frequent visits would not allow of our suffering a morsel of rubbish to be seen.

We eluded detection from this by throwing out of the window, which overlooked the Scarpe, every handful of rubbish that we got from our mine. Desfosseux had besides found means of ridding us of our fetters, and we worked with less fatigue and difficulty. One of us was always in the hole, which was already large enough to admit a man. We thought that we had at length terminated our labors and our captivity, when we discovered that the foundations, which we had imagined to be composed of common stone, were formed of masses of sandstone of large size. This compelled us to enlarge our subterranean gallery, and for a week we worked at it unremittingly. To conceal the disappearance of that one of us who might be at work when the guard went round, we had filled a vest and shirt with straw, and placed the figure in the posture of a sleeping man.

After fifty-five days and nights of unrelaxing toil, we at last so far completed our work that we had but one stone to remove and then should reach the river's bank. One night we determined on making an essay, and all appeared favorable to our design; the jailer had locked up earlier than usual, and a dense fog gave us a confident hope of avoiding the sentinel of the bridge. The shaken stone yielded to our efforts, and fell inside the aperture we had made;

but the water followed it at the same time as if impelled by the sluice of a mill. We had calculated our distance incorrectly, and the hole being made some feet beneath the level of the river, we were soon deluged. At first, we endeavored to plunge through the opening; but the rapidity of the current precluded all attempts, and we were compelled to call for help, or remain immersed in water for the whole night. At our cries the jailer and turnkeys ran to our assistance, and were greatly astonished at finding themselves mid-leg deep in water. All was soon discovered and the mischief repaired, whilst we were shut up singly in dungeons in the same gallery.

This catastrophe filled me with very sad reflections, from „which I was very soon aroused by the voice of Desfosseux, who told me, in slang terms, not to despair, but to take courage by his example. Desfosseux was certainly endowed with a strength of mind which nothing could depress. Cast half naked on the straw in a dungeon, where he could scarcely lie at length, loaded with thirty pounds weight of fetters, he yet sang with great vociferation, and was only devising means of escape, that he might again do some evil deed; and opportunity was not long wanting.

In the same prison with us were confined the jailer of the Petit Hotel of Lille, and the turnkey, Baptiste, both accused of having aided my escape for a bribe. The day of their trial having arrived, the jailer was acquitted, but Baptiste's sentence was deferred, the tribunal having decreed a fresh process, in which I was to be heard. Poor Baptiste then came to me, begging me to tell the truth. At first, I only gave him evasive answers; but Desfosseux having told me that the man might serve us, and that we must arrange terms with him, I promised to do what he wished; on which he made me vast professions of gratitude and offers of service. I took him at his word, and desired him to bring me a knife and two large nails, of which Desfosseux had told me that he had need, and in an hour I had them brought to me. On learning that I had procured them, Desfosseux made as many jumps as his fetters and his bounded space would allow. Doyenette equally gave himself up to the most excessive joy; and, as gayety is in general catching, I felt myself too in a mirthful mood, without exactly knowing why.

When these transports had a little subsided, Desfosseux desired me to look at the roof of my dungeon, and observe if there were not five stones whiter than the rest; and on my replying in the affirmative, he desired me to try the divisions with the point of my knife, which I did, and found the cement had been replaced by crumbs of bread, whitened with scraping; and Desfosseux told me that the prisoner who had been there before me, had done this to remove the stones and save himself, when he had been taken to another part of the prison. I then transferred the knife to Desfosseux, who employed himself with activity in opening a passage to my dungeon, when we were served similar to my predecessor. The jailer, having got wind of something, changed our dungeons, and placed us all three in a dungeon next to the scarpe, where we were chained together, so that the least movement of one of us was communicated to the others—a horrid punishment when prolonged, and which ends in a total deprivation of sleep. At the end of two days Desfosseux, seeing us dejected, resolved on using a means which he only resorted to on desperate occasions, and which he reserved as the preparatory step toward escape.

Like many of the galley slaves, he carried secretly about him a case full of files, with which he set to work, and in less than three hours our fetters fell off. We cast them through the grating into the river. The jailer coming to visit us the moment after to see if we were quiet, almost fell backward at finding us freed from our irons, and asked us what we had done with them; to which we only replied with jokes. The inspector of the prison arriving, together with an attendant bailiff named Hurtrell, we were compelled to undergo a fresh examination; and Desfosseux, who was much irritated, said, "You ask for our fetters? Well, the worms have eaten them, and will eat as many as you may load us with."

The inspector then suspecting that we had that famous herb which cuts iron, which no botanist had ever yet discovered, ordered us to strip and be examined from head to foot, and then again loaded us with irons, which were again cut off the following night, for the precious case was not discovered. This time we reserved to ourselves the pleasure of throwing them on the ground in the presence of the inspector and Hurtrel, the bailiff, who did not know what to think of it. The report spread through the city that there was in the prison a conjuror who took fetters off by only touching them. To cut short all these accounts, and particularly to avoid drawing the attention of the other prisoners to means of getting rid of their chains, the public accuser gave an order to shut us up and watch us with particular care—a recommendation which did not prevent us from quitting Douai sooner than they expected, or than we ourselves had the least idea of.

Twice a week we had leave to consult our counsel in the gallery, of which one door led to the court of justice, and I contrived to get an impression of the lock. Desfosseux made a key, and one fine day, whilst my counsel was engaged with another client, accused of two murders, we all three got out without being seen. Two other gates which opposed us were broken open in a twinkling, and the prison was soon left behind us. But yet I was uneasy. Six francs was our whole stock, and we could not get far with such a sum, which I told my companions, who looked at each other with a sinister smile; and on my repeating my observation, they told me that, on the next night, they intended to enter a house in the neighborhood with which they were well acquainted.

I had no intention of turning house-breaker, any more than when I was amongst the Bohemians. I had profited by the experience of Desfosseux in escaping, but never contemplated uniting myself with such a villain: and yet I was not desirous of entering into any explanation. By evening we had reached a village on the road to Cambrai; we had not eaten since our escape from prison, and were sorely pressed by hunger. It was absolutely necessary to get provisions in the village. The half-naked appearance of my companions might give rise to suspicion, and it was agreed that I should go for the food. I went to a public-house, where, after having taken some bread and brandy, I went out by a different door from that at which I had entered, directing my steps in the opposite direction to that in which I had left the two men whose company I was so greatly desirous of getting rid of. I walked all night, and only stopped at break of day to sleep a few hours on a haystack.

Four days afterward I reached Compeigne, on my way to Paris, where I trusted to find some means of existence until my mother could send me some succor. At Louvres, meeting a regiment of black hussars, I asked the quartermaster if I could enter, but he told me that they did not enlist; and the lieutenant, to whom I afterward applied, gave me the same reply, but touched by the embarrassment of my situation agreed to keep me to clean the extra horses which he was going to procure at Paris. A cap of a police officer and an old cloak which was given to me, enabled me to clear the barrier unquestioned, and I went to the military school with the detachment, which I afterward accompanied to the depot at Guise. On arriving in the city, I was presented to the colonel, who although suspecting me to be a deserter, engaged me under the name of Lannoy, which I assumed without being able to justify by any credentials. Concealed by my new uniform, and mingled with the rank of a numerous regiment, I thought myself secure, and began to think of making my way as a soldier, when an unfortunate accident again befell me.

On entering the barrack one morning I met a gendarme, who had left Douai for Guise. He had so frequently seen me, that he knew me at first sight and called to me. We were in the midst of the street, and thoughts of escape were useless, I therefore went up to him and boldly feigned to be glad to see him. He replied to me, but with an air that seemed to augur me no good. Whilst thus together, a hussar of my squadron, seeing me with the gendarme, approached and said to me, "Well, Lannoy, what are you doing with the round hats?"

"Lannoy!" said the gendarme with astonishment.

"Yes, it is a nom de guerre."

"Oh, we will see about that," said he, seizing my collar. I was compelled to follow him to prison, and my identity being confirmed, in opposition to my statements at the regiment, I was by a cursed chance again sent to Douai.

This sentence completely overpowered me, and the intelligence that reached me at Douai was not calculated to set me at rest. I heard that Grouard, Harbaux, Stofilet, and Boitel, had decided by lot that one of them should confess the execution of the forgery; but as this forgery could only be the work of one person, they determined on accusing me, thus punishing me for what I had said of them at my last examination; and I learnt besides, that the prisoner who could have corroborated my statement was dead. If anything could console me, it was that I had escaped in time from Desfosseux and Doyenette, who had been taken four days after our escape with their booty about them, in a mercer's shop in Ponte-a-Marcq. I soon saw them, and as they were astonished at my abrupt departure, I told them that the arrival of a gendarme at the public-house where I was purchasing provisions, had compelled me to fly with speed.

Again united, we formed new plans of escape, which the approach of our trials rendered of great importance to us.

One evening a convoy of prisoners arrived, four of whom, ironed, were placed with us. They were the brothers Duhesme, rich farmers of Bailleul, where they had enjoyed the best reputation, until an unexpected accident unfolded their real characters. These four persons, men of powerful strength, were at the head of a band of Chauffeurs, who had struck terror into the vicinity, without any person being able to identify them. The prattling of a little girl of one of the Duhesmes at last exposed the affair. This child, chatting at a neighbor's house, said that she had been very much frightened the night before. "And with what?" said the curious neighbor, "Oh, papa came home again with the black men." "The black men?" "Yes, the men who go out with papa every night, and come home in the daytime and count out money; my mother lights the candle, and my aunt Genevieve also, because my uncles are amongst the black men. I asked my mother one day what it was all about, and she said, 'Be discreet, my child, your father has a black hen who finds him in money, but it is only at night, and that he should not scare it, he makes his face as black as her feathers. Be silent, for if you tell anybody what you have seen, the black hen will never come again.'"

We may easily divine that it was not to visit the mysterious hen that the Duhesmes blackened their faces with smoke. The neighbor, who guessed as much, communicated her suspicion to her husband, who, in his turn, questioned the little girl, and convinced that the favorites of the black hen were Chauffeurs; he made a deposition, and on measures being taken, the band was apprehended, all disguised, as they were about to sally out on an expedition.

The youngest Duhesme had, in the sole of his shoe, a knife blade, which he had contrived to conceal on the road from Bailleul to Douai. Being told that I knew the way of the prison, he communicated this to me, asking me if it were not possible to effect an escape with its assistance. I was reflecting about it, when a justice of the peace, attended by gendarmes, came to make a strict search throughout our room, and about our persons. No one amongst us knowing the reason of this, I thought it prudent to hide in my mouth a small file which I had always about me, but one of the gendarmes having watched me, cried, "He is going to swallow it!" "Swallow what?" Everybody looked, and we then learnt that they wanted to find the seal which had served to stamp the forged orders for Boitel's liberation. Suspected, as we have just learnt, of having got it, I was transferred to the prison of the Town Hall, and thrust into a dungeon so chained that my right hand was confined to my left leg, and my left hand to my right leg. The dungeon was, moreover, so damp, that in twenty minutes the straw which they had thrown me was as wet as if it had been dipped in water.

I remained eight days in this frightful state, and when they found that it was impossible I could have got rid of the seal in the way suspected, I was ordered to the usual prison. On learning this intelligence, I pretended, as is often done under such circumstances, to be exceedingly weak and scarcely able to bear the light of day. The unwholesome state of the dungeon made this very probable, and the gendarmes fell completely into the snare, and carried their complaisance so far as to cover my eyes with a handkerchief, and then deposited me in a hackney-coach. On the road I took off the handkerchief, and opening the door, with a dexterity never yet surpassed, jumped out into the street; the gendarmes sought to follow, but, impeded by their sabers and jackboots, they had scarcely got out of the carriage when I was at a considerable distance I quitted the city instantly, and resolved on embarking, I reached Dunkirk with some money which my mother had transmitted to me. I there made friends with the supercargo of a Swedish brig, who promised to get me a berth on board.

While waiting for orders to sail, my new friend proposed that I should accompany him to Saint Omer, where he was going to get a large quantity of biscuit. I did not fear recognition in my sailor's clothes, and agreed, as it was impossible to refuse a man to whom I was under such great obligations. I went with him, but my turbulent character would not allow me to remain quiet in a pot-house row, and I was arrested as a riotous fellow and taken to the watchhouse. There they asked for my papers, of which I had none, and my answers inducing a belief that I might be an escaped prisoner, they sent me the next day to the central prison of Douai, without allowing me to bid adieu to the supercargo, who was doubtlessly much surprised at this occurrence. At Douai, they put me once more in the prison of the Town Hall where at first the jailer evinced much kindness toward me, which did not so however last. At the termination of a quarrel with the turnkeys, which I took too active a part, I was thrown into a dark cell under the tower. There were five of us, one of whom, a deserter sentenced to death, was talking of nothing but suicide, until I desired him not to think of that, but rather devise means of escape from this dismal hole, where the rats, which ran about like rabbits in a cornfield, eat our bread and bit our faces while we slept. With a bayonet, stolen from one of the soldiers of the national guard who did duty at the prison, we commenced working a hole in the wall, in a direction in which we heard a cobbler hammering his leather. In ten days, and as many nights, we penetrated six feet in depth and seemed to get nearer the cobbler's hammer. On the eleventh day, in the morning, on drawing out a brick, I saw daylight from a window which looked into the street, and gave light to a place where the jailer kept some rabbits.

This discovery inspired us with fresh courage, and the evening visit being concluded, we took from the hole all the loosened bricks, of which there were two courses, and placed them behind the dungeon door, which opened inward, so as to barricade it, and then set to work with so much industry, that daylight surprised us, when the hole, six feet large at the opening, was only two feet at the end. The jailer came with our allowances, and finding some resistance, opened the wicket, and saw the high pile of bricks, to his great astonishment. He desired us to open the door, and on our refusal the guard came, then the commissary of the prison, then the public accuser, then the municipal officers clothed with the tricolored scarfs. We held a parley, and during this time one of us continued working at the hole, which the darkness did not disclose. We might perhaps escape before the door was forced, when an unexpected event deprived us of our last hope.

The jailer's wife, in going to feed the rabbits, had observed rubbish scattered on the floor. In a prison, nothing is indifferent, and she carefully examined the wall, and although the bricks had been so replaced as to conceal the hole, she yet saw that they had been separated; and on calling for the guard, with a blow from the butt-end of a musket, our bricks were knocked out and we were discovered. On both sides they called to us to clear the doorway, or they would fire on us.

Entrenched behind the materials, we answered that the first who entered should be knocked on the head with bricks and irons. So much determination alarmed the authorities, and they left us for a few hours to calm ourselves. At noon, a municipal officer appeared at the wicket, which as well as the hole, had been sedulously guarded, and offered us an amnesty, which we accepted; but scarcely had we removed our chevaux-de-frise, when they attacked us with the butt-end of muskets, flat sides of sabers, and bunches of keys, even the jailer's mastiff joined the party; he jumped at me and bit me most severely all over. They then led us into the courtyard, where a body of fifteen men held us, lying on our faces, whilst they riveted our fetters. This job done, they cast me into a dungeon yet more horrible than that I had left, and it was not till the next day that the surgeon Dutilleul, (now keeper at the hospital of St. Maude) came to dress the bites and bruises which covered me.

I had scarcely recovered from this when the day of trial came, which my repeated escapes, and those of Grouard, who fled just as I was retaken, had deferred for eight months. The trial began, and I saw that I was lost; my companions accused me with an animosity, explained by my retarded confessions, which were useless to myself, and had not at all injured them. Boitel declared that I had asked him how much he would give to get out of prison. Herbaux confessed that he had forged the order, but not added the signatures, and said besides that I had persuaded him to forge it, and then taken it from him without his thinking it of the least importance. The jury thought that nothing indicated that I had materially aided the crime; all the charge against me was confined to allegations, without proof, that I had furnished the seal. However, Boitel, who remembered having begged for the forged order; Stofflet, who had brought it to the jailer; Grouard, who had at least assisted at the whole operation, were acquitted; whilst Herbaux and I were condemned to eight years' imprisonment.

This was the termination of the sentence, although many false reports were circulated through the malevolence and stupidity of enemies. Some say that I was sentenced to death for numerous murders; others state that I had long been chief of a band which robbed the diligences; the most moderate state that I was condemned to perpetual labor at the galleys for robbery and housebreaking; and it has been asserted that I (at a later period) incited wretches to crime that I might show my vigilance in pouncing upon them; as if there were not a sufficient number of the really guilty. Certainly false comrades, as are everywhere to be found, even among robbers, sometimes instructed me in the plans of their accomplices; certainly to confirm the intent whilst we prevented the crime, it was sometimes necessary to allow of a partial commission of a deed, for experienced rogues are never caught but in the very act: and I ask, is there anything in this which has the appearance of an inducement to do ill? This imputation emanated from the police, amongst whom I have some enemies; but the imputation fails before the publicity of judicial facts, which would not have failed in revealing the infamies with which I am charged; and it also fails before the operations of the brigade of safety, which I directed. It is not when proof is given that we have recourse to deception, and the confidence of the clever men who have preceded M. Delavau, in the office of chief magistrate, will acquit me of such wretched expedients. "He is a lucky fellow," said, one day, the police officers who had failed in an enterprise in which I succeeded, to M. Angles. "Well," said he, turning his back on them, "do you be lucky fellows too."

Parricide is the only crime of which I have not been charged, and yet I declare that I never was sentenced to, nor underwent, but the sentence which I have just mentioned. My pardon will prove this; and when I assert that I never aided in this miserable forgery, I should be believed, for it was at last but a prison joke, which, if proved, would at present only subject the offender to a sentence of corporal punishment. But it was not the suspected accomplice in a foolish forgery that was to be punished; it was the disorderly, rebellious, and impudent prisoner, the chief of so many plans of escape, of whom an example must be made and I was sacrificed.

CHAPTER VII

WORN OUT BY THE BAD TREATMENT OF EVERY species which I experienced in the prison of Douai, tormented by a watchfulness redoubled after my sentence, I took care not to make an appeal, which would keep me there some months. What confirmed me in my resolution was, the information that the prisoners were to be sent forthwith to the Bicêtre, and there, making one chain, to be sent on to the Bagne at Brest. It is unnecessary to say, that I relied on escaping on our route. As to the appeal, I was told that I could present a petition for pardon from the Bagne, which would have the same effect. We remained, however, some months at Douai, which made me regret bitterly that I had not made my petition for annulling the sentence.

At length the order of removal arrived, and, what would scarcely be credited from men doomed to the galleys, it was hailed with enthusiasm—so much were we tired of the torments of Marin, the jailer. Our new situation was not, however, much more satisfactory; the officer, Hurtrel, who accompanied us, I know not why, had ordered irons of a new construction, which fastened to each of our legs a ball of fifteen pounds weight, whilst we were secured two and two by a massive wrist-cuff of iron. Besides, the vigilance was extreme, and it was impossible to think of doing anything by address. An attack by main force could alone save us, and I proposed it to fourteen of my companions, who agreed on it, and it was settled that the project should be put in execution on our way through the forest of Compeigne. Desfosseux was of the party, and by means of fine saws which he had always securely secreted about him, our fetters were cut in three days; the plaster of a particular sort of gum prevented our keepers from perceiving the trace of the instruments.

On reaching the forest and gaining the appointed spot, the signal was given, the fetters fell from us, and we leaped from the carriages which enclosed us to try and gain the thicket, but the five gendarmes and the eight dragoons who escorted us charged sword in hand. We entrenched ourselves behind the trees, armed with the stones which are piled up to mend the roads, and with some weapons we had got hold of at the first moment of confusion. The soldiers hesitated for an instant, but, well-armed and well mounted, they soon made up their minds, and at the first charge two of our party fell dead, five more terribly wounded, and the others falling on their knees cried for mercy. Surrender was now imperative; and Desfosseux, myself, and some others who had escaped, got into the carriage, when Hurtrel, who had kept at a very respectful distance from the affray, came up to a poor wretch, who certainly did not hurry himself very much, and thrust his sabre through him. Such baseness enraged us; the prisoners who had not yet ascended the carriages took up stones, and but for the aid of the dragoons, Hurtrel would have been knocked on the head. The soldiers bid us desist before we brought down destruction on ourselves: and the thing was so evident, that we were compelled to lay down our arms, that is the stones. This circumstance, however, put a termination to the annoyances of Hurtrel, who never approached us but with fear and trembling.

At Senlis, we were placed in the temporary prison, one of the most horrible I ever tenanted. The jailer, exercising the office of streetkeeper, the prison was guarded by his wife. And what a creature was she! As we had made ourselves notorious, she thrust us into the most secret dungeons, convincing herself by previous personal examination that we had nothing about us that could aid escape. We were, however, trying the walls, when we heard her roar out, "Rascals, I am coming to you with my bastinado. I will teach you how to play music!" We took her at her word, and all desisted. The next day we reached Paris, and were lodged in the outer boulevards, and at four in the afternoon we got in sight of Bicêtre.

On reaching the end of the avenue which looks on the road to Fontainebleau, the carriages turned to the right, and entered an iron gate, above which I read mechanically this inscription: "Hospice de la vieillesse," (Hospital for the aged). In the forecourt, many old men were walking, clothed in gray garments. They were paupers, and stared at us with that stupid curiosity which results from a monotonous and purely animal existence; for it often happens that a person admitted into a hospital, having no longer his own subsistence to provide for, renounces the exercise of his narrow faculties, and ends by falling into a state of perfect idiocy. On reaching the second court, in which was the chapel, I remarked that the majority of my companions hid their faces with their hands or pocket-handkerchiefs. It may be supposed that they experienced some feelings of shame. No; they were only thinking of allowing their faces to be seen as little as possible, so that if opportunity presented, they might the more easily escape.

"Here we are," said Desfosseux to me. "You see that square building? That is the prison." We alighted at an iron door, guarded inside by a sentry. Having entered the office, we were only registered, our description being deferred until the next day. I perceived, however, that the jailer looked at us, Desfosseux and me, with a sort of curiosity, and I thence concluded that we had been recommended by the officer Hurtrel, who had preceded us a quarter of an hour from the time of the business of the forest of Compeigne. Having opened many low doors, guarded with iron plates, and the Birdcage Wicket, we were introduced to a large yard, where about sixty prisoners were playing at fives, and shouting so loudly as to sound all over the place. At our appearance their game ceased, and surrounding us, they examined with much surprise the irons which loaded us. It was, besides, to enter Bicêtre in the most favorable manner to be decked with such caparisons, for they estimated the deserts of the prisoner—that is to say, his boldness and talent for escape—by the precautions taken to secure him. Desfosseux, who found himself amongst friends, had no difficulty in introducing us as the most distinguished personages of the north. He did more; he particularly expatiated on my merits, and I was accordingly surrounded and made much of by all the worthies of the prison: Beaumont, Guillaume, Mauger, Jossat, Maltaise, Corun, Blondy, Troaflat and Richard, one of the parties concerned in the murder of a Lyons courier, never left me. As soon as my fetters were taken off, they took me to a drinking-shop, where for two hours I did justice to a thousand invitations, when a tall man with a police officer's cap, who they told me was the room inspector, took us to a large place called Le Fort Mahon, when we were clothed in the prison garb, consisting of a frock half gray and half black. The inspector told me I should be brigadier, that is, that I should preside at the giving out of the provisions amongst my table companions, and I had, in consequence, a good bed, whilst others slept on camp couches. In four days I was known to all the prisoners; but although they had the highest opinion of my courage, Beaumont, wishing to try me, picked a quarrel with me. We fought, and as he was an expert boxer, I was completely conquered. I, however, had my revenge in a room, where Beaumont, unable to display the resources of his art, had the worst of it. My first defeat, however, gave me a desire to be instructed in the mysteries of this art, and the celebrated Jean Gospel, the Saint George of boxing, who was at the Bicêtre with us, soon counted me among those of his pupils who were destined to do him the most honor.

The prison of the Bicêtre is a neat quadrangular building, enclosing many other structures and many courts, which have each a different name; there is the grand cour (great court), where the prisoners walk; the cour de cuisine (or kitchen court); the cour des chiens (or dog's court); the cour de correction (or court of punishment); and the cour des fers (or iron court). In this last is a new building five stories high; each story contains forty cells, capable of holding four prisoners.

On the platform, which supplies the place of a roof, was night and day a dog named Dragon, who passed in the prison for the most watchful and incorruptible of its kind; but some prisoners managed at a subsequent period to corrupt him through the medium of a roasted leg of mutton, which he had the culpable weakness to accept; so true is it, that there are no seductions more potent than those of gluttony, since they operate indifferently on all organized beings. To ambition, to gaming, and to gallantry, there are bounds fixed by nature; but gluttony knows nothing of age, and if the appetite sometimes opposes its inert power we are quits with it by a good fit of indigestion. However, the Amphytrions escaped while Dragon was swallowing the mutton; he was beaten and taken into the cour des chiens, where, chained up and deprived of the free air which he had breathed on the platform, he was inconsolable for his fault, and perished piecemeal, a victim of remorse at his weakness in yielding to a moment of gluttony and error.

Near the erection I speak of is the old building, nearly arranged in the same way, and under which were dungeons of safety, in which were enclosed the troublesome and condemned prisoners. It was in one of these dungeons that for forty-three years lived the accomplice of Cartouche, who betrayed him to procure this commutation! To obtain a moment's sunshine, he frequently counterfeited death so well that when he had actually breathed his last sigh, two days passed before they took off his iron collar. A third part of the building, called La Force, comprised various rooms, in which the prisoners were placed who arrived from the provinces, and were destined, like ourselves, to the chain.

At this period, the prison of Bicêtre, which is only strong from the strict guard kept up there, could contain twelve hundred prisoners; but they were piled on each other, and the conduct of the jailers in no way assuaged the inconvenience of the place: a sullen air, a rough tone, and brutal manners, were exercised toward the prisoners, and they were in no way to be softened but through the medium of a bottle of wine, or a pecuniary bribe. Besides, they never attempted to repress any excess or any crime, and provided that no one sought to escape, they might do whatever they pleased in the prison, without being restrained or prevented. Whilst men condemned for those attempts which modesty shrinks from naming, openly practiced their detestable libertinism, and robbers exercised their industry inside the prison, without any person attempting to check the crime or prevent the bestiality.

If any man arrived from the country well-clad, who, condemned for a first offense, was not as yet initiated into the customs and usages of prisons, in a twinkling he was stripped of his clothes, which were sold in his presence to the highest bidder. If he had jewels or money, they were alike confiscated to the profit of the society, and if he were too long in taking out his ear-rings, they snatched them out without the sufferer daring to complain. He was previously warned, that if he spoke of it, they would hang him in the night to the bars of his cell, and afterward say that he had committed suicide. If a prisoner, out of precaution, when going to sleep, placed his clothes under his head, they waited until he was in his first sleep, and then they tied to his foot a stone, which they balanced at the side of his bed; at the least motion the stone fell, and, aroused by the noise, the sleeper jumped up, and before he could discover what had occurred, his packet, hoisted by a cord, went through the iron bars to the floor above. I have seen, in the depth of winter, these poor devils, having been deprived of their property in this way, remain in the court in their shirts until someone threw them some rags to cover their nakedness. As long as they remained at Bicêtre, by burying themselves, as we may say, in their straw, they could defy the rigor of the weather; but at the departure of the chain, when they had no other covering than the frock and trousers made of packing-cloth, they often sank exhausted and frozen before they reached the first resting place.

It is necessary, by facts of this nature, to explain the rapid depravity of men whom it was easy to excite to honest feelings; but who, unable to escape the height of misery but by excess of wickedness, sought an alleviation of their lot in the real or apparent exaggeration of all species of crime. In society, we dread infamy; in the society of prisoners, there is no shame but in not being sufficiently infamous. The condemned prisoners are a distinct people; whoever is cast amongst them must expect to be treated as an enemy as long as he will not speak their language, and will not identify himself with their way of thinking.

The abuses I have mentioned are not the only ones; there are others even more terrible. If a prisoner were marked out as a false brother or as a sneak, he

73

was pitilessly knocked on the head, without any jailer interfering to prevent it. Matters came to such a pitch, that it was necessary to assign a particular division to those individuals, who, giving an account of their own doings, had made any mention of their comrades which they thought could in any way compromise them. On the other hand the impudence of the robbers, and the immoralities of their keepers, were carried to such an extent, that they prepared openly in the prison tricks of swindling and theft, which were to be perpetrated on quitting the walls of the prison. I will mention only one of these plans, which will suffice to evince the measure of credulity of the dupes and the audacity of the plotters. These latter obtained the address of certain rich persons living in the province, which was easy from the number of prisoners who were constantly arriving. They then wrote letters to them, called, in the slang language, "letters of Jerusalem," and which contained in substance what follows. It is useless to observe that the names of places and persons change according to circumstances.

"Sir,—You will doubtlessly be astonished at receiving a letter from a person unknown to you, who is about to ask a favor from you; but from the sad condition in which I am placed, I am lost if some honorable person will not lend me succor: that is the reason of my addressing you, of whom I have heard so much that I cannot for a moment hesitate to confide all my affairs to your kindness. As valet-de-chambre to the Marquis de I emigrated with my master, and that we might avoid suspicion we traveled on foot and I carried the luggage, consisting of a casket containing 16,000 francs in gold and the diamonds of the late marchioness. We were on the point of joining the army at, when we were marked out and pursued by a detachment of volunteers. The marquis, seeing how closely we were pressed, desired me to throw the casket into a deep ditch near us, so that it might not implicate us in case we were apprehended. I relied on recovering it the following night; but the country people. aroused by the tocsin which the commandant of the detachment ordered to be rung, began to beat the wood in which we were concealed with so much vigor, that it was necessary to think only of escape. On reaching a foreign province, the marquis received some advances from the prince of; but these resources soon failing, he resolved on sending me back for the casket thrown into the ditch. I was the more certain of finding it, as on the day after I had thrown it from me, we had made a written memorandum of the localities, in case we should be for any length of time without being able to return for it. I set out, and entering France, reached the village of without accident, near the spot where we had been pursued. You must know the village perfectly, as it is not three-quarters of a league from your residence. I prepared to fulfill my mission, when the landlord of the auberge where I had lodged, a bitter Jacobin and collector of national property, remarking my embarrassment when he proposed to drink to the health of the republic, had me apprehended as a suspected person; and as I had no passport, and unfortunately resembled an individual pursued for stopping the diligence, I was taken from prison to prison to be confronted with my pretended accomplices, until on reaching Bicêtre I was obliged to go to the infirmary, where I have been for two months.

"In this cruel situation, having heard mention of you by a relation of my master's who had property in your district, I beg to know if I cannot, through your aid, obtain the casket in question, and get a portion of the money which it contains. I could then supply my immediate necessities and pay my counsel, who dictates this, and assures me that by some presents I could extricate myself from this affair.

"Receive, sir, etc.

(Signed)"

N.

Out of one hundred such letters, twenty were always answered: and astonishment will cease when we consider that they were only addressed to men known by their attachment to the old order of things, and that nothing reasons less than the spirit of party. It testified besides to the person addressed, that unlimited confidence which never fails to produce its effect on self-love or interest. The person answered that they would agree to undertake to get the casket from its place of concealment. Another letter from the pretended valet-de-chambre, stating, that being entirely stripped, he had agreed with the keeper of the infirmary for a very small sum to sell the trunk, in which was, in the false bottom, the plan already alluded to. Then the money arrived, and they received sums sometimes amounting to twelve or fifteen hundred francs. Some individuals, thinking to give a profound proof of sagacity, came even from the remotest parts of their province to Bicêtre, where they received the destined plan which was to conduct them to this mysterious forest, which, like the fantastic forests of the romances of chivalry, fled eternally before them. The Parisians themselves sometimes fell into the snare; and some persons may still remember the adventure of the cloth seller of the Rue des Prouvaires, who was caught undermining an arch of the Pont Neuf, where he expected to find the diamond of the Duchess de Bouillon.

We may imagine that such maneuvers could not be effected but by the consent and with the participation of the keepers, since they received the correspondence of the treasure-seekers. But the jailer thought that by the increase of the money spent by the prisoners in viands and spirits, they being thus occupied would not think of escaping. On the same principle, he tolerated the making varieties of things in straw, wood and bone, and even false pieces of two sous, with which Paris was at one time inundated. There were also other crafts exercised; but these were done clandestinely. They made privately false passports with the pen, so well done as to pass current— saws for cutting iron, and false hair, which was of great service in escaping from the Bagne, the galley slaves being particularly recognizable by their shorn heads. These various articles were concealed in thin cases, which could be hid in the intestines.

As for me, always occupied with the idea of escaping from the Bagne, and reaching a seaport whence I could embark, it was night and day plotting the means of getting away from Bicêtre. I at length imagined that by breaking through the quadrangle of Fort Mahon, and reaching the water-courses made under it, we might by means of a short mine, get into the court of the idiots I have before alluded to, whence there would be no difficulty in reaching the outside. This project was executed in ten days and as many nights. During the whole time, the prisoners of whom we had any distrust were always accompanied by a trusty man; but we were obliged to wait until the moon should be on the wane. At length, on the 3rd of October, at two o'clock in the morning, we descended the water-course, thirty-three in number, provided with dark lanterns, and we soon opened the subterranean passage and reached the court of the idiots. We wanted a ladder, or something instead of it, to climb the walls, and at last got hold of a long pole, and we were going to draw lots to decide who should first climb up, when a noise of chains suddenly broke the silence of night.

A dog came out from a kennel placed in an angle of the court. We stood motionless, and held our breath, for it was an important moment. After having stretched himself out and yawned, as if he had only wanted to change place, the animal put one foot into his kennel as if about to return, and we then thought ourselves saved. Suddenly he turned his head to the place in which we were huddled together, and fixed on us two eyes which looked like burning coals. A low growling was then followed with barkings which sounded all over the place. Desfosseux wished to try and cut his throat, but he was of a size to render the issue of a contest doubtful. It appeared best to us to lie down in a large open space, which served as a walking-ground for the idiots; but the dog still kept up the concert, and, his colleagues having joined him, the din became so excessive, that the inspector Giroux, fancying something particular was passing amongst his lodgers, and knowing his customers, began his round by Fort Mahon, and almost fell backward at finding no one. At his cries, the jailers, turnkeys, and guard, all assembled. They soon discovered the road we had taken, and taking the same to get into the court of the idiots, they loosened the dog, who ran straight at us. The guards then entered the place where we were with fixed bayonets, as if about to carry a redoubt. They put handcuffs on us, the usual prelude of any important matter to be done in a prison; and we then returned, not to Fort Mahon, but to the dungeon, without, however, experiencing any bad treatment.

This attempt, the boldest of which the prison had for a long time been the theatre, threw the keepers into so much confusion, that it was two days before they perceived that one of the prisoners of Fort-Mahon was missing. It was Desfosseux. Knowing all his address, I thought him at a distance, when, on the morning of the third day, I saw him enter my dungeon, pale, exhausted and bleeding. When the door was closed on him he told me all his adventure.

At the moment when the guard had seized us he had squatted down in a sort of tub, probably used for baths, and hearing no noise, he had left his retreat; and the pole had aided him in climbing several walls; but yet he always got back to the idiots' court. Day was just breaking, and he heard footsteps going and coming in the buildings, for they are nowhere earlier than in hospitals. It was necessary to avoid the gaze of the turnkey, who would soon be in the courts; the wicket of a room was half open—he glided in, and was about with much precaution to roll himself in a large heap of straw; but what was his astonishment to see it occupied by a man naked, his hair disheveled, beard long, and eye haggard and bloodshot. The madman, for such he was, looked at Desfosseux with a fierce air, then made him a quick sign: and as he stood still, darted at him as if to attack him. A few caresses seemed to appease him; he took Desfosseux by the hand and made him sit down beside him, heaping all the straw around him in the manner and with the gestures of a monkey. At eight o'clock a morsel of black bread fell in at the door, which he took up, looked at, threw into a heap of dirt, and then picked it up and began to eat. During the day more bread was brought; but as the madman was asleep, Desfosseux seized and devoured it at the risk of being himself devoured by his terrible companion, who might have been enraged at the abstraction of his pittance. At twilight the madman awoke, and talked for some time with inconceivable volubility; night came on and his excitement sensibly increased, and he began to leap about and make hideous contortions, shaking his chains with a kind of pleasure.

In this appalling situation Desfosseux waited with impatience until the madman fell asleep, to go out at the wicket. About midnight, hearing him move no longer, he advanced first one leg and then the other, when he was seized by the madman with a powerful grasp, who threw him on the straw and placed himself before the wicket, where he remained till daylight, motionless as a statue. The next night another attempt, and another obstacle. Desfosseux, who grew distracted, employed his strength, and a tremendous struggle ensued; Desfosseux, being struck by his chains, and covered with bites and blows, was compelled to call for the keepers. They mistaking him at first for one of the madmen who had got loose, we're also about to put him in a cell; but he managed to make himself known, and at length obtained the favor of being brought back to us.

We remained eight days in the dungeon, after which I was put in the Chaussee, where I found a party of prisoners who had received me so well on my arrival. They were making good cheer and denied themselves nothing; for, independently of the money procured by the "letters of Jerusalem," they had got a supply from some females whom they knew, and who constantly visited them. Having become, as at Douai, the object of special vigilance, I still sought to escape: when at length the day arrived for the departure of the chain.

Chapter VIII

It was the 20th of November, 1797: all the morning we remarked a more than usual commotion in the prison. The prisoners had not left their cells, and the gates were every moment opened and shut with much noise: the jailers went to and fro with a busy air, and they were knocking off irons in the great court, of which the sound reached our ears. About eleven o'clock two men, clothed in blue uniforms, entered Fort, Mahon, where for eight days I had been replaced with the companions of my essay to escape: it was the captain of the chain and his lieutenant. "Well," said the captain, smiling in a kind of familiar way, "have we any return horses (fugitive galley-slaves)?"

And whilst he spoke all pressed about, trying who should testify the most respect to him. "Good-day, M. Viez: good-day, M. Thierry," resounded on all sides. These salutations were even repeated by the prisoners who had never seen either Viez or Thierry, but who, assuming an air of acquaintance, hoped to get some favor. It was no wonder if Viez was a little giddy with so much applause; but as he was accustomed to these homages it did not quite turn his brain, and he knew very well what he was about. He perceived Desfosseux. "Ah ha!" said he, "here is a darby cutter (one skilled in cutting off his chains), who has traveled before with us. I heard that you had a narrow escape of being a head shorter (guillotined at Douai), my boy. You escaped well, by Jove; for look you, it is better to go back to the meadow (Bagne) than let the executioner play at pitch and toss with your knowledge-box (head). Besides, my lads, let the world be quiet, and we shall get beef and celery." The captain had only begun his inspection and continued it, addressing similar jokes to all his "merchandise," for by that name he called the condemned prisoners.

The critical moment arrived, and we went into the Cours des Fers, where the house-surgeon came to us to examine if we were all in a state to bear the fatigues of a journey. We were all pronounced adequate, although some were in a most woeful plight. Each prisoner then puts off the prison livery, and assumes his own clothes; those who have none have a frock and trousers of packing-cloth, insufficient to protect them from the cold and damp. Hats and clothes, if at all decent, belonging to the prisoners, are torn in a particular way to prevent escape; they take, for instance, the border off the hat and the collar from the coat. No prisoner is allowed to retain more than six francs; the overplus is given to the captain, who gives it on the route in proportion as it is needed. This precaution is easily eluded by placing louis in large sous hollowed out.

These preliminaries adjusted, we went into the great court, where were the guards of the chain, better known as argousins, or galley-serjeants, who were for the most part men of Auvergne, water-carriers, messengers, or coalmen, who carried on their trade in the intervals between the journeys. In the midst of them was a large wooden chest, containing the fetters which are used in all similar expeditions. We were made to approach two and two, taking care to match us in height, by means of a chain of six feet in length, united to the cordon of twenty-six prisoners, who could thus only move in a body: each was confined to the chain by a sort of iron triangle, called the cravat, which, opening on one side by a turning screw, is closed on the other with a nail firmly riveted. This is the most perilous part of the operation; the most turbulent and riotous then keep quiet: for at the least movement, instead of falling on the anvil, the blows would break their skull, which every stroke of the hammer grazes. Then a prisoner comes with long scissors and cuts off the hair and whiskers of the prisoners, pretending to leave them irregular.

At five in the evening, the fettering was finished; the argousins retired, and the prisoners alone remained. Left to themselves, far from despairing, these men gave themselves up to all the tumults of riotous gayety. Some vociferated horrible jokes, echoed from all sides with the most disgusting shouts; others amused themselves by provoking the stupid laughter of their companions by beastly gestures. Neither the ears nor the modesty were even spared, all that was heard or seen was immoral and discordant. It is too true that, once loaded with fetters, the condemned thinks himself obliged to trample under foot all that is honored and respected by the society which has cast him off; there are for him no longer any restraints, but from material obstacles; his charter is the length of his chain, and he knows no law but the stick to which his jailer accustoms him Thrown amidst beings to whom nothing is sacred, he takes care how he testifies that steady resignation which betokens repentance; for then he would be the butt of a thousand jokes; and his keepers, troubled at his serious mood, would accuse him of meditating some plot. It is best, if he would keep them unsuspicious of his intentions, that he should always appear reckless and abandoned. A prisoner who sports with his destiny is never an object of mistrust; the experience of the greater part of the wretched beings who have escaped from the Bagne prove this. What is certain, is that with us, those who had the greatest interest in escaping were the least dejected; they were the leaders. When night came on, they began to sing. Imagine fifty scoundrels, the greater part drunk, all screeching different airs. In the midst of this din a "return horse" thundering out with the lungs of a Stentor, some couplets of the "Galley Slave's Complaint."

All our companions were not so happy; in the third cordon, composed of the least disorderly, we heard sobs, saw tears flowing; but these symptoms of grief, or, of repentance, were hailed by the shouts and threats of the two other cordons, where I figured in the first rank as a dangerous fellow, from my address and influence. I had near me two men—one a schoolmaster condemned for rape; and the other an ex-officer of health, sentenced for forging—who, without mirth or melancholy, talked together with a very calm and natural tone.

"We are going to Brest," said the schoolmaster.

"Yes," answered the officer of health, "we are going to Brest; I know the country, I passed through it when I was sub-aide-de-camp, in the 16th Brigade—a good country, upon my word—I shall not be sorry to see it again."

"Is there much amusement?" asked the pedagogue.

"Amusement!" said his companion, with an air of astonishment.

"Yes, amusement—I ask you, if we can procure any little pleasure if we are well treated,—if provisions are cheap."

"In the first place, you will be taken care of," replied the officer, "and well taken care of; for at the Bagne at Brest only two hours are needed to find all the beans in the soup, while at Toulon the search would take eight days."

Here the conversation was interrupted by loud cries, proceeding from the second division. They were knocking on the head three prisoners, the ex-commissary of war Lemiére, the staff-major Simon, and a robber named the Petit Matelot (little sailor), who were accused of having betrayed their comrades by information, or of having defeated some plot in prison. The person who had pointed them out to the vengeance of the galley slaves was a young man, who would have been a good study for a painter or an actor. With dilapidated green slippers, a hunting waistcoat destitute of buttons, and nankeen pantaloons, which seemed to defy the inclemency of the weather; his head-dress was a helmet without a peak, through the holes of which a tattered nightcap was visible.

In the Bicêtre, he was only known by the name of "Mademoiselle," and I learnt that he was one of those degraded wretches, who abandon themselves in Paris to a course of the most disgusting debaucheries. The argousins, who ran at the first noise, did not give themselves the least trouble to get the Petit Matelot from the hands of the galley slaves, and he died four days afterward of the blows he had received. Lemiére and Simon would also have perished but for my interference; I had known the former when in the roving army, where he had rendered me some service. I declared that it was he who had supplied me with the tools necessary for undermining the walls at Fort Mahon, and thenceforward they left him and his companion unmolested.

We passed the night on the stones in a church, then converted into a magazine. The argousins made regular rounds, to assure themselves that no one was engaged in fiddling (sawing their fetters). At daybreak we were all on foot; the lists were read over, and the fetters examined. At six o'clock we were placed in long cars, back to back, the legs hanging down outside, covered with hoar frost and motionless from cold. On reaching St. Cyr we were entirely stripped, to undergo a scrutiny which extended to our stockings, shoes, shirt, mouth, ears, nostrils, etc. It was not only the files in cases which they sought, but also for watch-springs, which enable a prisoner to cut his fetters in less than three hours. This examination lasted for upward of an hour, and it is really a miracle that one-half of us had not our noses or feet frozen off with cold.

At bedtime, we were heaped together in a cattle stall, where we laid so close that the body of one served for the pillow of the person who laid nearest to him, and if any individual got entangled in his own, or any other man's chain, a heavy cudgel rained down a torrent of blows on the hapless offenders. As soon as we had laid down on a few handfuls of straw, which had already been used for the litter of the stable, a whistle blew to command us to the most absolute silence, which was not allowed to be disturbed by the least complaint, even when, to relieve the guard placed at the extremity of the stable, the argousins actually walked over our bodies.

The supper consisted of a pretended bean soup, and a few morsels of half-moldy bread. The distribution was made from large wooden troughs, containing thirty rations: and the cook, armed with a large pot ladle, did not fail to repeat to each prisoner, as he served him, "One, two, three, four, hold out your porringer, you thief;" the wine was put into the same trough from which the soup and meat were served out, and then an argousin, taking a whistle, hanging to his buttonhole, blew it thrice; saying, "Attention, robbers, and only answer by a yes, or a no. Have you had bread?"

"Yes."

"Soup?"

"Yes."

"Meat?"

"Yes."

"Wine?"

"Yes."

"Then go to sleep, or pretend to do so."

A table was laid out at the door, at which the captain, lieutenant, and chief argousins, seated themselves to take a repast superior to ours; for these men, who profited by all occasions to extort money from the prisoners, took excellent care of themselves, and eat and drank abundantly. At this moment the stable offered one of the most hideous spectacles that can be imagined; on one side were a hundred and twenty men herded together like foul beasts, rolling about their haggard eyes, whence fatigue or misery banished sleep; on the other side, eight ill-looking fellows were eating greedily without, not for one moment losing sight of their carbines or their clubs. A few miserable candles, affixed to the blackened walls of the stable, cast a murky glare over this scene of horror, the silence of which was only broken by stifled groans, or the clank of fetters. Not content with striking us indiscriminately, the argousins made their detestable and brutal witticisms about the prisoners; and if a man, fevered with thirst, asked for water, they said to him, "Let him who wants water put out his hand."

The wretch obeyed, mistrusting nothing, and was instantly overwhelmed with blows. Those who had any money were necessarily careful; they were but very few, the long residence of the majority in prison having, for the most part, exhausted their feeble resources.

These were not the only abuses which marked the progress of the galley chain. To economize to his own profit the expenses of the journey, the captain generally made one of the cordons to go on foot. But this cordon was always that of the strongest men, that is, the most turbulent of the condemned. Woe to the females whom they met, or the shops which they came near. The women were assaulted in the grossest manner, and the shops stripped in a twinkling, as I saw at Morlaix, at a grocer's, who did not save even a loaf of sugar, or a pound of soap. It may be asked what the guards were about during the commission of this offense? The guards were pretending to be very busily preventing it, but without opposing any real obstacle to it, knowing that they would ultimately profit by the plunder; since the prisoners must sell their booty through their medium, or exchange with them for strong liquors. It was the same with the thefts made on the prisoners who were added to the chain in its passage; scarcely were they ironed, when their neighbors hustled them, and took from them all the little sums they might have.

Far from preventing or checking these spoliations, the argousins even suggested them, as I saw them do with an ex-gendarme, who had sewed up a few louis in his leather breeches. "Here is some fat!" said they, and in less than three minutes the poor devil was penniless. At such times the party attacked call out loudly for the argousins, who take good care not to approach until the robbery be perfected, and they thump, with heavy cudgels, the poor wretch who has been plundered. At Rennes, the bandits I am speaking of carried their infamy to such an extent as to despoil a sister of charity, who had brought us some tobacco and money, in a stall where we were to pass the night. The most crying of these abuses have disappeared, but many yet exist, which it will be difficult to root out, if we consider to what sort of men the conducting of the chain must be intrusted, and the materials they have to work upon.

Our toilsome journey endured for twenty-four days, and on reaching Pont-a-Lezen, we were placed in the depot of the Bagne, when the prisoners perform a kind of quarantine, until they have recovered from their fatigue, and it has been ascertained whether they have any contagious disease. On our arrival we were washed in pairs, in large tubs filled with warm water, and on quitting the bath our clothes were allotted to us. I received, like the others, a red frock or cassock, two pairs of trousers, two sailcloth shirts, two pairs of shoes, and a green cap; each garment and article, was marked with the initials GAL, and the cap had besides a tin plate, on which was the number of the entry in the register. When they had given us our clothing, they riveted an iron ring round the leg, but did not couple us.

The depot of Pont-a-Lezen, being a sort of lazaretto, there was not a very rigorous vigilance kept up. I was even told that it was easy to get out of the rooms and climb the outside walls. I learned this from a man named Blondy, who had once escaped this way from the Bagne at Brest, and hoping to profit by this information, I made arrangements to avail myself of the first opportunity. We sometimes had loaves given to us, weighing eighteen pounds each, and on quitting Morlaix, I had hollowed out one of these, and filled it with a shirt, a pair of trousers, and some handkerchiefs. It was a new kind of portmanteau, and passed unsuspected. Lieutenant Thierry had not given me to a special watch; on the contrary, having learned the grounds of my condemnation, he had told the commissary, when speaking of me, that with men as orderly as I was, he could manage the chain as easily as a girls' school. I had then inspired no mistrust, and looked about me to execute my project. I at first contemplated cutting through the wall of the room in which I was placed. A steel chisel, left by accident on the foot of my bed by a turnkey prisoner, who riveted the ankle cuffs, served me to make the opening, whilst Blondy cut my irons. This completed, my comrades made a figure of straw, which they put in my place, to deceive the vigilance of the argousins on guard, and soon, clothed in the garments I had concealed, I got into the courtyard of the depot. The walls which environed it were at least fifteen feet high, and to climb them I found I must get something like a ladder; a pole served as a proxy, but it was so heavy and so long that it was impossible for me to drag it over the wall, to aid my descent on the other side. After many trials, as vain as they were painful, I was compelled to risk the leap, in which I succeeded so badly, and came down with so much violence on my legs, that I could scarcely drag myself into a bush that was near. I hoped, that when the pain had somewhat abated, I could escape before daybreak, but it became more excessive, and my feet swelled so prodigiously, that I was compelled to give up all hopes of escape. I dragged myself along, as well as I was able, to the door of the depot, to return to my cell, thinking thereby to diminish the number of blows which would be assuredly bestowed upon me. A sister whom I asked for, and to whom I told all, had me conveyed into a room, where my feet were dressed. This excellent woman, who compassionated my lot, went to the commandant of the depot, and obtained my pardon by her solicitations, and at the end of three weeks, being completely recovered, I was conveyed to Brest

The Bagne is situated in the bosom of the bay; piles of guns, and two pieces of cannon, mounted at the gates, pointed out to me the entrance, into which I was introduced, after having been examined by the two guards of the establishment. The boldest of the condemned, however hardened, have confessed that it is impossible to express the emotions of horror excited by the first appearance of this abode of wretchedness. Each room containing twenty night camp-couches, called bancs (benches), on which lie six hundred fettered convicts, in long rows, with red garbs, heads shorn, eyes haggard, dejected countenances, whilst the perpetual clank of fetters conspires to fill the soul with horror. But this impression on the convict soon passes away, who feeling that here he has no cause to blush at the presence of anyone, soon identifies himself with his situation. That he may not be the butt of the gross jests and filthy buffoonery of his fellows, he affects to participate in them; he even exceeds them; and soon in tone and gesture this conventional depravity gets hold of his heart. Thus, at Anvers, an ex-bishop experienced, at first, all the outpourings of the riotous jokes of his companions; they always addressed him as Monseigneur, and asked his blessing in all their obscenities; at every moment they constrained him to profane his former character by blasphemous words, and, by dint of reiterating these impieties, he contrived to shake off their attacks; at a subsequent period he became the public-house keeper at the Bagne, and was always styled Monseigneur, but he was no longer asked for absolution, for he would have answered with the grossest blasphemies.

The inconveniences and abuses that existed at the prison of Brest when I was conducted thither, were additional inducements to make my sojourn as brief as possible. In such a situation, the first thing is to assure oneself of the discretion of the comrade with whom we may be coupled. Mine was a vine-cutter from Dijon, about thirty years old, condemned to twenty-four years' labor for forcible burglary; already half an idiot, misery and brutal treatment had completely stupefied him. Bowed beneath the stick, he seemed to have just preserved the instinct of a monkey or a dog, and thus answered the whistle of the galley-serjeants. He was of no use to me, and I was compelled to look out for a mate who would not fear or shrink from the prospective beatings which are always liberally bestowed on convicts suspected of favoring, or even conniving at the escape of the prisoner. To get rid of Bourguignon, I feigned indisposition, and he was yoked to another, as when I recovered, I was placed with a poor devil sentenced to eight years' labor for stealing chickens from a church.

He had not entirely parted with his senses, and the first time we were alone together said to me—"Listen, comrade; I can see you do not mean to live long at the public expense— be frank with me, and you will not lose by it." I told him that I intended to escape at the first opportunity. "Well," said he, "I advise you to bolt before the beasts of serjeants are quite acquainted with your phiz:—but have you any cash?" I told him that I had, and he then informed me that he could procure me other habiliments, but that I must buy a few utensils like one who meant to work out his time quietly. These utensils were two wooden bowls, a wine-keg, straps to support my fetters, and a small mattress stuffed with oakum. It was Thursday, the sixteenth day of my confinement at the Bagne, and on the Saturday evening I obtained sailor's clothes, which I immediately put on under my convict's frock. On paying the seller of them, I saw that he had about his wrists round cicatrices of deep burns, and I learnt, that being condemned to the galleys for life in 1776, he had been put to the torture at Rennes, without confessing the robbery of which he was accused. On the promulgation of the code of 1791, his sentence was commuted to twenty-four years' labor at the galleys.

The next day my division went out, at the cannon's signal, to work at the pump, which was always in motion. At the wicket, they examined, as usual, our manacles and clothing. Knowing this practice, I had pasted over my sailor's garb a bladder painted flesh color. As I purposely left my frock and shirt open, none of the guards thought of examining me more closely, and I got out unsuspected. Arrived at the basin, I retired with my comrade behind a pile of planks, and my fetters having been cut the previous evening, soon yielded. Having got rid of these, I soon threw off my galley-frock and trousers, and putting on under my leather cap a wig which I had brought from Bicêtre, and having given my comrade the trifling recompense which I had promised him, I disappeared, cautiously gliding behind the piles of timber.

CHAPTER IX

I PASSED THROUGH THE WICKET WITHOUT DIFFICULTY, and found myself in Brest, a place entirely unknown to me; and the fear that my doubt as to what road I should take might induce suspicion, increased my uneasiness. At length, after a thousand ins and outs, turnings and twistings, I reached the only gate of the city, where was always stationed an old galley guard named Lachique, who detected a convict by a look, a motion or a turn; and what rendered his observations more easy was, that whoever passed any time at the Bagne, dragged habitually and involuntarily that leg to which the fetter had been fastened.

However, it was necessary to pass this dreaded personage, who was smoking very sedately, fixing his hawk's eye on all who went in and came out. I had been warned, and determined to exercise all my effrontery. On getting up to Lachique, I put down a pitcher of buttermilk, which I had purchased to render my disguise the more complete, and filling my pipe, I asked him for a light. He gave it readily and with all the courtesy he was capable of, and after we had blown a few whiffs in each other's faces, I left him and went on my way.

I went straight forward for three-quarters of an hour, when I heard the cannon shots which were fired to announce the escape of a convict, so that the peasantry of the neighborhood may be informed that there is a reward of one hundred francs to be obtained by the lucky individual who may apprehend the fugitive. I saw many persons armed with guns and scythes scour about the country and beat every bush, and even the smallest tufts of heath. Some laborers appeared to take their arms out with them as a precaution, for I saw several quit their work with a gun which they took out of a furrow. One of these latter passed near me in a cross road which I had taken on hearing the report of the cannon, but they had no suspicion of me, for I was clad very well, and my hat being off, by reason of the heat, they saw my hair curled, which could not be the case with a convict.

I continued striking into all the byways, and avoiding towns and detached houses. At twilight I met two women, whom I asked about the road, but they answered me in a dialect which I did not comprehend, but on showing them some money, and making signs that I was hungry, they conducted me to a small village to a cabaret, kept by the garde-champetre (patrol), whom I saw in the chimney nook, decorated with his insignia of office. I was for a moment disturbed, but soon recovering myself, I said I wished to speak to the mayor. "I am he," said an old countryman with a woolen cap and wooden shoes, seated at a small table and eating an oaten cake. This was a fresh disappointment to me, who relied on escaping in my way from the cabaret to the mayor's house. However, I had the difficulty to contend with, and surpass in some way or other. I told the wooden-shoed functionary, that having lost myself on leaving Morlaix for Brest, I had wandered about, and asking him at the same time how far it was from this latter city, and expressing a desire to sleep there that evening—

"You are five leagues from Brest," said he, "and it is impossible to reach it this evening; if you will sleep here, I will give you a bed in my barn, and tomorrow you can start with the garde-champetre, who is going to carry back a fugitive convict whom we apprehended yesterday."

These last words renewed all my terrors, for by the tone in which they were uttered, I saw that the mayor had not credited the whole of my story. I, however, accepted his obliging offer; but after supper, at the instant we reached the barn, putting my hands in my pockets, I cried out with all the energy of a man in despair—

"Oh, heavens! I have left at Morlaix my pocketbook, with my passport and eight double louis. I must return this moment, yes, this very moment; but how shall I find my way? If the patrol, who knows the road, would go with me, we should be back in time in the morning to set out early with the galley slave."

This proposal routed all suspicions, for a man who wishes to escape seldom solicits the company he would fain avoid; on the other hand the garde-champetre, smelling a reward, had buttoned on his gaiters at the first word. We set out accordingly, and at break of day reached Morlaix. My companion, whom I had taken care to ply well with liquor on the road, was already pretty well in for it, and I completed him with some rum at the first pot-house we reached in the city. He stayed there to wait for me at a table, or rather under the table, and he might have waited long enough.

I asked the first person I met to direct me to Vannes, and on being told, I set out, as the Dutch proverb has it, "with my feet shod by fear." Two days passed without accident, but on the third, some leagues from Guemene, at the turning of the road, I met two gendarmes, who were returning from duty. The unexpected vision of yellow breeches and laced hats gave me uneasiness, and I made an effort to escape, when my two gentlemen desired me to halt, making at the same time a very significant gesture with their carbines. They came up to me, and having no credentials to show them, I invented a reply on the spur of the moment. "My name is Duval, born at l'Orient, deserter from the Cocarde frigate, now in the roadstead at St. Maly." It is useless to say, that I had learnt all this during my stay at the Bagne, where we had daily accounts from all parts. "What!" cried the thief, "you must be Auguste—son of father Duval, who lives at L'Orient, on the terrace near the Boule d'Or." I did not deny this, for it would have been worse to have been detected as a fugitive convict. "Parbleu!" added the brigadier, "I am sorry you are caught, but that cannot now be helped; I must send you to l'Orient or to St. Malo," I begged him not to send me to the former of these towns, not caring to be confronted with my new relations, in case they should desire to confirm the identity of my person. However, the quarter-master gave orders that I should be conducted thither, and the next day I reached l'Orient, when I was entered in the jailer's book, at Pontainau, the naval prison, near the new Bagne, which was to be peopled by convicts brought hither from Brest.

Being next day questioned by the commissary of the marine, I again declared that I was Auguste Duval; and that I had left my ship without permission, to go and see my parents. I was then led back to prison, where A found, amongst other sailors, a young man of l'Orient, accused of striking a lieutenant. Having talked some time with him, he said to me one morning, "My boy, if you will pay for breakfast, I will tell you a secret worth knowing." His mysterious air disturbed me, and made me anxious to know all; and after breakfast he said to me, "Trust to me and then I can extricate you. I do not know who you are, but I am sure you are not young Duval, for he has been dead these two years at St. Pierre, at Martinique. (I started.) Yes, he has been dead these two years, but no one knows it, so well are our colonial hospitals regulated. Now I can give you such statements about his family, that you may pass for him even with his parents, for he left home when he was very young. To make quite sure, you can feign a weakness of intellect, produced by sea toil and sickness. Besides, before Auguste Duval went to sea, he had a mark tattooed on his left arm, as most sailors have; I know it well; it was an altar with a garland on it. If you will remain a fortnight in the cell with me, I will mark you in a similar manner, so that all the world could not detect the imposture." My friend appeared frank and open-hearted, and I may account for the interest he took in me, by his desire to trick justice, a feeling that pervades the minds of all prisoners; for them to deceive it, mislead it, or delay it, is a pleasurable vengeance, which they willingly purchase at the expense of a few weeks' confinement. Here was such an opportunity, and the means were soon put in action. Under the windows of our room was a sentinel, and we began by pelting him with pieces of bread; and as he threatened to tell the jailer of us, we cared him to put his menaces into execution. On this, when he was relieved, the corporal, who was a meddling fellow, went to the office; and the next moment the jailer came to take us, without even telling us the reason of our removal. But we soon found it out on entering a sort of hole in the sunken ditch, very damp but tolerably light. Scarcely were we shut in, when my comrade commenced operations, in which he perfectly succeeded. It consisted only in pricking my arm with several needles tied together, and dipped in Indian ink and carmine. At the end of twelve days the wounds closed, so that it was impossible to tell how long they had been made. My companion also took advantage of this "leisure undisturbed," to give me additional details concerning the Duval family, whom he had known from childhood, and was in fact related to them, and instructed even in the minutest habitual trick of my Sosia.

These instructions were of unspeakable advantage to me when, on the sixteenth day after our detention in the dungeon I was taken out to be confronted with my father, whom the commissary of marine had sent for. My comrade had so well described him, that I could not be mistaken on perceiving him. I threw my arms about his neck; he recognized me; his wife, who came soon after, recognized me; a female cousin and an uncle recognized me; and I was so undoubtedly Auguste Duval, that the commissary himself was convinced of it. But this was not sufficient to procure my liberation; as a deserter from the Cocarde, I was to be sent to Saint Malo, where she had left several men at the hospital, and then be tried before the maritime court. To tell the truth I felt no alarm at this; certain that I should find means of escape on my journey, I set out at length, bathed with my parents' tears, and the richer by several louis, which I added to the stock already concealed about me.

Until we reached Quimper, where I was to be handed over to another guard, no opportunity presented of bidding adieu to the company of gendarmes who guarded me, as well as many other individuals, robbers, smugglers, or deserters. We were placed in the town jail, and on entering the chamber where I was to pass the night, I saw at the foot of the bed a red frock, marked on the back Gal, initials but too well known to me. There, covered with a tattered quilt, slept a man, whom, by his green cap decked with the tin plate numbered, I recognized as a galley slave. Would he know, would he betray me? I was in a spasm of fear, when the individual, awakened by the noise of bolts and bars, sat up in his bed, and I knew him to be a young fellow named Goupy, who went to Brest at the same time as myself. He was condemned to chains for life, for a forcible burglary in the environs of Bernai in Normandy; his father was a galley-serjeant at Brest, where most probably, he did not come first purely for change of air. Not wishing to have him continually before his sight, he had procured an order for his removal to the Bagne at Rochfort, and he was then on his road thither. I told him all my affairs, and he promised secrecy, and kept his promise the more faithfully, as it would have profited him nothing to betray me.

However, the guard did not start immediately, and fifteen days elapsed after my arrival at Quimper, without any mention of departure. This delay gave me the idea of penetrating the wall and escaping; but having found the impossibility of success, I managed so as to obtain the confidence of the jailer, and got an opportunity of executing my project by inspiring him with an idea of false security. After having told him that I had heard the prisoners plotting something, I pointed out to him the place in the prison where they had been at work. He made most minute search, and naturally enough found the hole I had made; and this discovery procured for me all his kindness. I sometimes found it overpowering, for the watch was kept so regularly that all my schemes were routed. I began to think of going to the hospital, where I hoped to be more fortunate in the execution of my projects. To give myself a high fever, it was only necessary to swallow tobacco juice for a couple of days, and then the doctors ordered my removal. On getting to the house, I got in exchange for my clothes a gray cap and cloak, and was then put along with the rest.

It was a part of my plan to remain for some time at the hospital, that I might know the ways in and out, but the illness caused by the tobacco juice would only last for three or four days, and it was necessary to find some recipe which would bring on another complaint; for, knowing no one in the place it was impossible for me to get a supply of tobacco juice. At Bicêtre, I had been taught how to produce those wounds and Bores, by means of which so many beggars excite public pity, and get those alms which cannot be worse bestowed. Of all these expedients, I adopted that which consisted in making the head swell like a bushel; first, because the doctors would certainly be mistaken; and then because it gave no pain, and all traces of it could be removed by the day following My head became suddenly of a prodigious size, and great was the talk thereof amongst the doctors of the establishment, who not being, as it appeared, blessed with a superabundance of skill knew not what to think of it. I believe some of them spoke of elephantiasis, or of dropsy in the brain. But, be that as it may, their brilliant consultation ended in the prescription most common in hospitals, of putting me on the most strict regimen.

With money, such orders did not fret me; but yet I had only gold, and changing that might awaken suspicion. However, I determined to try a liberated convict, who acted as infirmary helper; and this fellow, who would do anything for money, soon procured for me what I desired. On my telling him that I was desirous of getting out into the town for a few hours, he said, that if I disguised myself, it would not be difficult, as the walls were not very high. It was, he said, the way he and his companions got out when they wanted anything. We agreed that he should provide me with clothes, and that he should accompany me in my nocturnal excursion, which was to be a visit to sup with some girls. But the only clothes he could procure for me inside the hospital were much too small, and we were compelled to suspend operations for a time.

Just at this time, one of the sisters of charity passed by my bed, whom I had already watched in performing very mundane duties; not that sister Franchise was one of those dandified nuns who were ridiculed on the stage, before the young nuns were transformed into boarders, and the white handkerchief was replaced by the green apron. Sister Francoise was about thirty-four, a brunette, with a deep color, and her powerful charms created more than one unhappy passion, as well amongst the soldiers as the infirmary overseers. On seeing this seducing creature, who weighed perhaps nearly fifteen stone, the idea occurred to me that I would borrow for a short time her cloister garb. I spoke of it jestingly to my overseer but he took it as if meant seriously, and promised on the ensuing night to get a part of sister Franchise's wardrobe. About two in the morning, I saw him come with a parcel, containing a gown, handkerchief, stockings, etc., which he had carried off from the sister's cell whilst she was at matins. All my bedroom companions, nine in number, were soundly asleep, but I went out to put on my attire. What gave me the most trouble was the head-dress. I had no idea of the mode of arranging it, and yet the appearance of disorder in these garments, always arranged with a scrupulous nicety, would have infallibly betrayed me.

At length sister Vidocq finished her toilet, and we crossed the courts and gardens, and reached a place where the wall could easily be scaled. I then gave the overseer fifty francs, nearly all my store; he lent me a hand, and I was soon in the lonely spot, where I reached the country, guided by my indefinite directions. Although much encumbered with my petticoats, I yet walked so fast as to get on at least two leagues before sunrise. A countryman whom I met going to sell his vegetables at Quimper, and whom I questioned as to my road, told me that I was journeying toward Brest. This was not the way for me, and I made the fellow comprehend that I wished to go toward Rennes, and he pointed out to me a cross road leading to the high route to this city, which I immediately took, trembling at every moment, lest I should meet any of the soldiers of the English army, then lying in the villages between Nantes and Brest. About ten in the morning, on reaching a small hamlet, I inquired if there were any soldiers near, evincing much fear, which was real however, lest they should examine me, which would have led to a detection. The person whom I asked was a sacristan, full of chatter and inquisitiveness, who compelled me to enter a curate's house near at head, to take some refreshment.

The curate, an elderly man, whose face betrayed that bent violence so rare among the ecclesiastics who come into towns to blazon forth their pretensions and conceal their immorality, received me very kindly. "My dear sister," said he, "I was about to celebrate mass; as soon as that is over, you shall breakfast with us." I was then compelled to go to church and it was no trifling embarrassment for me to make the signs and genuflections prescribed to a nun. Fortunately, the curate's old female servant was at my side, and I got through very well by imitating her in every particular. Mass concluded, we sat down to table, and interrogatories commenced. I told the good people that I was going to Rennes to perform penance. The curate asked nothing more. The sacristan pressing me rather importunately to know why I was thus punished, I told him, "Alas, it was for curiosity!" This closed the little man's mouth. My situation was, however, one of difficulty, I was afraid to eat, lest I should betray too manly an appetite: and again, I more frequently said "M. le cure," than "my dear brother;" so that my blunders would have betrayed all, had I not terminated the breakfast. I found means, however, to learn the names of the villages of the district, and, strengthened by the blessings of the curate, who promised not to forget me in his prayers, I went on my way somewhat more accustomed to my new attire.

I met few people on my way, the wars of the revolution had depopulated the wretched country, and I traversed the villages whilst the inhabitants were all in bed. Arriving one night at a hamlet, composed of a few houses, I knocked at the door of a farmhouse. An old woman came to open it to me, and conducted me to a good-sized parlor. The family consisted of father, mother, a young lad, and two girls, from fifteen to seventeen years of age. When I went in, they were making a kind of cake of buckwheat flour, and were all around the frying pan. I expressed my desire for some refreshment. Out of respect to my sacred office, they gave me the first cakes, which I devoured without even feeling that they were so burning hot as to scorch my palate. I have often since sat down at sumptuous tables, where I have had abundance of most exquisite wines, and meats of the most delicate and delicious flavor, but I can never forget the cakes of the peasant of Lower Brittany.

On the termination of supper we had prayer, and then the father and mother lighted their pipes. Suffering greatly from agitation and fatigue, I expressed a wish to retire. "We have no bed to give you," said the master of the house, who had surely been a sailor, spoke very good French: "you shall sleep with my two girls." I observed to him, that going on a vow I must sleep on straw, adding that I should be contented with a corner in the stable. "Oh!" replied he; "in sleeping with Jeanne and Madelon you will not break your vow, for the bed is only made of straw. Besides, you cannot be in the stable, for that is already occupied by a tinker and two soldiers, who asked my leave to pass the night there." I could say nothing more; and but too glad to escape the soldiers, I reached the boudoir of the young ladies. It was a loft filled with cider apples, cheese, and smoked bacon: in one corner a dozen fowls were roosting, and lower down were hutched eight rabbits. The furniture consisted of a dilapidated pitcher, worm-eaten joint stool, and the fragment of a looking-glass; the bed, like all in that country, was only a chest shaped like a coffin, half filled with straw, and scarcely three feet wide.

Here was a fresh embarrassment for me; the two young girls undressed very deliberately before me, who had many and good reasons for seeming very shy. Independently of circumstances that may be guessed, I had under my female attire a man's shirt, which would betray my sex and my incognito. Not to be detected, I took out a few pins very slowly, and when I saw the two sisters had got into bed I overturned, as if by accident, the iron lamp which lighted us, and then took off my feminine habits without fear. On getting between the sail-cloth sheets, I laid down so as to avoid all unlucky detection. It was a tormenting night: for without being pretty, mademoiselle Jeanne, who could not stir without touching me, had a freshness and plumpness but too attractive for a man condemned for so long a period to the rigors of absolute celibacy; those who have ever been in a similar situation, will believe without difficulty that I could not sleep for a single instant.

I was motionless, with my eyes open like a hare in its form, when long before daylight I heard a knocking with the butt-end of a musket against the door. My first idea, like every man in similar circumstances, was that they had traced me, and were coming to apprehend me; but I did not know where to conceal myself. The blows were redoubled: and I then bethought me of the soldiers sleeping in the stable, which dissipated my fears. "Who is there?" said the master of the house, leaping up.

"Your soldiers."

"Well, what do you want?"

"Fire to light our pipes before we set off."

Our host then arose, and blowing up the fire left in the ashes, he opened the door to the soldiers. One of these, looking at his watch by the lamplight, said "It is half-past four o'clock. Come, let us go; the rations are in good order. Come, to the march, my lads." They went away, and our host, putting out the lamp, went to bed again. As for me, not wishing to dress myself in presence of my bed-fellows any more than undress myself, I immediately rose, and lighting the lamp, put on my woolen gown, and then going down on my knees in a corner, pretended to pray until the family should awake. I did not remain long in waiting. At five o'clock in the morning the mother cried from her bed, "Jeanne, get up, and get some soup ready for the sister, who wishes to depart early." Jeanne got up, and the buttermilk soup having been made and eaten with good appetite, I left the good persons who had so kindly welcomed me.

Having walked all day without flagging, I found myself at the close of the day in a village near the environs of Vannes, when I remembered I had been deceived by false or mistaken directions. I slept at this village, and the next day I went through Vannes at a very early hour. At the end of eight days' walk, I reached Nantes, and I inquired for Feydeau. When at the Bicêtre, I had learned from a man named Grenier, called the Nantais, that there was in this quarter a kind of auberge, where robbers met without fear of disturbance. I knew that by using a well-known name I should be admitted without difficulty; but I only remembered the address very vaguely, and scarcely knew how and where to find out the place. I adopted an expedient which succeeded. I went into many houses and asked for M. Grenier. At the fourth where I sought for this name, the hostess, leaving two persons with whom she was conversing, took me into a small room and said to me, "Have you seen Grenier? Is he still sick (in prison)?"

"No," answered I, "he is well (free);" and perceiving that I was all right with the mother of robbers, I told her unhesitatingly who I was, and how I was situated. Without replying, she took my arm, and opening a door let into the panel, made me enter a low room, where eight men and women were playing at cards and drinking brandy, etc.

"Here," said my guide, presenting me to the goodly party, much astonished at the appearance of a nun, "here is a sister come to convert you all." At the same time I tore off my handkerchief, and three of the party, whom I had met at the Bagne, recognized me. They were Berry, Bidaut Mauger and the young Goupy, whom I had met at Quimper. The others were fugitives from the Bagne of Rochefort. They were much amused at my disguise; and when supper had made us all jolly, one of the females put on my nun's habit, and her gestures and attitudes contrasted so strangely with this costume, that we all laughed till we cried, until the moment when we went to bed.

On waking, I found on my bed new clothes, linen, and in fact everything necessary for my toilet. Whence did they come? But this was of no consequence. The little money which I had not expended at the hospital at Quimper, where I paid dearly for everything, had been used on my journey; and without clothes, resources or acquaintances, I was compelled to wait until I could write to my mother; and in the meantime accepted all that was offered me. But one circumstance of a particular nature abridged my stay at the Feydeau. At the end of a week, my companions seeing me perfectly recovered from my fatigues, told me one evening that they intended on the next day to break into a house on the Place Graslin, and relied on my going with them. I was even to have the post of honor, that of working inside with Mauger.

But I did not intend to do this, and thought how I could make use of the circumstance to get away and go to Paris, where, near my family, my resources would not fail me; but it never entered into my calculations to enroll myself in a band of thieves; for although I had associated with robbers, and lived by my wits, I felt an invincible repugnance to enter upon on a career of crime, of which early experience had taught me the perils and risks. A refusal would, on the other hand, render me suspected by my new companions, who, in this retreat, secure from sight or hearing, could knock me on the head with impunity, and send me to keep company with the salmon and smelts of the Loire; and I had only one course to take, which was to get out as quickly as possible, and this I resolved on doing.

Having exchanged my new clothes for a countryman's frock and eighteen francs to boot, I left Nantes, carrying at the end of a stick a basket of provisions, which gave me at once the appearance of an inhabitant of the environs.

CHAPTER X

ON QUITTING NANTES, I WALKED FOR A DAY and two nights without stopping at any village, and my provisions were exhausted; still I went on haphazard, although decided on reaching Paris or the seashore, hoping to get to sea in some ship, when I reached the first habitation of a town which appeared to have been lately the scene of a combat. The greater part of the houses were nothing but a heap of rubbish, blackened by fire, and all that surrounded the place had been entirely destroyed. Nothing was standing but the church tower, whence the clock was striking the hour for inhabitants who no longer existed.

This scene of desolation presented at the same time the most whimsical occurrences. On the only piece of wall which remained belonging to an auberge, were the words "Good entertainment for man and horse;"—there the soldiers were watering their horses in the holy-water vessels;—farther on, their companions were dancing to the tune of an organ with the country women, who, ruined and wretched, had prostituted themselves to the Blues (Republicans) for bread. By the traces of this war of extermination we might have thought ourselves in the midst of the wilds of America, or the oases of the desert, where barbarous tribes were cutting each other's throats with blind fury. Yet there had only been, on both sides, Frenchmen: but every species of fanaticism made rendezvous there. I was in La Vendee, at Cholet.

The master of a wretched cabaret, thatched with broom, where I halted, gave me my cue, by asking me if I had come to Cholet for the next day's market. I answered in the affirmative, much astonished that one should be held in the midst of these ruins, and even that the farmers of the environs had anything to sell; but my host told me that scarcely anything was brought to this market but cattle from distant districts; on the other hand, although no one had yet done anything to repair the disasters of the war, the amnesty was nearly terminated by General Hoche, and if republican soldiers were still found in the country it was that they might keep down the Chouans (a Contraction of the word *chathaunt*, a screech-owl; a title given to parties of Vendeeans, and afterward to bands formed for plunder, who ravished the western part of France subsequently to 1793, and were called by this name because, like owls, they came out only at night), who were becoming formidable.

I went to the market early the next day, and thinking to take advantage of it, I accosted a cattle-dealer, whose face was familiar with me, asking him to listen to me for a moment. He looked at me with distrust, taking me probably for a spy, but I hastened to relieve his suspicions, telling him that it was only a personal affair. We then entered a hovel where they sold brandy, and I then told him that having deserted from the 36th demi-brigade to see my parents, who lived in Paris, I was desirous of getting some situation which would allow me to reach my destination without fear of arrest. This good fellow told me that he had no situation to offer me, but that if I would drive a drove of oxen as far as Sceaux, I might go with him. No proposal was ever accepted with more readiness, and I entered on my duty instantly, anxious to show my new master all the return I could testify for his kindness.

In the afternoon he sent me to carry a letter to a person in the town, who asked me if my master had desired me to take anything back with me; I said no. "Never mind," said the person, who was, I believe, a notary, "take him this bag with three hundred francs." I delivered this sum to the cattle dealer, to whom my punctuality gave confidence. We set out next day, and on the third morning, my master calling to me, said, "Louis, can you write?"

"Yes, sir."

"Reckon?"

"Yes, sir."

"Keep an account?"

"Yes, sir."

"Ah, well; as I must go out of the road to see some lean beasts, at St. Gauburge, you will drive the oxen on to Paris, with Jacques and Saturnin: you will be head man." He then gave me his instructions and left us.

By reason of my advancement, I no longer traveled on foot, which was a great relief to me; for the drivers of cattle are always stifled with the dust, or up to their knees in mud, which increases as they proceed. I was besides, better paid and better fed, but I did not abuse these advantages, as I saw many other head drovers do on the journey. Whilst the food of the animals was converted by them into pullets, or legs of mutton, or exchanged with the innkeepers, the poor brutes grew visibly thinner.

I behaved myself most faithfully, so that joining us at Verneuil, my master, who had preceded us, complimented me on the state of the drove. On reaching Sceaux, my beasts were worth twenty francs a head more than any others, and I had spent ninety francs less than my companions for my traveling expenses. My master, enchanted, made me a present of forty francs, and cited me as the Aristides of cattle drovers, and I was in some sort quite an object of admiration at the market of Sceaux, and, in return, my colleagues would willingly have knocked me on the head. One of them, a chap of Lower Normandy, famed for strength and skill, endeavored to disgust me with my avocation, by taking upon himself to inflict the popular vengeance upon me; but what could such a clumsy yokel do against the pupil of the renowned Gospel! The Low Norman cried craven, after one of the most memorable boxing matches of which the inhabitants of a fat cattle market ever preserved a remembrance.

My conquest was the more glorious, as I had testified much forbearance, and had only consented to fight when I would have been impossible to avoid it. My master, more and more satisfied with me, wished absolutely to engage me for a year, as foreman, promising me a small share of the profits. I had received no news of my mother; and here I found resources which I was about to seek at Paris; and, besides, my new dress disguised me so much that I felt no fear of detection in my frequent excursions to Paris. I passed, in fact, many persons of my acquaintance, who paid no attention to me. But one evening as I was passing along the Rue Dauphine, to get to the Barriere d'Enfer, someone tapped me on the shoulder. My first thought was to run for it, without turning round, being aware that, whoever thus stops you, relies on your looking back to seize you; but a stoppage of carriages choked up the passage. I therefore waited the result, and in a twinkling discovered that it was a false alarm.

The person who had so much alarmed me, was no other than Villedieu, the captain of the 13th chasseurs, with whom I had been intimately acquainted at Lille. Although surprised to see me with a hat covered with waxed cloth, a smock-frock, and leathern gaiters, he testified much pleasure at the meeting, and invited me to supper, saying that he had some marvelous narratives to tell me. He was not in his uniform, but this did not astonish me, as the officers commonly wore common clothes when staying in Paris. What struck me most was his uneasy air and excessive paleness. As he expressed a wish to sup out of the barriers, we took a coach, which conveyed us to Sceaux.

On reaching the Grand Cerf, we asked for a private room. We were scarcely served with what we asked for, when Villedieu, double-locking the door and putting the key in his pocket, said to me, with tears in his eyes, and with a wild air, "My friend, I am a lost man! lost! undone! I am pursued, and you must get me a habit similar to your own. If you want it, I have money, plenty of money, and we will start for Switzerland together. I know your skill at escapes, and you, and you only can extricate me."

The commencement did not place me upon a seat of velvet; already much embarrassed myself, I did not much care to place myself again in the way of being apprehended, and to unite my fortunes with those of a man hotly pursued might lead to my detection. This reasoning, which I made to myself, decided me on being wary with Villedieu; besides, as yet I did not know exactly what he wished to do. At Lille, I had seen him spending much more than his pay; but a young and handsome officer has so many ways of procuring money, that no one thinks any harm of that. I was then greatly astonished at the following details.

"I will not speak to you of those circumstances in my life which preceded your acquaintance with me; it will suffice to say, that as brave and intelligent as most, and backed with good interest, I found myself at the age of thirty-four, a captain of chasseurs, when I met you at Lille, at the Café de la Montagne. There I associated with an individual whose honest appearance prepossessed me in his favor, and our intimacy ripened into so close a friendship, that he introduced me to his house. It was one replete with comfort and elegance, and I received every attention and token of amity; so good a fellow was M. Lemaire, so charming a woman was Madame Lemaire. A jeweler, traveling about with his articles of trade, he made frequent absences of six or eight days; but still I visited his wife, and you may guess that I soon became her lover. Lemaire did not perceive, or would not perceive it. I led, to be sure, a most agreeable life, when one morning I found Josephine in tears. Her husband, she told me, had just been apprehended, with his clerk, for having sold unstamped plate, and as it was probable that his house would be soon visited, all its contents must be speedily removed. The most valuable goods were then packed in my portmanteau, and conveyed to my lodgings. Josephine then entreated me to go to Courtrai, where the influence of my rank might be of avail to her husband. I did not hesitate for a moment, for so deeply was I enamored of this woman that I would have given up the exercise of my faculties if I did not think as she thought, and wish what she wished.

"Having obtained my colonel's permission, I sent for horses and a post chaise, and set out with the express who had brought the news of Lemaire's arrest. I did not at all like this man's face, and what prejudiced him against me was to hear him and Josephine, and treat her with much familiarity. Scarcely had I got into the carriage, when he installed himself at ease in one corner and slept till we reached Berlin, where I stopped to take some refreshment. 'Captain, I do not wish to get out,' said he familiarly and rousing himself; 'be so good as to bring me a glass of brandy.' Much surprised at this tone, I sent what he asked for by the waiting-maid, who returned to me, saying that he would not answer her, but was asleep. I went to the chaise, where I saw my gentleman motionless in his corner, his face being covered with a handkerchief; 'Are you asleep?' said I in a low tone. 'No,' he replied, 'nor do I wish to be; but why the devil did you send a servant when I told you that I do not wish to face these gentry' I gave him his glass of brandy and we started again. As he did not appear disposed for sleep, I asked him carelessly his reason for preserving so strong an incognito, and concerning the business which led me to Courtrai, of which I knew no details. He then told me, that Lemaire was accused of belonging to a band of Chauffeurs, and added, that he had not told Josephine, for fear of increasing her affliction. We drew near Courtrai, and about four hundred paces from the town my companion called to the postilion to stop for an instant; he then put on a wig, concealed in the crown of his hat, stuck a large plaster on his left eye, took from under his waistcoat a brace of pistols, primed them, returned them to the belt under his vest, opened the door, jumped out and disappeared.

"All these maneuvers, which were perfect mysteries to me, only served to create great uneasiness. Could it be that Lemaire's arrest was only a pretext? Was he laying a snare for me? Did he wish me to play some part in an intrigue of any kind? I could not explain it to myself, nor think it was so. I was still very uncertain what to do, and was pacing the chamber, with long strides at the Hotel du Damier, where my mysterious companion had advised me to alight, when the door suddenly opened and I saw Josephine. At her appearance all suspicions vanished. Her abrupt entrance, her hurried journey made without me, and some hours after, whilst she might easily have had part of my chaise, and my protection, ought rather perhaps to have excited them. But I was in love, and when Josephine told me that she could not endure an absence, I thought her argument and explanation admirable and unanswerable. It was four o'clock in the afternoon, and Josephine dressed herself, and, going out, did not return until ten o'clock. She was accompanied by a man dressed like a peasant of Liege, but whose manner and expression of countenance did not agree with his costume.

"Some refreshments were brought in, and the servants then leaving us, Josephine immediately throwing herself on my neck, begged me to save her husband, repeating, that it only depended on me to do this. I promised all she asked, and then the pretended peasant, who had till this time been perfectly silent, spoke in very good language, and unfolded to me what I was required to do. Lemaire, he said, reached Courtrai, with several travelers, whom he did not know, and had only met on the road, when they were surrounded by a body of gendarmes, who summoned them to surrender. The strangers stood on the defensive, and pistol shots were exchanged, and Lemaire, who with his clerk, had remained neuter on the field of battle, had been seized without making any effort to escape, feeling a consciousness of innocence, and that he had nothing to fear. But very serious charges had been produced against him; he was unable to give a very precise account of his business in the district, because, said the assumed countryman, he was then smuggling; besides, they had found in a bush, two pair of pistols, which it was asserted had been thrown there by himself and clerk, at the moment they were apprehended; and, finally, a woman swore that she had seen him the week before on the road to Ghent, with the identical travelers, whom he said he had not met before the morning of the engagement with the gendarmes.

"'Under these circumstances,' added my peasant interlocutor, 'we must find means of proving first that Lemaire has only left Lille three days, and that he had been there for the entire month previously. That he never carries pistols. That before starting he received sixty louis from a person.'

"This confidence ought to have opened my eyes as to the nature of the steps required of me; but intoxicated with Josephine's caresses, I drove away all thoughts, and compelled myself not to think of what might be the results. We all three set out the same night for Lille, and on arriving I ran about all day making the necessary arrangements, and by evening all my witnesses were ready. Their depositions had no sooner reached Courtrai, than Lemaire and his clerk were set at liberty. We may imagine their joy; and it was in fact so excessive, that I could not help thinking that the case must have been critical indeed, if their liberation could occasion such transports. The day after his arrival, dining with Lemaire, I found in my napkin a rouleau of a hundred louis. I was weak enough to accept them, and from that hour my ruin was decreed.

"Playing high treating my comrades, and having habits of luxury, I soon spent this sum. Lemaire daily made me fresh offers of service, by which I profited to borrow several sums of him, amounting to two thousand francs, without being any the richer or more moderate. Fifteen hundred francs borrowed of a Jew, on a post-obit for a thousand crowns, and twenty-five louis which the quartermaster advanced me, disappeared with the same alacrity. At last I spent even a sum of five hundred francs, which my lieutenant had begged me to keep for him until the arrival of his horse-dealer, to whom he owed this sum. This I lost on one evening at the Café de la Montagne, with a man named Carrie who had already ruined half the regiment.

"The night that followed was a fearful one; agitated by the shame of having abused the confidence of the lieutenant, by squandering what was his little all, enraged at being duped, and tormented with the desire of still playing on, I was twenty times tempted to blow my brains out. When the trumpets sounded the turn out, I had not closed my eyes; it was my week, and I went out to go through the examination of the stables; the first person I met was the lieutenant, who told me that the horse-dealer had arrived, and he would send his servant for the five hundred francs. My agitation was so great that I answered I scarcely knew what, and the obscurity of the stable alone prevented him from observing my confusion. There was not a moment to lose, if I would not forfeit my good name with my superiors and brother officers.

"In this horrid situation I did not even think of applying to Lemaire, so much I already imagined had I abused his friendship; but I had no other resource, and, at length, I resolved on writing him a note, stating the embarrassment in which I was placed. He came to me instantly, and laying on the table two gold snuff-boxes, three watches, and twelve engraved spoons, he told me that he had no ready money at the moment, but that I could easily procure it by taking these valuables to the pawnbrokers, and he left them at my disposal. After overwhelming him with thanks, I sent the whole to be pledged by my servant, who brought me twelve hundred francs for them. I first paid the lieutenant, and then, led by my unlucky star, I flew to the Café de la Montague, where Carre, after much persuasion, was induced to give me my revenge, and the remaining seven hundred francs passed from my purse to his.

"Aghast at this stroke of fortune, I wandered for some time about the streets of Lille, whilst a thousand mad ideas flashed through my brain. It was in this mood that I imperceptibly drew near to Lemaire's house, which I entered mechanically: they were sitting down to dinner, and Josephine, struck by my extreme paleness, questioned me with interest concerning my affairs and my health. I was in one of those dejected moods whence the consciousness of his weakness makes the most reserved more communicative: I confessed all my extravagances, adding, that within two months I must pay more than four thousand francs, of which I had not a single sous.

"At these words Lemaire looked fixedly at me, with a gaze I can never forget all my life, be it long or short. 'Captain,' said he, 'I will not forsake you in your difficulties, but one confidence deserves another; nothing should be kept from a man who has saved you from ...' and with a horrid smile he passed his hand across his throat. I trembled and looked at Josephine. She was perfectly calm! It was a horrible moment! Without seeming to notice my perturbation, Lemaire continued his fearful confidence. I learned that he was out of Sallambier's band, and that, when the gendarmes had apprehended him near Courtrai, they were returning from a party of plunder in a country house in the vicinity of Ghent. The servants had defended themselves, and three had been killed, and two wretched women were hung up in a cellar. The valuables I had pawned were the produce of the robbery which had followed these atrocities! After having explained to me how he had been apprehended near Courtrai, whilst making off, Lemaire added, that henceforward it was only for me to repair my losses and better my fortune by accompanying him in two or three expeditions.

"I was annihilated! Up to this period the conduct of Lemaire, the circumstances of his arrest, the nature of the service which I had rendered him, appeared to me very suspicious; but I carefully drove from my thoughts all that could convert my suspicions into reality. As if tormented by a frightful nightmare, I waited till I should awake, and my waking was more horrible still.

"'Well,' said Josephine, with an inquiring tone, 'you do not answer—Ah! I see, we have lost your friendship; and I shall die!' She burst into tears; my head was in a whirl: forgetful of Lemaire's presence, I threw myself on my knees like a madman, crying out, 'I quit you? no, never, never!' Tears choked my utterance, and I saw a tear in Josephine's eyes, but she instantly resumed her firmness. For Lemaire, he offered us orange-flower water with as much calmness as a cavalier presents an ice to his partner at a ball.

"I was thus enlisted in this band, the terror of the departments of, the north, La Lys and L'Escaut. In less than fifteen days I was introduced to Sallambier, in whom I recognized the peasant of Liege: to Duhamel, Chopine, Calandrine, and the principal Chauffeurs. The first business in which I took a share was in the environs of Douai. Duhamel's mistress, who accompanied us, introduced us to the house, in which she had been waiting-maid. The dogs having been poisoned by a wood-cutter employed on the premises, we only waited until the family should be asleep to commence our operations. No locks could resist Calandrin, and we reached the drawing-room with the utmost silence. The family, consisting of the father, mother, great aunt, two young persons, and a relation on a visit, were playing at Buillotte. We only heard the words, 'Pass, I hold; I play Charlemagne,' etc.; when Sallambier, opening the door quickly, appeared, followed by ten men with blackened faces, and pistols and daggers in their hands. At this sight the cards fell from the hands of all; the females shrieked for mercy, until, with a motion of his hand, Sallambier compelled silence, whilst one of our band, jumping like a monkey on the mantelpiece, cut the ropes of the bells. The women fainted, but were not heeded. The master of the house alone retained some presence of mind. After having opened his mouth at least twenty times without uttering a word, he at length contrived to ask what we wanted?' Money' said Sallambier, whose voice seemed to me entirely changed; and taking the candle from the card-table, he made signs to the master of the house to follow him into the next room, where he knew that the money and jewels were deposited. It was precisely Don Juan preceding the statue of the Commandant.

"We remained in the dark, motionless at our posts, only hearing the stifled sobs of the females, the chink of money, and these words, 'More, more,' which Sallambier repeated from time to time in a sepulchral tone. At the end of twenty minutes he returned with a red handkerchief, tied together by the corners, and filled with pieces of money; the jewels were in his pockets. To neglect nothing, they took from the old aunt and the mother their ear-rings, as well as the watch of the relation who had so well chosen the time to make his visit. We set out at last, after having carefully locked up the whole party, without the servants, who had been for some time in bed, being at all disturbed or aware of the attack on the chateau.

"I had a share also in several other enterprises, more hazardous than that I now mention. We were resisted, or else the proprietors had concealed their money, and to make them produce it they were put to most dreadful tortures. At first they confined themselves to burning the soles of their feet with red-hot shovels; but adopting more expeditious measures, they began to tear out the nails of those who were obstinate, or blow them as large as balloons with bellows. Some of these unfortunates, having really no money as was supposed, died in the midst of these tortures. See, my friend, on what a career I had entered; I, an officer well born, for whom twelve years of active service, some exploits of bravery, and the testimony of my comrades, had created a universal esteem, which I had ceased to deserve for a very long time, and which I was about to lose forever."

Here Villedieu paused, and dropped his head upon his breast, like one overwhelmed by his recollections. I left him undisturbed for a moment, but the names he mentioned were too well known to me not to excite the most lively curiosity in my mind to hear the whole of his recital. A few glasses of champagne restored his energy, and he thus continued:—

"But crimes multiplied so alarmingly, that the gendarmes not being sufficiently powerful to check them, columns of the military were taken from the various garrisons. One was placed under my command. You may suppose that this measure had an entirely contrary effect to that intended; forewarned by me, the Chauffeurs avoided the places that I was to watch with my division. Thus matters went on worse than ever, and the authorities were at a loss what plans to adopt, when they learned that the majority of the Chauffeurs resided at Lille, and the order was given for redoubling the superintendence (surveillance) at the gates. We found means, however, to render all these precautions useless. Sallambier procured at a broker's of the town, who clothed a regiment, fifteen uniforms of the 13th Chasseurs, and disguised with them that number of Chauffeurs, who, with me at their head, went out at twilight, as if going on a detachment of a secret enterprise.

"Although this stratagem completely answered, I thought I perceived myself to be the object of particular surveillance. A report spread about that there were men in the vicinity of Lille disguised as horse chasseurs. The colonel appeared to mistrust me, and one of my brother officers was appointed alternately to direct the moving columns before entrusted to my charge alone. Instead of giving me the watchword, as to the other officers of the gendarmes, I was not informed of it until the moment of departure. At length I was so directly accused, that I was under the necessity of inquiring of the colonel, who, without any disguise, told me that I was reported to have communication with the Chauffeurs. I defended myself as well as I could, and thus matters remained, only that I left the service of the moving columns, which began to be so active that the Chauffeurs scarcely durst show themselves.

"Sallambier, unwilling to remain long in inaction, redoubled his audacity in proportion as obstacles multiplied about us. In one night he committed three robberies in the same district. But the proprietors of the first of the houses attacked, having divested themselves of their gags and bonds, gave the alarm. The tocsin was sounded for two leagues round, and the Chauffeurs only owed their safety to the fleetness of their horses. The two brothers Sallambier were hotly followed, and it was only on approaching Bruges that they distanced their pursuers. In a large village where they were, they hired a chaise and two horses, to go, as they said, some leagues, and return in the evening.

"A coachman drove them, whom, on getting to the water's edge, the elder Sallambier struck from behind with his knife, and knocked him from his seat. The two brothers then threw him into the sea, hoping that the waves might retain the corpse. Masters of the conveyance, they went on their journey, when, toward the close of the day, they met a countryman who bade them good evening. As they did not answer, the man approached, saying, 'Ah! Vandeck, do you not know me? It is I—Joseph.' Sallambier then told him that he had hired the carriage for three days without a conductor. The tone of this answer, the condition of the horses, covered with sweat, and which their master would never have let without a driver, all made the interrogator suspicious. Without prolonging the conversation, he ran to the adjacent village and gave the alarm. Seven or eight men on horseback pursued the carriage, which they soon perceived traveling slowly along. They increased their speed and overtook it. It was empty. Rather disappointed, they drove it into an auberge where they intended to pass the night; but scarcely were they seated, when a great noise was heard, occasioned by a crowd conveying before the magistrate two travelers accused of the murder of a man whom some fishermen had found with his throat cut on the seashore. All ran out, and Joseph recognized the individuals whom he had seen in the carriage, and which they had quitted because the horses could go no further. They (the two Sallambiers) appeared greatly disconcerted when confronted with Joseph. Their identity was soon settled. Under a suspicion that they might belong to some band of Chauffeurs, they were transferred to Lille, where they were recognized on reaching the Petit Hotel.

"There the elder Sallambier, pressed by the agents of police, denounced all his companions, and pointed out when and where they might be taken. In consequence of this information, forty-three persons of both sexes were "apprehended. Among them were Lemaire and his wife. At the same time an order of arrest was issued against me; but informed by a quartermaster of gendarmes, whom I had served, I escaped and reached Paris, where I have been these ten days. When I met you I was looking for the house of an old sweetheart, where I intended to conceal myself, or obtain some means of escape to a foreign country; but I am now easy, since I met with Vidocq."

CHAPTER XI

THE CONFIDENCE OF VILLEDIEU FLATTERED ME VERY MUCH; but yet I thought my rencontre with him might lead me into danger. I therefore told him a false tale when he inquired about my mode of life and domicile. For the same reason I took care not to be at the rendezvous which he had appointed for the next day; for it would have been attended with much risk to myself and no advantage to him. On leaving him, at eleven o'clock in the evening, I took the precaution of making many detours before I entered my auberge, for fear of being dogged by any police agents. My master, who had gone to bed, aroused me early in the morning to tell me to set out with him for Nogent le Rotrou, whence we were to proceed to his own farms, situated in the environs of this city.

In four days, we arrived at the termination of our journey, and although received in the family as a hardworking and faithful servant, I still persisted in the intention I had formed for some time of returning to my own country, whence I received neither information nor money. On returning to Paris with some cattle, I told my master of my determination, and he let me go with much reluctance. On quitting him, I entered a café in the Place du Chatelet, to procure a porter to fetch my luggage, and there taking up a newspaper, the first intelligence that met my eyes was an account of Villedieu's capture. He had not allowed himself to be taken before he had prostrated two of the agents of police, who had orders to apprehend him, and was himself severely wounded. On being executed, two months afterward, at Bruges, the last of eighteen, all his accomplices, he contemplated their headless and bleeding bodies as they fell one by one by his side with a calmness and fortitude that never wavered for an instant.

This circumstance gave me reason to be satisfied with the steps that I had taken. Had I stayed with the cattle dealer, I was under the necessity of coming twice a week to Paris, and the police, directing its attention against all plots and foreign agents, was assuming an extent and energy which might have brought detection on me, as they minutely watched individuals, who, perpetually called by business from the departments of the west, might serve as agents between the Chouans and their friends in the capital. I therefore set out without delay, and on the third day reached Arras, which I entered in the evening, at the time when the workmen were returning home from labor. I did not go directly to my father's house, but to one of my aunts, who informed my parents. They thought me dead, not having received any of my last letters; and I have never been able to discover how and by whom they were intercepted. Having related all my adventures at length, I asked the news of my family, which necessarily led to my inquiring for my wife. I was told that my father had for some time received her at his house, but that her conduct was so scandalous, that she had been disgracefully expelled thence. She was, I was informed, pregnant by an attorney, who supplied most of her wants," but that for some time nothing had been heard of her, and they had ceased to trouble themselves concerning her.

I gave myself no care about her, for I had matters of much greater import which demanded my attention. I might be discovered at any moment; and if apprehended at my parent's house they would be involved in difficulties. It was imperative on me to find an asylum where the vigilance of the police was not so active as at Arras, and I threw my eyes upon a village in the vicinity, Amber-court, where there resided a quondam Carmelite friar, a friend of my father, who agreed to receive me. At this period (1798) priests were compelled still to say mass in secret, although direct hostilities toward them had ceased. Father Lambert, my host, celebrated his divine functions in a barn; and as he had no assistance but from an old man, feeble and impotent, I offered to fulfill the duties of sacristan, which I did so satisfactorily, that one would have supposed it had been my calling all the days of my existence. I also became father Lambert's assistant in giving lessons to the children of the neighborhood. My skill in teaching made some noise in the district, for I had taken an excellent method to advance my pupils rapidly; I traced the letters with a lead pencil, which they wrote over with the pen, and the Indian-rubber effected the rest. The parents were delighted; only it was rather difficult for my scholars to perform without their master; but the Artesian peasants, however cunning in the common trans-actions of business, were good enough not to find this out.

This sort of life was rather agreeable to me. Clothed as a wandering friar, and tolerated by the authorities, I had no fear of detection or suspicion: on the other hand, my animal tastes, which I have always held in due consideration, were well supplied, the parents sending us perpetually beer, poultry, and fruit. I had in my classes some pretty peasant girls, who were very teachable. All went on well for some time, but at length a distrust of me was evinced; I was watched, and it was discovered that I pushed my instructions occasionally rather too far, and complaint was made to father Lambert, who told me of the charges against me, which I stoutly denied. The complainants were silenced, but redoubled their vigilance; and one night, when, impelled by classic zeal, I was about to give a lesson in a hay-loft to a female scholar about sixteen years of age, I was seized by four brewers' men, dragged into a hop ground, stripped of my clothes, and scourged, till the blood flowed copiously, with rods of nettles and thistles. The pain was so acute, that I lost my senses, and on reviving, found myself in the streets, naked, and covered with blisters and blood.

What was to be done? To return to father Lambert would be to incur fresh dangers. The night was not much advanced, and although eaten up with excess of fever, I determined to go on to Mareuil, to an uncle's house, and arrived there at two o'clock in the morning, worn out with fatigue, and only covered with a ragged mat which I had found near a pond. After having laughed unsparingly at my mishap, they rubbed my body all over with cream mixed with oil; and at the end of eight days I set out quite well for Arras, but it was impossible for me to remain there. The police might get information it some unlucky moment that I was there, and I therefore decided on starting for Holland, and fixing myself there, taking with me a supply of money, which enabled me to remain at my ease until something should occur that would employ me usefully.

I passed through Brussels (where I learnt that the Baroness d'l__ had settled in London), Anvers, and Breda, and then embarked for Rotterdam, in which city I put up at an inn that had been specially recommended to me. I there met with a Frenchman, who was remarkably attentive and civil to me, and frequently invited me to dinner. I received all his advances with mistrust, knowing that all means were resorted to by the Dutch government to recruit their navy. In spite of all my caution, my companion contrived to intoxicate me with a particular liquor, and on the next morning I awoke on board a Dutch brig of war. All doubt was at an end; intemperance had given me up as a prey to the "sellers of souls."

Lying near the shrouds, I was reflecting on my singular destiny, which multiplied so many incidents of my wayward career, when one of the crew, pushing me with his foot, desired me to rise and get on my sailor's clothes. I pretended not to understand him, and then the boatswain gave me the same orders in French. On my replying that I was not a sailor, since I had signed no agreement, he seized a rope's end to strike me with; on which, I grasped a knife belonging to a sailor, who was breakfasting at the foot of the mainmast, and, placing my back against a gun, I swore I would rip up the first man who should assault me. This occasioned much disturbance in the ship, and brought up the captain, who was a man about forty, of good appearance, and whose manners were free from that coarseness so usual with seafaring people. He listened to me with kindness, which was all he could do, for it was not in his power to change the maritime organization of his government.

We had then on board men whose inclinations and habits of life were so totally foreign from naval service, that the very idea of compelling them to enter it was essentially ridiculous. Of the two hundred individuals pressed like myself, there were not perhaps twenty who had ever set foot on shipboard before. The majority had been carried off by main force, or trepanned by drunkenness: they had inveigled others by a promise of a free passage to Batavia, where they wished to settle; amongst these were two Frenchmen, one a bookkeeper from Burgundy, and the other a gardener of Lemosin, who, it is evident, were admirably calculated to make sailors. To console us, the crew told us that, for fear of desertion, we should not go ashore for six months.

To me, who had so long intended to enter the navy, the situation was not so repugnant, if I had not been constrained to it, and if I had not had in perspective the slavery which threatened me; added to which, was the ill-treatment of the boatswain, who could not forgive my first essay with him. On the least false maneuver or mistake, the rope's end descended on my back in a style so argumentative and convincing, that I even regretted the cudgel of the galley-serjeant at the Bagne. I was in despair, and twenty times resolved to let fall from the maintop a wooden pulley on the head of my tormentor, or else to fling him into the sea when I was on the watch. I should certainly have done

one or the other of these, if the lieutenant, who had taken a liking to me because I taught him to fence, had not in some measure alleviated my sufferings. Besides, we were forthwith going to Helvoetslays, where the *Heindrack* lay, of whose crew we were to form a part, and in the passage an escape might be effected.

The day of transshipment came, and we embarked, to the number of two hundred and seventy, in a small sloop, manned by twenty-five sailors, and with twenty-five soldiers to guard us. The weakness of this detachment determined me to attempt to disarm the soldiers, and compel the sailors to conduct us to Anvers. One hundred and twenty of the recruits, French and Belgians, entered into the plot, and we resolved on surprising the men on guard at the moment their comrades were at dinner, whom we could then easily secure. This enterprise was executed with success as they suspected nothing. The commandant of the detachment was seized at the moment he was taking his tea, but was not at all maltreated. A young man of Tournai, engaged as super-cargo, and reduced to work as a sailor, explained to him so eloquently the motives that led to our revolt, as he called it, that he allowed himself to be conducted into the hold with his soldiers unresistingly. As for the sailors they were neutral: a man of Dunkirk only, who was in our plot, took the helm.

Night came on, and I wished to lie-to, lest we should encounter any guard ship, to which the sailors could make signals; but the Dunkirker obstinately refused, and we kept on our course, and at daybreak we were under the cannon of a fort near Helvoetsluys. The Dunkirker then announced his intention of landing to see if we could get on shore safely, and I saw then that we were sold; but it was impossible to recede. Signals had doubtlessly been made, and at the least movement the guns of the fort could blow us out of the water. It was compulsory, then, that we should await the event. Soon a boat, with twenty men on board, left the shore and approached the sloop. Three officers who were in it came on deck, without testifying any fear, although it was the scene of a busy struggle between our comrades and the Dutch sentry, who wanted to free the soldiery from the hold. The first word of the eldest officer was to ask for the ringleader, and all remaining mute, I spoke in French—that there had been no plot, but that it was by a simultaneous movement that we had resolved on throwing off the slavery imposed on us. We had ill-treated no one, as the captain and sailors could testify, who knew it was our intention to have left them in possession of the vessel after we had landed at Anvers."

I know not what effect my harangue produced, for I was not allowed to finish it; only, whilst we were piled up in the hold, in the place of the soldiers, whom we had confined there on the previous evening, I heard someone say to the pilot, "that more than one would swing at the yard-arm next morning." The sloop was then turned toward Helvoetsluys, and we reached that place the same day, at about four o'clock in the afternoon. In the roadstead was anchored the *Heindrack*. The commandant of the fort went in his cutter, and in an hour afterward I was conducted thither also. I found there assembled a sort of maritime council, who questioned me as to the particulars of the mutiny, and the part I had taken in it. I asserted, as I had already done to the fort governor, that having signed no articles of engagement, I thought myself justified in effecting my escape by any means that presented.

I was then ordered to retire, to make way for the young man of Tournai, who had seized the captain. We were looked on as the leaders in the enterprise, and we know that in such cases it is the ringleaders who undergo the punishment, and we were to suffer nothing more or less than hanging. Fortunately, the young man, who had had time for consideration, corroborated my statement, and asserted firmly that no one had suggested it, but that the idea had come across us all at the same moment; besides, we were quite sure of not being betrayed by our comrades, who showed much concern for us, and swore that if we were condemned, the ship on board which they should be placed should jump like a rocket—that is, that they would fire the powder-magazine, although they should be blown up with it; and these were lads who would have dared to do what they ventured to talk about. Whether they feared the results of these menaces, and the bad example that it would afford to the sailors of the fleet which had been recruited in a similar way—or whether the council held that we were entrenched behind a rampart of legitimate defense, in seeking to withdraw ourselves from a compulsory service, they promised to ask for our pardon from the admiral, on condition that we kept our comrades in due subordination, which appeared not to be their favorite virtue. We promised all that they desired, for nothing makes one so easy to be persuaded or to promise, as the feeling of a cord about one's neck.

These preliminaries agreed upon, our comrades were transferred on board the ship, and went between decks with the crew, whose complement they were to make up. All was done with the greatest order, neither was any complaint heard, nor was there the smallest disorderly symptom to be repressed. It is right to say that we were not ill-treated, as we had been on board the brig, where our old friend the boatswain did all with the rope's end in his hand. Besides, by giving the marines instruction in fencing, I was treated with some attention, and this even made bombardier, with a pay of twenty-eight florins per month. Two months passed away thus, whilst the vigilance of the English cruisers would not allow of our quitting anchorage. I became reconciled to my new employment, and had no thoughts of leaving it, when news was brought that the French authorities were searching for all Frenchmen who were forming part of the Dutch crews.

Researches, however, were continued; they stationed agents at the ports and taverns, who examined those men who landed by permission or otherwise. In one of my excursions, I was apprehended. I have long preserved my gratitude for it toward the ship's cook, who honored me with his personal animosity ever after I had found fault with his giving us swipes for beer, and stinking cod for fresh fish. Taken before the commanding officer, I said I was a Dutchman, and my knowledge of the language sufficed for me to keep up my assertion; and besides, I demanded to be taken back to my ship with a guard, that I might procure papers to substantiate my assertion, than which nothing could be more natural. A subaltern was ordered to accompany me, and we set out in the skiff that had conveyed me ashore. On getting near the ship, I made my friend, with whom I had been talking very familiarly, get up alongside first; and when I saw him entangled amongst the rigging, I thrust off suddenly from the ship's side, calling to the boat's crew to pull their hardest, and that they should have something to drink. We were cutting through the water while my subaltern friend was jostled about amongst the crew, who did not or pretended not to know him. On getting ashore, I ran to conceal myself in a house which I knew, determined on quitting the vessel, in which it would be difficult for me to appear without being apprehended. My flight would confirm all suspicions raised against me. and therefore the captain gave me his authority, tacitly, to do what I might think best for my own security.

A Dunkirk privateer, the *Barras*, Captain Fomentin, was in the roads. At this period, vessels of this kind were seldom overhauled, as they were in a measure a sort of asylum; and as it suited me to get on board it, I got a lieutenant, to whom I applied, to introduce me to Fomentin, who, on my own statement, admitted me on board as master-at-arms. Four days afterward, the *Barras* set sail for a cruise in the Sound. It was at the beginning of the winter of 1799, when the tempestuous weather destroyed so many vessels on the coast of the Baltic. Scarcely were we at sea, when a northerly wind rose, quite contrary to our destination. We were compelled to put about, and the roll of the ship was so great, that I was excessively ill; so much so, that for three days I could take nothing but weak brandy and water, and half the crew were in the same state, so that a fishing-boat might have taken us without our striking a blow.

At length the wind abated, and turned suddenly to the southwest; and the *Barras*, an admirable sailor, going ten knots an hour, all hands aboard soon recovered. At this moment, the man at the masthead cried out, "A sail on the larboard tack!" The captain took his glass, and declared it to be an English coaster, under a neutral flag, and which the squalls had separated from the convoy. We bore down on her, with the wind on our bow. At the second discharge of our guns she struck, before we could board her; and putting the crew down into the hold, we made for Bergen in Norway, where our cargo was soon disposed of.

I remained six months on board the *Barras*, and my share of the prizes was pretty considerable, when we went to lay up for a time at Ostend. We had scarcely got into the basin, when several police agents came on board to examine the papers of the crew; and I afterward learnt that they paid us this unusual visit, in order to detect a murderer who was supposed to be on board.

When my turn came for examination, I asserted that I was Auguste Duval, born at l'Orient; and added, that my papers were at Rotterdam, in the office of the Dutch marine department. No notice was taken, and I thought I had well got rid of the affair. When the three hundred men who were on board had been questioned, eight of us were called, and told that we must go to the register office, to give the requisite explanation. Not liking this, I turned off at the first angle of the street, and had already gained thirty yards on the gendarmes, when an old woman, who Was washing the steps of a house, put her broom between my legs and I fell. The gendarmes came up to me and put on handcuffs, besides belaboring me pretty well with the butts of carbines and the flat sides of swords, and I was conducted thus to the commissary, who, after hearing me, asked me if I had not escaped from the hospital of Quimper. I saw that I was caught, for there was equal danger as Duval or Vidocq. However, I decided on the first name, which offered less unfavorable chances of the two; since the road from Ostend to l'Orient is longer than from Ostend to Arras, and thus afforded more opportunities for escape.

CHAPTER XII

EIGHT DAYS ELAPSED, DURING WHICH I ONLY once saw the commissary, and was then sent with a party of prisoners, deserters, etc., who were to be conveyed to Lille. It was to be expected that the uncertainty of my identity would terminate on reaching a city where I had so often dwelt; and therefore, informed that we should pass through that place, I took such precautions that the gendarmes who had already conducted me did not recognize me; my features, concealed under a thick mask of dust and sweat, were, besides, completely filtered by the swelling of my cheeks, almost as large as those of the angels which on the frescoes of churches are seen blowing the trumpet of the last judgment. It was in this state that I entered the Egalite, a military prison, where I was to stay for some days, there to charm away the weariness of my seclusion.

I risked several visits to the canteen, in the hope that mingling with the visitors I might find an opportunity of escape. Meeting with a sailor whom I had known on board the *Barras*, I thought I might make him instrumental to my project. I asked him to breakfast with me, and our meal finished, I returned to my chamber, where I remained for three hours, reflecting on the means of recovering my liberty, when the jailor came to ask me to share the dinner which his wife had just brought him. The sailor, then, had a wife,—and the thought crossed me, that to elude the vigilance of the jailer, she might procure me female attire or some disguise. Full of this idea, I went down to the canteen and drew near the table, when I heard a piercing cry, and a woman fainted. It was my comrade's wife. I ran to raise her—Good heavens, it was Francine! Alarmed at my own imprudence, which had allowed an expression of astonishment to escape from me, I tried to repress the emotion which I had unavoidably testified. Surprised and astonished, the spectators crowded round us, and overwhelmed me with inquiries, and, after some moments of silence, I told them that it was my sister whom I had so unexpectedly met.

This incident passed without any consequences, and next day at early dawn we set off: and I was in consternation at finding that the convoy, instead of following as usual the road to Sens, took that of Douai. Why change the direction of our journey? I attributed this to some indiscretion of Francine. But I soon learnt that it resulted simply from the necessity of leaving at Arras some of the refractory prisoners from Cambrai.

Francine, whom I had so unjustly suspected, was awaiting me at our first halt. In spite of the gendarmes, she would speak to and embrace me. She wept bitterly, and joined my tears with hers. With what bitterness did she reproach herself for the infidelity which was the cause of all my misfortunes! Her repentance was sincere, and I sincerely forgave her: and when, on the order of the brigadier, we were compelled to separate, she slipped into my hands two hundred francs in gold as the only recompense in her power.

At length we reached Douai, and at the gate of the prison of the department a gendarme rang the bell. Who answered the summons? Dutilleul, the turnkey, who, after one of my attempts to escape, had dressed my hurts for a month afterward. He did not appear to know me. At the office I found another person whom I knew, the guard Hurtrel, in such a state of inebriety that I flattered myself his memory had entirely left him. For three days nothing was said to me; but on the fourth I was led before the examining magistrate, in the presence of Hurtrel and Dutilleul, and was asked if I were not Vidocq? I replied that I was Auguste Duval, which might be confirmed by sending to l'Orient; and besides, the motive of my apprehension at Ostend proved it, as I was only charged with having deserted from a ship of war. My straightforward tale seemed to weigh with the judge, who hesitated; but Hurtrel and Dutilleul persisted in asserting that they were not mistaken. Rausson, the public accuser, came to see me, and also said he knew me; but as I was not disconcerted, he remained in doubt, and to clear up the affair they devised a stratagem.

One morning I was told that a person wanted me at the office, and on going thither I found my mother, whom they had sent for from Arras; with what intention may be easily divined. The poor woman hastened to embrace me, but I saw through the snare, and putting her from me quietly, I said to the magistrate who was present, that it was an unmanly thing to give the unfortunate woman any hopes of seeing her son, when they were, at least, uncertain of their ability to produce him. My mother, who was put on her guard by a signal which I managed to communicate to her, pretending to examine me attentively, at length declared that a wonderful likeness had deceived her, and then retired, uttering many bitter reproaches against those who had taken her from home only to afford her but a fallacious joy.

The magistrate and turnkeys were then reduced to their original state of dubiety, when a letter which arrived from l'Orient seemed to put the matter beyond a doubt. It mentioned a drawing pricked on the left arm of Duval, who had escaped from the hospital at Quimper, as a thing which would at once dispel every doubt as to the identity of the individual detained at Douai. I was again summoned before the examining judge, and Hurtrel, already triumphing in his penetration, was present at the interrogation. At the first words I saw what was coming, and stripping my coat sleeve above my elbow, I showed them the drawing, which they scarcely expected to find, and which exactly coincided with the description sent from l'Orient. All were in the clouds again, and what yet made the situation more complicated, was that the authorities of l'Orient demanded me as a deserter from the fleet. Fifteen days were thus spent without any decision having been made concerning me; when, tired with the severities used toward me, and hoping to procure approbation, I wrote to the president of the criminal tribunal, declaring that I was really Vidocq. I had determined on this, under the idea that I should be sent forthwith to Bicêtre with a party, and that was actually the result. It was utterly impossible, however, for me to make the least effort to escape by the way, as I was guarded with unremitting vigilance.

I made my second entry at Bicêtre on the second of April, 1799, and there found some old prisoners, who, although galley slaves, had obtained permission to have their sentence to the Bagne remitted.

I saw at Bicêtre Captain Labbre, who, it may be recollected, supplied me, when at Brussels, with papers, by means of which I had deceived the Baroness d'l_____. He had been sentenced to sixteen years at the galleys, for being concerned in an extensive robbery committed at Ghent, at the house of Champon, the aubergiste. He was with us, to depart with the first chain, the near approach of which was disagreeably announced to us. Captain Viez, knowing the gentlemen who were to be confided to him, had declared, that to prevent any chance of escape, he would put us on wrist-cuffs and cellars until we reached Toulon. However, our promise induced him to forego this formidable project.

After the riveting of the fetters was done (in a similar way to that in which it had been performed at my first departure), I was put at the head of the first cordon, with Jossas, one of the most celebrated robbers of Paris and the provinces, better known as the Marquis de Saint-Armand de Faral, which he constantly bore. He was a man about thirty-six years old, with a gentlemanly appearance, and able to assume at will the most perfect suavity of manners. His traveling costume was that of a dandy leaving his bedroom for his boudoir. With pantaloons of silver-grey knit materials, he wore a waistcoat and cap trimmed with Astracan fur, of the same color, and the whole covered with a large cloak lined with crimson velvet. His expenditure equaled his appearance, for not contented with living sumptuously at the places of repose, he also supported three or four others of the cordon.

Jossas never had any education, but having entered when very young into the service of a rich colonel, whom he accompanied in his travels, he had acquired manners sufficiently good not to disgrace any circle. Thus his comrades, seeing him introduce himself into the first society, named him 'Passe-par-tout.' He was so completely identified with this character, that at the Bagne, when confined in double irons, and mingling indiscriminately with men of the most miserable appearance, he still kept up a portion of his grandeur, though disguised in a convict's cassock. Having provided himself with a splendid dressing-box, he bestowed an hour daily on his toilet, and was extremely particular about the appearance of his hands, which were certainly very handsome.

Jossas was one of those thieves of whom, fortunately, but few are now in existence. He meditated and prepared an enterprise sometimes as long as a year beforehand. Operating principally by means of false keys, he began by taking first the impression of the lock of the outer door. The key made, he entered the first part; if stopped by another door, he took a second impression, had a second key made; and thus in the end attained his object. It may be judged, that only being able to get on during the absence of the tenant of the apartment, he must lose much time before the fitting opportunity would present itself. He only had recourse to this expedient when in despair, that is, when it was accessible to introduce himself to the house; for if he could contrive to procure admittance under any pretext, he soon obtained impressions of all the locks, and when the keys were ready, he used to invite the persons to dine with him, and whilst they were at table, his accomplices stripped the apartments, from whence he had also contrived to draw away the servants, either by asking their masters to bring them to help to wait at table, or by engaging the attention of the waiting-maids and cooks by lovers, who were in the plot. The porters saw nothing, because they seldom took anything but jewels or money. If by chance any large parcel was to be removed, they folded It up in dirty linen, and it was thrown out of window to an accomplice in waiting with a washer-woman's wheelbarrow.

In society, where he passed as a Creole of Havana, he often met inhabit-ants of that place, without ever letting anything escape him which could betray him. He frequently led on families of distinction, to offer him the hand of their daughters. Taking care always, during the many conversations thereon, to learn where the dowry was deposited, he invariably carried it off, and ab-sconded at the moment appointed for signing the contract. But of all his tricks, that played off on a banker at Lyons, is perhaps the most astonishing. Having acquainted himself with the ways of the house, under pretext of arranging ac-counts and negotiations, in a short time an intimacy arose, which gave him the opportunity of getting the impression of all the locks, except that of the cash-chest, of which a secret ward rendered all his attempts unavailing. On the other hand, the chest being built in the wall, and cased with iron, it was impossible to think of breaking it open. The cashier, too, never parted from his key; but these obstacles did not daunt Jossas. Having formed a close intimacy with the cashier, he proposed an excursion of pleasure to Collonges; and on the day appointed they went in a cabriolet. On approaching Saint Rampert, they saw by the riv-erside a woman apparently dying, and the blood spouting from her mouth and nostrils; beside her was a man, who appeared much distressed, assisting her. Jossas, testifying considerable emotion, told him that the best method of stop-ping the effusion of blood was to apply a key to the back of the female. But no one had a key except the cashier, who at first offered that of his apartment. That had no effect. The cashier, alarmed at seeing the blood flow copiously, took out the key of his cash-chest, which was applied with much success be-tween the shoulders of the patient. It has been already guessed that a piece of modeling wax had been placed there previously, and that the whole scene had been preconcerted. Three days after the cash-box was empty.

Jossas spent money with the facility of a man who comes easily by it. He was very charitable; and I could cite many instances of his whimsical generosity. Amongst others, the following:—One day he penetrated into an apartment in the Rue du Hazard, which he had been informed would yield a rich booty. At first the wretchedness of the furniture surprised him, but the proprietor might be a miser. He went on searching, burst open all, broke everything, and only found in a desk a bundle of pawnbrokers' duplicates. He took from his pocket five louis, and placing them on the mantelpiece, wrote on the glass these words, "Payment for broken furniture;" he then retired, after closing the doors carefully, lest any other robbers, less scrupulous, should carry off what he had respected.

When Jossas set out with us for Bicêtre it was his third journey. He afterward escaped twice, was retaken, and died at the Bagne at Rochefort in 1806.

On our way to Montereau, I was witness of a scene which may as well be known. A convict named Mauger knew a young man of the city, who was believed by his parents to be sentenced to the galleys; and recommending his next neighbor to hide his face with his handkerchief, he told several persons he met on our way, that the person who thus concealed himself was the young man in question. The chain went onward, but scarcely were we a quarter of a league from Montereau, when a man, running after us, gave the captain fifty francs, produced by a collection made for the "man with the handkerchief." These fifty francs were in the evening distributed amongst the plotters of the scheme, without any other persons but themselves knowing the cause of such liberality.

At Sens, Jossas played another comedy. He had sent for a man named Sergent, who kept the auberge de l'Ecu; and on his arrival, this man testified the most excessive grief. "What!" he exclaimed, with tears in his eyes, "you here, my noble marquis! You, the brother of my old master! I who thought you on your return to Germany! Oh heavens! what a misfortune!" It may be guessed that in some expedition, Jossas, being at Sens, had passed himself for an emigrant, returned clandestinely, and the brother of a count with whom Sergei, had been cook. Jossas explained to him how, being apprehended with a forged passport at the moment he was gaining the frontier, he had been sentenced as a forger. The good aubergiste did not confine himself to empty lamentations, but sent the galley slave an excellent dinner, which I partook, with an appetite greatly contrasted with my wretched situation.

Save and except a tremendous chastisement inflicted on two convicts who had tried to escape at Beaume, nothing extraordinary occurred till we reached Chalons, when we were put on board a large boat, filled with straw, very similar to those which convey charcoal to Paris; the whole covered with a thick cloth. If, to cast a glance over the country, or breathe a purer air, a convict ventured to raise a corner, a shower of blows rained instantly on his shoulders. Although free from such treatment, I was not the less affected at my situation; scarcely could the gayety of Jossas, who was never downcast, avail in making me for a moment forget, that, on reaching the Bagne, I should be the object of special vigilance that must frustrate every hope of escape. This idea doubly depressed me when we reached Lyons.

On seeing the Baslie, Jossas said to me, "You are going to see something new." I saw, on the quays of the Seine, an elegant carriage, which seemed to be waiting the arrival of the boat. As soon as it came in sight, a female put her head from the window, and waved a white handkerchief. "It is she," said Jossas, who replied to the signal. The boat having been moored to the quay, the lady descended, and mixed in the crowd of lookers-on; I could not see her face, which was concealed by a very thick black veil. She remained there from four in the afternoon till evening, and the crowd then dispersing, Jossas sent Lieutenant

Thierry to her, who soon returned with a sausage, in which were concealed fifty louis. I learnt that Jossas, having made a conquest of this lady under his title of marquis, had informed her by letter of his condemnation, which he doubtlessly accounted for as he had done with the aubergiste at Sens. These sorts of intrigues, now very rare, were at this period very common. Ignorant of the stratagem plotted to deceive her, the veiled lady reappeared the next day on the quay, and remained there until our departure, to the great satisfaction of Jossas, who not only was recruited in finance, but was assured of an asylum in the event of effecting his escape.

We had nearly reached the termination of our navigation, when, two leagues from Pont St. Esprit, we were overtaken by one of those terrific storms so common on the Rhone. It was announced by distant rumblings of thunder. Soon afterward, the rain descended in torrents; gusts of wind, such as are only experienced under the tropics, blew down houses, uprooted trees, and drove the waves mountain high, which threatened at each moment to overwhelm us with destruction. At this moment the spectacle that presented itself was horrific; by the rapid flashes of lightning were to be seen two hundred men, chained so as to deprive them of the remotest hope of safety, and expressing by fearful cries the anguish of approaching death, rendered inevitable by the weight of their fetters: on their sinister countenance might be read the desire to preserve a life disputed by the scaffold, a life henceforward to be spent in misery and degradation. Some of the convicts evinced an absolute passiveness; many, on the contrary, delivered themselves up to a frantic joy. If any unfortunate wretch, mindful of his innocent youth, muttered out the fragment of a prayer, his next companion would perhaps shake his fetters, whilst he howled an obscene song, and the prayer expired in the midst of lengthened howls and shrieks.

What redoubled the general consternation was, the despair of the mariners, who seemed to have given all over for lost. The guards were not more confident, and even gave symptoms of an intention to quit the boat, which was visibly filling fast with water. Then matters took a fresh turn, and they urged on the argousins, crying, "Make the shore! let all make for shore!" The darkness, added to the confusion of the moment, affording an opportunity with impunity, the most intrepid of the convicts rose, declaring that no person should quit the boat until it reached the bank. Lieutenant Thierry was the only one who appeared to have preserved his presence of mind; he put on a bold front, and protested that there was no danger, as neither he nor the sailors had any intention of quitting the vessel. We believed him the more as the weather was gradually becoming more moderate. Daylight appeared, and on the surface of the waters, smooth as ice, there would have been nothing to recall the disasters of the night, if the muddy tide had not been strewn with dead cattle, trees, and fragments of furniture and houses.

Escaped from the tempest, we landed at Avignon, and were confined in the castle. There commenced the vengeance of the argousins: they had not forgotten what they were pleased to term our insurrection; refreshing our memories with it by blows from their cudgels, and then preventing the public from giving the convicts that assistance which the end of the journey prevented from passing through their hands. "Alms to these vagabonds!" said one of them, called father Lami, to some ladies who wished to bestow some aid: "it would be money lost. Besides, ask the captain."

Lieutenant Thierry, who ought not to be mentioned with such brutal and inhuman beings, and of whom I have already spoken, gave permission; but by a refinement of villainy, the argousins made the signal for departure before the distribution was finished. The rest of the journey had no features of interest; and at length, after thirty-seven days of most painful travel, the chain entered Toulon.

The fifteen carriages arrived at the port, and drawn up in front of the rope-yard, the convicts were ordered to alight, and were then escorted to the courtyard of the Bagne. On the way thither, those who had clothes worth anything made all possible haste to take them off and sell or give them to the crowd which assembled at the arrival of a new chain. When the clothing of the Bagne was distributed, and the manacles had been riveted, as I had seen it done at Brest, we were conveyed on board a cut-down frigate, called Le Husard, used as the floating Bagne. As soon as the convicts employed as writers, had written down our descriptions, the escaped convicts were riveted to the double chain. Their escape added three years additional confinement to the original sentence.

As I was thus circumstanced, I was sent to No. 3, where the most suspected convicts were placed. Lest they should find an opportunity for escaping in going to the harbor, they never went to labor. Always fettered to the "bang," lying on the bare plank, eaten up by vermin, and worn out by brutal treatment and want of nourishment and exercise, they presented a most lamentable appearance.

I found in the cell, all the most abandoned scoundrels that ever assembled at the Hague. I saw there one named Vidal, who even struck the convicts themselves with horror. Apprehended at fourteen years of age, in the midst of a band of brigands, whose crimes he participated, his age alone redeemed him from the scaffold. He was sentenced to imprisonment for twenty-four years; but scarcely had he reached the prison when, at the conclusion of a quarrel, he killed a comrade with a blow of his knife. A sentence of twenty-four years' hard labor was then substituted for that of imprisonment only. He had been for some years at the Bagne, when a convict was sentenced to death. There was not an executioner to be found in the city, and Vidal eagerly offered his services, which were accepted, and the execution was carried into effect, but they were compelled to put Vidal on the bench with the galley-guards, or else the convicts would have knocked him on the head with their fetters. The threats which menaced him did not prevent him from fulfilling his new office again, some time afterward. Besides, he undertook to administer the sentences of bastinado on the prisoners. At length, in 1794, the revolutionary tribunal having been installed at Toulon, after the taking of that town by Dugommier, Vidal was employed to carry their sentences into effect. He then thought he was liberated, but when the terror had ceased, he was remanded to the Bagne, where he was placed under a special surveillance.

On the same bench with Vidal was the Jew Deschamps, one of the principal of the party concerned in robbing the royal wardrobe, to the details of which the convicts listened with a sinister pleasure. At the enumeration of the diamonds and jewels carried off, their eyes sparkled, their muscles contracted by a convulsive motion; and by the expression of their countenances, inferences might unerringly have been drawn of the first uses they would have made of their liberty. This disposition was particularly discernible in those men only convicted of petty offenses, who were taunted and bantered as only having stolen objects of small value; and then, after estimating the plunder of the wardrobe at twenty millions of francs, Deschamps added, with an air of contempt toward a poor devil sentenced for stealing vegetables, "Ah! ah! this was cabbage."

From the moment when the robbery was perpetrated it became the subject of multiplied comments, which circumstances and agitation of mind rendered very singular. It was during the meeting of the representatives on the Sunday evening (16th of September, 1792), that Roland, minister of the interior, announced the event to the tribune of the convention, complaining bitterly of the insufficient surveillance of the agents and the military guards, who had forsaken their posts, under pretext of the "severity of the cold."

Some days afterward, Thuriot, who was one of the commission charged with searching out the matter, in his turn accused the minister of carelessness, who answered drily, that he had something else to do besides watching the wardrobe. The discussion rested here, but these debates had aroused the public attention, and the sole public theme was of guilty conclusions, and plots framed for robbery, of which the produce was devoted to keeping the police agents in pay; they went so far as to say, that the government had robbed itself; and what gave a consistency to such a report, was the reprieves granted on the 18th of October to some individuals condemned for this affair, and from whom confessions were expected.

However, on the 22d of February, 1797, in a report to the Conseil d'Anciens, on a proposal to grant a reward of five thousand francs to a Madame Corbin, who had facilitated the discovery of a great quantity of the plundered property, Thiebault declared, in the most formal manner, that this event was not the result of any political measure, and had all been incurred by the defective vigilance of the police, and by the mismanagement which pervaded every department of the administration.

At the beginning, the Moniteur had heated the imaginations of the most wary, by speaking of forty armed robbers, who had been surprised in the wardrobe. The truth is, that no one was surprised; and when they first discovered the loss of "the regent," the dauphin's coral, and a vast many other jewels, valued at seventeen millions of francs, for four successive nights, Deschamps, Bernard Salles, and a Portuguese Jew, named Dacosta, had in their turns entered the apartments, without any other arms than the tools requisite to extract the jewels, set in the plate, which they disdained to carry off; and thus they removed with the greatest precaution the magnificent rubies which formed the eye of the ivory fishes.

Deschamps, to whom belongs the honor of the invention, first got into the gallery by climbing a window, by means of a lamp-post, at the angle of the Rue Royale and the Place of Louis XV. Bernard Salles and Dacosta, who kept watch, were at first his only comrades; but on the third night, Bensit Naid, Philipponeau, Paumettes, Fraumont, Gay, Monton lieutenant of the National Guard, and Durand, called "Le Turc," a jeweler in the Rue Saint Sauveur, were added to the gang, as well as many first-rate "cracksmen," who had been, in a friendly way, invited to come and participate in the spoil. The rendezvous was at a billiard-room in the Rue de Rohan; and, besides, they made so little mystery of the robbery, that, the morning after the first booty, Paumettes, dining with some girls at a cook-shop in the Rue d'Argenteuil, threw on the table to them a handful of rose and small brilliant diamonds. The police, however, got no information. To detect the principal authors it was necessary that Durand, arrested for forging assignats, should confess to obtain his own pardon, and, on his information, "the regent" was discovered and seized at Tours, sewn up in the head-dress of a woman named Lebiene, who, unable to reach England in consequence of the war, was about to sell it at Bordeaux to a Jew, known to Dacosta. They had attempted to get rid of it in Paris, but the value of the gem, estimated at twelve millions of francs, would have awakened dangerous suspicions; they had also given up the idea of cutting the stone, lest the lapidary should betray them.

Before having been sentenced for the robbery of the wardrobe, Deschamps had been implicated in a capital affair, whence he was extricated, although guilty, as he boasted to us, by giving details not to be doubted. He had been concerned in the double murder of the jeweler Deslong and his servant maid, committed with his accomplice, the broker Fraumont.

Deslong had an extensive business, and besides private purchases, he also bartered diamonds and pearls; and as he was known to be an honest man, he often had valuable gems entrusted to him, either to sell or unset. He also frequented auctions, where Fraumont first knew him, who was constantly at sales to buy the ropes, altar cloths, and other pillaged church ornaments, which he burnt to get the metal from the gold lace. From the custom of meeting together so frequently in business, a sort of acquaintance sprang up between the two men, which soon became a closer intimacy. Deslong had no concealment with Fraumont, and consulted him in all his undertakings, informed him of the worth of all the deposits entrusted to him, and even confided to him the secret of a hiding-place in which he kept his most valuable articles.

Informed of all these particulars, and having free access at all times to Deslong's house, Fraumont conceived the project of robbing him whilst he and his wife were at the theatre, which they frequented. He wanted an accomplice to keep watch; and besides, it would have been dangerous for Fraumont, whom everybody knew, to be seen on the premises on the day of the robbery. He first selected a locksmith, a fugitive convict, who made the false keys necessary for entering Deslong's house; but this man being pursued by the police, was forced to leave Paris, and he then substituted Deschamps.

On the day fixed for the perpetration of the robbery, Deslong and his wife having gone to the Theatre de la Republique, Fraumont concealed himself at a vintner's to watch for the return of the servant maid, who usually took advantage of the absence of her master and mistress to go and see her lover. Deschamps went up to the apartment, and opened the door gently with one of his false keys. What was his astonishment to see in the hall the maidservant whom he thought absent (her sister, who was much like her, having in fact left the house a few minutes before I). At the sight of Deschamps, whose surprise made his countenance even more frightful, the girl let fall her work and shrieked. Deschamps sprang upon her, threw her down, seized her throat, and gave her five blows with a clasp-knife, which he had about him, in the right-hand pocket of his trousers. The unhappy creature fell bathed in blood, and whilst the death-rattle was yet sounding in her throat, the ruffian ransacked every corner of the room: but whether this unexpected event disturbed him, or that he heard some noise on the staircase, he only carried off some pieces of plate which came to hand, and returned to his accomplice at the vintner's, and told him the adventure. He (Fraumont) was much grieved, not at the murder of the servant, but at the little information and clumsiness of Deschamps, whom he reproached with not having discovered the secret closet which he had so plainly pointed out; and what put the capstone on his discontent was, that he foresaw that after such a catastrophe, Deslong would be more careful of his property, and it would be impossible ever again to get such an opportunity.

In fact, Deslong did change his lodging after this event, which inspired him with the most excessive fright, and the few persons whose visits he allowed were received with the greatest precaution. Although Fraumont did not present himself, yet he had no suspicion of him. How could he suspect a man who, if he had perpetrated the crime, would not have failed to have ransacked the closet, of which he knew the secret? Meeting him at the end of a few days on the Place Vendome, he pressed him strongly to come and see him, and became more intimate with him than ever. Fraumont then began plotting again; but, despairing of breaking open the new place of security, which, besides, was carefully guarded, he determined on changing his plan. Led to Deschamp's house, under pretense of bargaining for a large lot of diamonds, Deslong was assassinated and robbed of seventeen thousand francs, in gold and assignats, with which he had provided himself by advice of Fraumont, who dealt him the first stab.

Two days elapsed, and Madame Deslong, not seeing her husband return, who never made so long an absence without a previous intimation, and knowing that he had considerable property about him, no longer doubted but that some misfortune had befallen him. She then went to the police, they contrived to get hold of Fraumont and Deschamps; and the confession of the locksmith, which corresponded with the accounts of the robbery, and who was apprehended soon after, would have had an unpropitious termination for them, had not the authorities refused to give this man the liberty they had promised to reward him with; and the police agent, Cordat, who had been the go-between, unwilling that his promises should be broken, aided his escape on the way from La Force to the Palace. This circumstance removing the only witness who could be brought forward, Deschamps and Fraumont were set at liberty.

Condemned afterward to eighteen years' imprisonment for other robberies, Fraumont set out for the Bagne at Rochefort; but he was not yet out of courage, and by means of money, produced by his plunder, he had bribed several persons who were to follow the chain to aid his escape, in case he should attempt it, or even to carry him off by force, if need should be. The use he proposed to make of his liberty was to assassinate M. Delalande, high president of the tribunal which had condemned him, and commissary of the police of the Section de L'Unite, who had brought such overwhelming charges against him. All was ripe for the execution of this plot, when a common woman, who had learned the details from the lips of one of the accomplices, made a spontaneous confession, and measures were accordingly taken. The escort was informed of it; and when the chain left, Fraumont was put in extra chains, which were not removed until his arrival at Rochefort, where he was an object of special vigilance; and I was told that he died at the Bagne. As for Deschamps, who escaped from Toulon soon after, he was apprehended at the end of three years, as concerned in a robbery committed at Anteuil, sentenced to death by the criminal tribunal of the Seine, and executed at Paris.

In cell No. 3, I was only separated from Deschamps by a burglar named Louis Mulot, son of that Cornu who so long affrighted the people of Normandy, where his crimes are still unforgotten. Disguised as a horse-dealer, he frequented the fairs, watched the merchants who had large sums about them, and taking the crossroads, laid in wait for and assassinated them. Married, for the third time, to a young and pretty woman of Bernai, he had at first carefully concealed from her his infernal trade; but he was not slow in discovering that she was entirely worthy of him, and thenceforward she accompanied him in all his expeditions. Frequenting all the fairs as a peripatetic mercer, she easily introduced herself to the rich graziers of the valley of Auge, and more than one met his death at the appointed spot of gallant rendezvous. Often suspected, they brought forward alibis, always successful, and for which they were indebted to the fleetness of the excellent horses with which they were always provided.

In 1794, the Cornu family consisted of the father, mother, three sons, two daughters, and their lovers, all of whom had been habituated to crime from their earliest childhood, either in keeping watch or setting fire to barns, etc. The youngest, Florentine, having at first testified some repugnance, they had cured her delicacy by compelling her to carry in her apron, for two leagues, the head of a farmer of the environs of Argentin!

At a later period, entirely devoid of any tender scruples, she had, as her lover, the assassin Capelle, executed in 1802. When the family formed itself into a band of Chauffeurs to infest the country (Caen and Falaise) it was she who put to torture the wretched farmers, by putting a lighted candle under their armpits, or placing blazing tinder on their toes (whence the name of Chauffeurs or burners).

Hotly pursued by the police of Caen, and particularly by that of Rouen, who had apprehended two of the juniors of the family at Brionne, Cornu resolved on retiring for some time to the vicinity of Paris, trusting thus to elude inquiry. Installed with his family in a lone house, on the road to Sevres, he did not fear to take his walks in the Champs-Elysees, where he met nearly all the robbers of his acquaintance.

"Well, father Cornu," said they to him one day "what are you about now?"

"Oh, always administering the last consolation (assassination), my sons—the last consolation."

"That is droll, father Cornu; but discovery may ensue."

"Oh! No fear where no witnesses. If I had done for all the corn-threshers (farmers) whom I have only singed, I should have nothing to funk about now."

In one of his excursions, Cornu met an old comrade, who proposed to him to break into a villa, situated in the wood of Ville d'Avray. The robbery was committed and the booty shared, but Cornu found that he had been duped. On reaching the middle of the wood, he let fall his snuff-box whilst offering it to his companion, who stooped to pick it up, and at that very instant Cornu blew out his brains with a pistol-shot, plundered him, and regained his own house, where he told the tale to his family with bursts of laughter.

Apprehended near Vernon, at the moment he was breaking into a farm, Cornu was conducted to Rouen, tried before the Criminal Court, and sentenced to death. Soon after this, his wife, who was still at liberty, came every day to bring him food and console him. "Listen," said she to him one morning, when he appeared more dejected than usual, "listen, Joseph they say that death affrights you,—don't play the noodle, at all events, when they lead you to the scaffold. The lads of the game will laugh at you."

"Yes," said Cornu, "all that is very fine, if one's scrag was not in danger; but with Jack Ketch on one side, and the black sheep (clergyman) on the other, and the traps (gendarmes) behind, it is not quite so pleasant to be turned into food for flies."

"Joseph, Joseph, do not talk in this way; Iam only a woman, you know; but I could go through it as if at a wedding, and particularly with you, old lad! Yes, I tell you again, by the word of Marguerite, I would willingly accompany you."

"Are you in earnest?" asked Cornu. "Yes, quite in earnest," sighed Marguerite. "But what are you getting up for? What are you going to do?"

"Nothing," replied Cornu; and then going to a turnkey who was in the passage, "Roch," said he to him, "send for the jailer, I want to see the public accuser."

"What!" said his wife, "the public accuser! Are you going to split (confess)? Ah, Joseph, consider what a reputation you will leave for our children!"

Cornu was silent until the magistrate arrived, and he then denounced his wife; and this unhappy woman, sentenced to death by his confessions, was executed at the same time with him. Mulot, who told me all this, never repeated the narrative without laughing till he cried. However, he thought the guillotine no subject for joking; and for a long time avoided all crimes that could send him to rejoin his father, mother, one of his brothers, and his sister Florentine, all executed at Rouen. When he spoke of them, and the end they had made, he frequently said, "This is the fruits of playing with fire; they shall never catch me at such work:" and, in fact, his tricks were not so redoubtable: he confined himself to a species of robbery in which he excelled. His eldest sister, whom he had brought to Paris, aided him in all his enterprises. Dressed as a washerwoman, with a pannier at her back and a basket on her arm, she went to all the houses where there was no porter, and, knocking at the doors, if she learnt that the occupants were from home, she returned and told Mulot. Then he, disguised as a journeyman locksmith went with his bunch of picklocks, and opened the most complicated locks. Frequently, his sister, to avoid suspicion, with her apron and a modest cap on, and with the disturbed appearance of a nurse who had lost her key, aided his operations. Mulot, though he did not want foresight, was yet one day surprised in the very act, and soon after condemned to imprisonment.

CHAPTER XIII

I NEVER WAS SO WRETCHED AS AFTER MY ENTRY at the Bagne at Toulon. Cast at twenty-four years of age amongst the most abandoned wretches, and necessarily in contact with them, although I would have preferred a hundred times to be reduced to living in the midst of people infected with the plague; compelled only to see and hear degraded beings whose minds were incessantly bent on devising evil schemes, I feared the dire contagion of such vicious society. When, day and night, in my presence, they openly practiced the most vile and demoralized actions, I was not so confident in the strength of my own character as not to fear that I might become too much familiarized with such atrocious and dangerous conversation. In fact, I had resisted many dangerous temptations; but want, misery, and the thirst of liberty, will often involuntarily tempt us to a step toward crime. I had never been in any situation where it was more positively incumbent on me to attempt an escape, and henceforward all my ideas and thoughts were turned to the compassing of this measure.

Various plans suggested themselves, but that was not sufficient; for to put any of them into execution I must await a favorable opportunity, and until then patience was the only remedy for my woes. Fastened to the same bench with robbers by profession, who had already escaped several times, I was, as well as they, an object of special surveillance, which it was difficult to divert. In their cambrons (watch-boxes), at a short distance from us, the argousins were always on the lookout, and observed our least motions.

Father Mathieu, their chief, had the eyes of a lynx, and such a knowledge of the men he had to deal with, that he could tell at the slightest glance if they were scheming to deceive him. This old fox was nearly sixty years of age; but having a vigorous constitution, which seemed proof against the attacks of time, he was still hale and hearty. He was one of those square figures which never wear out. I have him now in my "mind's eye," with his little tail, his gray and powdered locks, and his face in wrinkles so congruous with the business of his calling. He never spoke without mentioning his cudgel; it was a never-ending theme of pleasurable recital to talk of the many bastinadoes he had inflicted personally, or ordered to be done. Always at war with the convicts, he knew every one of their tricks. His mistrust was so excessive, that he often accused them of plotting when they were not at all thinking of it.

It may be supposed that it was no easy matter to make a sop for this Cerberus. I tried, however, to procure his favor—an attempt in which no one had as yet succeeded; but I soon found that I had not essayed in vain, for I perceptibly gained on his goodwill. Father Mathieu sometimes talked to me—a sign, as the experienced told me, that I had made some way with him. I thought I might ask something from him on the strength of this, and I asked him to allow me to make children's toys with the pieces of wood brought in by the working convicts. He granted all I asked, provided I was steady; and the next day I began my work. My companions cut out roughly, and I finished the toys. Father Mathieu approved of my productions; and when he saw that I had assistance in my work, he could not forbear testifying his approbation, which he had not expressed for a long time previously.

"Well, well!" said he, "how I like people to amuse themselves; it would be well if you all did the same. It would pass time away, and with the profits you might purchase some small comforts."

A few days afterward the bench was a perfect workshop, where fourteen men, equally anxious to drive away ennui and earn a little money, worked away with much industry. We had all some goods ready, which were sold by the assistants of the convicts who gave us the materials. For a month our trade was very brisk, and every day we had abundant returns, not a sous of which was reserved. Father Mathieu had authorized us to appoint as our treasurer a convict named Pantaragat, who sold provisions in the room in which we were. Unfortunately there are goods which cannot be multiplied without the necessary balance between produce and consumption being destroyed. Toulon was replete with toys of every description, and we must henceforward sit with folded arms. No longer knowing what to do, I feigned a complaint in my legs, that I might be sent to the hospital. The doctor to whom I was recommended by Father Mathieu, whose protégé I had become, actually believed that I was unable to walk. When one would attempt to escape, it is impossible to manage better than to contrive to excite such an opinion.

Doctor Ferrant did not for an instant suspect me of an intent to deceive him. He was one of those disciples of Esculapius who think that bluntness is a part of their profession; but still he was a humane man, and behaved very kindly to me. The chief surgeon had also a liking for me, and to me he trusted the care of his surgery chest. I scraped his lint, rolled his bandages, and made myself generally useful, so that my willingness procured for me his kindness. Every one, even to the argousin of the infirmary, behaved well to me, although no one could exceed in sternness M. L'Homme (that was his name), whom they called, jokingly, "Ecce Homo," because he had been formerly a seller of psalms and canticles. Although I had been pointed out to him as a daring fellow, M. L'Homme was so much pleased with my good behavior, and still more with the bottles of mulled wine which I shared with him, that he perceptibly became more humanized. When I was pretty well assured that I should not excite his suspicions, I unmasked my battery, to overpower his vigilance, as well as that of his fellow-guards. I had already procured a wig and black whiskers, and had besides, concealed in my mattress, an old pair of boots, which, when well waxed, seemed as good as new; but that was only an equipment for my head and feet. To complete my toilet, I relied on the head surgeon, who used to lay on my bed his great-coat, hat, cane and gloves. One morning, whilst he was engaged in amputating an arm, I saw that M. L'Homme had followed him to assist in the operation, which was performed at the extremity of one of the wards. The opportunity for a disguise was admirable, and I hastened to complete it; and in my new costume, I went straight to the door. I had to pass through a crowd of

124

argousins; but I ventured boldly, and none of them appeared to pay any attention to me, and I already thought myself out of danger, when I heard a cry, "Stop him, stop him! a prisoner has escaped!" I was not more than twenty steps from the arsenal, and, without losing my presence of mind, I redoubled my speed, and having got to the door, I said to the guard, pointing to a person who was just entering the city, "Run with me; he has escaped from the hospital."

This would, perhaps, have saved me; but, just as I stepped over the wicket, I was seized by the wig, and on turning round, saw M. L'Homme; resistance would have been certain death; and I therefore quietly followed him back to the Bagne, where I was put to the double chain. It was evident that I was to undergo punishment, and to avoid it, I cast myself on my knees before the commissary, saying, "Oh, sir, do not let me be beaten; that is the only favor I ask; I would rather undergo three years' additional confinement." The commissary, however touching my petition might have been, could not keep his countenance; but told me, that he would pardon me on account of my boldness and ingenuity, on condition that I would point out the person who had procured me the disguise.

"You must be aware," I replied to him, "that the people who guard us are wretches who will do anything for money, but nothing in the world shall induce me to betray those who serve me."

Pleased with my frankness, he ordered me to be released from the double chain; and when the argousin murmured at so much indulgence, he desired him to be silent, adding, "You ought to like, rather than be angry with him, for he has just given you a lesson which you would do well to profit by." I thanked the commissary, and the next moment was conducted to the fatal bench to which I was to be fastened for the next six years. I then flattered myself with the hopes of returning to my trade of toy-making, but father Mathieu refusing me, I was compelled, unwillingly, to remain unemployed. Two months elapsed without any change in my circumstances, when, one night, being unable to sleep, there flashed through my brain one of those luminous ideas which only occur in darkness Jossas was awake, and I mentioned it to him. It may be surmised that he was always intent on effecting his escape, and he thought it admirably wonderful as I had devised it, and begged me not to fail putting it into execution. It will be seen that I did not neglect his advice. One morning, the commissary of the Bagne going his rounds, passed near me, and I begged leave to speak to him in private.

"What do you want?" said he.

"Have you any complaint to make? Speak, my man, speak out, and I will do you justice" Encouraged by the kindness of this language, I said, "Good sir, you see before you a second example of an honest criminal. You may perhaps remember that on coming here I told you that I was in my brother's place. I do not accuse him; I am even pleased at thinking he was ignorant of the crime imputed to him; but it was he, who, under my name, was condemned by the court at Douai; he escaped from the Bagne at Brest, and now, having reached

England, he is free, and I, the victim of a sad mistake, must submit to punishment. Alas! how fatal to me has been our resemblance!

"Without this circumstance, I should not have been taken to Bicêtre; the keeper would not have sworn to my person. In vain have I begged for an inquiry; it is because their testimony has been received, that an identity is allowed which does not exist. But the error is consummated, and I have much to bewail! I know that it is not with you to alter a decision from which there is no appeal, but it is a favor you may grant to me: to be sure of me, I am placed in a cell with suspected men, where I am with a herd of robbers, assassins, and hardened ruffians. At every moment I tremble at the recital of crimes which have been committed, as well as at the hopes of those who are plotting others, to be perpetrated the moment, if it ever arrives, that they shall get free from their fetters. Ah! I beg you, in the name of every sentiment of humanity, to leave me no longer amongst a set of such abandoned miscreants. Put me in a dungeon, load me with chains, do with me whatever you will, but do not leave me any longer with them. If I have endeavored to escape, it has been only that I might get away from such a sink of infamy. (At this moment I turned toward the convicts.) You may see, sir, how ferociously they gaze at me; they already prepare to make me repent of what I am saying to you; they paint, they burn, to bathe their hands in my blood; once more I conjure you, do not give me up to the vengeance of these atrocious monsters." During this discourse, the convicts were petrified with astonishment; they could not conceive that one of their comrades would thus upbraid them in their very teeth; the commissary himself did not know what to think of such a step; he was silent, and I saw that I had touched him deeply. Then throwing myself at his feet, with tears in my eyes, I added, "Pity me; if you refuse me, if you go without removing me from this room you shall never see me again." These words produced the desired effect. The commissary, who was a worthy man, had me unloosed in his presence, and gave orders that I should be placed with the working convicts. I was yoked with a man named Salesse, a Gascon, as knavish as a convict may be. The first time we were alone, he asked me if I intended to escape. "I have no thoughts of it," replied I, "I am but too glad that they allow me to work." But Jossas possessed my secret, and he arranged all for my escape. I had a plain dress which I concealed under my galley clothes without the knowledge even of my yoke-fellow. A moving screw had supplied the place of the rivet in my fetters, and I was ready to start. The third day after leaving my companions I went out to labor, and presented myself before the argousin.

"Get along, good-for-nought," said father Mathieu, "it is not time."

I was in the rope-room, and the place appeared propitious. I told my companion that I had a call of nature, and he pointed out some pieces of wood behind which I could go, and he was scarcely out of sight, when throwing off my red shirt, and taking out the screw, I ran toward the basin. The frigate La Meuron was then under repair, which had brought Bonaparte and his suite from Egypt. I went on board and asked for the master-carpenter, whom I knew to be in the hospital. The cook, whom I accosted, took me for one of the new

126

crew. I was rejoiced at this. I knew him to be a man of Auvergne, by his accent, I began conversing with him in his own provincial dialect, and in a tone of much assurance, although I was on thorns the whole time; for forty couples of convicts were at work close to us. They might recognize me in a moment. A cargo soon set off for the town, and I jumped into the boat, when, seizing an oar, I rowed away like an old sailor, and we soon reached Toulon. Anxious to reach the country I went to the Italian gate, but no one was allowed to go out without a green card given by the magistrates, and I was refused egress, and whilst I was thinking how I could get out, I heard the three reports of the cannon which announced my escape. At this moment a tremor pervaded all my limbs; already did I see myself in the power of the argosins, and all the police of the Bagne. I pictured myself in presence of the excellent commissary, whom I had so basely deceived. If I were taken, I must be lost. These sad reflections coming over me, I walked away in haste, and that I might avoid a crowd, betook myself to the ramparts.

On reaching a solitary spot, I walked very slowly like a man who, not knowing whither to bend his steps, is full of consideration, when a female accosted me, and asked me in provincial French what the hour was; I told her that I did not know; and she then began to talk of the weather, and concluded by asking me to accompany her home; it is only a few yards hence, she added, and no one will see us. The opportunity of finding a place of refuge was too propitious to be refused, and I followed my conductress to a sort of small inn, when I sent for some refreshment. Whilst we were conversing together, three other cannon shots were heard. "Ah," cried the girl, with an air of satisfaction, "there is a second escape today." "What !" said I, "my lass, does that please you? Should not you like to get the reward?" "I! why you cannot know much of me." "Bah, bah," I replied, "fifty francs are always worth earning, and I swear to you that if one of these fellows fall into my clutches."

"You are a wretch!" she said, making a gesture of indignation. "I am only a poor girl, but Celestine would never eat the bread earned by means so despicable." At these words, pronounced with an accent of truth which left no doubt on my mind of her sincerity, I did not hesitate to confide my secret to her. As soon as I had informed her that I was a convict, I cannot express how much she appeared interested in my fate. "Mon Dieu!" she said, "they are so much to be pitied; I would save them all, and have already saved many;" then, after pausing for an instant, as if to consider. "Let me manage it," she then added; "I have a lover who has a green card, I will borrow it from him, and you shall use it, and, once out of the city, you can deposit it under a stone which I will point out to you, and in the interim, as we are not in security here, I will take you to my apartments." On reaching this, she told me that she must leave me for, a moment, "I must tell my lover," she said, "and will speedily return." Women are sometimes most admirable actresses, and, in spite of her kind protestations, I feared some treachery. Perhaps Celestine was going to denounce me; she had not reached the street, when I ran down the staircase. "Well, well," cried the girl, "do you fear? If you mistrust me, come along with me." I thought it most prudent to watch her, and we walked away together, whither I knew not. Scarcely had we gone ten yards, when we met a funeral procession. "Follow the burial," said my protectress, "and you will escape;" and before I had time to thank her, she disappeared. The followers were numerous, and I mixed amongst the crowd of assistants, and, that I might not be thought a stranger at the ceremony, I entered into conversation with an old sailor, from whose communications I soon learnt how to utter a few well-timed remarks on the virtues of the defunct. I was convinced that Celestine had not betrayed me. When I left the ramparts behind me, which it had been of such paramount importance for me to pass, I almost wept for joy; but that I might not betray myself, I still kept up a strain of suitable lamentations.

On reaching the cemetery I advanced in my turn to the edge of the grave, and after having cast a handful of earth on the coffin, I separated from the company by taking a circuitous path. I walked on for many hours without losing sight of Toulon, and about five o'clock in the evening, just as I was entering a grove of firs, I saw a man armed with a gun. As he was well clad, and had a game-bag, my first thought was that he was a huntsman; but observing the butt of a pistol projecting from his girdle, I feared that I had met with one of those Provencals, who, at the sound of the cannon, always scour the country in search of the runaway galley slaves. If my fears were just, flight was unavailing; and it was, perhaps best to advance rather than retreat. This I did, and on approaching him sufficiently close to be on my guard in case he should show any hostilities, I asked him the road to his.

"Do you want the highroad or the byway?" said he, with peculiar emphasis.

"Oh, either, no matter which," I answered; hoping by my indifference to re-move his suspicions.

"In that case, follow this path, it leads to the station of the gendarmes; and if you do not like traveling alone, you can avail yourself of the escort."

At the word "gendarmes" I turned pale, and the stranger; perceiving the effect his words had produced, added, " Come, come; I see you are not over anxious to travel on the highway. Well, if you are not in a very great hurry, I will conduct you to the village of Pourieres, which is not two leagues from Aix."

He seemed so well acquainted with the localities, that I availed myself of this offer, and consented to follow him. Then, without stirring, he pointed out a clump of bushes, where he bid me await his joining me. Two hours passed before he finished his guard, and he then came to me. "Get up," said he.

I obeyed, and when I thought myself in the thickest of the wood, I found myself at the borders of it, about fifty paces from a house, in front of which were seated several gendarmes. At the sight of their uniforms, I started. "What ails you, man?" asked my guide; "do you think I would betray you? If you fear anything, take these and defend yourself;" at the same time offering me his pistols, which I refused. "Well, well;" he added, and squeezed my hand, to testify how much he was satisfied with my confidence.

Concealed by the bushes which skirted our path, we stopped I could not comprehend the motive of a halt so near the enemy. Our stay was protracted till nightfall when we saw approaching from Toulon a mail, escorted by four gendarmes who were relieved by the same number from the brigade whose vicinity had so much alarmed me. The mail proceeded on its journey, and was soon out of sight. My companion then taking my arm, said in an under-tone, "Let us start, nothing can be done today."

We then walked away in an opposite direction for about an hour, and my guide going up to a tree, clasped the trunk in his hands, and I saw that he was counting the number of notches just by a knife. "Good, good," he ejaculated with an air of satisfaction, which was to me inexplicable, and taking from his game-bag a piece of bread which he divided with me, he then gave me a bottle, whence I drank with pleasure. The collation could not have been more opportune, for I was in want of something to recruit my strength. In spite of the darkness, we walked so fast that I was tired, and my feet, long unused to exercise, had become so painful that I was going to declare it impossible for me to proceed further, when a village clock struck three. "Gently," said my guide, stooping and placing his ear on the ground; "do as I do, and listen; with this cursed Polish legion one must be always on the watch. Did you hear nothing?" I replied that I thought I heard the footsteps of a body of men. "Yes," he added, "it is they; stir not on your life, or we shall be taken." He had scarcely spoken, when a patrol guard came toward the thicket in which we were concealed. "Did you see anything, you fellows?" said someone in a low tone. "Nothing, serjeant."

"Parbleu! I thought so; it is as dark as an oven. This devil of a Roman, whom heaven's thunders crush! To make us travel all night like wolves in a wood! Ah, if ever I find him, or any of his gang!"

"Qui vive? (who goes there?)" cried a soldier, suddenly.

"What do you see?" said the sergeant.

"Nothing; but I heard a breathing on this side," and he indicated the spot where we were.

"Stuff! You are dreaming. You are so much alarmed about Roman, that you think that you always have him in your cartridge-box."

Two other soldiers asserted that they had heard the same.

"Hold your tongues," replied the serjeant. "I see there is nobody, and we must once more according to custom, return to Pourieres without having trapped our game. Come, my lads, it is time to be off." The patrol seemed disposed to retreat. "It is a ruse de guerre," said my companion. "I know they will beat the wood and return upon us in a semicircle."

It was now necessary that I should be firm and composed. "Are you fearful?" said my guide.

"This is no time for fear," I replied.

"Well then, follow me; here are my pistols; when I fire, do you the same, so that the four shots only sound like one report. Now, fire."

The four shots were fired, and we then ran cite all speed, without being pursued. The fear of falling into an ambuscade, had made the soldiers come to a halt, but we did not pause from our flight. On getting near an isolated hut, the stranger said to me, "It is now daylight, and we are safe," and then leaping the pales of the garden, he took a key from the hollow trunk of a tree, and opening the door of the cot we immediately entered.

An iron lamp, placed on the mantelpiece, lighted up a plain and rustic apartment. I only observed in a corner a barrel, containing, as I thought, gunpowder, and near it on a shelf was a quantity of gun-cartridges. A woman's attire placed on a chair with one of those large black hats worn by the Provencal peasants, indicated the presence of a sleeping female, whose heavy breathing reached our ears. Whilst I threw a rapid glance about me, my guide produced from an old trunk a quarter of a kid, some onions, oil, and a bottle of wine: he invited me to partake of a repast, of which I felt in the greatest need. He seemed very desirous of interrogating me, but I ate with so much appetite that I believe he felt a scruple of conscience in interrupting me. When I had finished, which was not whilst anything remained on the table, he led me to a sort of loft, assuring me that I was in perfect safety, and then left me before I could ask if he was going to stay in the hut; but scarcely had I stretched myself out on the straw when a heavy sleep took possession of all my faculties.

When I awoke I judged by the height of the sun that it was two o'clock. A female peasant, doubtlessly the same whose apparel I had seen, warned by my movements, showed her head at the opening of the door of my garret.— "Do not stir," said she in a Provencal dialect, "the environs are full of sapins (gendarmes) who are examining every place." I did not know what she meant by sapins but I guessed that it did not refer to anything very propitious for me.

At twilight I saw my new friend of the previous evening, who, after some trifling conversation, asked me point-blank who I was, whence I came, and whither I was going. Prepared for these unavoidable questions, I replied that I was a deserter from the ship Oran, then in the roadstead at Toulon, that I was going to Aix, whence I hoped to get to my own country.

"That is all very good," said my host. "I see who you are: but do you know who I am?"

"I' faith, to tell the honest truth, I first took you for a patrol; afterward I took you for a leader of smugglers—and cow I do not know what to think."

"You shall know, them. In our country we are brave enough, you see, but object to be made soldiers on compulsion, so we did not comply with the requisition when we could do anything to avoid it. The quota selected in Pourieres even refused to march at all when called upon. The gendarmes came to compel the refractory, and they resisted. Men were killed on both sides: and all the townsmen who participated in the affray betook themselves to the woods to escape a court-martial. We thus met, sixty in number, under the orders of M. Roman and the brothers Bisson de Tretz: if you like to remain with us I shall be glad, for last night's experience tells me that you are a man of mold, and I advise you not to be in any fear about gendarmes. Besides, we want for nothing, and run but little risk. The country people inform us of all that passes, and give us provisions. Come, will you join us?"

I did not judge it wise to reject the proposition: and, without reflecting on the consequences, I answered as he wished. I stayed two days at the hut, and on the third set out with my companion, armed with a carbine and two pistols. After many hours' walking over mountains covered with wood, we reached a hut larger than that we had quitted: it was the headquarters of Roman. I waited a moment at the door for my guide to announce me. He soon returned, and introduced me to a large apartment, where I saw about forty persons, the greater number of whom were grouped about a man who, by his appearance, half-rustic, half-citizen, might have passed for a rich country proprietor. I was presented to this personage, who said to me, "I am delighted to see you: I have heard of your coolness, and know your worth. If you will share our perils, you shall find friendship and freedom: we do not know you, but you have a face which would command friends everywhere. To sum up all, our men are honorable and brave—for probity and honor are our mottos." After this discourse, which could only be addressed to me by Roman, the brothers Bisson, and then all the troop, gave me the embrace of brotherhood.

Such was my reception in this society, to which its leader attributed a political intent; but it is certain, that after beginning, like the Chouans, to stop the diligences which conveyed the state moneys, Roman had begun to plunder travelers. The mutineers who composed his band had at first much reluctance in committing these robberies; but habits of an unsettled life, idleness, and especially the difficulty of returning to their homes, soon removed all scruples

The day after my arrival, Roman appointed me to conduct six men to the environs of Saint Maximin. I did not know the purport of the mission. About midnight, on reaching the borders of a small thicket that skirted the road, we ensconced ourselves in a ravine. Roman's lieutenant, Bisson de Tretz, recommended absolute silence. The wheels of a carriage were soon heard, and it passed us. Bisson looked out cautiously, and said, "It is the Nice diligence: that will not do for us: it has more soldiers than ducats." He then ordered us to retreat, and we regained the hut: when Roman, enraged at seeing us return empty-handed, swore loudly, exclaiming, "Well, well ! they shall pay for this tomorrow."

It was no longer possible for me to deceive myself as to the association to which I belonged: I had decidedly fallen in with that famous band of highwaymen who were spreading terror throughout Provence. If I fell into the hands of justice—a fugitive galley slave—I could hardly hope for that pardon which might be granted even to the troop with which I was mingled. Reflecting on all the difficulties of my situation, I was tempted to escape them by flight; but, so recently enrolled, how was it possible to evade the strict scrutiny with which they regarded me? On the other hand, to express any desire of withdrawing myself from the confederacy, would only have provoked a suspicion fatal to my purpose or safety. Might I not be considered as a spy, and be shot as such? Death and infamy threatened me whichever way I turned. In the midst of these perplexities to which I was a prey, my only idea was to sound the man who had first effected my introduction amongst my comrades; and, with as much apparent indifference as I could assume, I inquired if it would not be possible to obtain from our captain leave of absence for a few days? The man looked at me with an air of cunning and suspicion: "Yes, friend," said he, "such favors are sometimes obtained, when our chief knows well the person to whom he grants them." This said, he turned upon his heels, and left me to rack my brain anew for some happier device to effect my liberty than this had proved.

I had now been upward of eleven days with these bandits, each day more fully resolved to withdraw myself from the honor of their exploits, when one night that I had fallen asleep through excessive fatigue, I was suddenly aroused by an extraordinary noise; I listened, and discovered that the confusion which had broken my rest was occasioned by one of the troops having been robbed of a purse heavy with many years' booty: to my consternation I found that, as being the last comer amongst them, their suspicions were directed to me. They surrounded me and formally accused me of having stolen the purse; the cry was unanimously against me, and drowned my protestations of innocence; they insisted upon searching my person. I had lain down in my clothes, which a hundred hands were ready to strip off me. What were their surprise, anger, and astonishment, at perceiving on my shoulder the brand of a galley slave!

"A galley slave!" exclaimed the captain. "A galley slave amongst us! He can only be here as a spy; knock him on the head, or shoot him, that will be soonest done."

I heard the click of the muskets preparing to obey this last order.

"One moment," exclaimed the chief; "let him, before he dies, make restitution of the lost money."

"Yes," said I to him, "the money shall be restored, but on condition that you grant me a few minutes' private conversation."

He consented to listen to what I had to say, under the idea that now I should make a full confession; but the moment I found myself alone with him, I protested anew that I was entirely innocent of the affair, and suggested an expedient for discovering the culprit, the idea of which was drawn from a work I had read of Berquin's. My plan was acceded to, and the captain returned to his men, holding as many straws in his hand as there were individuals present. "Observe me well," said he to them; "the longest of these straws will fall into the hands of him who is guilty."

The drawing began, each man in silence plucked out a straw; but when it had concluded, the straws were returned to the captain, and his troop looked with curious eagerness for the result.

One alone was found shorter than the others. A man named Joseph d'Osiolles presented it. "You are then the thief!" exclaimed the captain. "Every straw was of the same length. You have shortened yours, and thus criminated yourself." Joseph was searched, and the stolen purse found hid in his belt.

My justification was complete; the whole troop acknowledged my innocence; and the captain, whilst he sought to excuse the violence to which I had been subjected, added, that I must no longer form part of his band. "It is a sad piece of ill luck for you," said he; "but you must feel that, having been at the galleys... "

He did not complete the sentence, but, putting fifteen louis in my hands, he compelled me to promise silence as to all I had seen or heard for the next twenty-five days.

I was prudent, and faithful to my engagement.

Chapter XIV

After the dangers I had undergone whilst remaining with Roman and his band, some idea may be formed of the joy which I experienced on quitting them. It was evident that the government, once determinately settled, would adopt the most efficacious measures for insuring the safety of the interior. The remains of the bands, which, under the name of "Chevaliers du Soleil, or the Compagnie de Jesus," owed their formation to a political reaction, deferred indefinitely, could not fail to be destroyed as soon as was desired. The only honest excuse for their brigandage—royalism—no longer existed; and although Hiver, Leprêtre, Boulanger, Bastide, Jansein, and other "sons of the family," made a boast of attacking the couriers, because they found their profit in it, it began to be no longer in good taste to think that it was quite correct to appropriate to oneself the money of the state.

All the them who had thought it a service to check, pistol in hand, the circulation of dispatches and the collection of the imposts, withdrew now to their firesides; and those who had profited by their exertions, or wished for other reasons to be forgotten, betook themselves to a distance from the scene of their exploits. In fact, order was re-established, and the time was at hand when robbers, whatever might be their pretext or motive, were no longer to be tolerated. I should not have been very desirous, under such circumstances, to have enrolled myself in a band of robbers, and, the infamy of such a procedure apart, I should have been kept from it by the certainty of being speedily brought to the scaffold.

But another thought animated me; I wished to avoid, at any cost, the opportunities and means of committing crimes; I wished to be free. I knew not how this wish was to be realized, nor did it matter; my determination was made, and I had, as they say, marked a cross on the prison. In haste to get at a considerable distance, I took the road to Lyons, avoiding the high ways, until I reached the environs of Orange; there I fell in with some Provencal wagoners, whose packages soon revealed to me that they were about to take the same road as myself. I entered into conversation with them; and as they appeared to me to be hearty, jovial fellows, I did not hesitate to tell them that I was a deserter, and that they would serve me materially if, to aid me in avoiding the vigilance of the gendarmes, they would agree to bestow their patronage on me. This proposal did not surprise them, and it even seemed as if they had suspected that I should claim their protection and secrecy. At this period, and particularly in the south, it was not rare to meet with fine fellows, who had left their colors, and committed themselves to the care of Heaven. It was then very natural to take my word, and the waggoneers received me kindly; and some money which I displayed, as if by chance, completed the interest which I had already excited. It was agreed that I should pass for the son of the person who had these conveyances in charge. I was accordingly clothed with a smock-frock, and was supposed to be making my first journey. I was decorated with ribbons and nosegays, emblems which at each public-house procured for me the congratulations of all the inmates.

A new "John of Paris," I filled my part very well; but the donations necessary to support it adequately made such inroads on my purse, that, on reaching the guillotine, where I was to leave my party, I had only twenty-eight sous left. Having wandered about for some time in the dirty and dark streets of the second city in France, I remarked, in the Rue des Quatre Chapeaux, a sort of tavern where, I thought that I might procure a supper commensurate with my finances. I was not mistaken; the supper was light enough, and soon dispatched. To remain hungry is indeed a disagreeable thing; and not to know where to find shelter for one's head is equally annoying.

When I had wiped my knife, which, however, had not been much engaged, I was reflecting that I must pass the night under the canopy of heaven, when at a table near to mine, I heard a conversation in that bastard German so much spoken in some districts of the Netherlands, and with which I was well acquainted. The speakers were a man and woman about to retire, and whom I found to be Jews. Informed that at Lyons as in many other towns, these people kept furnished houses, in which they received smugglers, I asked if they could direct me to a public-house. I could not have addressed myself to better persons; for they were lodging-keepers, and offered to become my hosts, which, on agreeing to, I accompanied them. Six beds were in the room in which I was placed, none of which were occupied, although it was ten o'clock, and I fell asleep under the idea that I should have no companions in my room.

On waking, I heard the following conversation in a slang language which was familiar to me.

"It is half-past six," said a voice, which was not unknown to me, "and you lie snoring still."

"Well, and what then? We wanted to break open the old goldsmith's shop last night, but he was on his guard, and we ought to have given him a few inches of cold steel, and then the blood would have flowed."

"Ah ha! but you fear the guillotine too much. But that is not the way to go to work to get the money."

"I would rather murder on the highway, than break open shops; the gendarmes are always at your heels."

"Well, then, you have got no booty; and yet there were snuff-boxes, watches, and gold chains enough. The Jew will have no business today."

"No; the false key broke in the lock, the citizens cried for help, and we had to run for it...."

"Holloa!" said a third person; "do not wag your tongues so fast; there is a man in bed who may be listening."

The advice was too late, but it silenced them, and I half opened my eyes to see the faces of my companions; but my bed being very low, I could not perceive them. I remained quiet, that they might suppose me asleep; when one of the speakers having arisen, I recognized him as an escaped prisoner from

Toulon, named Neveu, who had left some days before me His comrade jumped out of bed, and him I knew to be Cadet-Paul, another fugitive; a third, and then a fourth arose, and I knew them all then to be galley slaves.

I almost fancied myself in my room, No. 3. At length I got up from my bed, and scarcely had I put foot on the floor, when they all exclaimed ""Tis Vidocq!" They surrounded and congratulated me. One of the robbers, Charles Deschamps, who had escaped a few days after me, told me, that the whole Bagne were full of admiration at my boldness and success. Nine o'clock having struck, they conducted me to breakfast, where we joined the brothers Quinet, etc. They overwhelmed me with kindness, procured me money, clothes, and even a Mistress.

I was here situated precisely as I had been at Nantes, but I was not more desirous of following the profession of my friends than I had been in Bretagne; but until I had a remittance from my mother I must live somehow. I thought I might manage to support myself for a time without labor. I proposed most determinately only to receive subsistence from the robbers; but man proposes and God disposes. The fugitives, discontented that I, under various pretexts, always avoided joining their daily plundering parties, at once denounced me, to get rid of a troublesome witness, who might become dangerous. They imagined that I should escape, as a matter of course, and relied, that once known by the police, and having no refuge but with their band, I should then unite myself to their party. In this circumstance, as in all others of a similar kind, in which I have been found, if they were so desirous of my companionship, it was because they had a high opinion of my penetration, my adroitness, and particularly of my strength, —a valuable quality in a profession in which profit is too often attained by peril.

Arrested at Adele Buffin's, in the passage Saint Come, I was taken to the prison of Roanne, where I learnt from my examination that I had been sold. In the rage which the discovery threw me into, I took a sudden step, which was, in a measure, my introduction to a career entirely new to me. I wrote to M. Dubois, commissary-general of the police, requesting a private interview, and the same evening I was conducted to his private closet. Having explained my situation to him. I offered to put him in the way of seizing the brothers Quinet, then pursued for having assassinated the wife of a mason. I proposed, besides, to point out the means of apprehending all the persons lodging as well at the Jew's as at Caffin's, the joiner's. In return, I only asked for liberty to quit Lyons. M. Dubois had, doubtless, been before the dupe of such proposals, and I saw that he hesitated to trust me. "You doubt my word," said I to him. "Should you still suspect me if I should escape on my way back to prison, and return and surrender myself as your prisoner?" "No," he replied. "Well, then, you shall soon see me again, provided that you consent not to give my guards any additional orders for my security." He agreed, and I went away; but on arriving at the corner of the street, I knocked down the two tipstaffs, who had each an arm of mine, and regained the Hotel de Ville with all possible speed, where I found M. Dubois, who was greatly surprised at my prompt reappearance, but certain from that that he might rely on me, I was allowed to go at liberty.

The next day I saw the Jew, whose name was Vidal, who directed me to a house where, he said, my friends had gone to live, and thither I went. They knew of my escape; but as they had no idea of my understanding with the commissary general of police, and did not think that I knew who had directed the blow which struck me, they gave me a very cordial reception. During the conversation, I gathered details from the brothers Quinet, which I transmitted to M. Dubois the same evening, and who, convinced of my sincerity, reported my conduct to M. Ganier, secretary-general of the police. I gave this gentleman all necessary information, and must say that he acted his part with much tact and activity.

Two days before they commenced operations, as I had advised, on Vidal's house, I thought it expedient that I should be again arrested. I was again conducted to the prison of Roanne, where the next day Vidal, Coffin, and many others, whom they had caught in the same snare, were brought in. I was at first kept from communicating with them, because I had thought it best that I should be put "all secret." When I was released from it, at the end of several days, to join the other prisoners, I pretended much surprise at finding all the party there. None appeared to have the least idea of the part which I had played. Neveu alone regarded me with distrust, and on my demanding the cause, he said that by the way in which they had been pursued and interrogated, he could not help suspecting that I was the denouncer. I feigned much indignation; and fearing that this opinion might be disseminated, I assembled the prisoners, and informing them of Neveu's suspicions, I demanded if they thought me capable of selling my comrades? and on their answering in the negative, Neveu was compelled to apologize to me. It was important to me that these suspicions should be thus destroyed, for I knew that certain death would be my doom if they had been confirmed. There had been many instances at Roanne of this distributive justice, which the prisoners exercised toward one another. One named Moissel, suspected of having given information relative to a robbery of church plate, had been knocked on the head in the court without the assassin being detected. More recently, another individual, accused of a similar indiscretion, had been found one morning hung with a straw band at the bars of his window, and the perpetrator was never discovered.

In the meantime, M. Dubois sent for me to his closet, where, to avoid suspicion, the other prisoners were conducted with me, as if about to undergo an examination. I entered first, and the commissary-general told me that many very expert robbers had arrived at Lyons from Paris, and the more dangerous, as, being supplied with regular credentials, they might wait in safety for the opportunity of making some decided stroke, and then immediately go away. The names by which they were mentioned were then entirely new to me, and I told M. Dubois so, adding that possibly they might be false. He wished to release me immediately, that by seeing these individuals in some public place, I might assure myself whether I had ever seen them before; but I observed to him, that so abrupt a liberation would certainly compromise me with the prisoners, in case that the good of the service should require me again to be entered as prisoner on the jailer's books. The reflection appeared just; but it was agreed that they should devise a means of sending me away the next day without incurring suspicion.

Neveu, who was "amongst the prisoners, was also examined after me in the commissary's closet. After some minutes he came out in a rage, and I asked him what had happened.

"What do you think?" said he, "the old covey wanted life to turn nose on the cracksmen who have just arrived. If they find no one to blow them but me, they are all right."

"Why, I did not think you such a flat," said I, the idea flashing on my mind that I might turn this to advantage; "I have promised to blow the gang, and insure them a lodging in the stone jug."

"What! you turned nose? Besides, you are not fly to the gang."

"What matters that? I shall get out of quod, and show them my heels, whilst you are still clinking the darbies."

Neveu appeared struck with the idea, and expressed much regret for having refused the offers of the commissary-general; and as I could not get rid of him, I begged him to return to M. Dubois and recall his refusal. He agreed; and as I had arranged, we were one evening conducted to the great theatre; thence to the Celestins, where Neveu pointed out to me all the men. We then retired, escorted by the police agents, who kept close upon us. For the success of my plan, and to avoid suspicion, it was expedient to make the attempt to escape, which would at least confirm the hope which I had given to my companion, and I told him of my intention. On passing Rue Merciere, we entered abruptly into a passage, and closed the door; and whilst the officers ran to the other end, we went out quietly by the way we had entered. When they returned, ashamed of their stupidity, we were already at a considerable distance.

Two days afterward, Neveu, who was no longer wanted, and could not suspect me, was again arrested. I, knowing then the robbers whom we wanted, pointed them out to the police officers in a church, where they had one Sunday assembled, it the hope of making a good booty on the termination of the prayers. Being no longer useful to the authorities, I then quitted Lyons to go to Paris, where thanks to M. Dubois, I was sure of arriving in safety.

I set out on the Burgundy road by the diligence, which then only traveled by day. At Lucy-le-Bois, where I slept with the other travelers, I was forgotten; and on waking, learned' that the vehicle had been gone two hours. I trusted to overtake it, in consequence of the ruggedness of the road, which is very steep in these districts; but on reaching Saint Brice, I was convinced that it was too much in advance to allow of my overtaking it, and I accordingly slackened my pace. A person who was traveling in the same direction, seeing me in a great heat, looked attentively at me, and asked me if I had come from Lucy-le-Bois; and on my replying in the affirmative, our conversation rested there. This man stopped at Saint Brice, whilst I pushed on to Auxerre. Spent with fatigue, I entered an inn, where, after having dined, I desired to be conducted to a bed.

I slept for several hours, when I was awakened by a great noise at my door, at which some persons were knocking violently. I got up half-dressed, and my eyes, heavy from sleep, gazed, as I opened the door, on tricolored scarfs, yellow trousers, and red facings. It was the commissary of police, attended by the quartermaster and gendarmes, a sight which I could not see without some emotion. "See how pale he turns," said one of them; "it is he." I raised my eyes, and recognized the man who had spoken to me at Saint Brice; but nothing explained to me as yet, the motive of this sudden invasion.

"Let us proceed methodically," said the commissary; "five feet five inches (French measure), that is right; brown hair—eyebrows and beard, idem—common forehead—gray eyes—prominent nose—good-sized mouth—round chin—full face—good color—tolerably stout."

"It is he," said the quartermaster, the two gendarmes, and the man of Saint Brice.

"Yes, it is indeed," said the commissary, in his turn. "Blue surtout—trousers of gray cashmere—white waistcoat—black cravat."

This was my dress, certainly.

"Well, did I not tell you so?" said the officious guide of the police, exulting at my capture: "he is one of the robbers!"

The description tallied exactly with mine. But I had stolen nothing; and yet in my situation I could experience all the disquiets of having done so. Perhaps it was a mistake; perhaps also.... The party were transported with joy. "Peace!" said the commissary; and turning over the leaf, he continued, "We shall easily recognize his Italian accent. He has besides the thumb of the right hand injured by a shot."

I spoke, and showed my right hand, which was in a perfectly sound state. All the parties stared; particularly the man of Saint Brice, who appeared singularly disconcerted: as for me, I felt relieved of an enormous weight. The commissary, whom I questioned in my turn, told me, that on the preceding night a considerable robbery had been committed at Saint Brice. One of the suspected individuals wore clothes similar to mine, and there was a similarity of description. It was to this combination of circumstances, to this strange sport of fortune, that I was indebted for the disagreeable visit which I received. They made excuses, which I accepted with a good grace, very happy at getting off so well; but yet, in fear of some new catastrophe, I put myself the same evening into a packet-boat, which conveyed me to Paris, whence I started immediately for Arras.

CHAPTER XV

MANY REASONS, WHICH MAY BE DIVINED, did not allow of my proceeding at once to my paternal abode; and, alighting at the house of one of my aunts, I learnt the death of my father, which sad intelligence was soon confirmed by my mother, who received me with a tenderness widely contrasting with the treatment I had experienced during the two years of my absence. She was extremely anxious to keep me with her; but it was absolutely necessary that I should be constantly concealed, and I did not leave the house for three months.

At the end of that time, my confinement began to weary me, and I went out, sometimes under one disguise and sometimes under another. I thought I had not been recognized, when, suddenly a report spread through the town that I was there, and the police began to search for me, making constant visits to my mother, without, however, discovering the place of my concealment.

Secure in my retreat, out of which I thought it would be difficult to surprise me, I soon took fresh excursions. One day, on Shrove Tuesday, I even carried my daring to such an extent as to appear at a ball, in the midst of upward of two hundred persons. I was dressed as a marquis; and a female, with whom I had been on intimate terms, having recognized me, told another, who thought that she had a cause of complaint against me; so that in less than a quarter of an hour everybody knew under what disguise Vidocq was concealed. The report reached the ears of two police sergeants, Delrue and Carpentier, who were on duty at the ball; and the former, coming up to me, said in a low voice that he wished to speak with me in private; a refusal would have been dangerous, and I followed him into the court, where Delrue asked my name. I did not hesitate to give him a false one; and proposed politely that he should untie my mask if he doubted me. "I do not require that," said he, "but I shall not object to look at you." "Well, then, untie my mask, which has got entangled in my hair." Full of certainty, Delrue went behind me, and at that instant I upset him with a forcible motion of my body backward, and with a blow of my fist I sent his satellite rolling beside him on the earth. Without waiting until they arose, I fled with the utmost speed in the direction of the ramparts, relying on being able to climb over them, and get into the country: but scarcely had I run many paces, when I found myself in an alley which had been blocked up at one end since I had quitted Arras.

Whilst I was thus wandering out of my way, a noise of iron heels announced that the two Serjeants were at hand; and I soon saw them approach me, sword in hand. I was unarmed; and seizing the large house key, as if it had been a pistol, I presented it at them, and compelled them to make way for me. "Pass quietly, Francois," said Carpentier, with a tremulous voice, "do not play any nonsense with us." I did not want to be told a second time, and in a few minutes reached my retreat.

This adventure was noised about, and in spite of the efforts which the two serjeants made to conceal it, they were laughed at by everybody. What was most annoying to me was, that the authorities redoubled their vigilance, so that it was almost impossible for me to go out. I remained thus immured for two months, which to me seemed as many centuries. Being no longer able to endure it, I resolved on quitting Arras, and they made me up a pack of lace; and one fine night, provided with a passport, which Blondel, one of my friends, had lent to me, I set out. The description did not answer; but for want of a better, I was compelled to put up with that; and, in fact, no objection was made to me on my route.

I reached Paris. Whilst engaged in disposing of my commodities, I made indirectly some steps toward finding out if it were not possible to obtain some reversal of my sentence. I learnt that I must, in the first instance, give myself up as a prisoner, but I could never resolve on again mixing with the wretches whom I knew so well. It was not the confinement that I dreaded; I would willingly have submitted to have been enclosed alone between four walls; and what proves this is, that I then requested leave from the minister to finish the term of my sentence in the madhouse at Arras; but my application remained unanswered.

My lace was sold, but with so little profit that I could not think of turning to this trade as a mode of life. A traveling clerk, who lived in the Rue Saint Martin, in the same hotel as I did, and to whom I partly stated my situation, proposed that I should enter the service of a seller of finery, who visited the fairs. I procured the situation, but only kept it for ten months, as we had some disagreements which determined me again to return to Arras. I was not long in returning to my nightly excursions. In the house of a young person to whom I paid some attentions, I frequently met the daughter of a gendarme, and endeavored to learn from her all that was plotting against me. The girl did not know me; but as in Arras I was the constant subject of conversation, it was not extraordinary to hear her speak of me, and frequently in singular terms. "Oh," said she to me one day, "we shall soon catch that vagabond; there is our lieutenant who wants him too much not to catch him soon; I would bet that he would give a day's pay to get hold of him."

"If I were your lieutenant, and wanted to take Vidocq," replied I, "I would contrive that he should not escape me."

"You! Oh yes, you and everybody! He is always completely armed. You know they said that he fired twice at Delrue and Carpentier; and that is not all, for he can change himself into a bundle of hay whenever he likes."

"A bundle of hay!" cried I, surprised at the novel endowment assigned to me—"A bundle of hay! How?"

"Yes, sir; my father pursued him one day, and at the moment he laid his hand upon his collar, he found that he only held a handful of hay. He did not only say it, but all the brigade saw the bundle of hay, which was burnt in the barrack-yard."

I could not make out this history; but learnt afterward that the police officers, not being able to lay hold of me, had given circulation to this tale amongst the credulous citizens of Arras. With the same motive they obligingly insinuated that I was the double of a certain loup-garou, whose wonderful appearance froze with fear the superstitious inhabitants of the country. Fortunately, these terrors were not shared by some pretty women, whom I had interested in my favor; and if the demon of jealousy had not suddenly seized on one of the number, the authorities would not perhaps have given themselves so much trouble about me. In her anger she was indiscreet; and the police, who did not clearly know what had become of me, again learnt that I was certainly in Arras.

One evening as, without mistrust and only armed with a stick, I was returning through the Rue d'Amiens, on crossing the bridge at the end of the Rue des Goquets, I was attacked by seven or eight individuals. They were constables disguised; and, seeing my garments, were already assured of their prize, when, freeing myself by a powerful jerk, I leapt the parapet, and threw myself into the river. It was in December; the tide was high, the current rapid, and none of the policemen had any inclination to follow me; they thought, besides, that by waiting for me on the bank I should not escape them; but a sewer that I found enabled me to deceive them, and they were still waiting for me when I was at my mother's house.

Every day I experienced fresh dangers, and every day the most pressing necessities suggested new expedients for my preservation. However, at length, according to my custom, I grew weary of a liberty which the compulsion of concealment rendered illusory. Some nuns of the Rue had for some time harbored me; but I resolved on quitting their hospitable roof, and turned over in my mind the means of appearing in public without inconvenience. Some thousands of Austrian prisoners were then in the citadel, whence they went out to work with the citizens, or in the neighboring villages, and the idea occurred to me, that the presence of these strangers might be useful to me. As I spoke German, I entered into conversation with one of them, and inspired him with sufficient confidence to confide to me his intention of escaping. This project was favorable to my views; the prisoner was embarrassed with his Kaiserlik uniform, and I offered to exchange it for mine; and for some money which I gave him to boot, he was glad to let me have his papers also. From this moment I was an Austrian, even in the eyes of the Austrians themselves, who, belonging to the different corps, did not know all their body.

Under this new disguise, I joined a young widow, who had a mercery establishment in the Rue de ___; she found that I had ability, and wished that I would install myself at her house; and we soon visited the fairs and markets together. It was evident that I could not aid her, unless I could understand the buyers, and I formed gibberish, half Teutonic, half French, which they understood wonderfully well, and which became so familiar to me, that I insensibly forgot that I knew any other language. Besides the illusion was so complete, that after cohabiting together for four months, the widow did not suspect any more than the rest of the world, that the soi-disant Kaiserlik was one of the friends of her childhood. However, she treated me so well, that it was impossible to deceive her any longer; and one day I told her who I really was, and never was woman more astonished. But, far from its injuring me in her estimation, the confidence in some sort only made our intimacy the closer; so much are women generally smitten by anything that bears the appearance of mystery or adventure! And then, are they not always delighted with the acquaintance of a wicked fellow? Who, better than myself, can know how often they are the providence of fugitive galley laves and condemned prisoners?

Eleven months glided away, and nothing occurred to disturb my repose. The frequency of my being in the streets, my constant meetings with the police officers, who had not even paid attention to me, all seemed to augur the duration of this tranquility, when, one day as we were sitting down to dinner in the back shop, the faces of three gendarmes were visible through a glass door. I was just helping the soup; the spoon fell from my hands; but recovering soon from the stupor into which this unlooked-for visit had thrown me, I darted toward the door, which I bolted, and then jumping out of the window, I got into a loft, whence I gained the roof of the next house, and running down the staircase which led into the street, I found, on reaching the door, two gendarmes. Fortunately they were but novices, who did not know me: "Go up," said I to them, "the brigadier has got him, but he resists; go up, and lend your aid, whilst I run for the guard." The two gendarmes ascended quickly, and I made off."

It was plain that I had been sold to the police. My friend was incapable of such a black deed, but she had, without doubt, been guilty of some indiscretion. Now that the cry was raised against me, ought I to tarry longer at Arras? It would be in vain to say, that I would always remain in my place of concealment; I could not reconcile myself to a life so wretched, and I determined on quitting the city. My little lady mercer insisted on accompanying me; she had means of conveyance; her commodities were soon packed, and we set out together, and the police was informed last of the disappearance of a female, whose measures they ought not to have been in ignorance of. According to some old notions, they imagined that we should go toward Belgium, as if Belgium had still been the country of refuge; and whilst they were pursuing us in the direction of the. old frontier, we were quietly progressing toward Normandy, by crossroads, which my companion had obtained a knowledge of in her mercantile journeys.

It was at Rouen that we had made up our minds to fix our abode. Arrived in this city, I had with me the passport of Blondel, which I had procured at Arras: the description which it gave was so different from mine, that it was indispensably necessary to make myself a little more like it.

To achieve this it was necessary to deceive the police, now become the more vigilant and inquisitive, as the communications of the emigrants in England were made through the Normandy coast. Thus did I contrive it. I went to the town hall, where I had my passport vise for Havre. A visa was obtained without difficulty; it was sufficient that the passport was not entirely contradictory, and mine was not so. The formality gone through, I departed, and two minutes afterward I entered the office, and asked if any person had found a pocket-book. No one could give me any tidings of it, and then I was in despair; pressing business called me to Havre, and I wanted to start that very evening, but what was to be done without a passport?"

"Is it only that?" said a clerk. "With the register of the visa you can get a duplicate passport." This was what I needed; the name of Blondel was kept, but this time, at least, my description was correctly given. To complete the effect of my stratagem, not only did I set out for Havre, but I advertised my pocket-book by little bills stuck about, although it had only passed from my hands to that of my companion.

By means of this little bit of good management my reinstatement was complete; and, provided with fitting credentials, I had only to lead an honest life, and I actually began to think of it; and took, in Rue Mortainville, a repository for mercury and bonnets, in which we did so well, that my mother, whom I had informed secretly of my success, determined on coming to join us. For a year I was really happy; my business increased, my connections extended, my credit was established, and more than one banking-house in Rouen, may perhaps remember when the signature of Blondel was well respected in the place. At length, after so many storms, I thought I had reached port; when an incident, which I had never contemplated, involved me in a fresh series of vicissitudes. The lady mercer with whom I lived, this woman who had given me the strongest proofs of devotion and love, began to burn with other fires than those which I had kindled in her heart. I was desirous of persuading myself that she was not unfaithful, but the fault was so flagrant that the offender had not even the resource of those well-supported denials, which enable the convenient husband to persuade himself that he is not wronged. At another time, I would not have submitted to such an affront without putting myself into a transport of rage, but how time had changed me! Witness of my misfortune, I coldly signified my determination to separate; prayers, supplications, nothing could bend me; I was immutable. I might have pardoned her, it is true, if only out of gratitude: but who would convince me that she who had befriended me would break off with my rival? And might I not have cause to fear, that, in a moment of tenderness, she would compromise my safety by some disclosure? We then divided our stock of goods, and my companion quitting me, I never heard of her after.

Disgusted with my residence at Rouen, through this adventure, I took to my old trade of traveling merchant; my journeys comprised the circuit of Nantes, St. Germain, and Versailles, where, in a short time, I formed an excellent connection; my profits became sufficiently considerable to allow of my renting at Versailles, a warehouse, with a small apartment, which my mother inhabited during my journeys. My conduct was then free from any stigma; I was generally esteemed in the circle which I had formed; and again I hoped that I had overcome the fatality which so often cast me into the path of dishonor, whence all my efforts were now used to free myself, when, denounced by an early friend, who thus revenged himself for some disagreement we had once had together, I was arrested on my return from the fair of Nantes. Although I obstinately asserted that I was not Vidocq, but Blondel, as my passport proved, I was sent to

St. Denis, whence I was to be sent to Douai. By the extraordinary care taken to prevent my escape, I perceived that I was recommended; and a glance which I threw over the book of the gendarmerie, revealed to me a precaution of a very particular nature. I was thus designated—

"SPECIAL SURVEILLANCE."

"Vidocq (Eugene Francois), condemned to death for non-appearance. This man is exceedingly enterprising and dangerous."

Thus, to keep the vigilance of my guards on the alert, I was described as a great criminal. I set out to St. Denis in a car, pinioned, so that I could not move, and to Louvres the escort never took his eyes off me. These arrangements announced the rigors in store for me, and I roused all the energy that had already so often procured me my liberty.

We had been put into the clock-house of Louvres, now transformed into a prison, where they brought us two mattresses, a counterpane and sheets, which, cut and fastened together, would help us to descend into the churchyard. A bar was cut with the knives of three deserters confined with us, and at two o'clock in the morning I made the first attempt, and having reached the extremity of the rope, I perceived that it was nearly fifteen feet from the ground. Hesitation availed nought, and I let go, but, as in my fall at the ramparts at Lille, I sprained my left leg so severely, that I could scarcely walk. However, I attempted to climb the walls of the churchyard, when I heard the key turn quietly in the lock. I was the jailer and his dog, who had noses alike for following a scent.

The jailer at first passed beneath the cord without seeing it, and the mastiff near a ditch in which I lay, without smelling me. Having gone the round they retired, and I thought that my companions would follow my example; but no one appearing, I climbed the wall and got into the plain. The pain of my foot became more and more acute, but I bore the pain, and courage giving me strength, I made considerable progress. I had nearly advanced a quarter of a league, when I suddenly heard the sound of the tocsin. It was in the middle of May. At the earliest dawn, I saw several armed peasants go out of their dwellings and spread themselves over the plains. They were probably ignorant of what was the cause of disturbance, but my sore leg was a token that might make me suspected. My face was unknown. In all probability, the first persons who met me would secure my person. Had I been in full possession of my limbs, I could have distanced all pursuit. I must yield at present; and scarcely had I proceeded two hundred paces, when I was overtaken by the gendarmes, who were scouring the country in all directions, and who seized and conveyed me back to the cursed clock-house.

The unpropitious result of this attempt did not discourage me. At Bapaume we were placed in the citadel, an old police station, guarded by a detachment of conscripts of the 30th regiment of the line. One sentinel only was placed over us, and he was under the window, and near enough for me to enter into conversation with him, which I did. The soldier to whom I addressed myself appeared a good fellow enough, and I thought I could easily bribe him. I offered him fifty francs to let us escape whilst he was on guard. He refused at first; but by the tone of his voice, and by a certain twinkling of his eyes, I thought I saw his impatience to get such a sum, only that he was afraid of consequences. To encourage him I increased the dose, and showed him three louis, when he said he would aid us, at the same time adding that his round would be from midnight till two o'clock. Having made our arrangements, I commenced operations. The wall was pierced so as to allow us a free egress, and we waited until the opportunity should arrive. At length midnight struck. The soldier immediately announced to me that he was there, and I gave him the three louis, and then made the necessary dispositions. When all was ready I called out. "Is it time?" I said to the sentinel. "Yes; make haste," he answered, after a trifling hesitation. I thought it singular that he did not answer instantly, and imagining that his conduct was somewhat dubious, I listened. He seemed to be marching, and by the moonlight I also perceived the shadow of several men in the ditch, and had no longer any doubt but that we were betrayed. However, as I might have been mistaken, to make quite sure I took some straw, which I stuffed into some clothes, and put it at the aperture which we had made, and at the same instant a sabre blow, that would have cleft an anvil, informed me that I had well escaped, and confirmed me more and more in the opinion that we must not always trust to conscripts. The prison was soon filled with gendarmes, who drew up a statement of facts. They examined us, wishing very much to know all; and I declared that I had given the conscript three louis, which he flatly denied. He was examined, and on their being found in his shoes, he was put in the black hole.

As for us, we were threatened most menacingly; but as they could not punish us, they contented themselves with doubling the guard. There was now no method of escape, without one of those opportunities for which I watched incessantly, and which presented itself earlier than I expected. The next day was the day of our departure, and we had descended into the barrack-yard, which was in great confusion from the arrival of a fresh number of prisoners and a detachment of conscripts from Ardennes, who were going to the camp at Boulogne. The adjutants were squabbling with the gendarmes about room for forming three divisions, and making the muster-call. While each were counting their men, I glided cautiously in at the tail of a baggage-wagon just leaving the court, and thus passed through the city, motionless, and in as small a compass as possible, to elude detection. Once beyond the ramparts, I had only to steal away, and I seized the opportunity whilst the wagoner, thirsty, as these people always are, had gone into an alehouse to refresh himself; and whilst his horses awaited him on the road, I lightened his conveyance of a load of which he was not aware. I slept in a field of maize, and when night arrived, directed my steps eastward.

CHAPTER XVI

I TRAVELED THROUGH PICARDY TOWARD BOULOGNE. At this period, Napoleon had abandoned his intention of a descent on England, and was about to make war against Austria with his vast army, but had left many billions on the shores of the British Channel. There were in the two camps, that on the left and that on the right, depots of almost every corps, and soldiers of every nation in Europe.

The uniforms were various, and this variety might be useful in concealing me; but I thought that it would be bad policy to disguise myself by only borrowing a military garb. I thought for a moment of becoming actually a soldier, but then to enter a regiment it would have been necessary to have certain papers, which I had not. I then gave up the intention, and yet my abode at Boulogne was dangerous, until I should decide, on something.

One day that I was more embarrassed and more unquiet than usual, I met on the walks a serjeant of marine-artillery whom I had met at Paris, and who was, as well as myself, a native of Arras; but having embarked when very young in a ship of war, he had passed the greater portion of his life in the colonies, and on his return to his native country had learnt nothing of my doings. He only looked on me as a bon vivant; and a public-house row, in which I energetically espoused his cause, had given him a high opinion of my courage.

"What, is it you?" said he, "Roger Bontemps; and what are you doing at Boulogne?"

"What am I doing! why, seeking employment in the train of the army."

"Oh, you want employment; do you know that it is devilish difficult to get a berth now? But, if you will listen to my advice—, though this is not the place for such conversation; let us go to Galand's."

We then went to a sort of sutler's booth, which was modestly stationed in one of the angles of the street.

"Ah! good-day, Parisian," said the serjeant to the host. "Good day, father Dufailli—What will you have this morning?—a dram?—mixed or plain?"

"Five-and-twenty gods! papa Galand, do you take us for blackguards? It is the best pallet and super-excellent wine that we want, do you bear?"

Then addressing me, "Is it not true, old boy, that the friends of our friends are our friends? That you must agree to," and, taking my hand, he led me into a small room, where M. Galand admitted his favorite customers.

I was very hungry, and saw with lively satisfaction the preparations for a repast, of which I was to partake. A waiting-maid, from twenty-five to thirty years, well built, and with a face and good humor which such girls have who can constitute the felicity of a whole regiment, brought in the dishes. She was a native of Liege; lively, agreeable, chattering in her dialect, and uttering every moment such low witticisms as excited greatly the mirth of the serjeant, who was delighted with her.

"She is the sister-in-law of our host," said he to me; "what cat-heads she has! she is as plump as a ball and as round as a buoy—a dainty lass, upon my faith."

At the same time, Dufailli, pulling her about, began to play all sorts of naval tricks; sometimes drawing her on his knees, sometimes applying to her shining cheeks one of those hearty smacks which bespeak more love than discretion.

I confess I was annoyed at this coquetry, which delayed our meal, when Mademoiselle Jeannette (so was the nymph called) having abruptly broken from the arms of my Amphitryon, returned with part of a deviled turkey and two bottles, which she placed before us.

"Well done," said the serjeant; "here is wherewithal to moisten our food and increase the juices. I shall play my part. After that, we shall see; for here, my boy, it is all as I wish. I have only to make a signal. Is it not so, Jeannette? Yes, my comrade," continued he, "I am master here."

I congratulated him on so much good fortune, and we began to eat and drink with might and main. It was long since I had been at such a festival, and I played my part manfully. Abundance of bottles were emptied; and we were about, I believe, to uncork the seventh, when the serjeant went out, and Simon returned, bringing with him two new guests, a forager aid a serjeant-major. "Five-and-twenty gods! I like good fellowship," cried Dufailli. "By Jove, I have made two recruits. I know how to go recruiting; ask these gentlemen."

"Oh yes," said the forager, "he is a cock, father Dufailli, to invent plots to seduce conscripts; when I think of them, I remember my own adventure."

"Ah, you still remember that!"

"Yes, yes, my old lad, I remember it, and the major also, when you were deep enough to enlist him as secretary to the regiment."

"Well! has he not done well? A thousand thunders! is it not better to be the first accountable man in an artillery company than sit scratching away on paper in a study? What say you, forager?"

"I agree with you; but..."

But, but, you will tell me perhaps you, that you were happier when, with your old dog of a master, you were obliged to lay hold of the watering pot and make yourself dripping wet with throwing frogs' spawn over your tulips. We were going to embark at Brest on board *L'Invincible*, and you would only go out as a flower-gardener. 'Well then,' said I, 'go as flower gardener; the captain likes flowers; every man to his taste, but also every man to his trade;' and I carried on mine. I think I see you now; you were rather disappointed when, instead of employing yourself in cultivating marine plants, as you expected, you were sent to man the shrouds of a thirty-six: and when you were ordered to fire a bombshell—that was a nosegay for you! But no more of that; and let us drink a measure of wine. Come, lads, here's to our comrades."

I filled all the glasses, and the serjeant continued—

"You see that I am not wanted now, therefore let us make of all of us but a pair of friends. This is easily done; I have caught these nicely in my snare, but that is nothing; we recruiters of the marines are but fools to the recruiters of earlier days; you are still but greenhorns. Ah, you never knew Belle-Rose! He was the lad for taking in the knowing ones! Such as I am, I was not a thorough noodle, and yet he twisted me completely round his finger. I think I have already told you the tale; but at all events I will give it you again for the general good.

"Under the ancient regime, do you see, we had colonies, the Isle of France, Bourbon, Martinique, etc.; now they are ours no longer; we have only the Isle of Oleron left; it is little more than nothing; or, as somebody said, it is the foot of earth whilst we wait for the rest. The descent would have restored to us all the others; but bah, the descent—we must no longer think of that, that is settled; the flotilla will rot in the port, and they will make firewood of the hulls. But I am getting out of my latitude steering seaward, instead of landward; now then for Belle-Rose.

"As I told you, he was a spark who had cut his wisdom teeth and in his time young fellows were not of the same kidney with those of the present day.

"I had left Arras at fourteen, and been at Paris for six months, apprentice to a gunsmith, when one morning, my master desired me to carry to the colonel of the carbineers, who lived in the Place Royale, a pair of pistols which he had been repairing. I soon performed this commission, and unfortunately these cursed pistols should return eighteen francs to the shop, and the colonel counted out the money, adding a trifle for myself. So far, so good; but, lo and behold, in crossing a street I heard somebody knock at a window; I raised my eyes, supposing that I should see some acquaintance, who; what should I see but a Madame de Pompadour, who, with all her charms displayed, was tapping at a window, and who, by an inclination of her head, accompanied with a charming smile, invited me to go up to her. She might have been called a picture moving in its frame. A magnificent neck, a skin white as snow, a wide chest, and above all, a delightful countenance, combined to inflame me. I went upstairs four at a time, and on introducing myself to my princess, I found her a divinity. 'Approach, my little one,' said she to me, tapping my cheek lightly; 'you are going to make a little present, are you not?'

"I put my trembling hand into my pocket, and taking out the piece of money given to me by the colonel—

'Well, my child,' continued she, 'I think you are a lucky lad, and I am your countrywoman. Oh, you wish to treat your townswoman to a glass of wine.'

"The request was urged so sweetly, that I had no power of denial left, and the eighteen francs of the colonel were trenched upon. One glass produced another, that generated a third, which begot a fourth, and so on, until I was drunk with wine and delight. Night arrived, and I know not how, but I awoke in the street on a heap of stones at the gate of a hotel.

"My surprise was great on looking about me, and still more when, on looking in my purse, the birds were flown.

"How could I return to my master's? Where sleep? I determined to walk about till daybreak; I had only to kill time, or rather torment myself about the consequences of a first fault. I turned mechanically toward the Market of the Innocents. Mind how you trust your countrywomen! said I to myself. I am nicely fleeced! If I had only some money left—

"I confess that at this moment some droll ideas crossed my brain. I had often seen pasted upon the walls of Paris— 'Pocket-book Lost,' with one thousand, two thousand, or even three thousand francs' reward for the person who would bring it back. I thought I might find one of these, and looking carefully about me on the pavement, and walking like a man who is looking for something, I was seriously intent on the probability of finding so good a windfall, when I was aroused from my reverie by a blow of a fist, which encountered my back, 'What, my boy, you out so early this morning?' — 'Ah, is it you, Fanfan; and by what chance in this quarter at this hour?'

"Fanfan was a pastry-cook's apprentice, whom I knew, and in a moment he told me that he had left the oven for the last six weeks; that he had a mistress who fitted him out; that for a short time, he was from home, because the intimate friend of his mistress had chosen to sleep with her. 'As for the rest,' said he, 'I wink at it. If I pass a night here, I return to my haunt next morning, and recover myself during the day.' Fanfan the pastry-cook appeared to me a keen fellow; and thinking that he might devise some plan to extricate me from my embarrassment, I told him the whole of it.

"'Is that all?' said he. 'Come to me at mid-day at the public-house at the Barriere des Sergents; and I may give you some useful counsel: under any circumstances we'll dine together.'

"I was punctual at the rendezvous, and Fanfan did not keep me waiting; he was there before me, and on my entrance, I was led into a small room, where I found him seated before a tub of oysters, with a female on each side of him, one of whom, on perceiving me, burst out into a loud fit of laughter. 'Ah, what is that for?' said Fanfan. 'Oh, heaven, it is my townsman.'— 'It is my townswoman,' said I, confused. 'Yes, my little one, it is your townswoman. I was going to complain of the trick she had served me on the previous evening, but embracing Fanfan, whom she called her pet, she laughed more heartily than before, and I saw that the best thing I could do was to join in the laugh like a jolly fellow.

"'Well,' said Fanfan, pouring out a glass of white wine, and helping me to a dozen oysters, 'you see, you must never despair of Providence. We have some pigs feet on the gridiron, do you like pigs feet?' And before I could answer his question, they were put on the table. The appetite I displayed was so much in the affirmative, that Fanfan had no further occasion to ask my opinion of them. The Chablis soon put me in spirits, and I forgot the disagreeables which had given me such cause of dreading my master; and, as the companion of my townswoman had cast a gracious eye on me, I did not hesitate to make desperate love to her. By the honor of Dufailli! she was soon won, and gave me her hand.

"'You really love me then,' said Fanchette—so was my damsel named.—' Love you?' said I; 'why, if you like, we will be married.' 'That is right,' said

Fanfan, 'marry; and to commence, I will wed you at once. I marry you, my boy; do you understand? so embrace," and at the same time, he united our hands and drew our faces toward each other, 'Dear child,' said Fanchette giving me a second kiss without the aid of my friend, 'be easy; I will instruct you.'

"I was in paradise, and spent a delightful day. In the evening I went to bed with Fanchette, and we were mutually pleased with each other.

"My education was soon perfected. Fanchette was delighted at having met with a pupil who profited so well from her instructions, and recompensed me generously.

"At this period the Notables had just assembled, and they were good pigeons. Fanchette plucked them, and we shared the spoils. Each day we banqueted without limit. These Notables supplied our throats as well as exerting their own! And I had always a well-supplied purse.

"Fanchette and I denied ourselves nothing; but how brief are the moments of happiness! Oh, how brief!

"Scarcely had a month of this charming life elapsed, when Fanchette and my townswoman were apprehended and taken to prison. What had they done I do not know, but evil tongues said something about the abstraction of a repeating watch. I, who had no particular wish to make acquaintance with the lieutenant-general of police, thought it best to make as few inquiries as possible.

"This arrest was a blow which we had not looked for. Fanfan and I were overwhelmed at it. Fanchette was such a dear girl! and then how was I to carry on the war? My kettle was upset; farewell oysters, farewell Chablis, farewell hours of love! I should have stuck to my anvil; and Fanfan reproached himself for having quitted his patty-pans.

"We were walking sorrowfully on the Quai de la Ferraille, when we were suddenly aroused by a sound of military music, two clarionets, a large drum and cymbals. The crowd had gathered around this band, stationed in a car, above which floated colors and plumes. I think they were playing the air, 'Where can we find joys equal to those at home?' When the musicians had finished, the drums beat a roll, and a gentleman, covered with gold lace, got up and spoke, showing a large representation of a soldier in full uniform. 'By the authority of his majesty,' said he, 'I am here to explain to the subjects of the king of France the advantages which he offers in admitting them to his colonies. Young men who are around me, you must have heard of the land of Cocagne, and it is to India that we must go to find this fortunate country. There we must go if we would live in clover.

"'Would you have gold, pearls, or diamonds? The roads are paved with them; you have only to stoop and pick them up, and not even that, for the savages will collect them for you.

"'Do you love women? There they are for all tastes; negresses, who belong to all the world; then Creoles, white as you or I, and who dote to madness on white men, which is natural enough in a country where the men are all black;

and note particularly that every one of them is as rich as Croesus; which, between ourselves, is very advantageous in marriage.

"'Do you love wine? It is like the women, of all sorts; Malaga, Bordeaux, Champagne, etc. For instance—you must not often expect to meet with Burgundy, I will not deceive you, it will not bear sea carriage: but ask for any other that is made throughout the world, at sixpence a bottle, and believe me, you will find them but too happy to procure it for you. Yes, gentlemen, for sixpence; and that cannot surprise you, when you learn that sometimes one, two, or three hundred ships, loaded with wines, arrive at the same time in one single harbor. Picture to yourself the embarrassment of the captains; in haste to return, they quickly unload, and announce that they shall esteem it a favor from any who will empty the casks gratis.

"'That is not all. Do not you think it would be a sweet life always to have sugar in plenty? I have not mentioned coffee, lemons, pomegranates, oranges, pineapples, and the millions of delicious fruits which grow here as wild as they did in Paradise; and the liqueurs which are much esteemed.

"'If I were addressing women or children, I might expatiate on all these delicacies, but I am speaking to men.

"'Sons of family, I am not ignorant of the efforts usually made by parents to restrain young people from the path which must lead to fortune; but be more rational than the papas, and particularly the mammas.

"'Do not listen to them, when they tell you that the savages eat the Europeans with only a little salt. That was all very well in the days of Christopher Columbus and Robinson Crusoe.

"'Do not listen to them, when they endeavor to terrify you about the yellow fever. The yellow fever! Gentlemen, if it were as terrible as people say, there would be nothing but hospitals in the country; and God knows that there is not a single one.

"'Doubtless they will frighten you about the climate. I am too frank not to confess it—the climate is warm, but nature is so prodigal in giving refreshments, that, in truth, we must attend to the thing, or we should not perceive it.

"'They will alarm you about the sting of the mosquitoes, and the bite of rattlesnakes. But have you not slaves always about you expressly to drive away the former, and does not the noise of the latter sufficiently inform you of its approach?

"'They will talk to you of shipwrecks. Know that I have crossed the sea fifty-seven times; that I have again and again crossed the line; that I look on going from one pole to the other, like drinking a glass of water; and although on the ocean there is neither wooden sledges nor nurses, I think myself more secure on board a seventy-four, than in the inside of the coach to Auxerre, or on the conveyance from Paris to St. Cloud This must be enough to dissipate all fears. I might add a variety of delights. I might talk of the chase—sporting, fishing. Imagine to yourself forests, where the game is so tame that it never thinks of running away, and so timid that if you only call to it, it falls down! Imagine rivers and lakes, where fish are so abundant that they choke the waters. This is all very wonderful, but perfectly true.

"'I had nearly forgotten to talk to you of horses. Horses, gentlemen! You cannot take a step without meeting with thousands of them. You might call them flocks of sheep, only that they are larger. Are you fond of them? Do you like riding? Only take a rope in your pocket, which should be rather long, and you must make a running knot in it—you seize the moment when the animals are grazing and afraid of nothing; you then approach quietly, and make your choice; and when your choice is made, you throw the cord—the horse is yours; you have only to back him and lead him where you please and think proper; for, remember, that here every man is uncontrolled in his actions.

"'Yes, gentlemen, I repeat it, it is all true, very true; the proof is, that the king of France, his majesty Louis XVI, who can almost hear me in his palace, authorizes me on his part to offer you these advantages. Should I dare to lie so near to him?

"'The king desires to clothe you, the king wishes to support you, he wishes to make you rich men; in return, he asks but little from you; no labor, and good pay; good nourishment; to rise up and lie down at pleasure; exercise once a month, at the parade of St. Louis; this, for I will conceal nothing, cannot be dispensed with, unless you get leave, which is never refused. These obligations done, your time is your own. What more can you desire? A good engagement? you shall have it: but hasten, I advise you; tomorrow will perhaps be too late, the ships are about to start, and only wait for a fair wind to set sail. Hasten, then, near to Paris; hasten. If, perchance, you should grow tired of doing well, you shall have dismissal when you please; a bark is always in port, ready to conduct to Europe those who are homesick; it is expressly used for that purpose. Let those who desire to have further particulars, come to me; I have no occasion to tell my name; I am very well-known; my residence is only a few paces distant, at the first lamp, at the house of a wine merchant. Ask for M. Belle-Rose.'

"My situation made me attentive to this harangue, which I have remembered, although it is twenty years since I heard it, and I do not think that I forget a single word.

"It made no less impression on Fanfan, and we were consulting together, when a shabby-looking fellow, whom we had not at all offended, gave Fanfan a blow, which knocked his hat off. 'I will teach you,' said he, 'you puppy, to grin at me.' Fanfan was bewildered by the blow, and I defended him, when the blackguard raised his hand against me; we were soon surrounded, and the quarrel was growing warm, and the people flocked round, trying who should see most of it. Suddenly, someone separated the crowd; it was M. Belle-Rose. 'What is all this?' said he; and looking at Fanfan, who was crying, 'I think this gentleman has been struck— that cannot be put up with; but the gentleman is brave, and that will settle the business.' Fanfan was desirous of showing that he had done nothing wrong, and then that he had not been struck. 'It is all the same, my friend,' replied Belle-Rose; 'it cannot be settled that way.' 'Certainly,' said the bully, 'it cannot be decided in this way. The gentleman insulted me, and shall give me satisfaction; one of us must fall.'

"' Well, well, be it so; he will give you satisfaction,' replied Belle-Rose: 'I will answer for these gentlemen; what is your hour?'—'Yours.'—'Five in the morning, behind the bishop's palace;—I will bring weapons.'

"Upon this the blackguard retired; and Belle-Rose striking Fanfan on the stomach, heard some pieces chink in the waistcoat pocket, where he carried his money, the last relics of our former splendor. 'Really, my lad, I take an interest in you,' said he: 'you must come with me; our friend here must go with us;' and so saying, he gave me a poke, similar to that he had bestowed on Fanfan.

"M. Belle-Rose conducted us into the Rue de la Juiverie, to a wine merchant's, where he made us enter. 'I will not enter with you,' said he to us; 'a man like me must preserve decorum: I am going to pull off my uniform, and will join you in a minute. Ask for a red seal and three glasses.' He left us. 'A red seal,' said he turning round: 'mind the red seal.'

"We executed the orders of M. Belle-Rose, who was not long in returning, and whom we received cap-in-hand. 'Ah! my boys,' said he, 'put on your hats; no ceremonies between us; I am going to sit down: where is my glass? the first come, the first served. (He drank it down at a gulp.) I am devilish thirsty, and the dust sticks in my throat.'

"M. Belle-Rose poured out a second whilst he spoke, and then wiping his forehead with a handkerchief, he leant his two elbows on the table, and assumed a mysterious air, which began to disquiet us.

"'Ah! my young friends, it is tomorrow that we have to have the brush. Do you know," said he to Fanfan, 'that you have a devil to meet?—one of the best fencers in France: he pinked St. George.' 'He pinked St. George,' repeated Fanfan, looking most piteously at me. 'Ah! indeed, he pinked St. George; but that is not all,—he has a most unlucky hand.' 'And so have I,' said Fanfan. 'What, you too?'—'By Jove, I think a day never passed, when I was at my master's, that I did not break something, if only a plate or two.' 'Oh, you misunderstand me,' said Belle-Rose; 'we say that a man has an unlucky hand, when he always kills the man whom he fights.'

"The explanation was but too clear. Fanfan trembled in every limb, the sweat ran down his forehead in large drops, white and blue clouds pervaded the red cheeks of the pastry cook's apprentice, his face lengthened, his heart beat, and he would have suffocated, had he not heaved an enormous sigh.

"'Bravo!' cried Belle-Rose, taking his hand in his own, 'I like men who have no fear. You are not afraid.' Then, striking the table, 'Waiter, another bottle of the same; mind you, my friend here, pays. Get up a little, my friend; move yourself—stir about—stretch out your arm—circulate your blood—thrust out; that's it,—splendid! admirable! superb!' And during this time Belle-Rose emptied his glass. 'On the honor of Belle-Rose I could make a fencer of you. Do you know, you have an excellent idea of it. You would do well at it; there are more than four of our masters not so well made for it as you. What a pity you were never taught; but nothing is impossible, you have frequented the schools?'

'Oh, I swear not, replied Fanfan. 'Come, confess that you fight well.'—'No, not at all.'— 'No modesty; why conceal your talent that way, I can easily perceive it.'

'I protest to you,' said I, 'that he never handled a foil in his life.'

'Since you attest it, sir, I must believe; but, ah! you are two deep fellows; you must not teach old apes how to grin; tell me the truth, and do not fear that I would betray you: am not I your friend? If you have no confidence in me, I may as well go. Farewell, gentlemen,' continued Belle-Rose, with a provoked air, going toward the door, as if about to depart.

"'Oh, M. Belle-Rose, do not forsake us,' cried Fanfan. 'Rather ask my friend if I have deceived you. I am a pastry cook by trade, and I cannot help my fate. I have handled the rolling-pin, but,—'

"'I saw you had handled something,' said Belle-Rose. 'I like sincerity, such sincerity as yours; it is the chief of military virtues; with that we may go to any extent. I am sure you would make an admirable soldier. But that is not our present business. Waiter, a bottle of wine. Since you tell me you never did fight, I will believe nothing again—(after a moment's silence)—Never mind, my delight is to confer happiness on young people. I will teach you a thrust—a single thrust. (Fanfan stared.) You must promise me not to show it to anybody.'—' I swear it,' said Fanfan. "Well, you will be the first to whom I ever showed it. I must leave you! It is a thrust unequaled; one which I kept only to myself. Never mind, I will initiate you at daylight tomorrow.'

"From this moment Fanfan appeared less alarmed, and overpowered M. Belle-Rose with thanks. We drank a few more glasses, during a multitude of protestations on one side and gratitude on the other; and then, as it was growing late, M. Belle-Rose took leave of us like a man who knew the world. Before he left us he showed us a place where we could sleep. 'Say that you come from me,' said he, 'at Griffon's, in the Rue de la Mortellerie; sleep in peace, and you shall find all go well.' Fanfan paid the bill, and then Belle-Rose said, 'Good-night, tomorrow I shall come and wake you.'

"We went to Griffon's, where we procured beds. Fanfan could not close in eye, and was perhaps impatient to learn the thrust which M Belle-Rose had promised to teach him; or he might be frightened; perhaps he was.

"At the first peep of day the key turned in the lock, and someone entered. It was Belle-Rose. 'Come, boys; what, still asleep! Hear the muster-call, my lads,' cried he. In a moment we jumped up. When we were ready, he went out a moment with Fanfan, and they soon afterward returned. 'Let us go,' said Belle-Rose: 'mind, no nonsense; you have nothing to do but give the twisting thrust, and he will pink himself.'

"In spite of his lesson, Fanfan was not quite tranquil; and having reached the ground, he was more dead than alive. The adversary and his second had arrived already. 'Here we are,' said Belle-Rose, and taking the foils which he had given to me, and breaking off the buttons, he measured the blades. 'Neither of them is six inches longer than the other. Come, take this,' said he to M. Fanfan, giving him one of the foils.

"Fanfan hesitated; and on the second offer, seized the handle so clumsily that he let it fall. 'That is nothing,' said Belle-rose, picking it up, and putting it in Fanfan's hand; he then placed him opposite his adversary. 'Mind, guard! We shall see who will tickle his man.'

"' One moment,' said the second of the opponent; 'I have a question to ask first, sir,' said he, addressing Fanfan, who could scarcely support himself, 'are you either master or provost?'—'What do you say?' replied Fanfan, with the voice of a man half-dead. 'According to the laws of dueling,' responded the second, 'my duty compels me to summon you to declare on your honor, are you master or provost?' Fanfan was silent, and looked at Belle-Rose as if to ask him what he should say. 'Speak, sir,' said the second to Fanfan. 'I am— I am—I am only an apprentice,' stammered Fanfan. 'Apprentice means amateur,' added Belle-Rose. 'In this case,' continued the second, 'the gentleman amateur must undress; for our business is with his skin.'—'That is just,' said Belle-Rose, 'I did not think of that; he will undress himself: quick, quick, M. Fanfan, off with coat and shirt.'

"Fanfan cut a scurvy figure: the sleeves of his doublet were very tight, and he unbuttoned at one end and buttoned up at the other. When he had taken off his waistcoat, he could not undo the strings of the neck of his shirt, and was compelled to cut them; and at last, except his breeches, was as naked as a worm. Belle-Rose again gave him the foil. 'Now, my friend,' said he, 'mind your guard !' — 'Defend yourself,' cried his adversary; swords were crossed. Fanfan's blade shook and trembled; the other weapon was motionless. Fanfan seemed about to faint.

"'Enough,' suddenly cried Belle-Rose and the second, 'you are two brave fellows; enough, you must not cut each other's throats; be friends, embrace, and let there be no further dispute. Good God! all that is good need not be killed. But he is a gallant young lad. Be appeased, M. Fanfan.'

"Fanfan breathed again, and plucked up when his courage was mentioned; his opponent made some difficulty about consenting to an arrangement, but at length was softened; and they embraced, whilst it was agreed that the reconciliation should be completed by breakfasting at a drinking house near Notre Dame, where there was good wine to be had.

"When we reached the place, the breakfast was spread and ready.

"Before we sat down, M. Belle-Rose took Fanfan and myself aside. 'Well,' said he, 'you know now what a duel is; it is not an out of the way matter; I am content with you, my dear Fanfan, you behaved like an angel. But you must be great throughout: you understand me—you must not allow him to pay.'

"At these words Fanfan turned very red; for he knew the depth of our purse. 'Oh, good Lord, let the mutton boil,' added Belle-Rose, who saw his embarrassment. 'If you are out of cash I will take care of all that; here, do you want money? Will you have thirty francs?—or sixty? Amongst friends, that is nothing.' And so saying, he drew a dozen crowns from his pocket—'With you they are in good keeping, and will bring good luck.'

"Fanfan hesitated. 'Accept them, and pay me when you can. On these terms there can be no hesitation in borrowing.' I jogged Fanfan's elbow, as much as to say, 'Take it.' He obeyed; and we pocketed the crowns, touched at the kindness of Belle-Rose.

"He was soon, however, to skin us of them. Experience is a great teacher, and M. Belle-Rose was a deep fellow!

"Breakfast went off with spirit; we talked much of the avarice of parents—the brutalities of apprentices' masters—of the blessings of independence—the immense wealth amassed in the Indies: the names of the Cape, Chandernagor, were adroitly introduced; examples were quoted of the vast fortunes made by the young men whom Belle-Rose had recently engaged. 'It is not to boast,' said he, 'but I am not an unlucky fellow: it was I who enlisted little Martin; and now he is a nabob, rolling in gold and silver. I will bet that he has grown proud; and perhaps if he saw me would not recognize me. Oh, I have found many ingrates in my time! But what of that! It is the fate of man!'

"Our sitting was a long one. At the dessert, M. Belle-Rose again brought on the carpet the fine fruits of the Antilles: whilst he drank the wine. 'Cape wine forever,' said he: 'how delicious that is!' with the coffee he expatiated on the Martinique: when they brought the Cognac, 'Ah! ah!' said he, making a grimace, 'this is not equal to the rum, and still less the excellent pineapple of Jamaica;' they poured out some parfait amour; 'This is drinkable,' said he, 'but still it is not even small beer in comparison with the liqueurs of the celebrated Madame Anfous.'

"Belle-Rose was seated between Fanfan and myself, and during the whole repast took great care of us. He kept up the incessant song of 'Empty your glasses;' and he filled them incessantly. 'Who made you such half-wet birds?' said he at intervals. 'Come, another glass, look at me, and do as I do.'

"These phrases, and many others, had due effect. Fanfan and I were pretty well done up; he particularly. 'M. Belle Rose, is it very far to the colonies, Chandernagor, Seringapatam?—are they very far off?' he repeated, from time to time, and he already imagined himself embarked, so completely was he imbued with the flourishing accounts. 'Patience,' said Belle-Rose, at length, 'and we shall get there; and in the meantime I am going to tell you a story. One day when I was on guard at the governor's... '

'Hold your peace,' said Belle-Rose, putting his hand upon his mouth, 'it was only when I was the private,' he continued; 'I was quietly seated in front of my sentry-box, reposing on a sofa, when my negro, who carried my gun,—you must know that in the colonies every soldier has his male and female slave, as we might here have domestics of both sexes; only that you may do with them what you please; and if it be your pleasure, you may kill them as you would a fly; for you have power of life and death over them. As for the woman, you do what you please with her;—I was on guard, as I just told you, and my negro was carrying my gun.'

"M. Belle-Rose had scarcely got so far, when a soldier in full dress entered the room, and gave him a letter, which he opened in haste. 'It is from the minister of the marine,' said he; 'M. de Sartines tells me, that the service of the king summons me to Surinam. 'The devil!' added he addressing Fanfan and me, 'how awkward it is; I did not think of quitting so soon; but as they say, he who reckons without his host, reckons twice: never mind.'

"Belle-Rose then, taking his glass in his right hand, knocked several times on the table, and whilst the other guests withdrew, a waiting-maid entered. 'The bill, and send your master;' and the master came with the bill of our expenses. 'Astonishing, how soon it mounts up,' observed Belle-Rose, 'one hundred and ninety livres, twelve sous, six deniers! Ah! M. Nivet, do you want to skin us alive? Here is an item I will not pass by—four lemons, twenty-four sous. We only had three—reduction the first. Peste, papa Nivet, I am not surprised at your making a fortune. Seven half-glasses, that is very fine; but how do you make it out, when there were only six of us? I shall find other mistakes, I am convinced. Asparagus, eighteen livres; that is too much.'—

'In April,' said M. Nivet, 'and so early I' —

'Well, that is right, young peas, artichokes, fish, lettuces, strawberries, twenty-four livres—that is correct. The wine is fair enough: now I will add it up. Put down nought and carry one—the total is correct, deducting the twelve sous and the six deniers there remains one hundred and ninety livres. Well, will you give me credit for the amount, papa Nivet?'—

'Oh!' replied the landlord, 'yesterday, yes; today, no; credit on land as long you please, but once at sea, how am I to be repaid? At Surinam? Devil take the seagoing creditors. I tell you money I want, and you shall not go out till I am satisfied: otherwise I shall call the watch, and we shall then see." M. Nivet went out in an apparent rage.

"'He is a man of his word,' said Belle-Rose to us. 'But an idea strikes me; in great distresses, great remedies. Doubtlessly you have no greater wish than myself to be led before M. Lenoir between four guards. The king gives 100 francs a man for recruits; there are two of you, that makes 200 francs; sign your enrolments; I will go and get the cash, then return and free you. What say you?'

"Fanfan and I looked at each other in silence. 'What! do you hesitate? I had a better opinion of you. I, who would cut myself in quarters—and then I do not ask you to do an unpleasant thing. Heavens! that I was of your age, and knew what I know! We have always resources whilst we are young. Come,' he added, presenting the paper to us, 'now is your time to coin money; put your name at the bottom of this paper.'

"The persuasions of Belle-Rose were so pressing, and we were so fearful of the watch, that we signed. 'That is right,' said he, 'now I will go and pay; if you are vexed, there is always time: you will have nothing to do but return the money; but we shall not come to that. Patience, my friends, I will soon return.'

"Belle-Rose soon went out and quickly returned.

"'The embargo is removed,' said he, 'and now we are free to go or stay; but you have not yet seen Madame Belle-Rose, Irish. to introduce you to her: she is a woman with wit to the end of her nails.'

"M. Belle-Rose conducted us to his house; his lodging was not over brilliant—two rooms on the back of a mean-looking house a little distance from the Arch-Marion. Madame Belle-Rose was in a recess at the end of the second room, her head resting on a heap of pillows. Near her bed were two crutches: and at a little distance, a night table, a spitting-box, a shell snuff-box, a silver goblet, and a bottle of brandy nearly emptied. Madame Belle-Rose was about forty-five or fifty; she was attired in a stylish morning-gown, with top-knot, and head-dress of lace. Her face was distorted as we entered by a violent fit of coughing. 'Wait till she has done,' said Belle Rose to us; and at length, her cough ceasing, 'Can you talk, my duck?'—'Yes, my precious,' she answered, —'Well, you will oblige me by informing my friends here what fort'nes are made in the colonies,' —'Immense! M. Belle Rose, immense!'—'What alliances?—'What alliances? Superb! M. Belle Rose, superb! the meanest heiress has millions of piastres.'— 'What life do they lead?'—'The life of a prince, M. Belle-Rose.'

"'You see,' said the husband, 'I did not make her say so.' "The farce was thus performed. M. Belle-Rose offered us the refreshment of a glass of rum: we drank to his wife, and she drank to our good voyage. 'For, I suppose,' she added, 'that these gentlemen are ours. My dear fellow,' said she to Fanfan, 'you have the face they like in those parts; square shoulders, wide chest, well-made leg, nose a la Bourbon.' Then turning to me, 'And you, too; oh! you are well-limbed fellows', — 'And lads, too, who will not allow themselves to be trampled on,' added Belle-Rose; 'this gentleman has been at it already this morning.' 'What, already! I congratulate him. Come here, my dear sir, and let me kiss you; I always liked young fellows, that is my taste: everyone has their inclination. Do not be jealous, Belle-Rose.'

'Jealous of what? My friend behaved like a second Bayard, as I shall tell the regiment; the colonel shall know it, and advancement must follow—corporal at least, if not an officer. Ah, when you have the epaulette on your shoulders, you will be a noted brave man! Fanfan jumped for joy. As for me, sure that I was no less brave than he, I said to myself, 'If he advances, I shall not hang back.' We were both very happy.

"'I ought to tell you one thing,' pursued the recruiter; 'recommended as you are, you must excite jealousy; there are envious people everywhere; but remember that if they use a word of abuse, I shall take it up; once under my protection—enough. Write to me.'

'What!' said Fanfan, 'do not you go with us?'

'No,' replied Belle-Rose, 'to my great regret: the minister has need of me. I shall join you at Brest, tomorrow at eight o'clock I expect you here, not later: today I have no leisure to remain longer with you; duty must be done. Adieu till tomorrow.'

"We took leave of Madame Belle-Rose, who embraced us. Next day we were, at half-past seven, aroused by the bugs which lodged with us at Griffon's. 'Give me punctual men!' said Belle-Rose, when he saw us; 'I am one myself.' Then assuming a more serious air: 'If you have any friends and acquaintances, you have the rest of the day for leave-taking. Now this is your route; your allowance is three sous per league, with lodging, firing, and candle. You may start as soon as you like; that is no affair of mine; but do not forget, that, if you are found in the streets of Paris tomorrow evening, the police will conduct you to your place of destination.'

"This threat cut us up root and branch; but as we had baked, so we must brew; and we started. From Paris to Brest is a famous, long walk, but, in spite of blisters, we made ten leagues a day. We arrived at last, but not without having a thousand times cursed Belle-Rose. A month afterward we embarked. Ten years afterward, day for day, I was made corporal, and Fanfan also promoted; he was knocked on the head at St. Domingo, during Leclerc's expedition. He was a devil amongst the negro women. As for me, I have yet a steady foot and good eye; my chest is well lined, and I may have the luck to bury you all. I have passed many rough days in my life; been thrown from one colony to another; I have rolled my ball as I went, and I have not been a loser; never mind, the children of glee will never die;—and that, when they are no more here, they are to be found elsewhere," continued the Serjeant Dufailli, striking the pockets of his uniform; and then lifting up his waistcoat, exposed a leather belt, apparently well lined. "I say, there is yet butter in the churn, and yellow enough, too, without counting what we may chance to borrow from the English. The India Company owe me a balance still, which some three-masters will bring."—"In the meantime, all goes well with you, father Dufailli," said the forager. "Very well," said the serjeant-major. Yes, very well, indeed, thought I; determining to cultivate an acquaintance which chance rendered so propitious for me.

Chapter XVII

WHILST GIVING US THE SCENE OF THE RECRUITERS, father Dufailli had drunk at every sentence. He was of opinion that words flowed best when moistened. He might, to be sure, have used water; but he had a great horror of that, he said, ever since he fell into the sea, which was in it. Thus it happened, that partly through drinking and partly through talking, he got drunk imperceptibly. At last he reached a point, at which he found it impossible to express himself, but with the utmost difficulty; his tongue became what we call thick. And then the forager and sergeant-major retired.

Dufailli and I remained alone; he was asleep and leant on the table, and began to snore; whilst I coolly gave myself up to a train of reflections. Three hours elapsed, and he had not finished his sleep. When he awoke, he was quite surprised to find any one near him; at first, he looked at me as through a thick fog, which did not allow him to distinguish my features, but insensibly the vapor disappeared, and he recognized me, which was all he could do. He stumbled as he arose; and ordering a basin, of coffee, without milk, into which he emptied a salt-cellar, shallowed the liquid with small gulps; and baring got rid of his short sword, he took my arm, dragging me toward the door. My aid was most needful to him; it was the vine twining about the elm. "You are going to tow me," said he, "and I will pilot you. Do you see the telegraph? What does it say, with its arms in the air?"

"It makes signals that the *Dufailli* is lying-to."

"The *Dufailli*,—thousand gods! a ship of three hundred tons at least. Do not fear; all's right with *Dufailli*."

At the same time, without letting go my arm, he took off his hat, and placing it on the end of his finger, spun it round. "See my compass; attention— we go as the cockade points—whether the cape of the Rue des Precheurs! forward, march!" ordered Dufailli; and we took together the road to the lower town, after he had put you his hat with much noise.

Dufailli had promised to advise me, but he was not in a state to do it. I anxiously desired that he should recover his reason, but, unfortunately, the air and exercise produced a precisely opposite effect. On going down the main street, we were obliged to enter every public-house, with which the residence of the army had filled the place; everywhere made a stay, shorter or longer. I endeavored to make them as brief as possible. Each shop, Dufailli said, was a port, into which we must put, and each port increased the cargo, which he had already so much difficulty to carry. "I am as full as a beggar," said he to me, in broken words: "and yet I am not a beggar, for beggars never get drunk, do they, my boy?"

Twenty times I resolved on leaving him; but Dufailli, when sober, might aid me; I remembered his full girdle, and even without that, I knew well that he had other resources than his sergeant's pay. Having reached the church in the Place d'Alton, he took it into his head to have his shoes brushed, which, when done, he lost his balance in moving from the stool; and, thinking he would fall, I approached to support him, "What, countryman, don't fear because I make a reel or two; I have a sailor's foot." In the meantime the brush had given brightness to his shoes; and when they were completely blackened, "Come, the finishing touch," said Dufailli; "or is that for tomorrow?" At the same time he gave him a sous. "You will not make a rich man of me, sergeant." "What, do you grumble?—mind I don't kill you." Dufailli made a gesture, but his hat fell off, and, blown by the wind, rolled along the pavement; the shoe-black ran after it and brought it back. "It is not worth two-pence," cried Dufailli; "never mind, you are a good fellow." Then thrusting his hands into his pockets, he took out a handful of money; "Here, drink to my health."—"Thanks, my colonel," said the shoe-black, who proportioned his titles to the generosity he met with.

"I must now," said Dufailli, who seemed by degrees to recover his senses, "lead you into good quarters." I had made up my mind to accompany him wherever he went. I had witnessed his liberality, and I was not ignorant that drunkards are the most grateful persons possible to those who give them their company. I allowed myself then to be piloted as he wished, and we reached the Rue des Precheurs. At the door of a new house of elegant appearance, was a sentry and several soldiers. "This is it," said he. "What, here? Are you going to take me to the staff-major?"—"The staff-major! —nonsense; I say it is the beautiful and fair Magdelaine's; or, if you like it better, 'Madame quarante-mille hommes' (madam forty thousand men) as they call her."—"Impossible, Dufailli, you are under some mistake."—"Oh, I see double, do I? Is not that the sentinel?' Dufailli advanced while speaking, and asked for admittance. "Go back," said the quartermaster, roughly; "you ought to know well enough that this is not your day." Dufailli persisted. "Go away, I tell you," said the subaltern, "or I will take you to the black hole." This threat made me tremble all over.

Dufailli's obstinacy might be fatal to me, and yet it would not have been prudent to tell him my fears; at all events not where we then were; and I therefore only made some observations to him, which were however entirely lost upon him in his present state. "Let the fellow go and be, the sun shines equally for us all; liberty, equality, or death," he repeated, whilst struggling to escape the hold I kept on him that he might not commit himself in any way. "Equality, I tell you;" and in an attitude better conceived than described, he looked at me with that stupid no-meaning stare which a man has when he has "put an enemy into his mouth to steal away his brains," and reduce him to the level of a brute.

I was in despair, when at the cry, "Present arms!" followed by this warning, "Cannoneer, mind what you do; here is the adjutant, here is Bevignac;" he suddenly seemed quite to come to himself. A shower-bath falling from a height of fifty feet, upon a maniac's head, has not so sudden an effect in restoring his senses. The name of Bevignac made a singular impression of the soldiery, who had arranged themselves in front of the ground floor of the fair Magdelaine's house. They looked at one another without, as it seemed, daring to breathe, so

162

much were they alarmed. The adjutant, who was a tall, meagre-looking man, having arrived, began to count them, whilst he made motions with his cane. I never saw a face so deeply furrowed; on his thin and lank jaws were two small unpowdered curls; on the whole countenance might be traced a certain something, which declared that adjutant Bevignac was a perfect martinet, and determinately opposed to anything like a want of discipline. Anger was visible in his face, his eyes were bloodshot, and a horrible convulsion of his jaws announced that he was about to speak. "By the devil's nest! Well! All quiet! You know orders. None but officers! By Satan's nest! and every man in his turn." Then perceiving us and advancing toward us with uplifted cane, "What are you doing here, you serjeant of powder monkeys?" I thought he was about to strike us. "Oh, I see," he added. "It is nothing; only drunk;" addressing Dufailli. "Well, a jovial cup is excusable; go to bed, and do not let me meet you again."—"Yes, commandant," replied Dufailli, at this order, and we went away down the Rue des Precheurs.

There is no occasion to mention the profession of the fair Magdelaine le Picarde: it must have been already guessed. She was a tall woman about twenty-three years of age, remarkable for the bloom of her complexion, as well as the beauty of her figure. It was her boast, that she belonged to no one person. She devoted herself, from a principle of conscience, entirely and solely to the army—the whole army—but nothing but the army; fifer or field-marshal, all who wore the uniform, were equally well received by her; but she professed great contempt for what she called the snobs. There never was a citizen who could boast of her favors: she was somewhat tenacious with marines, whom she called "tar-buckets," and fleeced at pleasure, because she could not make up her mind to look on them as soldiers; and she used to say, that the navy filled her purse, and the army was her lover. This lady, whom I had occasion to visit at a subsequent period, was, for a long time, the delight of the camp, without her health being at all impaired, and was supposed to be rich. But whether Magdelaine (as I know) was not mercenary, or whether as the old proverb goes, "What is got over the devil's back is spent under his belly," Magdelaine died in 1812, at the hospital of Andres, poor, but true to her flag: but two years more, and, like any other nymph well-known in Paris, after the disaster of Waterloo, she would have had the grief of calling herself the "widow of the grand army."

It is very difficult to eradicate an idea from a brain troubled with the fumes of wine. Dufailli had resolved on finishing the day in female society, and nothing could turn him from it. Scarcely had we taken half-a-dozen steps, than looking back, "He has disappeared," said he, "come along, this way;" and, leaving my arm, he advanced toward a door, at which he knocked; and which, after a few minutes, was half opened, and an old woman's head appeared. "What do you want?"— "What do we want?" answered Dufailli; "don't you know me? Do not you recognize friends?"— "Ah! ah! it is you, father Dufailli; there is no room for you." "No room for friends! You're joking, mother; you are playing off some trick upon us."— "No, on the word of an honest woman; you know, my old lad, that no one is more welcome than yourself; but my eldest daughter is engaged, and so is Pauline; but we shall be glad to see you by and bye."— "Well, if it must be so, Mother Thomas," said Dufailli, putting a piece of money on his eye, "it cannot be helped, but you must get us something to drink meanwhile; you have some little spare corner to put us into."—"Ay, ay, always a wag, always a wag, father Dufailli; it is impossible to refuse your insinuating requests. Come! quick, quick, let no one see you coming in; hide yourselves there, my boys, and mum." Madame Thomas had placed us behind an old screen, in a low room, through which all persons going out must pass. We did not wait long alone. Mademoiselle Pauline came to us first, and, having whispered to her mother, came and sat down with us to a flask of Rhenish.

Pauline was not fifteen years of age, and yet she had already acquired the dissipated air, the bold look, the loose discourse, the hoarse voice, and the disgusting manners of the common courtesan. This early prey to dissipation was destined for my amusement, and was lavish in her endearments. Therese was better suited to the bald head of my companion, who waited until she should be at leisure; and, at length, the quick step of a hussar boot, garnished with spurs, announced that the cavalier was taking leave of his lady fair. Dufailli, who was somewhat impatient, rose abruptly from his seat, but his short sword getting between his legs, he fell, knocking down the screen, table, bottles, and glasses. "Excuse me, captain," he stammered out, whilst endeavoring to rise; "it was the fault of the wall."— "Oh, it is of no consequence," said the officer; who, although rather confused, very readily aided in lifting him up, whilst Pauline, Therese, and their mother, were seized with a fit of irrepressible laughter.

When Dufailli had recovered his feet, the captain departed; and, as the fall had produced no bruise nor wound, nothing checked our mirth. I shall throw a veil over the remaining scenes of this evening. We were in a place where Dufailli was well known, and my readers may guess the rest; suffice it to say, that about one o'clock in the morning, I was buried in profound sleep, when I was suddenly awakened by a most tremendous uproar. Without suspecting the cause, I dressed myself in haste, and some cries of "Guard! Guard! Murder! murder!" from the shrill lungs of Mother Thomas, warned me that the danger was not far off. I was unarmed, and ran immediately to Dufailli's room to ask for his tinder-box, of which I knew I should make a better use than he would. It was time, for our castle was invaded by five or six marines, who, sword in hand, were endeavoring to get our berths. These gentlemen were threatening, neither more nor less, than to force us to jump out of the windows; and, as they swore, besides, to put everything to fire and sword in the house, Mother Thomas, with her squeaking pipe, was pealing the tocsin of alarm with a noise that aroused the whole neighborhood. Although a man not easily frightened, I confess I felt a sensation of fear which I could not repress. The event, whatever it might be, would probably end seriously for me.

I was, however, determined to take a resolute part. Pauline earnestly urged me to shut myself up with her. "Fasten the bolt," said she. "I beseech you to fasten the bolt." But the garret in which we were was not impregnable. I might be blockaded; and preferred defending the approach to the place, rather than run the risk of being taken like a rat in a trap. In spite of Pauline's efforts to detain me, I attempted a sortie, and was soon engaged with the assailants. I darted amongst them from the end of a narrow gallery, and with so much impetuosity, that before they could recover themselves, upset, and thrust headlong from a ladder, by which they were attempting to gain an entrance, they were laid sprawling on the ground, bruised and wounded severely. Then Pauline, her sister, and Dufailli, to render the victory more decisive, flung upon them all that came to hand; chairs, tables, stools, and various items, which to list would be tedious. At every missile that struck them, the enemy, prostrate on the pavement, cried out with pain and rage. In a moment, the passage was filled. This nocturnal brawl could not fail to arouse all in the vicinity; and the night-guard, police agents, and patrol, entered the domicile of Madame Thomas;—there must have been at least fifty men, all armed, and making a tremendous hubbub. Madame Thomas endeavored to testify that her house was quite tranquil, but they would not hear her: and these words, some of which were pretty significant, reached our ears from the ground floor—"Take this woman off."— "Come, old, follow us; or shall we get a wheelbarrow to bundle you in, old duchess? Come, no nonsense." "Sweep off the whole party; take everyone; seize their arms. I will teach you, you blackguards, to make a row." From these words, pronounced in a provincial accent, and mixed with occasional interjections, which, like the garlic and pepper, are fruits of his country, we learnt that Adjutant Bevignac was at the head of the party. Dufailli had no inclination to get into his clutches; and, as for me, I had excellent reasons for wishing to escape. "The staircase—go up the staircase, and guard the passage," roared out Bevignac. But whilst he thus bellowed and vociferated, I had time to tie a sheet to the window-bar, and the obstacles which separated us from the armed force had not been removed, when Pauline, Therese, Dufailli, and myself, were already out of reach. This threat, "Do not trouble yourselves—I will follow you," which we heard at a distance, only moved our laughter. The danger was over.

We consulted as to where we should pass the night. Therese and Pauline proposed that we should quit the city, and make a pastoral excursion into the country. "No, no," said Dufailli; "let us go to Boutrois;" and this was agreed on. M. Boutrois, although it was an untimely hour, opened his doors with much politeness. "Ah," said he to Dufailli, "I learnt that you had received your prize-money, and you are both right and welcome to pay us a visit. I have some admirable claret. What will the ladies please to take? A two-bedded room, I see." At the same time M. Boutrois, armed with a bunch of keys, and with a candle in his hand, led us to the room destined for us. "You will find yourselves quite at home here. No one will disturb you; where we purvey for the lieutenant of the marine, the commandant in chief, and the commissary general of police, you know no one dares to interfere. Madame Boutrois now does not like a joke, so I shall take care and say that you are alone. Madame B. is a very good woman—a very good woman; but her manners, you see—her manners are very formal: and on this point she is strictness personified. Women here! If she had only the slightest suspicion of such a thing, she would think herself lost forever; she has such an opinion of the sex in general! Oh, mon Dieu! must we not live with the living—the jolly—the vivacious? I am a philosopher myself, provided—mind, I say provided—that there is no ground for scandal; and suppose there were, why everyone to his liking, as the elderly gentlewoman said when she embraced her cow; every person to his own way of thinking and doing; the only point being, that it does not offend or prejudice anyone."

M. Boutrois treated us to a great many more equally brilliant aphorisms; after which he told us that he had a well-stocked cellar, all of which was at our service. "As for the boiler," he added, "that at the present hour has got rather cool, but your worships have only to order, and in a brace of seconds all shall be ready." Dufailli ordered some claret, and a fire, although it was quite warm enough to have done without.

The claret was brought, five or six logs were cast on the fire, and an ample collation spread before us. Some cold poultry occupied the center of the table, and formed the resisting point of an unprepared repast where all had been calculated for an enormous appetite. Dufailli desired that nothing should be wanting; and M. Boutrois, sure of being well paid, was most complying. Therese and her sister devoured all with their eyes, and I was not in a bad humor for commencing the attack and carrying on the war.

Whilst I was cutting up the fowl, Dufailli tasted the claret. "Delicious, delicious!" he repeated, smacking his lips, and then began to drink heartily; and scarcely had we begun to eat, when an unconquerable drowsiness nailed him to his chair, where he snored away most comfortably until the dessert came in. He then woke, crying out, "the devil—it blows hard— where am I? Does it freeze? I feel a sort of an all-overish-I-don't-know-how-ishness." "Oh," cried Pauline, who took me for a sapper of the guards, "his supper has not well digested."— "Papa's legs and back are asleep," said Therese, in her turn, and opening a sort of sweetmeat box in which was some snuff, "Take a pinch, my venerable; that will clear your eyes" Dufailli took a pinch; and if I mention this circumstance, trifling in itself, it is because I have before neglected to say, that Pauline's sister was more than thirty, and from the simple fact that she took snuff like a lawyer or commissary's clerk, we may easily imagine that she was not in the freshness of youth and beauty.

However that may be, Dufailli made much of her. "I like the little thing," he said occasionally, "she is a good girl."

"Oh, that is nothing new," replied Therese, "whenever a vessel anchors in our roads, I have gone through the scrutiny of all the crew; and I defy any sailor to say, 'black's the white of my eye.' When one knows how to behave as one should, one—" "The wench says right," interrupted Dufailli. "I like her because she is open, and so I will give her a good turn."

"Ha ha," cried Pauline, laughing, and then addressing me, "And you, will you give me a similar turn?"

Thus ran our conversation, when we heard, coming from the road leading to the harbor, a body of men, whose boots made a great noise as they walked.

"Captain Paulet forever!" they cried out; "Captain Paulet forever!" The troop soon stopped in front of the hotel. "Hallo! father Boutrois, father Boutrois?" they roared out altogether. Some tried to force the door; others thumped with the knocker in a most energetic manner; some pulled the bell with incredible violence; and others threw stones at the shutters.

At this uproar I started, imagining that our asylum was to be again attacked; Pauline and her sister were not quite at ease; and at length somebody running hastily downstairs, four steps at a time, the door was opened, and there was a rush, as if the embankments of a ditch had given way. The torrent was headlong; a mixture of voices uttered sounds quite unintelligible to us. "Peter, Paul, Jenny, Eliza, house, everybody, wife, get up! By Jove, they sleep like dormice." One might have thought that the house was on fire. We soon heard doors opening and shutting; there was a noise of tables, an inconceivable uproar, a female servant who was bitterly complaining of indecent treatment, shouts of riotous laughter, and bottles rattling and breaking. Plates, dishes, and glass clashing together, and the winding-up of the jack, added to the din; a chinking of money, oaths in English and French occasionally heard amidst this infernal clatter, all made the place a perfect bedlam broke loose. "By Jove, it is Joy, or I never heard it before," said Dufailli. "What are all these rejoicings for? What does it all mean? Have they captured the Spanish galleon? But this is not the track for them."

Dufailli cudgeled his brain to make out the cause of all the uproar, which was to me equally inexplicable, when M. Boutrois, with a radiant face, entered, to ask leave to light a fire. "You do not know," said he, "that the *Revanche* has just come into port. Our Paulet has been carrying on the war in his old way; is he not a fortunate fellow? A capture of three millions (francs) beneath the very cannon of Dover."—"Three millions!" cried Dufailli, "and I not there!"—"Do you hear that, sister? Three millions!" added Pauline jumping like a young kid.

"Three millions!" echoed Therese, "I am delighted! We shall come in for a share!"— "Ah, woman, woman," interrupted Dufailli, "interest before all; you should rather think of your mother, who is perhaps at this moment in darkness and distress."—"Mother Thomas is an old..." added Therese. "Come, that is neat, very neat," observed Boutrois, "for a daughter. 'Honor thy father and thy mother, that thy days may be long,' — "I cannot swallow that three millions," said Dufailli. "Tell us, father Boutrois, all about it." Our host excused himself on the plea of business; "besides," he added, "I do not well know the particulars, and am in a great hurry."

The riot continued; I heard them ranging chairs, and the silence that followed betokened that their jaws were filled. As it was probable that there would be some suspension of these noises, I proposed that we should go to bed, which was agreed on; and as daybreak was near at hand, that we might not be disturbed by the light, and make up for lost time, we drew the curtains close.

However, we were not aroused so soon as I had anticipated: sailors eat fast and drink long. Songs which shook the very glasses, at length disturbed our repose; forty discordant voices joining in the chorus of the celebrated hymn of

Roland. "Devil take the singers!" cried Dufailli, "I had the most agreeable dream:—I was at Toulon: were you ever at Toulon, old fellow?" I answered Dufailli, that I knew Toulon, but could not see what relation there could be between his agreeable dream and that city. "I was a galley-slave," he replied, "and had just escaped." Dufailli perceived that this statement made an unpleasant impression on me, which I could not conceal. "Well, what is the matter with you, countryman? I had just escaped, and that's no bad dream, I think, for a prisoner. It was only a dream, to be sure; but that is not all, for I entered amongst the corsairs, and got as much gold as I could carry."

Although I have never been superstitious, I must confess I took Dufailli's dream as a prediction of my future lot; it was perhaps a warning from Heaven to determine the course I should pursue. However, said I to myself, at present I do not deserve Heaven's interposition, and perhaps I only fancy it. I soon made another reflection. It occurred to me, that the old serjeant might have been venting his suspicions of me, and the idea vexed me. I rose; and Dufailli saw that I had an air more serious than usual. "What ails you?" said he, "why, you look as moping as an owl."

"Has anybody sold you peas which you cannot boil?" asked Pauline, taking me by the arm, and swinging me round to disturb my reverie. "Is he in the doldrums?" inquired Therese. "Hold your tongue," replied Dufailli, "and speak when you have leave to do so; in the meantime, sleep, sluts, sleep, and do not move till we return."

He then beckoned me to follow him; and in obeying he conducted me to a little parlor, where we found Captain Paulet and his crew, the majority of whom were drunk with wine, and joy. As soon as we appeared, there was a unanimous shout of "Dufailli! Dufailli!"—"Hail to mine ancient!" said Paulet; and then offering my companion a seat beside him, added, "Anchor here, my old cock, we may well say that Providence is good. M. Boutrois, Boutrois, bring more 'bishops,' as if it rained wine. Come, we will have no sorrow here, from this time henceforward," he added, pressing Dufailli's hand. Paulet then looked attentively at me, and said, "I think I know you, we have met before; you have handled a marlin-spike, my hearty."

I told him that I had been on board the privateer "Barras," but that I did not recollect ever having met him before. "Well, then, we will make acquaintance now. I do not know," he added, "but you look like a jolly dog—a lad for all sorts of weathers, as we say. I say, my boys, has he not the look of a hearty chap? I like the cut of his jib. Sit here, on my right hand; by my fist, what a back and loins! Here are shoulders! You are just the lad for fishing for Englishmen." On finishing these words, he put on my head his red cap. "It does not look amiss on the lad," he added, with a knowing look, but in which there was much kindness.

I saw at once that the captain would not be sorry to number me amongst his crew. Dufailli, who had not yet become speechless, exhorted me most energetically to profit by the opportunity; this was the good advice he had promised me, and I followed it. It was agreed that I should go on a voyage, and that the next day I should go to the owner, M. Choisnard, who would advance me some money.

It must not be doubted but that I was well received by my new comrades; the captain had placed a thousand crowns to their credit at the hotel, and many of them had other resources in the city. I never witnessed such profusion. Nothing was too dear or delicate for the privateers. M. Boutrois, to satisfy them, was compelled to put the whole city and environs in requisition, and even dispatched couriers to nourish their luxurious palates, the duration of which was not limited to a single day. It was on Monday, and my companion was not sobered by the following Sunday; as for me, my stomach and head agreed delightfully, and neither received the slightest check.

Dufailli had forgotten his promise to the ladies, and I reminded him of it; and quitting our party for a moment, I returned to them, presuming that they were growing impatient at our absence. Pauline was alone, her sister had gone to 'earn what was become of their mother; she soon returned, and throwing herself on the bed, she exclaimed with an air of despair, "We are undone forever."

"What is the matter?" I asked.

"We are lost," she answered, with her face bathed in tears. "Two men have been carried to the hospital with broken ribs, a guard has been wounded, and the commandant has ordered the house to be shut up. What will become of us? Where can we find a home!"

"A home," said I, "you shall always find; but where is your mother?" Therese answered that her mother was first led to the guardhouse, and afterward to the city prison, and the report was that she would not very easily get out again.

This information gave me some uneasiness; Mother Thomas would be questioned, and perhaps had already been examined at the police office, or by the commissary-general; and she doubtless had mentioned, or would mention, Dufailli's name; and if he were questioned, I should be so also. It was important to prevent this: I returned with haste to concert with the sergeant the measures necessary to be pursued. Fortunately, he was not so far gone as not to hear reason. I talked only of the danger which threatened him; he understood me, and taking twenty livres from his pocket, "Here," said he, "is wherewithal to stop Mother Thomas's blabbing tongue;" and then calling a waiter to him, he gave him the money, desiring him to carry it forthwith to the prisoner. "He is the jailer's son," said Dufailli, "and has admittance everywhere; and, moreover, is a close and discreet lad."

Our messenger returned quickly, and told us that Mother Thomas, though twice examined, had mentioned no names, and had received the bribe with gratitude; vowing that she was determined, if she died for it, to say nothing that could injure us; and thus I was assured that I had nothing to fear on this head. "And as to the wenches, what must we do with them?" said I to Dufailli. "Oh, we must export them to Dunkirk, and I will pay the expenses," he replied; and we then returned to prepare them for their departure. At first they appeared astonished; but after some arguments, proving that it was the best method they could adopt, and that there was danger in remaining longer at Boulogne, they resolved to leave us. The next day we started them off, and the parting did not cost us much pain.

Mother Thomas recovered her liberty after six months' confinement; Pauline and her sister then returning to the maternal bosom, though torn from their native soil, renewed the courses of their former lives. I know not whether they made a fortune; it is not impossible. But for want of accurate information, I here end their history, and resume my own.

Paulet and his crew had scarcely noticed our absence before we rejoined them; we sang, drank, and ate without stirring, until midnight; thus confounding all repasts in one lengthened meal. Paulet and Fleuriot, his second in command, were the heroes of the feast; physically, as well as morally, they were the perfect antipodes of each other. The former was a stout, short man, strong-backed, square set, with a neck like a bull; wide shoulders, a full face, and his features like that of a lion, his aspect either fierce or gentle; in fight, he was pitiless, elsewhere he was humane and compassionate. At the moment of boarding, he was a perfect demon; in the bosom of his family, and with his wife and children, except a little roughness of manner, he was as mild as a dove; then he was the jolly, simple, bluff, and rough farmer; a perfect patriarch, whom it was impossible to discern in the pirate. Once on shipboard, his manners and language entirely changed, and he became harsh and coarse to excess; his will was as despotic that of an oriental pasha; abrupt and rude, he had an iron arm and will, and woe to him who opposed either. Paulet was a daring and good man, sensible though brutal; no one ever possessed more frankness and loyalty.

Paulet's lieutenant was one of the most singular beings I ever met with: endowed with a most robust constitution, although yet very young, he had tried it with every sort of excess; he was one of those libertines, who by dint of anticipating the pleasures of life's stores, spends his revenue before he gets it, eats his calf in the cow's belly. Headstrong, with vivid passions and a heated imagination, he had early abandoned himself to premature excesses. He had not reached his twentieth year, when the decay of his lungs, together with a universal sinking of his whole frame, had compelled him to quit the artillery, into which he had entered at eighteen years of age, and now this poor fellow had scarcely a breath of life in him; he was frightfully thin; two large eyes, whose blackness made more apparent the melancholy paleness of his complexion, were apparently all that remained of this carcass, in which, however, was a soul of fire. Fleuriot was not ignorant that his days were numbered. The most able physicians had pronounced his sentence of death, and the certainty of his approaching dissolution had suggested to him a strange resolution. This is what he told me upon the subject: "I served," said he, "in the fifth regiment of light artillery, where I was entered as a volunteer. The regiment was quartered at Metz. A gay life and hard work had exhausted me, and I was as dry as parchment. One morning the turnout was sounded, and we set off. I fell sick by the way, and received a hospital order; and a few days afterward, the doctors, seeing that I spit blood abundantly, declared that my lungs were not in a state to be subjected to the exercises of a horse, and consequently I was advised to enter the foot artillery; and scarcely was I well when I did so. I left one berth for another, the small for the large, the six for twelve, the spur for the spatter dash. I had no longer to gallop hard, but I had to turn my body about on the platform; to jump up and down like a goat, to roll gun-carriages about, to dig trenches, to strap up artillery gear, and worse than that, to carry on my back the internal knapsack, that eternal calf's skin which has killed more conscripts than the guns of Marengo. The calf's skin gave me a knock-down blow. I could not resist its attack. I offered myself to the depot, and was admitted. I had only to undergo the inspection of the general. He was that martinet Sarrazin. He came to me. 'I will wager that he is still weak-chested: are you not?' 'Consumption in the second degree,' replied the major. 'Is it so? I thought it. I said so. They are all narrow-shouldered, hollow-chested, thick-visaged. Show your legs. Why there are four campaigns in them yet,' continued the general, striking me on the calf. 'And now what would you? Your dismissal? You shan't have it. Besides,' said he, 'death only comes to him who pauses: go your way.' I wished to speak. 'Be gone,' repeated the general, 'and be silent.'

The inspection concluded; I went and threw myself on my camp-bed, and whilst I reclined on my four-feet-long mattress, reflecting on the harshness of the general, it occurred to me that I might find him more tractable if I were recommended by one of his brother officers. My father had been intimate with General Legrand, who was then at the camp at Ambleteuse, and I thought I might find a protector in him. I saw him, and he welcomed me as the son of an old friend, gave me a letter to Sarrazin, and sent one of his aide-de-camps to attend me. The recommendation was pressing, and I made sure of success. We arrived at the camp, and making for the general's abode, a soldier pointed it out to us, and we found ourselves at the gate of a dilapidated barracks, which bore no marks of being a general's residence; no sentinel, no inscription, no sentry-box. I knocked with my sabre-hilt, and a voice cried, 'Enter,' with the accent and tone of displeasure. A packthread, which I pulled, drew up a wooden latch, and the first object that met our eyes, on penetrating this asylum, was a woolen covering, under which, lying side by side on the straw, were the general and his negro. In this posture he gave us audience. Sarrazin took the letter, and having read it, without changing his position, he said to the aide-de-camp, 'General Legrand takes an interest in this young man. Well, what would he have? that I put him on half-pay? Oh! he cannot think of such a thing.' Then addressing me, 'How much fatter should you be, if I put you on half-pay? Oh, you have a fine prospect at home: if you are rich, to die gradually with over-nursing; if you are poor, to increase the misery of your parents, and finish your days in a hospital. I am a doctor for you: and my prescription is a bullet, and then your cure will follow: if you escape that, the knapsack will do for you, or marching and exercise will put you to rights; these are additional chances. Besides, do as I do, drink tar-water: that is worth all your jalaps, and gruels, and messes.' At the same time he stretched out his arms, he seized a large pitcher, which was near him, and filled a can, which he offered to me, and all refusal was in rain. I was compelled to swallow some of the nauseous stuff, as was also the aide-de-camp; the general drank after us, and his negro, to whom he handed the can, finished what was left.

"There was then no hope of his recalling the decision against which I had appealed, and we withdrew greatly discontented. The aide-de-camp returned to Ambleteuse and I to Fort Chatillon, which I entered more dead than alive. From this moment I became the prey to an apathetic sadness, which absorbed all my faculties: I then obtained an exemption from service: night and day I remained on my couch, indifferent to all around me; and I think I should have remained in that position till now, if one winter's night the English had not determined to burn our flotilla. An inconceivable fatigue, although I did nothing, seizing on my senses, had induced a profound sleep. Suddenly, I was aroused by the report of cannons. I arose, and through the panes of my window, I saw a thousand fires crossing each other in the air. On one side were immense trains of fire like rainbows; on the other side were vast stars, which seemed to grow larger and redder, and my first idea was that I saw fireworks. At length a noise like that of torrents, which precipitate themselves in cascades from the tops of rocks, gave me a sort of shuddering feeling: at intervals darkness usurped the place of the ruddy light, which I can only compare to daylight in hell. The very earth seemed scorched by it. I was already agitated by fever, and I thought my head was swelling larger and larger. The muster-call was beaten. I heard the cry 'To arms!' and on the ground the trampling of horses' feet. Terror seized me, and delirium possessed me. I got my boots, and tried to pull them on; it was impossible; they were too tight, my legs were entangled in them; I tried to pull them off again; I could not. During my exertions each moment increased my fears, all my comrades were dressed; the silence which reigned about me warned me that I was alone, and whilst, from all parts, persons were running together, without thinking of the law, I fled with haste across the country, carrying my clothes under my arms.

"Next day, I reappeared amidst all the people whom I found living. Ashamed of a cowardice at which I was myself astonished, I had trumped up a story, which, if I could ensure belief, would have given me the reputation of a hero. Unfortunately the tale was not swallowed so easily as I could have desired; no one was the dupe of my lies; sarcasms and rude jokes without end, were thrown out, until I almost burst with spite and rage; in any other circumstances I would have fought the whole regiment, but I was in a state of weakness, from which I did not rouse till the following night, when I recovered a little of my wonted energy.

"The English had again commenced the bombardment of the city, and were so close to the shore, that we could even hear their voices, and the balls of the thousand cannons on the coast passed over their heads. Movable batteries were then erected, which, to approach them as closely as possible, floated according to the ebb and flow of the tide. I was ordered to the command of a twelve-pounder, which having stationed at the extremity of the rafts, we

172

anchored. At that very moment a shower of bullets were directed at us: our howitzers were observed under the wagons and amongst the horses. It was evident that in spite of the obscurity of the night, we had become an object of aim to the enemy. We were about to return the compliment, and had altered the level of our gun, when my corporal, almost as much alarmed as I had been the previous evening, desirous of seeing if the trunnions had got loose in shifting the gun, placed his hand on them, and suddenly uttered a piercing shriek which was reechoed all along the bank. His fingers were crushed beneath twenty hundredweight of metal. He attempted to disengage them, but the incumbent mass only pressed the more heavily, and he was still held fast, and when enabled to disengage himself he fainted. A dram of brandy revived him, and I offered to lead him to the camp, which was no doubt set down as a pretext for absenting myself.

"The corporal and I walked away together; but at the moment of entering the artillery warren, which we had to cross, a burning hand-grenade fell between two chests filled with powder. The danger was imminent, and in a few seconds the whole ammunition would have blown up. By running away I could have escaped safely, but a change came over me, and death was no longer fearful. Quicker than lightning I seized on the metal tube whence brimstone and fiery matter were escaping, and attempted to extinguish the flame; but this being impossible, I carried it in my hand, blazing as it was, to a distance; and the instant I threw it on the earth, it burst with a violence that shivered the metal to pieces.

"There was a witness of this deed; my hands, my face, my burnt garments, the sides of the powder-boxes already blackened with fire, all testified my courage. I might have been proud, but I was only satisfied; my companions would henceforward have no right to taunt me with their offensive jokes. We went onward, and scarcely had we advanced a single step, when the whole atmosphere seemed one blaze of fire; the flames appeared in seven places at once, and the brilliant and horrible light seemed at the harbor; the slates cracked, whilst the roofs were burning, and we thought we heard the report of musketry. Some detachments, deceived by this, scoured about to discover the enemy. Nearer to us, at a short distance from the ship-building yard, clouds of smoke and flame rose from a thatch, whence the burning straw was driven in all directions by the wind. We heard a cry of distress—the voice of a child—which struck to my heart; it was perhaps too late, but I determined to attempt its rescue, and succeeded in restoring the infant to its mother, who having left it for an instant, was returning to it in an agony of distress.

"My honor was now redeemed, and cowardice could no longer be charged upon me. I returned to the battery, when every person congratulated me. A chief of a battalion promised me a cross, which he had, however, been unable to procure for himself for forty years, because he had always had the bad luck to get behind, and never in front of the cannon. I was now in a fair way of getting renown, and opportunities presented perpetually. There were mediators appointed between England and France to negotiate for peace. Lord

Lauderdale was in Paris as plenipotentiary, when the telegraph announced the bombardment of Boulogne, which was but the second act to the attack of Copenhagen. At this information, the emperor, indignant at the causeless renewal of hostilities, sent for Lord L., reproached him with the perfidy of his cabinet, and ordered him to quit France instantly. A fortnight afterward, Lord Lauderdale arrived here at the Canon d'Or. He was an Englishman, and the exasperated people were desirous of revenging themselves on him: they surrounded him, mobbed him, and pressed upon him; and in defiance of the protection of two officers who were attending him, they showered stones and mud upon him from all sides. Pale, trembling and faltering, the peer thought he was about to fall a sacrifice, when, sword in hand, I cleared my way through the rabble, crying, 'Destruction to whoever strikes him!' I harangued the multitude, dispersed them, and led the way to the harbor, where, without being subjected to further insult, he embarked on board a flag-of-truce-boat. He soon reached the English squadron, which the next evening renewed the bombardment. The following night we were again on the shore, and at one o'clock the English, after throwing a few Congreve rockets, suspended their firing; and I, worn out with toil, threw myself on a gun-carriage, and slept soundly. I know not how long my sleep lasted, but when I awoke I was up to my neck in water, my blood was frozen, my limbs stiffened, and my sight and memory bewildered. Boulogne had changed its situation, and I took the fire of the flotilla for that of the enemy. It was the commencement of a lengthened malady, during which I obstinately refused to go to the hospital. At length I was convalescent; but as I only recovered slowly, I was again named for the half-pay, and this time was reduced against my own wish, for I had now adopted the opinion of general Sarrazin.

"I had no longer any wish to die in my bed, and applying to myself the sense of the words, 'There is only death for him that pauses,'—that I might not pause, I commenced a career in which, without too painful labors, there is a never ceasing activity requisite. Persuaded that I have but a short time to live, I am determined to employ that time. I have turned privateer, and what risk do I run? I can but be killed, and have but little to lose; in the meanwhile I wanted for nothing, emotions of every sort; perils and pleasures; and now I never pause."

The reader will now judge what sort of men were Captain Paulet and his lieutenant. Scarcely had this latter a breath left in his body, and yet in fight, as everywhere else, he was the leader. Sometimes he was lost in dull thought, whence he roughly aroused himself, his head giving the impetus to his system, and he evinced a turbulence which was restrained by no bounds. There was no extravagance, no wild sally of which he was not capable; and in the reckless state of excitation, all was dared by him. He would have scaled heaven itself. I cannot tell all the pranks he played at the first banquet to which Dufailli had presented me. Sometimes he proposed one scheme, sometimes another; at length he bethought him of the theatre. "What do they play tonight?"

"'Misanthropy and Repentance.'"

"I prefer the 'Two Brothers.' Comrades! which of you is in a sniveling mood? The captain weeps every year at his festival, we fellows know nothing of such joys. They are confined to the fathers of families. Do you ever go to the play, captain? You should go; for there will be all the world there. All the fashionables, shrimp girls in silken gowns; the nobility of the land. Oh God! heaven itself is struck to see the sows in ruffles. Never mind; these radios must have their play, though it would be as well, if they understood French. Oh, do go and see them. I remember some ladies at the last ball, who being asked to dance, answered, 'I'm axed already.'"

"Come, come, will you never hold your gabble?" said Paulet to his lieutenant, whom none of the men had interrupted.

"Captain," he replied, "I have made a motion, and no one has answered me; nobody wants to snivel. Well, goodbye; I will go and blubber alone."

Fleuriot immediately went out, and the captain then commenced his eulogy. "He has," said he, "a burning brain, but for courage he is not equaled by any man under heaven." He then informed us how he was indebted to the daring of Fleuriot for the capture he had just made. The recital was animated and well told in spite of Paulet's manner, who had a strange way of pronunciation, and who informed us that he had knocked out the brains of a dozen Englishmen with a handspike. This evening advanced, and Paulet who had not seen his wife and children, was about to retire, when Fleuriot returned. He was not alone. "Captain," said he, entering, "what think you of this agreeable sailor I have just engaged? I think that red cap was never placed over a prettier countenance."—

"True," replied Paulet, "but is it a cabin boy you have brought us? He has no beard. Parbleu!" he added, raising his voice, "it is a woman!" Then continuing, with more strongly expressed astonishment, "If I am not mistaken, it is the Saint."

"Yes," replied Fleuriot, "it is Eliza, the amiable and better half of the manager of the company which now enchants Boulogne; she has come to congratulate us upon our late good fortune."—

"Madame amongst privateers!" said the captain, casting on the disguised actress a look of contempt but too expressive of his thoughts. "I complimented her taste; she will hear agreeable conversation; the devil must possess her! A woman, too!"—

"Come, come, captain," cried Fleuriot, "privateers are not cannibals, they will not eat her up. What harm is there in it?"—

"None; only the season is propitious for a cruise; my crew are all well, and we were in no want of madame to improve their health." At these words, significantly uttered, Eliza cast her eyes on the ground. "My dear girl, do not blush," said Fleurriot, "the captain is only jesting."—

"Not I, by Neptune; I never jest. I remember the Saint Napoleon, when the whole staff, beginning with Marshal Brune, was in commotion; there was no small battling in that day: madame knows all about it, the how, the when, the why, and the wherefore, and will not wish me to be more explicit."

Eliza, humbled by this language, did not repent however after having accompanied Fleuriot; during her agitation, she attempted to justify her appearance at the Lion d'Argent with that softness of tone, those insinuating manners, that mildness of countenance, which seems so foreign to licentious behavior; she talked of admiration, glory, valor, heroism, etc., that she might make way in Paulet's estimation; she appealed to his gallantry, and called him a "Chevalier Francais." Flattery has more or less influence over every mind, and Paulet's language became more polished; he excused himself as well as possible, obtained Eliza's pardon, and took leave of his comrades, recommending them to amuse themselves, though they was no fear of growing dull. As for me, I could not keep my eyes open, and I went to my bed, where I heard and saw nothing. Next day I arose, recruited and in spirits, and Fleuriot took me to the owner, who, on the strength of my appearance, advanced me a few five-franc pieces.

A week afterward, seven of our comrades were in the hospital. The name of the actress, Saint, had disappeared from the playbill, and we learnt that she had profited by the offer of part of a post-chaise belonging to a colonel, who, tormented by a thirst of gaming, even to the risking the very epaulets of his uniform, had gone off express to Paris.

I waited with anxiety the moment of our embarkation. The five-franc pieces of M. Choisnard were spent, and if they allowed me to live, they scarcely permitted me to cut any figure; besides, on shore I daily ran the risk of some unpleasant rencontre. Boulogne was infested with a great many bad fellows: Mansui, Tribout, Sale, were carrying on their trade in the port, where they despoiled the conscripts, under the orders of another thief named Canivet, who, in the face of the army and its commander, ventured to call himself the Decapitator. I think I still see the legend on his police cap, where were depicted a death's head, swords, and thigh bones crossed. Canivet was the collector, or rather lord-paramount, and had a large number of sub-agents, cabin-boys, and petty fellows, who paid him a tax for the privilege of thieving: he watched them incessantly, and if he suspected them of deceiving him, he generally chastised them with his sword. I thought it likely that in this gang there might be some fugitive from the galleys, and I feared recognition. My apprehensions were the better founded, as I had heard a report that many freed galley slaves had been placed either in the corps of sappers, or that of the military workmen in the fleet.

For some time nothing was talked of but murders, assassinations, robberies; and all those crimes were evidences of the presence of hardened villains, amongst whom, perchance, might be some with whom I had compulsorily associated when at Toulon. It was absolutely necessary to avoid them: for to come again in contact would have given me much trouble, from the difficulty of not compromising myself. Robbers are like women; when we would escape their vices and their society, they conspire to prevent it; all seek to retain the comrade who would fly from evil; and it is a glory for them to keep him in the abject state whence they themselves wish not to be emancipated, nor would allow others to escape. I recalled to mind the comrades who denounced me at Lyons, and the motives that induced them to have me apprehended. As my experience was fresh, I was very naturally inclined to profit by it, and be on my guard; and consequently went into the street as seldom as possible, and passed nearly all my time in the lower town, at Madame Henri's where the privateers boarded, and were accommodated with credit on the strength of their respective prizes. Madame Henri, supposing she had ever been a wife, was now a good-looking widow, and still attractive, though she owned to thirty-six: she had two charming girls, who, without forgetting themselves, yet gave hopes to every jolly lad whom fortune favored. Whoever spent his money in the house was a welcome guest, and he who squandered most was always first in estimation with the mother and daughters as long as his profusion lasted. The hand of these girls had been promised twenty times; twenty times had they been betrothed, and yet their reputation for virtue had never been blown upon. They were free in conversation, but reserved in manners; and although their purity of mind was not unsullied, yet no one could boast of having induced them to commit a *faux pas*. Yet how many naval heroes had been subdued by the power of their charms! How many aspirants, deceived by their unmeaning coquetries, had flattered themselves on a predilection which was to lead them to so much bliss! And then, how could one not be mistaken as to the real sentiments of these chaste Dianas, whose perpetual amiability seemed to give the preference to the person last looked upon?

The hero of today was feasted, fondled; a thousand little attentions were evinced, certain little peculiar privileges permitted,—a kiss, for instance, on the sly; a seducing glance of the eye; economical advice was freely bestowed, whilst seeking to procure something extravagant; they regulated the expenditure of his money, and as funds grew low, which was a matter of course, they learned the fact of approaching penury by the well-timed proffer of a temporary loan; it was rarely refused, and without evincing indifference or disgust, they only expected that necessity and love would send the inamorato to seek new perils. But scarcely was the wind in the sail of the ship of the lover, and he was calculating the happy chances which would ultimately lead to a marriage, and the small loan which he had vowed to return a hundred-fold, when already was his place filled by some other fortunate mortal; so that in Madame Henri's house the lovers were constantly succeeding each other, and her two girls were like two citadels, which, always besieged, and always on the point of surrender in appearance, yet never yielded. When one raised the siege, another attacked the spot; there was illusion for all, and nothing but illusion. Cecile, one of Madame Henri's daughters, had passed her twentieth year; she was a merry one, a great laugher, and would listen without blushing to the broadest joke; and denied only the final surrender of the fort. Hortense, her sister, was much like her, only younger, and her character more natural; she sometimes said strange things; but it seemed as if honey and orange flower water flowed in the veins of these two females, for they were so mild and gentle on all occasions. There was no inflammable material in their hearts, although they showed no repugnance to a pressing proposal, and evinced no astonishment at the familiarity of a sailor; yet be it said, they did not the less deserve the surname bestowed on the shepherdess of Vaucouleurs, as well as on a little town of Picardy.

It was at the fireside of this amiable family that I seated myself for a month, with a constancy that astonished myself, dividing my hours between piquet, cribbage, and mild ale. The inactivity of my life was irksome, but at last it ceased: Paulet was desirous of resuming his cruise, and we set sail; but the nights were not dark enough, and the days had become too long. All our captures were limited to a few poor coal gigs, and a sloop of no value; on board which we found Lord Somebody, who, in the hopes of regaining his appetite, had undertaken a sea voyage, accompanied by his cook. He was sent to spend his money and eat his trout at Verdun.

The dull season was at hand, and we had as yet made no prizes. The captain was as moody and dull as a country whipping-post. Fleuriot was entirely out of patience, swore and raved from morning till night, and from night till morning was in a tempest of rage; all the crew were quite out of sorts (to use a vulgar expression), and I think we were all in a humor which would have led us on to attack a first-rate man-of-war. It was midnight, and we had just left a small bay near Dunkirk, and was steering toward the English coast, when, by the light of the moon, which, bursting forth from the thick clouds, cast her brilliant rays on the waves, at a short distance we saw a sail. It was a brig of war which was plowing the glittering wave. Paulet instantly discerned it. "My lads," he cried, "it is our own; every man lie down on his face, and I will answer for our success." In an instant we boarded her. The English crew fought bravely, and a bloody struggle ensued on the deck. Fleuriot, who according to custom was the first to board, fell amongst the number of the dead. Paulet was wounded, but was avenged: and well avenged his lieutenant also. He struck down all who faced him, and never did I witness such a scene of slaughter. In less than ten minutes we were masters of the ship, and the tricolored flag was hoisted in the place of the red flag. Twelve of our crew had fallen in the action, in which an equal desperation was testified on both.

Amongst those who fell was one Lebel, whose resemblance to me was so striking that it daily caused the most singular mistakes. I called to mind that my "Sosia" had regular credentials, and it occurred to me that I should do wrong to let slip so favorable an opportunity. Lebel had become food for the fishes, and consequently had no further need of a passport which would stand me in the greatest stead.

The idea appeared to me admirable. I only had one cause of fear, which was that Lebel might have left his pocketbook with the owner of the privateer. I was overjoyed at discovering it about his person, and immediately took possession of it without being discovered by any person; and when they threw into the sea the sacks of sand in which the dead bodies were put that they might the more readily sink, I felt myself lightened of a great weight, thinking that at length I had got rid of that Vidocq who had played me so many scurvy tricks.

However, I was not completely assured, for Dufailli, who was our master-at-arms, knew my name. This circumstance annoyed me; and that I might have nothing to dread from him, I determined to let him into my secret by some pretended confidence. My precaution was useless. I called for Dufailli and sought him in every part of the vessel, but found him not; I went on board the *Revanche* and looked for him, called to him, but no answer was given; I went down to the powder room, but no Dufailli. What could have become of him? I went to the spirit-room; near a barrel of gin and some bottles I saw an extended body; it was he. I shook him, turned him on his back—he was breathless— livid— dead.

Such was the end of my protector; a congestion of the brain, a sudden apoplexy, or instantaneous choking caused by intoxication had terminated his career. Since the first creation of marine serjeants, never was there one who got drunk with such consistent regularity and unremitting perseverance. A single trait characterized him, and this prince of drunkards related the circumstance as the most delightful event of his life. It occurred on Twelfth-day. Dufailli had drawn king; and to honor his royalty, his comrades seated him on a handbar-row borne by four gunners. On each side of him were placed bottles of brandy for distribution; and elevated on this temporary palanquin, Dufailli made a halt before every booth in the camp, where he drank and made others drink, amidst overwhelming shouts. These rejoicings were so often repeated, that at last his head became giddy; and his ephemeral majesty, introduced to a public-house, swallowed, without scarcely tasting it, a pound of bacon, which he mis-took for Gruyere cheese. The meat was indigestible; and Dufailli, conducted back to his barrack, threw himself on his bed, when he soon began to experi-ence a most violent convulsion of the stomach, and In vain did he strive to repress the event that followed. This crisis over, he fell asleep, and was only awakened from his lethargic stupor by the growling of a dog and the noise of a cat who were quarreling in his room! O, dignity of human nature, where wert thou? Such were the lessons of temperance which the Spartans gave their chil-dren, by making their slaves drunken, and then pointing out the effect of their excesses to them.

I have delayed an instant, to give the last and finishing touch to my fellow-countryman. He is no more. Peace be to his manes! Returned on board the brig, where Paulet had left me with the captain of the prize and five men of the crew of the *Revanche*, scarcely had we closed the hatchways on our prisoners, than we began coasting our way into Boulogne: but the report of the cannon fired by the English before we had boarded had summoned one of their frig-ates, which bore down upon us, crowding all sail; and was soon so near that several shots passed over us, and we were pursued as far as Calais, when the swell of the sea becoming very great, and a stormy wind blowing on shore, we thought she would sheer off for fear of getting amongst the breakers; but she was no longer under control, and driven toward land had to contend at once with all the violence of the elements. To run aground was her only chance of safety, but that was not attempted. In a moment, the frigate was impelled beneath the crossfires of the Batteries de la Cote de Fer, of the jetty, and of Fort Rouge; and from every quarter there came a shower of bombs, chain-shot and grape. Amidst the horrible noise of a thousand shots, a cry of distress was heard, and the frigate sank without any possibility of succor being afforded.

An hour afterward it was daylight; and in the distance we saw several fragments floating. A man and woman were tied to a mast, and waved a handkerchief, which we saw just as we were doubling Cape Grenet. I thought we could rescue these unfortunate beings, and proposed the attempt to the commander of the prize: and on his refusal to allow us the use of the jolly-boat, in a rage I threatened to break his skull. "Well," said he, with a disdainful smile, and shrugging his shoulders, "Captain Paulet is more humane than you; he has seen them, but does not stir about it, because it is useless. They are there and we are here, and everyone for himself in bad weather; we have suffered quite loss enough, if it were only Fleuriot."

This answer restored me to my natural coolness, and made me understand that we ourselves were in greater danger than I had imagined. In fact, the waves evinced it; over our heads were gulls and divers, mingling their piercing cries with the shrill whistling of the north wind; in the horizon, darkening more and more, were long black and red streaks; the face of heaven was disfigured, and all betokened the impending tempest. Fortunately, Paulet had skillfully calculated time and distance; we failed in reaching Boulogne harbor, but found shelter and anchorage at Portel, not far from thence. On going ashore here, we saw lying on the strand the two unfortunates whom I would have succored; the flow of the tide had cast them lifeless on a foreign shore, on which we gave them burial. They had been lovers, perhaps, and I was touched at their fate; but other cares diminished my regrets. All the population of the village, women, children, and old men, were assembled on the coast. The families of a hundred and fifty fishermen were in despair at seeing their frail barks fired upon by six English ships of the line, whose solid hulks were furrowing the waves. Each spectator, with an anxiety more easily imagined than described, followed with his eyes the bark in which he was most interested, and according as it was sunk or escaped from peril, were cries, tears, lamentations, or transports of rapturous joy evinced. Mothers, daughters, wives and children, tore their hair, rent their clothes, threw themselves on the earth, uttering imprecations and blasphemies. Others, without thinking how much they insulted distress, without thinking of rendering thanks to heaven toward which their suppliant hands had been raised the instant before, danced, sung, and with faces shining through forgotten tears, manifested every symptom of the most overpowering joy. Fervent vows, the patronage of Saint Nicholas, the efficacy of his intercession, all was forgotten. Perhaps, next day, recollection might have returned and a little more compassion been evinced for a suffering neighbor; but during the storm egotism was paramount and, as I was answered, "Everyone for himself."

Chapter XVIII

I RETURNED TO BOULOGNE THE SAME EVENING; where I learnt that, in consequence of an order from the general in command, all the individuals who, in each corps, were marked as black sheep, were to be immediately arrested and sent on board the cruisers. It was a sort of press which was intended to purge the army, and to check its demoralization, which had increased to an alarming extent.

Thus I judged it best to quit the *Revanche* on board which, to repair the losses of the late owner did not fail to send some of the men whom the general had deemed it expedient to get rid of. Since Canivet and his myrmidons were no longer in the camp, I thought there could be no ill result if I again turned soldier. Furnished with Lebel's papers, I entered a company of gunners, then employed in coast service: and as Lebel had formerly been a corporal in this division, I obtained that rank on the first vacancy; that is, a fortnight after my enrolment.

Regular behavior, and a perfect knowledge of my duties, with which I was well acquainted, as an artillery-man of the old school, soon acquired for me the favor of my officers; and a circumstance which might have gone greatly against me still further conciliated them toward me.

I was on guard at the fort of Eure, during the spring tides, and the weather was excessively bad; mountains of water were dashed over the platform with so much violence, that the thirty-six pounders were shaken from the embrasures, and, at the dash of every wave, it seemed as if the whole fort was rent to pieces. Until the Channel should be calmer, it was evident that no ship would dare venture out; and night having come on, I did not station sentinels, but allowed the soldiers to remain in bed until next day. I watched for them, or rather I could not sleep, as I had no need of repose; when, about three in the morning, some words, which I knew to be English, struck on my ear; at the same time a knocking commenced at a door under the steps, leading to the battery.

I thought we were surprised, and immediately roused everybody. I put them under arms, and had already determined on selling my life dearly, when I heard a woman's voice, who supplicated our aid. I soon heard distinctly these words in French: "Open, we have been shipwrecked!" I wavered an instant, and then with due precaution and determination to sacrifice the first who on entering should betray any hostile intent, I opened the door and saw a woman, an infant and five sailors, all more dead than alive. My first care was to have them all placed before a roaring fire, for they were dripping with wet and almost motionless from cold. My men and I lent them shirts and clothing: and as soon as they were a little revived, they told us the accident to which their visit to us was attributable. Having sailed for the Havannah, in a three-masted vessel, and on the point of finishing a prosperous voyage, they had dashed upon the mole of our pier, and only escaped death by throwing themselves on our battery from the maintop. Nineteen of their crew amongst whom was the captain, had perished in the waves.

The sea still blockaded us for several days, without any boat daring to venture out to us. At the end of the time I was rowed on shore with my wrecked sailors, whom I conducted myself to the chief officer of the naval service, who congratulated me, as if I had taken so many prisoners. If it were so brilliant a capture, I could really have said that it had only caused me one single fright. However that may be, in the company it procured for me a very high opinion.

I continued to fulfill my duties with exemplary punctuality, and three months glided away, during which I had nothing but praise. This I determined always to deserve, but an adventurer's career was still to be my lot. A fatality which I was compelled to submit to unresistingly, and often unknowingly, perpetually threw me in contact with persons and things which were most in opposition to the destiny I was attempting to cut out for myself. It was to this singular fatality, that without being enrolled in the secret societies of the army, I was indebted for being initiated into its mysteries.

It was at Boulogne that these societies were first formed. The first of all was that of the Olympians, whose founder was one Crombat of Namur. It was at first only composed of a few young naval officers, but it rapidly increased, and all military men were admitted; principally, however, those of the artillery corps.

Nothing was more common at Boulogne than dueling; and the mania had extended even to the dull and peaceable Netherlanders of the flotilla, under the orders of Admiral Wehrwel. There was not far from the camp on the left, at the foot of a hill, a small wood, which could be passed at no hour without observing on the turf a dozen individuals engaged in what they called an affair of honor. It was here that a celebrated Amazon, the Demoiselle fell under the sword of a quondam lover, the Colonel, who, not recognizing her in her male attire, had accepted from her a challenge to single combat. The Demoiselle whom he had forsaken for another, had wished to perish beneath his hand.

One day I was casting my eyes on this scene of bloody encounter, from the extremity of the camp which peopled the extensive plain, when I saw at some distance from the little wood two men, one of whom was advancing toward the other, who was retreating across the plain. By the white trousers I knew the champions were Hollanders, and I paused a moment to look at them. Soon the assailant retrograded in his turn, and then, mutually alarmed, they both retreated, brandishing their sabers; one, plucking up a little courage, made a thrust at his adversary, and then pursued him to the brink of a ditch which he was unable to leap. Both then throwing down their swords, a pugilistic combat commenced between the heroes, who thus decided their quarrel. I was greatly amused at this comic duel, when I saw near a farm where we sometimes went to eat "codiau" (a kind of white soup made with flour and eggs), two individuals who, stripped to the skin, were already prepared, sword in hand, attended by their seconds, who were respectively a quartermaster of the tenth regiment of dragoons and a forager of artillery. The weapons soon crossed, and the

182

smaller of the two combatants, who was an artillery serjeant, skipped about in a very singular manner, and having traversed in a strange way at least fifty paces, I thought he must be infallibly run through, when in an instant he disappeared, as if the earth had opened and swallowed him up, and a loud burst of laughter succeeded. After the first shoutings of this noisy mirth, the seconds approached, and I observed that they stooped down. Impelled by a feeling of curiosity, I went toward the spot, and arrived just in time to help them in pulling out from a hole dug for the formation of a large hog trough, the poor devil whose sudden disappearance had so greatly astonished me. He was almost lifeless, and covered with mire from head to feet. The air soon brought him back to his senses, but he was afraid to breathe; he dared not open his eyes or mouth, so foul was the liquid in which he had been plunged. In this woeful plight, the first words that saluted his ears were jokes. Feeling disgusted at such unfeeling conduct, I yielded to my just indignation, and darted at his antagonist one of those significant glances which between soldier and soldier need no interpreter. "Enough," said he, "I am ready for you;" and scarcely was I on my guard, when on the arm which held the foil, to which I had opposed mine, I saw a tattooing which I thought was not unknown to me. It was the figure of an anchor, of which the stem was encircled by the folds of a serpent. "I see the tail," I exclaimed, "take care of the head;" and with this word of advice I thrust at my man, and hit him on the right breast. "I am wounded," he then said, "that is, first blood."—"It is," said I, "first blood;" and without another word I began to tear my shirt to stanch the blood that flowed from his wound. I necessarily exposed his breast, where, as I had judged, I saw the head of the serpent, which was delineated as if gnawing the extremity of his bosom.

Observing how earnestly I alternately examined his features, and this mark, my adversary seemed to grow uneasy; but I hastened to assure him, by these words, which I whispered in his ear: "I know you; but fear nothing, I am discreet, —"I know you too," he replied, squeezing my hand, "and I will be also silent." He who thus promised secrecy was a fugitive galley-slave from the Bagne of Toulon. He told me his assumed name, and stated that he was principal quartermaster of the tenth dragoons, where in expense he surpassed all the officers of his regiment.

Whilst this mutual recognition was taking place, the individual whose cause I had espoused as the champion of his wrongs, was endeavoring to wash off in a rivulet the thickest of the filth which covered him, and he soon returned to us; and all were now quiet and well behaved, so that there were no longer any grounds of difference, and the inclination for laughter was turned into an uncommon wish for reconciliation.

The principal quartermaster, whom I had wounded but slightly, proposed that we should ratify articles of peace at the Canon d'Or, where they had always ready excellent stewed eels and ready-plucked poultry. He there gave us a princely breakfast, which was kept up till supper came, for which his adversary paid.

On our separation, the quartermaster made me promise to meet him again, and the sergeant would not be contented unless I accompanied him home.

This serjeant was M. Bertrand, who lodged in the upper town, in the house of a superior officer. As soon as we were alone, he testified his gratitude with all the warmth of which he was capable; for after drinking, a coward who has been rescued from peril may evince some feeling. He made me offers of any kind of service, and as I would accept of none, he said; "You think, perhaps, that I have no influence; I should be but a paltry protector, certainly, comrade, if I had only the power of a subaltern; but that is because I do not wish to be otherwise. I have no ambition, and all the Olympians are like me; they despise the miserable distinction which rank confers." I asked who the Olympians were? "They are," he replied, "men who adore liberty, and seek equality: will you be an Olympian? For if so, say the word, and you shall be admitted instantly."

I thanked M. Bertrand, adding, that I did not see any necessity to enroll myself in a society to which the attention of the police would be drawn sooner or later. "You are right," he replied, and then with earnestness added, "Do not enter, for it will go badly with them." He then gave me details concerning the Olympians; and, as if impelled by the feeling of confidential communication which champagne so peculiarly excites, he told me, under the seal of secrecy, the object of his mission to Boulogne.

After this first interview, I continued to see M. Bertrand, who remained for some time in his office of 'spy,' until the period having arrived when he was sufficiently instructed, he asked and procured a month's leave of absence, being about, as he said, to obtain a considerable estate; but at the expiration of the month, M. Bertrand did not return, and the report spread that he had carried off the sum of 12,000 francs, which had been confided to his care by Colonel Aubry, for whom he was to have brought back an equipage and horses; another sum, destined for purchases on account of the regiment, had also been carried off by the active M. Bertrand. It was known that in Paris he had alighted at the Rue Notre ame des Victoires, at the Hotel de Milan, where he had pushed his credit to the very utmost extent.

All these particulars caused a mystification, of which even the sufferers by it dared not openly to complain. It was only settled that M. Bertrand had disappeared: he was tried and condemned, as a deserter, to five years labor. A short time afterward, an order arrived for the arrest of the principal Olympians, and for the dissolving of their society. But this order could be but partially enforced; as the leaders, aware that government was about to interfere with them, and cast them into the dungeons of Vincennes, or some other state prison, preferred death to a miserable existence, and five suicides took place on the same day. A serjeant-major of the twenty-fifth regiment of the line, and two other serjeants of another regiment, blew out their brains. A captain, who had the previous evening received his commission and a company, cut his throat with a razor. He lodged at the Lion d'Argent: and the innkeeper, astonished that he did not, as usual, come down to breakfast with the other officers,

184

knocked at his door. The captain was stooping over a large basin which he had placed to receive the blood; he put on his cravat hastily, opened the door, and fell dead in the effort of speaking. A naval officer, who commanded a brig laden with powder, set fire to it, which communicated to another brig, which also blew up. The earth shook for several miles round, and all the windows in the lower town were broken; the fronts of several houses on the harbor were shaken down; pieces of wood, broken masts, and fragments of carcasses, were hurled to a distance of eighteen hundred horses. The crews of the two ships perished. One man only was saved, and that most miraculously. He was a common sailor, and at the time of the explosion in the maintop; the mast to which he clung was carried almost to the clouds, and then fell perpendicularly into the basin of the harbor, which was dry, and planted itself to a depth of more than six feet. The sailor was found alive, but had lost both sight and hearing, which he never after recovered.

At Boulogne, these coincidences were the theme of general conversation. The doctors pretended that these simultaneous suicides were the result of a peculiar affection emanating from the atmosphere. They appealed, by way of proof, to an observation made at Vienna, where, the previous summer, a great many young girls, impelled by a sort of frenzy, had thrown themselves into the river on the same day.

Some persons thought they could explain what appeared most extraordinary in this circumstance, by saying, that most commonly one suicide, when very generally talked of, is followed by two or three others. In fact, the public understood the cause the less, inasmuch as the police, which feared to allow anything to appear that could characterize the opposition to the imperial regime, designedly circulated the wildest reports; and precautions were so well taken, that in this instance the name of Olympian was not once pronounced in the camps: but the real origin of these tragic events was in the denunciations of M. Bertrand. Doubtless, he was recompensed, although I know not in what manner; but what appears most probable is, that the minister of police, satisfied with his services, continued to employ him; for, some years afterward, he was in Spain, in the regiment of Isembourg, where, as a lieutenant, he was no less thought of than Montmorenci, Saint-Simon, and other offspring of some of the most illustrious houses of France, who had been placed in this corps.

A short time after the disappearance of M. Bertrand, my company was sent to St. Leonard, a small village, at a league from Boulogne. There our duties consisted in guarding a powder-magazine, in which was kept a large quantity of warlike stores and ammunition. The service was not arduous, but the fort was thought dangerous, as many sentinels had been murdered on duty; and it was thought that the English had a design of blowing up this depot. Some such attempts, which had taken place in various posts, left no doubt on the matter; and we had sufficient reason, therefore, for exercising unremitting vigilance.

One night, when it was my turn to keep guard, we were suddenly roused by the report of a musket, and everyone was instantly on foot. I hastened, according to custom, to relieve the guard, who was a conscript, of whose courage there was some doubt; and, on being questioned, I thought, from his answers, that he had been needlessly alarmed. I then went round the magazine, which was an old church; I had all parts and places examined, but nothing was observable—no trace of any person. Persuaded then, that it was a false alarm, I reprimanded the conscript and threatened him with the black hole. However, on the return of the relief-piquet, I interrogated him afresh; and, from the assured tone with which he asserted that he had seen some one, and by the details he gave, I began to think that his terror was not so causeless as I had imagined, and I consequently went out, and going a second time toward the magazine, of which I found the door ajar, I pushed it open, and on entering, my eyes were struck with the faint glimmering of a light which projected from between two rows of boxes filled with cartridges. I dashed along the passage, and on reaching the extremity, I saw a lighted lamp beneath the lowest cask, the flames of which already had smoked the wood, and a smell of turpentine pervaded the place. There was not a moment to lose, and without hesitation I overturned the lamp, and stamped out all the other appearances of sparks, etc. The profound darkness that ensued, guaranteed to me the certainty that I had prevented the explosion, but I was not at ease until the smell was entirely dissipated, and then I went away. Who was the incendiary? This I knew not; but there arose in my mind strong suspicions of the magazine keeper, and to arrive at the truth I went forthwith to his residence. His wife was then alone, and told me that, kept at Boulogne on business, he would sleep there, and would return on the next morning. I asked for the keys of the magazine, but he had taken them with him; and this removal of the keys confirmed me in the opinion that he was guilty: but, before I made any report, I again visited his house at ten o'clock, to convince myself, and he had not then returned.

An inventory, which was made the same day, proved that the keeper must have the greatest interest in destroying the depot entrusted to his care, as the only mode by which he could conceal the extensive robberies he had committed. Six weeks elapsed before we learnt what had become of him; and then some reapers found his dead body in a wheat-field, with a pistol lying beside him.

As it had been my presence of mind which had prevented the blowing up of the powder-magazine, I was, promoted to the rank of Serjeant; and the General, who desired to see me, promised to recommend me to the consideration of the ministry. As I thought I was now in a fair way to do well, I was very careful to lose, as Lebel, all the bad qualities of Vidocq, and, if the necessary duty of attending to the distribution of rations had not led me to Boulogne occasionally, I should have been a most exemplary fellow; but every time I went to the city, I had to visit the quartermaster-in-chief of dragoons, against whom I had espoused the cause of M. Bertrand: not that he exacted this from me, but I thought it needful to be on good terms with him. Then, however, the whole day was consecrated to Bacchus; and, in spite of myself, I lapsed from my good intentions of reform.

By the help of a supposititious uncle, a man of wealth and influence, whose property, he said, was secured to him, my old colleague of the Bagne, led a very agreeable life; and the credit he obtained, from the reputation of being a person of family, was unlimited. There was not a Boulognese citizen of wealth but cultivated the acquaintance of a personage of such distinction most sedulously. The most ambitious papas desired nothing more ardently than to have him for a son-in-law; and, amongst the young ladies, it was the general wish to catch him: thus he had facilities of dipping into the purses of the one and obtaining the good graces of the other. He had an equipment like a colonel—dogs, horses, and servants, and affected the tone and manners of a nobleman. He possessed, in a supreme degree, the art of throwing powder in people's eyes and making himself appear a man of consequence; so much so, that the officers themselves, who are generally so extremely jealous of the prerogatives belonging to an epaulet, thought it very natural that he should eclipse them. In any place but Boulogne, the adventurer would have been soon detected as a swindler, as he had not received any education; but in a city where the citizens of a recent establishment were as yet genteel in costume only, it was an easy matter to carry on such an imposition.

Fessard was the real name of this quartermaster, who was only known at the Bagne as Hippolyte. He was, I believe, from Low Normandy; and, with an exterior of much frankness, an open countenance, and the haughty air of a young rake, he combined that sly character which slander has attributed to the inhabitants of Domfront: in a word, he was a shrewd man of the world, and gifted with all that was necessary to inspire confidence. A rood of land in his own country would have been to him sufficient to have produced a thousand actions at law, and quite sufficient possession to have enabled him to make his fortune by ruining his neighbor; but Hippolyte really had nothing in the world, and unable to turn pleader, he became a swindler, then a forger, then we shall learn what, and must not anticipate.

Every time I visited the town, Hippolyte paid for dinner; and one day, between dessert and cheese, he said to me, "Do you know I am astonished at you;—to live in the country like an anchorite; to be content with a daily pittance; to have just twenty-two sous per diem. I cannot conceive how a person can endure such a lot; as for me, I would rather die at once. But you have your pickings somewhere, slyly; you are not the lad to live without some such additions." I told him that my pay sufficed for me; and besides, I was fed, clothed, and in want of nothing. "All very fine," he replied; "but yet we have some priggers here: you have no doubt heard of the 'Minions of the moon'—you must be one; and, if you like, I will quarter you;—take the environs of St. Leonard."

I was told that the army "de la Lune" was a band of malefactors, the leaders of whom were, up to this period, concealed from the scrutiny of the police. These brigands, who had organized a system of murder and robbery for a circuit of more than ten leagues, all belonged to various regiments. At night they ranged about the camps, or concealed themselves on the roads, making pretended rounds and patrols, stopping any person who presented the least hope of booty. That they might not be impeded, they provided themselves with uniforms of every denomination. At a time of need they were captains, colonels, generals, and used all the proper words of regimental order and discipline—passwords, countersigns, etc.; with which some trusty friend took care to inform them, from time to time, as they were altered.

From what I knew, the proposal of Hippolyte was well calculated to alarm me; for either he was one of the leaders of this army de la Lune, or he was one of the secret agents employed by the police to effect the breaking up of this army: perhaps he was both. My situation with him was most embarrassing, and the thread of my destiny was again entangled; nor could I, as at Lyons, extricate myself from this business by denouncing him: and then, what would it have availed me to have denounced him, had he been an agent?—This idea made me cautious of the mode in which I should reject his proposition, which I did by saying with firmness, that I was resolved to become an honest man. "Didn't you see," said he, "that I was only joking? and you take up the matter seriously; I only wanted to try you. I am charmed, my comrade, to find in you such a determination. I have formed a similar one," he added, "and am on the highway to it; and the devil shall not again turn me from it." Then, turning the conversation, we left all further mention of the army de la Lune.

Eight days after this interview, during which Hippolyte had made me this proposal, so promptly retracted, my captain, ongoing through the inspection, condemned me to four-and-twenty hours' confinement, for a spot which, he said, was on my uniform. This cursed spot, although I opened my eyes as widely as possible, I was unable to perceive; but be it as it may, I went to the guard-house without a murmur. Four-and-twenty hours soon pass away! The next morning would terminate my sentence:—when, at five o'clock in the morning, I heard the trot of horses, and soon afterward I heard the following dialogue:—

"Who goes there?—France.—What regiment?—The imperial corps of gendarmerie." At the word gendarmerie I felt an involuntary shudder, and suddenly my door opened and someone called "Vidocq."

Never did this name, falling suddenly on the ears of a troop of villains, disconcert them more effectually than it did myself at this moment "Come, follow us," cried out the officer; and to prevent any possibility of escape, he fastened a rope round me. I was instantly conducted to prison, where I had a tolerable bed, on paying for it. I found a numerous and goodly assemblage. "Did I not say so?" cried a soldier of artillery, whom, by his accent, I knew to be a Piedmontese. "We shall have all the camp. Here is another. I will bet my head that he owes his imprisonment to that thief of a quartermaster. Will no one cut that villain's throat?"

"Go, look for him, then, your quartermaster," interrupted a second prisoner, who also seemed to be a newcomer. "Whatever he may have done, he is now at a distance; he has made himself scarce a week since. But, my lads, you must own that he is a crafty chap. In less than three months, forty thousand francs in debt in the city. What a lucky dog! And then how many little boys and girls has he left behind?—I should be sorry to father all his flock. Six young ladies, daughters of our leading burgesses, are in a fair way of becoming mammas! Each thought she had him to herself; but he seems to have cut his heart into small pieces, and shared it amongst them!" –"Oh! yes," said a turnkey, who was preparing my bed, "he has spent like a prodigal, and now must mind what he is about; for, if they catch him, handcuffs are the word. He is marked as a deserter. He will be caught, I think."

"Do not make too sure," I replied; "they will catch him as they caught M. Bertrand."— "Well, suppose he should be taken," resumed the Piedmontese, "would that prevent my being guillotined at Turin? Besides, I repeat it, I will bet my head."— "What does the fool say about his head?" cried a fourth. "We are here in prison, and as it was to be, what consequence through whose means?" This reasoner was right. It would have been useless to lose oneself in a field of conjectures, and we must all have been blind not to have recognized Hippolyte as the author of our arrest. As for me, I could not be deceived, for he was the only person in Boulogne who knew that I had escaped from the Bagne.

Many soldiers of different ranks came against their will to fill up the chamber in which were assembled the principal readers of the army de la Lune. Very seldom in the prison of so small a town, was there seen a more singular assemblage of delinquents; the "provot," that is the elder of our room, named Lelievre, was a poor devil of a soldier, who, condemned to death three years before, had perpetually before him the chance of the termination of the respite, by virtue of which he still existed.

The Emperor, to whose mercy he had been recommended, had pardoned him; but as the pardon had not been registered, and as the indispensable official papers had not been transmitted to the chief judge, Lelievre continued a prisoner; and all that could be done in favor for this unfortunate being, was to suspend the execution until the moment when an opportunity should present itself of again calling the Emperor's attention to his case. In this state, in which his life was uncertain, Lelievre deliberated between the hope of freedom and the fear of death; he laid down to sleep with the one and awoke with the other. Every evening he thought himself sure of his liberty, and every morning he expected to be shot; sometimes gay even to folly, sometimes dull and spiritless, he never enjoyed a moment of equable calm. If he played a game of draughts or matrimony, he paused in the midst of it, threw down the cards, and striking his forehead with his clenched hands, jumped up from his seat, and raving like a madman, he ended by flinging himself on his bed, where, lying on his face, he remained for hours in a state of mental depression. The hospital was Lelievre's house of pleasure; and if he got wearied, he went there for consolation from sister Alexandrine, who had a most tender heart, and sympathized with all the wretched. This compassionate sister was deeply interested in the prisoner, and Lelievre deserved it, for he was not a criminal but a victim; and the sentence against him was the unjust result of a feeling but too common in councils of war, that the innocent should even suffer if there are disorders to repress. The conscience and humanity of judges ought to be silent when necessity calls for exemplary punishment. Lelievre was one of the few of those men who, steeled against vice, can without danger to their morality remain in contact with the most contaminated. He acquitted himself of his duties of steward (prevot) with as much equity as if he had been endued with all the powers of a licensed magistrate; he never let off a newcomer, but explained to him his duties as a prisoner, endeavoring to render as easy as possible the firs, days of his captivity; and rather might be said to do the honors of the prison than to enforce his authority.

Another character also attracted the regard and affection of the prisoners, Christiern, whom we called the Dane. He did not speak French, and only understood by signs; but his intelligence seemed to penetrate our very thoughts; he was melancholy, thoughtful, and gentle; in his features there was a mixture of nobleness, candor, and sadness, which insinuated and touched at the same time. He wore a sailor's dress; but the flowing curls of his long black hair, his snowy white linen, the delicacy of his complexion and manners, the beauty of his hand, all announced a man of exalted condition. Although the smile was often on his lips, yet Christiern appeared a prey to the deepest sorrow; but he kept his grief to himself, and no one knew even the cause of his detention. One day he was summoned whilst he was engaged in tracing on the glass with a flint the drawing of a fleet, which was his sole amusement, except occasionally sketching the portrait of a female, whose resemblance he seemed delighted to be perpetually depicting. We saw him go out; and soon afterward being brought back, scarcely was the door closed upon him, than taking from a leather bag a prayer-book, he was soon engrossed in its perusal. At night he slept as usual until daybreak, when the sound of a drum warned us that a detachment was entering the prison yard, and he then dressed himself hastily, gave his watch and money to Lelievre, who was his bedfellow; and having frequently kissed a small crucifix which he always wore round his deck, he shook hands with all of us. The jailer, who was present, was very deeply affected; and when Christiern left us, said, "They are going to shoot him; all the troops are assembled, and in less than a quarter of an hour all his misfortunes will terminate This sailor whom you all took for a Dane, is a native of Dunkirk; his real name is Vandermot; he served in the corvette *Hirondelle*, and was taken prisoner by the English, and placed in the hold of a prison ship with many others; when, exhausted with breathing infectious air and almost starving, he consented to a proposal of being removed from this living tomb, on condition that he would embark in a vessel belonging to the East India Company. On the return of the ship it was captured by a privateer, and Vandermot was brought here with the rest of the crew. He was to have been sent to Valenciennes, but at the moment of departure, an interpreter interrogated him, and it was found by his answers that he was not conversant with the English language; this gave rise to suspicions, and he declared that he was a subject to the king of Denmark; but as he had no proof of this assertion, it was decided that he should remain here until the whole affair should be cleared up. Some months elapsed, and Vandermot seemed to have been forgotten, when one day a woman and two children came to the jail, and asked for Christiern. 'My husband!' she cried, seeing him. 'My wife! my children!' he exclaimed, embracing them with ardor. 'How imprudent you are!' said I in a whisper to Christiern! 'It is well that only I am with you!' I promised to be secret, but it was useless. In the joy of having news from his wife, to whom he had written, and who thought him dead, had shown his letters to her neighbors, and some of the most officious amongst them had already denounced him—the wretches! it is their deed which this day destroys him. For some old howitzers which the ship mounted, they have treated him as one taken in arms against his country. Are not such laws unjust?

"Yes, yes, the laws are unjust," said a number of fellows who were sitting round a bed, playing at cards, and drinking spirits. "Come, push round the glass," said one, handing it to his neighbor. "Holla!" said a second, who remarked the air of consternation expressed in Lelievre's features, and shook his arm; "do not put yourself in a fright about it! His turn today, ours tomorrow."

This conversation, horribly prolonged, degenerated into unfeeling jokes, until the sound of a drum and fifes, which the echo of the river repeated in various quarters, indicated that the detachments of various corps were marching back to the camp. A death-like silence pervaded the prison for several minutes, and we thought that Christiern had already undergone his sentence; but at the instant when his eyes were covered with the fatal bandage, and on his knees he awaited the execution of his sentence, an aide-de-camp had stopped the fire of the musketry. The prisoner again saw the light of heaven, and was to be restored to his wife and children, whose prayers and supplications to Marshal Brune had been the means of saving his life. Christiern, led back to confinement, was still full of joy, as he had been assured of his speedy freedom. The emperor had been petitioned for his pardon, and the request, made in the name of the marshal himself, was so generously urged, that it was impossible to doubt of success.

The return of Christiern was an event on which we did not fail to congratulate him: we drank to the health of the returned prisoner; and the arrival of six new prisoners, who paid their entrance fees with much liberality, was an additional incentive to rejoicing. These men, whom I had known as a part of Paulet's crew, were sentenced to a few days' confinement, as a punishment for having, in boarding a prize, in defiance of the articles of war, plundered the English captain. As they had not been compelled to refund, they brought their guineas with them, and spent them freely. We were all satisfied: the jailer, who collected even to the very smallest portions of this golden shower, was so pleased with his new guests, that he relaxed his vigilance, although there were in one room three prisoners under sentence of death, Lelievre, Christiern, and the Piedmontese Orsino, a chief of Barbets, who having encountered near Alexandria a detachment of conscripts marching toward France, had got into their ranks, where he had supplied the place and name of a deserter. Orsino, whilst serving under this flag, had conducted himself irreproachably, but had marred all by an indiscretion. A price was set upon his head in his own country, and the sentence was to be put into execution at Turin. Five other prisoners were under the weight of charges of the gravest nature. Four were marines;

two of them Corsicans and two Provencals, charged with the assassination of a woman, from whom they had stolen a golden cross and silver buckles; the fifth had been, as well as they, of the army de la Lune, and to him were attributed very peculiar powers: the soldiers asserted that he could render himself invisible, and metamorphose himself as he pleased; he had, besides, the gift of ubiquity; in fact, he was a sorcerer; and that because he was humpbacked, facetious, severe, a great tale-teller, and, having been a sharper all his days, was clever in many tricks of legerdemain. With such company, most jailers would have used the greatest precaution; but ours considered us as only skillful practitioners, and constantly associated with us. Besides, for ready cash, he provided for all our wants, and had no idea that we could have any wish to leave him; and he was correct to a certain point; for Lelievre and Christiern had not the least wish to escape; Orsino was resigned; the marines did not anticipate a very severe sentence; the sorcerer relied on the insufficiency of evidence; and the privateers, always drinking, felt no sort of melancholy. I alone nourished the idea of getting away; but that I might not be suspected, I affected to be undisturbed; and so well did I conceal my intent, that it seemed that if the prison were my natural element, and all thought that I was as comfortable there as a fish in water. I did not drink but on one occasion— that of Christiern's return amongst us. That night we were all somewhat in liquor, and about two in the morning I felt a burning thirst which seemed to inflame my whole body; and on getting out of bed half awake, I groped about for the pitcher, and on drinking I found a most horrible mistake; I had taken one vessel for another, and was almost poisoned.

By daybreak I had scarcely repressed the violent commotions of my stomach, when one of the turnkeys came to tell us that there was some work to be done: as this afforded an opportunity for getting a little air, which I thought would revive me, I offered myself as substitute for a privateer, whose clothes, I put on; and crossing the courtyard, I saw a subaltern officer of my acquaintance, who came in with his cloak on his arm. He told me that he was sentenced to a month's imprisonment for having created an uproar in the theatre, and had just been entered on the prison book. "In that case," said I, "you can begin your work at once here is the trough." The subaltern was accommodating, and did not require a second hint; and whilst he very readily went to work, I passed boldly by the sentinel, who, fortunately for me, took no notice of me.

Leaving the prison, I made my way into the country, and did not stop till I reached the bridge of Brique, where I paused in a small ravine, whilst I reflected on the best mode of escaping pursuit; and at first resolved on going to Calais, but my unlucky stars suggested my return to Arras. In the evening I went to sleep in a barn in which travelers rested. One of them, who had left Boulogne three hours after me, told me that the whole city was plunged in grief at the execution of Christiern. "It is the only thing they can talk about," said he. "It was expected that the emperor would pardon him, but the telegraph signaled that he was to be shot. He had once narrowly escaped, but today he has suffered. It was piteous to hear him cry, 'Pardon, pardon,' whilst endeavoring to raise himself after the first fire, amidst the howlings of some dogs behind him, whom the shots had struck. It went to the very heart, but yet they finished their work. It was his destiny!"

Although this information caused me great affliction, I could not help thinking that Christiern's death would effect a diversion in favor of my escape; and as he told me nothing which seemed as if I had been missed on the general master-call, I thought myself in security. I reached Bethune without mishap, and went to lodge with an old regimental acquaintance, who received me kindly. But however prudent one may be, there are always some unexpected occurrences; I had preferred the hospitality of a friend to a lodging at an auberge, and I had thereby placed myself in the jaws of danger; for my friend was recently married, and his wife's brother was one of those obstinate brutes, whose hearts, insensible to glory, only desire inglorious peace. As a natural consequence, the abode I had chosen, as well as those of all the young fellow's relations, were frequently visited by gendarmes; and these very agreeable gentlemen invaded the residence of my friend long before daybreak, and, without any respect to my slumbers, demanded to see my papers. For want of a passport I endeavored to enter into certain explanations with them, which was but lost labor. The brigadier, after viewing me attentively, cried out, "I am not mistaken, 'tis he; I have seen him at Arras; 'tis Vidocq!" I was compelled to confess, and in less than a quarter of an hour found myself in the prison of Bethune.

Perhaps, before I proceed, my readers will not be sorry to learn the fate of my companions in captivity, whom I had left at Boulogne; and I can satisfy their curiosity with respect to some of them. We have learnt that Christiern was shot, brave, good fellow as he was! Lelievre, who was equally worthy, lingered on between hope and fear till the year 1811, when the typhus fever terminated his existence. The four sailors, the murderers, were one night liberated, and sent to Prussia, where two of them received the cross of honor under the walls of Dantzic; and the sorcerer was released without any sentence having been passed. In 1814 he called himself Collinet, and was the quartermaster of a Westphalian regiment, of which he hoped to get the chest for his own peculiar profit. This adventurer, not knowing how to dispose of his booty, went on the wings of haste to Burgundy, where, in the neighborhood, he fell in with a troop of Cossacks, who compelled him to surrender, and give an account of himself. This was the last day of his life, for they ran him through with their lances.

My stay at Bethune was brief; for the day after my capture I was forwarded to Douai, whither I was conducted under good escort.

Chapter XIX

I HAD SCARCELY SET MY FOOT IN PRISON, when the attorney-general Rauson, whom my repeated escapes had irritated against me, appeared at the grating, and said, "What, Vidocq has arrived! Have they put him in fetters?"

"What have I done, sir," said I, "that you should wish to be so severe with me? Is it a great crime because I have so frequently escaped? Have I abused the liberty which I hold so precious? When I have been retaken, have I not been found exerting myself to procure honorable modes of livelihood? I am less guilty than unfortunate! Have pity on me; pity my poor mother; or if I am condemned to return to the Bagne, she will die!"

These words pronounced with accents of sincerity, made some impression on M. Rauson, who returned in the evening, and questioned me at length of the mode of my life since I had left Toulon; and as in proof of what I told him I offered indubitable testimony, he began to evince some kindness toward me. "Why do you not draw up," said he, "an application for pardon, or at least for a commutation of the sentence? I will recommend you to the chief justice." I thanked the magistrate for his proffered kindness to me, and the same day a barrister of Douai, M. Thomas, who took a real interest in me, brought for my signature, a petition, which he had been so kind as to draw up for me.

I was in expectation of the answer, when one morning I was sent for to the police office. Imagining that it was the decision of the minister which was to be communicated to me, and impatient to know it, I followed the turnkey with the haste of a man who anticipates agreeable intelligence. I relied on seeing the attorney-general, but my wife appeared, accompanied by two strangers. I endeavored to guess the purport of her visit, when, with the most unembarrassed tone in the world, Madame Vidocq said to me, "I have come to tell you that the sentence of our divorce has been pronounced. I am going to be married again, and therefore I have judged it best to go through this formality. The clerk will give you a copy of the judgment for perusal."

Except obtaining my freedom, nothing could be more agreeable to me than the dissolution of this marriage, as I was forever disembarrassed from a creature whom I loathed. I do not know if I had sufficient command of myself to restrain my joy, but certainly my countenance must have betokened it; and if, as I have cogent reasons to believe, my successor was present, he retired with a conviction that I did not at all envy him the treasure he was about to possess.

My detention at Douai was painfully prolonged. I was in suspense for five whole months, and nothing arrived from Paris. The attorney-general had evinced much interest for me, but misfortune engenders distrust, and I began to fear that he had led me on with a vain hope, that I might form no plans of escape before the departure of the galley slaves; and struck with the idea, I again plotted deeply-laid projects for escape.

The gaoler, named Wettu, viewing me as gained over and peaceable, showed me various little favors; we frequently dined together tête-à-tête in a small room with one window, which looked on to the Scarpe. It struck me, that with the aid of this opening, which was not grated, someday, after dinner, I could easily take French leave and depart; only it was absolutely necessary that I should secure some disguise, which when I had effected my escape, would effectually conceal me from all pursuit. I confided my intentions to some friends, and they provided for me the uniform of an artillery officer, of which I resolved to avail myself at the very first opportunity. One Sunday evening I was at table with the jailer, and the agent Hurtrel; the wine had made them very merry, for I had pushed it about briskly.

"Do you know, my hearty," said Hurtrel to me, "that it would have been no safe business to have put you here seven years ago. A window without bars! By Jove, I would not have trusted you."—

"And further, Hurtrel," I replied, "one should be made of cork to risk a plunge from such a height; the Scarpe is very deep for a person who cannot swim."

"True," said the gaoler; and there the conversation rested, but my determination was taken. Some friends arrived, and the gaoler sat down to play with them, and fixing on the moment when he was most intent on his game, I threw myself into the river.

At the noise of my fall, all the party ran to the window whilst Wettu called loudly to the guard and turnkeys to pursue me. Fortunately, twilight rendered it scarcely possible to discern objects; and my hat, which I had thrown designedly on the bank, seemed to indicate that I had immediately got out of the river, whilst I had continued swimming toward the water-gate, under which I passed with great difficulty, in consequence of being very cold, and my strength beginning to fail. Once out of the city, I gained the bank, my clothes full of water, not weighing less than a hundred weight; but I had made up my mind not to delay, and pushed on at once for Blangy, a village two leagues from Arras. It was four in the morning; and a baker, who was heating his oven, gave me leave to dry my garments, and supplied me with food. As soon as I was dried and refreshed, I started for Duisans, where the widow of an old friend of mine, a captain, resided. A messenger was to bring to me there the uniform which had been provided for me at Douai; and no sooner had I obtained it, than I went to Hersin, where I stayed a few days with a cousin of mine. The advice of my friends, which was very rational, urged me to depart as quickly as possible; and as I learnt that the police, convinced that I was in the vicinity, were beating up every quarter, and were approaching the place of my abode, I determined not to wait for them.

It was evident that Paris only could afford me refuge; but to get to Paris it was indispensable I should pass through Arras, where I should be infallibly recognized. I cogitated on the means of obviating this danger; and prudence suggested to me to get into the wicker calash of my cousin, who had a famous horse, and was the cleverest fellow in the world for his knowledge of the crossroads. He pledged himself, on the reputation of his talent as a guide, to carry me in safety by the ramparts of my native town; and I wanted no more at his hands, trusting to my disguise to effect the rest. I was no longer Vidocq, unless I was examined very closely; and on reaching the bridge I saw, without the least alarm, eight horses belonging to gendarmes, tied to the door of a public-house I confess I would rather have avoided them but it faced me, and it was only by fronting it boldly that I could hope to escape detection. "Come on," said I to my cousin; "here we must make an essay! Get down; be as quick as you can, and call for something." He immediately alighted, and entered the public-house with the air of a man who had no dread of the eye of the brigade. "Ah!" said they, "it is your cousin Vidocq that you are driving?"—"Perhaps it may be," he answered, with a laugh: "go and see." A gendarme did approach the calash, but rather from curiosity than suspicion. At the sight of my uniform, he respectfully touched his hat, and said, "Your servant, captain;" and soon afterward mounted his horse with his comrades. "Good journey," cried my cousin, cracking his whip; "if you lay hold of him, perhaps you will write us word."—"Go your way," said the quartermaster, who commanded the troop, "we know his haunt; Herein is the word; and tomorrow by this time, he will be again between four walls."

We continued our journey very quietly, but yet one thing made me somewhat uneasy; my military dress might expose me to some difficulties which would have an unpleasant result. The war with Prussia had begun, and there were but few officers in the interior, unless they were confined there by some wound. I determined on carrying my arm in a sling as an officer who had been disabled at Jena; and if any questions were asked, I was prepared to give all particulars on this subject, which I had learnt from the bulletins; and to add those which I could pick up by hearing a multitude of accounts, some true and some false, from witnesses either ocular or not. In fact, I was quite *au fait* concerning the battle of Jena, and could speak to all comers with perfect knowledge of the subject; nobody knew more of it than I did. I acquitted myself in admirable style at Beaumont, when the weariness of our horse, which had conveyed us thirty-three leagues in a day and a half, compelled us to halt. I had already began conversing in the inn, when I saw a quartermaster of gendarmes go straight up to an officer of dragoons, and ask for his papers I went up to the quartermaster and asked him the motive of this precaution. "I asked him for his route," he answered, "because when everyone is with the army, a healthy officer would not be left in France."

"You are right, comrade," said I, "duty must be performed;" and at the same time, that he might not take a fancy to ask me a similar question, I asked him to dine with us; and during the meal I so far gained his confidence, that he requested me, on reaching Paris, to use my interest in procuring him a change of quarters. I promised him all he asked, which much pleased him; as I was to use my own influence, which was great, and that of others still more powerful. We are generally prodigal in bestowing that which we have not. However it may be, the flask circulated rapidly; and my guest, in the enthusiasm of having secured an interest which was so desirable to him, began to talk that voluble nonsense which usually precedes drunkenness, when a gendarme brought him a packet of dispatches. He opened them with an unsteady hand, and attempted to read them, but his eyes refused their office, and he begged me to peruse them for him. I opened a letter, and the first words which struck my sight were these: "Brigade of Arras." I hastily read it, and found that it was advice of my traveling toward Beaumont, and adding that I must have taken the diligence of the Silver Lion. In spite of my agitation, I read the letter to him, omitting or adding particulars as I pleased. "Good! very good!" said the sober and vigilant quartermaster; "the conveyance will not pass until tomorrow morning, and I will take due care." He then sat down with the intention of drinking more, but his strength did not equal his courage, and they were obliged to carry him to bed, to the great scandal of all the lookers-on, who repeated with much indignation, "What! the quartermaster! a man of rank, to behave so shamefully!"

As might be conjectured, I did not wait the uprising of the man of rank; and at five o'clock got into the Beaumont diligence, which conveyed me safely to Paris, where my mother, who had remained at Versailles, rejoined me. We dwelt together for some months in the faubourg Saint Denis, where we saw no one, except a jeweler named Jacqueline, whom I was compelled, to a certain extent, to make my confidant, because he had known me at Rouen under the name of Blondel. It was at his house that I met a Madame de B, who holds the first rank in the affections of my life. Madame de B or Annette, for so I call her, was a very pretty woman, whom her husband had abandoned in consequence of his affairs turning out unfortunate. He had fled to Holland, and had not been heard of for a considerable time. Annette was then quite free; she pleased me; I liked her wit, understanding, kindly feeling, and ventured to tell her so; she saw soon, and without much trouble my assiduity and regard; and we found that we could not exist without each other. Annette came to live with me, and as I resumed the trade of a traveling seller of fashionable commodities, she resolved to accompany me in my perambulations. The first journey we undertook together was excessively fortunate. I learnt, however, at the moment I was leaving Melun, from the landlord of the inn at which I had put up, that the commissary of police had testified some regret at not having examined my papers; but what was deferred was not ended, and that at my next visit, he meant to pay me a visit. The information surprised me, for I must consequently have been in some way an object of suspicion. To go on might lead to danger, and I therefore returned to Paris, resolving not to make any other journeys, unless I could render less unfavorable the chances which combined against me.

Having started very early, I reached the faubourg Saint Marceau in good time; and at my entrance, I heard the hawkers bawling out, "that two well-known persons were to be executed today at the Place de Greve." I listened, and fancied I distinguished the name of Herbaux. Herbaux, the author of the forgery which caused all my misfortunes? I listened with more attention, but with an involuntary shudder; and this time the crier, to whom I had approached, repeated the sentence with these additions: "Here is the sentence of the criminal tribunal of the department of the Seine, which condemns to death the said Armand Saint Leger, an old sailor, born at Bayonne, and Cesar Herbaux, a freed galley slave, born in Lille, accused and convicted of murder," etc.

I could doubt no longer; the wretch who had heaped so upon my head was about to suffer on the scaffold. Shall I confess that I felt a sentiment of joy, and yet I trembled? Tormented again, and agitated with a perpetually renewing uneasiness, I would have destroyed all the population of the prison and Hughes, who having been the means of casting me into the abyss of misery, had kept me there by their vile disclosures. It will not excite wonder, when I say that I ran with haste to the palace of justice to assure myself of the truth; it was not mid-day, and I had great trouble in reaching the grating, near which I fixed myself, waiting for the fatal moment.

At last four o'clock struck, and the wicket opened. A man appeared first on the stage, it was Herbaux. His face was covered with a deadly paleness, whilst he affected a firmness which the convulsive workings of his features belied. He pretended to talk to his companion, who was already incapacitated from hearing him. At the signal of departure, Herbaux, with a countenance into which he infused all the audacity he could force, gazed round on the crowd, and his eyes met mine. He started, and the blood rushed to his face. The procession passed on, and I remained as motionless as the bronze railings on which I was leaning; and I should probably have remained longer, if an inspector of the palace had not desired me to come away. Twenty minutes afterward, a car, laden with a red basket, and escorted by a gendarme, was hurried over the Pont-au-Change, going toward the burial ground allotted for felons. Then, with an oppressed feeling at my heart, I went away, and regained my lodgings, full of sorrowful reflections.

I have since learnt, that during his detention at the Bicêtre, Herbaux had expressed his regret at having been instrumental in getting me condemned, when innocent. The crime which had brought this wretch to the scaffold was a murder committed in company with Saint Leger, on a lady of the Place Dauphine. These two villains had obtained access to their victim under pretext of giving her tidings of her son, whom they said they had seen in the army.

Although, in fact, Herbaux's execution could not have any direct influence over my situation, yet it alarmed me, and I was horror-stricken at feeling that I had ever been in contact with such brigands, destined to the executioner's arm; my remembrance revealed me to myself, and I blushed, as it were, in my own face. I sought to lose the recollection, and to lay down an impassable line of demarcation between the past and the present; for I saw but too plainly, that the future was dependent on the past; and I was the more wretched, as a police, who have not always due powers of discernment, would not permit me to forget myself. I saw myself again on the point of being snared like a deer. The persuasion that I was interdicted from becoming an honest man drove me to despair; I was silent, morose and disheartened. Annette perceived it, and sought to console me; she offered to devote herself for me, pressed me with questions, and my secret escaped me; but I never had cause to regret my confidence. The activity, the zeal and presence of mind of this woman, became very useful to me. I was in want of a passport, and she persuaded Jacquelin to lend me his; and to teach me how to make use of it. She gave me the most complete accounts of her family and connections. Thus instructed, I set out on my journey, and traversed the whole of Lower Burgundy. Almost everywhere I was examined as to my passport, which, if they had compared it with my person, would have at one disclosed the fraud: but this was nowhere done, and for more than a year, with trifling exceptions not worth detailing, the name of Jacquelin was propitious to me.

One day that I had unpacked at Auxerre, and was walking peaceably on the quay, I met one Paquay a robber by profession, whom I had seen at the Bicêtre, where he was confined for six years. I would rather have avoided him, but he addressed me abruptly, and from his first salutation, I found that it would not be safe to pretend no acquaintance with him. He was too inquisitive about what I was doing; and as I saw from his conversation that he wished me to join him in his robberies, I thought it best, to get rid of him, to talk of the police of Auxerre, whom I represented as very vigilant, and consequently much to be dreaded. I thought I saw that my information made an impression on him, and I colored the picture still higher, until at length, after having listened with much, but unquiet attention, be suddenly cried, "Devil take it! it appears that there is nothing to be done here: the packet-boat will start in two hours, and if you like, we will be off together."—"Agreed," said I; "if you are for starting I am your man, " I then quitted him, after having promised to rejoin him immediately that I should have made some preparations which were necessary. How pitiable is the condition of a fugitive galley slave, who, if he would not be denounced or implicated in some evil deed, must be himself the denouncer. Returned to the public-house, I then wrote the following letter to the lieutenant of the gendarmerie, whom I knew to be on the hunt for the authors of a robbery lately committed at the coach office:—

Sir,

A person who does not wish to be known, informs you, that one of the authors of the robbery committed at the coach office in your city, will set out by the packet boat to go to Soigny, where his accomplices most probably are. Lest you should fail, and not arrest him in time, it would be the best for two disguised gendarmes to go on board the packet boat, with him, as it is important that he should be taken with prudence, and not allowed to get out of sight, as he is a very active man.

This missive was accompanied by a description so minute that it was impossible to mistake him. The moment of departure arrived, and I went on the quays, taking a circuitous route, and from the window of a public-house where I stationed myself, I perceived Paquay enter the packet boat, and soon afterward the two gendarmes embarked, whom I recognized by a certain air which may be seen, but cannot be described. At intervals they handed a paper to each other which they perused, and then cast their eyes on the man, whose dress, contrary to the usual garb of the robbers, was in a bad condition. The boat moved on, and I saw it depart with the more pleasure, as it carried with it Paquay, his propositions, and even his discoveries, if, as I did not doubt, he had the intention of making any.

The day after this adventure, whilst I was taking an inventory of my merchandise, I heard an extraordinary noise, and, looking from the windows, I saw Thierry and his satellites guarding a chain of galley slaves! At this sight, so terrible and inauspicious for me, I drew back quickly, but in my haste I broke a pane of glass, and suddenly attracted all looks toward me. I wished myself in the bowels of the earth. But this was not all; for, to increase my disquietude, somebody opened my door; it was the landlady of the Pheasant, Madame Gelat. "Here, M. Jacquelin, come and see the chain passing," she cried, "Oh, it is long since I saw such a fine one, there are at least one hundred and fifty, and some of them famous fellows! Do you hear how they are singing?"

I thanked my hostess for her attention, and pretending to be much busied, told her that I would go down in an instant. "Oh, do not hurry yourself," she answered, "there is plenty of time, they are going to sleep here in our stables. And then if you wish to have any conversation with the commandant, they will put him in the chamber next to you."

Lieutenant Thierry my neighbor! At this intelligence I know not what passed in my mind; but I think that if Madame Gelat had observed me she would have seen my countenance grow pale, and my whole frame tremble with an involuntary shudder. Lieutenant Thierry my neighbor! He might recognize me, detest me; a gesture might betray me; and it was therefore expedient to avoid a rencontre if possible. The necessity of completing my inventory was an excuse for my apparent want of curiosity. I passed a frightful night, and it was not until four o'clock in the morning when the departure of the infernal procession was announced to me, that I breathed freely again.

He has never suffered who has not experienced horrors similar to those into which the presence of this troop of banditti and their guards threw me. To be again invested with those fetters which I had broken at the cost of so much endurance and exertion, was an idea which haunted me incessantly. I was not the sole possessor of my own secret, for there were galley slaves everywhere, who, if I sought to flee from them, would infallibly betray me; my repose, my very existence, was menaced on all sides, and at all times. The glance of an eye, the name of a commissary, the appearance of a gendarme, the perusal of a sentence, all aroused and excited my alarm. How often did I curse the perverse fate, which, deceiving my youth, had smiled at the disorderly license of my passions; and that tribunal which, by an unjust sentence, had plunged me into a gulf whence I could not extricate myself, nor cleanse myself of the foul imputations which clung to me; and those institutions which close forever the door of repentance! I was excluded from society, and yet I was anxious to give it proofs of good conduct; I had given them; and I attest my invariably honorable behavior after every escape, my habits of regularity, and my punctilious fidelity in fulfilling all my engagements.

Now some fears arose in my mind concerning Paquay, in whose arrest I had been instrumental; and, on reflection, it seemed that I had acted inconsiderately in this circumstance; I felt a forewarning of some impending evil, and the presentiment was realized. Paquay, when conducted to Paris and then brought back to be confronted at Auxerre, learned that I was still in that city; he had always suspected me of having denounced him, and determined on his revenge. He told the jailer all he knew concerning me, and he reported it to the authorities; but my reputation for probity was so well established in Auxerre, where I remained for three months at a time, that, to avoid an unpleasant business, a magistrate, whose name I will not disclose, sent for me, and gave me notice of what had occurred. There was no occasion for me to avow the truth, my agitation revealed all, and I had only strength to say, " Sir, I seek to be an honest man." Without any reply, he went out and left me alone. I comprehended his generous silence, and in a quarter of an hour I had lost sight of Auxerre; and from my retreat I wrote to Annette, to inform her of this fresh catastrophe. But to remove suspicion, I recommended her to stay for a fortnight at the "Pheasant," and to tell everybody that I was at Rouen, making purchases, and on the expiration of the time she was to rejoin me at Paris, where she arrived at the day appointed. She told me that the day after my departure, disguised gendarmes had called at my warehouse, intending to arrest me, and that not finding me, they had said that they did not mind, for they should discover me at last.

They continued their search; and this deranged all my plans, for, masked under the name of Jacquelin, I saw myself reduced to quit it, and once more renounce the industrious trade which I had created.

No passport, however good, could protect me through the districts which I usually traveled over; and in those where I was unknown, my unusual appearance would most probably excite suspicion. The crisis was horridly critical. What could I do? This was my only thought, when chance introduced me to a tailor of the Cour Saint Martin, who was desirous of selling his business. I treated with him, persuaded that I could nowhere be so safe as in the heart of a capital, where it is easy to lose oneself amid the crowded population. Eight months elapsed, and nothing disturbed the tranquility enjoyed by my mother, Annette, and myself. My trade prospered, and every day augmented it; nor did I confine myself, as my predecessor had done, to the making up of clothes, but traded also in cloths, and was perhaps on the road to fortune, when one morning all my troubles were renewed.

I was in my warehouse, when a messenger came to me, and said I was wanted at a coffee house in the Rue Aumaire, and thinking that it was some matter of business, I immediately went to the place appointed. I was taken into a private room, and there found two fugitives from the Bagne at Brest; one of them was that Blondy who aided my unfortunate escape from Pont-a-Luzen. "We have been here these ten days," said he to me, "and have not a sous.

Yesterday we saw you in a warehouse, that we learnt was your own, which gave us much pleasure; and I said to my friend, 'Let us now cast off all care;' for we know that you are not the man to leave old comrades in difficulty."

The idea of seeing myself in the power of two ruffians, whom I knew capable of the wildest deeds, even of selling me to the police to make profit out of me, although they injured themselves, was overwhelming. I did not fail to express my pleasure at seeing them, adding, that I was not rich, and regretting that it was only in my power to give them fifty francs. They appeared content with this sum; and on leaving me, expressed their intention to depart at once for Chalons-sur-Marne, where they said they had business. I should have been but too fortunate had they at once quitted Paris, but on bidding me adieu, they promised soon to see me again, and I remained tormented with the dread of their return. Would they not consider me as a milch-cow, and make the most of their power over me? Would they not be insatiable? Who could answer that their demands would be limited to my means? I already saw myself the banker of these gentlemen, and many others; for it was to be presumed, that, in conformity with the custom of these thieves, if I satisfied them they would introduce their friends to me, who would also draw upon me, and I should only be on good terms with them till my first refusal, and after that, they would without doubt serve me a villainous trick. With such bloodhounds let loose upon me, it may be imagined that I was but ill at ease! It must be allowed that my situation was an unpleasant one, but it was crowned with a rencontre which made it still worse.

It may or may not be remembered that my wife, after her divorce, had married again, and I thought she was in the department of the Pas-de-Calais, entirely occupied in being happy and making her new husband so, when, in the Rue du Petit-Carreau, I met her, face to face; and it was impossible to pass her, for she at once recognized me. I spoke to her, without alluding to the wrongs she had done me; and as the dilapidation of her dress evinced that she was not in very flourishing circumstances I gave her some money. She perhaps imagined that it was an interested generosity, but it certainly was not. It never occurred to me that the ex-madame Vidocq would denounce me. In truth, in recurring at a later period to our old wrangles, I thought that my heart had only given me prudential suggestions, and then approved of what I had done: it appeared most proper that this female, in her distress, should rely on me for some assistance. Detained in or far from Paris, I was anxious to relieve her misery. This should have been a consideration to determine her to preserve silence; and I at least thought so. We shall see whether or not I was deceived in my expectation.

The support of my ex-wife was an expense to which I reconciled myself; but of this charge I did not as yet know the whole weight. A fortnight had elapsed since our interview; when one morning I was sent for to the Rue de L'Echiquier, and ongoing there, at the bottom of a court, in a ground floor room, very clean, but meanly furnished, I saw again not only my wife, but also her nieces and their father, the terrorist Chevalier, who had just been freed from an imprisonment of six months, for stealing plate. A glance was sufficient to assure me that I had now the whole family on my hands. They were in a state of the most complete destitution; I hated them and cursed them, and yet could do nothing better than extend my hand to them. I drained myself for them, for to have driven them to despair would have brought on my own ruin; and rather than return to the power of the police, I resolved on sacrificing my last sous.

At this period it seemed as if the whole world was leagued against me; I was compelled to draw my purse-strings at every moment, and for whom? Tor creatures who, looking on my liberality as compulsory, were prepared to betray me as soon as I ceased to be a certain source of reliance. When I went home from my wife's, I had still another proof of the wretchedness affixed to the state of a fugitive galley slave. Annette and my mother were in tears. During my absence, two drunken men had asked for me, and on being told that I was from home, they had broken forth in oaths and threats which left me no longer in doubt of the perfidy of their intentions. By the description which Annette gave me of these two individuals, I easily recognized Blondy and his comrade Deluc. I had no trouble in guessing their names; and besides, they had left an address, with a formal injunction to send them forty francs, which was more than enough to disclose to me who they were, as there were not in Paris any other persons who could send such an intimation. I was obedient, very obedient; only in paying my contribution to these two scoundrels, I could not help letting them know how inconsiderately they had behaved. "Consider what a step you have taken," said I to them; "they knew nothing at my house, and you have told all; my wife, who carries on the concern in her name, will perhaps turn me out, and then I must be reduced to the lowest ebb of misery."— "Oh, you can come and rob with us," answered the two rascals.

I endeavored to convince them how much better it was to owe an existence to honest toil, than to be in incessant fear from the police, which sooner or later catches all malefactors in its nets. I added that one crime generally leads to another; that he would risk his neck who ran straight toward the guillotine; and the termination of my discourse was, that they would do well to renounce the dangerous career on which they had entered.

"Not so bad!" cried Blondy, when I had finished my lecture, "not so bad! But can you in the meantime point out to us any apartment that we can ransack? We are, you see, like Harlequin, and have more need of cash than advice," and they left me, laughing deridingly at me. I called them back, to profess my attachment to them, and begged them not to call again at my house. "If that is all," said Deluc, "we will keep from that."— "Oh yes, we'll keep away," added Blondy "since that is unpleasant to your mistress."

But the latter did not stay away long: the very next day at nightfall he presented himself at my warehouse, and asked to speak to me privately. I took him into my own room. "We are alone?" said he to me, looking round at the room in which we were; and when he was assured that he had no witnesses, he drew from his pocket eleven silver forks and two gold watches, which he placed on a stand. "Four hundred francs for this would not be too much—the silver plate and the gold watches. Come, tip us the needful." "Four hundred francs!"

said I, alarmed at so abrupt a total; "I have not so much money."—" Never mind—go and sell the goods." — "But if it should be known?" "That's your affair; I want to be ready; or if you like it better, I'll send you customers from the police office—you know what a word would do. Come, come, the cash, the chink, and no gammon." I understood the scoundrel but too well: I saw myself denounced, dragged from the state into which I had installed myself, and led back to the Bagne. I counted out the four hundred francs.

CHAPTER XX

I WAS A RECEIVER OF STOLEN GOODS! A criminal, in spite of myself! But yet I was one, for I had lent a hand to crime. No hell can be imagined equal to the torment in which I now existed. I was incessantly agitated; remorse and fear assailed me at once day and night; at each moment I was on the rack, I did not sleep, I had no appetite, the cares of business were no longer attendee to, all was hateful to me. All! No, I had Annette and my mother with me. But should I not be forced to abandon them? Sometimes I trembled at the thoughts of my apprehension, and my home was transformed into a filthy dungeon; sometimes it was surrounded by the police, and their pursuit laid open proofs of a misdeed which would draw down on me the vengeance of the laws. Harassed by the family of Chevalier, who devoured my substance; tormented by Blondy, who was never wearied with applying to me for money; dreading all that could occur, that was most horrible and incurable in my situation; ashamed of the tyranny exercised over me by the vilest wretches that disgraced the earth; irritated that I could not burst through the moral chain which irrevocably bound me to the opprobrium of the human race; I was driven to the brink of despair, and, for eight days, pondered in my head the direst purposes.

Blondy, the wretch! Blondy was the especial object of my wrathful indignation; I could have strangled him with all my heart, and yet I still kept on terms with him, still had a welcome for him. Impetuous and violent as I was by nature, it was astonishing how much patient endurance I exercised; but it was all owing to Annette. Oh! How I prayed with fervent sincerity, that, in one of his frequent excursions, some friendly gendarme might drive a bullet through Blondy's brain! I even trusted that it was an event that would soon occur; but every time that a more extended absence began to inspire me with the hope that I was at length freed from this wretch, he again appeared, and brought with him a renewal of all my cares.

One day I saw him come with Deluc and an ex-clerk, named St. Germain, whom I had known at Rouen; where, like many others, he had barely the reputation of an honest man. St. Germain, who had only known me as the merchant Blondel, was much astonished at the meeting; but two words from Blondy explained my whole history—I was a thorough rogue. Confidence then replaced astonishment: and St. Germain, who at first had frowned, joined in the mirth. Blondy told me, that they were going all three to set out for the environs of Senlis, and asked me for the loan of my wicker car, which I made use of when visiting the fairs. Glad to get rid of these fellows on such terms, I hastily wrote a note to the person who had charge of it. He gave them the conveyance and harness, and away they went; whilst for ten days I heard nothing of them, when St. Germain reappeared. He entered my house one morning with an alarmed look, and an appearance of much fatigue. "Well," said he, "my comrades have been seized."— "Seized!" cried I, with a joy which I could not repress, but assuming all my coolness, I asked for the details, with an affectation of being greatly concerned. St. Germain told me, in a few words, that Blondy and Deluc had only been apprehended because they traveled without credentials. I did not believe anything he said, and had no doubt but they had been engaged in some robbery; and what confirmed my suspicions was, that, on proposing to send them some money, St. Germain told me that they were not in want of any. On leaving Paris, they had fifty francs amongst them; and certainly with so small sum, it would have been a difficult matter to have gone on for a fortnight; and yet how was it that they were still not unprovided? The first idea that flashed through my brain, was, that they had committed some extensive robbery, which they wished to conceal from me; but I soon discovered that the business was of a still more serious nature.

Two days after St. Germain's return, I thought I would go and look at my car; and remarked, at first, that they had altered its exterior appearance. On getting inside, I saw on the lining of white and blue striped line, red spots recently washed out; and then opening the seat, to take out the key, I found it filled with blood, as if a carcass had been laid there! All was now apparent, and the truth was exposed, even more horrible than my suspicions had foreboded. I did not hesitate; far more interested than the murderers themselves in getting rid of all traces of the deed, on the next night I took the vehicle to the banks of the Seine, and having got as far as Bercy, in a lone spot, I set fire to some straw and dry wood, with which I had filled it, and did not leave the spot until the whole was burnt to ashes.

St. Germain, to whom I spoke of the circumstances, without adding that I had burnt my carriage, confessed that the dead body of a wagoner, assassinated by Blondy, between Louvres and Dammartin, had been concealed in it, until they found an opportunity of throwing it into a well. This man, one of the most abandoned villains I ever encountered, spoke of the deed as if it were a most harmless action; and a laugh was on his lips while he related the facts with the most unembarrassed and easy tone. I was horrified, and listened with a sort of stupefaction; and when he asked me for the impression of the lock of an apartment with which I was acquainted, I reached the climax of my terrors. I made some observations, to which he replied, "What is that to me?—business must be done. Because you know him! Why that is the stronger reason; you know all the ways of the house; you can guide me, and we will share the produce!—Come, it is no use refusing; I must have the impression." I pretended to yield to his arguments. "Such scruples as these—hold your tongue!" replied St. Germain; "you make me sweat (the expression he used was not quite so proper). But come—all is agreed, and half the plunder is yours." Good God! what an associate! I had no cause to, rejoice at Blondy's mishap; I really got rid of a fever and fell into an ague. Blondy would yield to persuasion on certain terms, but St. Germain never; and he was even more imperious in his demands. Exposed to see myself compromised from one moment to another, I determined to see M. Henry, chief of the division of security in the prefecture of police. I went to him; and having unfolded my situation to him, declared that if he would tolerate my residence at Paris, I would give him exact information of a great many fugitive galley slaves, with whose retreats and plans I was well acquainted.

M. Henry received me with much kindness; but having for a moment reflected on what I had said, answered that he could not enter into any terms with me. "That should not prevent your giving the information," he continued, "and we can then judge how useful it may be; and perhaps..."—"Ah, sir, no perhaps, that would risk my life. You are not ignorant of what those individuals are capable whom you denounce; and if I must be led back to the Bagne after some part of an accusation has stated that I have made communications to the police, I am a dead man."—"Under these circumstances, let us speak no further on the subject;" and he left me, without even asking my name.

I was deeply grieved at the ill success of my proposition. St. Germain was about to return and demand the performance of my promise. What was I to do? Ought I to inform the individual, that we were about to rob him together? If it had been possible to have avoided accompanying St. Germain, it would not have been so dangerous to have given such notice; but I had promised to assist him, and had no pretext for getting off from my promise, and I waited for him as I should have done for a sentence of death. One, two, three weeks passed in these perplexities, and at the end of this time I began to breathe again; and when two months had elapsed, was perfectly at my ease, thinking that he had been apprehended, as well as his two companions. Annette (I shall always remember it) made a nine days' vow, and burnt at least a dozen wax candles in token of joy. "I pray to heaven," she sometimes said, "that they may continue where they are." The torment had been of long duration, but the moments of calm were brief, and they preceded the catastrophe which decided my existence.

The 3rd of May, 1809, at daybreak, I was awakened by several knocks at my warehouse door; and going down to see, was on the point of opening the door, when I heard some voices in conversation in a low tone. "He is a powerful man," said one; "we must be wary!" There was no doubt concerning the motives of this early visit, and I returned hastily to my chamber, told Annette what had passed, and opening the window, whilst she entered into conversation with the officers, I glided out in my shirt, by a door which opened on the staircase, and soon reached the upper story; at the fourth I saw an open door and entered, looked about me, listened, and found I was alone. In a recess in the wall was a bed, hidden by a ragged crimson damask curtain. Pressed by circumstances, and sure that the staircase was guarded, I threw myself beneath the mattress; but scarcely had I lain down when someone entered, whom I recognized to be a young man named Fosse, whose father, a brass-worker, was lying in an adjacent room and a dialogue thus began:—

SCENE THE FIRST

FATHER, MOTHER, AND SON

Son. "What do you think, father? They are looking for the tailor—they want to seize him—all the house is in an uproar. Do you hear the bell? Hark! hark! they are ringing at the watchmaker's."

Mother. "Let them ring—do not you meddle in business that does not concern you;—(to her husband) Come, father, dress; they will soon be here."

Father. (Yawning, and, as I imagined, rubbing his eyes.) "The devil fetch them—what do they want with the tailor?"

Son. "I do not know, father; but there are lots of them— bailiffs and gendarmes, and a commissary is with them."

Father. "Perhaps it is nothing at all."

Mother. "But what can they want with the tailor? What can he have done?"

Father. "What can he have done? Since he sells cloth, he may have made clothes of English goods."

Mother, "He may have employed foreign goods! You make me laugh at you. Do you think he would be apprehended for that?"

Father. "Yes, I think they would apprehend him for that, and the continental blockade."

Son. "Continental blockade! What do you mean by that father? What has that to do with the matter?"

Mother. Oh! yes! Tell us then, what will be the end of this; and let us know the truth of it all."

Father. "The meaning of all this! that perhaps they will make the tailor a head shorter."

Mother. "Good God! poor man! I am sure they will take him away—criminals, like him, are not guilty; and if it only depended on me, I know I would hide them all in my chemise."

Father. "Do you not know the tailor is a large fellow?— he has a famous body of his own."

Mother. "Never mind, I would hide him. I wish he would come here. Do you remember the deserter?"

Father. "Hush, hush! Here they come."

SCENE THE SECOND

ENTER THE COMMISSARY, GENDARMES, AND THEIR ATTENDANTS.

At this moment the commissary and his staff, having traversed the house from top to bottom, reached the fourth story.

Commissary. "Ah! the door is open. I beg pardon for disturbing you, but the interest of society demands it. You have a neighbor, a very bad man, a man who would kill either father or mother."

Wife. "What, Monsieur Vidocq?"

Commissary. "Yes, madam, Vidocq; and I charge you, in case you or your husband have given him shelter, to tell me without delay."

Wife. "Ah, Monsieur le Commissaire, you may look everywhere, if you please. We give shelter to anyone who—"

Commissary. "Ah, you should beware, for the law is very severe in this particular. It is a subject on which there is no joking! You would subject yourselves to very severe punishment; for a man condemned to capital punishment, it would be nothing less than"

Husband (quickly). "We are not afraid of that, Monsieur Commissaire."

Commissary. "I believe you, and rely on you. However, that I may have nothing to reproach myself with, you will permit me to make a slight search, just a simple formality. (Addressing his attendants)—Gentlemen, are the egresses well-guarded?"

After a very minute search of the inner room, the commissary returned to that in which I was. "And in this bed," said he, raising the tattered damask curtains, whilst at my feet I felt one of the corners of the mattress shake, which they let fall carelessly, "there is no Vidocq here. Come, he must have made himself invisible; we must give over the search." It may be imagined that I felt overjoyed at these words, which removed an enormous weight from my mind. At length all the alguazils retired, the brass-worker's wife attending them with much politeness, and I was left alone with the father and son, and a little child, who did not think that I was so near them. I heard them pitying me; but Madame Fosse soon ran up the staircase, four steps at a time, until she was quite out of breath, and I still was the theme of conversation.

SCENE THE THIRD. THE HUSBAND, WIFE, AND SON.

Wife. "Oh, my God! my God! how many people there are in the street. Ah! they say fine things about M. Vidocq! they talk much, and all sorts of things. However, there must be some of it true; never so much smoke without some fire. I knew very well that this Monsieur Vidocq was a proud chap for a master tailor. His arms were crossed much more frequently than his legs."

Husband. "There you go, like all the rest, with your suppositions; you are a slanderous woman now. Besides, it is no business of ours; and suppose that it did concern us, of what do they accuse him, what do they chatter about? I am not curious."

Wife. "What do they chatter about! Why, the very thoughts on it make me tremble, when they say he is a man condemned to death for having killed a man I wish you could hear the little tailor who lives lower down."

Husband. "Oh, he speaks from a professional jealousy."

Wife. "And the porteress at No. 27, who speaks of what she knows well, says, that she has seen him go out every evening with a thick stick, so well disguised that she did not know him."

Husband. "The porteress says that?"

Wife. "And that he went to lay wait for the people in the Champs Élysées."

Husband. "Are you growing foolish?"

Wife. "Ah, is that foolish? The cook-shopman, perhaps is foolish, when he says that they were all robbers who came in, and that he had seen M. Vidocq with some very ill looking fellows."

Husband. "Well! who had ill looks after?"

Wife. "After all, he is, said the commissary to the grocer, a worthless man; and worse than that, for he added, that he was a vile criminal, and justice could not get hold of him."

Husband. "And you talk nonsense; you believe the commissary because he is beating up our quarters; but I will never be persuaded that M. Vidocq is a dishonest man. I think on the other hand that he is a good fellow, a punctual man. Besides, whatever he may be, it is no business of ours; let us meddle with our own affairs, and time wags onward:— we must to work; come quickly, to work, to work."

The sitting was adjourned; father, mother, son, and little daughter, all the Fosse family, went away, and I remained locked up, reflecting on the perfidious insinuations of the police, who, to deprive me of the aid of my neighbors, represented me as an infamous villain. I have often seen, subsequently, this species of tactics employed, the success of which is always founded on atrocious calumnies and measures revolting because unjust; clumsy, because they produce an effect entirely contrary to that which is expected; for those persons who would exert themselves personally in the apprehension of a thief, are prevented from fear of struggling with a man, whom the feeling of crime and the prospect of a scaffold drive probably to despair.

I had been shut up for two hours; there was no noise either in the house or in the street, and the groups had dispersed; I was beginning to take courage, when I heard a key thrust into the lock, and whilst I again squatted beneath the coverlid, the father, mother, son and daughter, Fosse entered.

The father and son were quarreling, and by the interference of the mother I had no doubt but blows would arise, when, throwing aside the tattered curtains, I made my appearance in the midst of the astonished family. It may be imagined how much the good folks were surprised. Whilst they were looking at me without saying a word, I told them as briefly as possible how I had got among them; how I had concealed myself under the mattress, etc. The husband and wife were astonished that I had not been stifled in my place of concealment; they pitied me, and with a cordiality not uncommon amongst people of their class, offered me refreshments, which were necessary after so painful a morning.

It may be supposed that I was on thorns during the progress of the whole affair; I perspired copiously; at any other moment I should have been amused;

but when I reflected on the inevitable results of a discovery, none less than myself could appreciate the burlesque of my situation.

After the reception afforded me by the Fosse family, it was probable that I should have no reason to repent of having waited patiently for results. However, I was not yet fully assured; this family was not well off, and it might happen that the first impression of kindness and compassion, which the most perverse persons sometimes evince, would give place to the hope of obtaining some reward by surrendering me to the police; and then supposing my hosts to be what is called "stanch," yet an indiscreet expression might betray me. Without being endowed with much penetration, Fosse guessed the secret of my uneasiness, which he succeeded in dissipating by protestations too sincere to be doubted.

He undertook to watch over my safety, and began by disclaiming any return for his kindness, and then informed me that the police agents had fixed themselves in the house and the adjoining streets, and intended to pay a second visit to all the lodgers of the house. On these statements, I judged that it was imperative on me to get away, for they would doubtlessly this time ransack all the apartments.

The Fosse family, like many other of the working people of Paris, used to sup at a wine shop in the vicinity, where they carried their provisions, and it was agreed that I should seize on that moment to go out with them. Until night, I had time to form my plans, and was first occupied with thinking how I should obtain intelligence of Annette, when Fosse undertook this for me. It would have been the height of imprudence to have communicated directly with her, and he thus contrived it. He went into the Rue de Grammont, where he bought a pie into which he introduced the note that follows:—

"I am in safety. Be careful of yourself, and trust no one. Do not attend to promises from persons who have neither the intention nor the power of serving you. Confine yourself to these four words: 'I do not know.' Play the fool, which will be the best proof of your sense. I cannot meet you; but when you go out, always go through the Rue St. Martin and the Boulevards. Mind, do not return; I will answer for all."

The pie, entrusted to a messenger of the Place Vendome and addressed to Madame Vidocq, fell, as I had foreseen, into the hands of the agents, who allowed it to be delivered, after having read the dispatch; and thus I attained two ends at once, that of deceiving them, by persuading them that I was not in that quarter, and that of assuring Annette that I was out of danger. My expedient succeeded, and I was more calm in making preparations for my retreat. Some money, which I had snatched from my night-table, served to procure me pantaloons, stockings and shoes, a frock, and a blue cotton cap, intended to complete my disguise. When supper-hour came, I left the room with all the family, carrying on my head, as a precaution, a large dish of mutton, the appetizing fumes of which sufficiently explained the intent of our excursion. My heart did not beat less anxiously when I met, face to face, on the second floor, a police officer, whom I did not at first perceive, as he was ensconced in a corner. "Put out your candle," cried he abruptly to Fosse. "Why?" replied he, who had only taken a light that it might not awaken suspicion. "Go along and ask no questions," said the fellow, blowing out the candle himself. I could have hugged him! In the passage we met several of his comrades, who, more polite than he, made way for us to pass. At length we got out, and the moment we turned the angle of the street, Fosse took the dish from me, and we parted. That I might not attract attention, I walked very slowly to the Rue des Fontaines; but when once there, I did not amuse myself, as the Germans say, in counting my buttons, but directed my steps toward the Boulevard of the Temple, and running rapidly, reached the Rue de Bondy, without thinking of asking where I was.

However, it was not enough to have escaped a first pursuit, for doubtless other searches more active would be instituted. It was necessary to mislead the police, whose numerous bloodhounds, according to custom, would leave all other business, and occupy themselves solely in hunting for me. At this juncture, I resolved to make use of those persons for my safety whom I considered as my denouncers. These were the Chevaliers, whom I had seen on the previous evening, and who in conversation had dropped some of those words which make no impression at the time, but which we reflect upon afterward. Convinced that I had no terms to keep henceforward with these wretched beings, I determined to avenge myself on them, whilst I compelled them to refund all that I could enforce from them. It was on a tacit understanding that I had obliged them; and they had violated the faith of treaties, even against their own interest; they had done wrong; and I intended to punish them for having mistaken their own interest.

The road is not far from the Boulevards to the Rue de l'Echiquier, and I fell like a bombshell on Chevalier's domicile, whose surprise at seeing me at liberty confirmed my suspicions. He pretended at first an excuse for going out; but, double locking the door, and putting the key in my pocket, I seized on a knife lying on the tables and told my brother-in-law that if he uttered a cry it was all over with him and his family. This threat could not fail to produce the due effect: I was with people who knew me, and who feared the violence of my despair. The women were more dead than alive, and Chemlier, petrified and motionless as the stone vessel on which he leant, asked me, with a faint voice, what I wanted from him? "You shall know," answered I.

I began by asking for a complete suit of clothes, with which I had provided him the month previously, and he gave it to me: I made him also give me a shirt, boots, and a hat; all of which having been purchased with my means, my demand was only for restitution. Chevalier did all this with a stern look, and I thought I read in his eyes the meditation of some project; it might be that he intended to let his neighbors know by some means the embarrassment into which my presence threw him, and prudence demanded that I should insure a retreat in case of a nocturnal visit. A window looking on the garden, was closed by two iron bars: I ordered Chevalier to take one of them out; and as, in spite of my directions, he was exceedingly awkward about it, I took the work in hand myself, without his perceiving that I had laid down the knife which had inspired him with so much fear. The operation ended, I again took up the weapon: "And now," said I to him and the terrified women, "you may go to bed." As for me, I was hardly inclined to sleep, and threw myself into a chair, where I passed a very agitated night. All the vicissitudes of my life passed in review before me, and I did not doubt that a curse hung over me: in vain did I fly from crime, crime came to seek me; and this fatality, against which I struggled with all the energy of my character, seemed to delight in overturning my plans of conduct, in incessantly placing me in contact with infamy and imperious necessity.

At break of day, I roused Chevalier, and asked him what money he had, and on his replying that he had only a few pieces of money, I desired him to take four silver knives and forks, which I had given him, to take his permit of residence, and to follow me. I had no need of him, but it would have been dangerous to leave him at home; for he might have informed the police, and directed them on my route, before I had concerted my plans. Chevalier obeyed, and I was not very fearful of the women, as I took so precious a hostage with me; and as, besides, they did not precisely partake of his feelings. I contented myself on going out by double-locking the door, and we reached the Champs Elysees by the most deserted streets of the capital, even in daytime. It was four o'clock in the morning, and we met nobody. I carried the knives and forks, which I took good care not to trust to my companion, as I wanted to get off without inconvenience in case he should turn upon me or create a disturbance. Fortunately he was very quiet, for I had the terrible knife, and Chevalier, who never reasoned, felt persuaded that at the least motion he should make, I would stab him to the heart; and this salutary dread, which he felt the more deeply as it was not undeserved, kept him in check.

We walked for some time in the environs, and Chevalier, who did not fore-see how this was to end, walked mechanically beside me, like one bewildered and idiotic. At eight o'clock, I made him get into a coach, and conducted him to the passage of the wood of Boulogne, where he pledged in my presence, and under his own name, the four knives and forks, on which they lent him a hundred francs. I took the sum, and, satisfied with having so conveniently recovered in a lump what he had extorted from me in detail, I got into the coach with him once more, which I stopped at the Place de la Concorde. There I alighted, after having given him this piece of advice, "Mind and be more circumspect than ever; if I am arrested, whoever is the cause, look to yourself." I desired the coachman to drive on to Rue de l'Echiquier, No. 23; and to be sure that he took no other direction, I remained for a short time on the watch; and then, jumping into a cabriolet, I went to the clothes man of the Croix Rouge, who gave me the clothes of a workman in exchange for my own. In this new costume, I walked toward the Esplanade des Invalides, to learn if it were possible to pur-chase a uniform of this establishment. A wooden-legged man, whom I questioned, directed me to Rue St. Dominique, where, at a broker's, I should find a complete outfit. This broker was, it appeared, a chattering fellow. "I am not inquisitive," said he—(that is the preamble to all impertinent inquiries)—

"You have all your limbs; I presume the uniform is not for yourself." "It is," said I; and as he testified astonishment, I added that I was going to act in a play.

"And in what piece?" "In L'Amour Filial."

The bargain concluded, I immediately set out for Passy, where, at the house of a friend, I hastened to effect my metamorphose. In less than five minutes I was converted into the most maimed of invalids; my arm laid over the hollow of the breast, and kept close to my body by a girth and the waist-band of my breeches, had entirely disappeared; some ribbons introduced into the upper part of one of the sleeves, the end of which was hung to a button in front, joined a stump admirably deceptive, and which made the disguise most efficient; a dye which I used to stain my hair and whiskers black, perfected my disguise, under which I was so sure of misleading the physiognomical knowledge of the observers in the quartier St. Martin, that I ventured there that evening. I learned that the police not only still kept possession of my abode, but were making an inventory of the goods and furniture. By the number of officers whom I saw going and coming, it was easy to perceive that the search was prosecuted with a renewal of activity very extraordinary at this period, when the vigilant administration was not too zealous, unless it were in cases of political arrests. Alarmed at such an appearance of investigation, anyone but myself would have judged it prudent to leave Paris without delay, at least for a time. It would have been best perhaps to allow the storm to blow over; but I could not resolve on forsaking Annette in the midst of her troubles, caused by her attachment to me.

At this time she must have suffered much; shut up in the depot of the prefecture, she was placed in solitary confinement for twenty-five days, whence she was only taken to be threatened with being left to rot in St. Lazarre, if she would not confess the place of my retreat. But with a dagger at her breast, Annette would not have betrayed me. It may be judged how deeply I was grieved to learn her wretched situation, and yet be unable to deliver her. As soon as it depended on me, I hastened to aid her. A friend to whom I had lent a few hundred francs, having returned them to me, I begged him to retain a portion of the sum; and full of hope that the term of her detention would soon expire, since after all, they had only to reproach her with having lived with a fugitive galley slave, I prepared to quit Paris, determining, if she was not set at liberty before my departure, that I would let her know, by some means, where I had betaken myself. I lodged in the Rue Tiquetonne, at the house of a currier, named Boudin, who undertook for a compensation, to get for himself a passport which he would give to me. We were exactly alike; he, like me, was fair, with blue eyes, colored complexion, and by a singular chance, had on his upper lip a slight cicatrix. He was however shorter than I was, and to increase his height so as to reach mine, he put two or three packs of cards in his shoes. Boudin had recourse to this expedient; so that, although I could use the strange faculty I had of reducing my height four or five inches, at pleasure, the passport which he procured did not need that I should have recourse to this curtailment of my fair proportions. Provided with this, I was congratulating myself on a resemblance which insured my liberty, when Boudin (after I had been at his house eight days) confided to me a secret which made me tremble. He was a forger of false money, and, to give me a sample of his skill, coined in my presence eight five-franc pieces, which his wife passed the same day. It may be believed that the confidence of Boudin alarmed me.

At first I argued that actually from one moment to another, his passport would become but a bad recommendation in the eyes of the gendarmes; for from the trade he carried on, Boudin must, sooner or later, be the object of an arrest; besides, the money I had given him was but a rash adventure, and it must be confessed that I had but a small chance of advantage in personating such a character. This was not all; considering that this state of suspicion, which in the opinion of the judge and of the public is always inseparable from the condition of a fugitive galley slave, was it not likely that if Boudin were appre-hended as a corner, I should be considered as his accomplice? Justice has committed many errors! Condemned once, though innocent, who would an-swer that I should not a second time be similarly sentenced? The crime which had been wrongfully imputed to me, inasmuch as it pronounced me a forger, was nominally the same species of crime as that which Boudin had committed. I saw myself sinking beneath a weight of presumptive evidence and appear-ances, such as, perhaps, my counsel, ashamed of undertaking my defense, would conceive necessary to impel him to throw me on the pity of my judges. I heard my death sentence pronounced. My fears redoubled when I learnt that Boudin had an associate, a doctor, named Terrier, who frequently came to his house. This man had a most hanging look, but it seemed to me that, on only looking at him, all the police officers in the world would have suspected and watched him. Without knowing him, I should have thought that in following him it would be impossible not to attain the knowledge of some perpetrated or intended crime. In a word, he was a bird of ill-omen to everyplace he en-tered: and persuaded that his visits would bring mischief to the house, I persuaded Boudin to give up a business so hazardous as that he followed; but the most cogent reasons prevailed not with him; all I could obtain by dint of entreaty was, that to avoid giving rise to the search which would certainly be-tray me to the police, he would suspend the making and the passing of money as long as I should remain with him; but this promise did not prevent my dis-covering him two days afterward hard at work. This time I thought it best to address his fellow laborer, to whom I represented, in the most glaring colors, the danger which he ran. "I see," answered the doctor, "that you are one of those cowardly fellows of whom there are so great a number. Suppose we are de-tected, what then? There are many others who make their exit at the Place de Greve, and we are not there yet; for fifteen years I have used these 'chambers gentlemen' as my bankers, and nobody has yet doubted me; it will do yet. And besides, my friend," he added, in an ill-humored tone, "do you meddle with your own affairs."

After the turn which this discussion took, I saw that it would be superfluous to continue it, and that I should do wisely to be on my guard, feeling still more the necessity of quitting Paris as speedily as possible. It was Tuesday, and I purposed starting on the following day; but having learnt that Annette would be set at liberty at the end of the week, I proposed deferring my departure until her release, when on Friday, about three o'clock in the morning, I heard a light knock at the street door. The nature of the rap, the hour, and circumstance, all combined to make me think that they were coming to take me; and saying nothing to Boudin, I went out on the staircase, and getting to the top, I got hold of the gutter, and climbing on the roof, hastened to conceal myself behind a stack of chimneys.

My presentiments had not deceived me, and in an instant the house was filled with police agents, who searched everywhere. Surprised at not finding me, and doubtless informed by my clothes, left near my bed, that I had escaped in my shirt, which would not allow me to go far, they imagined that I could not have escaped by the usual way. For want of cavaliers to send in pursuit of me, they sent for some bricklayers, who went all over the roof, where I was found and seized, without the nature of the place allowing me to offer any resistance, which could only have been done at the risk of a most perilous leap. Except a few cuffs, which the agents bestowed on me, my arrest offered nothing remarkable. Conducted to the prefecture, I was interrogated by M. Henry, who remembering perfectly the offer I had made him some months previously, promised to do all in his power to ease my situation; but still I was taken to the Force, and thence to Bicetre, to await the departure of the next chain of galley slaves.

Chapter XXI

I BEGAN TO GROW WEARY OF ESCAPES and the sort of liberty they procured for me; I did not wish to return to the Bagne; but I preferred a residence at Toulon to that in Paris, if I were compelled to submit to such creatures as Chevalier, Blondy and company. I was in this mood in the midst of a considerable number of these supporters of the galleys, whom I had had but too many opportunities of knowing, when several of them proposed that I should help them in trying for a run through the court of the Bons Pauvres.

At any other time the project would have made me smile. I did not decline it; but I studied it like a man who considered localities, and so as to preserve for myself that preponderance which my real successes procured for me, and those which were attributed to me—I might say those which I attributed to myself; for as soon as we live amongst rogues, there is always an advantage in passing for the most wicked and the most clever; and such was my well-established reputation, wherever there were four prisoners at least three had heard of me;—not at all an extraordinary thing, for there were galley slaves who assumed my name.

I was the general to whom all the deeds of his soldiers is attributed; they did not cite the places I had taken by assault, but there was no jailer whose vigilance I could not escape, no irons that I could not break through, no wall that I could not penetrate. I was less famed for courage and skill, and it was the general opinion that I was capable of any deed of renown in case of need. At Brest, at Toulon, at Rochefort, in fact everywhere, I was considered amongst robbers as the most cunning and most bold. The most villainous sought my friendship, because they thought there was still something to be learnt from me, and the greatest novices collected my very words as instructions from which they could gather profit.

At Bicêtre, I had a complete court, and they pressed around me, surrounded me, and made tenders of services and kind offers, and expressed regards of which it would be difficult to form an idea. But now, this prison glory was hateful to me: the more I read the souls of malefactors, the more they laid themselves open to me, the more I pitied society for having nourished in its bosom such offspring. I no longer felt that sentiment of the community of misfortune which had formerly inspired my breast; cruel experience and a riper age had convinced me of the necessity of withdrawing myself from these brigands, whose society I loathed, and whose language was an abomination to me. Decided, at any event, to take part against them for the interest of honest men, I wrote to M. Henry to offer my services afresh, without any other condition than that of not being taken back to the Bagne, resigning myself to finish the duration of my sentence in any prison that might be selected.

My letter pointed out so fully the information I could supply, that M. Henry was struck with it: only one consideration balanced with him; it was the example of many accused or condemned persons, who, having engaged to guide the police in its searches, had only given but trifling information or had even finished themselves by being detected in criminal deeds. To this powerful argument, I opposed the cause of my condemnation, the regularity of my conduct after my escapes, the constancy of my endeavors to procure an honorable existence, and finally I produced my correspondence, my books, my punctuality and credit, and I called for the testimony of all persons with whom I had transacted business, and particularly of my creditors, who had all the greatest confidence in me.

These facts and documents militated strongly in my favor. M. Henry submitted my proposal to the prefect of the police M. Pasquier, who decided on granting it. After a residence of two months at Bicêtre, I was removed to the Force; and, to avoid suspicion, it was stated amongst the prisoners, that I was kept back in consequence of being implicated in a very bad affair, which was to be inquired into. This precaution joined to my renown, put me entirely in good odor. Not a prisoner dared to breathe a doubt of the gravity of the charge against me. Since I had shown so much boldness and perseverance to escape from a sentence of eight years in irons, I must of necessity have a conscience charged with some great crime, capable, if I should be discovered as the author, of sending me to the scaffold. It was then whispered and at last stated openly at La Force, in speaking of me, "He is a cutthroat!" And as, in the place where I was confined, an assassin inspires great confidence, I took care not to refute an error so useful to my plans. I was then far from seeing that an imposture, which I allowed freely to be charged upon me, would be thence perpetuated; and that one day, in publishing my memoirs, it would be necessary to state that I had never committed murder.

The engagement I had entered into was not so easily fulfilled as may be supposed. A multitude of robbers were then preying on the capital, and it was impossible to furnish the slightest indication of the principal of them; it was only on my ancient renown that I could rely for obtaining any information of the staff of these Bedouins of our civilization; it availed me, I will not say beyond, but equal to what I could desire.

At this period there was in Paris a band of fugitive galley slaves, who daily perpetrated robberies, without any hope being entertained of putting a termination to their plundering. Many of them had been apprehended, and acquitted for want of evidence; obstinately entrenched in absence of witnesses, they had long braved the attempts of justice, which could neither oppose to them the testimony of the commission of crime, nor proofs of guilt. To surprise them properly, it would have been necessary to know their domicile; and they were so well concealed that discovery seemed impossible. Amongst them was one named France (called Tormel), who on coming to La Force, had nothing more urgent than to ask me for ten francs to pay his footing, and I was not inclined to refuse his demand. He soon came to join me, and feeling obliged to me, did not hesitate to give me his confidence. At the time of his arrest he had concealed two notes of a thousand francs from the police, which he gave me, begging me to advance him money, from time to time, as he needed it. "You do not know me," said he, "but these bills speak for me; I trust them to you because I know they are better in your hands than in mine: some time or other we will change them, which now would be difficult, and we must wait." I agreed with France as he wished; I promised to be his banker, as I risked nothing.

Apprehended for violent burglary at an umbrella shop in the passage Feydeau, France had been often interrogated, and constantly declared that he had no residence. However, the police had learnt that he had an abode; and it was the more interesting to learn it, as it would lead to the discovery of instruments of robbery, as well as a great quantity of stolen goods. It was a detection of the highest importance, since it would adduce most material proofs. M. Henry told me that he relied on me for obtaining this information; I maneuvered accordingly, and soon learnt that at the time of his arrest, France was at the corner of the Rue Montmartre and the Rue Notre Dame des Victoires, in an apartment let by a female receiver of stolen goods, named Josephine Bertrand.

These proofs were positive, but it was difficult to make use of the information without betraying my share in the business to France, who, having only confessed to me, could only suspect me of betraying him. I, however, succeeded; and so little did he suspect that I had abused his confidence, that he told me all his troubles, in proportion as the plan which I had concerted with M. Henry progressed. Besides, the police were so arranged, that they seemed only to be guided by chance, and thus were the arrangements made.

They gained over to their interest one of the lodgers of the house which France had inhabited; and this lodger told the landlord, that, for about three weeks, no movement was seen in the apartment of Madame Bertrand J and this awakened and afforded a wide field for conjecture. It was remembered that a person went frequently in and out of this apartment; his absence was talked of, and it was a matter of astonishment that he was not seen: the word disappearance was mentioned, and thence the necessity of the intervention of the commissary; then the opening of the door in presence of witnesses; then the discovery of a great quantity of stolen property belonging to the neighborhood, and many of the instruments made use of to consummate these robberies. The next inquiry was, what had become of Josephine Bertrand? and all the persons were visited to whom she had referred when she hired the apartments, but nothing could be learnt of this woman; only that a girl, named Lambert, who had succeeded her in the apartment of the Rue Montmartre, had just been apprehended; and as this girl was known as France's mistress, it was conjectured that these two had a common residence. France was in consequence conducted to the spot, and recognized by the neighbors. He pretended that he had been taken by surprise, and that they were mistaken, but the jury before whom he was taken decided otherwise, and he was condemned to the galleys for eight years.

France once convicted, it was easy to follow up the traces of his comrades, two of whom were named Fossard and Legagneur. They were watched, but the negligence and want of address in the officers enabled them to escape the pursuit which I directed. The former was a man the more dangerous, as he was very skillful in making false keys. For fifteen months he seemed to defy the police, when one day I learnt that he resided with a hairdresser in the Rue du Temple, facing the common sewer. To apprehend him from home was almost impossible, for he was skillful in disguises, and could detect an officer a hundred paces off; on the other hand, it would be better to seize him in the midst of his professional apparatus, and the produce of his robberies. But the undertaking presented obstacles: Fossard never answered when they knocked at his door, and it was most likely that he had a means of egress, and facilities for getting over the roofs. It appeared to me, that the only mode of seizing him was, to profit by his absence and hide in his lodging. M. Henry was of my opinion; and the door being broken open in the presence of a commissary, three agents placed themselves in a closet adjoining a recess. Nearly seventy-two hours elapsed, and nobody arrived; at the end of the third day, the officers having exhausted their provisions, were going away, when they heard a key turn in the lock, and Fossard entered. Immediately two of the officers, in conformity with their instructions, darted from the closet and threw themselves upon him; but Fossard, arming himself with a knife which they had left on the table, frightened them so, that they themselves opened the door which their comrade had closed; and, having turned the key upon them, Fossard quickly descended the staircase, leaving the three agents all the leisure necessary for drawing up a report, in which nothing was wanting, except the circumstance of the knife, which they were very cautious in mentioning.

Before being sent to the Conciergerie, France, who had never ceased to think me stanch, recommended one of his friends to me, named Legagneur, a fugitive galley slave, arrested in the Rue de la Mortellerie, at the moment when he was executing a robbery by the aid of false keys; and this man, deprived of all resource in consequence of the departure of his comrade, was thinking of sending for the money which he had deposited with a receiver of stolen goods in the Rue St. Dominique, at the Gros Caillou. Annette, who came constantly to see me at La Force, and sometimes ably abetted me in my pursuits, was charged with the commission; but either from distrust, or a desire to retain it for himself, the receiver received the messenger very ungraciously; and as she insisted, he threatened her with an arrest. Annette returned to tell us that she had failed in her errand. At this information Legagneur would have denounced the receiver, but that was only the first impulse of anger. Growing more calm, he judged it most fitting to defer his vengeance; and, moreover, to make it turn to his profit. "If I denounce him," said he to me, "not only shall I get nothing by it, but he may contrive to appear not at all in fault. It will be best to wait until I get out, and then I will make him squeak." Legagneur, having no further hope from his receiver, determined to write to two accomplices, Marguerit and Victor Desbois, renowned robbers. Convinced of this old truism, that small presents preserve friendship, in exchange for the aid he asked from them, he sent them the impressions of the locks which he had taken for his own private use. Legagneur again had recourse to the mediation of Annette, who found the two friends at the Rue Deux Ponts, on a wretched ground floor, a place where they never met without taking great previous precaution. It was not their residence. Annette, whom I had desired to do all in her power to learn this, had the sense not to lose sight of them. She followed them for two days, under different disguises; and, on the third, informed me that they slept in the small Rue St. Jean, in a house with gardens behind. M. Henry, to whom I communicated this circumstance, arranged all the necessary measures which the nature of the place required; but his officers were not more courageous, nor more skillful, than those from whom Fossard had escaped. The two robbers saved themselves by the garden, and it was not till some time afterward that they were apprehended in the Rue St. Hyacinthe St. Michel.

Legagneur having been in his turn conducted to the Conciergerie, was replaced in my room by the son of a vintner at Versailles, named Robin, who, united with the thieves of the capital, told me, in our conversations, their arrangements, as well concerning all that had been done, as of their present state and intended plans. He it was who pointed out to me the prisoner Mardargent as a fugitive galley slave, whilst he was only detained in custody as a deserter; for this latter crime he had been sentenced to twenty-four years' labor at the galleys: he had passed some time in the Bagne; and by the help of my notes and recollections, we were soon excellent friends: he fancied (and he was not mistaken) that I should be delighted to meet again my old companions in misfortune: he pointed out several amongst the prisoners, and I was fortunate enough to send back to the galleys a considerable number of those individuals whom justice, for want of the necessary proofs for their conviction, might have let loose upon society.

Never had any period been marked with more important discoveries than that which ushered in my debut in the service of the police; although scarcely enrolled in this administration, I had already done much for the safety of the capital, and even for the whole of France. Were I to relate half my successes in my new department, my reader's patience would be exhausted; I will simply make mention of an adventure which occurred a few months before I quit the prison, and which deserves to be rescued from the general oblivion.

One afternoon, a tumult arose in the court, which terminated in a violent pugilistic combat; at this hour in the day such occurrences were very frequent. The two champions were Blignon and Charpentier (called Chante a l'heure). A violent quarrel had arisen between them; when the action had ceased, Chante a l'heure, covered with contusions, entered the drinking shop to have his bruises fomented. I was there engaged at my game of piquet. Chante a l'heure, irritated with his defeat, was no longer master of himself, and as the brandy he had called for to wash his hurts, found its way almost unconsciously to his mouth instead, he became proportionably energetic; until at last his mind could no longer contain the angry burst of his feelings. "My good friend," said he to me, (for you are my very good friend), do you see how this beggar of a Blignon has served me; But he shall not go off scot-free!"

"Oh, never heed him," I replied; "he is stronger than you, and you must mind what you are about. Do you wish to be half killed a second time?"

"Oh, that is not what I mean. If I choose, I can put a stop to his beating me, or anyone else again. I know what I know!"

"Well, and what do you know?" cried I, struck by the tone in which he pronounced these last words.

"Yes, yes," answered Chante a l'heure, highly exasperated; "he has done well in driving me to this: I have only to blab, and his business is settled."

"Nonsense; hold your tongue," said I, affecting not to believe him: "you are both birds of a feather. When you owe anyone a spite, you have only to blow at his head, and he would instantly fall."

"You think so, do you?" said Chante a l'heure, striking the table. "Suppose I told you that he had slit a woman's weasand!"

"Not so loud, Chante a l'heure; not so loud," said I, putting my finger significantly on my lips. "You know very well that at La Force walls have ears; and you must not turn nose against a comrade."

"What do you call turning nose?" replied he, the more irritated in proportion as I feigned a wish to stop him from speaking; "when I tell you that it only depends on me to split upon him in another case."

"That is all very well," I replied; "but to bring a man before the bigwigs, we must have proofs!"

"Proofs! Does the devil's child ever want them? Listen. You know the little shopkeeper who lives near the Pont Notre Dame?"

"An old procuress, mistress of Chatonnet, and wife of the hump-backed man?"

"The same! Well, three months ago, as Blignon and I were blowing a cloud, quietly, in a boozing ken of the Rue Planche-Mibray, she came there to us. 'There's swag for you, my lads,' said she, 'not far off, in the Rue de la Sonnerie! You are boys of mettle, and I will put you on the lay. An old dowager who has been pocketing lots of blunt, a few days since, received fifteen or twenty thousand francs, in notes or gold; she often comes home in the darkey, and you must slit her windpipe; and when you have prigged the chink, fling her into the river.'

At first we did not relish the proposition, and would not hear of it, as we never cared to commit a murder, but the old hag so pestered us by telling us that she was well feathered, and that there was no harm in doing for an old woman, that we agreed to it. It was settled that the process should give us notice of the precise time and hour. However, I felt very I-don't-know-how-ish about it; because, you see, when you are not used to a job of the kind, you feel queerish a bit. But, never mind, all was settled; when next morning, at the Quatre-Cheminées, near Sevres, we met with Voivenel and another pal. Blignon told the business to them, at the same time stating his objection to the murder. They thereupon proposed to give us a hand, if we chose. 'Agreed,' replied Blignon: 'where there is enough for two, there is enough for four:' thus we settled it, and they were to be in the rig with us. From that time Voivenel's pal never let us rest, and was impatient for the arrival of the moment. At length, the old

Mother Murder-love told us all was ready. It was a thick fog on the night of the thirtieth of December. 'Now's the time!' said Blignon. Believe me or not, as you like; but on the word of a thief I would have backed out, but I could not; I was drawn on, and dogged the old woman with the others; and, in the evening, when, having as we knew received a considerable sum, she was returning from the house of M. Rousset, a person who let out carriages, in the Alley de la Pompe, we did for her. It was Voivenel's friend who stabbed her, whilst Blignon, having blinded her with his cloak, seized her from behind. I was the only one who did not dabble in her blood; but I saw all, for I was put on the lookout: and I then learnt, and saw, and heard enough to give that scoundrel Blignon his passport to the guillotine.

Chante a l'heure then, with an insensibility which exceeds belief, detailed to me all the minutest circumstances of this murder. I heard this abominable recital to the close, making incredible efforts to conceal my indignation; for every word which he uttered was of a nature to make the hair stand on end of even the least susceptible person. When the villain had finished retracing, with a horrible fidelity, the agonies of his victim, I urged him anew not to break off his friendship with Blignon: but at the same time I dexterously threw oil on the fire I appeared solicitous to extinguish. My plan was to lead Chante a l'heure to make a public confession of the horrible revelation to which rage and revenge had spurred him on. I was further desirous of being enabled to furnish justice with those means of conviction which would be necessary to punish the assassins. It remained in uncertainty; possibly, after all, this affair was merely the fruits of an overheated brain, and Chante a l'heure, when no longer under the influence of wine and vengeance, might disavow all recollection of it. However the business might terminate, I lost no time in dispatching to M. Henry a report, in which I explained the affair, as well as the doubts I myself entertained of its veracity; he was not long in replying to my communication," that the crime I alluded to was but too true. M. Henry begged I would endeavor to procure for him the precise account of everything which had preceded and followed this murder; and the very next day my plans were laid to obtain them. It was difficult to procure the arrest of any of the guilty party, without their suspecting the hand which directed the blow; but in this dilemma, as well as in many others in which I had been placed, chance came to my assistance. The following day I went to awaken Chante a l'heure, who still suffering from the intemperance of the preceding night, was unable to quit his bed; I seated myself beside him, and began to speak of the state of complete intoxication in which I had seen him, as well as of the indiscreet actions he had committed.

The reproof appeared to astonish him; but when I repeated a few words of the conversation we had held together, his surprise redoubled, and as I had foreseen, he protested the impossibility of his having used such language; and whether he had effectually lost his recollection, or whether he mistrusted me, he tried hard to persuade me that he had not the slightest remembrance of what had passed. Whether he at this moment spoke the truth, or not, I profited by it to tell him that he had not confined his confidential communications to one alone, but had spoken of all the circumstances of the murder in a loud tone, in the presence of several prisoners who were sitting near the fire, and had heard all that had passed as well as myself. "What an unlucky fellow I am!" cried he, with every sign of sincere distress. "What have I done? What is to be done to extricate myself from the situation in which it places me?" — "Nothing is more simple," said I: "if you should be questioned as to the scene of yesterday, you can say, 'Upon my word, when I have taken too much, I say or do anything; and if I happen to have a spite against a man, I do not know what I might invent about him.'"

Chante a l'heure took all this 'or genuine advice; but on the same morning, a man named Pinson, who passed for a great sneak, was conducted from La Force to the office of the prefect; this exchange could not have occurred more opportunely for my project, and I hastened to acquaint Chante a l'heure with it, adding that all the prisoners believed that Pinson was only removed in the expectation of his making some very important discoveries.

At this intelligence he appeared thunderstruck: "Was he one of those who were present when I was talking the other night?" asked he with strong anxiety. I replied that I had not particularly observed; he then communicated to me more frankly his fears, and I obtained from him fresh particulars, which, sent off without delay to M. Henry, caused all the accomplices in this murder to fall into the hands of justice; die shopkeeper and her husband were of the number. They were all committed to solitary confinement; Blignon and Chante a l'heure in the new building, the others in the infirmary, where they remained a very long time. The public authorities had inquired into it, and I no longer troubled myself with the affair. Nothing material resulted from the investigation, which had been badly begun from the first, and finally the accused were pardoned. My abode at Bicêtre and La Force embraced a point of twenty-one months, during which not a single day passed without my rendering some important service. I believe I might have become a perpetual spy, so far was everyone from supposing that any connivance existed between the agents of the public authority and myself. Even the porters and keepers were in ignorance of the mission with which I was entrusted. Adored by the thieves, esteemed by the most determined bandits, I could always rely on their devotion to me; they would have been torn to pieces in my service, a proof of which occurred at Bicêtre, where Marilargent had several severe battles with some of the prisoners who had dared to assert that I had only quitted La Force to serve the police. Coco-Lacour and Goreau, prisoners in the same jail as incorrigible thieves, with no less ardor and generous intrepidity undertook my defense.

M. Henry did not allow the print to remain in ignorance of the numerous discoveries effected by my sagacity. This functionary, to whom I was represented as a person on whom he might depend, consented at last to put an end to my detention. Every measure was taken that it might not be known that I had recovered my liberty; they sent to fetch me from La Force, and carried me from thence without neglecting any of their rigorous precautions. My handcuffs were replaced, and I ascended the wicker car with the private understanding that I was to escape on the road, and I was not slow in profiting by this permission. The same night my flight was made known, and all the police were in search of me. This escape caused much noise, particularly at La Force, where my friends celebrated it with rejoicings, drank to my health, and wished me a safe and prosperous journey.

Chapter XXII

As a secret agent of government, I had duties marked out, and the kind and respectable M. Henry took upon himself to instruct me in their fulfillment; for in his hands were entrusted nearly the entire safety of the capital: to prevent crimes, discover malefactors, and to give them up to justice, were the principal functions confided to me.

By thieves, M. Henry was styled the Evil Spirit; and well did he merit the surname, for with him, cunning and suavity of manners were so conjoined as seldom to fail in their purpose. Among the coadjutors of M. Henry, was M. Bertaux, a cross-examiner of great merit. The proofs of his talent may be found in the archives of the court. Next to him, I have great pleasure in naming M. Parisot, governor of the prisons. In a word, M. Henry, Bertaux, and Parisot, formed a veritable triumvirate, which was incessantly conspiring against the perpetrators of all manner of crimes; to extirpate rogues from Paris, and to procure for the inhabitants of that immense city a perfect security.

So soon as I was installed in my new office of secret agent, I commenced my rounds, in order to take my measures well for setting effectually to work. These journeys, which occupied me nearly twenty days, furnished me with many useful and important observations, but as yet I was only preparing to act, and studying my ground.

One morning I was hastily summoned to attend the chief of the division. The matter in hand was to discover a man named Watrin, accused of having fabricated and put in circulation false money and bank notes. The inspectors of the police had already arrested Watrin, but, according to custom, had allowed him to escape. M. Henry gave me every direction which he deemed likely to assist me in the search after him; but unfortunately he had only gleaned a few simple particulars of his usual habits and customary haunts; every place he was known to frequent was freely pointed out to me; but it was not very likely he would be found in those resorts which prudence would call upon him carefully to avoid; there remained therefore only a chance of reaching him by some by-path. When I learnt that he had left his effects in a furnished house, where he once lodged, on the boulevard of Mont Parnasse, I took it for granted that, sooner or later, he would go there in search of his property; or at least that he would send some person to fetch it from thence; consequently, I directed all my vigilance to this spot; and after having reconnoitered the house, I lay in ambush in its vicinity night and day, in order to keep a watchful eye upon all comers and goers. This went on for nearly a week, when, weary of not observing anything, I determined upon engaging the master of the house in my interest, and to hire an apartment of him, where I accordingly established myself with Annette, certain that my presence could give rise to no suspicion.

I had occupied this post for about fifteen days, when one evening, at eleven o'clock, I was informed that Watrin had just come, accompanied by another person. Owing to a slight indisposition, I had retired to bed earlier than usual; however, at this news I rose hastily, and descended the staircase by four stairs at a time; but whatever diligence I might use, I was only just in time to catch Watrin's companion; him I had no right to detain, but I made myself sure that I might, by intimidation obtain farther particulars from him. I therefore seized him, threatened him, and soon drew from him a confession, that he was a shoemaker, and that Watrin lived with him, No. 4, Rue des Mauvais Garcons. This was all I wanted to know: I had only had time to slip an old great coat over my shirt, and without stopping to put on more garments, I hurried on to the place thus pointed out to me. I reached the house at the very instant that some person was quitting it: persuaded that it was Watrin, I attempted to seize him; he escaped from me, and I darted after him up a staircase; but at the moment of grasping him, a violent blow which struck my chest, drove me down twenty stairs. I sprung forward again, and that so quickly, that to escape from my pursuit he was compelled to return into the house through a sash window.

I then knocked loudly at the door, summoning him to open it without delay. This he refused to do. I then desired Annette (who had followed me) to go in search of the guard, and whilst she was preparing to obey me, I counterfeited the noise of a man descending the stairs. Watrin, deceived by this feint, was anxious to satisfy himself whether I had actually gone, and softly put his head out of window to observe if all was safe. This was exactly what I wanted. I made a vigorous dart forward, and seized him by the hair of his head: he grasped me in the same manner, and a desperate struggle took place; jammed against the partition wall which separated us, he opposed me with a determined resistance. Nevertheless, I felt that he was growing weaker; I collected all my strength for a last effort; I strained every nerve, and drew him nearly out of the window through which we were struggling: one more trial and the victory was mine; but in the earnestness of my grasp we both rolled on the passage floor, on to which I had pulled him: to rise, snatch from his hands the shoemaker's cutting knife with which he had armed himself, to bind him, and lead him out of the house, was the work of an instant.

Accompanied only by Annette, I conducted him to the prefecture, where I received the congratulations first of M. Henry, and afterward those of the prefect of police, who bestowed on me a pecuniary recompense. Watrin was a man of unusual address; he followed a coarse, clumsy business, and yet he had given himself up to making counterfeit money, which required extreme delicacy of hand. Condemned to death, he obtained a reprieve the very hour that was destined for his execution; the scaffold was prepared, he was taken down from it, and the lovers of such scenes experienced a disappointment. All Paris remembers it. A report was in circulation that he was about to make some very important discoveries; but as he had nothing to reveal, a few days afterward he underwent his sentence.

Watrin was my first capture, and an important one too; this successful beginning awoke the jealousy of the peace officers, as well as those under my orders; all were exasperated against me, but in vain; they could not forgive me for being more successful than themselves. The superiors, on the contrary, were highly pleased with my conduct; and I redoubled my zeal to render myself still more worthy their confidence.

About this period a vast number of counterfeit five-franc pieces had got into general circulation; several of them were shown me; whilst examining them, I fancied I could discover the workmanship of Boudin (who had informed against me) and of his friend, Dr. Terrier. I resolved to satisfy my mind as to the truth of this; and in consequence of this determination, I set about watching the steps of these two individuals; but as I durst not follow them too closely, lest they might recognize me, and mistrust my observation, it was difficult for me to obtain the intelligence I wanted. Nevertheless, by dint of unwearied perseverance, I arrived at the certainty of my not having mistaken the matter, and the two corners were arrested in the very act of fabricating their base coin; they were shortly after condemned and executed for it. It has been publicly asserted, in consequence of a report set on foot by the inspectors of the police, that Dr. Terrier had been led away by me, and that I had in a manner placed in his hands the instruments of his crime.

Let the reader remember the reply which this man made to me, when, at Boudin's house, I sought to persuade him to renounce his guilty industry, and he will judge whether Terrier was a man to allow himself to be drawn away.

CHAPTER XXIII

IN SO POPULOUS A CAPITAL AS THAT OF PARIS, there are usually a vast many places of bad resort, at which assemble persons of broken fortune and ruined fame; in order to judge of them under my own eye, I frequented every house and street of ill fame, sometimes under one disguise and sometimes under another; assuming indeed all those rapid changes of dress and manner which indicated a person desirous of concealing himself from the observation of the police, till the rogues and thieves whom I daily met there firmly believed me to be one of themselves; persuaded of my being a runaway, they would have been cut to pieces before I should have been taken; for not only had I acquired their fullest confidence, but their strongest regard; and so much did they respect my situation, as a fugitive galley slave, that they would not even propose to me to join in any of their daring schemes, lest it might compromise my safety.

All however did not exercise this delicacy, as will be seen hereafter. Some months had passed since I commenced my secret investigations, when chance threw in my way St. Germain, whose visits had so often filled me with consternation. He had with him a person named Boudin, whom I had formerly seen as a restaurateur in Paris, in the Rue des Prouvaires, and of whom I knew no more than that trifling acquaintance which arose from my occasionally exchanging my money for his dinners. He however seemed easily to recollect me, and, addressing me with a bold familiarity, which my determined coolness seemed unable to subdue.

"Pray," said he, "have I been guilty of any offense toward you, that you seem so resolved upon cutting me?"

"By no means, sir," replied I; "but I have been informed that you have been in the service of the police."

"Oh, oh, is that all?" cried he, "never mind that, my boy; suppose I have, what then? I had my reasons; and when I tell you what they were, I am quite sure you will not bear me any ill will for it."

"Come, come," said St Germain, "I must have you good friends; Boudin is an excellent fellow, and I will answer for his honor, as I would do for my own. Many a thing happens in life we should never have dreamt of, and if Boudin did accept the situation you mention, it was but to save his brother: besides, you must feel satisfied, that were his principles such as a gentleman ought not to possess, why, you would not find him in my company."

I was much amused with this excellent reasoning, as well as with the pledge given for Boudin's good faith; however, I no longer sought to avoid the conversation of Boudin. It was natural enough that St. Germain should relate to me all that had happened to him since his last disappearance, which had given me such pleasure.

After complimenting me on my flight, he informed me that after my arrest he had recovered his employment, which he however was not fortunate enough to keep; he lost it a second time, and had since been compelled to trust to his wits to procure a subsistence. I requested he would tell me what had become of Blondy and Deluc?

"What," said he, "the two who slit the wagoner's throat? Oh, why the guillotine settled their business at Beauvais."

When I learnt that these two villains had at length reaped the just reward of their crimes, I experienced but one regret, and that was, that the heads of their worthless accomplices had not fallen on the same scaffold.

After we had sat together long enough to empty several bottles of wine, we separated. At parting, St. Germain having observed that I was but meanly clad, inquired what I was doing, and as I carelessly answered that at present I had no occupation, he promised to do his best for me, and to push my interest the first opportunity that offered. I suggested that, as I very rarely ventured out for fear of being arrested, we might not possibly meet again for some time. "You can see me, whenever you choose," said he; "I shall expect that you will call on me frequently." Upon my promise to do so, he gave me his address, without once thinking of asking for mine.

St. Germain was no longer an object of such excessive terror as formerly in my eyes; I even thought it my interest to keep him in sight, for if I applied myself to scrutinizing the actions of suspicious persons, who better than he called for the most vigilant attention? In a word, I resolved upon purging society of such a monster. Meanwhile, I waged a determined war with all the crowd of rogues who infested the capital. About this time robberies of every species were multiplying to a frightful extent: nothing was talked of but stolen palisades, outhouses broken open, roofs stripped of their lead; more than twenty reflecting lamps were successively stolen from the Rue Fountaine au Roi, without the plunderers being detected.

For the whole month, the inspectors had been lying in wait in order to surprise them, and the first night of their discontinuing their vigilance the same depredations took place. In this state, which appeared like setting the police at defiance, I accepted the task which none seemed able to accomplish, and in a very short time I was enabled to bring the whole band of these shameless plunderers to public justice, which immediately consigned them to the galleys.

Each day increased the number of my discoveries. Of the many who were committed to prison, there were none who did not owe their arrest to me, and yet not one of them for a moment suspected my share in the business. The thieves of my acquaintance looked upon me as their best friend and true comrade; the others esteemed themselves happy to have an opportunity of initiating me in their secrets, whether from the pleasure of conversing with me, or in the hope of benefiting by my counsels. It was principally beyond the barriers that I met with these unfortunate beings.

One day when I was crossing the outer Boulevards, I was accosted by St. Germain, who was still accompanied by Boudin. They invited me to dinner; I accepted the proposition, and over a bottle of wine they did me the honor to propose that I should make a third in an intended murder.

The matter in hand was to dispatch two old men who lived together in the house which Boudin had formerly occupied in the Rue des Prouvaires. Shuddering at the confidence placed in me by these villains, I yet blessed the invisible hand which had led them to seek my aid. At first I affected some scruples at entering into the plot, but at last feigned to yield to their lively and pressing solicitations, and it was agreed that we should wait the favorable moment for putting into execution this most execrable project. This resolution taken, I bade farewell to St. Germain and his companion, and (decided upon preventing the meditated crime) hastened to carry a report of the affair to M. Henry, who sent me without loss of time to obtain more ample details of the discovery I had just made to him. His intention was to satisfy himself whether I had been really solicited to take part in it, or whether, from a mistaken devotion to the cause of justice, I had endeavored to instigate those unhappy men to an act which would render them amenable to it. I protested that I had adopted no such expedient, and as he discovered marks of truth in my manner and declaration, he expressed himself satisfied. He did not, however, omit to impress on me the following discourse upon instigating agents, which penetrated my very heart. Ah, why was it not also heard by those wretches, who since the revolution have made so many victims! The renewed era of legitimacy would not then in some circumstances have recalled the bloody days of another epoch.

"Remember well," said M. Henry to me, in conclusion, "remember that the greatest scourge to society is he who urges another on to the commission of evil. Where there are no instigators to bad practices, they are committed only by the really hardened; because they alone are capable of conceiving and executing them. Weak beings may be drawn away and excited: to precipitate them into the abyss, it frequently requires no more than to call to your aid their passions or self-love; but he who avails himself of their weakness to procure their destruction, is more than a monster—he is the guilty one, and it is on his head that the sword of justice should fall. As to those engaged in the police, they had better remain forever idle, than create matter for employment."

Although this lesson was not required in my case, yet I thanked M. Henry for it, who enjoined me not to lose sight of the two assassins, and to use every means in my power to prevent their arriving at the completion of their diabolical plan. "The police," said he, "is instituted as much to correct and punish malefactors, as to prevent their committing crimes; but on every occasion I would wish it to be understood, that we hold ourselves under greater obligations to that person who prevents one crime, than to him who procures the punishment of many."

Conforming with these instructions, I did not allow a single day to pass without seeing St. Germain and his friend Boudin. As the blow they meditated was to procure them a considerable quantity of gold, I concluded that I might, without overacting my part, affect a degree of impatience about it. "Well," said I to them, every time we met, "and when is this famous affair to take place?"—

"When!" replied St. Germain, "the fruit is not yet ripe; when the right time comes," added he, pointing to Boudin, "my friend there will let you know." Already had several meetings taken place, and yet nothing was decidedly arranged; once more I hazarded the usual question, "'Hello again!" said St. Germain, "my good friend, now I can satisfy your natural curiosity; we have fixed upon tomorrow evening, and only waited for you to deliberate upon the best way of going to work." The meeting was fixed a little way out of Paris. I was punctual to the time and place, nor did St. Germain keep me waiting. "Hark ye," said he, "we have reflected upon this affair, and find that it cannot be put into execution for the present. We have, however, another to propose to you; and I warn you, you must say at once, without any equivocation, 'yes' or 'no.' Before we enter upon the object of my coming hither, it is but fair I should let you into a little confidential story respecting yourself, which was told to me by one Carre, who knew you at La Force. The tail runs, that you only escaped its walls upon condition of serving the police as its secret agent!"

At the words "secret agent," a feeling almost approaching to suffocation stole over me, but I quickly rallied upon perceiving that, however true the report might be, it had obtained but little faith with St. Germain, who was evidently waiting for my explanation or denial of it without once suspecting its reality. My ever-ready genius quickly flew to my aid, and without hesitation I replied, that I was not much surprised at the charge, and for the simple reason that I myself had been the first to set the rumor afloat." St. Germain stared with wonder.

"My good fellow," said I, "you are well aware that I managed to escape from the police whilst they were transferring me from La Force to Bicêtre. Well! I went to Paris and stayed there until I could go elsewhere. One must live, you know, how and where one can. Unfortunately, I am still compelled to play at hide and seek, and it is only by assuming a variety of disguises that I dare venture abroad, to look about and just see what my old friends are doing; but in spite of all my precautions, I live in constant dread of many individuals, whose keen eyes quickly penetrate my assumption of other names and habits than my own; and who having formerly been upon terms of familiarity with me, pestered me with questions I had no other means of shaking off, than in insinuating that I was in the pay of the police; and thus I obtained the double advantage of evading, in my character of 'spy,' both their suspicions and ill will, should they feel disposed to exercise it in procuring my arrest."

"Enough—enough," interrupted St. Germain; "I believe you; and to convince you of the unbroken confidence I place in you, I will let you into the secret of our plans for tonight: At the corner of the Rue d'Enghein, where it joins the Rue Hautville, lives a banker, whose house looks out upon a very extensive garden; a circumstance greatly in favor both of our expedition and our escape after its completion. This same banker is now absent, and the cash-box, in which is a considerable sum in specie, besides bank notes, etc., is only guarded by two persons. Well, you can guess the rest. We mean to make it our own by the law of possession, this very evening. Three of us are bound by oath to do the job, which will turn out so profitably. But we want another: and now that you have cleared your character and given scandal the lie, you shall make the fourth. Come, no refusal;—we reckon on your company and assistance, and if you refuse you are a regular set-down sneak."

I was as eager in accepting the invitation, as St. Germain could possibly be in giving it: both Boudin and himself seemed much pleased with my zeal. Who my remaining coadjutor was, I knew not, but my surmises on the subject were soon settled by the arrival of a man, a perfect stranger to myself, named Dubenne. He was the driver of a cabriolet, the father of a large family, and a man, who, more from weak than bad principles, had allowed himself to be seduced by the temptations of his guilty companions. Whilst a mixed conversation was going on between them, my thoughts were busily at work upon the best method of causing them to be taken in the very act they were then discussing. What was my consternation to hear St. Germain, at the moment we all rose to pay our score, address us in these words:—

"My friends, when a man runs his neck into the compass of a halter, it behooves him to keep a sharp lookout. We have this day decided upon playing a dangerous, but as I take it, a sure game; and in order that the change may be in our favor, I have determined upon the following measure, which I think you will all approve. About midnight, all four of us will obtain access into the house in question. Boudin and myself will undertake to manage the inside work, whilst you two remain in the garden, ready to second us in case of surprise. This undertaking, if successful, will furnish us with the means of being at our ease for some time; but it concerns our mutual safety that we should not quit each other till the hour for putting our plan into execution."

This finale, which I feigned not to hear, was repeated a second time, and filled me with a thousand fears that I might not be able to withdraw myself from the affair, as I had intended. What was to be done? St. Germain was a man of uncommon daring, eager for money, and always ready to purchase it, either with his own blood or that of others; however, it was as yet but ten o'clock in the morning; I hoped that, during the long interval between that hour and midnight, some opportunity would present itself of dexterously stealing away and giving information to the police. Meanwhile, I made not the slightest objection to the proposition of St. Germain, which was indeed the best pledge we could separately have of the good faith of the others. When he perceived that we were all agreed, Saint Germain, who, by his energy, his talent for plotting, and carrying his schemes into execution, was the real head of the conspiracy, expressed his satisfaction, and added further—

"This unanimity is what I like; and I beg to say, that for myself I will leave nothing undone to merit the continuance of so flattering a consent to my wishes and opinions."

It was agreed that we should take a hackney-coach, and proceed together to his house, situated in the Rue St. Antoine. Arrived there, we ascended into his chamber, where he was to keep us under lock and key until the instant of departure. Confined between four walls, in close converse with these robbers,

I knew not what saint to invoke, and what pretext to invent, to effect my escape. St. Germain would have blown out my brains at the least suspicion; and how to act or what was to be done, I knew not. My only plan was to resign myself to the event, be it what it might; and this determination taken, I affected to busy myself with the preparatives for our crime, the very sight of which redoubled my perplexity and horror. Pistols were laid on the table, in order to have the charges drawn and to be properly reloaded. Whilst they underwent a strict scrutiny, St. Germain remarked a pair which seemed to him no longer able "to do the state any service;" he laid them aside—

"Here," said he, "these toothless barkers will never do; whilst the rest of you are loading and priming your batteries, I will get these changed for others more likely to aid our purpose." As he was preparing to quit the room, I bade him remember that, according to our contract, none of us could quit the place without being accompanied by a second, "Right—quite right," replied he; "I like people not only to make, but to keep engagements; so come with me."

"But," said I, "these other two gentlemen?"

"Oh!" laughed St. Germain, "they shall be kept out of harm's way till our return;" so saying, he very coolly double-locked the door upon them, and then taking me by the arm, led me to a shop from which he generally supplied himself with what he required for his various expeditions. Upon the present occasion, he purchased some balls, powder, flints, exchanged the old pistols for new ones, and then declaring his business completed, returned with me to his house. On entering, I felt a fresh thrill of horror, from perceiving how earnestly and yet calmly the wretch Boudin was occupied in sharpening two large dinner-knives on a hone—the sight froze my blood, and I turned away in disgust.

Meanwhile the time was passing away; one o'clock struck, and no expedient of safety had yet presented itself. I yawned and stretched, feigning weariness, and going into an apartment adjoining the one in which we had assembled, threw myself on a bed, as if in search of repose; after a few instants, I appeared still more fidgety with this indolence, and I could perceive that the others were not less so than myself. "Suppose we have a glass of something to cheer us," cried St. Germain. "An excellent idea!" I replied, almost leaping for joy at the unexpected opening it seemed likely to afford my scheme; "a most capital thought—and by way of helping it, if you can manage to send to my house, you may have a glass of Burgundy, such as cannot be met with every day." All declared the thought a most seasonable relief to the ennui which was beginning to have hold of them, now that all their work of preparation was at an end; and St. Germain without further delay dispatched his porter to Annette, who was requested to bring the promised treat herself. It was agreed that nothing relative to our plan should be uttered before her, and whilst my three companions were indulging in rough jokes upon the unexpected pleasure thus offered them, I carelessly resumed my place on the bed, and whilst there traced with a pencil these few lines—

"When you leave this place, disguise yourself; and do not for an instant lose sight of myself, St. Germain, or Boudin. Be careful to avoid all observation; and, above all, be sure to pick up anything I may let fall, and to convey it as directed." Short as was this hurried instruction, it was, I knew, sufficient for Annette, who had frequently received similar directions, and I felt quite assured that she would comprehend it in its fullest sense. It was not long before she joined us, bringing with her the basket of wine. Her appearance was the signal for mirth and gayety. She was complimented by all; and as for myself, under the semblance of thanking her for her ready attendance with an embrace, I managed to slip the billet into her hand: she understood me, took leave of the company, and left me far happier than I had felt an hour before.

We made a hearty dinner, after which I suggested the idea of going alone with St. Germain to reconnoiter the scene of action, in order to be provided with the means of guarding against any accident. As this seemed merely the counsel of a prudent man, it excited no suspicion; the only difference in his opinion and mine was that I proposed taking a hackney coach, whilst he judged it better to walk. When we reached the part he considered most favorable for scaling, he pointed it out to me; and I took care to observe it so well, that I could easily describe it to another, without fear of any mistake arising. This done, St. Germain recollected that we had all better cover our faces with black crape, and we proceeded toward the Palais Royal, for the purpose of buying some; and whilst he was in a shop, examining the different sorts, I managed to scrawl hastily on paper every particular and direction which might enable the police to interfere and prevent the crime. St. Germain, whose vigilance never relaxed, and who had, as much as possible, kept his eye upon me with calm scrutiny, conducted me to a public-house, where we refreshed ourselves with some beer: quitting this place, we walked again homeward, without my having been enabled to dispose of the billet I had written; when, just as we were re-entering his odious den of crimes, my eye caught sight of Annette, who, disguised in a manner that would have effectually deceived every other but myself, was on the watch for our return. Convinced that she had recognized me, I managed to drop my paper as I crossed the threshold; and relieved, in a great measure, of many of my former apprehensions, I committed myself to my fate.

As the terrible hour for the fulfillment of our scheme approached, I became a prey to a thousand terrors. Despite the warning I had sent through Annette, the police might be tardy in obeying its directions, and might perhaps arrive too late to prevent the consummation of the crime. Should I at once avow myself, and in my real character, arrest St. Germain and his accomplices? Alas! What could I do against three powerful men, rendered furious by revenge and desperation? And besides, had I even succeeded in my attempt, who could say that I might be believed, when I denied all participation with them, except such as was to further the ends of justice. Instances rose to my recollection, where, under similar circumstances, the police had abandoned its agents, or, confounding them with the guilty wretches with whom they had mingled, refused to acknowledge their innocence. I was in all the agony of such reflections, when St. Germain roused me, by desiring I would accompany Debenne, whose cabriolet was destined to receive the expected treasure of money-bags, and was for that purpose to be stationed at the corner of the street. We went out together, and, as I looked around me, I again met the eye of my faithful Annette, whose glance satisfied me that all my commissions had been attended to. Just then, Debenne inquired of me the place of rendezvous. I know not what good genius suggested to me the idea of saving this unhappy creature. I had observed that he was not wicked at heart, and that he seemed rather drawn toward the abyss of guilt by want and bad advice, than by any natural inclination for crime. I hastily assigned to him a post, away from the spot which had been agreed on; and, happy in having saved him from the snare, rejoined St. Germain and Boudin at the angle of the boulevard St. Denis. It was now about half-past ten, and I gave them to understand that the cabriolet would require some time in getting ready; that I had given orders to Debenne, that he should take his station in the corner of the Rue du Faubourg Poissonniere, ready to hasten to us at the slightest signal. I observed to them, that the sight of a cabriolet too near to the place of our labors might awaken suspicion; and they agreed in thinking my precautions wisely taken.

Eleven o'clock struck—we took a glass together in the fauxbourg St. Denis, and then directed our steps toward the banker's habitation. The tranquility of Boudin and his infamous associate, had something in it almost fiend-like: they walked coolly along, each with his pipe in his mouth, which was only removed to hum over some loose song.

At last we arrived at the part of the garden wall it had been determined to scale, by means of a large post, which would serve as a ladder. St. Germain demanded my pistols;—my heart began to beat violently, for I fully expected that, having by some ill chance penetrated my real share in the affair, he meant that I should answer for it with my life; resistance would have been useless, and I put them into his hands; but, to my extreme relief, he merely opened the pan, changed the priming, and returned them to me. After having performed a similar operation on his own pistols and those of Boudin, he set the example of climbing the post; Boudin followed; and both of them, without interrupting their smoking, sprung into the garden; it became my turn to follow them: trembling, I reached the top of the wall; all my former apprehensions crowded back upon me. Had the police yet had time to lay their ambuscade? Might not St. Germain have preceded them? These and a thousand similar questions agitated my mind. My feelings were, however, wrought up to so high a pitch, that, in the midst of such a moment of cruel suspense. I determined on one measure, namely, to prevent the commission of the crime, though I sank in the unequal struggle However, St. Germain, seeing me still sitting astride on the top of the wall, and becoming impatient at my delay, cried out, "Come, come down with you." Scarcely had he said the words, than he was vigorously attacked by a number of men. Boudin and himself offered a desperate resistance. A brisk firing commenced—the balls whistled—and, after a combat of some minutes, the two assassins were seized, though not before several of the police had been wounded. St. Germain and his companion were likewise much hurt. For myself, as I took no part in the engagement, I was not likely to come to any harm:

nevertheless, that I might sustain my part to the end, I fell on the field of battle, as though I had been mortally wounded. The next instant, I was wrapped in a covering, and in this manner conveyed to a room where Boudin and St. Germain were; the latter appeared deeply touched at my death; he shed tears, and it was necessary to employ force to remove him from what he believed to be my corpse.

St. Germain was a man of about five feet eight inches high, with strongly developed muscles, an enormous head, and very small eyes, half closed, like those of an owl; his face, deeply marked with the smallpox, was extremely plain; and yet, from the quickness and vivacity of his expression, he was by many persons considered pleasing. In describing his features, a strong resemblance would suggest itself to those of the hyena and the wolf, particularly if the attention were directed to his immensely wide jaws, furnished with large projecting fangs; his very organization partook of the animal instinct common to beasts of prey; he was passionately fond of hunting; the sight of blood exhilarated him: his other passions were gaming, women, and good eating and drinking. As he had acquired the air and manners of good society, he expressed himself, when he chose, with ease and fluency, and was almost always fashionably and elegantly dressed; he might be styled a "well-bred thief." When his interest required it, no person could better assume the pleasant mildness of an amiable man; at other times he was abrupt and brutal. His comrade Boudin was diminutive in stature, scarcely reaching five feet two inches; thin, with a livid complexion; his eyes dark and piercing and deeply sunk in his head. The habit of wielding the carving-knife, and of cutting up meat, had rendered him ferocious. He was bow-legged; a deformity I have observed among several systematic assassins, as well as among many other individuals distinguished by their crimes.

I cannot remember any event of my life which afforded me more real satisfaction than the taking of these two villains. I applauded myself for having delivered society from two monsters, at the same time that I esteemed myself fortunate in having saved Debenne from the fate that would have befallen him, had he been taken with them. However, the share of self-satisfaction produced by the feeling of having been instrumental in rescuing a fellow-creature from destruction, was but a slight compensation for the misery I experienced at being in a manner compelled, by the stern duties of the post I filled, either to send a fresh succession of victims to ascend the scaffold, or to mount it myself. The quality of "secret agent" preserved, it is true, my liberty, and shielded me from the dangers to which, as a fugitive galley slave, I was formerly exposed; true, I was no longer subjected to the many terrors which had once agitated me; but still I was not pardoned; and until that happy event took place, the liberty I enjoyed was but a precarious possession, which the caprice of my employers could deprive me of at any moment. Again, I was not insensible to the general odium attached to the department I filled. Still, revolting as were its functions to my own choice and mind, it was a necessary evil, and one from which there was no escape. I therefore strove to reconcile myself to it by arguments such as these:—Was I not daily occupied in endeavoring to promote the welfare of society? Was I not espousing the part of the good and upright against the bad and vicious? And should I by these steps draw down upon me the contempt of mankind? I went about dragging guilt from its hidden recesses, and unmasking its many schemes of blood and murder: and should I for this be pointed out with the finger of scorn and hatred? Attacking thieves, even on the very theatre of their crimes, wresting from them the weapons with which they had armed themselves, I boldly dared their vengeance; and did I for this merit to be despised? My reason became convinced; and my mind, satisfied with the upright motives which guided me, regained its calmness and self-command; and thus armed, I felt that I had courage to dare the ingratitude and obloquy of an unjust opinion respecting me and my occupation.

CHAPTER XXIV

THE THIEVES WHO HAD EXPERIENCED A TEMPORARY panic at the many arrests which had successively fallen with unexpected vengeance on many of their party, were not long in reappearing more numerous and more audacious than ever. Amongst their number were several fugitive galley slaves, who having perfected in the Bagnes a very dangerous sort of trade, and ready invention, had come to exercise it in Paris, where they soon rendered themselves dreaded by all parties.

The police, exasperated at their boldness, resolved upon putting an end to their career. I was accordingly commanded to seek them out, and further orders were given to me to arrange a plan of action with the peace officers, by which they might be at hand whenever I deemed it likely they could affect the capture of any of these ruffians. It may be easily guessed how difficult my task must be; however, I lost no time in visiting every place of ill-fame, both in the metropolis and its environs.

In a very few days, I had gained the knowledge of all the dens of vice where I might be likely to meet with these wretches. The barrier de la Courtille, those of the Combat and de Menilmontant were the places of most favorite resort; they were, in a manner, their headquarters, and woe to the agent who had shown himself there, no matter for what reason; he would assuredly have had his brains beaten out. The gendarmes were equally in dread of this well-known and formidable association, and carefully abstained from approaching it. For my own part I felt less timidity, and ventured without hesitation into the midst of this herd of miserable beings. I frequented their society; I became to outwardly resemble one of themselves, and soon gained the advantage of being treated with so much confidence as to be admitted to their nocturnal meetings, where they openly discussed the crimes they had committed, as well as those they meditated. I managed so skillfully, that I easily drew from them the particulars of their own abode, or that of the females with whom they cohabited.

I may go still further, and assert that so boundless was the confidence with which I had inspired them, that had any one of their members dared to express the shadow of a suspicion respecting me, he would have been punished on the spot. In this manner, I obtained every requisite information; so that, when I had once indicated any fit object for arrest, his conviction and condemnation became matters of course. My researches, "intra muros," were not less successful. I frequented every tennis court in the environs of the Palais Royal, the Hotel d'Angleterre, the boulevards of the Temple, and in fact the whole city. Not a day passed in which I did not affect some important discovery. Nothing escaped me, either relating to crimes which had been committed, or were in contemplation. I was in all places; I knew all that was passing or projecting; and never were the police idly or unprofitably employed, when set to work upon my suggestions.

M. Henry openly expressed his surprise as well as satisfaction at my zeal and success; it was not so with many of the peace officers and sub-agents of police; for, little accustomed to the hard duty and constant watchfulness my plans induced, they openly murmured. Some of them, in their anxiety to be rid of the irksomeness of my direction, were cowardly enough to betray the secret of the disguise under favor of which I had so skillfully maneuvered. This imprudent act drew down upon them severe reprimands, without having the effect of making them more circumspect, or more devoted to the public good.

It will be readily understood, that associating as I constantly did with the vilest and most abandoned, I must as a matter of course, be repeatedly invited to join in their acts of criminal violence; this I never refused at the moment of asking, but always formed some plea for failing to attend the rendezvous for such purposes. These men of crimes were generally so absorbed in their villainous machinations, that the most flimsy excuse passed current with them: I may even say, that frequently it did not require the trouble of an excuse to deceive them. Once arrested, they never troubled themselves to find out by what means it had been effected; and had they even been more awake, my measures were laid too ably for them to have arrived at the chance of suspecting me as the author of it: indeed, I have often been accosted by some of the gang to communicate the sorrowful tidings of the apprehension of one of their number, as well as to beg my advice and assistance in endeavoring to procure his release.

Nothing is more easy, when once on good terms with a thief, than to obtain a knowledge of the persons to whom he disposes of his stolen property. Perhaps the recital of the means I adopted to rid Paris of one of these dangerous characters may not be uninteresting to the reader.

For many years the police had had its eye upon him, but as yet had not been able to detect him in any positive act of delinquency. His house had undergone repeated searches without any effect resulting from the most diligent inquiry; nothing of the most trifling nature could be found to rise in evidence against him. Nevertheless, he was known to traffic with the thieves; and many of them who were far from suspecting my connection with the police, pointed him out to me as a stanch friend, and a man on whom they could depend. These assertions respecting him were not sufficient to effect his conviction; it would be requisite to seize him with the stolen articles in his possession. M. Henry had tried every scheme to accomplish this; but whether from stupidity on the part of the agents employed by him, or the superior address of the receiver of stolen property, all his plans had failed. He was desirous of trying whether I should be more successful. I willingly undertook the office, and arranged my plans in the following manner:—Posted near the house of the suspected dealer in stolen property, I watched for his going out, and following him when he had gone a few steps down the street addressed him by a different name to his own. He assured me I was mistaken; I protested to the contrary; he insisted upon it I was deceived, and I affected to be equally satisfied of his identity, declaring my perfect recognition of his person as that of a man who for some time had been sought after by the police throughout Paris and its environs. "You are grossly mistaken," replied he, warmly; "my name is So-and-so, and I live in such a street." "Come, come, friend," said I, "excuses are useless. I know you too well to part with you so easily." "This is too much," cried he; "but at the next police station I shall possibly be able to meet with those who can convince you that I know my own name better than you seem to do." This was exactly the point at which I wished to arrive. "Agreed," said I; and we bent our steps toward the neighboring guardhouse. We entered, and I requested he would show me his papers: he had none about him. I then insisted upon his being searched, and on his person were found three watches and twenty-five double Napoleons, which I caused to be laid aside till he should be examined before a magistrate. These things had been wrapped in a handkerchief, which I contrived to secure; and after having disguised myself as a messenger, I hastened to the house of this receiver of stolen goods, and demanded to speak with his wife. She, of course, had no idea of my business, or knowledge of my person; and seeing several persons besides herself present, I signified to her that my business being of a private nature, it was important that I should speak to her alone; and in token of my claims to her confidence, produced the handkerchief, and inquired whether she recognized it. Although still ignorant of the cause of my visit, her countenance became troubled, and her whole person was much agitated as she begged me to let her hear my business. "I am concerned," replied I, "to be the bearer of unpleasant news; but the fact is, your husband has just been ar-rested, everything found on his person has been seized, and from some words which he happened to overhear, he suspects he has been betrayed; he therefore wishes you to remove out of the house certain things you are aware would be dangerous to his safety if found on the premises; if you please, I will lend you a helping hand, but I must forewarn you that you have not one moment to lose."

The information was of the first importance; the sight of the handkerchief, and the description of the objects it had served to envelop, removed from her mind every doubt as to the truth of the message I had brought her, and she easily fell into the snare I had laid to entrap her. She thanked me for the trouble I had taken, and begged I would go and engage three hackney coaches, and return to her with as little delay as possible. I left the house to execute my com-mission; but on the road I stopped to give one of my people instructions to keep the coaches in sight, and to seize them, with their contents, directly when I should give the signal. The vehicles drew up to the door, and upon re-entering the house, I found things in a high state of preparation for removing. The floor was strewn with articles of every description: time-pieces, candelabra, Etruscan vases, cloths, cashmeres, linen, muslins, etc. All these things had been taken from a closet, the entrance to which was cleverly concealed by a large press, so skill-fully contrived, that the most practiced eye could not have discovered the deception. I assisted in the removal, and when it was completed, the press hav-ing been carefully replaced, the woman begged of me to accompany her, which I did, and no sooner was she in one of the coaches, ready to start, than I suddenly pulled up the window, and at this previously concerted signal, we were immediately surrounded by the police. The husband and wife were tried at the assizes, and, as may be easily conceived, were overwhelmed beneath the weight of an accusation, in support of which there existed a formidable mass of convincing testimony.

Some persons may perhaps blame the expedient to which I had recourse in order to free Paris from a receiver of stolen property, who had been for a long time a positive nuisance to the capital. Whether it be approved of or not, I have at least the consciousness of having done my duty; besides, when we wish to overreach scoundrels who are at open war with society every stratagem is allowable by which to affect their conviction, except endeavoring to provoke the commission of crime.

CHAPTER XXV

NEARLY ABOUT THE SAME TIME IN WHICH THE event mentioned in the last chapter occurred, a gang had formed itself in the Faubourg St. Germain, which was, more particularly, the scene of its exploits. It was composed of individuals who acted under the guidance of a captain named Gueuvive, alias Constantin, shortened by abbreviation into Antin; for the same custom exists amongst thieves as amongst bullies, spies, and informers, of being called only by the last syllable of the Christian name.

Gueuvive, or Antin, was a fencing master, who after having served as bully to the lowest prostitutes, and for the humblest wages, was competing in his present character the many vicissitudes of his ill-spent life. It was well known that he was capable of any action, however bad, and although murder had never been proved against him, yet few doubted his willingness to shed blood, if by so doing he could reap the most trifling advantage. His mistress had been murdered in the Champs Élysées, and suspicions were strongly directed against him as the author of the crime. However this may be, Gueuvive was a man of enterprising character, extreme boldness, and possessed of the most unblushing effrontery; at least, this was the estimate formed of him by his companions, amongst whom he enjoyed a more than common celebrity.

For some time, the attention of the police had been directed to this man and his associates, but without being enabled to secure any of them, although each day teemed with fresh accounts of their continued attacks upon the property of the citizens of Paris. At length it was seriously resolved to put an end to the misdeeds of these plunderers, and I received, in consequence, orders to go in search of them, and to endeavor to take them in the very fact. I accordingly provided myself with a suitable disguise, and that every evening opened the campaign in the Faubourg St. Germain, frequenting every place of ill-fame in it.

About midnight, I went to the house of a person named Boucher, in the Rue Neuve Guillemain, where I took a glass of brandy with some common girls; and whilst sitting with them, I heard the name of Constantin pronounced at the table adjoining mine. I at first imagined he was present; but upon cautiously questioning one of the girls, she assured me he was not; although, added she, "he seldom fails being here every day to meet his numerous friends." From the tone in which she spoke I fancied I could perceive that she was perfectly conversant with the habits of these gentry, and in the hope of drawing further particulars from her, I invited her to sup with me. The offer was accepted, and by the time I had well plied her with liquor, she gave me the information I required, and with the more readiness, as from my dress, actions, and expressions, she had set me down in her own mind as one of the light-fingered brethren. We passed a part of the night together, and I did not quit her till she had fully explained to me the different haunts of Gueuvive.

The next day, at twelve o'clock, I repaired to the house of Boucher, where I again met my companion of the preceding night. I had scarcely entered when she saw me, and immediately addressing me, cried, "Now is your time if you wish to speak with Gueuvive; he is here;" and she pointed to an individual from twenty-eight to thirty years of age, neatly dressed, although but in his waist-coat; he was about five feet six inches high, extremely good-looking, fine black hair and whiskers, regular teeth, in fact, precisely as he had been described to me. Without hesitation, I addressed him requesting he would oblige me with a little tobacco from his box. He examined me from head to foot, and inquired "if I had served in the army."

I replied that I had been in a hussar regiment, and soon, over a glass of good drink, we fell into a deep conversation upon military affairs.

Time passed while we were thus engaged, and dinner was talked of; Gueuvive declared that I should make one in a party he had been arranging, and that my company would afford him much pleasure. It was not very prob-able I should refuse: I accepted his invitation without further ceremony; and we went away together to the Barriere du Maine, where four of his friends were awaiting his arrival. We immediately sat down to the dinner-table, and as I was a stranger to all, the conversation was very guarded. However, a few cant words which occasionally escaped them, soon served to convince me that all the members of this charming society were cracksmen (thieves).

They were all very curious to hear what I did for my living; and I soon fudged a tale which satisfied them, and induced them not only to suppose I came from the country, but likewise that I was a thief on the lookout for a job. I did not explicitly state these particulars, but affecting certain peculiarities which betray the profession, I allowed them to perceive that I had great reasons for wishing to conceal my person.

The wine was not spared, and so well did it loosen every tongue, that be-fore the close of the repast, I had learned the abode of Gueuvive, as well as that of his worthy coadjutor, Joubert, and the names of many of their comrades. At the moment of our separating, I hinted that I did not exactly know where I should procure a bed, and Joubert immediately offered to give me a night's lodging with him, and conducted me to the Rue St. Jaques, where he occupied a back room on the second floor; there I shared with him the bed of his mistress, the girl Cornevin.

We conversed together for some time, and before we fell asleep, Joubert overwhelmed me with questions; his object was to sift out my present mode of existence, what papers I had about me, etc. His curiosity appeared insatiable, and in order to satisfy it, I contrived either by a positive falsehood, or an equiv-ocation, to lead him to suppose me a brother thief. At last, as if he had guessed my meaning, he exclaimed, "Come, do not beat about the bush any longer; I see how it is, you know you are a prig." I feigned not to understand these words; he repeated them; and I, affecting to take offense, assured him that he was greatly mistaken, and that if he indulged in similar jokes, I should be compelled to withdraw from his company. Joubert was silenced, and nothing further was said till the next day at ten o'clock, when Gueuvive came to awaken us.

It was agreed that we should go and dine at La Glaciere. On the road Gueuvive took me aside and said, "Hark ye, I see you are a good fellow, and I am willing to do you a service if I can; do not be so reserved then, but tell me who and what you are." Some hint I had purposely thrown out having induced him to believe that I had escaped from the Bagne at Toulon, he recommended me to observe a cautious prudence with my companions, "for though they are the best creatures living," said he, "yet they are rather fond of chattering."— "Oh," replied I, "I shall keep a sharp lookout, I promise you; besides, Paris will never do for me, I must be off; there are too many sneaking informers about for me to be safe in it."—"That's true," added he, "but if you can keep Vidocq from guessing at your business, you are safe enough with me, who can smell those beggars as easily as a crow scents powder."—

"Well," said I, "I cannot boast of so much penetration, yet I think, too, that from the frequent description I have heard of this Vidocq, his features are so well engraved in my recollection, that I should pretty soon recognize him, if I came unexpectedly in his way."—"God bless you!" cried he, "it is easy to perceive you are a stranger to the vagabond: just imagine now, that he is never to be seen twice in the same dress; that he is in the morning perhaps just such another looking person as you; well, the next hour so altered, that his own brother could not recognize him; and by the evening, I defy any man to remember ever having seen him before. Only yesterday, I met him disguised in a manner that would have deceived any eye but mine, but he must be a deep hand if he gets over me; I know these sneaks at the first glance, and if my friends were as knowing as myself, his business would have been done long ago."—"Nonsense," cried I, "everybody says the same thing of him, and yet you see there is no getting rid of him."—"You are right," replied he, "but to prove that I can act as well as talk, if you will lend me a helping hand, this very evening we will waylay him at his door, and I'll warrant we'll settle the job, so as to keep him from giving any of us further uneasiness."

I felt curious to learn whether he really was acquainted with my residence, and promised readily to join his scheme, and accordingly, about the dusk of the evening, we each tied up in handkerchiefs a number of heavy ten-sous pieces, in order to administer to this scamp of a Vidocq a few effectual blows the moment he should issue from his house. Having fastened the money in a hard knot at the corner of our handkerchiefs, we set out, and Constantin, who seemed just in the humor for the task he had undertaken, led the way to the Rue Neuve St. Francois, and stopped before a house, No. 14,—my exact abode. I could not conceive how he had procured my address, and must confess the circumstance gave me great uneasiness, whilst it redoubled my wonder that being so well acquainted with my dwelling, he should appear to have so little knowledge of my person. We kept watch for several hours, but Vidocq, as may be well imagined, did not make his appearance. Constantin was nighly enraged at this disappointment. "We must give it up for tonight," said he at length, "but the first time I meet the rascal, by heavens, he shall pay doubly for keeping me waiting now!"

At midnight we retired, putting off the execution of our project till the ensuing night. It was amusing enough to see me thus assisting in laying an ambuscade for myself to be caught in. The readiness with which I embarked in the scene quite won the goodwill of Constantin, who, from this moment, treated me with the greatest confidence; he even invited me to make one in a projected plan for robbing a house in the Rue Cassette. I agreed to join the party, but declared that I neither could nor would venture out in the night without first going home for the necessary papers which would serve me in case of our scheme failing, and our getting into the hands of the police. "In that case," replied he, "you may as well just keep watch for us, whilst we do the job." At length the robbery took place, and as the night was excessively dark, Constantin and his companions wishing to hurry faster than the absence of all light permitted them, had the boldness to take down a lamp from before a door, and to carry it before them. Upon their return home, this watch light was placed in the middle of the room, whilst they seated themselves around it to examine and divide their booty. In the midst of their exultation at the rich results of their expedition, a sudden knocking was heard at the door; the robbers, surprised and alarmed, looked at each other in silent dread. This was a surprise for which they were indebted to me. Again the knocking was heard. Constantin then by a sign commanding silence, said in a whisper, "'The police; I am sure of it." Amidst the confusion occasioned by these words, and the increased knocking at the gate, I contrived, unobserved, to crawl under a bed, where I had scarcely concealed myself, when the door was burst open, and a swarm of inspectors and other officers of the police entered the room. A general search took place, even the bed where the mistress of Joubert slept did not escape: they stuck their sticks both over and under the bed which served as my hiding place without discovering me, but that, of course, I was prepared for.

The commissioner of the police drew up a procés-verbal, an inventory of the stolen property, and it was packed off with the five thieves to the prefecture. This operation completed, I quit my hiding place, and found myself alone with the girl Cornevin, who was all astonishment at my good fortune, the reason of which she was far from suspecting. She urged me to remain where I was." What are you thinking of?" said I. "Suppose the police return! No, no! let me get away now the coast is clear, and I promise to join you at l'Estrapade." I sought my own house to procure the repose I so greatly needed, and at the hour agreed on, went to fulfill my appointment with Cornevin, who was expecting me. It was on her I depended to procure a complete list of all the friends and associates of Joubert and Constantin; and as I stood rather high in her good graces, she soon furnished me with the desired information; so that in less than a fortnight, thanks to an auxiliary, I contrived to introduce amongst the gang, I succeeded in causing them to be arrested in the very commission of their crimes. There were eighteen in all, who, with Constantin, were condemned to the galleys.

At the moment when the chain to which they belonged was about to set out, Constantin having perceived me, became perfectly furious, and broke out into the most violent imprecations and invectives; but, without feeling any offense at his gross and vulgar appellations, I contented myself with approaching him and saying coolly, "that it was very surprising how a man like him, who knew Vidocq, and could boast of the precious faculty of 'smelling out an informer as far off as a crow scents powder,' should have allowed himself to be done in that manner." This was a knockdown blow to Constantin; he could make no reply, but with an air of sullen confusion, turned away from me and was silent.

Chapter XXVI

I WAS NOT THE ONLY SECRET AGENT OF THE POLICE; a Jew named Gaffré was my coadjutor; he had been employed before me by the police, but as our principles did not agree, we did not long go on with harmony together.

Gaffré was the only secret agent with a salary. I was no sooner united with him than he tried to get rid of me; I pretended not to see through his intention, and if he contemplated my destruction, I resolved, on my side, to defeat his plans. I had a dangerous game to play: Gaffré was wily as a snake. When I knew him he was called the high-priest of thieves. He had begun at eight years of age; at eighteen he was whipped and marked on the place du Vieux-Marche, at Rouen. His mother, who was mistress of the famous Flambard, chief of the police in that city, had endeavored to save him; but although one of the handsomest Jewesses of her time, the magistrates would grant nothing to her charms; Gaffré was too capable; Venus in person could not have prevailed upon · his judges. He was banished. However, he did not quit France, and when the revolution burst forth, he was not slow in assuming the old course of his exploits in a band of chauffeurs, amongst whom he figured under the name of Caille.

Like the majority of his confederates, Gaffré had completed his education in the prisons, and then he had become a universal genius, that is to say, there was no species of gigging in which he was not fully expert. Contrary to custom, he adopted no special or particular line of conduct; he was essentially the man of the moment; nothing came amiss to him from cutting a windpipe to drawing a wipe (assassination to pocket-picking). This general aptitude, this variety of contrivance, had enabled him to amass a small sum. He had, as they say, shot in the locker, and could live without working; but people of Gaffré's profession are industrious, and although he was liberally paid by the police, he kept on adding to his accumulations the produce of some unlawful exactions, which did not prevent him from being much considered in his quarter, when, with his acolyte Francfort, another Jew, he had been named captain of the national guards.

Gaffré was afraid that I should supplant him, but the old fox was not cunning enough to hide his apprehensions; I watched him, and was not slow in discovering that he was maneuvering to get me into a snare. I appeared to be blindly led by him, and he chuckled internally at his anticipated victory; when, wishing to catch me in a plot which I saw through, he was himself taken in the net, and in the end shut up for eight months in the depot.

I never allowed Gaffré to surmise that I had suspected treachery, and he continued to dissemble the hatred which he bore toward me, and that so well, that we were apparently the best friends in the world. I was on the same terms with many robbers who were secret agents, and with whom I had associated during my detention. These latter detested me heartily, and although we kept smiling countenances toward each other, they flattered themselves that they should pay me off some day. Goupil, the Saint George of pugilism, was amongst those who afforded me their friendship, and, constantly attached to my person, filled the office of tempter; but he was not more fortunate nor more adroit than Gaffre. Compere, Manigant, Corvet, Bouthey, Leloutre, also tried to catch me tripping: but I was invulnerable, thanks to the advice of M. Henry.

Gaffré having recovered his liberty, did not renounce his design of ruining me. With Manigant and Compere he plotted to get me condemned; but persuaded that having once defeated him he would not leave me, but return to the charge with vigor, I was incessantly on my guard. I awaited him firmly, when one day that a religious solemnity had attracted a vast crowd to Saint Roch, he announced to me that he had orders to attend there with me. "I shall take Compere and Manigant with us," he added, "as we learn that at this moment there are many strange robbers in Paris, and they will point out to us all they know." "Take whom you please," I answered, and we set out. When we reached our destination, there was a considerable crowd; the service we were upon did not require that we should all unite at one point. Manigant and Gaffre went first. Suddenly, in the place they were, I remarked an old man, who, by being pressed against a pillar, did not know where to put his head; he did not cry out, from respect to the sacred place, but his whole person was disarranged and his wig knocked awry: he lost his footing; his hat, which fell off, and which he anxiously followed with his eyes, was rolled from place to place, sometimes from and sometimes toward him. "Gentlemen, I beseech you, I beg of you," were the only words which he pronounced in a most piteous tone; and, holding in one hand a gold-headed cane and in the other his snuff-box and pocket-handkerchief, he shook his hands in the air, as if he would have reached the ceiling with them. I found he had lost his watch, but what could I do? I was too far distant from the old gentleman; besides my advice would be too late; and then Gaffré, was he not also witness of the scene? and although he said nothing, he doubtless had some motive for it. I adopted the wisest plan, and was silent to see what would ensue, and during the space of two hours, the duration of the ceremony, I had an opportunity of observing five or six of these concerted squeezes, and saw Gaffré and Manigant always in them. The latter, who has since undergone a confinement of twelve years in the Bagne at Brest, was at this period the most expert pickpocket in the capital; he excelled in extracting the money from a person's pocket and transferring it into his own; with him the transmutation of metals was reduced to a simple displacing, which he effected with incredible talent.

The short stay in the church of St. Roch was not particularly productive; however, without including the old man's watch, he had stolen two purses and some other articles of value.

After the ceremony had terminated, we went to dine at a coffee-house; the worthies paid the expenses, and nothing was spared; we drank deeply, and at the dessert they confided to me what I could not fail to have known. At first, they only mentioned the purses, in which they found a hundred and seventy-five francs in hard cash. The bill paid, there remained a surplus of one hundred francs, of which they handed me over twenty as my portion, counseling me to be silent and discreet. As money has no name, I thought there was no reason for a refusal.

The party appeared enchanted at having thus initiated me, and two flasks of Beaune were emptied to celebrate the occasion. No mention was made of the watch, nor did I allude to it; not only that I might appear ignorant of it, but I was also all eyes and ears, and was not slow in learning that it was in Gaffre's possession. I then began to assume the appearance of a drunken man, and shamming a call of necessity, I desired the waiter to lead me where I wished to go. He conducted me out, and when alone I wrote with a pencil this note:—

"Gaffré and Manigant have just stolen a watch in the church of Saint Roch; in an hour, unless they change their intention, they will cross the market of St. Jean. Gaffré carries the spoil."

I hastily descended, and whilst Gaffré and his confederate thought me engaged up five flights of stairs, I got into the street, and dispatched a messenger to M. Henry. I went back again without loss of time, and my absence had not been of long duration. When I entered I was out of breath, and as red as a turkey cock. They asked me if I felt better.

"Yes, a great deal," I stammered out, and falling nearly under the table.

"Steady, boys, steady," said Manigant.

"He sees double," observed Gaffré.

"He is done up," added Compere, "quite done up, but the air will revive him."

They gave me some sugar and water. "Go to," I cried out. "What! water for me, water for me!"

"Yes, it will do you good."

"Do you think so?"

I extended my hand, but instead of seizing the glass, I upset and broke it. I then played a few silly drunken tricks, which amused the party, and when I judged that M. Henry had received my dispatch, and taken measures accordingly, I insensibly came to myself.

On going out, I saw with pleasure that our route was not changed. We went towards the market of St. Jean, and there saw a file of soldiers. When I saw them sitting at the door, I did not doubt but that they were there in consequence of my message, and the less so as I observed Menager the inspector following us. When we passed they approached us, and, taking us politely by the arm, invited us to enter the guardhouse. Gaffré could not imagine what this meant, but supposed the soldiers were in error. He wished to argue the point. They desired him to obey, and he was compelled quietly to submit. They began with me, but found nothing; when they came to Gaffré's turn he was not at all easy. At length the fatal watch was produced from his fob: he was a little disconcerted but at the moment of his examination, and particularly when he heard the commissary say, "Write: a watch set with brilliants," he turned pale and looked at me. Had he any suspicion of what had passed? I do not think so, for he was convinced that I did not know of the robbery of the watch; and besides, he was sure that, if I had known it, as I had not left them, I could not have turned nose.

Gaffré, on being questioned, pretended that he had bought the watch: they were persuaded that this was a lie, but the person who was robbed not being present to claim his property, it was not possible to condemn him. He was, however, confined for a time in Bicêtre, and then sent under surveillance to Tours, whence at a later period he returned to Paris. This villain died there in 1822.

At this period, the police had so little confidence in their agents, that there was no kind of expedient to which they had not recourse to prove them. One day Goupil was let loose upon me, and came with a singular proposal.

"You know Francois, the publican," said he to me.

"Yes, and what of that?"

"If you will help me, we will draw a tooth or two from him."

"How?"

"Why he has very frequently addressed the prefecture, to obtain permission to keep open house during part of the night, which request has always been denied; and I have given him to understand that it only depends upon you to procure what he is so anxious to have."

"You are wrong, for I can do nothing."

"You can do nothing! Very true, certainly! Oh you can do nothing, but you can buoy him up with the hope that you can do it."

"That is true, but wherein would be the benefit to him?"

"Say the benefit to us. Francois, if well managed, would bleed well. He is already told that you are the man who is 'all in all' in the administration; he has a good opinion of you, and so no doubt he will tip freely on the first requisition."

"Do you think he will part with the blunt?"

"I am sure, my boy, he will shell out six hundred francs as easily as a penny; we shall handle the ready, that is the main thing, and we can afterward leave him to his reflections."

"Well, but he will be enraged."

"Never mind, let him do his worst; but give yourself no trouble, I will provide for all. No black and white work (writing) mind; you know the proverb, 'Writings are men, words but women.'"

"True as gospel; no receipt for cash in hand, and yet we can safely pocket."

"Certainly, he who sows should reap: and no labor no profit. Meanwhile I will go and see how the land lies, and sound the old boy."

Goupil then took my hand, and shaking it heartily, he added, "I am now going straight to Francois, I will tell him you will call in the evening; I shall fix the hour for eight o'clock, but do not come till eleven, because (as you must say) you will have been delayed; at midnight we shall be told to go out, you must appear to comply with this formality, and Francois will seize the opportunity of urging his request. You are a man of experience, and know how to play your cards. Farewell for the present."

"Adieu," I replied, and we separated. Scarcely, however, had we turned our backs on each other than Goupil returned.

"Oh!" said he, "you know that very frequently the feathers are more valuable than the bird; I want a pluck at the feathers, otherwise" and he assumed a peculiar attitude, opening his enormous mouth, holding his hands about six inches from the ground, as if he was about to scrape the pavement, and completing the menace by drawing back his body and advancing his legs, in which the mobility of his feet were not the least comical part of his attitude.

"All's right," said I to Goupil, "you shall not swallow me. We will divide,—it is a bargain."

"On the word of a thief."

"Yes, make yourself easy."

Goupil immediately took the road to Courtille, where he very frequently went, and I that of the prefecture of police, when I informed M. Henry of the proposals made to me. "I hope," said he, "that you will not lend yourself to the plot." I protested that I was not at all inclined to do so, and he evinced his pleasure at my free communication. "Now," he added, "I will give you a proof of the interest that I take in you;" and he arose to reach from his chest a packet of papers, which he opened. "You see it is full, and they are all reports against you: they are in abundance, but yet I employ you, because I do not believe one word of what they say."

Gaffre and Goupil having failed in their plans for my destruction, Corvet resolved to try his success in the same way. One morning when I was in want of some particular information, I went to the house of this agent, whose wife was also attached to the police. I found both man and wife at their lodging, and although I only knew them from having once or twice co-operated with them in some unimportant discoveries, they gave me the information I required with so much goodwill, that, like a man who has the feelings of good fellowship toward those with whom he has associated, I offered to regale them with a bottle of wine at the nearest cabaret. Corvet alone accepted the proffer, and we went together and seated ourselves in a private room.

The wine was excellent; we drank one, two, three bottles. A private room and three bottles of wine led on to confidence. About an hour afterward, I thought I perceived that Corvet had some proposal to make, and at length he somewhat suddenly said, "Listen, Vidocq (and he knocked his glass on the table with some emphasis,) you are a jolly lad, but you are not open amongst friends; we know well enough that you are a fellow workman, but you're a deep file: we two might do a fine stroke of business."

I pretended not to comprehend him.

"Nonsense, come, come," he replied, "no gammon, that will not go down with me, I know you are a cunning fellow; although I don't know your place of work, I will speak to you as I would to my own brother, if I think I may depend upon you. It is all very well to serve the police, but there is nothing to be made out of it, and a crown changed is a crown spent and gone. Now if you will keep counsel, there is a job or two which I have in my eye which we will do together, and which will not hinder us from doing our friends a good turn."

"How," said I, "would you abuse the confidence placed in you? That is not right, and I am sure that if it were known at the prefecture, they would give you two or three years of it at Bicêtre."

"Ah! you are like all the rest," replied Corvet, "you are going to be mealy-mouthed and squeamish; you are delicate, are you? Come, come, we know one another."

I testified much astonishment at his holding such language to me, and added that I was fully persuaded that he only said so to try me, or perhaps lay a snare for me.

"A snare!" cried he, "a snare to bring you into trouble, I had rather put my own neck in jeopardy; you must be mad to suppose it. I do not beat about the bush; when I say anything, it is blunt and straightforward; with me there is no back door; and as a proof that all is not as you believe, I will tell you that no later than this evening I am going to work. I have already laid my plan, the keys are made, and if you will come with me, you shall see how I will do the job."

"I doubt you have either lost your senses, or you wish to entangle me in your net."

"What, do you not give me any credit for better feelings? (Elevating his voice.) I tell you then you shall not have a finger in the pie. What more would you have? I shall take my wife with me, it will not be the first time, but it will be the last if you choose to make it so. With two men there is always a resource at hand. The business of today regards you nothing; you will wait for us in the coffee house at the corner of the Rue de la Tabletterie. It is almost facing where we are going to work, and as soon as you see us come out, do you follow; we will sell the booty, and we will go snacks. After that you will no longer distrust us. What think you?"

There was so much appearance of sincerity in this discourse, that I really hardly knew how to act with Corvet. Did he want an accomplice, or did he seek a means of destroying me? I have still my doubts on this point; but in either case Corvet was a manifest rogue.

By his own confession, his wife and he committed robberies. If he had spoken the truth, it was my duty to deliver him up to justice; if on the contrary, he had lied, in the hope of entrapping me into a criminal action to denounce me, it was only right to prosecute the plot to its termination, that I might show to the authorities that to tempt me was labor in vain.

I had endeavored to dissuade Corvet from his design, but when I saw that he persisted, I feigned to allow myself to be seduced.

"Well then," I said, "since it must be so, I accept the proposal."

He instantly embraced me, and the rendezvous was fixed for four o'clock, at a vintner's. Corvet returned home, and as soon as he had left me I wrote to M. Allemain, commissary of police in the Rue Cimetiere St. Nicholas, to inform him of the robbery which was to be perpetrated in the evening. I gave him, at the same time, all the necessary information for seizing on the culprits in the very commission of their crime.

I was at my post at the agreed hour; Corvet and his wife were not long after me, and after drinking a bottle or two of wine to cheer them in their work they proceeded on their enterprise. A moment afterward, and I saw them enter a courtyard in the Rue de la Haumerie. The commissary had so well contrived that he apprehended the two at the moment, when laden with booty, they left the apartment they had ransacked. This couple were condemned to ten years' confinement.

During the trial Corvet and his wife asserted that I had tempted them to the robbery. Certainly in the line I had pursued, there was nothing that could be construed into such a temptation; besides in a robbery I do not see how there can be any provocation possible. A man is honest or he is not: if he be honest, no consideration can be sufficiently powerful to determine him on committing a crime: if he be not, he only wants the opportunity, and is it not evident that it will offer itself sooner or later?

Chapter XXVII

IN 1810, ROBBERIES OF A NEW KIND AND inconceivable boldness suddenly awakened the police to the knowledge of the existence of a troop of malefactors of a novel description.

Nearly all the robberies had been committed by ladders and forcible entries; apartments on the first and even second floor had been broken into by these extraordinary thieves, who, till then, had confined themselves to rich houses; and it was evident that these robbers must have had a knowledge of the localities, by the method of their burglaries.

All my efforts to discover these adroit thieves were without success, when a burglary, which seemed almost impracticable, was committed in the Rue Saint-Claude, near the Rue Bourbon-Villeneuve, in an apartment on the second floor above the "entresol," in a house in which the commissary of police for the district actually resided. The cord of the lantern which hung at his house-door had served for a ladder.

A nose-bag (a small bag in which corn is put for horses to feed from when on the coach-stand) had been left on the spot, which gave rise to a surmise that the perpetrators might be hackney-coachmen, or at least that hackney-coaches had been employed in the enterprise.

M. Henry directed me to make my observations amongst the coachmen, and I discovered that the nose-bag had belonged to a man named Husson, who drove the fiacre No. 712. I reported this: Hasson was apprehended, and from him we obtained information concerning two brothers, named Delzeve, the elder of whom was soon in the hands of the police; and on his interrogation by M. Henry, he made such important discoveries as led to the apprehension of one Metral, a room-cleaner in the palace of the Empress Josephine. He was stated to be the receiver of the band, composed almost entirely of Savoyards, born in the department of Leman. The continuation of my search led to my securing them all, twenty-two in number, who were subsequently condemned to imprisonment.

These robbers were for the greater part messengers, room-cleaners, or coachmen; that is, they belonged to a class of individuals proverbial for honesty, and who from time immemorial had been celebrated for probity throughout Paris; in their district they were all considered as honest men, incapable of appropriating to themselves the property of another; and this opinion contributed to render them the more formidable, as the persons who employed them, either in sawing wood or in any other kind of work, had no distrust of them, and gave them free ingress and egress everywhere, and at all times. When it was known that they were implicated in a criminal affair, they were not believed to be guilty; and I myself, for some time, hesitated in my opinion. However, evidence was adduced which was against them, and the ancient renown of the

Savoyards, in a capital in which they had resided unsuspected for ages, was blasted never again to flourish.

During the year 1812 I had rendered to justice the principals of the band; but Delzéve, the younger, had baffled all efforts to capture him, and bid defiance to the pursuits of justice, when, on the 31st of December, M. Henry said to me, "I think, if we manage well, we can get hold of the crab Ecrevisse (Delzéve's cognomen); tomorrow will be new year's day, and he will be sure to visit the washerwoman, who has so often given him an asylum, as well as his brother; I have a presentiment that he will be there this evening, or during the night, or certainly early in the morning."

I was of the same opinion; and M. Henry ordered me to go with three officers, and place ourselves on the watch near the washerwoman's house, who lived in the Rue de Gresillon.

I received this command with a satisfaction which is always with me a presage of good luck. Attended by the three inspectors, I went, at seven o'clock in the evening, to the appointed spot. It was bitterly cold, the ground covered with snow, and never had winter been more severe.

We stationed ourselves in ambuscade; and, after many hours, the inspectors, nipped with cold, and unable any longer to endure it, proposed that we should quit our station. I was half-frozen, having no covering but the light garment of a messenger. I made some remarks to them; and, although it would have been infinitely more agreeable to me to have retired, we determined to remain till midnight. Scarcely had the hour agreed upon struck, than they claimed of me the fulfillment of my promise, and we quitted our post, which we had been ordered to keep till daybreak.

We went toward the Palais Royal; a coffee house was open, which we entered to warm ourselves, and having taken a bowl of hot wine we separated, each to go to his own home. As I went toward mine, I reflected on what I was doing.— "What!" said I to myself, "so soon forget instructions which have been given to me; thus to deceive the confidence of my superior; it is an unpardonable baseness! My conduct not only seems reprehensible, but I think that it even deserves the most severe punishment." I was in despair at having complied with the wishes of the inspectors; and resolute in repairing my fault, determined to return alone to the post assigned and pass the night there, even if I died on the spot. I then returned and ensconced myself in a corner, that I might not be seen by Delzéve, in case he should come.

For an hour and a half I remained in this position, until my blood congealed, and I felt my courage weakening, when suddenly a luminous idea shone upon me. At a short distance was a dunghill, whose smoke betrayed a state of fermentation: this depot is called the lay-stall: I ran toward it; and having made a hole in one corner, sufficiently deep to admit me up to my waist, I jumped into it, and a comfortable warmth soon re-established the circulation of my blood. At five in the morning, I was still in my lurking place, where I did very well, except from the fumes which invaded my nostrils. At length the door of the house, which was the one pointed out to me, opened to let out a woman, who did not shut it after her. Instantly, and without noise, I leaped from the dung heap and entering the court looked about me, but saw no light from any part.

I knew that Delzéve's associates had a peculiar way of whistling for him; it was the coachman's whistle, and known to me; I imitated it; and, at the second attempt, I heard someone exclaim, "Who calls?"

"It is the 'chauffeur' (a coachman from whom Delzéve had learnt to drive) who whistles for the crab."

"Is it you?" cried the same voice, which I knew to be Delzéve's.

"Yes; the chauffeur wants you. Come down."

"I am coming—wait a minute."

"It is very cold," I replied; "I will wait for you at the public-house at the corner; make haste—do you hear?"

The public-house was already open; for on new year's day, they have custom betimes. But I was not tempted to drink; and that I might trap Delzéve, I opened the side door, and then letting it shut with violence, without actually going out, I concealed myself under a flight of steps. Soon afterward Delzéve came down, and on perceiving him I jumped at him, seized his collar, and holding a pistol to his breast, told him he was my prisoner. "Follow me," I said, "and make the slightest signal at your peril; besides, I am not alone."

Dumb with surprise, Delzéve made no answer, but followed me mechanically. I fastened his hands, and he was then incapacitated from either resisting or flying from me.

I hastened to convey him away, and the clock struck six as we entered the Rue du Rocher; a hackney coach was passing, which I hailed, but the man seeing me covered with dirt, hesitated, until I offered him double hire; and led by that he condescended to take us up, and we were soon rolling over the pavement of Paris. To make assurance doubly sure, I tightened the wrist-cuffs, lest, having come to himself, he might have rebelled; and although, in a personal conflict, I should have been sure of victory, yet, as I contemplated bringing him to confession, I was unwilling to have any quarrel; and blows, which would have been inevitably the result of rebellion, would decidedly have produced this result.

Delzéve felt aware of the impossibility of escape, and I endeavored to make him hear reason; that I might completely wheedle him, I offered him some refreshment, which he accepted; and the coachman having procured as some wine, we kept driving about and drinking without any determined plan.

It was still early, and persuaded that it would be advantageous to prolong our tête-à-tête, I proposed to Delzéve, that we should go and breakfast in a place where we could have a private room. He was then quieted; and appearing hopeless of escape, accepted my offer, and I took him to the Cadran Bleu; but before we got there he had already told me many pieces of important information as to the number of his accomplices still at large in Paris; and I felt convinced that, at table, he would make a "clean breast of it." I made him understand that the only way to propitiate the favor of justice was to confess all he knew; and to fortify his resolution in this case, I used some arguments of a peculiar philosophy, which I have always employed with success in consoling criminals; and at length, he was perfectly disposed to do all I wished, when the coach reached the cook-shop. I made him go upstairs first, and when I had ordered the breakfast, I told him that, being desirous of eating my meal at my ease, I must confine him as I wished. I agreed that he should be left sufficiently unshackled to exercise his arms at the game of knife and fork; and at table, no one could desire greater freedom. He was not at all offended at the proposition, and I thus contrived it:—with two napkins I tied each leg to the foot of his chair, three or four inches from the bar, which prevented him from attempting to rise without the risk of breaking his head by a fall.

He breakfasted with much appetite, and promised to repeat before M. Henry, all that he had confessed to me. At noon we left the café, Delzéve being well primed with wine, and getting into a coach, quite friends and on good terms with each other, we reached the prefecture ten minutes afterward. M. Henry was then surrounded by his police officers, who were paying him the compliments of the new year's day. I entered and addressed this salutation to him:—"I have the honor to wish you a happy and prosperous year, and to present to you the redoubtable Delzéve."

"This is, indeed, a new year's gift," said M. Henry to me, when he perceived the prisoner, and then turning to the officers of peace and security: "It would be a desirable thing, gentlemen, that each of you should have a similar present to offer to your prefet." Immediately afterward he gave me the order for conducting Delzéve to the depot, saying, with much kindness, "Vidocq, go and take some repose; I am much satisfied with your conduct."

Chapter XXVIII

IT IS VERY RARE THAT A FUGITIVE GALLEY SLAVE escapes with any attention of amendment; most frequently the aim is to gain the captive, and then put in practice the vicious lessons acquired at the Bagnes, which, like most of our prisons, are schools in which they perfect themselves in the art of appropriating to themselves the property of another. Nearly all celebrated robbers only became expert after passing some time at the galleys. Some have undergone five or six sentences before they became thorough scoundrels; such as the famous Victor Desbois, and his comrade Mongenet, called Le Tambour (Drummer,) who, during various visits to Paris committed a vast many of those robberies on which people love to descant as proofs of boldness and address.

These two men, who for many years were sent away with every chain, and as frequently escaped, were once more back again in Paris; the police got information of it, and I received the orders to search for them. All testified that they had acquaintances with other robbers no less formidable than themselves. A music mistress, whose son, called Noel with the Spectacles, a celebrated robber, was suspected of harboring these thieves. Madame Noel was a well-educated woman and an admirable musician; she was esteemed a most accomplished performer by the middle class of tradespeople, who employed her to give lessons to their daughters. She was well known in the Marias and the Quartier Saint Denis, where the polish of her manners, the elegance of her language, the gentility of her dress, and that indescribable air of superiority which the reverses of fortune can never entirely destroy, gave rise to the current belief that she was a member of one of those numerous families to whom the Revolution had only left its hauteur and its regrets.

To those who heard and saw her without being acquainted, Madame Noel was a most interesting little woman; and besides, there was something touching in her situation; it was a mystery, and no one knew what had become of her husband. Some said that she had been early left in a state of widowhood; others that she had been forsaken; and a third affirmed that she was a victim of seduction. I know not which of these conjectures approaches nearest the truth, but I know very well that Madame Noel was a little brunette, whose sparkling eye and roguish look were softened down by that gentle demeanor which seemed to increase the sweetness of her smile and the tone of her voice, which was in the highest degree musical. There was a mixture of the angel and demon in her face, but the latter perhaps preponderated; for time had developed those traits which characterize evil thoughts.

Madame Noel was obliging and good, but only toward those individuals who were at issue with justice; she received them as the mother of a soldier would welcome the comrade of her son. To insure a welcome with her, it was enough to belong to the same "regiment" as Noel with the Spectacles; and then, as much for love of him and from inclination perhaps, she would do all in her power to aid, and was consequently looked upon as a "mother of robbers." At her house they found shelter; it was she who provided for all their wants; she carried her complaisance so far as to seek "jobs of work" for them; and when a passport was indispensably requisite for their safety, she was not quiet until by some means she had succeeded in procuring one. Madame Noel had many friends among her own sex, and it was generally in one of their names that the passport was obtained. A powerful mixture of oxygenated muriatic acid obliterated the writing; and the description of the gentleman who required it, as well as the name which it suited his purpose to assume, replaced the feminine description. Madame Noel had generally by her a supply of these accommodating passports, which were filled according to circumstances, and the wants of the party requiring such assistance.

All the galley slaves were children of Madame Noel, but those were the most in favor who could give her any account of her son; for them her devotion was boundless; her house was open to all fugitives, who made it their rendezvous; and there must be gratitude even amongst them, for the police were informed that they came frequently to Mother Noel's for the pleasure of seeing her only; she was the confidante of all their plans, all their adventures, all their fears; in fact, they communicated all unreservedly, and never had cause to regret their reliance on her fidelity.

Mother Noel had never seen me; my features were quite unknown to her, although she had frequently heard of my name. There was then no difficulty in presenting myself before her, without giving her any cause for alarm; but to get her to point out to me the hiding place of the men whom I sought to detect, was the end I aimed at, and I felt that it would be impossible to attain it without much skill and management.

At first, I resolved on passing myself off as a fugitive galley slave; but it was necessary to borrow the name of some thief, whom her son or his comrades had mentioned to her in advantageous terms. Moreover, a little resemblance was positively requisite, and I endeavored to recollect if there were not one of the galley slaves whom I knew had been associated with Noel with the Spectacles, and I could not remember one of my age, or whose person and features at all resembled mine. At last, by dint of much effort of memory, I recalled to mind one Germain, alias "the Captain," who had been an intimate acquaintance of Noel's, and although our similarity was very slight, yet I determined on personating him. Germain, as well as myself, had often escaped from the Bagnes, and that was the only point of resemblance between us: he was about my age, but a smaller-framed man; he had dark brown hair, mine was light; he was thin, and I tolerably stout; his complexion was sallow, and mine, fair, with a very clear skin; besides, Germain had an excessively long nose, took a vast deal of snuff which, begriming his nostrils outside, and stuffing them up within, gave him a peculiarly nasal tone of voice. I had much to do in personating Germain; but the difficulty did not deter me; my hair, cut a la mode des bagnes, was dyed black, as well as my beard, after it had attained a growth of eight days; to embrown my countenance I washed it with white walnut liquor; and to perfect the imitation, I garnished my upper lip thickly with a kind of coffee-grounds, which I plastered on by means of gum arabic, and thus became as nasal in my twang as Germain himself. My feet were doctored with equal care; I made blisters on them by rubbing in a certain composition, of which I had obtained the receipt at Brest. I also made the marks of the fetters; and when all my toilet was finished, dressed myself in the suitable garb. I had neglected nothing which could complete the metamorphosis;— neither the shoes nor the marks of those horrid letters GAL. The costume was perfect; and the only thing wanting was a hundred of those companionable insects which people the solitudes of poverty, and which were, I believe, together with locusts and toads, one of the seven plagues of old Egypt. I procured some for money; and as soon as they were a little accustomed to their new domicile, which was speedily the case, I directed my steps toward the residence of Madame Noel, in the Rue Ticquetonne.

I arrived there, and knocking at the door, she opened it: a glance convincing her how matters stood with me, she desired me to enter, and on finding myself alone with her, I told her who I was. "Ah, my poor lad," she cried, "there is no occasion to tell me where you have come from; I am sure you must be dying with hunger!"—

"Oh yes," I answered, "I am indeed hungry; I have tasted nothing for twenty-four hours." Instantly, without further question, she went out, and returned with a dish of hog's puddings and a bottle of wine, which she placed before me. I did not eat, I actually devoured; I stuffed myself, and all had disappeared without my saying a word between my first mouthful and my last. Mother Noel was delighted at my appetite, and when the cloth was removed she gave me a dram. "Ah, mother," I exclaimed, embracing her, "you restore me to life; Noel told me how good and kind you were:" and I then began to give her a statement of how I had left her son eighteen days before, and gave her information of all the prisoners in whom she felt interested. The details were so true and well-known, that she could have no idea that I was an impostor.

"You must have heard of me," I continued; "I have gone through many an enterprise, and experienced many a reverse. I am called Germain, or the captain; you must know my name."

"Yes, yes, my friend," she said, "I know you well; my son and his friends have told me of your misfortunes; welcome, welcome, my dear captain. But heavens! what a state you are in: you must not remain in such a plight. I see you are infested with those wretched tormenting beasts, but I will get you a change of linen, and contrive something as a comfortable dress for you."

I expressed my gratitude to Madame Noel; and when I saw a good opportunity, without giving cause for the slightest suspicion, I asked what had become of Victor Desbois and his comrade Mongenet. "Desbois and Le Tambour? Ah! my dear, do not mention them, I beg of you," she replied; "that rogue Vidocq has given them very great uneasiness; since one Joseph (Joseph Longueville, an old police inspector), whom they have twice met in the streets, told them that there would soon be a search in this quarter, they have been compelled to cut and run, to avoid being taken."

"What," cried I with a disappointed air, "are they no longer in Paris?"

"Oh, they are not very far distant," replied Mother Noel; "they have not quitted the environs of the 'great village' (Paris): I dare say we shall soon see them, for I trust they will speedily pay me a visit. I think they will be delighted to find you here."

"Oh, I assure you," said I, "that they will not be more delighted at the meeting than myself; and if you can write to them, I am sure they would eagerly send for me to join them"

"If I knew where they were," replied Mother Noel, "I would go myself and seek for them to please you; but I do not know their retreat, and the best thing for us to do is to be patient and await their arrival."

In my quality of a newcomer, I excited all madame Noel's compassion and solicitude, and she attended to nothing but me. "Are you known to Vidocq and his two bull-dogs, Levesque and Compere?" she inquired.

"Alas! yes," was my reply; "they have caught me twice."

"In that case, then, be on your guard: Vidocq is often disguised; he assumes characters, costumes, and shapes to get hold of unfortunates like yourself."

We conversed together for two hours, when Madame Noel offered me a foot-bath, which I accepted; and when it was prepared, I took off my shoes and stockings, on which she discovered my wounded feet, and said, with a most commiserating tone and manner, "How I pity you; what must you suffer! Why did you not tell me of this at first? you deserve to be scolded for it. And whilst thus reproaching me, she examined my feet; and then pricking the blisters, drew a piece of worsted through each, and anointed my feet with a salve which she assured me would have the effect of speedily curing them.

The bath concluded, she brought me some clean linen; and, as she thought of all that was needful, added a razor, recommending me to shave. "I shall then see," she added, "about buying you some workman's clothes, as that is the best disguise for men who wish to pass unnoticed; and besides, good luck will turn up, and then you will get yourself some new ones."

As soon as I was thoroughly cleansed, mother Noel conducted me to a sleeping-room, a small apartment which served as the workshop for false keys, the entrance to which was concealed by several gowns hanging from a row of pegs. "Here." said she, "is a bed in which your friends have slept three or four times; and you need not fear that the police will hunt you oat; you may sleep secure as a dormouse."

"I am really in want of sleep," I replied, and begged her permission to take some repose, on which she left me to myself. Three hours afterward I awoke, and on getting up we renewed our conference. It was necessary to be armed at all points to deceive Madam Noel; there was not a trick or custom of the Bagnes with which she was not thoroughly informed; she knew not only the names of all the robbers whom she had seen, but was acquainted with every particular of the life of a great many others; and related with enthusiasm anecdotes of the most noted, particularly of her son, for whom she had as much veneration as love.

"The dear boy, you would be delighted to see him!" said I.

"Yes, yes, overjoyed."

"Well, it is a happiness you will soon enjoy; for Noel has made arrangements for an escape, and is now only awaiting the propitious moment."

Madame Noel was happy in the expectation of seeing her son, and shed tears of tenderness at the very thoughts of it.

In the course of conversation, mother Noel asked me if I had any affair (plan of robbery) in contemplation; and after having offered to procure me one, in case I was not provided, she questioned me on my skill in fabricating keys. I told her I was as adroit as Fossard. "If that be the case," she rejoined, "I am easy, and you shall be soon furnished; for as you are so clever, I will go and buy at the ironmonger's a key which you can fit to my safety lock, so that you will have ingress and egress whenever you require it."

I expressed my feelings of obligation for so great a proof of her kindness; and as it was growing late, I went to bed reflecting on the mode of getting away from this lair without running the risk of being assassinated, if perchance any of the villains whom I was seeking, should arrive before I had taken I he necessary precautions.

I did not sleep, and arose as soon as I heard Madame Noel lighting her fire; she said I was an early riser, and that she would go and procure me what I wanted. A moment afterward she brought me a key not cut into wards, and gave me files and a small vice, which I fixed on my bed; and as soon as my tools were in readiness, I began my work in presence of my hostess, who seeing that I was perfectly conversant with the business, complimented me on my skill; and what she most admired was the expedition of my work; for in fact, in less than four hours, I had perfected a most workmanlike key, which I tried, and it fitted most accurately. A few touches of the file completed the instrument; and, like the rest, I had the means of unobstructed entrance whenever I wished to visit the house.

I was Madame Noel's boarder; and, after dinner, I told her I was inclined to take a turn in the dusk, that I might find whether "a job" I contemplated was yet feasible, and she approved the suggestion, at the same time recommending me to use all caution. "That thief of a Vidocq," she observed, "is a thorn in one's path; mind him;—and, if I were you, before I made any attempts, I would wait until my feet were well." "I shall not go far," I replied; "nor stay away long." This assurance of a speedy return seemed to quiet her fears. "Well then, go," she said; and I went out limping.

So far all succeeded to my most sanguine wishes; it was impossible to stand better with mother Noel; but, by remaining in her house, who would guarantee that I should not be knocked on the head? Might not two or three galley slaves arrive together, recognize me and attack me? Then farewell to all my plottings; and it was incumbent, that, without losing the fruit of my friendship with mother Noel, I should prepare myself for the contingent danger. It would have been the height of imprudence to have given her cause to think that I had any motives for avoiding contact with her guests, and I consequently endeavored so to lead her on, that she should herself suggest to me the necessity of quitting her house; that is, that she should advise me no longer to think of sleeping in her domicile.

I had observed that Madame Noel was very intimate with a fruit-seller who lived in the house; and I sent to this woman one of my agents named Mancean, whom I charged to ask her secretly, and yet with a want of skill, for some accounts of Madame Noel. I had dictated the questions, and was the more certain that the fruit woman would not fail to communicate the particulars, as I had desired my man to beg her to observe secrecy.

The event proved that I was not deceived; no sooner had my agent fulfilled his mission, than the fruit woman hastened to Madame Noel with an account of what had passed; who, in her turn, lost no time in telling me. On the lookout at the steps of the door of her officious neighbor, as soon as she saw me, she came to me, and, without further preface, desired me to follow her, which I did; and on reaching the Place des Victoires, she stopped, and looking about her to be assured that no one was in hearing, she told me what had passed:—

"So," said she, in conclusion, "you see, my poor Germain, that it would not be prudent for you to sleep at my house; you must even be cautious how you approach it by day."

Mother Noel had no idea that this circumstance, which she bewailed so greatly, was of my own planning; and, that I might remove all suspicion from her mind, I pretended to be more vexed at it than she was, and cursed and swore bitterly at that blackguard Vidocq, who would not leave us at peace. I deprecated the necessity to which I was reduced, of finding a shelter out of Paris, and took leave of Madame Noel, who wishing me good luck and a speedy return, put a thirty-sous piece into my hand.

I knew that Desbois and Mongenet were expected; and I was also aware that there were comers and goers who visited the house, whether Madame Noel was there or not; and she was often absent, giving music lessons in the city. It was important that I should know these gentry; and to achieve this, I disguised several of my auxiliaries, and stationed them at the corners of the street, where, mixing with the errand boys and messengers, their presence excited no suspicion.

These precautions taken, that I might testify all due appearance of fear, I allowed two days to pass before I again visited Madame Noel: and this period having elapsed, I went one evening to her house, accompanied by a young man, whom I introduced as the brother of a female with whom I had once lived: and who, having met me accidentally in Paris, had given me an asylum. This young man was a secret agent, but I took care to tell Mother Nole that he had my fullest confidence, and that she might consider him as my second self: and as he was not known to the spies, I had chosen him to be my messenger to her whenever I did not judge it prudent to show myself. "Henceforward," I added, "he will be our go-between, and will come every two or three days, that I may have information of you and your friends."

"I' faith," said Mother Noel, "you have lost a pleasure; for twenty minutes sooner, and you would have seen a lady of your acquaintance here."

"Ah! Who was it?"

"Mongenet's sister."

"Oh! indeed; she has often seen me with her brother."

"Yes; when I mentioned you, she described you as exactly as possible:—'a lanky chap,' said she, 'with his nose always grimed with snuff.'"

Madame Noel deeply regretted that I had not arrived before Mongenet's sister had departed; but certainly not so much as I rejoiced at my narrow escape from an interview which would have destroyed all my projects; for if this woman knew Germain, she also knew Vidocq; and it was impossible that she could have mistaken one for the other, so great was the difference between us! Although I had altered my features so as to deceive, yet the resemblance which, in description, seemed exact, would not stand the test of a critical examination, and particularly the reminiscences of intimacy. Mother Noel then gave me a very useful warning, when she informed me that Mongenet's sister was a very frequent visitor at her house. From thenceforward I resolved that this female should never catch a glimpse of my countenance; and to avoid meeting with her, whenever I visited Madam Noel, I sent my pretended brother-in-law first, who, when she was not there, had instructions to let me know it, by sticking a wafer on the window At this signal I entered, and my aide-de-camp betook himself to his post in the neighborhood, to guard against any disagreeable surprise. Not very far distant were other auxiliaries, to whom I had confided Mother Noel's key, that they might come to my succor in case of danger; for, from one instant to another, I might fall suddenly amongst a gang of fugitives, or some of the galley slaves might recognize and attack me, and then a blow of my fist against a square of glass in the window was the signal which was to denote my need of assistance, to equalize the contending parties.

Thus were my schemes concerted, and the finale was at hand. It was on Tuesday, and a letter from the men I was in quest of, announced their intended arrival on the Friday following; a day which I intended should be for them a black Friday. At the first dawn, I betook myself to a wine vault in the vicinity, and, that they might have no motive for watching me, supposing, as was their custom, that they should traverse the street several times up and down before they entered Madame Noel's domicile, I first sent my pretended brother-in-law, who returned soon afterward, and told me that Mongenet's sister was not there, and that I might safely enter.

"You are not deceiving me?" said I to my agent, whose tone appeared altered and embarrassed, and fixing on him one of those looks which penetrated the very heart's core, I thought I observed one of those ill-suppressed contractions of the muscles of the face which accompany a premeditated lie: and then, quick as lightning, the thought came over me that I was betrayed— that my agent was a traitor. We were in a private room, and, without a moment's hesitation, I grasped his throat with violence, and told him, in presence of his comrades, that I was informed of his perfidy, and that if he did not instantly confess all, I would shoot him on the spot. Dismayed at my penetration and determined manner, he stammered out a few words of excuse, and falling on his knees confessed that he had discovered all to Mother Noel.

This baseness, had I not thus detected it, would probably have cost me my life, but I did not think of any personal resentment; it was only the interest of society which I cared for and which I regretted to see wrecked when so near port. The traitor, Manceau, was put in confinement, and, young as he was, having many old offenses to expiate, was sent to Bicêtre, and then to the Isle of Oleron, where he terminated his career. It may be conjectured that the fugitives did not return to the Rue Ticquetonne; but they were, notwithstanding, apprehended a short time afterward.

Mother Noel did not forgive the trick I had played her; and, to satisfy her revenge, she, one day, had all her goods taken away; and when this had been effected, went out without closing her door, and returned, crying out that she had been robbed. The neighbors were made witnesses, a declaration was made before a commissary, and Mother Noel pointed me out as the thief; because, she said, I had a key of her apartments. The accusation was a grave one, and she was instantly sent to the prefecture of police, and the next day I received the information. My justification was not difficult, for the prefet, as well as M. Henry, saw through the imposture; and we managed so well, that Mother Noel's property was discovered, proof was obtained of the falsity of the charge, and, to give her time for repentance, she was sentenced for six months to St. Lazarre. Such were the issue and the consequences of an enterprise, in which I had not failed to use all precaution; and I have often achieved success in affairs, in which arrangements had been made, not so skillfully concerted or so ably executed.

Chapter XXIX

AFTER HAVING UNDERGONE SEVERAL SENTENCES, two fugitives of the isles named Goreau and Florentin, called Chatelain (governor), of whom I have already spoken, were detained at Bicêtre, as incorrigible robbers. Weary of confinement in these cells, where they were buried alive, they sent to M. Henry a letter, in which they offered to give such information as should lead to the apprehension of several of their comrades, who were daily perpetrating robberies in Paris Fossard, sentenced for life, who had frequently escaped from the Bagnes, was the one marked out as the most dangerous. "He was," they wrote, "unequaled for intrepidity, and must be attacked with caution; for always armed to the teeth, he had resolved on blowing out the brains, of that police agent who should be sturdy enough to attempt to arrest him."

The heads of the police asked nothing better than to free the capital from such a daring thief, and their first idea was to employ me in discovering him, but the informers having suggested to M. Henry that I was, too well known to Fossard and his concubine not to defeat an operation which must be most delicately effected, it was decided that the affair should be entrusted to the skill of some police officers. To them therefore were given all the necessary instructions to regulate their searches; but, either they were not lucky, or they did not especially approve a rencontre with Fossard, who was "armed to the teeth," for he continued his exploits, and the numerous complaints to which his activity gave rise, and announced, that in spite of their apparent zeal, these gentlemen, as usual, made more noise than work.

The result was, that the prefet, who preferred doings to sayings, sent for them one day, and reprimanded them in a manner which must have been severe, to judge by the discontent which they could not help testifying.

They had just received this official proof of disapprobation, when I happened to meet, in the market of Saint-Jean, M. Yvrier, one of the officers in question, whom I saluted, and he thereupon accosted me, almost bursting with rage, saying, "Ah! there you are, Mr. Do-so-much; you are the cause of our having been reprimanded about that Fossard, the fugitive galley-slave, who they say is in Paris. If we are to believe monsieur le prefet, there is no one but you who can do anything. 'If Vidocq,' said he to us, 'had been ordered to this business, we should have had this fellow apprehended long ago.' Well, then, let us see, M. Vidocq; set your wits to work to find him, you who are so very clever, and prove that you have all the talent they say you have."

M. Yvrier was an old man, and it was respect for his safe which checked my reply to his impertinence; and although I was wounded by the tone of his address, I did not care to show it, contenting myself with replying, that I had not then the leisure to occupy myself about Fossard, that he was a capture I should reserve till the first of January that I might have a suitable new year's gift, for M. le prefet, as the previous year I had brought the famous Delzéve.

"Go on your way," replied M. Yvrier, irritated at this boast; "the event will show what you are; a presumptuous fellow, who creates difficulties to show his skill in surmounting them;' and he left me, grumbling out from between his teeth some other epithets and qualities which I neither understood nor heeded.

After this scene, I went to M. Henry's private room, to whom I related it. "Ah! they wince—they are angry, are they?" said he, laughing; "so much the better; it proves that they defer to your ability. I see," added M. Henry, "that these gentlemen are like the eunuchs of a seraglio; they cannot do themselves, and would not allow others to be doing." He then gave me the following particulars:—

"Fossard lives in Paris, in a street leading from a marketplace to a boulevard, on what story his apartments are, is unknown; but the windows may be recognized by having yellow silk curtains and other curtains of embroidered muslin. In the same house resides a little hump-backed woman, a seamstress, and intimate with the female who lives with Fossard."

These particulars were, it may be seen, not sufficiently definite to lead at once to the spot we wished to discover.

I was in doubt as to what steps I should first take; but as I had generally found that, in all my undertakings, it was from females that I gleaned my information, whether women or girls, I soon determined on the disguise which was best adapted to my purpose. It was apparent that I must assume the guise of a very respectable gentleman, and consequently, by means of some false wrinkles, a pig-tail, snowy-white ruffles, a large gold-headed cane, a three-cornered hat, buckles, breeches and coat to match,—I was metamorphosed into one of those good sexagenarian citizens, whom all old ladies admire. I had the precise appearance and air of one of those rich old boys of the Marias, whose rubicund and jolly countenance proves the ease of his circumstances, and the desire to bestow charity on those who need it, by way of a recompense to fortune. I was very sure that the hump-backed women would set their caps at me; and I had the appearance of so good a man, that it was impossible they would make any attempts at deceiving me.

Thus disguised I went into the streets, gazing upward to discover all the curtains of the prescribed color. I was so much occupied with this investigation, that I was entirely lost to all around me. Had I been a little less substantial-looking I might have been taken for a metaphysician, or perhaps for a poet who was seeking a couplet in the region of the chimney pots; twenty times I narrowly escaped the cabriolets; on all sides the cry of "Gare! Gare!" (mind, mind) assailed me, and then on turning round I was under the wheel, or else close beside a horse; sometimes, whilst I was wiping the dirt from my sleeve, a lash of a whip came across my face, or, if the driver were less brutal, it was some such salutation as this:— "Out of the way, old dunny-head," or else, "Come, what are you at, old stupid!"

My work was not to be completed in a single day, even as far as the yellow curtains went; I marked down more than one hundred and fifty in my memorandum book, which gave choice enough in all conscience. Might not the curtains, behind which Fossard was concealed, have been taken down and re-placed by white, green, or red ones? However, if chance was against me she might yet throw out some favorable hint for my guidance; and I took courage, although it is a somewhat painful task for a sexagenarian to ascend and de-scend a hundred and fifty staircases, consisting at least of seven hundred and fifty stories—to take more than thirty thousand steps, or twice the height of Chimborazo; but as I felt my breath good, and my legs strong, I undertook the task, sustained by the same hope as that which impelled the Argonauts to sail in quest of the golden fleece. It was my hump-backed lady that I sought; and in my ascents, in how many landing places have I not stood sentinel for hours together, in the persuasion that my lucky star would shine upon her? The heroic Don Quixote was not more ardent in the pursuit of his Dulcinea. I knocked at the doors of all the seamstresses; I examined them one after another, but no humps; they were all perfectly formed: or if by chance they had a projection, it was not a deviation of the spine, but one of those temporary exuberances which resolve themselves into maternity.

Thus passed several days without presenting to my longing eyes the object of my search, and I was heartily tired of my job, for every night my back ached past bearing, and yet the work was to be recommenced the next morning. I dared ask no questions; for although then some charitable soul might have put me on the right scent, yet I might get into danger; and at last, fatigued with this unsatisfactory mode of search, I determined to adopt another.

I have remarked that hump-backed women are generally very inquisitive and great chatterers; they are generally the news distributers of the district, and if not, they are then the registers of petty slanders, and nothing passes with which they are not acquainted. Impressed with this idea, I concluded that, un-der pretext of getting her little requisites supplied, the unknown humpy lady, who had already cost me so much trouble, would not fail, any more than many others, to come and have her wonted gossip at the milkman's, the baker's, the fruiterer's, the mercer's, or the grocer's. I resolved therefore to station myself at the doors of several of these chattering shops; and as every humpy woman, anxious for a husband, makes a great parade of her abilities as a clever caterer, I was persuaded that mine would be on foot early in the morning, and that I ought, to see her, to station myself at an early hour at my post of observation, and accordingly I went there at daybreak.

I first employed myself in considering how best to take my measures. To what milk-woman would a hump-backed lady give the preference? Certainly to her who had most gossip, and sold cheapest. There was one at the corner of the Rue Thevenot, who seemed to me to combine these two qualities; she had about her a great number of small cans, and from the midst of her circle did not cease to talk and serve, serve and talk. Her customers blabbed away to their hearts' content, and she chattered as indefatigably as her customers; but this was not of any consequence to me; I had pitched upon an admirable and likely spot, and was determined not to lose sight of it.

On going to my second watch in the evening, I impatiently awaited the arrival of my female Aesop, but there were only young girls, well made, slender, with good figures, easy appearance, neatly attired, and not one of them that was not as straight and upright as the letter I. I was beginning to despair, when at length my star beamed on the horizon; I saw the Venus, the prototype of all humped women! Ye gods! how handsome she appeared; and how splendid was the contour of that prominent feature for which I had so anxiously watched: her adorable hump! I gave myself time to contemplate this protuberance, which naturalists should, I think, take into consideration, and enumerate an additional race in the human species. I thought I was gazing on one of those fairies of the middle ages, in whom a deformity of this kind was "a double charm." This supernatural being, or rather extra-natural, approached the milk-woman, and having gossiped for some time, as I had anticipated, she took her cream; she then entered the grocer's; then paused a moment at the tripe-shop, where she procured some lights, probably for her cat; and then her stores provided, she turned off in the Rue du Petit Carreau, down the gateway, to a house of which the ground floor was occupied by a working turner. I cast my eyes instantly on the windows, but, alas! no yellow curtains met my longing, lingering look. I however made the reflection which had before suggested itself, that curtains, of whatever shade, have not the immobility of an original hump: and I resolved not to retire until I had some converse with the enchanting little lump of deformity, whose appearance had so truly enchanted me. I surmised that, in spite of my disappointment with regard to one of the main circumstances described for my guidance, yet that a conversation would elicit some useful information to lighten my path.

I determined to ascend the staircase; and on getting up to the first landing place, inquired for "a little lady rather deformed."—"Oh, it is the seamstress you want," was the reply, attended by a significant grin. "Yes, the seamstress I want; a person who has one shoulder somewhat higher than the other." Again I was laughed at, and her apartment pointed out as on the third story. Although her neighbors were very complaisant, I was rather nettled at their chuckling and laughing; it was exceedingly impolite; but such was my tolerance, that I freely pardoned the expression of their mirth; and was not that commendable in me? It preserved the character I had assumed. The door was shown to me; I knocked, and it was opened by my darling little Humpa herself; and after fifty apologies for the visit, I begged her to give me a few moments' audience, adding that I had personal business to discuss with her.

"Mademoiselle," said I, with a solemn tone, after she had seated me opposite to herself, "you are ignorant of the motive which has led me hither; but when you shall know it, perhaps the step I have taken will excite your interest."

The hump-backed damsel thought I was going to make an open avowal; the color rushed to her cheeks, and her look became animated, although she cast her eyes on the ground. I continued—

"Doubtless you will be astonished that at my age one can be as deeply enamored as at twenty years old."

"Ah, sir, you are still young," said the amiable Humpins, whose mistake I would not allow to be prolonged.

"Why, pretty well for that," I added, "but it is not of that I would speak. You know that in Paris it is not an uncommon for a man and woman to live together without the benediction of Holy Mother Church."

"What do you take me for, sir, to make such a proposal to me?" cried the little Humpetta, without giving me time to finish my sentence. I smiled at her mistake, and continued:

"I have no intention to make any such proposition; I only request that you will have the goodness to give me some information respecting a young lady, who, I am told lives in this house with a gentleman who passes for her husband"—"I know nothing at all about it," answered my little lady very snappishly.

I then gave her a tolerably accurate description of Fossard and the demoiselle Tonneau, his lady.

"Ah, I now know," said she; "a man of your figure and size, about thirty or five-and-thirty years of age, a good-looking gentleman; the lady, a pretty brunette, beautiful eyes, lovely teeth, charming mouth, superb eyelashes, dark brows, nose a little turned up, with a most engaging and modest demeanor. They did live here, but they have removed." I entreated her to give me their new address; and on her reply that she did not know it, I weepingly besought her to aid in the recovery of an ungrateful creature, whom I still fondly, dotingly loved, despite her perfidy.

The seamstress was touched. The tears I shed moved her tender heart; and feeling that I had gained ground, I became more and more pathetic. "Ah! her infidelity will cause my death: pity, commiserate a wretched husband; I conjure you, do not conceal from me her retreat and I shall owe you more than life."

Your hump-backed women are compassionate; moreover a husband is in their eyes so inappreciable a treasure; and as they are not possessed of one, they cannot imagine how anyone can be unfaithful; and thus my seamstress held adultery in utter abhorrence. She sincerely pitied me, and said she would do all in her power to serve me. "Unfortunately," she added, "their goods having been removed by porters not belonging to the district, I am completely ignorant of where they have gone or what has become of them; but would you like to see the landlady?" As I had no doubt of her sincerity, I went to see the landlady, but all I learnt from her was, that they had paid for the term agreed on, and had not left any tidings of their new abode.

Except having discovered Fossard's old lodging, I was no forwarder than at first; but I would not abandon the quest without exhausting every chance and inquiry that would suggest itself. Usually the porters of the various districts know each other; and I interrogated those of the Rue de Petit Carreau, to whom I introduced myself as a wronged husband; and one of them pointed out to me a comrade who had aided in the removal of my rival's goods and chattels.

I saw this individual and told him my concerted story; but he was a cunning chap, and intended to trick me. I pretended not to perceive it; and, as a recompense for promising that he would conduct me the next day to the place where Fossard had pitched his tent, I gave him two five-franc pieces, which were spent the same day at the Courtille, in company with the lady he "protected."

This interview was on the 27th of December, and we were to meet again the next day; and to fulfill my assertion of the 1st of January, there was not much time to lose. I was punctual at the rendezvous; and the porter, whom I had caused to be watched by some agents, was also to the time and place. Some more five-franc pieces changed masters from my purse to his, and I paid for his breakfast. We then started and we arrived at a very pretty house, at the corner of the Rue Duphot and that of Saint Honore. "Now," said he, "we must ask the vintner just by if they are still here." He wanted me to regale him again. I did not refuse; and we entered the shop, where we emptied a bottle of good wine: I then left him, fully assured of the residence of my pretended wife and her seducer. I had no further occasion for my guide, and dismissed him with a mark of my gratitude; but to be sure that he did not betray me, in the hope of being doubly paid, I ordered the agents to watch him closely, and to prevent his returning to the vintner's. As well as I can remember, to prevent all possibility of his so doing, they put him in the guardhouse: in such cases, we are not over particular; and, to be sincere, it was I who put him in the stone doublet, which was but a just retaliation. "My friend," I said to him, "I have left with the police a note of five hundred francs, destined to reward the man who shall successfully aid me in recovering my wife. It is now yours; and I will give you a note which will enable you to secure it;" and I gave him a small note to M. Henry, who on perusal, said to a police officer, "Conduct this gentleman to the chest." The chest was in this instance the Sylvestre Chamber (a place of confinement), where my friend the porter, had a little time for salutary reflection.

I was not certain of Fossard's residence, but yet relied on the indications given to me, and I was provided with the necessary power for his apprehension. Then the "richard du Marais" (the rich old man of the Marais) was suddenly metamorphosed into a coalman; and in this costume, under which neither the mother who bore me, nor any of the agents of the police, who saw me daily, could have recognized me, I employed myself in studying the ground on which I should so shortly be compelled to maneuver.

The friends of Fossard—that is, his denouncers—had advised that the agents employed in his apprehension should be warned that he was always provided with a dagger and pistols, one of which latter, with double barrels, was concealed in a cambric handkerchief which he always held in his hand. The information called for precaution; and besides, from the known desperation of Fossard's character, it was certain that, to avoid a confinement worse than death, he would not hesitate about a murder. I felt no anxiety to become his victim; and thought that it would sensibly diminish my chance of peril, if I came to a previous understanding with the vintner whose tenant Fossard was. The vintner was a good fellow enough, but the police is always in such ill odor, that it is no easy matter to procure the assistance of honest men. I determined to bring him over to my side, by making it much to his interest to do so. I had visited his house several times in my double disguise, and had leisure to make myself acquainted with all the localities, as well as with the sort of visitors who came there, I then went in my usual dress, and accosting the man, told him I wished to speak with him in private. He took me into a small room, when I thus addressed him:—

"I have to inform you, from the police, that a plan is formed to rob your house; the thief who has devised the means, and who probably intends perpetrating the robbery himself, lodges in your house; the female who lives with him comes sometimes behind your counter, sees your wife, and whilst conversing with her, has contrived to get the impression of the key which opens the door by which the proposed entry is to be made. All is arranged; the alarm is to be cut with nippers whilst the door is ajar; once inside, they will ascend quickly to your chamber; and if they have any suspicion that you are awake, as it is a perfect ruffian who concerts the project, there is no need for me to tell you what will ensue."

"They will cut our throats," said the alarmed vintner, and then called his wife to communicate the intelligence—"Oh, my love, what a world we live in—trust nobody! That Madame Hazard, who seemed too good to have a sin to confess—would you believe it—actually contemplates the cutting of our throats! This very night they will come and settle the business."

"No no, be quiet," I replied, "not this night; the till is not full enough, they wait until the fitting time; but if you are discreet and will second me, we will defeat them."

Madame Hazard was Mademoiselle Tonneau, who had assumed the name by which Fossard was known in the house; and I desired the vintner and his wife, who were gladly led by me, to treat their lodgers as usual. It need not be asked how willingly they followed my instructions; and it was agreed between us that to see Fossard go out, and to be able to decide on the best time to seize on him, I should ensconce myself in a small closet under the stairs.

At an early hour on the 29th of December, I betook myself to my station; it was desperately cold, the watch was a protracted one, and the more painful as we had no fire: motionless, however, and my eye fixed against a small hole in the shutter, I kept my post. At last about three o'clock, he went out; I followed, gladly, and recognized him; for up to that period I had my doubts. Certain now of his identity, I wished at that moment to put into execution the order for his apprehension; but the officer who was with me said he saw the terrible pistol. That I might authenticate the fact I walked quickly and passed Fossard: and then returning, saw clearly that the agent was right. To attempt to arrest him would have been useless, and I resolved to defer it; and on recalling to mind that a fortnight before I had flattered myself with the prospect of apprehending Fossard on the 1st of January, I was not displeased at the delay; but till then my vigilance was not to be relaxed for a single instant.

On the 31st of December, at eleven o'clock, when all my batteries were charged and my plans perfect, Fossard returned, and without distrust ascended the staircase shaking with cold; and twenty minutes after, the disappearance of the light indicated that he was in bed. The moment had now arrived. The commissary and gendarmes, summoned by me, were waiting at the nearest guardhouse until I should call them, and then enter quietly; we deliberated on the most effectual mode of seizing Fossard without running the risk of being killed or wounded; for they were persuaded that, unless surprised, this robber would defend himself desperately.

My first thought was to do nothing till daybreak, as I had been told that Fossard's companion went down very early to get the milk; we should then seize her, and after having taken the key from her, we should enter the room of her lover; but might it not happen, that contrary to his usual custom, he might go out first! This reflection led me to adopt another expedient.

The vintner's wife, in whose favor, as I was told, M. Hazard was much prepossessed, had one of her nephews at her house, a lad about ten years of age, intelligent beyond his years, and the more desirous of getting money as he was a Norman. I promised him a reward on condition that under pretense of his aunt's being taken suddenly ill, he should go and beg Madame Hazard to give him some Eau de Cologne. I desired the little chap to assume the most piteous tone he could; and was so well satisfied with a specimen he gave me, that I began to distribute the parts to my performers. The denouement was near at hand. I made all my party take off their shoes, doing the same myself, that we might not be heard whilst going up stairs. The little sniveling pilot was in his shirt; he rang the bell—no one answered; again he rang:— "Who's there?" was heard—"It is I, Madame Hazard; it is Louis: my poor aunt is very bad, and begs you will be so very obliging as to give her a little Eau de Cologne—Oh! she is dying!"

The door was opened; and scarcely had Mademoiselle Tonneau presented herself, when two powerful gendarmes seized on her, and fastened a napkin over her mouth to prevent her crying out. At the same instant, with more rapidity than the lion when darting on his prey, I threw myself upon Fossard, who, stupefied by what was doing, and already fast bound and confined in his bed, was my prisoner before he could make a single movement, or utter a single word. So great was his amazement, that it was nearly an hour before he could articulate even a few words. When a light was brought and he saw my black face, and garb of a coalman, he experienced such an increase of terror, that I really believed he imagined himself in the devil's clutches. On coming to himself, he thought of his arms, his pistols and dagger, which were upon the table; and turning his eyes toward them, he made a struggle, but that was all; for reduced to the impossibility of doing any mischief, he was passive, and contented himself with "chewing the cud of sweet and bitter fancy."

On searching the domicile of this formidable brigand, great quantities of jewels were found; diamonds and cash to the amount of eight or ten thousand francs. Fossard having recovered his spirits, told me that under the marble of the chimney-piece were ten notes of a thousand francs each. "Take them," said he: "we will divide, or you shall take as much as you please." I took the notes, and getting into a fiacre, we soon reached M. Henry's office, where we deposited the booty found in Fossard's apartments. On making out the inventory, when we came to the last item, the commissary, who had accompanied me in the enterprise, said, "It now only remains to conclude the procés-verbal."

"Stay, one moment," I cried, "here are ten thousand francs which the prisoner has handed over to me." I displayed this sum, to the great regret of Fossard, who gave me one of those looks which would say, "This is a turn I will never forgive."

Fossard entered early on a career of crime. Born of reputable parents, he had received a good education; his friends had done all in their power to divert him from his vicious courses, but in spite of good advice, he had thrown himself headlong into the vortex of bad company. He began by stealing trifling articles; but soon after, having acquired a decided taste for such pursuits, and blushing, no doubt, at being confounded with ordinary robbers, "petty larceny knaves," he adopted what the gentlemen style, a "distinguished line." The famous Victor Desbois and Noel with the Spectacles, who now honor the Bagne at Brest with their distinguished presence, were his associates; and they committed together those robberies which led to their imprisonment for life. Noel, whose talents as a musician, and in his quality of a teacher of the piano-forte, got access to all the rich houses, took impressions of the keys, which Fossard then fabricated. It was an art in which he defied Georget and all the locksmiths in the world to surpass him: however complicated the lock, however ingenious and difficult the secret, nothing resisted the efforts of his skill.

It may be easily conceived what advantage he made of such a pernicious talent; being, moreover, a man who could insinuate himself into the company of honest persons, and then dupe them. Besides, he was a close and frigid character, to which he added courage and perseverance. His comrades regarded him as the prince of thieves; and in fact amongst the "tip-top cracksmen" that is, in the aristocracy of robbers, I never knew but Cognard, Pontis, Comte de St. Helene, and Jossas, who were at all comparable to him.

After I had reinstated him at the Bagne, Fossard often attempted to escape. Some liberated prisoners who have lately seen him, have assured me that he only longs for liberty, that he may avenge himself on me. They say he has threatened to kill me. If the accomplishment of this kind intention depended solely on him, I am sure he would keep his word, if it were only to give a proof of his intrepidity. Two circumstances that have been told me, will give some idea of the man.

One day Fossard was about to commit a robbery in an apartment on the second story: his comrades, who were watching without, were stupid enough to allow the proprietor to ascend the staircase, and he, on putting the key into the door, opened it, went through several rooms, and on getting to an inner closet, saw the thief at work; but Fossard, putting himself on the defensive, escaped.

A window was open near him, and, darting out of it, he fell into the street without injury, and disappeared as swift as lightning.

Another time, whilst he was escaping, he was surprised on the tiles of Bicêtre, and fired at. Fossard, never disconcerted, continued to walk along without stopping or hastening his steps, and getting to that side which looks into the fields, he slid down. The fall was enough to have broken a hundred necks, but he received no hurt; only the slide was so rapid that his clothes were rent in shreds.

CHAPTER XXX

I DO NOT THINK THAT AMONGST THE READERS of these Memoirs one will be found who, even by chance, has set foot at Guillotin's, an unsophisticated adulterer of wines, whose establishment, well known to the most degraded classes of robbers, is situated opposite to the Cloaque Desnoyers, which the raff of the Barriére call the drawing-room of la Courtille. A workman may be honest to a certain extent and venture in, en passant, to papa Desnoyers. If he be awake, and keep his eye on the company, although a row should commence, he may, by the aid of the gendarmes, escape with only a few blows, and pay no one's scot but his own. At Guillotin's he will not come off so well, particularly if his toggery be over spruce, and his pouch has money in it.

Picture to yourself, reader, a square room of considerable magnitude, the walls of which, once white, have been blackened by every species of exhalation. Such is, in all its simple modesty, the aspect of a temple consecrated to the worship of Bacchus and Terpsichore. At first, by a very natural optical illusion, we are struck at the confined space before us, but the eye, after a time, piercing through the thick atmosphere of a thousand vapors which are most inodorous, the extent becomes visible by details which escape in the first chaotic glimpse. It is the moment of creation, all is bright, the fog disappears, becomes peopled, is animated, forms appear, they move, they are agitated, they are no illusory shadows, but, on the contrary, essentially material, which cross and recross at every moment. What beatitudes! What a joyous life! Never, even for the Epicureans, were so many felicities assembled together. Those who like to wallow in filth, can find it here to their hearts' content: many seated at table, on which, without ever being wiped away, are renewed a hundred times a day the most disgusting libations, close in a square space reserved for what they call the dancers. At the further end of this infected cave there is, supported by four worm-eaten pillars, the sort of alcove, constructed from broken-up ship-timber, which is graced by the appearance of two or three rags of old tapestry. It is on this chicken coop that the music is perched: two clarionets, a hurdy-gurdy, a cracked trumpet, and a grumbling bassoon—five instruments whose harmonious movements are regulated by the crutch of Monsieur Double-Croche, a lame dwarf, who is called the leader of the orchestra. Here all is in harmony—the faces, costumes, the food that is prepared; a genteel appearance is scouted. There is no closet in which walking-sticks, umbrellas, and cloaks are deposited; the women have their hair all in confusion like a poodle dog, and the kerchief perched on the top of the head, or in a knot tied in front, with the corners in a rosette, or, if you prefer it, a cockade, which threatens the eye in the same manner as those of the country mules. As for the men, it is a waistcoat with a cap and falling collar, if they have a shirt, which is the regulated costume; breeches are not insisted on; the supreme bon ton would be an artillery man's cap, the frock of a hussar, the pantaloons of a lancer, the boots of a guardsman in fact the cast-off attire of three or four regiments, or the wardrobe of a field of battle; and there is no out and outer thus attired but is the fancy man of these ladies, who adore the cavalry, and have a decided taste for the dress of the whole army; but nothing so much pleases them as mustachios, and a broad red cap adorned with leather the same color.

In this assembly, a beaver hat, unless napless and brimless, would be very rare; no one ever remembers to have seen a coat there, and should any one dare to present himself in a great coat, unless a family man, he would be sure to depart skirtless, or only in his waistcoat. In vain would he ask pardon for those flaps which had offended the eyes of the noble assembly; too happy would he be if, after having been bandied and knocked about with the utmost unanimity as a greenhorn, only one skirt should be left in the hands of these youthful beauties.

Desnoyers' is the resort of the lower orders; but before stepping over the threshold of the cabaret of Guillotin, even the canaille themselves look twice; as in this repository are only to be seen prostitutes with their bullies, pickpockets, and thieves of all classes, some prigs of the lowest grade, and many of those nocturnal marauders who divide their existence into two parts, consecrating it to the duties of theft and riot. It may be supposed that slang is the only language of this delightful society: it is generally in French, but so perverted from its primitive signification, that there is not a member of the distinguished "company of forty" who can flatter himself with a full knowledge of it, and yet the "dons of Guillotin's" have their purists; those who assert that slang took its rise in the East, and without thinking for a moment of disputing their talent as Orientalists, they take that' title to themselves without any ceremony, as also that of Argonauts, when they have completed their studies under the direction of the galley-serjeants, in working, in the port of Toulon, the dormant navigation on board a vessel in dock. If notes were pleasing to me, I could here seize the opportunity of making some very learned remarks. I should, perhaps, go into a profound disquisition, but I am about to paint the paradise of these bacchanalians; the colors are prepared—let us finish the picture.

If they drink at Guillotin's, they eat also, and the mysteries of the kitchen of this place of delights are well worthy of being known. The little Father Guillotin has no butcher, but he has a purveyor; and in his brass stew pans, the verdigris of which never poisons, the dead horse is transformed into beef a la mode; the thighs of the dead dogs found in Rue Guenegaud become legs of mutton from the salt marshes; and the magic of a piquant sauce gives to the staggering bob (dead born veal) of the cow-feeder the appetizing look of that of Pontoise. We are told that the cheer in winter is excellent, when the rot prevails; and if ever bread were scarce in summer during the "massacre of the innocents," mutton was to be had here at a very cheap rate.

In this country of metamorphoses the hare never had the right of citizenship; it was compelled to yield to the rabbit, and the rabbit—how happy the rats are!

"O fortunati nimium – si norint."

It was the domine of St. Mande who taught me this quotation; he told me it was Latin, perhaps it may be Greek or Hebrew;—no matter, I leave it, come what may, to the will of God; but still, if the rats could ever have seen what I have seen, unless they had been an ingrate and perverse race, they would have opened a subscription for the erection of a statue to the Liberator, little Father Guillotin.

One evening, led by my inclination, which a good Frenchman always follows, I went out; in my road I accidentally pushed against a door, it gave way, and, by the freshness of the air, I found I was in a court; the place was propitious, and I groped along until I made a trip over some paving stones which had been left in the way. I stretched out my arms to recover myself, and whilst with one hand I grasped hold of a post, I seized with the other something very soft and very long, I was in darkness, but fancied I saw several sparks shining, and by the touch I thought I recognized a certain velvet appendage of a quadruped's vertebral column. I kept hold of a bunch of it, and drawing it through my hand, there remained a packet of spoils, with which I entered the room at the very moment when M. Double-Croche, pointing out the figures to the dancers, was howling out "la queue du chat"—(the cat's tail).

It needs not to be asked how very a propos this was; there was throughout the assembly a general mewing, but it was only a joke; the lovers of fricassee mewed like the rest, and, after having taken their caps off, they said, "Come on, here is the good stuff! Covered by cat skin, and fed on cats, we shall not soon be in want; the mother of tom cats is not yet dead."

Father Guillotin consumed generally more oil than cotton, but I can, nevertheless, affirm, that, in my time, some banquets have been spread at his cabaret, which, subtracting the liquids, could not have cost more at the Café Riche or at Grignon's. I remember six individuals, named Draincourt, Vilattes, Pitroux, and three others, who found means to spend 166 francs there in one night. In fact, each of them had with him his favorite bella. The citizen no doubt pretty well fleeced them, but they did not complain, and that quarter of an hour which Rabelais had so much difficulty in passing, caused them no trouble; they paid like grandees, without forgetting the waiter. I apprehended them whilst they were paying the bill, which they had not even taken the trouble of examining. Thieves are generous when they are caught "i' the vein.' They had just committed many considerable robberies, which they are now repenting in the Bagnes of France.

It can scarcely be believed that in the center of civilization, there can exist a den so hideous as the cave of Guillotin; it must be seen, as I have seen it, to be believed. Men or women all smoked as they danced, the pipe passed from mouth to mouth, and the most refined gallantry that could be offered to the nymphs who came to this rendezvous, to display their graces in the postures and attitudes of the indecent Chahut, was, to offer them the pruneau, that is, the quid of tobacco, submitted or not, according to the degree of familiarity, to the test of a previous mastication. The peace officers and inspectors were characters too greatly distinguished to appear amongst such an assemblage, they kept themselves most scrupulously aloof, to avoid so repugnant a contact; I myself was much disgusted with it, but at the same time was persuaded, that to discover and apprehend malefactors it would not do to wait until they should come and throw themselves into my arms; I therefore determined to seek them out, and that my searches might not be fruitless, I endeavored to find out their haunts, and then, like a fisherman who has found a preserve, I cast my line out with a certainty of a bite.

I did not lose my time in searching for a needle in a bottle of hay, as the saying is; when we lack water, it is useless to go to the source of a dried up stream and wait for a shower of rain; but to quit all metaphor, and speak plainly—the spy who really means to ferret out the robbers, ought, as much as possible, to dwell amongst them, that he may grasp at every opportunity which presents itself of drawing down upon their heads the sentence of the laws. Upon this principle I acted, and this caused my recruits to say that I made men robbers; I certainly have, in this way, made a vast many, particularly on my first connection with the police.

On a particular afternoon I had a presentiment that a visit to Guillotin's would not be without its results. Without being superstitious, I know not why, I have always followed these inspirations; I put my wardrobe in requisition, and, after having suited myself so as not to bear any appearance of being a green-horn, I left my house with another secret agent, named Riboulet, a downy cove, whom all the houris of the boozing kens claimed as their chevalier, as did also the milliners' girls, who considered him as a complete kiddy. For such an excursion, a woman was an indispensable portion of the baggage, and Riboulet had one who just suited us: she passed as his mistress, and was a common woman, called Manon la Blonde, on whom he assured me that reliance could be placed. In two seconds she rent her woolen stockings in twenty places, tore the edges of her red cloak, begrimed her shawl, trod her shoes down at the heel, disheveled her locks, and gave to the kerchief with which she graced her brows that inde-scribable appearance which was necessary. She was highly delighted with the character she had to perform.

Thus attired and prepared, we set out together, arm-in-arm, toward la Courtille. On reaching the cabaret, we seated ourselves at a table in the corner, that we might the more easily watch whatever should pass. Riboulet was one of those men whose very appearance commanded instant attention; he had not spoken nor had I, but yet we were instantly attended to.

"You see," said he, "the cove knows the game o'day, the lush (wine), meat, and salad."

I asked if we could not have a matelote of eels.

"Snakes," cried Manon, "do you want; cag-mag and snivelers (stinking meat and onions) would be as good."

I said no more, and we began to eat with as much appetite as if we had never been initiated into the mysteries of Papa Guillotin's cookery.

During the repast, a noise at the door attracted our attention. It proceeded from some conquerors who made their triumphal entry: men and women, six in number, forming three couples of individuals whose "human face divine" was most tremendously disfigured: they had all scratched countenances and black eyes; by the bloody disorder of their attire, and the freshness of their dilapidations in face and garments, it was easy to perceive that they were the heroes of some spree, in which on both sides the quarrel had been decided by fisticuffs. They approached our table.

One Of The Heroes.—"By your leave, my trumps, is there room for us on this here seat?"

I.—"We shall be squeezed a little, but never mind" (making room).

Riboulet (addressing me).—"Come, my covey, make room for the gentlemen."

Manon (to the fresh arrivals).—"Are these ladies with you?"

One Of The Heroes.—"Vat is it you say? (turning to her friends) vat does he say?"

Her Pal.—"Hold your jaw, Titine (Celestine), the lady said nothing to affront you."

The whole party seated themselves.

A Hero.—" Halloo! come here, daddy Guillotin; a little black father, four year old, for eight mag." (A four-quart jug for eight sous.)

Guillotin. —"Coming, coming."

The Waiter (with the jug in his hand). "Thirty-two mag, if you please."

"I'll give you two and thirty kicks of the ____, you're chaffing us, my rum 'un."

Waiter.—"No, my knowing ones, but it's the custom, or, if you like, the way of this here house."

The wine was poured into all the glasses, and they also filled ours. "Excuse the liberty," said the Ganymede of the party.

"Oh, there's no harm done," replied Riboulet.

"You know one politeness requires another."

"But you are too polite."

"Oh no, drink away, nunky pays for all."

"You are right, my boys, so push the wine about."

We did push it about, and so well that about ten o'clock in the evening all the sympathy left between us was manifested by protestations, sight being lost; and by those explosions of drunken tenderness which develop all the infirmities of the human heart.

When the hour of parting had arrived, our new acquaintances, and particularly the softer sex, were completely drunk. Riboulet and his mistress were only somewhat elevated, as well as myself; they had preserved their senses, but to appear all in unison, we pretended to be so tipsy as to be unable to walk; formed into a phalanx, because in that way the gusts of wind are less to be feared, we left the theater of our pleasures. Then, that we might neutralize, by the aid of a chant, the reeling tendencies of our troop, Riboulet, with a voice whose echoes vibrated in every court and alley, began to sing, in the most finished slang of his time, one of those ballads with a chorus, which are as long as today and tomorrow.

"As from ken to ken I was going,
Doing a bit on the prigging lay;
Who should I meet but a jolly blowen.

Tol lol, lol lol, tol dirol lay;
Who should I meet but a jolly blowen,
Who was fly to the time o'day.

"Then his ticker is a-going,
With his onions, chain, and key.
Next slip off his bottom clo'ing,
And his gingerbread topper gay.

"Next slipt off his bottom clo'ing,
And his gingerbread topper gay.
Then his other toggery stowing,
All with the swag, I sneak away.

"Then his other toggery stowing,
All with the swag, I sneak away;
'Tramp it, tramp it, my jolly blowen,
Or be grabbed by the beaks we may.

"'Tramp it, tramp it, my jolly blowen,
Or be grabbed by the beaks we may;
And we shall caper a-heel-and-toeing
A Newgate hornpipe some fine day.

"'And we shall caper a-heel-and-toeing,
A Newgate hornpipe some fine day;
With the mots, their ogles throwing,
And old Cotton hamming his pray.

"'With the mots their ogles throwing.
And old Cotton humming his pray;
And the fogle-hunters doing."

Riboulet having been safely delivered of his fourteen couplets, Manon la Blonde was desirous of evincing the powers of her lungs. "Now for another!" said she.

The chorus, which we took up, as it were, was repeated eight or ten times, in a manner which almost broke the windows of the house about us. After this burst of bacchanalian hilarity, the first fumes of wine, which are usually most potent, beginning somewhat to dissipate, we entered into conversation. The chapter of confidences, according to custom, opened by interrogatories. I did not require to be much questioned, but went beyond the communications which they desired to know: a stranger in Paris, I had only known Riboulet in prison at Valenciennes, when he was sent back to his regiment as a deserter; he was a college chum, (a fellow-prisoner), whom I had met again. As to the rest, I took care to represent myself in colors which charmed them: I was a thorough out-and-outer. I know not what I had not done, and was ready to do anything. I unbosomed myself that they might unbosom as freely in their turn; it is a tactic which has often been successful with me: the party soon chattered like magpies, and I became as well acquainted with all their doings as if I had never been separated from them. They told me their names, residences, exploits, misfortunes, hopes; they had met a man who was really worthy of their confidence. I returned it, I suited them, and all was said.

Such explanations always make a man thirsty, more or less; all the liquorshops in our road were visited: more than a hundred toasts were drunk in honor of our new convention, and we were not to separate again. "Come along with us, come," they said, and they were so pressing, that, quite unable to refuse their importunities, I agreed to go to their abode, Rue des Filles-Dieu—No. 14, where they lodged in a furnished house. Once in their abode, it was impossible to refuse a share of their bed: it is difficult to describe what good fellows they were; and so was I, and they were the better convinced of it, as, during an hour, whilst I pretended to be sleeping, my friend Riboulet passed a eulogy on me, in a low tone of voice, of which not even half was true, or I should have richly merited a sentence for ten times the term of my natural life.

At last, Riboulet had so completely placed me in good odor with our hosts, that about break of day they proposed to me to go out upon a job with them, a robbery which they had planned in the Rue de la Verrerie. I had only just time to warn the chief of the second division, who made his arrangements so well, that they were apprehended with the property about their persons. Riboulet and I remained on the lookout, to give alarm in case of danger, as the thieves believed, but, in fact, to see if the police were on their posts.

When they passed near us, all three in a coach, whence they could not see us, "Well!" said Riboulet, "there they are, taken in the very act." They were also condemned; and if the names of Debuire, Rolé, and Hippolyte, called la Biche, are still on the muster-roll at the Bagnes, it is the result of an evening passed at Guillotin's amongst the children of the sun.

Chapter XXXI

Thieves frequently fell into my clutches when I least expected them; it was said that their evil genius impelled them to come and find me. It must be confessed that those who thus flung themselves into the wolf's throat, were horribly unlucky or infernally stupid. When I saw with what facility the majority of them gave themselves up, I was really astonished that they should have chosen a profession in which, to avoid perils, so many precautions are necessary; some of them were such good-natured fellows, that I considered as almost miraculous the impunity which they had enjoyed up to the moment when they met me, and paid the reckoning of their crimes. It is incredible that any individuals created expressly to fall into any plot or snare, should have awaited my coming to the police to be caught.

Before my time, the police was either most clumsily arranged, or else I was singularly fortunate; under any circumstances it is, as they say, "give a man luck and fling him into the sea." The following recital is in point. One day, toward twilight, dressed like a workman of the dockyards, I was seated on the parapet of the Quai de Gevres, when I saw coming toward me an individual whom I knew to be one of the frequenters of the Petite Chaise and the Bon Puits, two cabarets of renown for robbers.

"Good evening, Jean Louis," said this person, accosting me.

"Good evening, my lad."

"What the devil are you doing there? You look as if you were fucking?"

"What do you mean, my boy? When the belly grumbles the mouth mumbles."

"What, the cupboard empty! that is not right for you, who are one of the family."

"Very true, but 'tis so."

"Come along, then, let us have a quart at Niguenac's; I have twenty browns left, and we will see how far they will go."

He conducted me to a vintner's, and called for a bottle, and then, leaving me for an instant, returned with two pounds of potatoes. "Here," he said, putting them smoking hot upon the table, "here are some gudgeons caught with a spade in the fields of Sablons; they are not fried though."

"These are oranges, but we want some salt."

"Salt, my lad, that will not ruin us."

The salt was brought, and although an hour before I had made an excellent dinner at Martin's, I fell on the potatoes, and devoured them as if I had not tasted food for a couple of days.

"You peg away," said he, "as if you would crash your ivories (teeth); one would think that you were tucking in at a regular spread."

"Oh, my lad, all that goes down the gullet fills the belly."

"Very true, very true."

Mouthful followed mouthful with prodigious rapidity, and I did nothing but peel and swallow: I cannot tell how it was that I was not literally crammed, but my stomach had never been more complaisant. At last my task was done, my comrade offered me a quid, and thus addressed me:

"On the word of a man, and as true as my name is Masson, and is the same as my father's, I have always considered you a hearty blade; I know you have been unfortunate, I have been told so, but the devil's hoof is not always at the poor man's door, and if you like, I can put you on a good scent."

"That would not, perhaps, suit me, for my rigging is not over and above excellent."

"True! I see, I see, (looking at my clothes, which were rather tattered), it seems that at this moment you are not the luckiest cove in the world."

"Very right; I have most urgent need of a new fit out."

"In that case come with me; I have a locksmith's daughter with which I shall clear out an apartment this evening."

"Tell me all about it, for I must learn the particulars before I can join you in it."

"What a flat you are; there is no occasion for you to be fly."

"Oh! that is all true as gospel, and I am your man, only you can explain in two words."

"Now, hold your gab, I tell you, my plan is settled, and the booty sure: the fence's ken (receiver's house) is only a stone's throw off. As soon as prigged, so soon disposed of; it is a good haul, and you shall have your whack."

"Come, then, let us be off."

Masson conducted me to the Boulevard Saint Denis, which we traversed until we came to a heap of stones. There he stopped, looking about him to see that no one was watching, and then going up to the pile, he took off several lumps, put his hand into the cavity and fished up a bunch of keys.

"I have now all the herbs of Saint John," said he, "and we will go together to the corn market."

On reaching the place, he pointed out to me, at a small distance, and almost opposite the guardhouse, the house which he intended to enter.

"Now, my boy," said he, "do not go far distant, wait for me, and keep your weather-eye open; I am going to see if the mot has mizzled" (if the woman of the house has gone out).

Masson opened the sidedoor, but no sooner had he shut it after him than I ran to the post, where making myself known to the chief, I hastily told him that a robbery was then committing, and that no time was to be lost, if they would secure the robber with the property in his possession. Having done this, I returned to the place where Masson had left me. Hardly had I got there when some person, advancing toward me, said,

"Is it you, Jean Louis?"

"Yes, it is me," was my reply, testifying my astonishment that he had returned empty handed.

"Oh, say nothing about it; a devil of a neighbor came up the staircase and deranged my plans; but what is deferred is not lost. Minute follows minute and the mutton is boiled at last, as you will see; one must not compromise oneself."

He then left me again, and was not long in reappearing with a very large bundle, under the weight of which he was almost sinking. He passed me without uttering a word: I followed, and walking in close files, two guards, armed only with the bayonet, followed him also, making the least possible noise.

It was necessary to know where he deposited his booty. He entered a shopkeeper's at the Rue du Tour (the death's head), where he only stopped a moment.

"It was heavy," said he, on coming out, "and I have still a good cast to haul in."

I allowed him to go on, and returning again to the room he had before entered, he completed the gutting of it; and scarcely had ten minutes elapsed before he descended the second time, carrying on his head a bed, mattresses, quilts, curtains, and sheets. He had not had time to make a good bundle of them, and on crossing the threshold, being stopped by the narrowness of the door, and unwilling to drop his prey, he stumbled and almost fell, but, recovering himself, he began his journey, beckoning me to follow him. At a turn of the street he came up to me, and said, in a low voice,

"I think I shall go back the third time, if you will go up with me, as we can then get down the window-curtains and blinds."

"Agreed," said I; "when one sleeps on straw, curtains are a luxury."

"A luxury, indeed," said he smiling, "but no time must be lost in chatter, do not go far away and I will hail you as I pass."

Masson went on his way, but at a short distance from where we had met we were both stopped. We were first conducted to the guardhouse, and afterward to the commissary, who interrogated us.

"There are two of you," said the public officer to Masson, (pointing to me,) "who is this man? I suppose a thief like yourself."

"Who is this man? Do I know him? Ask himself; When I shall have seen him once more, that will be the second time."

"You must not tell me that there is no collusion between you, for you were met together."

"There is no collusion, my worthy commissary: he was going on one side of the way, I was coming on the other, just as he was passing close beside me, something slid from me, it was a pillow; I told him of it, and he stooped to pick it up, and just then the guard came up, and nabbed us both: this is why I am now before you, and I wish I may die if it is not the actual truth. Ask him if it is not."

The story was not badly imagined, and I took care not to deny what Masson said, but follow in his track: at length the commissary appeared convinced. "Have you any papers?" he inquired. I showed a permission of residence, which was pronounced correct, and my dismissal was instantly ordered. An evident satisfaction pervaded the features of Masson, when he heard the words Allez-vous coucher (go to bed) addressed to me: it was the formula of my liberty, and he was so much rejoiced at it, that any person must have been blind not to perceive it.

The robber was still kept, and nothing remained but to lay hands on the female receiver before she had disposed of the property entrusted to her. An immediate search was made, and, surprised in the midst of most material evidence which condemned her, the death's head was carried off from her trade at the moment when she least expected it.

Masson was taken to the prefecture of police, and the next day, according to the custom of thieves, from time immemorial, when a brother laborer is grabbed, I sent him a two-penny brown loaf, a hock of bacon, and a frame. I was told that he felt obliged by the attention, but had not the slightest suspicion that he who sent him the tribute of the fraternity was the cause of his mishap. It was only at La Force that he learnt that Jean Louis and Vidocq were the same person, and then he devised a singular means of defense; he asserted that I was the author of the robbery with which he was charged, and that, wanting his aid to remove the property, I had gone to seek him; but this long story stated to the court would not bear him out, and Masson in vain pleaded his innocence: he was sentenced to incarceration.

A short time afterward I was assisting at the preparation for the departure of the chain of galley slaves, when Masson, whom I had not seen since his apprehension, saw me through the grating.

"Ha!" said he to me, "Monsieur Jean Louis: and so it was you who got me into the stone jug. Oh! if I had known that you were Vidocq, I would have made you pay for the oranges?"

"You are a well-wisher of mine, then; you who made me the proposal of accompanying you?"

"Very true, but you never told me that you were a nose."

"If I had told you so I should have betrayed my trust, and that would not have prevented you from doing the job; you would only have chosen another pal."

"But you are not the less a rascal; I, who was so kind to you! Now, I would rather remain here as long as my life continued in my body, than be free, as you are, and equally dishonored."

"Every man to his taste."

"That is very fine! your taste—a nose, a spy—very fine, truly!"

"Why, it is as respectable a trade as thieving; besides, but for us what would the honest me do?"

At these words he burst into a loud fit of laughter.

"Honest men! Honest men!" he repeated, "you really make me laugh when I am in no grinning mood. Honest men! what would become of them? do not trouble yourself, for it cannot concern you; when you are at the meadow (Bagne) again, you will sing to a different tune."

"Oh! he will return there," said one of the prisoners who was listening to us.

"He," cried out Masson, "we do not want him; luck to the jolly boys! that's the thing."

Every time that my duties called me to Bicêtre I was sure that I should have to put up with such reproaches as I received from Masson. I seldom entered into discussion with the prisoner who apostrophized me, but I was not always silent, for fear that he might suppose, not that I despised him, but that I was afraid of him. Being in the presence of some hundreds of malefactors who had all, more or less, to complain of me, since they had all been apprehended by me, it may be supposed that it was necessary to evince some firmness, but the firmness was never more requisite than on the day when I first made my appearance in the midst of this horrible population.

I was no sooner the principal agent of the police of safety, than, most jealous of the proper fulfillment of the duty confided to me, I devoted myself seriously to acquire the necessary information. It seemed to me an excellent method to class, as accurately as possible, the descriptions of all the individuals at whom the finger of justice was pointed. I could thereby more readily recognize them if they should escape, and at the expiration of the sentence it became more easy for me to have that surveillance over them that was required of me. I then solicited from M. Henry authority to go to Bicêtre with my auxiliaries, that I might examine, during the operation of fettering, both the convicts of Paris and those from the provinces, who generally assemble on the same chain M. Henry made many observations to turn me from a step of which the advantages did not seem to him proportioned to the imminent danger to which I should thereby expose myself.

"I am informed," said he to me, "that the prisoners have conspired to play you some mischievous trick. If you persist — if you go at the departure of the chain, you will afford them an opportunity which they have long anxiously awaited: and, by my honor, whatever precautions you may take, I will not insure your safety." I thanked this gentleman for the interest which he testified for me, but at the same time insisted that he should accord me the permission I asked for, and he at length gave me the order which it was necessary for me to obtain.

On the day of fettering I went to Bicêtre with some of my agents; I entered the court, and instantly a most tumultuous uproar ensued, mingled with cries: "Down with the spies! down with the villain! down with Vidocq!" were heard from all the windows, where the prisoners, mounted on each other's shoulders, with faces pressed against the bars, were collected in groups. I advanced a few paces, and the vociferations redoubled; the whole place resounded with invectives and threats of destruction uttered with accents of fury; it was a most infernal sight to look at the visages of these cannibals, on which were manifested, by horrible contortions, the thirst of blood and the desire of vengeance. There was throughout the whole prison a most frightful uproar; I could not restrain an impulse of terror, and reproaching myself with my imprudence, was almost tempted to beat a retreat; but suddenly my courage mounted.

"What!" said I to myself, "thou hast not trembled when thou hast attacked the villains in their dens; they are here under bolts and bars, and art thou now scared? Courage; if thou must perish, at least make head against the storm, and let them not think they have intimidated thee!"

This return to a resolution more suited to the opinion which should really be formed of me, was so rapid as to leave no opportunity for any person to remark my weakness; I soon recovered all my courage, and, no longer burthened by a shadow of fear, walked boldly forward with my eyes fixed on the windows, and advanced to those of the lower story. At this moment a new burst of rage was evinced by the prisoners. They were not men, but ferocious beasts that were roaring; it was a tumult, a noise; it might have been thought that Bicêtre was about to be rent from its foundations, and that the walls of its cells were actually gaping open. In the midst of this outrageous din, I made a signal that I wished to speak: a dead silence ensued after the tempest, and they listened.

"Scum of the mob," I said, "why do you howl thus? It was when I grabbed you that you should, not have cried out, but defended yourselves. Shall you be any better for thus reproaching me? You treat me as a spy; well! I am a spy, but so are you also, for there is not one amongst you who has not offered to sell his comrade to me, in the hopes of thereby obtaining an impunity which I would not grant you; I rendered you to justice because you were culpable. I have not spared you I know; what motives have I for doing so? Is there any one here whom I ever knew when a freeman who can reproach me with ever having been his accomplice? Besides, even if I have been a thief, tell me, what does it prove but that I am more skillful or fortunate than you, since I have not been caught in the fact, I defy the most malicious to show a tittle of evidence to prove that I have been accused of robbery or swindling. It is useless to seek for twelve o'clock at three in the morning; oppose me by a single fact, one solitary truth, and I will confess myself the greatest rogue amongst you all. Is it the profession that you disapprove? Let those who blame me most for this tell me frankly, whether they do not a hundred times a day desire to be in my place?"

This harangue, during which no one interrupted me, was followed by hooting and shouting. Soon afterward vociferations and roarings began again, but I felt no sensation but that of indignation, and transported with anger, I became bold even beyond my strength. They announced that the convicts were about to be led into the court of fetters; I went to post myself in the passage, at the moment when they came to the call; and determined on selling my life dearly, I awaited until they should try to accomplish their threats. I confess that, in my mind, I desired much that one of them should attempt to lay hands upon me, so greatly did the desire of vengeance animate me. Ill-fated was the man who would have dared to assail me! but not one of these wretches made the least attempt, and I had only to endure the scowling look, to which I responded with that assurance which always disconcerts the enemy. The call terminated, a low murmur was the prelude to a fresh uproar: they vomited forth imprecations against me; "Let him come on then, he remains at the gate," the convicts bellowed forth, adding to my name the grossest epithets. Driven to extremity by this insolent defiance, I entered with one of my agents, and went into the midst of two hundred robbers, the majority of whom were arrested by me: "Come on, my friends! courage," cried they in the cells in which they were shut up; "look at the pig, kill him, and let us hear no more about him."

Now or never was the time:—"Now, gentlemen," said I to the galley slaves, "kill him, you see that they advise you well; try." I do not know what revolution of opinion actuated them, but the more I 'was in their power, the more they became appeased. At the termination of the fettering, those men who had sworn to exterminate me, were so much softened that many of them begged me to render them slight services. They had no reason to repent of having taxed my kindness, and the next day, at the hour of departure, after having thanked me, they bade me a cordial farewell. All was changed from black to white; the most mutinous of the previous evening had become supple, respectful at least in appearance, and almost overpoweringly so.

This was an experimental lesson of which I never lost the remembrance. It proved to me that, with persons of this stamp, we can only be potent when resolute: to keep them respectful, it is enough to have awed them once. From this period, I never allowed the chain to quit unless I attended the fettering of the convicts, and with very few exceptions, I was never afterward insulted. The convicts were accustomed to see me; if I did not go, it seemed as if they missed something, and in fact, nearly all of them had some commission to give me. From the moment they fell under the control of civil death, I was, in a measure, their testamentary executor. With a small portion resentments were not obliterated, but a thief's vengeance is not lasting. For eighteen years, that I have carried on the war with thieves, little or great, I have often been menaced; many galley slaves, celebrated for their intrepidity, have made oaths to assassinate me as soon as they should be at liberty if — they have all perjured themselves, and will continue to do so. Am I asked why? It is, that, at first, the only affair for a robber is to rob: that alone occupies him. If he cannot do otherwise, he will kill me to get my purse, that is his "vocation"—he will kill me to do away with a testimony which would destroy him, this is again a part of his business: —he will kill me to avoid punishment;—but when the punishment is inflicted, what purpose would it answer? Robbers do not lose time in assassination.

CHAPTER XXXII

ONE NIGHT, HALF OF WHICH HAD BEEN SPENT in the obscure lurking places of the Halle, hoping to fall in with some thieves who, in the overflow of that good nature which two or three glasses of liquor, offered at a fitting time, produce, allow themselves to be pumped, as to their past doings, those now in hand, and those meditated,—I was retiring, very much discomposed at having, to the detriment of my stomach, swallowed from pure vexation a good number of small glasses of that diluted spirit to which vitriol gives the strength and flavor, when at the corner of the Rue des Coutures Saint Gervais, I saw several individuals squatted in the embrasures of the doors.

By the light of the lamps, I easily distinguished beside them packets which they were endeavoring to squeeze into a smaller compass, but the suspicious whiteness of which could not fail to attract attention. Bundles at this hour of the night, and men who seek an obscure shelter when no water was falling;—a prodigious portion of perspicuity was not wanting to find, in such a combination of circumstances, all the characteristics of a suspicious occurrence. I made up my mind I hat they were thieves, and the bundles the booty which they had just obtained.

"Good," said I to myself, "let us evince no suspicions, but follow the procession when it sets forth, and if it passes by the corps de garde, catch is the word; on the other hand I will see them to their homes, take the address, and send the police after them." I thereupon made up my mind, without appearing to be troubled with what was behind me, but scarcely had I advanced ten paces when someone calls, "Jean Louis!" it was the voice of a man named Richelot, whom I had often met at various thieves' haunts I stopped naturally.

"Ah! good evening, Richelot," said I, "what the devil are you doing here at this time of the morning? Are you alone? You look frightened."

"Well I may be, I have narrowly escaped being nabbed on the boulevard du Temple."

"Nabbed! and why?"

"Why? here, come this way; do you see our friends with the bundles?"

"I am awake; you are loaded with swag (plunder)."

I approached them; and the whole party instantly rising, as soon as they were on their feet I recognized Lapierre, Commery, Lenoir, and Dubuisson; they all four hastened to assure me how glad they were to see me, and to extend the hand of friendship to me.

Commery. "Ah! we narrowly escaped; my heart still thumps, put your hand upon it, feel how it goes tick-tack."

Vidocq. "That is nothing."

Lapierre. "Oh! we have had a fright in real earnest; I know very well that when I saw the greens (the Parisian guards, whose uniform was green), my heart jumped bang into my mouth."

Dubuisson. "And just above the marketplace were the dragoons of Paris, whom we met nose to nose on horseback just by the theatre."

Vidocq. "What spoonies you are! you should have had a drag to whisk off the swag in. You are but greenhorns."

Richelot. "Greenhorns, if you like; but we had no means of conveyance, and we have therefore chosen the back streets."

Vidocq. "And where are you going? If I can assist you in any way...."

Richelot. "If you will pilot us, and give us your company as far as the Rue Saint Sebastien, where we are going to deposit the swag, you shall have your whack."

Vidocq. "With pleasure, my boys."

Richelot. "Well, then, go first, and spy if you twig any coves or beaks."

Richelot and his companions took up their bundles, and I went forward. Our progress was fortunate and we reached the door of the house without interruption, each of us taking off our shoes to make no noise as we went upstairs. We reached the landing-place on the third story; they were awaiting us. A door opened softly, and we entered a vast chamber dimly lighted, of which the tenant was a shipwright's man, who had already been before the police. Although he did not know me, my presence seemed to trouble him, and whilst he was helping to conceal the bundles under the bed, I heard him ask a question in a low voice, which I could guess by the reply, which was spoken in a louder tone.

Richelot. "It is Jean Louis, a good fellow; be quiet, he is stanch."

The Tenant. "That's all right; there are nowadays so many noses and sneaks, that we should be fly to every cove."

Lapierre. "Oh be easy! be easy! I can answer for him as for myself: he is a friend and a Frenchman."

The Tenant. "Since it is all right, I will trust him, and upon the strength of it we will have a shove in the mouth all round."

He got on a sort of stool, and lifting his hands up to the shelf of an old cupboard, he took out a full bladder.

"Here's the stuff, brandy, and nothing but some of my own prigging. Come, Jean, you shall begin."

Vidocq. "With all my heart (pouring forth into a green glass and drinking). It is capital out and out tipple, which cheers as it goes down—now it is your turn, Lapierre; come, sluice your ivories."

The glass and bladder passed from hand to hand, and when each had drank enough we threw ourselves on the bed until the morning. At daybreak we heard in the streets the cry of the sweep.

Richelot (jogging his neighbor). "Ah! Lapierre, we must go to the fence."

Lapierre. "Let me sleep, do."

Richelot. "Come, come, stir your stumps."

Lapierre. "Go by yourself, or take Lenoir."

Richelot. "You had better come, as you have already dealt with the old woman, and can make a super bargain."

Lapierre. "Let me alone, I am sleepy."

Vidocq. "My G—, what sluggards you are! I will go, if you will tell me where."

Richelot. "You are right, Jean Louis, but the fence has never seen you and will not deal for the sway but with us. But if you like we will go together."

Vidocq. "Yes, we two, and then another time she will know my phiz."

We went. The fence lived in Rue de Bretagne, No. 14, in the house of a sausage maker, who appeared the owner of it. Richelot entered, and asked if Madame Bras was at home. Yes, was the answer; and after having gone through the passage, we went up the stairs to the three pair. Madame Bras had not gone out, but actuated by a principle of honor, she would not take in any property by daylight. "At least," said Richelot to her, "if you cannot take the goods now, give us earnest; come, it is a good haul, and you know we deal all upon the square."

"You say very true, but I cannot allow myself to be compromised by a pair of good eyes; come in the evening, then all cats are grey." Richelot tried by every effort to extract some coin from her, but she was inexorable, and we retired without having obtained any thing. My companion cursed, swore, stormed, till it did one's heart good to hear him.

"Well," said I to him, "one would imagine that you had lost every thing. Why vex yourself? If she will not, another will; come with me to my fence, I am sure she will lend us four or five crowns."

We went to the Rue Neuve-Saint-Francois, where I had fixed my domicile. By a low whistle, I made Annette understand that I wanted her, and she quickly descended and came to us at the corner of the old Rue due Temple." "Good-day, Madame." "Good-day, Jean Louis."

"If you are inclined to be obliging, lend me twenty francs, and this evening you shall have them again."

"Yes, this evening! if you gain any thing you will go to la Courtille."

"No, I assure you I will be punctual." "May I believe you? I will not refuse you then; come with me, whilst your friend waits for you at the cabaret at the corner of the Rue de L'Oseille."

On being alone with Annette I gave her the requisite instructions, and when I found that she clearly understood them, I rejoined Richelot in the cabaret; "Here," said I to him, showing the twenty francs, "is what you may call a mot, and nothing but a good one."

"Parbleu, won't she post the blunt for the whole of the swag."

"I think not. She is only a fence for metal, tickers, and frippery."

"It is a pity, for she is an out-and-out mot, and just such a one as would suit us well."

After finishing our bottle, we set out to regain the lodging, where we found ready a Normandy goose of first-rate quality, and some other prog. I produced the money, and as it was intended for further supplies for the victualling office, our host went out for a dozen of wine and some bread. We were all so sharp-set that the provisions seemed only to appear and then vanish instantly. The bladder of brandy was drained to the last drop. Our meal terminated, it was proposed to open the packets. They contained most beautiful linen sheets, shirts of extraordinary fineness, gowns with superbly worked borders, cravats, stockings, etc., all damp and wet. The thieves told me that they had taken the booty from one of the largest houses in the Rue de L'Echiquier, where they had introduced themselves by a window, of which they had broken the bars.

The inventory concluded, I proposed that we should make different lots, and not sell them all in the same place. I insinuated that they would give as much for each lot as for the whole in a lump, and that two sales were better than one. My comrades were of the same opinion, and made two divisions of the booty. It then became a matter of question as to how to get rid of them; they were sure of the sale of one lot, but wanted a purchaser for the second. A clothes-seller, called Pomme Rouge, in the Rue de la Juiverie, was the man whom I pointed out to them. He had long been pointed out to me as a regular fence,—goods taken in and no questions asked. Here was an opportunity of putting him to the test, and I was unwilling that it should escape, for if he were caught, the result of my plans would be infinitely more agreeable; for instead of only one fence, I should cause the arrest of two, and thus I should kill three birds with one stone.

It was agreed that they should make an offer to my man, but nothing could be done till dark, and what was to keep us from ennui till then? What could we converse about? Amongst robbers the communion of martyrs had not mental resources sufficient to keep up conversation for more than a quarter of an hour. What can be done? Prigs do nothing, unless at work, and when at work they do nothing. But yet it was necessary to kill time; we had still some money before us, wine was voted for by acclamation, and we again commenced our libations to Bacchus. The sons of Mercury drink fast and long, but yet one cannot always be drinking. If, indeed, topers were like the buckets of the Danaides, open at one end and with holes at the other, disgust would not proceed from plenitude! Unfortunately, each man has his capacity, and when, between the bladder and the brain, the wave, whose place of exit is too narrow, remounts toward its source, there is no need to say, my worthy friend, that if we would avoid unpleasant consequences we must stop: this our companions did. As they thought they had need of their head for some later period, and as a thick cloud already began to spread over the osseous vault which covers the potent ruler of all our actions, that they might not lose all guidance, they insensibly ceased to make a funnel of their mouths, and only opened them to talk. What was the nature of their conversation? The talk, which they would have been much posed to keep up on any other subject, turned on their comrades who were at the Bagne, or in prison. They also spoke about spies.

"Talking of spies," said the shipwright, "you must have heard of the celebrated rogue who has turned nose, that Vidocq; do any of you fellows know him?"

Altogether (myself in chorus). "Yes, yes, but only by name."

Dubuisson. "I know they talk a good deal about him. They say he comes from the Bagne, where he was sentenced for twenty-four years."

The Shipwright. "You are wrong, you flat. This Vidocq is a prig, who was sentenced for life for his many escapes. He was allowed to be set at liberty because he promised to blow the gaff, and that is the reason that he stops at Paris. He is a deep file; when he wants to trap a covey he tries to make friends with him, and, as soon as he has done that, he slips some swag into his cly and then all is done; or else he leads him on to some job that he may be caught at work. He it was who floored Bailli, Jacquet, and Martinet. Oh G, yes it was he! let me tell you how he did them."

Altogether. (myself in chorus). "Did them, well said, my lad."

The Shipwright. "Whilst drinking together with another like himself, you know him, the rip Riboulet, Manon's fancy man."

All. "Manon la Blonde's?"

The Shipwright. "Yes, she. They were speaking of one thing and another, Vidocq says, as he had just left the Bagne, he wanted to find some friends to prig. The others are caught in the net. He tickles them so well that he leads them to a spot of work, in the Rue Grand Zurleur. It was thought that he would blow the gaff to the police, and so he did. They were all taken, and in the meantime the rascal escapes with his comrade. This is his plan for catching good fellows. It was he who brought all the chauffeurs to be kissed by the headsman's daughter after having been their leader."

Every time the narrator paused we refreshed ourselves with a glass of wine. Lapierre, profiting by one of these pauses, spoke thus.

"What, is it that cock-and-bull story? He talks like a magpie. He is chaffing us. Do you think such gammon amuses us? I like to amuse myself."

The Shipwright. "What the deuce will you do, then? If we had any books (cards), we might handle them a bit."

Lapierre. "I'll tell you what we will do, act a play."

The Shipwright. "Go it then, M. Tarma (Talma)."

Lapierre. "Do you think I can play by myself?"

Richelot. "We will help you, but what shall be the piece?"

Dubuisson. "The play of Caesar; you know there is one of that name, who says, the first who was king had a happy lot."

Lapierre. "Oh, none of that blarney; let us play the piece of Vidocq, caught, after having sold his brethren like Joseph."

I scarcely knew what to make of this singular business: however, without being at all disconcerted, I cried out suddenly, "I will play Vidocq; they say he is a stout chap, and it will suit me."

"You're stout," said Lenoir, "but he is much stouter."

"That is no matter," observed Lapierre, "Jean Louis is not a bad representation, he weighs his weight."

"Come, then, we don't want so much jaw about it," said 'Richelot, lifting a table into one corner of the room. "You Jean Louis, and you Lapierre stand there: Lenoir, Dubuisson, and Etienne (the shipwright), go to the other end: they shall be the friends, and I will seat myself on the bed and be the people."

"What people?" inquired Etienne. "Why the audience, if you like. The ship-wright is a booby."

"I am a spectator too."

"No, you stupid ass, I am. You are a friend, take your place, the play is going to begin."

We imagine ourselves in a public-house at La Courtille; each talks. I get up, and, under a pretext of asking for some tobacco, enter into conversation with the friends at the other table, I speak a little slang, they find me a downy cove, and give me a knowing look, which I return, and it is found we are all lads of the same profession. They follow the customary usages of society,—a glass more than necessary. I complain of being without a job of work. They complain, and we all complain together. We commence to be very full of mutual compassion and sympathy; I curse the beaks, they curse them too; I swear at the bigwigs of my quarter who persecute me; my friends look at each other, consult each other's eyes, and deliberate upon the opportunity offered by, or the disadvantages of, my acquaintance. They take my hand, they press it, I consent: it is agreed that they may rely on me. Then comes the proposal—the character I play is that which, with but few variations, I always have played—I only alter a little, but putting the stolen goods into the pockets of my friends. Then was heard the unanimous applause, accompanied by shouts of laughter. "Well done, well done," cried the actors and the witness of this scene.

"Well done, certainly," said Richelot, "but see the sun is setting and it is time to tramp; the play can finish in the drag, or elsewhere, when we have done with the fence; I will go and get a jarvey, if you fellows like?"

"Yes, yes, let us be off."

The drama was progressing well, we were approaching the climax, but it was doomed to be a very different one from that anticipated by these gentlemen, for the catastrophe was not in accordance with the title of the piece. We all got into a hackney-coach, and desired the coachman to stop at the corner of the Rue de Bretagne and the Rue de Tourraine. Bras, one of the fences, was waiting at a short distance. Dubuisson, Commery, and Lenoir, alighted, taking with them the portion of the merchandise which we had agreed to sell. Whilst they were agreeing about the price, I saw, on looking from the window, that Annette had fulfilled my intention. Persons whom I saw, some with their noses in the air, as if seeking for some number, others walking about like idlers, were not in this quarter, I thought, without some motive.

After ten minutes of expectation, we were rejoined by our comrades who had been to Bras. They had brought away one hundred and twenty-five francs for things worth at least six times as much; but it was of no consequence, they were not sorry to realize what they were in haste to enjoy.

There remained those bundles which we had reserved for Pomme Rouge. On reaching Rue de la Juiverie, Richelot said to me, "Come, you must go and bargain, you know the downy fence."

"That will not do," I replied, "I owe him money, and we have had a row about it."

I owed Pomme Rouge nothing, but we had seen each other, and he knew that I was Vidocq. It would, therefore, have been imprudent to show myself, and I left my friends to arrange these matters, and on their return, as the appearance of Annette in the vicinity of the shop gave me the certainty that the police was on the qui vive, I proposed to discharge the coach and go and sup in the cabaret of the Grand Casuel, on the Quai Pelletier, at the corner of the Rue Blanche Mibray.

After the visit to Pomme Rouge we were richer by eighty francs, and the sum at our disposal was so considerable, that we might give way to some excess without fear of distressing ourselves, but we had no time to expend it, for scarcely had we got our glasses in hand when the guard entered, followed by a posse of inspectors. At the sight of the veterans and the spies, all their countenances fell, and the general feeling was "we are caught." Thibault, the peace-officer, asked us for our papers; some had none, and others were not correct, mine were amongst these latter. "For the charge of all these sparks," said the peace-officer, "safe bind, safe find." We were tied two and two, and conducted to the commissary. Lapierre was coupled with me. "Have you good legs?" I said to him in a low tone. "Yes," was his reply, and when we reached the top of the Rue de la Tannerie, taking out a knife I had concealed up my sleeve, I cut the cord. "Courage, Lapierre, courage!" I cried. With a blow of my elbow I prostrated the veteran who had taken me by the arm; darted away, and with a few leaps reached a small alley leading to the Seine. Lapierre followed me, and we reached the Quai des Ormes together.

They lost all traces of us, and I was very glad to have escaped without being recognized. Lapierre was equally rejoiced, for not having had any time for reflection, he was far from suspecting any sinister motives in me; but, in fact, if I favored his escape, it was in the hope of introducing myself, under his auspices, into some other band of thieves. By fleeing with him I removed all suspicions that himself or his companions might have conceived, and kept up the good opinion which they had of me. In this way I hoped to make new discoveries, for as I was a secret agent I was as desirous of acting as quietly as possible.

Lapierre was free, but I kept him in sight, and was ready to give him up the moment he was no longer useful to me.

We continued running toward the hospital, where at length we stopped, and entered a cabaret to recover breath and rest ourselves. I ordered a measure of wine to refresh us. "Here, lad," said I to Lapierre, "here is a comforter."

"Oh yes, it is hard work."

"And difficult to keep up, is it not?"

"Nothing can drive the idea from my mind.

"What?"

"Here, let us drink."

And no sooner had he emptied his glass than he became more pensive; "No, no," he repeated, "nothing can drive the idea from my mind —"

"What do you mean? tell me."

"Well, then, I will tell you."

"You are right: but first you will do well to take off the stockings you have on your feet, and the cravat about your neck."

As it seemed to me that I perceived in the eyes of my friend that dark scowl of mistrust which, if one does not take care, increases so rapidly, I was glad to testify one of those marks of interest, the effect of which is to reassure a suspicious mind: such was my aim in advising him to remove from his attire, some articles of small value, which during the overhauling of the booty, his associates and himself had immediately applied to their own use.

"What shall I do with them?" said Lapierre.

"Throw them into the river."

"I'll not be such a fool! the silk stockings are quite new, and the cravat has never been hemmed."

"Silly nonsense."

"You want to laugh at me, my boy; throw away your own first."

I begged him to observe that I had nothing on that could compromise me. "You are like the hares," I added, "you lose your memory as you run; do you not remember that there was no cravat for me, and with trousers like these (touching those I wore) would you have me wear women's stockings?"

He took off the stockings which, folded up, he enveloped in the cravat.

Thieves are at the same time misers and spendthrifts: he felt the necessity of removing these convicting articles out of sight, but his heart bled at the thoughts of not making a profit by them. It is because the produce of robbery is often so dearly paid for, that the sacrifice of it is always painful.

Lapierre was most anxious to sell his stockings and cravat, and we went together to the Rue de la Bucherie to offer them to a shopkeeper, who gave us forty-five sous for them. Lapierre appeared to have made up his determination since the catastrophe of Grand Casuel; yet he was constrained in his manners, and if I may judge of what was passing in his mind, in spite of my efforts to re-establish myself in his opinion, I was strongly suspected. Such feelings were not very favorable to my projects, and persuaded that henceforward I must not temporize, but bring matters to a speedy termination, I said to Lapierre, "If you like we will go and sup at Place Maubert."

"I will, if you please," was the reply.

I took him to the Deux Freres, where I called for wine, pork-chops, and cheese. At eleven o'clock we were still at table, everybody had retired, and they brought us in a bill which came to four francs fifteen centimes. I immediately cried out, "My five-franc piece! my five-franc piece! where can it be?" I rummaged all my pockets and searched myself from head to feet. "My God! I must have lost it in running: look, Lapierre, if you have it!"

"No, I have only my forty-five sous, and not a dump besides."

"Look for it, I am going to try and arrange with the people." I offered the cabaretier two francs fifty centimes, promising to bring him the remainder on the morrow; but he would not listen to me. "Ah! you think," said he, "that you may come and have all you want here, and then pay me with monkey's allowance."

"But," I observed to him, "it is an accident which might happen to the most honest man."

"That's all my eye! When one is low in cash we are trickish or so; a cup of wine, or so, one would not mind, but it is no go to have a whole supper on tick."

"Oh, never mind, old lad; if it accommodates good fellows, never mind."

"Come, come, not so much jaw; pay me, or I'll fetch the guard."

"The guard! that for the guard and you too," accompanying the words with a gesture of contempt much used by common people.

"Ah, you vagabond! it is not enough to carry off my property!" cried he, doubling his fist and thrusting it in my face, "Do not strike me," I replied to his apostrophe, "do not strike me, or..."

He advanced toward me, and I instantly hit him a blow. A quarrel and uproar followed, which Lapierre thinking would come to serious consequences, judged it best to mizzle; but on the very moment when he was about to make off and leave, me to extricate myself as best I might, the waiter seized him by the throat and cried out thieves.

The guardhouse was nigh, the soldiers came in, and for the second time in that day, we were placed between two ranges of those candles of Maubeuge whose wicks have a smell of gunpowder. My comrade endeavored to prove to the corporal that he was not in fault, but the veteran was immovable, and we were shut up in the guardhouse. Lapierre became silent and sad as a brother of La Trappe, he did not even unclose his teeth. At length, about two o'clock in the morning, the commissary went his round, and asked to see the persons in confinement. Lapierre first appeared, and was told he might go if he would pay the bill. I was called in my turn, and on entering the room recognized M. Legoix. The recognition was mutual, and in two words I explained to him what I had done; I told him the place where the stockings and cravat had been sold, and whilst he hastened to seize on these articles, which were requisite to convict Lapierre, I returned to him. He was no longer silent.

"The bandage has fallen," said he. "I see what is done, it was all a plot."

"What! you are laughing at me, but I will speak frankly. Yes, it is done, and it is a plot, but it was you who got us into the trap."

"No, my friend, it was not me; I do not know who, but I suspect you more than any one else."

At these words I grew angry, he furious: to threats succeeded blows, and we proceeded to fight until we were separated. As soon as we were parted I found my five-franc piece; and as the cabaretier had not reckoned the thump I gave him, it was enough for me not only to satisfy all his demands, but also to offer to the corps de garde, I will not say the stirrup cup, but that small drop of farewell token which the snob always pays willingly. This tribute paid, there was no further reason for my detention, and I started off without paying my adieu to Lapierre, who was now known; and the next day I learned that the most complete success had crowned my efforts. The two fences, Bras and Pomme Rouge, had been surprised in the midst of ample proofs of the nefarious traffic which they carried on; the robbers had been apprehended with the property which they had instantly applied to their use, and they were compelled to confess; Lapierre alone had tried denial of the facts, but confronted with the shopkeeper of Rue de la Bacherie, he was decidedly and positively recognized—the stockings and cravat were his accusers. The whole gang, robbers and receivers, were sent to La Force, in the expectation of judgment; there they soon learnt that the comrade who had played the part of "Vidocq caught," was in fact, "Vidocq the catcher." Great was their surprise; how they must have commended the admirable talents of the comedian! The sentence confirmed, all were ordered to the Bagne. The evening before their departure I was present when they were fettered, and, on seeing me, they could not forbear smiling.

"Behold your work, you villain," said Lapierre, "you are content, no doubt."

"I have, at least, no reproach to make against myself, I did not advise you to steal. Did you not make up to me? Why be so confiding? When a man exercises a profession like yours, he ought to be more on his guard."

"It is all well," said Commery, "you are sure to be at the galleys again yourself."

"In the meantime a good journey to yourself. Keep my place for me, and if ever you return to Pantin (Paris) do not play at such dangerous games again."

After this reply they conversed together, and Bichelot said, "Well, well! I owe him a turn."

"As for you," replied the shipwright, "you brought him amongst us. Since you knew him, you ought to have known that he was a nose."

"Ah, yes! it was Bichelot who brought it upon us," sighed Pomme Rouge, who was being fettered, and nearly had his head broken by the hammer which was riveting his collar.

"Do not move," said the smith, roughly. "It was he, it was he," replied the fence, "who floored us, and but for him."

"Stand steady, you fool, and mind your eye." These were the last words I heard, but as I went away I saw, by certain gestures, that the colloquy grew warmer. What are they saying! I know not.

Chapter XXXIII

IN 1812, A PROFESSED THIEF, NAMED HOTOT, who had long sought to be reinstated as a secret agent, in which employment he had been engaged previously to my admission into the police, came to offer his services to me for the fete of Saint Cloud. It is known as one of the most celebrated of the environs of Paris, and that, led by the concourse of persons, pickpockets assemble there in large bodies.

It was on Friday that Hotot was brought to me by a comrade. This step appeared to me the more extraordinary, as I had previously given information against him which had led to his being brought before the court of assizes. Perhaps he only desired to connect himself with me that he might the more readily play me some ill turn: such was my first thought, but I received him kindly, and even testified my satisfaction that he had not doubted my wish to be of service to him. I evinced so much apparent sincerity in my proffers of goodwill toward him, that it was impossible for him to conceal his intentions from my penetration. A sudden change, which overspread his whole face, convinced me instantly that, in accepting his offer, I was favoring some plans which he was not willing to confide to me. I saw his internal congratulations at having duped me. But be that as it might, I feigned to have the utmost confidence in him, and it was agreed that on the following Sunday, he should go, at two o'clock, and post himself near the principal basin, that he might point out the thieves of his acquaintance, who, he told me, would come to work at that spot.

On the day appointed, I went to Saint Cloud with the only two agents I then had under my command. On arriving at the destined place, I looked out for Hotot; I walked backward and forward, looked about me on all sides, but no Hotot. At length, after waiting for an hour and a half, my patience being worn nearly threadbare, I dispatched one of my staff to the principal walk, desiring him to endeavor to find an auxiliary whose want of punctuality was as suspicious as his zeal.

My agent searched for an entire hour, when, wearied with exploring every hole and corner of the garden and park, he returned and told me that he could not find Hotot. The moment afterward, I saw my man himself running toward me, bathed in perspiration. "You do not know," said he to us, "that I had just got hold of six prigs, but they saw you, and instantly mizzled. I am sorry, for they swallowed the bait; but what is deferred is not lost, and I shall have them yet."

I pretended to take all this for gospel, and Hotot was convinced that I had not any doubt of his veracity. We spent the greater portion of the day together, and only separated about twilight. I then went to the gendarmes' station where the peace officers told me that many watches had been stolen in a direction precisely opposite to that in which, by the advice of Hotot, our watch was kept. It was then plain to me that he attracted us to one point that he might the more easily work in another. It is an old stratagem in the tactics of diversion and false information given by thieves, that they may have less fear of the police.

Hotot, whom I took good care not to reproach in any way, imagined that he had completely gulled me; but if I said nothing, I did not think the less, and increasing my show of friendship toward him, whilst he was meditating a renewal of his Saint-Cloud trickery, I was on the alert to catch him tripping at the first opportunity. Our friendship being still very close, the opportunity presented itself earlier than I had even dared to hope.

One morning I suddenly determined to make a visit to Hotot. We were near where he resided. I proposed to my comrade of the watch to accompany me; and on his assenting, we went to Hotot's, where, on knocking, he opened the door and appeared surprised to see us: "What a wonder at this early hour."

"Are you astonished?" said I; "we come to have a glass with you."

"Oh! you are welcome;" and then jumping into bed, "Where is the liquor?"

"Gaffre will be so kind as to fetch it."

I put my hand into my pocket, and as Gaffre as a Jew, was less careful of his trouble than his money, he willingly undertook the commission and went out for that purpose. During his absence I remarked that Hotot had the air of a man who has gone to bed later than usual; the room was, besides, in a very extraordinary state of disorder. His clothes, rather torn than taken off, seemed to have had a heavy soaking; and his shoes were covered with white clay, which was still wet. Not to have concluded from all these indications that Hotot had but recently returned, would not have been Vidocq. For the moment I thought nothing more of it, but my fancy soon wandered into the wide field of conjecture, and I conceived suspicions which I took care not to evince; I would not even appear curious, that is to say indiscreet, and, for fear of disquieting my worthy friend, I did not ask him a single question. We spoke of the rain and the fine weather, but more of the fine weather than the rain, and when we had nothing left to drink, we went away.

Once out of the house, I communicated to Gaffre the remarks I had made; "I am much deceived," I added, "or he has been abroad all night; there has been something in the wind."

"I think so too, for his clothes are still wet, and his shoes covered with mud! He has not been walking in the dust."

Hotot hardly thought that we were talking of him, but yet his ears must have tingled. "Where has he been? What has he done?" we inquired of each other; perhaps he has joined some gang. Gaffre was no less puzzled than myself, and we were compelled to think that Hotot might be honest after all.

At twelve o'clock, we went to make our report of the transactions of the night; our account was not very interesting; nothing has occurred was the whole contents. "Ah!" said M. Henry to us, "the people in the faubourg Saint Marceau are all honest; I had much better have sent you to the boulevard Saint Martin; it appears that the lead robbers have renewed their work; they carried off more than four hundred and fifty pounds from a house newly built. The watchman, who pursued without catching them, says, they were four in number. The robbery was effected during the heavy shower of last night."

"During the heavy shower! parbleu!" I cried, "you know one of the robbers."

"Who is he?"

"Hotot."

"He who joined the police, and who asked leave to enter it?"

"The same."

I told M. Henry of my suspicions and remarks, and as he was convinced that I was correct, I went out instantly that I might with all possible speed convert what was at present but presumptive evidence into proof positive. The commissary of the quarter in which the robbery had been effected, went with me to the spot, and we found in one place on the ground the deep imprint of two nailed shoes, and the earth had been indented by the weight of a man. These traces could afford precise indications; and precautions were taken that they should not be effaced. I felt perfectly assured that they were exactly fitted to Hotot's shoes, and taking Gaffre with me to him, that I might verify my suspicions without alarming the culprit, I devised the plan which was thus executed. On getting to Hotot's residence we made a tremendous noise at the door.

"Get up, get up, we have brought the poultry." He arose, turned the key, and we stumbled into the room like men somewhat stupid with liquor.

"Hallo!" said Hotot, "allow me to pay my respects to you. You have been warming the oven early this morning."

"Yes, and we have come to you," I replied, "to finish the baking. You are very cunning," I added, showing him in its covering a purchase which we had made as we came along. "Guess what we have in here."

"How can I guess?" Then tearing the corner of the paper, I exposed the claws of a bird.

"Ah! sacre dieu!" he cried, "it is a turkey."

"Yes, a brother of yours, and, as you see, it is by its feet that we know this sort of animal: do you understand me now?"

"What does he say?"

"I say it is roasted."

"Oh! it should be baked with venison fat"

"Venison fat! here look at it."

I handed the bird to him, and whilst he examined and turned it over and over, Gaffre stooped down, picked up his shoes, and put them in his hat.

"Well, and what did you give for this bit of hollow?"

"Seven bob, a kick and eight mag."

"The d___! Seven shillings and ten pence. About the price of a pair of shoes."

"Exactly so, my boy," said the pilferer, rubbing his hands.

"Here is plenty to bite at; and how well it smells, quite deliciously, it is perfectly tempting! We will soon settle his business."

"Who carves? I cannot."

"Well, then, we will help you; is there a knife in the box?"

"Yes, look in the drawer."

I found a knife, and then sought an excuse to send Gaffre out "Oh, by the way," said I, whilst I laid the cloth, "you can oblige me by going to my house, and saying, that they need not wait dinner for me."

"Very well, and then you will be off without me; that is no go; I shall not cut my stick until I have had some grubbery."

"But we cannot eat without drinking."

"Well, then, I will have the liquor produced."

He opened the window, and called to winter. "And now," he added, "you cannot play me any trick."

Gaffre was like the majority of police agents, and, except being treacherous, a good enough fellow; but a perfect gourmand. With him the belly superseded all other business; and thus, although he had obtained possession of the shoes, which was the main point in the affair, I saw I could not induce him to leave the place until he had his share of the eatables I hastened, therefore, to cut up the bird, and when the wine arrived, "Come to the table," I cried to my gastronomist, "make haste and cram your fill."

Hotot's bed was his table, and without any forks but those of father Adam, we made to the god who is within us, that is the god of Venus, a sacrifice in the manner of the ancients. We ate like ogres, and the repast was quickly terminated. "Now," said Gaffre, "I can toddle. I know not if you are like me, but when the sun shines in my stomach, I am good for nothing; when the chest is full it is a different matter."

"Well, then, mizzle."

He took his hat, and disappeared.

"Now he is gone," said Hotot, with the tone of a man who is not sorry to be left alone with another for some time. "Well, my friend Jules, is there never to be a vacancy for Hotot?"

"Patience, patience, all will come in good time."

"It is only for you to say a good word for me, and M. Henry would listen, if you would"

"It must not be today, then, for I expect a good rowing; Gaffre will not escape, for we have not sent in our report these two days."

This lie was not without its purpose; it was not necessary that Hotot should think I had been informed of the robbery in which I believed him a participator; he was without mistrust, and I kept him in that security; and, for fear he should think of getting up, I led the conversation to those points which most interested him. He spoke to me successively of many affairs. "Ah!" he said, sighing, "if I were certain of entering the police again, with a pay of ten or fifteen bob a day, I could give such information! I know now of a burglary, which would be a welcome disclosure to M. Henry."

"Do you?"

"Yes, three robbers, Berchier called Bicêtre, Caffin, and Linois, whom I will give up to him in the actual fact, as sure as you and I make two."

"If you can, why don't you? That would be an excellent beginning."

"I know it, but"

"Are you afraid to make yourself seem visible in the business? If you perform services, I will do my best to insure your admission."

"Ah, my friend, you pour balm into my mind; you will procure my admission."

"Oh that will be easily effected."

"Come then, a bumper to luck," cried Hotot, transported with joy.

"Yes, let us drink to your approaching reception."

"And the sooner the better."

Hotot was enchanted, and already laid down a line of conduct; he had his dreams of happiness, and there was in his very legs those inquietudes of hope which are produced by the prospect of coming pleasure. I was afraid lest he should quit his bed, when at length some person knocked at the door; it was Gaffre, holding in his hand a small bottle of brandy, which Annette had given to him. "Traffic," said my Israelite colleague as he entered, in that Hebrew slang, which was doubtless the favorite language of our patron, Monsieur Judas. As I pique myself on being a Hebraist of the first order, I instantly comprehended him, and saw how to play my cards. Whilst I was pouring out for the neophyte the nectar of a policeman, Gaffre replaced the shoes. We continued to chat and drink, and before we parted, I learnt that the plunder of the lead was that of which Hotot proposed to point out the perpetrators. The father Bellemont, a blacksmith of the Rue de la Tannerie, was the fence whom he mentioned to me.

As these details were interesting, I told Hotot that I should instantly communicate them to M. Henry, and recommended him to find out the place where the three thieves slept. He promised to point out the house, and when we had agreed upon preliminaries, we separated. Gaffre had not left me. "Well!" said he, "it is he, the shoes fit precisely, and the impression is very deep. In leaping from the window he must have fallen with all his weight." This was the signification of the word traiffe; and now I had only to take measures accordingly. I had already explained Hotot's conduct to myself, and I readily conceived the part he wished to play. In the first place, it was clear that he committed the robbery with the intention of making his profit by it, but he was chasing two hares at once; by pointing out his accomplices he attained his second object, that of making himself of consequence in the eyes of the police, that he might thereby be re-established in their employ. I trembled to think of the consequences of such a combination. "Wretch," said I to myself, I will contrive that he may have the recompense of his crime, and if the unhappy creatures who have aided him in his expedition are convicted, it is but just that he should be a partaker of their sentence. I did not hesitate to believe him the most guilty of the whole, and from what I knew of his character, it seemed most probable to me that he had led them on to it, only to contrive a job; I even went so far as to think that it was possible that he alone had committed the robbery, but thought it advisable to accuse of his own crime those individuals whose misconduct made them suspected characters. In each of these suppositions, Hotot was a great rogue, and I determined to rid society of him.

I knew that he had two mistresses, one Emilie Simonet, who had several children by him, and with whom he lived as a husband; the other Felicite Renaud, a common girl, who doted upon him. I thought I could contrive to attain my ends by setting these rivals at loggerheads, and by their mutual jealousy light the flambeau that was to show him to justice. Hotot was watched, and in the afternoon I learned that he was in the Champs Elysée with Felicite. I went to him there, and taking him aside, told him that I required him on an affair of extreme importance.

"You must know," said I, "you are to be apprehended and taken to prison, where you must pump a cove that we shall nab this evening. As you will be in quod before him, he will not take you for a sneak, and when he is brought in, you can easily plant yourself upon him."

Hotot accepted the proposition with joy. "Ah!" he exclaimed, "I am then a spy once more! You may rely on me, but I must first take leave of Felicite." He went toward her, and as the hour of nocturnal seductions, or padding the paved for the amorously disposed, was nigh, she was not angry with him for leaving her so soon.

"Now you have got rid of the mot, I will give you instructions. You know the little ken on the boulevard Montmartre in front of the Theatre des Varieties?"

"Yes, Brunet's."

"Well, go there and seat yourself at the further end of the room with a bottle of beer, and when you see two of the inspectors of the officer of peace, Mercier, enter—you know them?"

"Know them! do you ask me such a question, who am an old trooper?"

"Well, as you know them it will be all right: when they come in, make them a sign that it is you, that they may not mistake you for any other person."

"You be easy, they will not mistake me."

"You know it will be disagreeable if they should lay hands on some unlucky citizen."

"Oh! there shall be no mistake, I shall be there, and then the signal agreed on. The signal will do all."

"You understand clearly?"

"Yes, do you take me for a fool? I will not give them the trouble to take a second glance."

"All right, they shall have the countersign, and as soon as they perceive you, they will know what they are to do: they will arrest and convey you to the station of Lycee, where you will stay two or three hours, and then the youth you are to pump, having already seen you there, will not be surprised to meet you again at the depot."

"Give yourself no uneasiness; I will do the trick so well, that I will defy the most downy cove to discover that I am not situated exactly like himself. Besides, you will see how cleverly I do my work, to the very letter."

He seemed so hearty in the business, that I was really sorry at being compelled to deceive him thus, but, reflecting on his conduct toward his comrades, the feeling of pity which I had momentarily experienced was dissipated, never to return. He gave me his hand, and we parted; he walked with all the velocity of eager satisfaction; the earth seemed scarcely to bear him. On my part, no less swift than he, I flew to the prefecture, where I found the inspectors I had mentioned to him; one of them was named Cochois, now a watchman at Bicêtre; I told them what they were to do, and followed them. They entered the house.

Scarcely had they crossed the threshold, when Hotot, faithful to the orders I had given him, pointed to himself with his finger, like a man who says, "It is me." At this signal the inspectors went up to him, and asked for his letters of protection. Hotot, as proud as Artabanes, answered that he had none. "Then you must come with us," was the immediate rejoinder, and to prevent him from running away, if he should be so inclined, they secured his hands with cords. During this operation, a sort of internal content overspread the face of Hotot: he was happy to find himself caught; he blessed his bonds; he contemplated them almost with love, for, as he believed, all this preparation was but a ceremonious form; and in fact, like some philosopher of antiquity, he could boast of being free in his chains; and he said in a low voice to the inspectors, "Devil fetch me if I run! The mauleys and trotters are tied: you could not do more to secure a regular workman."

It was about eight in the evening when Hotot was brought to the guardhouse: at eleven o'clock they had not brought in the person from whom he was to extract confession, and the delay began to appear extraordinary to him. Perhaps the individual might have escaped the pursuit of justice, or, perhaps, he had already confessed. In that case the aid of a sneak was useless; I know not what conjectures the prisoner formed, I only know that at length, tired with waiting, and thinking they had forgotten him, he asked the sergeant of the guard to inform the commissary of police that he was still there. "If he be there, let him remain there," said the commissary, "it is no business of mine." This answer transmitted to Hotot awakened no other idea than that of a negligence of the inspectors. "If I had my supper now," he added, with the comico-serio accent of that lachrymose gayety which is less touching than laughable. "They are making sport of me, perhaps they are stuffing away in some comfortable corner, whilst I am supping here with Duke Humphrey." Twice or thrice he called, sometimes the corporal, sometimes the serjeant, to relate his griefs to them; he did not even leave the officer of the guard alone, but supplicated him to allow of his being set at liberty. "I will return, if necessary," he added; "what do you risk, since I was only grabbed for a particular purpose?"

Unfortunately the officer, who told us all these particulars next day, was one of those incredulous personages whose obstinacy is not to be shaken. Hotot was only tormented by his appetite; now, with persons who think there is such a thing as remorse, this might have been construed into presumptive innocence, but with those who trust only to lock and key— fatality had included this officer in the number; and, besides, not having any power to act for himself, however desirous of so doing, he drew the bolt upon Hotot, who, unable to obtain anything from the inspectors, made his moan in the following broken and interrupted soliloquy, which, heard through the door, excited mirth, by his alternatives of grotesque resignation and impatience.

"Oh! I say, though, it is coming it a little too strong to keep me here all night!—impossible—they are coming—no; no more an inspector than I am a king—what the deuce keeps the brutes? If I were behind them I would apply a quickener —if it is not their fault, to be sure, nothing can be said. They certainly planted me for the purpose—yet, why don't they bring in the cove—perhaps he has done them. If he be not caught in the fact they can do nothing with him. There is no fun in all this, though, to me, who have not tasted food since I arose. Come, gentlemen, as soon as you please, at your earliest convenience—I am quite ready—but we can't always have our own way. What a devil of an unlucky go for me! It plays the deuce with my stomach; I want to eat, and have nothing. How my belly cries cupboard. This is a nice new year's present, I must confess. Do they want to try my appetite? A very excellent method, certainly—fasting is good for young people. Never mind, never mind, it will not kill me this time, and I shall breakfast all the better in the morning. I will wager they are guzzling away at some cabaret, the brutes! If I were near them—this is a good joke, certainly, an admirable farce. In the name of all the devils in h—, and the saints in the calendar! Well, why put yourself out, my boy? Hunger makes the wolf leave the woods—get out, get out yourself, boy, it is easy enough—if I had but my turkey of this morning—if my friend Jules were here—he does not know, ah! if he knew."

Hotot said, as the people say, "if the king knew:" but whilst he was deploring my ignorance, and so very far from foreseeing the consequences of an arrest, which he supposed pretended, I, exploring the little streets in the neighborhood of the Place du Chatelet, had joined Emilie Simonet, in one of those low haunts where, to suit light purses, a landlady keeps liquors and lasses, both tending to the same end and serving for the same purposes. Here the liquors are like the secret entrance of the lottery-office, a means of deceiving the spy: the shame-faced lover enters, under the pretext of taking a glass of wine, and is doubly poisoned. It is to this sort of blind coffee shop that the refuse of prostitutes crowd, and heap their favors on the beastly drunkard, or make terms with the poverty of their customer. More than one devant beauty, now reduced to her calico petticoat, her coarse apron, and wooden shoes,— unless she prefers philosophes (shoes of fifteen, twenty, or twenty-five pence), here boasts of the tradition almost forgotten, though recent, of those charms which procured for her the cashmere and splendid veil which she displayed in the cavalcades of Montmorency, or else in the elegant tilbury which conveyed her to Bagatelle. I have seen many of these vicissitudes, and to give one of the million examples, there was a friend of Emilie, named Caroline, who had been the mistress of a Russian prince. In her days of splendor, a hundred thousand crowns a year did not pay the expenses of her establishment; she had equipages, horses, lackeys, courtiers; she had been very handsome, but her beauty had entirely faded. She was Emilie's companion, and even more degraded than her. Constantly muddled by liquor, she never had a lucid interval. The lady of the house, who provided her attire, for Caroline had no longer a rag of her own, watched her as closely as a cat does a mouse, lest she should sell her clothes. A hundred times she had been found at some low hole of vice, naked as a worm: she had drunk away every article of dress, even to her chemise. Such is the sad condition of these wretched creatures, almost all of whom have had, at one time of their lives, a run of good luck; after having the means of literally rolling in money, they feel the want of a crust to stop the cravings of hunger, and those palates on which the delicacies of Tortoni palled, find a relish in the potatoes of La Greve. It is in this catalogue of courtesans that are to be found those damsels who form the delight of the paviors, messengers, and water-bearers; kept by the libertines of this laborious class, whose liberalities form their main chance, they, in their turns, when not smitten by some fencing master or street-singer, support the thieves, or, at least, if they are in good keeping, by way of return, they comfort them during their dungeon woes, and in the dead season of the year.

The comrades of the princess Caroline, Emilie Simonet, or Madame Hotot, was one of this stamp: hers was a kind heart perverted; I met her at Mother Bariole's. Mother Bariole, a good woman, if there was ever one, and as honest as it was possible in her profession, had a sort of consideration amongst the debauched beings who infest these places in double capacities; these revolting porticos of a sanctuary, where, braving all disgust, lust and misery caress each other by turns. For nearly half a century her establishment was the providence and last refuge of those daughters of Lais, whom the consequences of their fall from virtue, and time, so swift in his outrages, have cast headlong under the same control as the stream and the bank: it is the old seraglio, where no one must penetrate who desires to rejoice his mind by delightful images: here is no enchantress! The Armida of the Chausse d'Antin is bit a hideous troll, who, alternating between a prison and a hospital, exhausts, in her own person, the vicissitudes of a career, whose last hope must be to die on a dunghill. In this asylum, the luxury of the Rue Vivienne is superseded by the trumpery of the temple: and she who, during the ephemeral triumph of her attractions scarcely budded, disdained the first fruits of the fashion, finds still wherewithal to deck herself in that faded finery, which, falling lower and lower, has at length reached the wardrobe of Mother Bariole. Thus we see a broken-down prag of the hackney drag assume, with pride, the harness which humiliated him in the days when his well-fed carcass formed the glory of a splendid equipage. If the comparison fails in the nobleness of idea, it is just in fact.

It would be a curious history, and profitable to morality, to have the narrative of some of Mother Bariole's nymphs: it might be to the purpose to add to it the biography of this venerable matron, who, placed for fifty years in the very centre of blows from fists, kicks from feet, thrusts from swords, etc., has passed through the whole period without a single scratch; the friend of the police, the friend of the thieves, the friend of the soldiery, in fact, everybody's friend, she has preserved herself invulnerable in the midst of storms innumerable, and of the thousand and one battles of which she has been a spectator. Sabine or Roman when the combat commenced, woe to him who touched a hair of the mother's head! Her counter was like the holy arch, it was the neutral territory which even the flying bottles respected. This is, indeed, being loved! Not one of the Sabines who would not have shed her blood for her.

It was a glorious sight to see her in the morning, as they were all thronging round her to tell their dreams about the lottery; and at the approach of quarter-day, when the savings destined to pay the rent were insufficient, because the money-box had been broken open, the poor girls would work themselves ill to make up the deficit! What misery if the abbess, to satisfy her landlord, was compelled to spout her silver mugs! In what could she then warm the little sugared wine which she drank with her Swiss, or her gossip, when chatting together, and deploring the hardship of the times, nose to nose, and with elbows on the table, they soothed their sorrows with a cup of comfort. This dear Mother Bariole, how often she sent to the Mont-de-Piete for the militia of good conduct to regale them with oysters and white wine! How generous, the inspectors found her, and how compassionate the thieves! The confidence of the latter she never betrayed. With what interest did she listen to the wailings of those who were out of work, and, sending a sprat to catch a herring, if she augured well of the fortune of any one of them, under the guise of friendship she handed over the cup of consolation; nay, even the creature on tick, if the unemployed cracksman was likely soon to be flush. "Work, my children," she said to the laborers of all classes, "to be welcome to me you must always be doing." She did not advise the soldiery in the same way, but gained their affections by attentions that were endless; she cursed the police with them, and to perfect their pleasure, in case of a disturbance, she never sent for the guard until the last extremity. She detested colonels, captains, adjutants, sub-lieutenants, in fact, all epaulettes; but then she doted on worsted lace, and nothing could equal her affection for subalterns in general, and particularly those who were well-looking; she was a mother to them all. "Ah, my darling!" I have heard her often say, "when you return with the serjeant you will be a major."

"Yes, mother Bariole, and between the hours of parade the house shall be merry."

Madame Bariole is still alive, but since I am not now called on to visit her, I know not if her establishment be supported on the same system. At the time I knew her, she had all the love for me which a spy could ever have expected from her. She was delighted when I asked for Emilie Simonet, who was her favorite. Mother Bariole thought I was about to throw the handkerchief in her harem.

"You cannot ask me for any one whom I would more readily give to you."

"Is she, then, your favorite?"

"What do you mean? I like women who take care of their children: if she had put them out of the way, I would never have looked at her again. Those poor little things did not ask to be born: why should not Christians have as much natural affection as animals? Her last is my godchild, the very image of Hotot, the very spit of him. I wish you could see her, she grows like a mushroom; she will be no fool: there will be no occasion to teach her anything; she will know everything"

"She is forward, indeed."

"Yes, and pretty: a little love. I let her only be until she is as old as a fifteen-sous piece, and I know she will bring her mother in as much money as she can carry. With a daughter, one always has a resource."

"Certainly."

"Yes, yes, the good God will bless her, Emilie; and then she has not, for a long time, had any mishap with the men."

"Does the good God meddle with these things?"

"Ah, certainly; you chaps are unbelievers, you believe in nothing."

"You have some religion, then, mother Bariole."

"I hope I have: I do not like priests, but that is all the same. It is not eight days since I had a nine days' devotion made at Sainte Genevieve for a safe passage of some liquor from Brussels, and the butt arrived safe and sound."

"And the end of the wax candle, have you burnt that?"

"Hold your tongue, you heathen."

"I will lay a bet that you have some Easter cake at your bed-head."

"A little, my boy! people should not live like brutes."

Bariole, who did not like to be thwarted about her creed, began to call to Emilie.

"Come, make haste," she cried; "wait, my son, I am going to see if she has finished."

"That's right, for I am in a hurry." Emilie soon appeared with a corporal of artillery, who, without looking behind him, immediately took leave of her.

"Since he did not ask for his dram," observed Bariole, "we will put it back into the bottle."

"I will drink it," said Emilie.

"No, no, Lisette."

"You joke, it is paid for" (drinking).

"Ah! there are flies in it."

"That will make your heart gay," I cried.

"So it will, well said, Is it you, Jules? what are you doing in this quarter?"

"I heard you were here, and said to myself, I must see Hotot's wife; I will have a drop with her."

"Agatha," called Bariole, "bring a pint;" and Agatha, according to custom, pretending to go down into the cellar, went out by the back door to the vintner's, whence she brought a flask, of which she reserved three parts, and by baptizing the rest, obtained the quantity required.

"This is not adulterated," said Emilie to me, whilst I poured it out into her glass, "see, it makes bubbles on the top, which is a good sign; I will drink again."

I pleased her much by giving her plenty of drink, but that was only the first step toward gaining her confidence; and wishing to reach, insensibly, to the catalogue of her complaints against Hotot, I managed so skillfully, that the change of conversation did not give her any suspicion. I first began by deploring my own lot, and these girls, when lamentations are made which have any relation to their own, are never slow in joining chorus: I have seen many of them, before the second pint has been emptied, burst into tears and weep like Magdalenes; at the third, I became their best friend; then there was no further restraint, all that was heaviest upon their hearts came forth with a sudden explosion; it was that moment of overflowing confidence, when the exordium is always, "The world is full of troubles, everyone has his own." Emilie, who had, during the day, tolerably well washed down her griefs, was not slow in commencing her tale of woe on the subject of her rival and Hotot's infidelities.

"Is he such a rover, your Hotot? fellows like him do not deserve to have wives. To leave such a woman as you for a Felicite! between ourselves; if I had to make a choice, I give you my word that I would give you the preference.'

"Come, Jules, you are buttering me down. You are trying it on! I know well enough that Felicite is the better looking; but if I am not so swell, I have my heart in the right place. You saw it when I used to take the scran to Lorcefé (La Force); that is the time to judge if one is true or not."

"That is true, you took every care of him, I was witness to that."

"Now, Jules, have I not done all a woman could do for him? The blackguard, one can scarcely keep one's temper! I did it to the injury of my trade. I am sure that no one could say a word against me; a married wife and all could not have done more."

"What is it you say? she would not have done so much!"

"To be sure not, but, it is not only that; he knows how disposed I am to have children—whilst he had been fifteen months in quod, did I have a young one without him? Is not that virtue? and now he would deprive me altogether. My shoe knows what I have undergone, and would tell long tales if it could speak; did it not have those ten-sous pieces which passed under the very nose of Bariole? He ought to remember them; but cut off the rope from a rogue's neck and – "

"You are right! It was not Felicite, then, who gave them to him?"

"Felicite! she would sooner have eaten him. But it is always those that they love best" (she sighed and drank, sighed and drank, sighed and drank again). "Since we two are together, tell me have you seen them together lately? tell me the truth, and on the word of Emilie Simonet, which is my real name, may every drop which has entered, and shall enter my lips, turn to poison, may I die on the spot, or may be nabbed when easing the next call I make a plant upon, if I open my mouth to him about it."

"Why should I tell you? you women are all blabs."

"On my word and honor" (assuming a solemn air and tone), "by the ashes of my father, who is as dead as you are alive."

This Homeric form of speech is no longer in use, except amongst the priestesses of Venus. Whence it came to them I know not. Had some washerwoman's daughter sworn by the ashes of her mother—but by the ashes of my father! The words are even more formidable than the prophetic nebula? which alarmed Fontenelle: they comprise an entire monograph! In the mouth of a woman who would seem to be honest, they are always a bad augury, whatever be her appearance or real situation; without running the risk of deceiving her, one can say, "I know you, beautiful mask." This oath, considering the quality of the persons who use it, has always appeared to me so burlesque, that it has never been uttered in my presence without exciting in me an irresistible impulse to laugh.

"Laugh away, laugh away," said Emilie to me, "it is laughable enough, is it not? Come now, be quiet: it is true, there is no pleasure with him, he believes nothing. May I be the greatest wretch under the canopy of heaven: by all that I hold dearest in life; by the life of my child, which is an oath I never make; may all the miseries of life befall me if I speak of you to him." At the same time pulling forward the thumb of her right hand, the nail of which, scraping against her upper teeth, escaped with a slight noise—she added, crossing herself as she spoke, "Now, Jules, it is sacred: now it is all as right as if a notary had signed articles between us."

During this conversation our pint measure had been frequently filled, and the more the Penelope of Hotot drank, the more pressing she became, and the more solemnly pledged herself to silence.

"Indeed, my boy Jules, you should tell me, when I promise you that he shall know nothing of it."

"Ah! you are such a good wench that I can keep nothing from you; but I forewarn you, do not nose, if so, take care of yourself. I would not be the death of you, but Hotot is my friend, you know."

"There is no danger, and when any one tells me a thing (pointing to her breast) it is there—it is death."

"Well, then, I went this evening to the Champs Elysees and there saw your man with Felicite; they were quarreling at first; she declared that he had you in his room in the Rue Saint Pierre aux Boeufs. He swore that he had not. and that he no longer kept up any connection with you. You know that when she was by I could not do otherwise than say as he did. They made it up, and, afterward, from some words they let fall, I think he passed the night before last with Felicite at the Place du Palais Royal."

"Oh, then, you're wrong, for he was with his friends. With Caflin, Bicêtre and Linois; Hotot told me that."

"What did he tell you?"

"He forbade me speaking of it; that is just like him, and then afterward, if any accident should happen to him he would fan me well."

"Oh, don't be alarmed; I am not the man to bring a friend into a scrape; if I am a spy, I have my feelings about me still."

"I know, my dear Jules, that you were compelled to enter the police, or else return to the Bagne."

"It is all the same, police or not, I am all right still; and if I had any one to lay my clutches on, Hotot is not the man."

"You are right, my boy, never snitch upon comrades: and now my lad of mettle, tell me, where did he go with the most!"

"Do you wish to know? They went to roost at Bicêtre's. I cannot give you the address, for I did not ask for it."

"Oh! gone to Bicêtre! right as my hand, right as a trivet —I will go and stir them up."

"I will go with you,—is it far off?"

"You know the Rue du Bon Puits?"

"Yes."

"Well! it is then at Lahire's, on the fourth pair of stairs. Now she shall carry my ten commandments in her face. Jules, have you a gig Hard piece? let me have it that I may mark the soles of her feet with it."

"I have not one."

"Never mind, I have my key in my handkerchief. Oh I'll kick up a h— of a row. I thought something would turn up this morning, for I had three knaves in my hand of cards."

"Listen to me, don't be too much in haste. That will not be the plan to find if they be there or not. You can trust to me, let me have my way: if I remain, you will know what it means—that I have found the birds at roost."

"That's a good idea, let us be sure before we begin to make an uproar."

We reached the Rue du Bon Puits, and I entered, when having assured myself that Bicêtre was in his lair, I rejoined Emilie, whose brain was actually turned by wine and jealousy.

"Well, now, see how unlucky we are! they have just left with Bicêtre and his wife, to go and sup at Linois's. I asked where, but they could not inform me."

"P'r'aps they would not; but that is of no consequence, none at all. I know where Linois hangs out, at his mother's. Come with me, you shall go and ask her, that they may have no suspicion of any thing."

"Oh! you will take me from place to place till morning!"

"What, Jules, do you refuse me? Ah, my dear boy, don't refuse, you shall have no reason to repent it—I will give you as many kisses as you like."

How could a kiss, and such a kiss, be resisted? I went to' the Rue Jocquelot, and then I climbed to the sixth story, where I saw Linois, who did not know my name.

"I am looking for Hotot," I said to him; "have you seen him?" "No," was the reply; and as he was in bed, I retired, after having wished him goodnight.

"We have the luck of it! I have again been thrown off my scent: they have been here, but have now gone off to seek for Caffin to stand some wine. Where does Caffin pitch his tent?"

"Why, I should be puzzled to tell you, but as he is a petticoat hunter, I am sure we shall find him amongst the women in the Place au Veaux. Come along."

"Why we shall traverse the four corners of Paris. It is getting late, and I have no time to spare."

"Pray, Jules, do not leave me, the inspectors will perhaps grab me."

As compliance was useful, I did not persist in my refusal I went with Emilie to the Place aux Veaux, and from ken to ken, taking draughts of courage in each cabaret, we flew onward to the place where I hoped to perfect my informations. We flew, I say, though the expression is rather strong, in spite of the weight on my arm; Emilie, very much intoxicated, had much difficulty to put her feet on the ground. But the more she staggered, the more communicative she became, so that she disclosed to me the most secret thoughts of her faithless swain. I learnt from her all that I required to know concerning Hotot, and I had the satisfaction of convincing myself that I was not deceived in judging him capable of directing the thieves whom he proposed to give up to the police. Emilie hoping to discover Hotot, and I to discover Caffin, when a girl named Louison la Blagueuse, whom we met, told us that he was with Emilie Taquet, and that he would pass the night either at Bariole's or at Blondin's, who was also an encourager of loves. "Thank ye, my little one," said Simonet to the sister Cyprian, who gave us this welcome information.

"It is just so," she continued, "Bicêtre is with his wife, Linois and Caffin are with theirs, Hotot is with Felicite, every Jack has his Jill; the wretch! he shall have my life or I will have his; I don't mind being killed (grinding her teeth and tearing her hair); Jules, do not leave me. I will massacre them, my friend, I will massacre them!"

During this ebullition of vengeance, we were still going forward, until at length we reached the corner of the Rue des Arcis. "What are you doing, Melie?" grunted out a harsh voice, and a female approached us. "It is the petite Madelon," cried Emilie.

"Ah, my lass! how are you? I am on the lookout: have you seen Caffin this evening?"

"Caffin, do you say?"

"Yes, Caffin."

"They are at Mother Bariole's."

No hour is unfitting that can be turned to its purpose. Besides, Emilie was one of the house. We went in and learnt that Caffin was there, but that Hotot had not made his appearance. On this intelligence, Madame Hotot imagined that they wished to deceive her.

"Yes, you encourage his vice," she said to Bariole; "give me my man, you old...."

I do not remember the epithets she heaped upon her, but there was, for a quarter of an hour, an incessant firing, supported by a succession of glasses of tape poured upon the wine which had already fermented jealousy to its height. "Will you cease with your bullying?" interrupted Bariole, who was an excellent trumpeter. "Your man! your man! he is at the mill, and the devil may fetch him. Did you put him into my keeping? He is a fine kiddy. Everybody's man! Such fellows as he are to be picked up—. You think he is with Caffin, then go and see: go to Taquet's chamber."

Emilie did not allow her to say so twice, but went to convince herself, and returned. "Well," said Bariole, "are you satisfied now?"

"There is no one there but Caffin."

"Did I not tell you so?"

"Where is the brute, where is the monster?"

"If you like," I said to her, "I will take you to him."

"Oh, pray do, I beg of you, Jules."

"It is a long distance from here, at the Hotel d'Angleterre."

"Do you think he is there?"

"I am sure of it; he went to pass an hour or two, and wait until Felicite has finished her evening, and then he will go and meet her in the Rue Froid Manteau."

Emilie did not doubt but that I had exactly guessed the fact, and would not delay a moment; she was bursting with rage, but would give me neither peace nor quiet until I had consented to undertake to go with her to the Hotel d'Angleterre. The transit appeared long, for I was the knight of a lady whose centre of gravity, vacillating excessively, gave me much trouble to keep my own equilibrium; however, half carrying the belle, I reached the Rue St. Honore, and the very door of the haunt where she trusted to find her man. We went through the rooms, and without fear of disturbing the amorous tête-à-têtes, glanced our eyes over each closet which was ranged on both sides of the corridor. Hotot was not there, and the rival of Felicite was transported beyond bounds; her eyes were starting from their orbits, her lips covered with foam; she wept, she stormed, she was an epileptic, a demoniac; with disheveled hair, pale, her features frightfully and spasmodically contracted, and the sinews of her neck stretched by passion, she presented the hideous appearance of one of those corpses to whom galvanism has restored motion. Terrible effects of love and brandy, jealousy and wine! Yet in the crisis which thus agitated her, Emilie did not lose sight of me, but, clinging to my arm, swore never to quit me until she had unkenneled the ingrate who had thus tormented her.

But there was now no more that I wished to learn, and for some time I had been endeavoring to rid myself of her, and make her understand that I was going to inquire if Felicite had returned, which was soon done, as she lived in a house where there was a doorkeeper. Emilie, who had received so much complaisance from me, could but be pleased with my offer, and I went out without any attempt on her part to follow me; but instead of performing the commission I had undertaken, I went to the corps de garde of the Chateau d'Eau, when making myself known to the chief officer, I begged him to arrest and keep her in the closest confinement. It certainly pained me to push matters to this extremity, for after all she had evinced it will be agreed that Emilie deserved a better fate, but this night she certainly passed in the guardhouse. How painful it is sometimes to perform strict duty! No one knew better than myself where was the beloved whom she was cursing; was I not necessarily deprived of the satisfaction of proving him innocent when she supposed him guilty? Perhaps, before I proceed further, it may not be useless to say why I had caused Hotot to be apprehended. It was that he might not have time to exculpate himself by the removal of all traces of his share in the robbery, or in bargaining for his safety with the police. But the tender Emilie, why imprison her? Had I not to dread her return to Bariole's, where, in the loquacity of intoxication, she might utter reminiscences which would put Caffin on his guard? It may be objected that she was not in a state even to keep herself upright; I will not dispute that; but the reader must remember that, from the experience of children and drunkards, certain philosophers have been induced to think that men (and women of course included) were originally quadrupeds. Emilie, even on four paws, could have regained her domicile, and then her tongue would soon have returned, and my measures must infallibly have been betrayed.

After all these precautions, Hotot being already in my clutch, I had only to secure his three accomplices, and I knew where to prick for them all. I took two agents with me, and soon afterward presented myself at Bariole's in the name of the law.

"Ah!" said the mother, "when I saw you bring your body here, I feared all was not right. What will these gentlemen take?" she added, addressing my two aide-de-camps. "You will take something to be sure, what shall it be? from the small bottle that I keep for friends?" and whilst speaking, she stooped to rummage in her counterdraw, whence she took, from amongst a parcel of millinery, an old gilt flask which contained the precious liquid. I am obliged to hide it, or with these girls—ah! people are much to be pitied who have to deal with women. I vow, if ever I can get a means of living—how happy they are who have an income to live upon! See, I have not enough to provide myself with an armchair. Here is one like a skeleton, we can see its bones."

"Oh! come tell us about your sofa; it has beautiful hair, and one leg in the air most gracefully," said a young girl, who, when we entered, was sleeping on a table in the corner of the room; "it is like Philemon and Baucis?"

"What, is that you, little Real? I did not see you. What are you chattering about with your Philemus and Baucou. Of what are you talking about?"

"I said," replied Fifine, "that it is like the Sybil's tripod." Good, good, it is the tripe man's armchair; you shall not say so of it any longer. I will have it new stuffed. You see she has had an education, and is not an ignorant beast like us: see what it is to have parents. But I know enough to carry on the war. Come, come, Fifine, draw the cork of this bottle and have a drop."

"You are very kind, ma'am."

"Do not tell any of the others."

The glass was poured out, and a double row of pearls were formed on the surface of the Cognac.

"It is delicious; I say it is in the Costico Barbaro," observed Fifine.

"Well, gentlemen," resumed Bariole, "shall we leave a drop for the Capuchins? Fill, I drink to you. Here's to you, my men; here we are all in perfect harmony, and yet we must die some day! It is so pleasant to agree when friends meet! Ah! my God, yes we must die, and that pains me, and yet we have all toil and trouble on this earth; it is too much for me, there's not a minute when the idea does not pass through my mind; but let us live honestly, that is the main thing, and then we can always walk with our heads up.—Let us not be led into temptation. In my case, die when I may, no one can reproach me with wronging them of the value of a pin's head. But what leads you here at this hour, my children? Not for my girls; they are all quiet; if you want a sample, look at her (pointing to Fifine). But, by-the-by, Jules, what have you done with Melie?"

"I'll tell you presently; give us a candle."

"I will bet you want Caffin. Good riddance; I assure you he is a regular fancy man."

"And a woman thumper, too!" added Fifine.

"We don't often see the color of his blunt," said Bariole.

"See, Jules, on this slate are the expense and earnings of his wife; she cannot get enough for the fellow. If Paris could be cleared of such vagabonds, we should be better off." She offered to lead me to the pensioner's chamber, but as I knew the way as well as she did, I declined the offer. "The second door," she said, "with the key in it." I could not mistake, and entering the room told Caffin he was my prisoner.

"Well! well! what's the row?" said he, waking; "what is it you, Jules, who have nabbed me?"

"What do you mean? I am no conjuror, and if you had been snitched, I should not have come to disturb your sleep."

"What, at the old game? but it won't do; old birds are not caught with such chaff."

"Just as you please, it is you own affair; but if what they say be true, your fortune is told: you are bound for a trip to the Bagne."

"Yes, believe that and drink water, you will never be full."

"Well, then, if you must have it all to convince you, listen. I have no interest in pumping you. I repeat that I could not have guessed your haunt had I not been told that you filched some double tripe (lead) on the boulevard Saint-Martin, when you narrowly escaped the watch, or you would not have needed my visit. Are you fly now? Out of the quartette that made the gang, one has blown the gaff. Guess the nose and I will tell you."

Caffin reflected for a moment, and then lifting his head up like a horse who rears, "Jules," he said, "I perceive one of the party has started, take me to the bigwig, and I'll make a clean breast won't too. There is no harm in peaching when others have nosed first. It is another thing with you, who are a spy by compulsion, for I know that if you could make the good hit, you would give the police the go-by."

"As you observe, my boy, if I had known what I now know, I should not have been amongst them; but when our senses leave us, we do many things we cannot undo."

"Where are you going to take me to?"

318

"To the station of the Place du Chatelet; and if you will tell the facts, I will inform the commissary."

"Yes, tell him to come; I will trap that Hotot, for it is only he who could have blown us."

The commissary came. Caffin confessed the crime, but at the same time did not fail to accuse Hotot, whom he pointed out as his only accomplice. He was not a false brother. His two friends showed the same friendship; surprised in bed, and interrogated separately, they could not do otherwise than confess their guilt. Hotot, whom they accused of their misfortune, was the only one whom each inculpated. In spite of this nobility of feeling, worthy of being cited with the fine traits of "Active Morality," this generous trio were sent to the galleys, and the traitor Hotot accompanied them. He is now at the Hague, where, most probably, he does but talk about the most curious particulars of his apprehension.

Emilie Simonet was released after six hours' captivity. When set free, she was half paralyzed by the bumpers she had quaffed; she could no longer understand, speak, or see, nor had she preserved the least recollection of what had passed. When the first rays of light broke in upon her, she asked for her lover, and on the reply of one of her companions that he was at La Force, "Miserable man!" she exclaimed, "what had he to do with taking lead from roofs, had he not all that man could wish for with me?" Afterward. the unfortunate Emilie showed herself inconsolable, and the exemplary model of a grief that was daily poisoned; if in the morning she was only maudlin, by evening she was dead— drunk! Terrible effects of love and brandy, of brandy and love!

A theft of small extent has supplied me with an opportunity of sketching a hideous picture; and yet the sketch is very imperfect and far from the abominable reality, from which the powers that be, who are bound to promote all that is good and civilized, will deliver us, when to them it seemeth best. To permit these sinks of corruption wherein the people plunge body and soul, and which are never closed, is an insult to morality, an outrage upon nature, and a crime against humanity. Let not these pages be accused as licentious; they are not the recitals of Petronius, which add fuel to the already inflamed imagination, and make proselytes to impurity. I describe immorality, not to extend its influences, but to make them abominated. Who that has read this chapter, is not horrified at the vices it depicts, since they produce the last degree of brutalization?

Chapter XXXIV

Amongst professed robbers, there were but few who did not consider it fortunate to be consulted by the police for information, or employed in some enterprise. Nearly the whole of them would have been cut into quarters to evince their zeal, under the persuasion that they thereby obtained, if not entire immunity, at least some little allowance. Those who most feared its powers were always most ready to serve it.

I recall, as a case in point, the adventure of a liberated galley slave, called Boucher, alias Cadet Poignon. For more than three weeks I had been on the lookout for him, when by chance I met him at a cabaret in the Rue Saint Antoine, at the sigra of the Bras d'Or. I was alone, and he was in a large company. To attempt to seize him *ex abrupto* would been to risk a failure, for he could have defended himself, and insured assistance. Boucher had been an agent of police. I had known him as such, and we were on very good terms together. It occurred to me that I would accost him in a friendly manner, and give him a specimen of my craft. On entering the cabaret, I went directly up to the table where he was sitting, and offered him my hand, saying, "Good day, friend Cadet."

"Ah, Jules, my boy, will you have anything? Call for a glass, or take mine."

"Yours is good; there is no gall on your lips. (I drank.) I want to say a word in your ear."

"With pleasure, old fellow; I am with you."

He rose, and, taking him by the arm, I said, "Do you remember the little sailor who was in the chain with you?"

"Yes, yes, a little fat, short chap, who was in the second string, wasn't he?"

"Exactly so, at least so I think. Should you know him again?"

"As well as if I saw my own father. I think I see him now, on Bench No.13, making straps for the conies' darbies.'"

"I have just apprehended a chap, who I think is he, but am not sure. By chance I went to the guardhouse at Birague, and as I went I out saw you enter here. Parbleu! said I to myself, that is lucky; here's Cadet, and he will tell me if I am right or not."

"I am quite ready, my boy, if I can oblige you: but before we go, we will have a glass or two. My friends, (to his companions,) do not be impatient; it is only the affair of a minute, and I will be with you again instantly."

We started, and on reaching the guardhouse door, politeness required that I should go first, and I did the honors. He went to the bottom of the room, looked sharply about him, but sought in vain for the individual of whom I had spoken to him.

"Where," said he, "is this fagot (galley slave) that I am to look at?"

I was then near the door, and saw placed against the wall the fragments of a looking-glass, such as is usually found in most guardhouses for the use of the dandies of the garrison, and calling to Boucher, I showed him the shattered reflector.

"Here," I said, "look here."

He looked, and turning toward me, said,

"Ah, Jules, you are chaffing me. I see only you and myself in the glass; but the man, the arrested man, where is he?"

"You must know that there is no man arrested here but yourself. See the order for your apprehension."

"Ah! this is a villainous trick."

"Don't you know that the most crafty man is he who prospers best in this world?"

"The most crafty, certainly; but it will do you no good to trap honest fellows in this way."

I had obtained the liberty of two celebrated female thieves, on condition of their serving the police faithfully. They had already given proofs of their skill in this way; but employed without salary, and compelled to plunder for an existence, they were taken again in very act of robbery. The sentence they underwent was that of which I abridged the duration.

Sophie Lambert and the girl Domer, alias La Belle Lise, were thenceforward in direct communication with me. One morning they came to tell me that they were certain of procuring the apprehension of one Tominot, a dangerous fellow, whom we had long been searching for. They were going, they declared, to breakfast with him, and he was to rejoin them in the evening at a vintner's in the Rue Saint-Antoine. Under other circumstances I might have been duped by these women; but Tominot had been arrested by me the previous evening, and it was a rather difficult matter for them to breakfast with him. I was nevertheless determined to try how far they would push the imposture, and promised to accompany them to their rendezvous. I went accordingly, but as may be supposed, no Tominot appeared up to ten o'clock, when Sophie, pretending impatience, asked the waiter if a gentleman had not inquired for them.

"Him you breakfast with?" said he. "He came at dusk, and desired me to say that he could not be with you this evening, but would not fail in the morning."

I had no doubt that the waiter was an accomplice, who had received his instructions; but I evinced no suspicion, and determined on seeing what these ladies would do next. For an entire week they took me sometimes to one place, sometimes to another, where we were always to find Tominot, but who of course never appeared. At length, on the 6th of January, they swore they would lead me to him. I waited for them, but they appeared without him, and gave me such good reasons, that I could not be angry; on the contrary, I evinced much satisfaction at the measures they had adopted; and to prove how well contented I was with them, I offered to give them a twelfth cake. They accepted the offer, and we went to the Petit Broc, in the Rue de la Verrerie. We drew for king and queen, and the royalty fell to Sophie's share, who was a queen in all her glory. We eat, drank, laughed, and when the moment of separation approached, it was proposed to consummate our gayety by a few bumpers of brandy; but a vintner's brandy,— stuff! It was good enough for the ladies of the fish-market; but I scorned to use my queen in that way. At this period I was established as a distiller in the Tourniquet Saint-Jean, and I offered to go to my house and fetch them a drop of the right sort. At this offer the party jumped for joy, and desiring me to return as quickly as possible, I set out, and two minutes afterward I appeared with a half bottle of Cognac, which was emptied in a twinkling. The flask being dried, I exclaimed, "Come, I have been a good boy to you—you must now do me a service."

"Both, my friend Jules," cried Sophie; "let us see what it is."

"Why this it is. One of my agents has apprehended two lady thieves; it is thought they have at home a great many stolen articles; but to make the search we must find their abode, and they refuse to give it. They are now at the guardhouse of Saint-Jean; if you go there you must try and pump them. An hour or two will suffice for you to draw them, and it will be easy work to two such deep baggages as you."

"Be easy, my dear Jules," said Sophie to me; "we will perform the commission. You know you can trust to us, and you might send us to the world's end if it could serve you: at least I can speak for myself."

"And for me, too," said La Belle Lise.

"Well, then, you must convey a line to the officer on guard, that he may know you."

I wrote a note, which I sealed, gave it to them, and we went out together. At a short distance from the market of Saint-Jean we separated, and whilst I remained on the watch, the queen and her companion went to the guardhouse. Sophie entered first, and presented the billet to the serjeant, who on reading it, said, "All right, here you both are. Corporal, take four men with you, and conduct these ladies to the prefecture." This order was given conformably to a note I had sent to the serjeant on going out to get the brandy; it was thus written:

"Monsieur the officer on guard will send under sure and good escort, to the prefecture of police, the females Sophie Lambert and Lise Domer, apprehended by order of M. le Prefet."

These ladies must have made singular reflections, and doubtless guessed that I was wearied with being made their plaything. Be that as it may, I went to see them at the depot next day, and asked them what they thought of the trick!

"Not bad," replied Sophie, "not bad; we had not stolen, though." Then addressing Lise, "It is your fault; why did you pretend to seek for a man who was already caught?"

"Did I know it? Ah, if I had I promise you besides,
what do you mean? He is caught, and they can accuse him."

"That is all very fine; but tell us, Jules, how long will they keep us at Saint Lazare?"

"Six months at least."

"Only that?" they cried out together.

"Six months is nothing," added Sophie: "it is soon passed. Well, my sweet lad, we are at the disposal of the present."

They had a month less than I had told them, and as soon as they were at liberty, came to bring me fresh information; and this time they were true. One remarkable peculiarity is, that female thieves are usually more incorrigible than males. Sophie Lambert could never persuade herself to renounce her habitual crime. From the age of ten she had entered on the career of theft; and when only twenty-five years of age had spent more than a third of her life in prison.

A short time after my entrance into the service of the police I apprehended her, and she was sentenced to two years' imprisonment. It was principally in furnished houses that she exercised her culpable industry; no one was more skillful in deceiving the vigilance of the porters, nor more fruitful in expedients to escape their questions. Once introduced, she halted at each landing to make a survey. If she saw a key in any door, she turned it without noise; and if the person who occupied the apartment was sleeping, no matter how lightly, Sophie had a hand still lighter, and in no time, watches, jewels, money, all found their way to her game-bag, the name she gave to a secret pocket under her apron. If the tenant of the room was awake, Sophie had excuses enough ready, declaring that she had made a mistake. Then if he awoke during the operation, without being at all disconcerted, she ran to the bed, and embracing him, exclaimed, "Ah, my poor little Mini, let me kiss you! Ah! sir, I ask pardon. What! is not this Number 17? I thought I was at my lover's."

One morning a person, whose apartment she was ransacking, having suddenly opened his eyes, perceived her near his drawers. He made an exclamation of surprise, and Sophie immediately began to play her scene; but the gentleman was not to be deceived, and was determined to profit by the pretended mistake; if Sophie resisted, a sound of money produced by the struggle, might betray the motive of her visit;— if she yielded the peril might be still greater. What was to be done? for any other than herself the conjecture would have been very embarrassing. Sophie was not cruel, and by the aid of a lie removed all difficulty, and the individual satisfied with what passed, allowed her to retire. He only lost at his game his watch, his purse, and six spoons

This woman was a daring creature; twice she ran headlong into my snares, but, after her liberation, in vain did I try to entrap her; there was no watching which she did not baffle, so completely was she on her guard. But what I could not effect by my utmost efforts, to take her flagrant delicto, I owed to a circumstance entirely fortuitous.

Having left my home at daybreak, I was crossing the Place du Chatelet, when I met Sophie face to face. She accosted me with much ease. "Good-day, Jules, whither are you bound so early? I will wager that you are going to catch some poor rook."

"Perhaps so; but certainly you are not the person; but where are you going?"

"I am going to Corbiel to see my sister, who's about to establish me in a house. I am weary of the stone jug. I am getting reformed; will you have a drop of ..."

"Willingly; I will stand treat, and we will have it at Lepretre's."

"Well, do as you like, but make haste, lest I lose the diligence; you will go with me, won't you? it is only to the Rue Dauphine."

"Impossible, I have business at La Chapelle, and am already late. All I can do, is take a small glass standing."

We went to Lapretre, and after a word or two, and a glass, took my leave.

"Adieu, Jules, good luck!"

Whilst Sophie trudged away from me, I turned down the Rue de la Haumerie, and ran to hide myself in the corner of the Rue Blanche Mibray; there I saw her file off toward the Pont-au-Change, walking very fast, and looking behind her at every instant. I felt assured that she feared being followed, and thereupon determined to pursue her. I gained the bridge of Notre Dame, and crossing it rapidly, reached the quay in time not to lose sight of her. On reaching the Rue Dauphine, she actually entered the office of the Corbiel coaches; but, persuaded that her departure was but a ruse to deceive me as to the intention of her early appearance, I ensconced myself in a corner, whence I could observed her motions. Whilst thus on the watch, a coach passed, in which I installed myself, and promised an extra fee to the coachman if he would follow a female whom I should point out to him. For the moment we were stationary; the diligence started, but there was no Sophie there I would have betted my life; but some minutes afterward she came to the office door, looked about on all sides, and then started off toward the Rue Christine. She entered into several furnished houses, and by her air, I could perceive that no opportunity had offered, but as she persisted in exploring the same quarter, I drew the natural inference that she had not maneuvered successfully, and as I was persuaded that she had not yet finished, I took care not to interrupt her. At length she entered (in the Rue de la Harpe) a fruiterer's, and a moment afterward appeared, carrying a large washerwoman's basket, which seemed heavy. She walked, however, very fast, and soon reached the Rue Mathurins-Saint-Jacques, and then that of Maçons Sorbonne. Unfortunately for Sophie, there is a passage which communicates with the Rue de la Harpe and the Rue des Macon, and there, after having alighted, I hastened to hide myself, and when she reached the end of the alley I came forth, and we met face to face. On seeing me she changed color, and attempted to speak, but was so much agitated that she could not utter a word. However, she came to herself gradually, and pretending to be in a great rage, said to me:—

"You see a woman in a passion; my laundress, who was to have brought my linen to the diligence, failed in her promise; I have just fetched it from her, and am going to convey it to a friend; that has prevented me from going to Corbeil."

"Just my case; on going to La Chapelle, I met a person who told me that my man was in this quarter, and that brought me here."

"So much the better; wait for me, I am going a few steps hence with my basket, and we will have a chop together."

"That I have no objection to; I, but what do I hear?"

Sophie and I stood thunderstruck at hearing piercing cries issue from the basket; I lifted up the linen that covered it, and saw—a child of two or three months old, whose roaring would have split the tympanum of a dead man.

"Well!" said I to Sophie, "the brat is yours, I suppose. Tell me, is it a girl, or a boy?"

"Well, I am caught again. I shall remember this, and if ever I am asked why, I shall answer, Oh, nothing, a childish affair. Another time when I steal linen I will first look at it."

"And this umbrella, whose is it?"

"Oh! my God, yes—. As you see; I had, however, wherewithal to shelter myself; but when chance is against you, it is in vain to attempt it."

I conducted Sophie to M. de Presne's, commissary of police, whose office was in the neighborhood. The umbrella was kept as a convicting evidence. As to the child, whom she had unwittingly carried off, it was instantly returned to its mother. The thief had a sentence of five years' imprisonment. It was, I believe, the fifth or sixth sentence she had undergone; she is still in the hands of justice, and I should not be surprised if she remains at Lazare for life. Sophie thought the trade she carried on a very natural one, and its repression, when unavoidable, she looked upon as an accident. Prison had no horrors for her, far from it; she was, in a manner, in her sphere. Sophie had contracted those inclinations, more than strange, which are not justified by the example of Sappho of old, and under lock and key the opportunities of abandoning herself to these shameful depravities were more frequent; it was not without a motive, as we see, that she had so little liberty. If she were apprehended, it caused her but trifling pain, as she consoled herself by perspective pleasures. This woman was a strange character, as we may judge. A woman named Gillion, with whom she lived in culpable intimacy, was taken whilst committing a theft. Sophie, who aided her, escaped, and had nothing to fear; but unable to endure a separation from her friend, she had herself denounced, and was not happy until she heard the sentence read which was to reunite them for two years. The majority of these creatures make a sport of prison; I have seen many, sentenced for a crime which they had committed alone, accuse a comrade, and she, although innocent, a merit of resigning herself to her sentence.

Chapter XXXV

A SHORT TIME BEFORE THE FIRST INVASION, M. Senard, one of the richest jewelers of the Palais Royal, having gone to pay a visit to his friend the Cure of Livry, found him in one of those perplexities which are generally caused by the approach of our good friends the enemy. He was anxious to secrete from the rapacity of the cossacks first the consecrated vessels, and then his own little treasures.

After much hesitation, although in his situation he must have been used to interments, Monsieur le Cure decided on burying the objects which he was anxious to save, and M. Senard, who, like the other gossips and misers, imagined that Paris would be given over to pillage, determined to cover up, in a similar way, the most precious articles in his shop. It was agreed that the riches of the pastor and those of the jeweler should be deposited in the same hole.

But, then, who was to dig the said hole? One of the singers in church was the very pearl of honest fellows, father Moiselet, and in him every confidence could be reposed. He would not touch a penny that did not belong to him. For thirty years, in his capacity of cooper, he had the exclusive privilege of bottling off the wine of the presbytery, which was the best that could be procured. Churchwarden, sexton, butler, ringer, factotum of the church, and devoted to his vice-regent, for whom he would have risen any hour of the night, he had all the qualities of an excellent servant, without including his discretion, intelligence, and piety. In so serious a conjecture it was plain that they could not fix better than on Moiselet, and he was the chosen man.

The hole, made with much skill, was soon ready to receive the treasure which it was intended to preserve, and six feet of earth were cast on the specie of the Cure, to which were united diamonds worth 100,000 crowns, belonging to M. Senard, and enclosed in a small box. The hollow filled up, the ground was so well flattened, that one would have betted with the devil that it had not been stirred since the creation. "This good Moiselet," said M. Senard, rubbing his hands, "has done it all admirably. Now, gentlemen cossacks, you must have fine noses if you find it out!" At the end of a few days the allied armies made further progress, and clouds of Kirguiz, Kalmucs, and Tartars, of all hordes and all colors, appeared in the environs of Paris. These unpleasant guests are, it is well known, very greedy for plunder: they made, everywhere, great ravages; they passed no habitation without exacting tribute: but in their ardor for pillage they did not confine themselves to the surface, all belonged to them to the centre of the globe; and that they might not be frustrated in their pretensions, these intrepid geologists made a thousand excavations, which, to the regret of the naturalists of the country, proved to them, that in France the mines of gold or silver are not so deep as in Peru. Such a discovery was well calculated to give them additional energy; they dug with unparalleled activity, and the spoil they found in many places of concealment, threw the Croesuses of many cantons into perfect despair. The cursed cossacks! But yet the instinct which so surely led them to the spot where treasure was hidden, did not guide them to the hiding place of the Cure. It was like the blessing of heaven, each morning the sun rose and nothing new; nothing new when it set.

Most decidedly the finger of God must be recognized in the impenetrability of the mysterious inhumation performed by Moiselet. M. Senard was so fully convinced of it, that he actually mingled thanksgivings with the prayers which he made for the preservation and repose of his diamonds. Persuaded that his vows would be heard, in growing security he began to sleep more soundly, when one fine day, which was, of all days in the week, a Friday, Moiselet, more dead than alive, ran to the Cure's.

"Ah, sir, I can scarcely speak."

"What's the matter, Moiselet?"

"I dare not tell you. Poor M. le Cure, this affects me deeply, I am paralyzed. If my veins were opened not a drop of blood would flow.

"What is the matter? You alarm me."

"The hole."

"Mercy! I want to learn no more. Oh, what a terrible scourge is war! Jeanneton, Jeanneton, come quickly, my shoes and hat."

"But, sir, you have not breakfasted."

"Oh, never mind breakfast."

"You know, sir, when you go out fasting you have such spasms."

"My shoes, I tell you."

"And then you complain of your stomach."

"I shall have no want of a stomach again all my life. Never any more—no, never—ruined."

"Ruined—Jesus Maria! It is possible. Ah! sir, run then —run—."

Whilst the Cure dressed himself in haste; and, impatient to buckle the strap, could scarcely put on his shoes, Moiselet, in the most lamentable tone imaginable, told him what he had seen.

"Are you sure of it?" said the Cure; "perhaps they did not take all."

"Ah, sir, God grant it, but I had not courage enough to look."

They went together toward the old barn, when they found that the spoliation had been complete. Reflecting on the extent of his loss, the Cure nearly fell to the ground. Moiselet was in a most pitiable state; the dear man afflicted himself more than if the loss had been his own. It was terrific to hear his sighs and groans. This was the result of a love to one's neighbor. M. Senard little thought how great was the desolation at Livey. What was his despair on receiving the news of the event! In Paris the police is the providence of people who have lost any thing. The first idea, and the most natural one, that occurred to M. Senard was, that the robbery had been committed by the Cossacks, and, in such a case, the police could not avail him materially; but M. Senard took care not to suspect the cossacks.

One Monday that I was in the office of M. Henry, I saw one of those little abrupt, brisk men enter who, at the first glance, we are convinced are interested and distrustful: it was M. Senard, who briefly related his mishap, and concluded by saying, that he had strong suspicions of Moiselet. M. Henry thought also that he was the author of the robbery, and I agreed with both. "It is very well," he said, "but still our opinion is only founded on conjecture, and if Moiselet keeps his own counsel we shall have no chance of convicting him. It will be impossible."

"Impossible!" cried M. Senard, "what will become of me? No, no, I shall not vainly implore your succor. Do not you know all 't Can you not do all when you choose? My diamonds! my poor diamonds! I will give one hundred thousand francs to get them back again."

"You may safely offer double, for if the robber has taken due precautions, we can do nothing in the business."

"Ah! sir, you drive me to despair," replied the jeweler, weeping warm tears, and throwing himself on his knees before the chief of the division. "A hundred thousand crowns' worth of diamonds! if I must lose them, I shall die with grief. I beseech you to have pity upon me."

"Have pity—that is easy for you to ask: but if your man is not excessively crafty, by setting some skillful agent to watch and circumvent him, we may perhaps obtain the secret from him."

"How shall I evince my gratitude to you? I care not for money: fifty thousand francs shall be the reward of him who succeeds."

"Well, Vidocq, what think you of it?"

"The affair is difficult," I answered to M. Henry, "but I will undertake it, and shall not be surprised if I come out of it with honor."

"Ah!" said M. Senard, squeezing my hand affectionately, "you restore me to life; spare nothing I beseech you, Monsieur Vidocq; go to any expense requisite to arrive at a fortunate result. My purse is open to you, whatever be the sacrifice. Well, do you think you will succeed?"

"Yes, sir, I do."

"Well, recover my casket, and there are ten thousand francs for you, yes, ten thousand francs. I have said it, and will not recede from my word."

In spite of the successive abatements of M. Senard, in proportion as he believed the discovery probable, I promised to exert every effort in my power to effect the desired result. But before any thing could be undertaken, it was necessary that a formal complaint should be made; and M. Senard and the Cure, thereupon, went to Pontoise, and the declaration being consequently made, and the robbery stated, Moiselet was taken up and interrogated. They tried every means to make him confess his guilt; but he persisted in avowing himself innocent, and, for lack of proof to the contrary, the charge was about to be dropped altogether, when, to preserve it for a time, I set an agent of mine to work. He, clothed in a military uniform, with his left arm in a sling, went with a billet to the house where Moiselet's wife lived. He was supposed to have just left the hospital, and was only to stay at Livry for forty-eight hours; but a few moments after his arrival, he had a fall, and a pretended sprain suddenly occurred, which put it out of his power to continue his route. It was then indispensable for him to delay, and the mayor decided that he should remain with the cooper's wife until further orders.

Madame Moiselet was one of those good, jolly, fat personages, who have no objection to living under the same roof with a wounded conscript, and bore all the joking about the accident which delayed the young soldier at her house; besides, he could console her in her husband's absence, and, as she was not thirty-six years of age, she was still at that time of life when a woman does not despise consolation. This was not all—evil tongues reproached Madame Moiselet with not liking wine—after it had been drunk; that was her local reputation! The pretended soldier did not fail to caress all the weak points by which she was accessible: at first he made himself useful, and then, to complete the conciliation of the good graces of his hostess, from time to time he loosened the strings of his tolerably well-filled purse to pay for his bottle of wine.

The cooper's wife was charmed with so many little attentions. The soldier could write, and became her secretary; but the letters which she addressed to her dear husband, were of a nature not to compromise her—not the least expression that can have a twofold construction—it was innocence corresponding with innocence. The secretary pities Madame Moiselet and commiserates the prisoner, and, to provoke disclosures, he makes a parade of that extensive morality, which allows of every means of enriching oneself; but Madame was too deep to be duped by such language, and constantly on her guard. At length after a few days' experience, I was convinced that my agent, in spite of his talent, would draw no profit from his mission. I then resolved to maneuver in person, and, disguised as a traveling hawker, I began to visit the environs of Livry. I was one of those Jews who deal in every thing— clothes, jewels, etc. etc.; and I took in exchange gold, silver, jewels, in fact, all that was offered me. An old female robber, who knew the neighborhood perfectly, accompanied me in my tour: she was the widow of a celebrated thief, Germain Boudier, called Father Latuil, who, after having undergone half-a-dozen sentences, died at last at Saint Pelagie. She had been confined for sixteen years in the prison of Dourdans, where the semblance of modesty and devotion which she assumed, had caused her to be called the Nun. No one was a better spy over woman, or could easier tempt them by the lures of ornaments and gewgaws. She had what is called the gift of the gab in the highest degree. I flattered myself that Madame Moiselet, seduced by her eloquence, and by our merchandise, would bring out the store of the Cure's crowns, some brilliant of the purest water, nay, even the chalice or paten, in case the bargain should be to her liking. My calculation was not verified; the cooper's wife was in no haste to make a bargain, and her coquetry did not get the better of her. Madame Moiselet was the phoenix of women. I admired her, and, as there was no temptation which she did not resist, convinced that I should lose my time by attempting to play any stratagem off upon her, I resolved to try my chance with her husband.

The Jew hawker was soon metamorphosed into a German servant; and under this disguise I began to ramble about the vicinity of Pontoise, with a design of being apprehended. I sought out the gendarmes, whilst I pretended to avoid them; but they, thinking I wished to get away from them, demanded a sight of my papers. Of course I had none, and they desired me to accompany them to a magistrate, who, knowing nothing of the jargon in which I replied to his questions, desired to know what money I had; and a search was forthwith commenced in his presence. My pockets contained some money and valuables, the possession of which seemed to astonish him. The magistrate, as curious as a commissary, wished to know how they came into my hands; and I sent him to the devil with two or three Teutonic oaths, of the most polished kind; and he to teach me better manners another time, sent me to prison.

Once more the iron bolts were drawn upon me. At the moment of my arrival, the prisoners were playing in the prison yard, and the jailer introduced me amongst them in these terms, "I bring you a murderer of the parts of speech; understand him if you can."

They immediately flocked about me, and I was accosted with salutations of Landsman and Meinheer without end. During this reception, I looked out for the cooper of Livry. I thought he must be a sort of clownish looking tradesman, who, joining in the concert of salutes, which were addressed to me, had called me Landsman in that soft silky tone, which is always acquired by those church rats who are wont to live on the meats of the altar. He was not over fat; but that was constitutional with him, and, his leanness apart, he was glowing with health: he had a narrow forehead, small brown eyes sunk in his head, an enormous mouth, and although, in detailing his characteristics, some of a very sinister kind might be seen, the whole had that gentle air which would tempt the devil to open the gates of Paradise; besides, to complete the portrait, this personage was at least four or five generations, behindhand in costume, a circumstance which, in a country where the Gerontes can make reputation for honesty, always establishes a presumption in favor of the individual.

I know not why I had pictured to myself that Moiselet should have the refinement of roguery, which, to give itself the appearance of honesty, and to conciliate the confidence of old men, dresses itself like them. In the absence of other more characteristic signs, a pair of spectacles on a prominent nose, large buttons on a coat of light hue and square cut, short breeches, a three-cornered hat of the old school, and clocked stockings, would have instantly attracted my attention. The air and face were correspondent, and I had every reason to believe that I had guessed correctly. I wished to assure myself.

"Mossie, Mossie," I said, addressing the prisoner, who seemed to think I said Moiselet, "now, Mossie Fine Hapit (not knowing his name, I so designated him, because his coat was the color of flesh), sacrement, ter teufle, no tongue to me; yer Francois, I misraple, I trink vine; faut trink for gelt, black viue."

I pointed to his hat, which was black; he did not understand me; but on making a gesture that I wanted to drink, he found me perfectly intelligible. All the buttons of my great coat were twenty-franc pieces; I gave him one: he asked if they had brought the wine, and soon afterward I heard a turnkey say,

"Father Moiselet, I have taken up two bottles for you." The flesh-colored coat was then Moiselet. I followed him into his room, and we began to drink with all our might. Two other bottles arrived; we only went on in couples. Moiselet, in his capacity of chorister, cooper, sexton, etc., was no less a sot than gossip; he got tipsy with great goodwill, and incessantly spoke to me in the jargon I had assumed.

"I like the German much," said he; "you can remain here, my jolly Kinserlique." And the jailer coming in to drink with us, he desired him to make me a bed beside his.

"Are you content, Kinserlique?"

"As content as you."

"Do you trink much?"

"I trink all times."

"All times! a good comrade;" and more wine was ordered

Matters progressed well; after two or three hours such as these, I pretended to get stupid. Moiselet, to set me to rights, gave me a cup of coffee without sugar; after coffee came glasses of water. No one can conceive the care which my new friend took of me; but when drunkenness is of such a nature it is like death—all care is useless. Drunkenness overpowered me, I went to bed and slept, at least Moiselet thought so; but I saw him many times fill my glass and his own, and gulp them both down. The next day, when I awoke, he paid me the balance, three francs and fifty centimes, which, according to him, remained from the twenty-franc piece. I was an excellent companion; Moiselet found me so, and never quitted me. I finished the twenty-franc piece with him, and then produced one of forty francs, which vanished as quickly. When he saw it drunk out also, he feared it was the last.

"Your button again," said he to me, in a tone of extreme anxiety, and yet very comical.

I showed him another coin. "Ah, your large button again;" he shouted out, jumping for joy.

This button went the same way as all the other buttons, until at length, by dint of drinking together, Moiselet understood and spoke my language almost as well as I did myself, and we could then disclose our troubles to each other. Moiselet was very curious to know my history, and that which I trumped up was exactly adapted to inspire the confidence I wished to create.

"My master and I come to France—I was tomestic—master of mein Austrian marechal—Austrian with de gelt in family. Master always roving, always gay, goint regiment at Montreau. Moutreau oh, mein Gott, great, great pattle—many sleep no more but in death. Napoleon coom—poum, poum go gannon. Prusse, Austrian, Rousse all disturb. I, too, much disturb. (Jo on my ways with master mein, with my havresac on mein horse—poor teufel was I—but there was gelt in it. Master them say, 'Galop, Fritz.' I called Fritz in home mein Fritz galop to Pondi—there halt Fritz—place havresac not visible and if I get again to Yarmany with havresac, me rich becomen, mistress mein rich, father mein rich, you too rich."

Although the narrative was not the cleverest in the world, father Moiselet swallowed it all as gospel; he saw well that, during the battle of Montereau, I had fled with my master's portmanteau, and hidden it in the forest of Bondy. The confidence did not astonish him, and had the effect of acquiring for me an increase of his affection. This augmentation of friendship, after a confession which exposed me as a thief, proved to me that he had an accommodating conscience. I thenceforward remained convinced that he knew better than any other person what had become of the diamonds of M. Senard, and that it only depended on him to give me full and accurate information.

One evening, after a good dinner, I was boasting to him of the delicacies of the Rhine: he heaved a deep sigh, and then asked me if there were good wine in that country.

"Yes, yes," I answered, "goot vine and charming girls."

"Charming girls, too!"

"Ya, ya!"

"Landsman, shall I go with you?"

"Ya, ya, me grat content."

"Ah, you content, well! I quit France, yield the old woman (he showed me by his fingers that Madame Moiselet was three-and-thirty), and in your land I take little girl no more as fifteen years."

"Ya, bien, a girl no infant: ah! you is a brave lad."

Moiselet returned more than once to his project of emigration: he thought seriously of it; but to emigrate, liberty was requisite, and they were not inclined to let us go out. I suggested to him that he should escape with me on the first opportunity—and when he had promised me that we would not separate, not even to take a last adieu of his wife, I was certain that I should soon have him in my toils. This certainty was the result of very simple reasoning. Moiselet, said I to myself, will follow me to Germany: people do not travel or live on air: he relies on living well there: he is old, and, like King David, proposes to tickle his fancy with some little Abishag of Sunem. Oh, father Moiselet has found the black hen; here he has no money, therefore his black hen is not here; but where is she? We shall soon learn, for we are to be henceforward inseparable.

As soon as my man had made all his reflections, and that, with his head full of his castles in Germany, he had so soon resolved to expatriate himself, I addressed to the king's attorney-general a letter, in which, making myself known as the superior agent of the Police de Surete, I begged him to give an order that I should be sent away with Moiselet, he to go to Livry, and I to Paris.

We did not wait long for the order, and the jailer announced it to us, on the eve of its being put into execution; and I had the night before me to fortify Moiselet in his resolutions. He persisted in them more strongly than ever, and acceded with rapture to the proposition I made him of our effecting an escape from our escort as soon as it was feasible.

So anxious was he to commence his journey, that he could not sleep. At daybreak, I gave him to understand that I took him for a thief as well as myself.

"Ah, ah, grip also," said I to him, "deep, deep Francois, you not spoken, but thief all as von."

He made me no answer; but when, with my fingers squeezed together a la Normande, he saw me make a gesture of grasping something, he could not prevent himself from smiling, with that bashful expression of Yes, which he had not courage to utter. The hypocrite had some shame about him, the shame of a devotee. I am understood.

At length the wished-for moment of departure came, which was to enable us to accomplish our designs. Moiselet was ready three whole hours beforehand; and to give him courage, I had not neglected to push about the wine and brandy, and he did not leave the prison until after having received all his sacraments.

We were tied with a very thin cord, and on our way as made me a signal that there would be no difficulty in breaking it. He did not think that he should then break the charm which had till then preserved him. The further we went on, the more he testified that he placed his hopes of safety in me: at each minute he reiterated a prayer that I would not abandon him: and I as often replied, "Ya, Francois, I not leave you." At length the decisive moment came, the cord was broken. I leaped a ditch, which separated us from a thicket. Moiselet, who seemed young again, jumped after me; one of the gendarmes alighted to follow us, but to run and jump in jack-boots and with a heavy sword was difficult; and whilst he made a circuit to join us, we disappeared in a hollow, and were soon lost to view.

A path into which we struck led us to the wood of Vaujours. There Moiselet stopped, and having looked carefully about him, went toward some bushes. I saw him then stoop, plunge his arm into a thick tuft, whence he took out a spade; arising quickly, he went on some paces without saying a word; and when we reached a birch tree, several of the boughs of which I observed were broken, he took off his hat and coat, and began to dig. He went to work with so much goodwill, that his labor rapidly advanced. Suddenly he stooped down, and then escaped from him that ha! which betokens satisfaction, and which informed me, without the use of a conjuror's rod, that he had found his treasure. I thought the cooper would have fainted; but recovering himself, he made two or three more strokes with his spade, and the box was exposed to view. I seized on the instrument of his toil, and suddenly changing my language, declared in very good French, that he was my prisoner.

"No resistance," I said, "or I will cleave your skull in two."

At this threat he seemed in a dream; but when he knew that he was gripped by that iron hand which has subdued the most vigorous malefactors, he was convinced that it was no vision. Moiselet was as quiet as a lamb. I had sworn not to leave him, and kept my word. During the journey to the station of the brigade of gendarmes, where I deposited him, he frequently cried out:

"I am done—who could have thought it? and he had such a simple look, too!"

At the assizes of Versailles, Moiselet was sentenced to six months' solitary confinement.

M. Senard was overpowered with joy at having recovered his hundred thousand crowns' worth of diamonds. Faithful to his system of abatement, he reduced the reward one-half; and still there was difficulty in getting five thousand francs from him, out of which I had been compelled to expend more than two thousand: in fact, at one moment I really thought I should have been compelled to bear the expenses myself.

CHAPTER XXXVI

A SHORT TIME AFTER THE DIFFICULT AFFAIR which proved so fatal to the cooper, I was employed to detect the authors of a nocturnal robbery, committed by climbing and forcible entry into the apartments of the Prince de Conde, in the Palais Bourbon. Glasses of a vast size had disappeared, and their abstraction was effected with so much precaution, that the sleep of two guard-dogs, who supplied the place of a watchman, had not been for a moment disturbed. The frames in which these glasses had been were not at all injured: and I was at first tempted to believe that they had been taken out by looking-glass makers or cabinet makers; but in Paris these workmen are so numerous, that I could not pitch on any one of them whom I knew with any certainty of suspicion. Yet I was resolved to detect the guilty, and to effect this I commenced my inquiries.

The keeper of a sculpture gallery, near the Quineaux of the Invalids, gave me first the information by which I was guided. About three o'clock in the morning, he had seen near his door several glasses in the care of a young man, who pretended to have been obliged to station them there whilst waiting for the return of his porters, who had broken their hand-barrow.

Two hours afterward, the young man having found two messengers, had made them carry off the glasses, and had directed them to the side of the Fountain of the Invalids. According to the keeper, the person he saw was about twenty-three years of age, and about five feet and an inch (French measure). He was clothed in an iron-gray great-coat, and had a very good countenance. This information was not immediately useful to me, but it led me to find the messenger, who, the day after the robbery, had carried some glasses of large size to the Rue Saint-Dominique, and left them at the little Hotel de Caraman. These were, in all probability, the glasses stolen, and if they were, who could say that they had not changed domicile and owner?

I had the person who had received them pointed out to me, and determined on introducing myself to her; and that my presence might not inspire her with fear, it was in the guise of a cook that I introduced myself to her notice. The light jacket and cotton nightcap are the ensigns of the profession; I clothed myself in such attire, and fully entering into the spirit of my character, went to the little Hotel de Caraman, where I ascended to the first floor. The door was closed; I knocked, and it was opened to me by a very good-looking young fellow, who asked me what I wanted. I gave him an address, and told him that having learnt that he was in want of a cook, I had taken the liberty of offering my services to him.

"My dear fellow, you are under a mistake," he replied, "the address you have given me is not mine, but as there are two Rues Saint Dominique, it is most probably to the other that you should go."

All Ganymedes have not been carried off to Olympus, and the handsome youth who spoke to me had manners, gestures, and language, which united to his appearance, convinced me in an instant with whom my business lay. I instantly assumed the tone of an initiate in the mysteries of the ultra-philanthropists, and after some signs which he perfectly understood, I told him how very sorry I was that he did not want me.

"Ah, sir," I said to him, "I would rather remain with yon, even if you only gave me half what I should get elsewhere; if you only knew how miserable I am; I have been six months out of place, and I do not get a dinner every day. Would you believe that thirty-six hours have elapsed and I have not taken anything."

"You pain me, my good fellow; what, are you still fasting? Come, come, you shall dine here."

I had really an appetite capable of giving the lie I had just uttered all the semblance of truth; a two-pound loaf, half a fowl, cheese, and a bottle of wine which he had procured, did not make long sojourn on the table. Once filled, I began again to talk of my unfortunate condition.

"See, sir," said I, "if it be possible to be in a more pitiable situation. I know four trades, and out of the whole four can not get employ in one, tailor, hatter, cook; I know a little of all, and yet cannot get on. My first start was as a looking-glass setter."

"A looking-glass setter!" said he abruptly; and without giving him time to reflect on the imprudence of such an exclamation, I went on.

"Yes, a looking-glass setter, and I know that trade the best of the four; but business is so dead that there is really nothing now stirring in it."

"Here, my friend," said the young man, presenting to me a small glass, "this is brandy, it will do you good; you know not how much you interest me. I can give you work for several days."

"Ah! sir, you are too good, you restore me to life; how, if you please, do you intend to employ me?"

"As a looking-glass framer."

"If you have glasses to fit, pier, Psyche, light of day, joy of Narcissus, or any others, you have only to entrust me with them, and I will give you a cast of my craft."

"I have glasses of great beauty; they were at my country house, whence I sent for them, lest the gentlemen Cossacks should take a fancy to break them."

"You did quite right; but may I see them?"

"Yes, my friend."

He took me into a room, and at the first glance I recognized the glasses of the Palais Bourbon. I was ecstatic in their praise, their size; and after having examined them with the minute attention of a man who understands what he is about, I praised the skill of the workman who unframed them, without injury to the silvering.

"The workman, my friend," said he, "the workman was myself; I would not allow any other person to touch them, not even to load them in the carriage."

"Ah! sir, I am very sorry to give you the lie, but what you tell me is impossible; a man must have been a workman to undertake such work, and even the best he of the craft might not have succeeded."

In spite of my observation, he persisted in asserting that he had no help, and as it would not have answered my purpose to have contradicted him, I dropped the subject.

A lie was an accusation at which he might have been angry, but he did not speak with less amenity, and after having given me his instructions, desired me to come early next day, and begin my work as early as possible.

"Do not forget to bring your diamond, as I wish you to remove those arches, which are no longer fashionable."

He had no more to say to me, and I had no more to learn. I left him, and went to join my two agents, to whom I gave the description of the person, and desired them to follow him if he should go out. A warrant was necessary to effect his apprehension, which I procured; and soon afterward, having changed my dress, I returned with the commissary of police, and my agents to the house of the amateur of glasses, who did not expect me so soon. He did not know me at first, and it was only at the termination of our search, that examining me more closely, he said to me:—

"I think I recognize you; are you not a cook?"

"Yes, sir," I replied; "I am cook, tailor, hatter, looking glass setter, and, moreover, a spy, at your service."

My coolness so much disconcerted him, that he could not utter another word.

This gentleman was named Alexandre Paruitte. Besides the two glasses, and two chimeras in gilt bronze, which he had stolen from the Palais Bourbon, many other articles were found in his apartments, the produce of various robberies. The inspectors who had accompanied me in this expedition undertook to conduct Paruitte to the depot, but, on the way, were careless enough to allow him to escape, nor was it until ten days afterward that I contrived to get sight of him, at the gate of the embassador of his highness the Sultan Mahmoud, and I apprehended him at the moment he got into the carriage of a Turk, who apparently had sold his odalisques.

I am still at a loss to explain how, in spite of obstacles, which the most expert robbers judged insurmountable, Paruitte effected the robbery which twice compelled me to see him. He was steadfast in his assertion of having no companions; for on his trial, when sentenced to irons and imprisonment, no indication, not even the slightest, could be elicited, encouraging the idea that he had any participators.

About the time when Paruitte carried off the glass from the Palais Bourbon, some thieves effected an entrance in the Rue de Richelieu, No. 17, in the Hotel de Valois, when they carried off considerable property, belonging to Marechal Boucher, valued at thirty thousand francs. All was fish that came to net, from the plain cotton handkerchief to the glittering uniform of the general. These gentlemen, accustomed to clear off all before them, had even carried off the linen intended for the laundress. The system, which has its rise in a desire not to leave a fraction of anything to the person robbed, is very dangerous for the thieves, for it compels them to make minute researches, and occasions delay, which sometimes terminates most unpropitiously. But on this occasion they had worked with perfect security; the presence of the general in his apartment had been a guarantee that they would not be troubled in their enterprise, and they had emptied the wardrobes and trunks with the same security as a broker who is making an inventory after a death. How, I shall be asked, could the general be present? Alas! he was—but when one plays an active part at a good dinner, can the result be doubted!

Without hatred, without fear, without suspicion, we pass gaily from Beaune to Chambertin, from Chambertin to Clos-Vougeot, from Clos-Vougeot to Romanée; then after having thus overrun all the wines of Burgundy and discussed their various merits, we come to Champagne and the flatulent Ai, and but too happy is that guest, who, full of the joys of the delicious pilgrimage, does not get so far muddled as to be unable to find his way home. The general, after a banquet of this kind, had still preserved his reasoning powers entire, at least I think so, but had returned excessively sleepy; and as in that state one is more anxious to tumble into bed, than to close a window, he had left his open for the convenience of comers and goers. What imprudence! I know not if he had agreeable dreams, but I remember, that in his statement of the transaction, he deposed that he had awakened from his sleep like a little St. John.

I was very desirous of detecting the insolents who had perpetrated this robbery attended with circumstances so aggravating. In the absence of all indications by which I might endeavor to trace a path for myself, I allowed myself to be led by that inspiration which has so seldom deceived me. The idea suddenly struck me, that the thieves who had introduced themselves at the general's might belong to the gang of one Perrin, a blacksmith, who had long been pointed out to me as a most audacious fence. I began by surveying the approaches to Perrin's domicile, which was in the Rue de la Sonnerie, No.1; but after several days' watching, nothing occurred to guide me, and I felt convinced that to arrive at any satisfactory result, I must have recourse to stratagem.

I could not go direct to Perrin as he knew me, but I instructed one of my agents, who would not be suspected. He went to see him, and they conversed on various topics; at length touching on robberies,—

"I' faith," said Perrin, "no bold hits are now made."

"What do you mean?" replied the agent, "I think those who were at the general's, in the Hotel de Valois, have no cause for complaint; when I learn that in his full-dress uniform there was concealed a sum of twenty-five thousand francs in banknotes."

Perrin had so much cupidity and avarice, that had he been possessor of the dress, this lie, which revealed to him riches of which he had not dreamt, would necessarily make an impression of joy, which he would be unable to dissemble; if the uniform had passed into other hands, and he had already disposed of it, a contrary feeling would betray itself. I had foreseen this alternative. Perrin's eyes did not sparkle, no smile was seen upon his lips: in vain did he seek to disguise his trouble, the feeling of his loss so sorely smote him, that he began to dash the floor with his foot, and tear his hair most furiously: "Ah, mon Dieu, mon Dieu!" he cried, "these events always befall me, must I forever be wretched?"

"Well, what do you mean? Did you buy it?"

"Yes, yes, I bought it, as you ask me, but I sold it again."

"Do you know to whom?"

"Certainly I do: to a man in the Rue Feydeau, that he might burn the lace."

"Oh, do not despair, there is a remedy still left, if the melter be an honest man."

Perrin gave a jump. "Twenty-five thousand francs burnt! Twenty-five thousand francs! That is not picked up every day; why was I in such haste about it?"

"Well, if I were you, I should try to get back the embroidery before it is put in the melting pot. If you like, I will go to the melter, and tell him that having had a good offer for it from one of the theatres, you are desirous of buying it back again. I will offer him a premium, and probably he will not make any difficulty about it."

Perrin thought the plan admirable, accepted the proposition with eagerness, and the agent, desirous of rendering him a service, ran to give me an account of what had passed. Then, taking search warrants, I made a descent upon the melter. The embroidery was untouched; I gave them to the agent to convey to Perrin, and at the instant when he, impatient to seize on the notes, gave the first cut with his scissors to release the presumed treasure, I appeared with the commissary. We found at Perrin's evidences of the illicit trade which he carried on; an abundance of stolen property was found in his stores. Conducted to the depot, he was examined; but, at first, only gave very vague replies, whence no intelligence could be collected.

After his imprisonment in La Force, I went to see him, and ask him for information, but could only get from him some few indications; he knew not, he asserted, the names of the persons who constantly dealt with him. However, the little he told me, aided me in forming suspicions. I had a considerable number of suspicious characters marched out before him, and, on his detection of them, they were put on their trials. Twenty-two were sentenced to irons, and amongst them was one of the authors of the robbery on General Boucher. Perrin was, tried and convicted of receiving the stolen booty, but in consequence of the utility of the information he had given, only the minimum of punishment was pronounced against him.

A short time afterward, two other fences, the brothers Perrot, in the hopes of clemency from the judge, followed the example of Perrin, not only in making confessions, but deciding several other prisoners or pointing out their accomplices. From their statements I brought into the power of justice two famous robbers, named Valentine and Rigaudi, alias Grindesi.

Never, perhaps, were there so many of those gentry, who unite the professions of thief and chevalier d'industrie, as in the year of the first restoration. One of the most skillful and most enterprising was Winter de Sarre-Louis.

Winter was only twenty-six, and was one of those handsome brown fellows, whose arched eyebrows, long lashes, prominent nose, and rakish air, have such charms for a certain class of females. Winter had, moreover, that good carriage, and peculiar look, which belong to an officer of light cavalry, and he therefore assumed a military costume, which best displayed the graces of his person. One day he was a hussar, the next a lancer, and then again in some fancy uniform. At will he was chief of a squadron, commandant, aide-de-camp, colonel, etc.; and to command more consideration, he did not fail to give himself a respectable parentage; he was by turns the son of the valiant Lasalle, of the gallant Winter, colonel of the grenadiers of the imperial horseguard; nephew of the general Comte de Lagrange, and cousin-german to Rapp; in fact, there was no name which he did not borrow, no illustrious family to which he did not belong. Born of parents in a decent situation of life, Winter had received an education sufficiently brilliant to enable him to aspire to all these metamorphoses; the elegance of his manner, and a most gentlemanly appearance, completed the illusion.

Few men had made a better debut than Winter. Thrown early into the career of arms, he obtained very rapid promotion; but when an officer he soon lost the esteem of his superiors, who, to punish his misconduct, sent him to the Isle of Rho, to one of the colonial battalions. There he so conducted himself as to inspire a belief that he had entirely reformed. But no sooner was he raised a step, than committing some fresh peccadillo, he was compelled to desert in order to avoid punishment. He came thence to Paris, where his exploits as swindler and pickpocket procured him the unenviable distinction of being pointed out to the police as one of the most skillful in his two-fold profession.

Winter, who was what is termed a downy cove, plucked a multitude of pigeons, even in the most elevated classes of society. He visited princes, dukes, the sons of ancient senators, and it was on them or the ladies of their circle that he made the experiments of his misapplied talents. The females particularly, however squeamish they were, were never sufficiently so to prevent themselves from being plundered by him. For several months the police were on the lookout for this seducing young man, who, changing his dress and abode incessantly, escaped from their clutches at the moment when they thought they had him securely, when I received orders to commence the chase after him, to attempt his capture.

Winter was one of those Lovelaces who never deceive a woman without robbing her. I thought that amongst his victims I could find at least one, who, from a spirit of revenge, would be disposed to put me on the scent of this monster. By dint of searching, I thought I had met with a willing auxiliary, but as these Ariadnes, however ill-used or forsaken they may be, yet shrink from the immolation of their betrayer, I determined to accost the damsel I met with cautiously. It was necessary before I ventured my bark, to take soundings, and I took care not to manifest any hostility toward Winter, and not to alarm that residue of tenderness which despite ill-usage, always remains in a sensitive heart. I made my appearance in the character of almoner of the regiment which he was thought to command, and as such was introduced to the mistress of the pretended colonel. The costume, the language, the manner I assumed were in perfect unison with the character I was about to play, and I obtained to my wish the confidence of the fair forsaken one, who gave me unwittingly all the information I required. She pointed out to me her favored rival, who, already ill-treated by Winter, had still the weakness to see him, and could not forbear making fresh sacrifices for him.

I became acquainted with this charming lady, and to obtain favor in her eyes, announced myself as a friend of her lover's family. The relatives of the young giddy pate had empowered me to pay his debts; and if she could contrive an interview with him for me, she might rely on being satisfied with the result of the first. Madame was not sorry to have an opportunity of repairing the dilapidations made on her property, and one morning she sent me a note, stating that she was going to dine with her lover the next day at the Boulevard du Temple, at La Galiote. At four o'clock I went, disguised as a messenger, and stationed myself at the door of the restaurant's; and after two hours' watch, I saw a colonel of hussars approach. It was Winter, attended by two servants. I went up to him, and offered to take care of the horses, which proffer was accepted. Winter alighted, he could not escape me, but his eyes met mine, and with one jump he flung himself on his horse, spurred him, and disappeared.

I thought I had him, and my disappointment was great; but I did not despair of catching my gentleman. Sometime afterward I learnt that he was to be at the Café Hardi, in the Boulevard des Italiens. I went thither with some of my agents, and when he arrived all was so well arranged, that he had only to get into a hackney-coach, of which I paid the fare. Led before a commissary of police, he asserted that he was not Winter; but, despite the insignia of the rank he had conferred on himself, and the long string of orders hanging on his breast, he was properly and officially identified as the individual mentioned in the warrant which I had for his apprehension.

Winter was sentenced to eight years' imprisonment, and would now be at liberty but for a forgery which he committed while at Bicêtre, which, bringing on him a fresh sentence of eight years at the galleys, he was conducted to the Bagne at the expiration of his original sentence, and is there at present.

This adventurer does not want wit: he is, I am told, the author of a great many songs, much in fashion with the galley slaves, who consider him as their Anacreon. I append one of his productions:

"Happy the days when I worked away,
In my usual line in the prigging lay;
Making from this and that and t'other,
A tidy living without no bother.
When my little crib was stored with swag,

And my cry was a veil-lined money-bag.
Jolly was I, for I feared no evil,
Funked at nought, and pitched care to the devil.

"I had, besides my blunt, my blower,
'So gay, so nutty, and so knowing;
On the very best of grub we lived,
And sixpence a quartern for gin I gived:
My toggs was the sporting'st blunt could buy,
And a slap-up out and outer was I.
With my mot on my arm and my tile on my head,
That ere's a gem man, everyone said.

"A-coming away from Vauxhall one night,
I cleared out a muzzy covey quite,
He'd been a strutting away like a king,
And on his digit he sported a ring,
A di'mond sparkle, flash, and knowing.
Thinks I, I'll watch the way he's going,
And fleece my gem man neat and clever,
Or, at least, I'll try my best endeavor.

A'ter the singing and fireworks vas ended,
I follows my gem man the way he bended,
In a dark corner I trips up his heels.
Then for his tattler and reader I feels;

I pouches his blunt, and I draws his ring.
Prigged his buckles and every thing,
And saying, 'I thinks as you can't follow, man,'
I pikes me off to likey Solomon.

"Then it happened d'ye see that my mot,
yellow a-bit 'bout the swag I'd got,
Thinking that I should jeer and laugh,
Although I never tips no chaff,
Tries her hand at the downy trick,
And prigs in the shop, but precious quick
'Stop thief was the cry, and she was taken.
I cuts and runs and saves my bacon.

"Then says he, says Sir Richard Birnie,
'I adwise you to nose on your pals, and turn the
Snitch on the gang, that'll be the best way
To save your scrag.' Then, without delay,

He so prewailed on the treach'rous varmint,
That she was noodled by the Bowstreet varmint.
Then the beaks they grabbed me and to pris'n I was dragg'd,
And for fourteen years of my life I was lagg'd.

"My mot must now be growing old,
And so am I, if the truth be told;
But the only way to get on in the world
is to go with the stream and however we're twirled,
To bear all rubs: and even ye suffer
To hope for the smooth even we feels the rougher,
Though very hard, I confess it appears,
To be lagged, for a lark, for fourteen years."

Winter, when I apprehended him, had many associates in Paris, and the Tuileries was the notorious place where the most daring and celebrated thieves assembled, who recommended themselves to public veneration by impudently bedecking themselves with all the crosses of the orders of knighthood. In the eyes of an observer who can discern accurately, the Chateau was then less a royal residence than a haunt infested by these thieves. There congregated a crowd of galley slaves, pickpockets, and swindlers of every class, who presented themselves as the old companions in arms of Charette, La Roche, Jaquelin, Stoflet, Cadoudal, etc. The days of review and court assemblies witnessed the gathering of these pretended heroes. In my office of superior agent of police, I judged it my duty to keep a strict look, out after these royalists of circumstances. I stationed myself in their way, either in or out of the apartments, and was soon fortunate enough to restore several of them to the Bagne.

One Sunday, accompanied by one of my auxiliaries, I was on the watch on the Place du Carousel; we saw, going out from the Pavilion de Flore, a person whose costume, not less rich than elegant, attracted the attention of every person. This personage must be a great lord: had he not been covered with orders, he would have been recognized by the delicacy of his embroidery, the grace of his feather, the sparkling knot of his sword; but in the eyes of the police officer all is not gold that glitters. The agent with me, in drawing my attention to this splendid signor, observed that there was a striking likeness between him and one Chambreuil, with whom he had been at the Bagne at Toulon. I had seen Chambreuil, and I went to station myself so as to see this person face to face; and in spite of the dress a la Francaise, the breeches a L'Angleterre, the laced neckerchief and ruffles, I instantly recognized the ex-galley slave; it was in fact, Chambreuil, a notorious forger, who had obtained much celebrity by his escapes from the galleys. His first sentence was about the period of the successful campaigns in Italy. At this time he followed the army, that he might the more easily imitate the signatures of the purveyors. He had a decided talent for this kind of imitation; but having been too prodigal of his abilities in this way, he had ended by procuring for himself three years' imprisonment. Three years soon pass away.

Chambreuil could not, however, reconcile himself to his prison; he escaped, and fled to Paris, where he put into circulation a vast many notes of his own fabrication. This industry was converted into a crime; and, again placed on his trial, he was found guilty, and sent to Brest, where, by virtue of his sentence, he should have passed eight years. Chambreuil again escaped; but as forgery was his constant resource, he was apprehended a third time, and appended to the chain, which was sent to Toulon. Scarcely had he arrived there, when he again endeavored to elude the vigilance of his keepers; but apprehended and sent back to the Bagne, he was placed in the too celebrated room, No. 3, where he passed his time, increased by three years.

During this detention, he endeavored to amuse himself by dividing his leisure between denouncement and swindling, which were no less to his taste than his other pursuit. His choice, however, was forged letters, which, on his leaving the Bagne, brought on him two years' imprisonment in the prison of Embrun.

Chambreuil had just arrived there, when the Duke d'Angouleme happened to be passing through the city. Chambreuil caused a petition to be presented to this prince, in which he stated that he was an old Vendean, a devoted servant, whose royalism had drawn down persecution upon him. He was immediately set at liberty, and soon afterward began to use his freedom as heretofore.

When we recognized him, it was easy to judge by the figure he cut that he was in a good vein of fortune. We followed him in an instant, to convince ourselves that it was indeed he; and as soon as all doubt was removed, I accosted him, declaring that he was my prisoner. Chambreuil thought then to impose upon me, by spitting in my face a tremendous series of qualities and titles, which he asserted belonged to him. He was nothing less than director of the police of the Chateau, and chief of the royal stud of France; whilst I was an insolent scoundrel, whom he was to punish instantly. In spite of threats, I persisted in making him get into a hackney-coach; and as he made some difficulty about it, we compelled him by main force.

In presence of M. Henry, M. le Director of the Police of the Chateau was not at all disconcerted; on the contrary, he assumed a tone of arrogant superiority, which actually alarmed the chief of the prefecture. They all thought that I had committed a blunder

"I will never put up with such an audacious insult," cried Chambreuil; "it is an outrage for which I will have ample reparation. I will let you know who I am, and we will see if you will dare to use toward me those arbitrary measures, which even the minister would not venture to employ."

I actually thought the moment had arrived when they would apologize to him, and reprimand me. They did not doubt but that Chambreuil was an old galley slave, but they were afraid they had offended in him some powerful man, on whom court favors were lavished. However, I asserted, with so much energy, that he was only an impostor, that they could not avoid giving a warrant to search his residence. I was to assist the commissary in this operation, at which Chambreuil was to be present; and on the road he whispered to me:

"My dear Vidocq, there are in my secretary some papers, which it is important to me to keep from inspection; promise me that you will get them, and you shall have no cause to repent it."

"I promise you."

"You will find them under a double lock, of which I will tell you the secret."

He told me how I was to proceed; and I found the papers in the place he had pointed out, which I kept to add to those which confirmed the propriety of his apprehension. Never had a forger so carefully arranged the materials of his swindling. There were found at his house a quantity of printed papers, some with this inscription, Haras de France, others with the Police du Roi; sheets a la Telliere bearing the titles of the minister of war, statements of services, brevets, diplomas, and a register of correspondence, always open as if by accident, that any looker-in might the more easily be deceived,—were among the documents, proving the high functions which Chambreuil took upon himself. He was supposed to be on terms of intimacy with the most distinguished personages; princes, and princesses wrote to him: their letters and his were transcribed beside each other, and what appears very strange is, that he is in correspondence with the prefect of police, whose reply was to be found in his lying register, on the margin of one of his missives.

The light afforded by the search so well corroborated my assertion respecting Chambreuill, that they did not hesitate sending him to La Force, there to await his trial.

Before the tribunal it was impossible to induce him to confess that he was a galley slave, which I persisted in calling him. He produced, on the contrary, authentic certificates, which stated that he had not left La Vendee since the year two. The judges were for a time in doubt how to decide between him and me, but I added so many and such powerful proofs in support of my assertion, that, his identity being recognized, he was sentenced to hard labor for life, and imprisoned in the Bagne of L'Orient, where he was not slow in resuming his old profession of denouncer. At the period of the assassination of the Due de Berry, in concert with one Gerard Carette, he wrote to the police that he had information to give respecting this fearful transaction. Cambreuil was known, and not credited; but some persons, absurd enough to believe that Louvel had accomplices, demanded that Carette should be brought to Paris. This was complied with, and Carette came, but nothing was elicited from him which threw any additional light on the subject.

The year 1814 was one of the most remarkable of my life, principally on account of the important captures which followed one another. Some of them gave rise to most whimsical incidents, and as I am in a vein I will relate one or two.

During a period of three years, a man of almost gigantic stature had been pointed out as the author of a vast many robberies committed in Paris. By the portraits which the sufferers drew of this individual, he could be no other than

Sablin, an excessively skillful and enterprising thief, who, freed from many successive sentences, (two of which were in fetters), had resumed his old trade with all the experience of the prisons. Many warrants were issued against Sablin, and the cleverest agents of police set upon him, but in vain; he escaped all pursuit, and if they had notice that he had appeared in any spot, by the time they arrived no trace of him remained. All the police officers being wearied by the useless pursuit of this invisible person, the task devolved on me to seek out and secure him, if possible. For fifteen months, I neglected no opportunity of endeavoring to meet him, but he never made his appearance in Paris for more than a few hours at a time, and as soon as the robbery was effected, he was away again without our being able in any way to trace him.

Sablin was in a manner known only to me, and I, therefore, was the person whom he most feared to meet. As he could see me afar off, he took good care to keep out of my way, and I never once got sight even of his shadow.

However, as lack of perseverance is not my fault, I at length learnt that Sablin had just taken up his residence at Saint Cloud, where he had hired an apartment. At this news, I set out from Paris, so as not to reach there until midnight. It was in the month of November, and the weather very bad. When I entered Saint Cloud, all my clothes were ringing wet: I did not take the trouble of drying them; and in my impatience to learn if I had been put on a false scent, I obtained, on talking about newcomers, some news, which was that a female, whose husband, a foreign merchant, was five feet ten inches (French measure), had recently occupied a certain house pointed out to me.

Five feet ten inches (French measurement) is not a common height even for Patagonians; and I no longer doubted but that I had at last found the actual domicile of Sablin. But as it was too late to present myself, I deferred my visit until the next day; and that I might be certain that my man did not escape me, I resolved, in spite of the rain, to pass the night before his house. I was in ambuscade with one of my agents, and at break of day, the door being opened, I glided quickly into the house that I might take a survey, and see if it were time to commence work. Scarcely had I put a foot on the first stair, when I paused—someone was descending. It was a woman whose features and painful step betokened a state of suffering. On seeing me, she shrieked and went back again: I followed, and entering with her into an apartment of which she had the key, heard myself announced in these words, pronounced in accents of horror, "Here is Vidocq." The bed was in an inner room, toward which I darted. A man was in bed—he raised his head: it was Sablin;—I flung myself upon him, and before he could recognize me I had handcuffed him.

During this operation the lady, having fallen into a chair, groaned very bitterly; she writhed, and appeared tormented by horrid pains.

"What is the matter with your wife?" I inquired of Sablin.

"Do you not see that she is in labor? All night she has been in the same state. When you met her, she was going out to Mother Tiremonde's (the midwife)."

At that moment the groans redoubled.

"My God! My God! I can move no longer, I am dying; pray have pity on me; relieve my sufferings! give me help!"

Soon only half-choked sounds were heard. Not to be touched at such a situation would have evinced a heart of marble. But what could I do? It was evident that a midwife was needed, but who was to go in search of her? Two were not too many to guard a fellow of Sablin's strength. I could not go out, nor could I determine on leaving a woman to die; and between humanity and duty, I was the most embarrassed man in the world. Suddenly, a historical anecdote, well told by Madame de Genlis, occurred to me: I recalled to mind the "Grand Monarque" performing the office of accoucheur to Lavalliere. Why, said I, should I be more delicate than he? Come, quick, a doctor: I am one. I immediately took off my coat, and in less than twenty-five minutes Madame Sablin was delivered: it was a boy, a fine boy, to which she gave birth. I swaddled the infant, after having made the toilet of his first ingress, or first egress, for I believe that in this instance the two expressions are synonymous; and when the ceremony was over, on looking at my work, I had the satisfaction to find that both mother and child were doing "as well as could be expected."

Then I had to fill out a form; the entry of the little newcomer on the register of the civil magistrates. We were all anxious: I offered to be subscribing witness; and when I had signed, Madame Sablin said to me, "Ah! Monsieur Vidocq, since you are here, there is another service you could render us."

"What?"

"I dare scarcely name it."

"Speak, if it be in my power..."

"We have no godfather; would you be kind enough to stand for the boy!"

"Certainly, as well as another; where is the godmother?"

Madame Sablin begged us to call in one of her neighbors; and as soon as all was in readiness, we went to church, accompanied by Sablin, whose escape I had rendered impossible. The honors of this sponsorship did not cost me less than fifty francs, and yet there was no christening feast.

In spite of the vexation which Sablin necessarily experienced, he was so deeply penetrated by my proceedings, that he could not forbear testifying his gratitude.

After a good breakfast, which was brought to us in the chamber of the lying-in lady, I conducted her husband to Paris, where he was sentenced to five years' imprisonment. Being master turnkey at La Force, where he underwent his sentence, Sablin found in this employment not only a means of living well, but also that of saving, at the expense of the prisoners and the persons who visited them, a small fortune, which he proposed to share with his wife; but at the period of his liberation, my friend Madame Sablin, who also had a partiality for the property of others, was expiating her crime at Saint Lazare. If the isolation consequent on the incarceration of his mate, Sablin, like many others, turned to evil courses, that is, having one evening in his pocket the fruits of his savings, which he had turned into specie, he went to the gambling table, and lost the whole. Two days afterward, he was found suspended in the wood of

Boulogne; he had selected as the instrument of his death one of the trees in the Allee des Voleurs.

It was not, as may have been seen, without much trouble that I was able to render Sablin up to justice. Certainly if all my searches had been of necessity as tedious and difficult, I could not have accomplished them: but success generally attended me, and sometimes was so close at hand, that I myself was amazed at it.

A few days after my adventure in Saint Cloud, the Sieur Sebillotte, a vintner in the Rue de Charenton, No. 145, complained of having been robbed. According to his statement, the thieves had effected an entrance by climbing, between seven and eight o'clock in the evening; had carried off twelve thousand francs in cash, two gold watches, and six silver spoons. There had been force used externally and internally. All the circumstances were so extraordinary, that the veracity of M. Sebillotte was somewhat doubted, and I was ordered to clear the affair up. A conversation I had with him convinced me that his complaint comprehended only plain facts.

M. Sebillotte was a landlord; he was in easy circumstances, and out of debt; consequently I could not detect in his situation a shadow of a motive which might lead me to believe that the robbery of which he complained was false; and yet it was of such a nature that, to commit it, the persons of the house must have been perfectly well known to the thieves. I asked M. Sebillotte what persons frequented his cabaret; and when he had mentioned some, he said,

"That is nearly all, except chance customers, and those strangers who cured my wife; on my word we were very lucky to have met with them! the poor thing had been suffering these three years, and they have given her a remedy which has done her much good."

"Do you often see these strangers?"

"They used to come here, but since my wife is better, we only see them occasionally."

"Do you know what they are? Perhaps they may have observed—"

"Ah! sir," cried Madame Sebillotte, who joined in the conversation, "do not suspect them, they are honest, I have proof of that."

"Yes, yes!" added the husband, "she has proof, which she will tell you: you will hear. Tell the gentleman, my dear."

Then Madame Sebillotte began her recital in these terms:—

"Yes, sir, they are honest, or I will be burnt alive. Well, you must know, it is not more than a fortnight ago, it was just a week after the term, I was counting out some money, when one of the females who is with them came in; it was she who had given me the remedy, from which I have had so much relief; and, I must tell you, she would not accept a sous for it, quite the contrary. You must suppose that I was very much pleased at seeing her; I made her sit down beside me, and whilst I was laying out the money in parcels of a hundred francs, she saw one on which was a large man leaning on two young ones, with a skin on his shoulders like a savage, holding a club: 'Ah!' said she, 'have you many like these?' 'Why,' said I. 'Because, you must know, that is worth a hundred and four sous. As many as you have, my husband will take at that price, if you will lay them aside.' I thought she was jesting; but in the evening I was never more surprised than to see her return with her husband. We looked over the money together, and as we found amongst it three hundred pieces of a hundred sous, like those she had pointed out, I let him have them, and he gave me a premium of sixty francs. You may judge after that if they are honest people or not, since they might if they had liked, have had them coin for coin."

By the work we know the workmen. The last sentence of Madame Sebillotte informed me what sort of people were those honest creatures whose eulogy she made; nor did I need more to be assured that the robbery, the authors of which I sought to detect, had been committed by the Bohemians. The matter of exchange was quite in their way; and then Madame Sebillotte, in describing them, only confirmed me more and more in my preconceived opinion.

I soon left the couple, and from that moment all dark complexions were looked at by me with suspicion. I was thinking how and where I should be most likely to fall in with some of the persons I wanted, when passing along the Boulevard du Temple, I saw, seated in a cabaret, called La Maison Rustique, two persons, whose copper-hued skin and foreign look awoke in my mind reminiscences of my sojourn at Malines. I entered; who should I see but Christian, with one of his pals, whom I also knew. I went up to them, and presenting my hand to Christian, saluted him by the name of Coroin. He looked at Ae for a moment, and then my features becoming known to dim, "Ah," he cried, jumping on my neck with transport, "my old friend."

So long a period had passed since we met, that, of course, after the customary compliments, we had many questions to ask and reply to mutually. He wanted to know why I left Malines; and without intimating my intentions to him, I trumped up a story which passed current.

"All right, all right," said he; "whether true or not, I credit it: besides, I find you again, and that is the main point. Ah! all our old cronies will rejoice to see you. They are all in Paris. Caron, Langarin, Ruffler, Martin, Sisque, Mich, Litle; even old mother Lavio is with us; and Betche too, little Betche."

"Ah, yes, your wife."

"How pleased she will be to see you. If you will be here at six o'clock the union will be complete; we are to meet here, and to go to the theatre together. You shall be of the party; but we will not part now. You have not dined?"

"No."

"Nor I either; we will go to Capucin."

"If you like; it is close at hand."

"Yes, only two steps, at the corner of the Rue d'Angouleme."

This vintner and cook, whose establishment bears a grotesque image of a disciple of Saint Francis as a sign, then enjoyed the favor of the public, in whose eyes quantity is always more valued than quality; and then for the holiday keepers on Sunday and Saint Monday,—for those jolly fellows, who carry on the war the whole week, is not very pleasant to have a place where, without faring badly or offending any person, they may appear in all sorts of garbs, with any growth of beard, and in every state of intoxication?

Such were the advantages which offered themselves at Capucins, without mentioning the large snuff box always open on the citizen's counter, at the service of whosoever, in passing, wished to refresh his nostrils with a pinch. It was four o'clock when we installed ourselves in this spot of liberty and joy The space was long till six o'clock. I was impatient to return to the Maison Rustique, where Christian's companions were to meet. After the repast we rejoined them; there were six, in accosting whom Christian spoke in their peculiar language. They instantly surrounded, hailed, embraced, welcomed me with acclamation: pleasure sparkled in their eyes.

"No play, no play," cried the wanderers, with unanimous voice.

"You are right," said Christian, "no play; we will go to the theatre another time; let us drink my boys, let us drink."

"Let us drink," echoed the gipsies. Wine and punch circulated freely. I drank, laughed, talked, and carried on my trade. I watched their countenances, motions, actions, and nothing escaped me. I recalled to myself some indications furnished by Monsieur and Madame Sebillotte; and the history of the hundred sous pieces, which had only been the first slight groundwork of a conjecture, became the basis of confirmed conviction.

Christian, or his mates, I could no longer doubt were the authors of the robbery announced to the police. How did I commend the casual glance made so a propos at the interior of La Maison Rustique! But it was not all to have detected the guilty; I waited until their brains were properly heated by the alcoholic applications; and when the whole party was in a state when one candle was enough to show two persons, I went out, and running hastily to the Theatre de la Gaite, informed the officer on duty that I was with some thieves, and arranged with him that in an hour or two at the latest he should apprehend us all, men and women.

These instructions given, I returned quickly. My absence had not been remarked; but at ten o'clock the house' was visited, the peace officer presented himself, and with him a formidable body of gendarmes and agents. They secured each of u« separately, and then conducted us to the guardhouse.

The commissary had preceded us; he ordered a general search. Christian, who called himself Hirch, in vain endeavored to conceal M. Sebillotte's six silver spoons; and his companion, Madame Villemain, (the title the lady gave herself,) could not preserve in secret, from the rigid search she underwent, the two gold watches mentioned in the complaint. The others were also compelled to produce money and jewels, which were taken from them.

I was anxious to know the opinion of my ancient comrades on this matter. I thought I read in their eyes that they did not in the least distrust me; nor was I mistaken, for scarcely had we reached the violin, (the watch-house,) than they made me excuses for having been the involuntary cause of my arrest.

"It was not purposely done," said Christian, "but who the devil could have expected such a thing? You were quite right to say that you knew nothing about us: be quiet and we will not say a word to the contrary; and as nothing has been found on your person to put you in any danger, you may be certain they will not long detain you."

Christian then recommended discretion to me, as to his real name, as well as those of his companions.

"Although," he added, "the recommendation is superfluous, since you are not less interested than we, in keeping silence on this score."

I offered to the gipsies to use the first moments of my liberty in their service; and in the hope that I should not be kept long in durance, they told me their domicile, so that in getting out I might inform their comrades. About midnight the commissary sent for me, under pretense of examining me, and we instantly went to the Marche Lenoir, where dwelt the famous Duchesse and three other pals of Christian, whom we apprehended by virtue of a warrant, and after a search which produced all necessary proofs for their conviction.

This band consisted of twelve persons, six men and six women; they were all condemned, the former to irons, the latter to close confinement. The vintner of the Rue de Charenton recovered his jewelry, plate, and the greater portion of his money.

Madame Sebillotte was overjoyed. The specific of the Bohemians had the effect of rendering her health less precarious, the information of the twelve thousand francs regained perfectly restored it, and doubtless the experience she had was not lost upon her; she remembered that, once in her life, she had nearly been a great loser, by having sold five-franc pieces for a hundred and four sous. "A burnt child dreads the fire."

This meeting with the gipsies was almost miraculous; but in the course of eighteen years that I have been attached to the police, it has happened more than once that I have been casually brought in contact with persons whom in my early days I had known.

A propos of occurrences of this kind, I cannot resist the desire of mentioning in this chapter one of the thousand absurd complaints which it was my lot to receive daily; this in particular procured for me a very singular renewal of acquaintance.

One morning whilst I was occupied in drawing up a report, I was told that a lady of respectable appearance desired to see me: she wishes to speak with you on an affair of importance. I ordered that she should be admitted instantly. She entered.

"I have to beg pardon for disturbing you; you are Monsieur Vidocq?"

"Yes, madame; and in what can I be of service to you?"

"Oh, you can aid me materially, sir; you can restore to me appetite and sleep. I neither rest nor eat. Ah, how wretched is it to be gifted with excessive sensibility. Ah I sir, how I pity persons of our sentiment! I swear to you that it is the most distressing qualification that heaven can bestow! He was so well brought up, so interesting. If you had known him, you could not have forborne loving him— Poor dear!"

"But, madame, condescend to explain; you may perhaps suffer by a causeless delay, and lose precious time."

"He was my only comfort—"

"Well, madame, what is it?"

"I have not power to tell you."

She put her hand into her reticule, and thence produced a paper which she gave me with averted eyes, saying: "Read, read."

"These are printed papers you have given me: you must have made some mistake."

"Would that I did, sir; would to heaven that I did. I beseech you to cast your eyes over the number 32, and 40; my grief forbids me to after more! Ah! how cruel is my fate. (Tears fell from her eyes, the words expired upon her lips, she was convulsed by sobs, and could with apparent difficulty prevent them suffocating her.) I am strangled! I am choking! I feel something swelling in my throat. Ah! ah! ah! ah!"

I handed a seat to the lady, and whilst she abandoned herself to her sorrow, I turned over two or three leaves, until I reached No. 32, 40, under the head of lost property; the page was moist with tears; I read:

"A small spaniel, with, long silvery silken hair, dropping ears: he is perfectly trimmed; a mark of fire above each eye; physiognomy excessively animated, the tail trumpet fashion, forming the bird of paradise. His natural disposition is very endearing; will eat nothing but the white of a chicken, and answers to the name of Garcon, pronounced with mildness. His mistress is in despair: fifty francs' reward will be given to whosoever will bring him to the Rue de Turenne, No. 23."

"Well, madame! what am I to do for Garcon? Dogs are not under my control. I see that he was a most amiable creature."

"Ah, sir, amiable! that is the exact word," sighed the lady, in accents that penetrated the very heart; "and his intelligence could not be surpassed; he never left me. Dearest Garcon! Would you believe it, that during the holy exercises, he had a more devout look than myself? In truth, he was generally admired, his appearance alone was a lesson to mankind. Alas, alas! on Sunday last we were going to the sacrament, I was carrying him under my arm; you know these little creatures have perpetual wants—at the moment we were entering the church, I put him on the ground, that he might do as he wished; I went onward, not to disturb him, and when I returned—no Garcon. I called: Garcon, Garcon! —he had disappeared. I left the Benedictine to run after him; and, judge of my misery, I could not find him. This is the business that has induced me to trouble you today, to entreat that you would have the excessive kindness to have a search made for him. I will pay all that is needful; but take care he is not ill-used. I am sure the fault has not been his."

"Indeed, madame, whether he is in fault or not is no concern of mine; your complaint is not of that nature to which I am allowed to attend; if we were to give our time to dogs, cats, and birds, there would be endless work."

"Well, sir; since you talk in that tone, I shall address his excellency. If there is no respect shown to persons who think well—do you know I belong to the congregation, and that—"

"You may belong to the devil for me—"

I could not finish my speech: a deformity which I observed suddenly in the devout mistress of Garcon, produced from me a sudden fit of laughter, which entirely disconcerted her.

"Am I an object of mirth?" she said; "laugh away, sir, laugh away."

When my sudden gayety had a little abated, I said:—

"Forgive, madame, this impulse, which I could not control; I did not know at first with whom I was conversing, but now I know how I should behave. Do you really deplore the loss of Garcon?"

"Ah! sir, I cannot survive it."

"You have never then experienced a loss which more sensibly affected you?"

"No, sir."

"Yet you have had a husband in this world, you had a son, you have had lovers—"

"I, sir! how dare you—"

"Yes, Madame Duflos, you have had lovers; you have really had them. Do you remember a certain night at Versailles?"

At abuse words she looked at me attentively for a moment; the color came to her cheek.

"Eugene?" she cried, and instantly hastened from the room.

Madame Duflos was a milliner whose clerk I had been for some time, when, to hide from the search of the police at Arras, I had concealed myself in Paris. She was a droll sort of woman; she had a fine head, bold eye, good eyebrows, majestic forehead; her mouth, elevated at the corners, was large, but adorned with thirty-two teeth of dazzling whiteness; her hair of a beautiful black, and aquiline nose, above a tolerably well-furnished moustache, gave to her physiognomy an air which would have been imposing, if her bosom, placed between two humps, and her neck plunged into these double shoulders, had not suggested the idea of a female Punch.

She was about forty when I first saw her: her appearance was most studiously attended to, and she gave herself the airs of a queen; but from the height of the chair whereon she was perched, so that her knees were elevated above the counter, she seemed less like a Semiramis than the grotesque idol of some Indian pagoda. When I saw her on this species of throne, I had much difficulty to be serious; but I preserved the gravity which circumstances demanded, and had just sufficient command over myself to convert into salutations of the most respectful kind a strong disposition to do entirely otherwise. Madame Duflos took from her bosom a large eyeglass, through which she viewed me, and when she had taken my dimensions from head to foot,

"What is your pleasure, sir?" said she.

I was about to reply, but a clerk who had undertaken to present me, having told her that I was the young man of whom he had spoken, she looked at me again, and asked me what I knew of business. Of business I was utterly ignorant; I was silent; she repeated the question, and as she evinced some impatience, I was forced to explain.

"Madame," I said, "I know nothing of the business of fashions, but with zeal and perseverance, I hope to give you satisfaction, particularly if assisted by your advice."

"Well, I like that; I wish people to be frank with me, I receive you; you shall fill Theodore's situation."

"I am at your orders as soon as you please, madame."

"Well, then, I engage you at once; from this very day you may begin on trial."

My installation was at once effected. In my situation as junior clerk, I had the task of arranging the magazine and workroom, where about twenty young girls, all very pretty, were employed in fashioning gewgaws, destined to tempt the provincial coquettes. Thrown amongst this bed of beauties, I thought myself transported to a seraglio, and, looking sometimes at the brown and sometimes at the fair, I thought of circulating the handkerchief pretty freely, when, on the morning of the fourth day, Madame Duflos, who had no doubt seen something not quite to her satisfaction, sent for me to her room.

"M. Eugene," she said, "I am much displeased with you; you have been here but a very short time, and already begin to form criminal designs upon my young people. I tell you that will not do for me at all, at all, at all."

Overwhelmed by this merited reproach, and unable to imagine how she had guessed my intentions, I could only stammer out a few unconnected words.

"You would have considerable difficulty in justifying yourself," she added, "but I know very well, that at your age we cannot repress our inclinations: but these girls must not be thought of in any way; in the first place, they are too young; then, again, they have no fortune; a young man should have some person who can assist him, some person of sense and reason."

During this moral lesson, Madame Duflos, carelessly extended on an easy couch, rolled about her eyes in a way that would infallibly have led to an overpowering burst of laughter from me, had not her head-woman entered very opportunely to tell her that she was wanted in the workroom.

Thus terminated this interview, which proved to me the necessity of being on my guard. Without renouncing my intentions, I only appeared to look on the young women with Indifference, and was skillful enough to set her penetration at default; she watched me incessantly, spied my gestures, my words, my looks; but she was only astonished at one thing— the rapidity of my progress. I had only passed one month's apprenticeship and could already sell a shawl, a fancy gown, a cap or a bonnet, as well as the most experienced hand. Madame was delighted, and had even the kindness to say, that, if I continued as attentive to her lessons, she did not despair of making me the cock of the mode.

"But," she added, "mind, no familiarity with the pullets: you understand me, M. Eugene; you understand me. And I have also another thing to recommend to you, that is, not to neglect your personal appearance, nothing is so genteel as a well-dressed man. Besides, I will undertake to provide your dress for the present; let me do so, and you will see if I will not make a little Love of you."

I thanked Madame Duflos, but as I feared with her extraordinary taste she might make of me some such a Cupid as she was herself a Venus, I told her that I wished to spare her the care of a metamorphosis which appeared to me impossible; but that if she would confine herself to her kind advice, I should receive it with gratitude, and seek to profit by it.

Sometime afterward Madame Duflos told me, that intending as usual to go to the fair of Versailles with some goods, she had decided that I should attend her. We started the next day, and forty-eight hours afterward were established at the Champ-de-Foire. A servant who had attended us slept in the shop; as for me, I lodged with Madame, at the auberge; we had ordered two rooms, but in consequence of the influx of strangers, we could only have one: resignation was compulsory. In the evening, Madame had a large screen brought, with which she divided the room into two, so that we each had our own apartment. Before we went to bed, she preached to me for an hour. Afterward, we went upstairs: Madame entered her division, I wished her good evening, and in two minutes was in bed. Soon sighs began to escape her, doubtless caused by the fatigue which she had experienced during the day; she sighed again, but the candle was out, and I went to sleep. Suddenly, I was interrupted in my first nap, I thought some one pronounced my name; I listened.

"Eugene."

It was the voice of Madame Duflos. I made no reply.

"Eugene," she called again, "have you closed the door properly?"

"Yes, Madame."

"I think you mistake; look, I beg of you, and see if the bolt is properly secured; we cannot be too careful in these auberges."

I did as desired, and returned to my bed. Scarcely was I laid once more on my left side than Madame began to complain.

"What a miserable bed! I am eaten up by the bugs, it is impossible to close an eye! And you, Eugene, have you any of these insupportable insects?"

I turned a deaf ear to the question.

"Eugene, answer me; have you any of these bugs, as I have?"

"On my word, madame, I have not yet found any."

"You are very fortunate then, and I congratulate you; as for me, I am devoured by them, I have bites of such a size! If it goes on in this way, I shall pass a sleepless night."

I kept silence, but was compelled to break in when Madame Duflos, exasperated by her sufferings, and not knowing how, between the biting and itching, to relieve herself, began to cry out with all her strength.

"Eugene! Eugene! Do get up, I beseech you, and be so good as ask the innkeeper for a light, that we may drive away these cursed animals. Make haste I entreat you, my friend, for I am in hell."

I went down, and came up again with a lighted candle, which I put on the table near the lady's bed. As I was but lightly clad, that is to say, with my flags flying in the wind, I retired as quickly as possible, as well out of respect to the modesty of Madame Duflos, as to escape the seductions of an elegant negligée, in which there appeared to me to be some design. But scarcely had I got round the screen, when Madame Duflos gave a piteous shriek.

"Ah! what a size, what a monster, I can never have the courage to kill it: how it runs, it will get away. Eugene! Eugene! come here, I supplicate you."

I could not retreat, but, like a second Theseus, I risked all and approached the bed.

"Where, where," said I, "is this Minotaur, let me exterminate him?"

"I conjure you, Eugene, not to jest in that way—there, there, see how it runs: did you see it on the pillow? how it goes down the bed—what swiftness! it seems to know the fate you have in store for it."

In vain did I use all diligence; I could neither catch nor even see the dangerous animal. I looked and felt everywhere to discover its hiding place. I made every possible exertion to find it, but in vain. Sleep overpowered us in our endeavors; and if, on waking, by a return to the past, I was led to reflect that Madame Duflos had been more fortunate than Potiphar's wife, I had the pain of thinking that I had not had all the virtue of Joseph.

From this time I had the job of watching every night that Madame was not tormented by bugs. My service by day was rendered much easier. Considerations, anticipations, little presents—nothing was spared; I was, like the conscript of Charlet, nourished, shod, clothed, and put to bed at the expense of the princess. Unfortunately, the princess was somewhat jealous, and her rule a little despotic. Madame Duflos asked nothing more but that, in more senses than one, I should amuse myself like a hump-backed man; but she went into most tremendous fits of rage if I even glanced at another woman. At last, worn out by this tyranny, I declared one evening that I would free myself from it.

"Ah! you will leave me then," said she, "we will see about that."

Then arming herself with a knife, she darted at me to plunge it in my heart. I seized her arm, and her rage being appeased, I agreed to remain, on condition that she would be more reasonable. She promised; but, from the next day, curtains of green taffety were placed over the windows of the room in which I was placed, as Madame had thought it fit to intrust me exclusively with keeping her books. This proceeding was the more vexatious, as I had then no prospect of any control over the work room.

Madame Duflos was most ingenious in isolating me from the rest of the world; every day there was a new precaution for my security. At last my slavery was so rigorous, that every person saw through the tenderness of which I was the object. The shop girls, who liked nothing better than teasing Madame, came to speak to me every instant, sometimes with one excuse, sometimes another;

poor Madame Duflos was tormented to death by it! how pitiable! Every hour in the day she poured forth her reproaches on me; and never gave one instant's intermission. I could not for any length of time remain easy under such a despotism. To avoid a burst which in my situation, might have involved me (I had then just escaped from the Bagne,) I secretly took a place by the diligence, and absconded.

How little did I then think, that, after a lapse of twenty years, I should meet again in the police office, my little Humpina of the Rue Saint Martin: the proverb would have it so: two mountains never meet.

Chapter XXXVII

For upward of four months a great number of murders and highway robberies had been committed on all the roads conducting to the capital, without its having been possible to discover the perpetrators of these crimes. In vain had the police kept a strict watch upon the actions of all suspected persons—their utmost diligence was fruitless; when a fresh attempt, attended with circumstances of the most horrible nature, supplied them with hints from which they could at length anticipate bringing the culprits to justice.

A man named Fontaine, a butcher, living at La Courtille, was going to a fair in the district of Corbeil, carrying with him his leather bag, in which was safely deposited the sum of fifteen hundred francs; he had passed the Cour de France, and was walking on in the direction of Essonne, when, at a trifling distance from an auberge where he had stopped to take some refreshment, he came up with two very well-dressed men. As evening was approaching, Fontaine was not sorry to obtain fellow travelers; he therefore addressed the two strangers, who were not slow in returning the salutation, and a conversation soon arose between them.

"Good-evening, gentlemen," said he to them.

"The same to you," replied they.

"We shall soon have night overtake us," resumed the butcher.

"We shall, indeed, sir," answered one of the two pedestrians, "and at this season of the year we must not reckon upon much assistance from the twilight."

"I should care very little about it," added Fontaine, "but unfortunately, I have still a considerable distance to walk tonight."

"And where may you be proceeding to, if it be not too impertinent a question?"

"Where am I going? Why, to Miller, to purchase sheep."

"In that case, if agreeable to you, we may as well join company; my friend and self are proceeding to Corbeil on business, so that chance has been most favorable to us."

"Agreed!" exclaimed the butcher, "things could not have fallen out better; nor shall I be slow in profiting by it; for, in my humble opinion, when one has money about one, traveling in good company is far more pleasant than being quite alone."

"You have money about you, then?"

"You are right there, my friend, and a pretty considerable sum, too."

"Well, we likewise have large sums; but we were informed that we ran no risk, as this part of the country was considered perfectly safe."

"Indeed; I am glad to hear it; but, were it otherwise, I have something here (showing a huge stick) that would make a tolerable resistance; besides, I think the most daring thieves would hardly have the courage to attack three such formidable antagonists as we should make."

"No, no; they would not dare to meddle with us."

Conversing thus, the trio reached the door of a small house, which the branch of juniper, decorating the entrance, designated as a cabaret. Fontaine proposed to his companions to take a bottle together. They entered; procured some Beaugency at eight sols the flask, and seated themselves to enjoy it. The cheapness of the wine—its harmless nature—their meeting with it at a time when weariness had begun to steal over at least one of the party—were so many reasons for lengthening their stay.

At last they rose to depart; and a general emulation arose as to who should defray the reckoning. Nearly an hour, during which more than one fresh bottle was discussed, passed in this amicable dispute; which, being at last yielded in favor of Fontaine, completed the elevation of his spirits, and raised him to the highest pitch of gayety. Under similar circumstances, what man could have harbored suspicion?

Poor Fontaine, delighted at having met with such agreeable companions, thought he could not do better than take them as guides for the remaining part of his journey; and in full confidence of their integrity, abandoned himself to their guidance along the byroad they were then traveling. He walked on, therefore, with one of his newfound friends, whilst the second followed close behind. The night was very dark, scarcely allowing the travelers to distinguish one step before the other; but guilt, with its lynx-like eye, can penetrate the thickest gloom; and while Fontaine was unsuspectingly following the path recommended by his companion, the one who remained behind him struck him over the head a violent blow with his cudgel, which made him reel: surprised, but not intimidated, he was about to turn round to defend himself, when a second blow, more fatal than the first, brought him to the ground: immediately the other robber, armed with a short dagger, threw himself upon him, and ceased not to deal out murderous wounds, until he believed his victim had ceased to exist.

Fontaine had yielded after a long and desperate struggle, and lay as apparently lifeless as his assassins would have had him. They quickly stripped him of the contents of his moneybag with which they made off, leaving him weltering in his blood. Happily, it was not long before a passenger, attracted by his groans, came to his succor, and discovered the wretched man, whom the freshness of the night air had recalled to his senses.

After having rendered him what assistance was in his power, the stranger hastened to the nearest hamlet in search of further aid—information was immediately dispatched to the magistrates of Corbeil—the attorney-general arrived without delay at the place of crime, and commenced the most diligent inquiries respecting the slightest circumstances attending it. Eight-and-twenty wounds, more or less deep, bore ample testimony how much the murderers had feared that their victim should escape them. Spite of the cruelty of their intention, Fontaine was yet able to utter a few words, although his extreme exhaustion from loss of blood rendered him unable to give all the particulars which were necessary for the ends of justice. He was removed to the hospital, and at the end of two days, so favorable a change took place, that he was pronounced out of danger.

The most minute exactitude had been observed in removing the body. Nothing had been neglected which might lead to the discovery of the assassins. Accurate impressions were taken of the footmarks; buttons, fragments of paper dyed in blood were carefully collected: on one of these pieces, which appeared to have been hastily torn off to wipe the blade of a knife found at no great distance from it, were observed some written characters, but they were without any connecting sense, and, consequently, unable to afford any information likely to throw a light on the affair. Nevertheless, the attorney-general attached a great importance to the explanation of these fragments; and, upon more narrowly exploring the spot where Fontaine had been lying, a second morsel was picked up, which presented every appearance of being part of a torn address; by dint of close examination, the following words were deciphered.

—A Monsieur Rao—
—Marchand de vins, bar—
—Roche—
—Cli—

This piece of paper seemed to have formed part of a printed address; but of whose address? It was at present wholly impossible to make out. However that may be, as no circumstance is too slight to deserve notice in the absence of more substantial proofs, notes were carefully made of everything that might be hereafter available information. The magistrates assembled on this occasion received the thanks their extreme zeal and ability so fully merited. So soon as they had fulfilled this part of their mission, they returned with all haste to Paris, in order to concert further plans with the judicial and administrative authority. At their desire, I had immediate conference with them, and furnished with a procés-verbal prepared by them, I opened the campaign against the assassins. Their victim had sufficiently described them; but how could I place implicit reliance on information proceeding from such a source?

Few men in imminent danger can preserve sufficient presence of mind to take accurate views of all that is passing; and upon the present occasion I was more inclined to doubt the testimony of Fontaine, from the extreme nicety with which he detailed the most trifling particulars; he related, that during the long struggle he had with the assailants, one of them had fallen on his knees, uttering a cry of pain, and that he heard him moaning and complaining to his accomplice of suffering extreme pain. Similar remarks to this, which he pretended to have made, appeared to me very extraordinary, considering the state in which he was found. I could not bring myself to believe that he himself felt quite assured of the correctness of his reminiscences. I determined, nevertheless, to turn them to the best account I could; but still I required a more definite point to start from. The torn address was, in my estimation, an enigma, which must first be solved; and, to effect this, I racked my brains day and night, and at last felt satisfied, that excepting the name (respecting which I had but few doubts) the perfect address would run thus:

A Monsieur,
Marchand de vins,
Barriére Rochechouart.
Chaussée de Clignancourt.

It was therefore evident that the assassins were in league with a wine-merchant of that neighborhood;—perhaps the wine merchant himself was one of the perpetrators of the crime. I set my plans to work, so as to know the truth as quickly as possible; and before the end of the day I was satisfied that I had been right in directing my suspicions toward an individual named Raoul. This man had become known to me under very unfavorable auspices; he passed for one of the most daring traffickers in contraband goods, and the cabaret kept by him had long been marked out as the rendezvous where a crowd of suspicious persons nightly celebrated their riotous orgies. Raoul had moreover married the sister of a liberated galley slave, and I was informed that he was linked in with persons of both sexes, of characters as desperate as their fortunes. In a word, his reputation was that of a loose and profligate man; and whenever a crime was denounced, if he had not positively participated in it, all thought themselves warranted in saying to him, "If it were not done by yourself, at least it was the work of your brother, or some of your relations."

Raoul, however, contrived to anticipate every scheme laid for entrapping him, either through his own sagacity, or the hints of his associates, I resolved, as a first step, to keep a careful watch over all the approaches to the cabaret; and I charged my agents to observe, with a scrutinizing eye, the different persons who frequented it, in order to ascertain whether, amongst the number, there might not be found one who was wounded in the knee. While my spies were at the post I had assigned to them, my own observations soon informed me that Raoul was in the constant habit of receiving at his house one or two persons of infamous character, with whom he seemed upon terms of the closest intimacy. The neighbors affirmed that they were frequently seen going out together, that they made long absences, and that it was universally believed that the greater part of honest Raoul's profits were those drawn from his dealings in contraband goods. A wine merchant who possessed the greatest facility of observing what was going on in Raoul's domicile, told me that he had often observed these worthy friends stealing from the house in the gloom of the evening, and returning at an early hour the following morning, apparently exhausted with fatigue, and splashed up to the neck. I further learned that he had set up a target in his garden, and was constantly practicing firing with a pistol Such were the particulars I gathered respecting this notable character from all who knew anything of him. At the same time my agents brought me the intelligence of their having observed at the house of Raoul a man, whom, for many reasons, they had surmised to be one of the assassins we were in search of. This person had first attracted their suspicions by a halt in his gait, proceeding not so much from habitual lameness, as from recent injury: and upon further examination of his person and dress, both were found in close agreement with the description given by Fontaine of one of the robbers. My agents further informed me that the man in question was generally accompanied by his wife; and that both appeared on the best possible terms with Raoul. My emissaries had succeeded in tracing their abode, which was on the first floor of a house situated on the Rue Coquenard; and here, in the apprehension of giving the slightest hints of their suspicions to the suspected party, their investigations had rested.

These particulars strengthened all my conjectures, and I was no sooner in possession of them, than I determined to go myself, and watch near the house that had been described to me It was now night, and I was compelled to defer my purpose till the coming morn; however, before the sun had risen, I was Op the lookout on the Rue Coquenard. I remained there without perceiving anything worthy of notice till four o'clock in the afternoon, and was beginning to grow impatient of the little success our plans seemed likely to realize, when my · agents pointed out to me an individual, whose features and name suddenly occurred to my memory. "See! there he is," cried they; and scarcely had my eyes glanced over him, than I recognized a person named Court, whom, from previous circumstances, fresh in my recollection, I instantly set down as one of the assassins I was in search of. His principles, which were of the most abandoned nature, had drawn down upon him, on many important occasions, severe consequences. He had just been punished by a six months' imprisonment for some fraudulent act, and I well-remembered having arrested him once before for a highway robbery. In a word, he was one of those degraded beings, who, like Cain, bore on his forehead the stamp of shame and death.

Without being much of a prophet, one might boldly have predicted that this man was destined to a scaffold. One of those presentiments, which have never deceived me, told me that he had at length reached the term of that perilous career to which a blind fatality had conducted him. However, not wishing to hazard success by precipitancy, I inquired, with all possible caution, what were his means of procuring a subsistence. No one could satisfy me; and it appeared a notorious truth, that he was never known either to possess a shilling, or to have any ostensible method of earning one. The neighbors, when questioned, assured me that he led a most dissolute life, and. in fact, was considered as a person of extremely bad connections and pursuits; his very looks would have condemned him in a court of justice; and for my own self, who had such powerful reasons for concluding both himself and his confederate Raoul to be finished rogues and highwaymen, it may be readily supposed I lost no time in applying for warrants for their apprehension. The necessary papers were no sooner asked for than given; and the very next morning, almost before daylight appeared, I repaired to the house where Court lodged; having ascended the stairs till I reached the landing place on the first floor, I knocked at his door.

"Who is there?" asked a voice from within.

"Who should it be but Raoul?" said I, imitating the voice of the latter; "come, come, friend, open the door."

"Well, don't be in a hurry then," answered he; and listening, I could distinctly hear the hasty movements of someone preparing to unfasten the door, which was no sooner unclosed, than, believing he was speaking to his friend Raoul, "Well," exclaimed he, "what news? anything fresh turned up?"

"Yes, yes," replied I, "I have a thousand things to say to you;" but by this, through the glimmer of morning twilight, he discovered his error, and cried out in a voice expressive of the greatest alarm, "Bless me, if it is not Monsieur Jules!" (This was the name which I was generally called by common women and thieves.)

"M. Jules!" replied the wife of Court, still more alarmed than her husband.

"Suppose it is M. Jules," said I, "why should that frighten you? The devil is never so black as he is painted."

"To be sure," observed the husband; "M. Jules is a good fellow; and although he nabbed me once, never mind, I owe him no ill-will for it."

"I know that, my regular," said I; "besides, why should you be angry with me? Is it my fault if you do a bit of moonlight?"

"Moonlight! Ah!" replied Court, with the accent of a man who felt himself all at once relieved of the weight of a mountain; "moonlight, oh, M. Jules, if it were so, you know very well I should make no secret of it with you; however, you are welcome to look about you, and see what is to be seen."

Whilst he was every moment becoming more tranquil as to the nature of my visit, I proceeded to turn over everything in the apartment, in which I found a pair of pistols ready loaded and primed; some knives: clothes which appeared to have been recently washed; with several other articles, all of which I seized.

There now only remained to put the finishing stroke to my expedition, by arresting both husband and wife; for, to have allowed either of them to remain at large, would have insured the destruction of my plan for entrapping Raoul, who would have learned from them sufficient to defeat my scheme. I therefore conducted them both to the station in the Place Cadet. Court, whom I had pinioned, relapsed all of a sudden into his original terror, and became gloomy and pensive. The precautions taken by me rendered him uneasy, and his wife appeared to participate in his terrible reflections. Their consternation was complete, when, upon our arrival at the guardhouse, they heard me give orders that they should be kept apart and carefully watched, I directed that they should be plentifully supplied with food; but they were neither hungry nor thirsty.

Whenever Court was questioned on the subject, a mournful shake of the head was the only answer returned; and eighteen hours elapsed without his opening his lips. His eyes were fixed and heavy, and his whole countenance rigid and immovable. This impassibility convinced me but too well that he was guilty. Under similar circumstances I have almost always observed the two extremes, a profound silence, or an extreme volubility.

Court and his wife being in a place of safety, my next business was to seize Raoul. I immediately repaired to his cabaret; he was not at home. The waiter left in charge of the house told me that he had slept at Paris, where he possessed a small country-house; but that being Sunday, he would be sure to return quite early.

This absence of Raoul was a mischance I had not calculated upon, and I trembled, lest on his way home the whim might have seized him of calling upon his friend Court. In that case he would of course have learned his arrest; and the knowledge of that might put him too much on his guard to enable me to lay hold of him. I feared likewise that he might have had a view of our expedition from the Rue Coquenard; and my apprehensions were redoubled when the waiter told me that his master's country house was in the Fauxbourg Montmartre. He had never been at it, and could not point out the road to me, but he believed it was in the close vicinity of the Place Cadet. Every additional particular I derived from him redoubled my fears, and led me to attribute the unusual absence of Raoul from his business to his having got a scent of my intentions toward him.

At nine o'clock he had not returned; and the waiter, whom I questioned as closely as I could do, without allowing him to see into my designs, appeared all wonder and uneasiness that his master should thus delay his return upon so busy a day as Sunday invariably was with him. Even the servant, who was busied in preparing the breakfast I had ordered for myself and my agents, expressed her surprise at her master, and still more her mistress, being so much less exact to their usual hour for appearing than she had ever known them. "If I only knew where to send to," said the poor woman, "I would certainly inquire whether any accident can have befallen them." Although fully persuaded that her fears were without foundation, I felt as much at a loss as the whole household to guess the reason of his non-appearance. Twelve o'clock struck, still no tidings had reached us, and I began really to believe that the train had blown up, when the waiter, who had for the last half hour been posted sentry before the door, came running toward me, crying out, "Here he is, here he comes!"

"Who wants me?" asked Raoul, as he entered. But scarcely had his foot crossed the threshold, than, recognizing me, he exclaimed, "Bless me, Jules! why what brings you in our neighborhood this morning?" He had evidently not the slightest suspicion that it was on his account I had come, and I endeavored to lead him still further from guessing the true nature of my visit. "So, friend!" said I, "you are a liberal, are you?"

"A liberal!"

"Yes, even so; and you are further accused but this is no place for conversation. Can I speak to you alone?"

"Certainly; step up to the room on the first floor, and I will follow you in a minute."

I did so, after having by signs instructed my agents to keep a strict eye over Raoul, and to take him into custody if he discovered the least disposition to quit the house. However, the unhappy man had no intention of escape, for in a very few minutes he joined me, and, with a look and manner expressive of jovial content, desired I would let him into the mighty mystery of my proceedings.

"Well, then," said I, "now that we can converse without interruption, I will frankly explain the cause of my present visit. But tell me first, can you not partly guess it?"

"Not I, upon my honor."

"You have already experienced great inconveniences on account of those singing clubs, which you have persisted in holding in your cabaret, spite of the formal prohibition issued by the police against them. Information has been given that every Sunday there are meetings held at your house, at which seditious toasts and songs libeling the government are permitted. Not only is it known that you countenance the assembling of a mass of suspicious characters, but it is understood that this very day a more than usual number is expected to collect within these walls from twelve to four o'clock. You see there is no blinding the police as to your goings on. This is not all; you are further accused of having in your possession a vast quantity of disloyal and immoral songs, which are so carefully concealed by you that my orders were not to appear before you except in a disguise, that would have prevented your recognizing my person, and to defer my operations till the gentlemen of the singing club should have opened their meeting. I am truly concerned to be charged with so very unpleasant a mission. Had I been apprized that you were the person alluded to, I should most certainly have declined the office: for with you, what would a disguise avail me?"

Raoul smiled. "I think, Master Jules," said he, "I should have been much amused at seeing you attempt to deceive me that way."

"Still," continued I, "it is better for you that I should be employed on this business than a stranger; you know very well that I have no ill-will against you. So take my advice, and give me up every song in your possession; and further to dispel the present doubts against you, refuse admission to every person whose presence here might, in the most trifling degree, compromise your safety."

"Upon my word," said Raoul, "I had no notion before how deep a politician you were."

"Why, as to that, friend," cried I, "a little of everything is a useful trade, and I for one find that if I desire to get on in this world, I must be able to ride on any saddle."

"Well," replied Raoul, "you can't help it, master Jules, but as true as my name is Clair Raoul, I swear to you that I am wrongly accused. People have surely gone mad! I, who think of nothing but just how to earn a bit of honest bread! What a world is this! Nothing but envy and spite against those who seem likely to meet with any thing like success!— however, M. Jules, if you doubt my word, you can easily judge for yourself—just make up your mind to stay here with your people; observe us well throughout the day, and form your own opinions of our principles and loyalty."

"Agreed," said I, "but hark ye, friend Raoul, no gammon if you please; you are just the chap to destroy all these objectionable songs, and nothing would be easier than for you to give a hint to your company, that would effectually silence the dingers from committing themselves in my hearing."

"Who do you take me for, sir?" exclaimed Raoul, with quickness. "I am incapable of such conduct; if I promise you to let every thing proceed as if you were not present, nothing could induce me to deviate from it; you can either believe me or not, at your pleasure, but to convince you of my honor in the business, you shall remain by my side the whole of the day; I pledge myself not to breathe one word respecting you to a living soul, not even to my wife when she comes home, so that you may be very sure;—however, you will, I hope, see no objection to my attending to my customers as usual."

"Assuredly not; let every thing go on as usual, and to lull all suspicion, I don't care if I lend you a helping hand."

"Your offer is too agreeable to be refused," replied Raoul: "so, if you please, M. Jules, we will proceed to work at once."

"Come on then," said I, and we descended the stairs together. Raoul prepared his huge carving knife, and, with my sleeves tucked up, and a napkin fastened before me, I aided him in carving the veal, which, with the accompaniment of sorrel sauce, was destined for the banquet of the Luculluses of the cabaret. From the veal we proceeded to the mutton; we set out some dozens of chops in the most tempting manner, and trimmed up the leg, that delicate morsel so generally relished and longed for. I next assisted in preparing some turkeys for the spit, after which we cleared away the litter, and repaired to the wine cellar, where I made myself equally useful, by helping my companion to manufacture genuine wine at six sols the flask.

During this operation I was quite alone with Raoul, who passed me off to everyone as his most intimate friend. I stuck as close to him as his very shadow and he himself appeared as unable to dispense with me as with his large carving knife. I must confess that several times I trembled lest he should suspect the motive of my watching him so closely; had he done so, he would certainly have murdered me, and I must have perished beneath his violence, without any human creature being able to assist me; happily he saw in me only a familiar of the political inquisition, and as to the seditious imputations urged against him, he was perfectly at his ease.

Up to four o'clock I continued my assistance as second in office, when the commissary of police, whom I had informed of the affair, arrived. I was on the ground floor, when I perceived him at a distance, and hastening to him, I begged he would not make his appearance for a few minutes. I then returned to Raoul, and affecting to be exceedingly angry, "The devil take them!" cried I, "the police have just sent to me to say that our business lies at your house in Paris, and that we must remove thither instantly."

"Oh, if that be all," said Raoul, "let us go there at once."

"Yes," replied I, "and when we are there we shall be ordered back again here; faith, they do not stand very nice as to the trouble they give us with their contradictory orders! If I were in your place, since we are in your house, I would send to request the commissary of police to allow your premises to be searched; it would be a convincing argument that you were wrongly accused."

Raoul applauded this advice as most excellent, did as I recommended, and having obtained the commissary's consent, the strictest search took place, without, however, its producing anything to criminate him.

"Well," cried he (when the whole was concluded), with that tone of exultation which might have sprung from a man of conscious integrity; "well, gentlemen, I hope you are now satisfied. Upon my word, I do not think myself at all well used to be suspected and searched in this manner. Why, you could not have done more had I committed murder!"

The assurance with which the latter part of the sentence was pronounced really startled me, and for a moment I repented of having ever suspected him, but the many reasons I had for concluding him guilty quickly effaced my regret. Still it was frightful to consider that a robber and a murderer like himself, whose hands were yet reeking with the blood of his victim, could, without a shudder, utter words which thus recalled his guilt. Raoul was calm and almost triumphant in his manner; and when we were seated in the hackney-coach which was to transport us to Paris, an indifferent spectator might have supposed he was proceeding to a festival; he rubbed his hands, and said with all the glee imaginable, "I am thinking how my wife will be astonished at seeing me return to her in such good company." It happened to be his wife who opened the door; at the sight of us her countenance underwent not the slightest alteration; she presented us with seats, but as we had but little time to lose, the commissary and myself immediately set to work to perform our task of examining the house. Raoul did not appear desirous of quitting us for a moment, but guided us through our search with the utmost complaisance.

In order to give a coloring to the story I had first told him, we affected the greatest solicitude respecting his papers; he gave me the key of his escritoire. I seized upon a bundle of papers, and the first upon which I cast my eyes was a direction, part of which had been torn off. Instantly the shape of the torn fragment, on which was written the address found on the place of murder, and affixed by the magistrates of Corbeil to their procés-verbal, occurred to my recollection. The piece now before me had evidently formed part of it. The commissary to whom I communicated my opinion coincided with me in it. Raoul had at first seen us take up the note and examine it, with perfect indifference: possibly, he might not himself recollect, just at that moment, its fatal signification; but as he observed our scrutiny more and more directed to it, his memory evidently refreshed him with its full force; his countenance changed in an instant; the muscles of his face contracted; a ghastly paleness came over him; and springing toward a drawer in which were his loaded pistols, he endeavored to seize them; when, by an equally rapid movement, my agents and myself threw ourselves upon him, and soon deprived him of all power of resistance.

It was nearly midnight when Raoul and his wife were conducted to the prefecture;—Court arrived there a quarter of an hour afterward. The two accomplices were separately confined. Up to this period there had been nothing but presumptive evidence against them; I therefore undertook to obtain their own confession whilst they remained in their first stupor. It was on Court that I first employed my eloquence. I worked him, as it is called, in every possible way. I used every species of argument to convince him that it was to his own interest to make a full avowal.

"Take my advice," said I to him, "declare the truth of the matter; why should you persist in endeavoring to conceal what is known to every one? you will find, by the very first question put to you at your examination, that your judges are much better informed than you think for—death has not sealed the lips of all the persons you have attacked. Many of those you believed your victims will produce overwhelming proofs against you; you may be silent, if you please, but your silence will not prevent your condemnation: public execution is not all you expose yourself to; think of the punishments and severity with which your obstinacy will be visited; justly irritated against you, the magistrates will show you no mercy up to the hour of your execution; you will be watched, tormented, worse even than by the tortures of a slow consuming fire: if you persist in your obstinate refusal to make a full confession, your prison will be a perfect hell to you. On the contrary, by avowing your past iniquities, expressing sorrow and contrition for them, and meeting your fate with resignation (since you cannot hope to escape from it), you will at least have a chance of exciting the pity of mankind, and the humane consideration of those appointed to try you."

I had carefully forborne mentioning to Court of what murder he was accused; fully impressed with the idea of his having been accessary to more than one, I avoided specifying that of which he then stood charged. I hoped that, by using only vague words, and refraining from every precise detail, I might be enabled to draw him on to the confession of other crimes besides the one for which he was then in custody.

"Well, then," said he, "since you advise it, I will acknowledge that it was I who murdered the traveling poulterer.— Why, his soul must have stuck faster to his body than I guessed it would, poor devil!—and did he really come back to life after such a dressing as I gave him I'll tell you, M. Jules, how the thing happened, and I wish I may die if I tell a lie about it:—A number of Normans were returning home, after having sold their wares at Paris. I fancied they must be loaded with money, and in consequence lay in wait for them. I stopped the first two who came by, but found little or nothing upon them. I was at that time in the most extreme necessity: want drove me on to the deed, for my wife was destitute of everything, and the thoughts of her wretched state wrung my heart. At last, whilst I was giving myself up to despair, I heard the noise of wheels: I hastened to meet it; it was a poulterer's cart; the poor wretch was half asleep when I called to him to deliver up his purse. He emptied his pockets. I felt in them myself, but his whole possessions were eighty francs!—eighty francs!

what was that to me who was in debt to every one? I owed two quarters' rent, and my landlord was hourly threatening to turn us out of doors. To heighten my misery, I was dubbed by other creditors equally merciless. What was I to do with this paltry supply of eighty francs? Rage took possession of me. I seized my pistols, and, without one moment's reflection, discharged them both at my gentleman's heart. A fortnight afterward I learned that he still lived! you may imagine, therefore, that my present situation does not surprise me; for, since the moment I have been describing to you, I have never enjoyed one hour's peace, in the fear of his paying me off sooner or later."

"Your fears were well founded," said I, "but this unfortunate dealer in poultry is not your only victim; what do you expect from the butcher whom you pierced through and through with your knife, after having carried off his purse?"

"Oh, as to that," exclaimed the villain, "may God receive his soul! I will answer for it, that if he witnesses against me. it can only be at the last judgment."

"You are mistaken, the butcher did not die of his wounds, any more than the former victim you were speaking of."

"Ah, so much the better," cried Court.

"No, he lives; and I must warn you that he has pointed out both you and your accomplices, in a manner too distinct to admit of any mistake."

Court endeavored to persist in affirming that he had no accomplices; but he became weary of his own falsehood, and at length admitted that Clair Raoul had participated in the crime for which he was accused. I urged him (but in vain) to name others as well; he maintained the same story, and I was compelled to content myself with what I had already drawn from him; however, in the fear of his retracting, I summoned the commissary, in whose presence Court repeated, and even enlarged upon what he had previously told me.

To have brought Court to an acknowledgment of his crime, and to obtain from him a written declaration of it, was no doubt an important point gained; but a more difficult battle remained to be fought ere Raoul could be persuaded to follow his example. To effect this, I stole softly to the room in which he was confined. He was sleeping: and, stepping cautiously in the fear of awaking him, I placed myself beside him, and whispered gently in his ear, in the hope of leading him, as under the influence of a dream, to answer the questions thus put to him. Without raising the low tone in which I had first addressed him, I interrogated him as to the particulars of the murder. Some unintelligible words escaped him, but it was impossible to make any sense of them. This scene lasted for nearly a quarter of an hour, when, on my asking him, "What became of the knife with which you murdered your victim?" he gave a sudden start, uttered some inarticulate sounds, and plunging from the bed on which he was lying, opened his wild and glaring eyes full upon me, as if he dreaded the apparition of some horrid vision.

From the terror and astonishment with which he continued to regard me, even after he had recognized my person, it might easily be perceived that he dreaded my having been the witness to his late severe internal struggle, and I could readily see in his eyes the eagerness with which he sought to divine how far his restless guilty conscience had betrayed him during his unquiet slumbers. A cold perspiration covered his face, he was deathly pale, and whilst he endeavored to force a smile, his teeth chattered and ground together in spite of him; he presented an exact representation of a damned spirit in all the tortures of an agonizing conscience—a second Orestes pursued by the furies. Ere the last vapors of his uneasy dreams had passed away, I wished to turn the circumstance to account; it was not the first time I had called the nightmare to my aid.

"You appear," said I to Raoul, "to have had a frightful dream; you have been talking a great deal, and seemed to be in great pain; I could not bear to see you suffer so much, and woke you to dispel the anguish and remorse to which you seemed a prey. Do not feel displeased at this language—it is in vain to dissimulate further; the confessions of your friend, Court, have informed us of everything—justice is in full possession of every circumstance relative to the crime whereof you are accused. Do not seek to palliate your participation in it, —the evidence of your accomplice cannot be invalidated by any thing you can say; if you seek to save yourself by a system of denial, the voice of your unhappy associate will confound you in the presence of your judges; and if that be not sufficient, the butcher whom you murdered near Milly will appear as your accuser."

At these words I steadily examined the countenance of Raoul; a slight discomposure was observable in his features, but it soon passed away, and recovering himself, he replied with firmness:

"M. Jules, you are trying to entrap me; you only throw away your time; you are deep and cunning, but I know my own innocence. As to what you say of Court, you will not persuade me that he is guilty; still less do I believe that he can have implicated my name, when there exists not the slightest appearance of probability of his doing so."

I again declared to Raoul that it was useless for him to seek to conceal the truth from me—"Well, then," said I, "if nothing else will do, you shall be confronted with your friend; we shall then see whether you will venture to persist in denying the facts he has sworn to."

"Let him come," cried Raoul, "I do not ask for anything better; I am confident that Court is incapable of a bad or dishonorable action. Why should he accuse himself of a crime he has not committed, and implicate me in it for mere wantonness? unless indeed he has lost his senses, which is not very likely. Hark ye, M. Jules, I am so certain of what I assert, that if he says he committed this murder, and that I had a share in it, I consent to pass for the greatest scoundrel that ever walked the earth. I will acknowledge, as true, whatever he may say; and I further engage, either to clear my innocence through his means, or to ascend the same scaffold with him. I do not dread the guillotine, whether its blow descend for this or any other offense; if Court confirms what you have said, be it so—all is over—the veil is raised, and two heads will fall at once."

I quitted him in these dispositions, and went to propose the interview with his comrade: the latter, however, refused, declaring that after the confession he had made, he had not the courage to encounter Raoul.—"Since I have regularly signed and attested my deposition," said he, "let it be read to him, it will suffice to convince him; besides he will recognize my writing."

This repugnance, which I was far from expecting, vexed me so much the more, as I have frequently known the thoughts of a man arraigned of crime to change in an instant from one opinion to the opposite extreme. I exerted all my influence to overcome Court's objections, and at length succeeded in deciding him to act as I wished. After a trifling delay, the two friends found themselves in each other's presence: they embraced: and the ingenuity of Court suggested to him a ruse by which to palliate his having involved his coadjutor in his acknowledgment of guilt: and this, without having originated in, my advice, materially assisted my plans:—"Friend Raoul," cried Court, "I am informed you have followed my example, and made a full confession of our unfortunate crime. It was the very best thing we could either of us do; for, as M. Jules observes, there are too many convincing proofs against us, to make further denial of any avail."

The person to whom these words were addressed stood for an instant as if petrified with astonishment; but, quickly gathering his spirits,—"Faith, M. Jules!" exclaimed he, "you have managed well—we are both completely drawn! Now, then, as I am a man of my word, I will keep that I gave you by concealing nothing;" and immediately he began a recital which fully confirmed that of his associate. These new revelations having received the usual forms of law, I remained in conversation with the two assassins, who bore their part in it with inexhaustible mirth and hilarity, the general effect of confession with the greatest criminals. I supped with them, and although they ate heartily they drank very moderately. Their countenances had resumed their usual calmness, and no vestige was perceptible of the late catastrophe; they looked upon it as a settled thing, that by their confession they had undertaken to pay their debt to offended justice.

After supper I informed them we should set out in the night for Corbeil. "In that case," said Raoul, "it is not worth while going to bed;" and he begged of me to procure him a pack of cards. When the vehicle which was to convey us was ready, they were as deeply engaged in their game of piquet as any two peaceful citizens of Paris could have been.

They ascended the carriage without appearing to suffer the least emotion at so doing, and we had scarcely reached the Barriere d'Italie, when they were happily asleep and snoring, nor had they aroused themselves, when, at eight o'clock in the morning, we entered Corbeil.

Chapter XXXVIII

THE NOISE OF OUR ARRIVAL WAS QUICKLY SPREAD ABROAD, and the inhabitants flocked to have a view of the assassins of the butcher whose story had excited so much commiseration. I was equally an object of curiosity to them, and was pleased with the present opportunity of learning the opinion entertained of me at the distance of six leagues from Paris. I hastened to mingle in the crowd assembled before the prison, from whence I could easily overhear the most amusing observations: "There he is, that is he!" exclaimed the spectators, raising themselves on tiptoe every time the wicket opened to allow ingress or egress to any of my agents.

"Look, look! do you see him?" said one of them, "that little hop-o'-my-thumb there, scarcely five feet high."

"Stuff! a shrimp like that! I could put fifty such in my pocket."

"Shrimp as you call him, he is more than a match for you; he is a first rate boxer, and has a sort of a back throw that would astonish you."

"All fudge, I dare say; do you suppose he is the only one that knows a good thing?"

"No, no!" bawled out a second spectator, "this is he, this tall slender fellow with the red hair."

"What a lath!" cried out the next bystander, "why, with one hand in my pocket, I could double him in two."

"You could?"

"Yes, I could!"

"And do you fancy that he would allow you to lay your fingers upon him? No, no! you have mistaken your man; he comes sometimes as if meaning to speak amicably to one, and just the moment you least expect it, comes a dig in the breadbasket, or, as he may happen to prefer, a conk on the head, which will make you see fifty candles at once."

"The gentleman who spoke last is perfectly right," said an old citizen, eyeing me through his spectacles; "this Vidocq is a most extraordinary character; I have been told that when he wishes to seize a man, he has a certain blow, which once aimed never fails to deprive the person against whom it is directed of all power of resistance."

"And I have been told," said a carman, joining in the conversation, "that he never goes without large clouts in the soles of his shoes, and whilst he is giving you a punch of the head, he breaks the shins with a kick a thousand times heavier than any horse."

"Mind where you are walking, you great clod-hopper," exclaimed a young girl, whose corns the clumsy carman had been most unceremoniously stamping on.

"Just a little treat for you, my pretty one," replied the rustic. "Never mind trifles like that, you are not quite killed. I dare say if Vidocq were to give you a gentle taste of the heel of his boot upon your favorite toe, you might indeed call out."

"Indeed, I should like to see him dare to do so."

"Ah! he would spoil your dancing, I can promise you— but who is that coming from the prison? Look!"

At this instant I addressed the carman. "I hope," said I, "that the sparkling eyes of my pretty neighbor here would insure her safety from Vidocq, wicked as he may be."

"Yes, yes," rejoined the carman, "I believe he is vastly civil to the women. I have been told that he is a merry fellow enough with them, and bears an excellent reputation; although many a pretty girl has lost hers through the honor of his good company." These words were accompanied by a loud horse laugh, in which the rest of the company joined.

"What is the matter there?" cried some who were not sufficiently nigh the scene of action to understand the cause of the burst of voices which assailed their ears.

"Hats off!"

"Do you observe that man in the wig?"

"Are those the murderers?"

"There he is! there he is!"

"Who? who?"

"Do not crowd so dreadfully."

"Take your hands off, you blackguard.""

"Knock him down! down with him!"

"How wrong of females to risk their lives by coming to a scene like this."

"Here, climb up on my shoulder."

"Down there, you are not made of glass."

"Are they all mad to make such a noise?"

"Oh, it is nobody after all, only a guardsman."

"Are there any of the spies amongst them?'

"Spies? Yes, four, I have been told."

By the time these different exclamations were ended, the flux and reflux of the multitude had borne me away to the midst of a fresh group, where a dozen gossips were busily conversing of me in the following manner:

First Gossip. (This speaker appeared, by his silvery locks, of venerable age.) "Yes, sir, he was condemned to the galleys for a hundred and one years—commuted from sentence of death."

Second Gossip. "A hundred and one years! Bless me, why that is more than an age!"

An Old woman. "The Lord be good unto me, what is that you favored me by saying? A hundred and one years! indeed, as the other gentleman observed, that is rather more than a day!"

Third Gossip. "No, no; something more than a day indeed! upon my credit, a tolerably long lease of it."

Fourth Gossip. "And so he had committed murder, had he?"

Fifth Gossip. "Why, did not you know that? Bless you, he is a villain loaded with every sort of crime; he has been guilty of every enormity by turns, each of which has merited the guillotine; but he is a deep rascal, and has managed to keep his head on his shoulders, to the surprise of every one."

Another Gossip. (In what order his speech was made I do not now remember; I recollect only that he was dressed in black, and from the style of his dress and hair I concluded him to be one of the churchwardens of the parish.)

The Fleur De Lis. "No, better still! I am informed by my friend the commissary, that this Vidocq always accustoms himself to wear a ring round his leg—is it not strange?"

Myself. "Come, do not seek to gammon us with your stories of rings; do you suppose we could not perceive it, if it were worn as you say?"

The Gossip In Black. (Gravely) "No, sir, you could not see it; in the first place, you are not to imagine it an iron ring of four or five pounds weight. No, it is a golden ring, as light as possible, and nearly imperceptible. Ah! indeed, if like me he wore short knee-breeches, you would soon discover it, but those trousers hide everything, Trousers, indeed! an absurd fashion. We may thank the Revolution for that introduction, as well as for cropped heads, haired a la Titus, as they term it, which no longer leave it possible to discover a gentleman from one who has tugged at the galleys. I only ask you, gentleman, whether if this Vidocq were to introduce himself amongst you, you would feel particularly flattered by his company?"

"Pray," asked the old woman who had before spoken, "is it true that he was publicly branded?"

"Certainly, madam; that too with a red-hot iron on both shoulders. I will answer for it that if he were stripped, you would read the mark in all its brightness."

A gendarme, who had been seeking me amongst the spectators, approached me, and, gently touching my shoulder, said, "M. Vidocq, the king's solicitor has been inquiring for you, and wishes to see you immediately." It was really ridiculous to see how every countenance changed at these words. "What! Can it be Vidocq?" exclaimed my late audience, with lengthened faces. "Vidocq! Vidocq!" shouted out others, and immediately all was fighting, struggling, and confusion, to endeavor to force a passage for the eager looks of those who were not sufficiently near to gratify their eyesight with a view of the so much coveted monster, for such they certainly expected to find me. Some even climbed on the shoulders of their neighbors to satisfy themselves as to whether I really was a human creature or not; of this I had convincing proofs by the following flying remarks which reached my ears:

"Bless me! light complexion! I fancied him quite dark. I heard he was ill-looking. I see nothing so very ugly about him. What a strange manner of walking he has!"

These and similar observations were made by the crowd, whose sole interest now seemed centered in noting down every particular relative to my personal appearance. So great was the concourse of gazers, that I had much difficulty in forcing my way along to the procurer. This magistrate wished me to conduct the accused persons before the interrogating judge. Court, whom I first led thither, appeared intimidated at finding himself in the presence of so many persons; I exhorted him to seep up his courage, and to confirm his confessions. This he did without any great difficulty, as far as related to the assassination of the butcher; but when questioned on the subject of the poulterer, he retracted all his previous declarations, and it was impossible to lead him to confess that he had had any other accomplices than Raoul. This latter, when introduced into the chamber, unhesitatingly confirmed every fact mentioned in the procés-verbal, which had been drawn up after his arrest. He related in full detail, and with the most imperturbable sang froid, all that had passed between the unfortunate Fontaine and his murderers, up to the moment of his striking the first blow at his victim.

"The man," said he, "was only stunned by the two blows he received from a stick; when I saw that they had not sufficed to bring him to the ground, I drew near, as if to support him, holding in my hand the knife which is lying upon that table;" pronouncing these words, he sprang toward the desk, abruptly seized the instrument of his crime, made two steps backward, and rolling his eyes, sparkling with fury, he assumed a menacing attitude. This movement, which was wholly unexpected, filled with terror all who were present: the sous prefet was nearly fainting, and I myself underwent some alarm. Nevertheless, I felt the necessity of concealing from Raoul the effect he had produced, and I even sought to attribute his violent gesture to a good motive. "Gentlemen!" cried I, smiling, "what is it you fear? Raoul is incapable of acting like a coward, and abusing the confidence reposed in him; he merely took up the knife, the better to explain his share in the business." "Thanks, M, Jules!" cried he, delighted with my explanation, and quietly laying down the knife on the table, he added, "I only wished to show you how I made use of it."

To complete the preliminaries, it only remained to confront the accused with Fontaine; the surgeon was applied to ascertain whether the sick man was sufficiently recovered to bear so trying a scene, and he having replied in the affirmative, Court and Raoul were taken to the hospital. Introduced into the apartment occupied by the butcher, their eyes eagerly sought their victim. Fontaine, with his head and face nearly covered with bandages, and his whole person wrapped in linen cloths, was indeed scarcely to be recognized; but beside him were displayed the clothes and shirt worn by him on the night he was so cruelly assaulted. "Ah! poor Fontaine!" cried Court, falling on his knees at the foot of the bed, decorated by these bloody trophies; "forgive the miserable wretches who have reduced you to this condition; that you still survive is a striking interposition of Providence, who has been pleased to preserve you the better to punish us as our crime deserves."

Whilst he was expressing himself thus, Raoul, who had likewise knelt down, preserved a deep silence, and appeared plunged in the deepest affliction.

"Stand up, both of you, and look the sick man in the face;" said the judge who accompanied them. They rose up—

"Take those murderers from my sight!" shrieked Fontaine, "their countenances and voices are but too familiar to me."

This recognition, and the manner of the culprits, was more than sufficient to establish the fact of Court and Raoul having been the actors in this frightful tragedy: but I was firmly persuaded that they had other crimes, besides this, with which to reproach themselves, and that, in order to commit them, there must have been more than two in number. This was a secret of the greatest importance. I determined to exert myself to the utmost to come to the truth; and not to quit them till I induced them to unload their consciences by a full confession of their past misdeeds. On our return to the prison after this meeting, I caused supper to be served for the accused and myself. The porter inquired whether he should place knives on the table.

"Yes, yes!" cried I, "set knives to each gentleman, by all means."

My two guests ate their meals with as great an appearance of appetite, as though they had been the most honest men breathing. When they had drunk a few glasses of wine, I dexterously brought back the conversation to the subject of their crime.

"You are not naturally bad fellows," said I to them. "I'll engage that you have been led into all this by some scoundrel or other; why not own it? From the confession and repentance you displayed at the sight of Fontaine, it is easily seen that you would willingly recall, at the price of your own blood, the violence he received at your hands. And do you not consider that by concealing your accomplices, you are responsible for all the crimes they may commit. Many persons who have come forward to depose against you, have declared that you were at least four in number in all your expeditions."

"They were mistaken then," exclaimed Raoul; "I give you my word of honor, M. Jules, that they were; we were never more than three, the other is an old officer of the customs, named Pons Gerard; he lives just on the frontier, in a little village between Capelle and Hirson in the department of the Aisne; but if you think to catch him, I must warn you that he is not to be caught napping, he always sleeps with one eye open whilst the other is shut."

"No!" said Court, "it would be no easy job to nab him, and if you do not set your wits to work, you will only get your labor for your pains."

"Oh, he is a queer hand, indeed," cried Raoul; "you are no bungler yourself, M. Jules, but ten like you would not frighten him; at any rate, you must be on your guard if he gets scent of your being in search of him; he is not far from Belgium, and will soon be off; if you surprise him, he will make a desperate resistance, so try if you cannot manage to take him asleep."

"Yes, if you could find out that he ever does sleep," added Court.

I made strict inquiries as to the usual habits of Pons Gerard, and obtained a full description both of them and his person. As soon as I had learned every particular requisite for being secure of identifying my man, thinking to stamp the confession I had just elicited with all possible authenticity, I proposed to the two prisoners to write off immediately for a magistrate to receive their depositions. Raoul instantly took up his pen, and when his letter was completed, I carried the letter myself to the king's solicitor; it was conceived in the following terms:—

"Sir,—Being now in a frame of mind more suitable to our unhappy condition, and resolving to profit by the advice you bestowed upon us, we have come to the resolution of acknowledging to you every crime of which we are guilty, and to point out to you a sharer in them, whose name is at present unknown to you. We entreat of you, therefore, to have the kindness to visit us in our prison, in order to receive our depositions."

The magistrate lost no time in acceding to their request, and Court, as well as Raoul, repeated before him all that they had previously told me of Pons Gerard.

This latter now occupied all my thoughts, and as it would not do to allow him time to learn the destruction of his comrade's schemes, I instantly obtained an order to arrest him.

CHAPTER XXXIX

DISGUISED AS A DEALER IN HORSES, I set out with my agents, Clement and Goury, who passed for my ostlers; and such was the diligence used by us, that, in spite of the severity of the season and the badness of the roads (for it was in the midst of winter), we arrived at La Capelle on the evening of the following day, which happened, fortunately for my purpose, to be the eve of a large fair. Having traversed the country more than once during my military career, I required but a very short time to arrange my plan of action, and to assume the dialect of the place.

All the inhabitants to whom I spoke of Pons Gerard described him to me as a robber, who subsisted only by fraud and rapine; his very name was sufficient to excite universal terror, and the authorities of the place, although daily furnished with proofs of his enormities, durst take no steps to repress them. In a word, he was one of those terrible beings who compel obedience from all who surround them. For my own part, little accustomed to draw back from a perilous enterprise, these particulars only stimulated me the more to enter upon the undertaking.

My vanity was piqued to accomplish a task which appeared to vie in difficulty with the labors of Hercules, but did I know that success would attend my arduous attempt? As yet I was ignorant of many essential points, but trusting for the best, I sat down to breakfast with my agents, and when we had sufficiently fortified our stomachs, we set out in search of the hardened accomplice of Court and Raoul. These latter had pointed out to me a lone auberge as the favorite haunt of Pons. This house was the rendezvous of a nest of smugglers, and the woman who kept it, considering Pons as one of her best customers, felt great interest in all that concerned him. So well had this auberge been described to me, that I required no further directions to find it; I therefore repaired thither with my two companions, and entering, seated myself without any ceremony, assuming the tone and manner of one well used to the ways of the house.

"Good-day to you, mother Bardou, how goes all with you?"

"The same to you, my good friends, and many of them. You are welcome to my poor place; thank God, we are all pretty comfortable, thanks for your inquiry. What would you please to have, gentlemen?"

"Dinner, dinner! my good soul; we are starving with hunger."

"You shall have it directly, sirs;—please to step into the next room, where you will find a good fire."

"Whilst she was employed in laying the cloth, I drew her into the following conversation:—

"I begin to fancy, my good hostess, that you have forgotten my features."

"Wait a little till I have time to look well at you."

"Why what a memory you must have to forget how I used to come with Pons to your house last winter! many a time have we paid you a moonshine visit."

"Bless me! now I begin to recollect."

"To be sure you do, look again."

"Oh! now I remember you perfectly."

"Well, how is our jolly cove Gerard? How is he a getting on? quite strong and hearty, eh!"

"I' faith is he, he was here only this morning, and took a glass or two on his way to Lanare house, where he had employment."

Of this house, or of its situation, I was utterly ignorant; nevertheless, as I had given myself out as a person well acquainted with the neighborhood, I was careful not to betray myself by risking any inquiry. Still I trusted that, without directly asking the question, I should be enabled to lead my voluble friend, by indirect means, to the point at which I wished to arrive. Accident favored me, for scarcely had we swallowed a few mouthfuls of our dinner, than Mother Bardou entered the room. "You were talking of Gerard just now," said she, "his daughter has just called in."

"Indeed! which of the daughters?"

"The youngest."

I rose immediately, and running up to the child, embraced her before she had time even to look at me; and rapidly naming each member of her family, made many and warm inquiries after their health. When she had replied to them, I cut short the parley by giving her a trifle of money, and recommending her to hasten home, whither I would accompany her, as I was extremely anxious to present myself to her excellent mother; beckoning to my companions, we left the house, following the footsteps of our little guide, who, surprised at the novelty of the rencontre, was making with all speed for the dwelling of her mother. No sooner, however, had we got out of sight of the auberge, than I called to the girl, "Hark ye, my little one, do you know the place they call Lanare house?"

"It stands just down there," said she, pointing with her finger to the other side of the Hirson.

"Well, then, I'll tell you what you shall do; just run on and let your mother know that you have met three particular friends of your father, and that we shall return to sup with him. So that she may as well have it already for four of us. That's right—make the best of your way; good-evening, my pretty maid."

The daughter of Gerard pursued her way, and we were not slow in following the road she had described to us, which brought us nearly facing the house we sought, but no persons were to be seen about, and upon questioning a countryman whom we met, he informed us that Pons was at work with a number of laborers at a short distance from thence; we proceeded onward, and having gained an eminence, obtained a view of about thirty men employed in repairing the high road. Gerard, by virtue of his office of overseer, was in the midst of this group. We advanced within fifty steps of the workmen, when I made my agents observe an individual whose countenance and general appearance exactly corresponded with the description we had received of the ferocious Pons; although we entertained no doubt of his being the man, we durst not attempt to seize him, for should his companions undertake his rescue, we, of course, should come off but badly, and even his single arm, when impelled by the fear of being taken prisoner, might be more than a match for my small party. Our situation was embarrassing enough, yet had we displayed the least symptom of it, Gerard would either have made us pay dearly for our temerity in daring to attack him, or he would escape our grasp by a hasty retreat to the frontier. Never had I felt a greater need of prudence and self-possession. I consulted with my agents, two firm and intrepid men. "Act as you think proper," said they, "and rest assured of our seconding you in whatever steps you may take."

"Well then," cried I, "follow me, and do nothing till a fit opportunity arrives; perhaps we may turn out the more cunning party of the two, although the enemy may have the advantage of superior strength."

I walked directly up to the individual whom I supposed to be Gerard, my two companions keeping at a little distance. The nearer I approached, the more assured did I feel that I had not mistaken my man: thus convinced, and without further hesitation, I hurried up to Pons, and embracing him with every demonstration of regard, exclaimed, "Pons, my good fellow, how are you! how is your excellent wife, and all your family? quite well, I trust?"

Astonished at this unexpected salutation, Pons remained in silent examination of my face for some minutes: "Devil take me," said he at last, "if I know who or what you are; where the deuce did you spring from?"

"What!" said I, "not recollect me? Am I then indeed so much altered?"

"Not I; I do not remember ever seeing you in all my life; can't you just tell me your name? Stay, now I look again, I feel certain that I have met that face of yours somewhere or other, although where I have seen you is more than I can tell."

"I am a friend to Raoul and Court," said I, whispering in his ear, "and am sent to you by them."

"Ah!" cried he, pressing my hands warmly in both of his, and turning to the workmen who were gazing in wonder at this unexpected change of his reception of me, "I must have lost my senses, I think, not to remember one of my best friends! Not to recognize my dear friend! the devil must have flown away with my memory. My dear fellow, let me embrace you;" and, suiting the action to the word, he gave me such an emphatic hug as well-nigh stifled me.

During this scene my agents had insensibly advanced nearer to the spot where we stood. Pons perceiving them, inquired if they belonged to me?" They are two of my ostlers," said I.

"I thought so, but you must stand greatly in need of refreshment, and those gentlemen yonder would, I dare say, have no objection to a glass of something good—what say you?"

"With all my heart. A bottle of your best wine will do us no harm."

"Well, then, let us go; but in this cursed place, which produces nothing but wolves, there is nothing to be had; however, if you don't mind walking over to Hirson (which, to be sure, is a good league from hence), we shall get as good a bottle of wine as ever was uncorked."

"Come along, then, let us go to Hirson."

Pons bade adieu to his comrades, and we set out together. As we walked along, I could not help confessing that the immense strength of this man did not appear to have been at all exaggerated by Raoul or Court; he was but of mid-dling height, probably not more than five feet four inches at the utmost, but square-built, and exhibiting every indication of muscular power. His swarthy face, embrowned still more by a constant exposure to the sun and wind, was distinguished by deeply marked features, expressive of energy and determina-tion; he had enormous limbs, and a strong, sinewy throat, in strict accordance with the whole of his robust frame; in addition to this he wore immense whisk-ers, and a more than usual quantity of beard; his hands were short, thick, and covered with hair, even to the fingers' ends; the harsh and pitiless air seemed to belong to a countenance which might exhibit a mechanical relaxation of the risible muscles, but had never once smiled from an internal feeling of benevo-lence or goodwill.

Whilst I was intently occupied in making these observations, I could per-ceive that Pons was regarding me with equal attention; at last stopping suddenly, as if to take a closer view, he exclaimed: "Why you really are a very fine fellow, and fill out your clothes as well as I have ever seen a man! I think you and I should make an excellent pair, for I am none of the slightest figures any more than yourself; not like that little hop-o'-my-thumb," added he, point-ing to Clement (who was the smallest man amongst my agents): "why I could swallow a dozen such as he at my breakfast."

"Don't flatter yourself," said I; "you might not find it so easy a task as you may fancy."

"Very possibly," replied he; "these undersized chaps are frequently all nerve and muscle."

After these trifling remarks, Pons inquired after his friends. I told him that they were quite well; but that not having seen him since the affair of Avesnes, I had left them very uneasy as to what had become of him. (The affair at Avesnes was a murder. When I alluded to it, his countenance exhibited not the slightest emotion.)

"Well, and what brings you to this part of the country?" asked he; "are you after a bit of moonshine, eh?"

"You have just hit it, my friend," said I. "My business here is to endeavor to dispose of a string of broken-down horses, which are famously doctored up for taking in the knowing ones. Our friends told me that you could lend me a help-ing hand."

"Ah, to be sure, you may depend on me," protested Pons.

With this sort of conversation we reached Hirson, where we halted at the house of a clockmaker who sold wine. We were soon placed round a table; our wine was brought, and, whilst we were drinking it, I led the conversation back to Court and Raoul. "Poor fellows," said I, "I fear that at this present moment they are very queerly situated."

"How so?" asked he.

"Why, I did not wish to tell you all at once; but the fact is, they are in considerable trouble; they have been arrested, and I greatly fear that they are now in prison."

"On what account?"

"Of that I am ignorant; all I know is, that I was breakfasting with Court and Raoul, when the police broke in upon us, and, after closely interrogating us all three, they allowed me to go about my business. As for our two poor friends, they were detained in solitary confinement; nor would you have learned their misfortune, had not Raoul, in returning from his examination, managed to whisper a few words to me unobserved, begging of me to warn you to be on your guard, for that they had been closely questioned as to their acquaintance with you. I cannot give you any further particulars."

"And who arrested you?" inquired Pons, who seemed thunderstruck at the intelligence.

"Vidocq."

"Oh! the scoundrel, the scamp! But who is this Vidocq, of whom we hear so much? I have never been able to meet him face to face; once only I perceived him following an individual into the house of Causette. I was told it was him, but I forget all about him; and I would cheerfully give half-a-dozen bottles of wine to anyone who would procure me a good stare at him."

"Bless you, it is easy enough to meet with him," replied I; "he is always about in one place or another."

"Well, I would advise him to keep out of my reach," exclaimed Pons. "If he were here, I'll engage he would pass the worst quarter of an hour he ever experienced in his life."

"Oh! You are like all the rest of them, talking of what you would do; and yet, if he were before you at this moment, you would sit perfectly still, and be the first to offer him a glass of wine." (At the time I was saying this I held out my glass, which he filled.)

"I! I offer him wine! May a thousand devils seize me first!"

"Yes, you, I say, would invite him to drink with you."

"I tell you I would die sooner."

"Then you may die as soon as you please, for I am Vidocq, and I arrest you!"

"How, how; what is this?"

"Yes, I arrest you!" and approaching my face to his, "I tell you, villain, I arrest you, you are done; and if you dare to misstep, I will tweak off your rascally nose. Clement, handcuff this worthy gentleman."

The astonishment of Pons defies description. Every feature appeared distorted, his eyes starting from their sockets, his cheeks quivering, his teeth chattered, and his hair stood on end; by degrees these symptoms of a general convulsion, which had affected only the upper part of his frame, gave way to a fresh revulsion of nature. After his arms were fastened, he remained for nearly half an hour motionless, and as though petrified. His lips were apart, and his tongue glued to the palate of his mouth; and it was only after repeated efforts that he succeeded in detaching it; in vain his parched and swollen tongue sought a moisture, which the dried-up lips were unable to afford, and the countenance of the ruffian exhibited alternately the pale, livid, cadaverous hues of a corpse; at last, recovering from his lethargy, Pons articulated these words:—

"What, are you Vidocq? Ah, had I but known it when you first spoke to me, I would have rid the earth of such a sneaking beggar."

"Well," said I "I thank you all the same for your kind intentions; meanwhile, as you have fallen into the trap, you owe me the six bottles of wine you promised to whoever would show you Vidocq, and you cannot deny my having done so. Another time, I advise you not to tempt the devil."

The gendarmes who were called in after the arrest of Pons, could scarcely credit their eyes; during the search we had been directed to make throughout his house, the mayor of the place begged to see us, that he might express his grateful sense of the service we had rendered to the whole province.

"You have," said he, "delivered us from a frightful scourge, from a wretch who was our torment and dread."

All the inhabitants joined in expressing their joy at the capture of their late foe, as well as their astonishment at the ease with which it had been effected.

The search over, we removed to sleep at La Capelle. Pons was closely handcuffed to one of my agents, who had orders not to quit him night or day; at our first halt, I caused him to be undressed, in order to ascertain whether or not he had any concealed arms about him. When he was stripped, I really doubted his belonging to the human race; the whole of his body was covered with a thick bushy glossy hair; he might, indeed, have been mistaken for the Hercules Farnese, enveloped in the skin of a bear.

Pons appeared perfectly tranquil, nor did any thing more than common arise till the following day when I ascertained that, during the night, he had eaten more than a quarter of a pound of tobacco. I had, from previous observation, noticed, that men who are greatly accustomed to the use of either tobacco or snuff, make an immoderate use of it in times of great peril or emergency. I knew well that a pipe is never more quickly consumed than when in the hands of a condemned criminal, whether it be immediately after receiving his sentence, or on the eve of its being put into execution; but I had never yet seen a prisoner, situated as Pons was, introduce into his stomach a substance, which taken in so large a quantity, might produce the most fatal effects. I very much feared that he would suffer from his excess, and even suspected he had committed it in the hope of its acting as poison. I, therefore, took from him what tobacco he had remaining, and gave orders that it should only be dealt out to him in small doses, and this on condition that he would engage only to chew it. Pons yielded with a tolerably good grace to this regulation; he ceased to devour his tobacco, although I never had any reason to suppose he had experienced the slightest inconvenience from what he had previously taken.

Chapter XL

I RETURNED DIRECTLY TO PARIS, AND THEN PROCEEDED with Pons to Versailles, where Court and Raoul were confined; immediately upon my arrival I went to see them.

"Well," said I to them, "our man is taken!"

"You have caught him!" exclaimed Court, "so much the better."

"But," inquired Raoul, "tell us how you managed to cage him, you must have had a fine business to tame so fierce a creature."

"He fierce!" said I, "on the contrary, he has been gentle as a lamb."

"What, did he make no defense? Ha! Raoul, do you hear that? he did not even defend himself!"

"The particulars you gave me of him," said I, "were not thrown away upon me."

Before quitting Versailles, I wished to show my sense of the kindness of the prisoners in thus aiding me in the capture of the ferocious Pons, and accordingly invited them to dine with me. My invitation was accepted with the most lively satisfaction, and during the remainder of the time we passed together, not the least gloom or sadness could be observed on their countenances; they appeared entirely resigned to their fate, and even their language seemed to have undergone some change, indicative of better feelings having resumed their empire over their minds.

"It must be confessed, my friend," said Court, "that we were following a rascally trade."

"Oh!" returned the other, "do not mention it; it makes no one rich in the end but the executioner."

"And that is not the worst part of it—to be in continual misery from constant alarm—never to know one moment's tranquility—to tremble at the sight of a stranger."

"True, indeed! I used to fancy I saw spies or disguised gendarmes in all who approached me, and the least noise, nay, my own shadow, would sometimes frighten me out of my senses."

"And, for my part, if I perceived myself an object of notice to any person, I instantly supposed he was taking down the description of my person, and the blood would rush to my face with such impetuosity as to suffuse my eyeballs with a guilty blush."

"Little indeed are the pangs of remorse and the terrors of a guilty conscience guessed by those who are innocent of crime; for my own part, rather than endure them as I have done for years past, I would blow out my brains."

"I have two children, but if I thought they were likely to tread in the steps of their unhappy father, I would implore of their mother to strangle them."

"Ah, my friend! had we but employed half the care and reflection in doing well it has cost us to prosecute our wicked schemes, we might now be enjoying a very different lot, and anticipating far brighter prospects than those before us."

"Well, well! 'tis useless repining; I suppose it was our fate."

"Don't tell me that; there is no such thing as fate; we are the workers of our own destinies, depend upon it; and I do not seek such a weak excuse for my crimes; no, I acknowledge that to a love of bad company alone I may attribute my being the wretch I am; do you not remember how, after every fresh act of wickedness, I sought to drown the whispers of a reproachful conscience by drunken excess? I felt as though the weight of a mountain was upon me, and had I swallowed gallons it would have been insufficient to remove it."

"And, for my part, I used to feel as though I had the hot iron gnawing my very vitals; if I fell into a short sleep, a thousand devils seemed dancing around me; sometimes I fancied myself discovered in clothes dyed in blood, burying the corpse of a victim; or stopped whilst in the act of conveying it away on my shoulders: shuddering I have awoke, bathed in perspiration, wrung from me by the horrid visions of my tortured spirit; drops of agony, which might have been gathered in spoonfuls, stood upon my aching brow; in vain have I sought by any change of position to taste a quiet sleep; turning upon my pillow, which seemed filled with thorns, even the pressure of my nightcap has appeared to my throbbing brain like the sharp points of an iron band, which drove its rugged teeth through my temples."

"Ah! I know well what all this is, I have felt as though a thousand needles were piercing every nerve."

"Possibly what you have described may be what is generally styled remorse."

"Remorse or not, it has been a fiery torment—a torment, M. Jules, which I am weary of;—I can bear it no longer, and it is time to end my misery. Some persons might owe you a grudge for the part you have acted toward us, but for my part I consider that you have done us a service; what say you. Raoul?"

"Since our confession, I feel as though I were in Paradise in comparison with my former sufferings. I know that we have a trying scene to go through, but our poor victims suffered as much at our hands, and it is but fair that we should serve as examples to others."

At the moment of separating from them, Raoul and Court begged of me to do them the kindness to come and see them directly they had received their sentence; this I promised, and I kept my word. Two days after they had been condemned to death, I went to them. When I entered their dungeon, they both uttered a cry of joy, and made its gloomy walls echo with the joyful welcome of their "liberator," as they termed me. They assured me that my visit afforded them the greatest pleasure they were capable of receiving, and entreated me to bestow on them one friendly embrace, in token of my forgiveness of their past, and satisfaction at their present conduct. I had not the heart to refuse them. They were fastened to a camp bed, with their hands and feet heavily fettered. I advanced toward them, and they pressed me in their arms with all the warmth and enthusiasm with which the sincerest friends would welcome each other after a long separation. A friend of mine, who was present at this interview, experienced considerable alarm at seeing me in a manner entirely at the mercy of two assassins.

"Fear nothing," said I.

"No, no," exclaimed Raoul, "fear nothing, there is little chance of our wishing to injure our good friend, M. Jules."

"M. Jules !" cried Court, "no, indeed, he is our only friend; and what is more, he does not forsake us now!"

As I was leaving them, I perceived two small books lying beside them, one of which was half open, and was entitled Christian Meditations.

"You have been reading, my friends," said I; "is religion a favorite study with you?"

"Oh no," said Raoul, "I know very little about it; these books were left us this morning by a clergyman who has been to visit us. I have just opened them, and certainly if people would follow the precepts they contain, the world would be better than it now is."

"Yes, so I think," said Court, "I am beginning to see that religion is not such a humbug as I once thought it; depend upon it we were not sent into the world to live and die like brutes."

I congratulated the new converts upon the happy change which had taken place in them.

"Who would have thought, two months back," resumed Court, "that I should suffer myself to be noodled by a priest!"

"And you know," rejoined Raoul, "my contempt for them and their sermons; but when men stand in our present awful extremity, it becomes them to look well about them; not that death alarms me; I care as little for it as I do for this cup of water. You will see whether I dread merely leaving this world, M. Jules."

"Ah yes!" said Court to me, "you must come."

"I will do so, I promise you."

"Honor."

"I pledge you my honor, I will be present."

The day appointed for the execution I repaired to Versailles. It was ten o'clock in the morning when I entered the prison; the two unhappy men were deeply engaged with their confessors. They no sooner perceived me, than precipitately rising, they approached me.

Raoul (taking my hand). "You do not know what pleasure the sight of you affords me, my friend; we were just preparing to leave this world with a clear conscience."

Myself. "Pray do not let me interfere with so sacred and important a duty."

Court. "You disturb us, M. Jules! surely you are jesting."

Raoul. "Our time draws to a close; we have but a poor ten minutes before us. (Turning to the ministers.) These gentlemen will excuse us."

Raoul's Confessor. "Proceed, my son, proceed."

Court. "There are but very few in the world like M. Jules; nevertheless he it was who caged us—but that is nothing."

Raoul. "If he had not done so, someone else would."

Court. "Yes, and some person, in all probability, who would not have treated us half so well."

Raoul. "Ah, M. Jules! I shall never forget all your kindness to me."

Court. "No friend could have done more."

Raoul. "And to come and witness the last concluding scene into the bargain."

Myself (offering him some snuff in the hope of changing the conversation). "Come, my friend, take a pinch, you will find it very good."

Raoul (taking a hearty pinch). "Not so bad; (he sneezes several times;) this is notice to quit, is it not, M. Jules?"

Myself. "I fear you may indeed look upon it as such."

At this moment Raoul opened the box, which he had taken into his own hands, looked at it attentively, and offering it to Court, inquired his opinion of it. "It is a fine thing of the sort, is it not, Court? tell me of what material it is composed?"

Court (turning away and shuddering). "It is gold."

Raoul. "You are right to avert your eyes from the sight of that fatal metal, which has caused the ruin of man since its first introduction; alas! we are melancholy instances of the pernicious effects it has produced."

Court. "To say that for such trash we should draw down so much trouble and suffering upon ourselves; how much better had we devoted our time to honest labor. We had both of us excellent parents; what are we now but a disgrace to them and our families?"

Raoul. "That is not my greatest grief at this awful moment. Think of the gentlemen whose wizands we have cut! the unfortunate beings! my heart bitterly reproaches me for their sufferings."

Court (embracing him). "But you sincerely repent of your past offenses, and are about to pay with your own life for those lives you have taken.—'He who sheddeth man's blood, by man shall his blood be shed.' I think that was what the worthy father here was reading to me as M. Jules entered."

Court's Confessor. "Come, my children, time is hastening on."

Raoul. "It is all in vain; the Supreme Being (if there really be one) can never pardon such guilty wretches as we are."

Court's Confessor. "God's mercy is inexhaustible. Jesus Christ dying on the cross interceded with his Father for the penitent thief."

Court. "May he be pleased to intercede for us likewise."

One Of The Confessors. "Raise your soul to God, my children, prostrate yourselves in humble prayer before him."

The two sufferers looked at me as if to discover what they ought to do. They appeared to fear my ridiculing any devotional feelings as the result of cowardice or weakness.

Myself. "Let no false shame prevent you from obeying the reverend father."

Raoul (to his comrade). "My friend, let us recommend our souls to our Maker."

Both Raoul and Court kneeled down, and remained for about a quarter of an hour in that position. They seemed rather collected than absorbed. The clock struck half-past eleven, they looked at each other, and both speaking together exclaimed, "In half an hour it will be all over with us." As they pronounced these words I saw that they wished to speak with me, I therefore drew aside, and they approached me. "M. Jules," said Court, "we would beg a last favor in addition to those we already owe you."

"What is it? depend upon my readiness to perform whatever you may require."

"We have each of us a wife in Paris—My kind wife! The thought of her breaks my heart—it overcomes me!"—tears filled his eyes, his voice became inarticulate, and he could not proceed.

"Come, Court," said Raoul, "what is the matter with you? Come, never play the baby; after all, you astonish me! can you be the brave fellow I took you for? Have not I a wife as well as you? Come, my boy, courage!"

"'Tis over now," resumed Court; "what I had to say to M. Jules was respecting some commissions we would fain in trust him with for our poor widows."

I pledged my word for the exact fulfillment of their desires; and when they had made known their wishes, I renewed the assurance of their being strictly performed.

Raoul. "I was quite sure that you would not refuse us."

Court. "Ah, M. Jules, how can we hope to repay your kindness?"

Raoul. "If what our ghostly friend here asserts be true, we shall meet in another and a better world."

Myself. "I trust so; and sooner perhaps than we at present think for."

Court. "Ah, 'tis a journey that must be taken sooner or later. We are upon the eve of our departure."

Raoul, "M. Jules, is your watch correct?"

Myself. "I believe it is too fast." (I drew it from my pocket.)

Raoul. "Let us see—twelve o'clock."

Court. "The hour for our execution: heavens! how the time gallops on!"

Raoul. "Look, the large hand is just about to overtake the small one! We shall never be weary of talking with you, M. Jules, but still we must part;—here take these prattlers we have no further need of them." (The prattlers were the books I have before described.)

Court. "And these two crucifixes, take them also; they will at least serve to remind you of us."

A noise of carriages was heard, the two culprits turned pale.

Raoul. "It is a wise plan to repent of our sins, but what if I determine to die game!—No; let me not turn bravado as many have done, but meet my fate with the courage of a man and the resignation of a sinner."

Court. "Well said, my friend, let us be firm, yet contrite."

The executioner arrived at the moment for ascending the fatal cart, and the sufferers bade me adieu.

"You have just embraced two death's heads," said Raoul, as he followed his friend.

The procession moved on toward the place of punishment. Raoul and Court were intently listening to their confessor, when all at once, I saw them start;—a voice never to be forgotten had struck upon their ear; it was that of Fontaine, who, recovered from his wounds, had mingled with the spectators; animated by the spirit of vengeance, he abandoned himself to the most ferocious expressions of joy. Raoul recognized him, and casting a look toward me full of contempt and pity for the unmanly exultation displayed by the man to whom he was making all the atonement in his power, he seemed to express that the presence of Fontaine was unpleasant and painful to him. As the vindictive butcher had taken his station close by me, I lost not an instant in compelling him to withdraw, and by a slight movement of the head, both Raoul and his companion testified their grateful sense of this attention to their wishes.

Court was first executed; even when he had ascended the scaffold his eye sought mine, as if to inquire whether I was satisfied with him. Raoul displayed equal firmness; he was in the very prime of life; twice did his head rebound upon the fatal plank, and the blood spirted out with so much violence as to cover the spectators even at the distance of twenty paces!

Such was the end of these two men, whose villainy was less the effect of natural depravity than the consequence of having associated with dissolute characters, who in the very bosom of society, form a distinct race, possessing their own principles, virtues and vices. Raoul, only thirty-eight years of age, tall, active, agile and vigorous; his eyebrows were high and arched, his eyes small, lively and of a sparkling black; his forehead, without being depressed, retreated backward a little, and his ears, which stood out from his head, appeared as though grafted upon two protuberances, like the generality of the Italians, whom he likewise resembled in the olive tint of his complexion. Court possessed one of those countenances which defy the rules of physiognomy; he had a half-squint with one eye, and the whole of his features could be said to boast of neither a good nor a bad expression; unless the sharp angles and projecting cheek bones might be construed into an indication of ferocity. Probably these symptoms of a bloodthirsty disposition had developed themselves through the constant murders and other atrocious acts in which he was constantly engaged. Court was forty-five years of age, and from his youth he had been continually involved in guilty courses: to have gone on so long with impunity must have required a more than ordinary supply of boldness and cunning.

The commissions intrusted to me by the two murderers were of a nature to prove that their hearts were yet accessible to good feeling. I discharged them with punctuality; as to the presents which they made me, I have preserved them, and can still show the books and the two crucifixes.

Pons Gerard, whom it was impossible to convict of the murder, was sentenced to perpetual hard labor.

THE END